Understanding Emotions

To Simon, Grant, Hannah, Natalie, and Serafina

Keith Oatley
Dacher Keltner
Jennifer M. Jenkins

Understanding Emotions

Second Edition

Blackwell
Publishing

© 2006 by Keith Oatley, Dacher Keltner, and Jennifer M. Jenkins

BLACKWELL PUBLISHING
350 Main Street, Malden, MA 02148-5020, USA
9600 Garsington Road, Oxford OX4 2DQ, UK
550 Swanston Street, Carlton, Victoria 3053, Australia

The right of Keith Oatley, Dacher Keltner, and Jennifer M. Jenkins to be
identified as the Authors of this Work has been asserted in accordance with
the UK Copyright, Designs, and Patents Act 1988.

First edition published 1996 by Blackwell Publishers Ltd
Second edition 2006 by Blackwell Publishing Ltd

5   2009

Library of Congress Cataloging-in-Publication Data

Oatley, Keith.
    Understanding emotions.—2nd ed. / Keith Oatley, Dacher Keltner, Jennifer M.
Jenkins.
       p. cm.
    Includes bibliographical references and index.
    ISBN 978-1-4051-3102-5 (hardcover : alk. paper)
    ISBN 978-1-4051-3103-2 (pbk. : alk. paper)
    1. Emotions.   I. Keltner, Dacher.   II. Jenkins, Jennifer M.   III. Title.

    BF531.O19 2006
    152.4—dc22

          2005029123

A catalogue record for this title is available from the British Library.

Set in 10.5/12.5pt Garamond
by Graphicraft Limited, Hong Kong
Printed and bound in Singapore
by Markono Print Media Pte Ltd

The publisher's policy is to use permanent paper from mills that operate
a sustainable forestry policy, and which has been manufactured from
pulp processed using acid-free and elementary chlorine-free practices.
Furthermore, the publisher ensures that the text paper and cover board used
have met acceptable environmental accreditation standards.

For further information on
Blackwell Publishing, visit our website:
www.blackwellpublishing.com

Short Contents

Contents

Figures

Tables

Preface

The strange thing about life is that though the nature of it must have been apparent to everyone for hundreds of years, no one has left any adequate account of it. The streets of London have their map; but our passions are uncharted.

Virginia Woolf, *Jacob's Room*

According to written and oral traditions people have been interested in emotions for thousands of years. In most societies emotions are at the center of popular understandings of psychology. In working on the second edition of our textbook, it has become clear that in research, too, emotions have now moved into their proper place, at or near the center of our understandings of the human mind and of relationships in the social world.

In writing the second edition of *Understanding Emotions*, we welcome Dacher Keltner who is not only a delight to work with but who brings fresh insights in this field. We hope you like the second edition, which maintains many of the features of the first. You will see Dacher's influence in updating and creating a more systematic organization that makes it easier for students and instructors to use this text in courses on emotions. Dacher's widely respected research on emotions and relationships is evident in this edition. We have also responded to our colleagues' suggestions for updating this book and have considered the many exciting advances in the field of emotions.

Changes in this edition include:

- Coverage of research approaches and "what is an emotion" have been streamlined into a single chapter (Chapter 1).
- A new section, *Integrating Evolutionary and Cultural Approaches to Emotion,* provides a cohesive synthesis of these approaches (Chapter 3).
- Studies of new expressions (love, desire) as well as new systems of communication (touch, music) appear in the chapter on expression (Chapter 4).
- A new chapter (5) offers discussion of bodily changes and the autonomic nervous system in emotions.
- A section has been added on subjective well-being and happiness (in Chapter 14).

- Updated references throughout reflect current research and data, including research on the central nervous system and affective neuroscience.
- A new design and pedagogical features include new integrated boxes such as *Historical Landmarks*, and *Historical Figures*, updated tables, boldfaced terms, and end-of-chapter summaries.
- Terms that indicate salient concepts are set in bold type. Where the terms are technical they are explained in the Glossary towards the end of the book.

Science depends on entering the tradition of what has gone before. As Robert Burton, a contemporary of Shakespeare, said in his famous work, *The Anatomy of Melancholy*: Each of us is able to see further by standing on the shoulders of giants. Our job as writers is to present some of what can be seen from this position, and to evaluate theories and evidence. You as a reader can then evaluate what we say in relation to what else you know, and can take part in the debate that is the social process of science, the means by which understanding is increased.

This book is intended for anyone with an interest in emotions, to show how far conceptualization and research have progressed toward understanding. The book, and we would claim the whole topic, extends across psychology, neuroscience, psychiatry, biology, anthropology, sociology, literature, and philosophy. Although some have argued that emotions are too heterogeneous for systematic study, the fact that we can write a textbook shows – we believe – that from a complex field, order is emerging.

An introduction to human emotions without a point of view would be dull and largely incomprehensible. The quantity of publications in the field makes it impossible to be exhaustive. We have therefore chosen studies and ideas that we believe are representative, hoping to convey a sufficient image for you to think productively. So, as well as an overall story, there is a story line for each chapter. Where there are controversies we discuss them, or at least indicate them so that you can look at the field from different points of view. But we have also worked to produce a coherent book. Although ours is not the only point of view, we think that by seeing that there is a coherent perspective in this area, you the reader will be able to agree, or to disagree, or to modify it. Knowing that any piece of evidence is not conclusive on its own but that each can provide a step toward exploring an idea, we hope that an integrated picture will take shape for you the reader, with concepts and ideas you can modify and apply to your own interests.

We have done our best to be fair-minded in our treatment of evidence, but our knowledge is necessarily incomplete and our views are necessarily biased toward our own interests and conceptualizations. Our interest is in thinking of emotions in cognitive, evolutionary, and developmental terms, in understanding their role in mediating everyday social interaction, and in seeing what goes wrong in the states known as emotional disorders. We see emotions as based on biological processes, elaborated in our close relationships, and shaped by culture. Like the skilled action when you write your signature, an emotion has a biological basis of components and constraints. It also has a history of individual development. It is only fully understandable within an interpersonal and cultural context.

We write about emotions in the Western tradition. This does not imply universality of Euro-American assumptions, but we do imagine that most of our readers are either members of that tradition or are conversant with it. We believe that by characterizing and identifying with this tradition, the ideas and findings that have substance within it can be seen clearly. We, and others, can form understandings based in that tradition and then understand better other culturally distinctive ways of thinking.

As well as a general introduction to the area, the book is designed for use as a textbook for a course on emotions for second- to fourth-year undergraduates, or for master's level students. But it is a textbook of a particular kind. Most textbooks in psychology nowadays are compendia of many things to be remembered and a few to be conceptualized. By contrast, I. A. Richards (1925) said that a book is "a machine to think with" (p. 1). We have written our book to encourage your thinking. Our conclusions make up our narrative thread. But by offering you sufficient detail of the evidence from which we draw our conclusions we hope to make it possible for you too to draw your conclusions.

The 14 chapters of this book can be covered in semester-long courses at the rate of one a week, perhaps with one or two chapters omitted according to the judgment of the instructor. For full-year courses, each chapter can be divided. Throughout, we keep in mind both the issue of prompting understandings of emotions and practical applications in clinical psychology, psychiatry, health care, education, and the issues of organizations. We envisage that many instructors who use the book will supplement it with readings that they provide. At the end of each chapter we offer some suggestions for further reading, typically reviews and books.

We have tested our ideas and coverage by attending to the currents of publications in the field, which has its own journals, its international society for research, its review volumes, its handbooks. We have drawn on results of a survey that one of us (KO) conducted with members of the International Society for Research on Emotions, on the most important new work on emotions since the first edition of this textbook. Also, we have received feedback from colleagues in North America and Europe to advise us on the balance, representativeness, content, and accuracy of our presentation. One of us (DK) has used the draft of the new book in an undergraduate course.

An Instructor's Manual with lecture notes and teaching tips is available upon request. Please visit www.blackwellpublishing.com/oatley.

Acknowledgments

As with any book, particularly a textbook, we the authors are not the only ones who brought this object into being. This text is a reflection of the work of many people: researchers and thinkers, our teachers, our students and our colleagues. We would like to thank once more those who assisted with the first edition of this text. In addition the following have contributed to this edition. We thank Jennifer Beer, Leslie Greenberg, Matt Hertenstein, Raymond Mar, Chris Oveis, and Nancy Stein, who have read chapters and offered suggestions. Raymond Mar has also helped with the finding of pictures. Mollie McNeil has helped with indexing. Others who have offered suggestions for this new edition, and help of various kinds, include Agneta Fischer, Nico Frijda, Marc Lewis, Phil Johnson-Laird, Batja Mesquita, Stephanie Shields, and a number of anonymous reviewers who gave advice on improvements that could be made from the first edition. We thank Christine Cardone, Executive Editor, and Sarah Coleman, Associate Development Editor, at Blackwell in Malden, Massachusetts, who have been wonderfully helpful and encouraging throughout. We thank Annette Abel, our copy editor, and Kitty Bocking who did the picture research, who have both been superb, as well as Leanda Shrimpton and Janey Fisher at Blackwell in Oxford, England.

The editor and publisher gratefully acknowledge the permission granted to reproduce the copyright material in this book:

M. D. S. Ainsworth & S. M. Bell, "Fig 2 Frequency of crying in the 'Strange Situation' test" in "Attachment, exploration, and separation: Illustrated by the behavior of one-year-olds in a strange situation," p. 58 from *Child Development* 41(1). The Society for Research in Child Development, Inc., 1970. Copyright © 1983 by Child Development. Reprinted by permission of Blackwell Publishing Ltd.

Rita L. Atkinson, Richard C. Atkinson, Edward E. Smith, & Daryl M. Bem, "Figs 2.6–7 Exploded view of human brain & human brain as if sliced in the midline," pp. 42–3 from *Introduction to Psychology,* 10th edn. Wadsworth, 1989. Copyright © 1989. Reprinted with permission of

Wadsworth, a division of Thomson Learning: www.thomsonrights.com. Fax 800 730 2215.

R. A. Baron, "Table 3 Positive and negative items mentioned in interview by interviewers in happy or despondent mood" in "Interviewer's mood and reaction to job applicants," p. 920 from *Journal of Applied Social Psychology* 17. V. H. Winston & Son, Inc., 1987. Copyright © V. H. Winston & Son, Inc., 360 South Ocean Boulevard, Palm Beach, FL 33480. Adapted by permission of V. H. Winston & Son, Inc. All rights reserved.

L. Berkowitz, S. Cochran, & M. Embree, "Rewards and punishments," pp. 687–700 from *Journal of Personality and Social Psychology* 40, 1981. Copyright © 1981 by Journal of Personality and Social Psychology. Reprinted by permission of the American Psychological Association and the author.

G. H. Bower, "Fig 4 Results of Bower's study of memories," p. 133 from *American Psychologist* 36. American Psychological Association, 1981. Copyright © 1981 by American Psychologist. Reprinted by permission of the American Psychological Association and the author.

Neil Carlson, "Fig 3.21: The autonomic nervous system and the target organs and functions served by the sympathetic and parasympathetic branches," p. 90 from *Foundations of Physiological Psychology*, 6th edn. Boston, MA: Allyn & Bacon, 2004. Copyright © 2004 by Pearson Education. Reprinted by permission of the publisher.

J. F. Cohn & E. Z. Tronick, "Fig 1 State transition diagrams for infants where mothers were normal or depressed" in "Three-month-old infant's reaction to simulated maternal depression," p. 189 from *Child Development* 54. The Society for Research in Child Development, Inc., 1983. Copyright © 1983 by Child Development. Reprinted by permission of Blackwell Publishing Ltd.

R. J. Davidson, "Fig 6 EEG activation" in "Anterior cerebral asymmetry and the nature of emotion," p. 145 from *Brain and Cognition* 20. Academic Press, Inc., 1992. Copyright © 1992 by Brain and Cognition. Reprinted by permission of Elsevier.

N. L. Etcoff & J. J. Magee, "Fig 1 Series of faces in equal increments from happy to sad" in "Categorical perception of facial expressions," p. 231 from *Cognition* 44. Elsevier Science Publishers, 1992. Copyright © 1992 by Cognition. Reprinted by permission of Elsevier.

Julian Jaynes, "Fig 5.5 Chimeric faces," p. 120 from *The Origin of Consciousness in the Breakdown of the Bicameral Mind*. London: Penguin Books Ltd. Copyright © 1976, 1990 by Julian Jaynes. Reprinted by permission of Houghton Mifflin Company and The Penguin Group UK. All rights reserved.

J. M. Jenkins & M. A. Smith, "Psychiatric symptoms in children whose parents had good or conflictual marriages" in "Factors protecting children living in disharmonious homes: Maternal reports," p. 64 from *Journal of the American Academy of Child and Adolescent Psychiatry* 29. Williams & Wilkins for figure. Copyright © 1990 by Journal of the American Academy of Child and Adolescent Psychiatry. Reprinted by permission of Lippincott, Williams and & Wilkins.

D. M. Mackie & L. T. Worth, "Fig 11.1 Attitude change in happy and neutral moods" in "Feeling good but not thinking straight: the impact of positive mood on persuasion," p. 206 from J. P. Forgas, *Emotion and Social Judgments*, 1991. Copyright © 1991 by Elsevier. Reprinted by permission of the publisher.

D. Morris, P. Collett, P. Marsh, & M. O'Shaughnessy, "Two coarse gestures of contempt," p. 107 in 1st edn of *Understanding Emotions from Gestures: Their origin and distribution.* London: Cape, 1979 Copyright © 1979 by D. Morris, P. Collett, P. Marsh & M. O'Shaughnessy. Reprinted by permission of The Random House Group Ltd.

K. Oatley, "Fig 30.1 The differentiation of normal emotions from depressive breakdowns" in "Life events, social cognition and depression," p. 552 from S. Fisher & J. Reason, *Handbook of Life Stress, Cognition and Health*, John Wiley & Sons, 1988. Copyright © 1988 by John Wiley & Sons Limited. Reprinted by permission of the publisher.

S. Scarr & P. Salapatek, "Fig 3.5 Fear of visual cliff, dogs, noises, and jack-in-the-box" in "Patterns of fear development during infancy," pp. 64–5 from *Merrill Palmer Quarterly* 16. Wayne State University Press, 1970. Copyright © 1970 by Merrill Palmer Quarterly. Reprinted by permission of Wayne State University Press.

R. M. Seyfarth & D. L. Cheney, "Three different kinds of fearful response by vervet monkeys" in "Meaning and mind in monkeys," p. 124 from *Scientific American* 267 (Dec.). Scientific American, Inc., 1992. Copyright © 1992 by Patricia J. Wynne. Reprinted by permission of the illustrator.

M. Sherif, "Hostility towards an outgroup" in "Experiments in group conflict," p. 58 from *Scientific American* 195. Scientific American, Inc., 1956. Copyright © 1956 by Sarah Love.

C. E. Vaughn & J. P. Leff, "Fig 1 Schizophrenic patients relapsing, as a function of High and Low Expressed Emotion of families" in "The influence of family and social factors on the course of psychiatric illness: A comparison of schizophrenic and depressed patients," p. 132 from *British Journal of Psychiatry* 129. Royal College of Psychiatrists, 1976. Copyright © 1976 by The British Journal of Psychiatry. Reprinted by permission of the journal.

Every effort has been made to trace copyright holders and to obtain their permission for the use of copyright material. The publisher apologizes for any errors or omissions in the above list and would be grateful if notified of any corrections that should be incorporated in future reprints or editions of this book.

PART I

Perspectives on Emotions

Approaches to Understanding Emotions

Figure 1.0 Young girl in hat, from Darwin (1872).

CHAPTER 1

Why is every critical moment in the fate of the adult or child so clearly colored by emotion?
Lev Vygotsky, 1987, p. 335

Contents

Introduction

Imagine you could flip a switch in your nervous system that would shut down your experience of emotions. No more tongue-tied embarrassment around a romantic interest. No more saying something in anger that you later regret. No more anxiety that interferes with your ability to do as well as you can. Would you choose to flip this switch, and be free of emotion?

If you would, you are in good company. For over two thousand years, many thinkers have argued that our emotions are base and destructive, and that the more noble reaches of human nature are achieved when our passions are controlled by our reason. Others have warned of the perils of particular emotions: so, for instance, it has often been thought that anger is always destructive to the self and to social relations. The West's most prominent early theorists of emotions, the Epicureans and Stoics (Nussbaum, 1994; Sorabji, 2000), whose influence has continued for more than 2,000 years, thought that emotions are irrational and damaging.

In this book, you will read about a different view, one that has emerged in the recent study of human emotions, the view that emotions serve important functions especially in our social lives. This does not mean that emotions are always rational. It does mean that we can make sense of emotions. As we work through the subject, you will find modest answers to old questions. Where do emotions come from in our evolutionary history? How are emotions different in different cultures? Where do emotions come from in our bodies and brains? What happens when we express our emotions? How can we cultivate emotions in our relationships, and through the life course? When are emotions dysfunctional? What is happiness?

In this introductory chapter, we lay foundations for answering these questions. We first look at early treatments of emotion, from Darwin to Aristotle, which set the stage for many of the traditions in the empirical study of emotion. We then look at how the study of emotion emerged in psychology and social science. Finally, we look at some attempts at defining emotions.

Nineteenth-century founders

We begin by looking at three theorists: Darwin, James, and Freud, who laid foundations not just for our understanding of emotions but for the whole fields respectively of evolutionary biology, psychology, and psychotherapy.

Charles Darwin: the evolutionary approach

> *Our descent, then, is the origin of our evil passions!! –*
> *The Devil under form of Baboon is our grandfather!*
> **Charles Darwin, notebook, cited in Gruber & Barrett, 1974, p. 289**

In 1872, Charles Darwin, the central figure in modern biology, published the most important book on emotions yet written – *The Expression of the Emotions in Man and Animals* (1872). Earlier, in *The Origin of Species* (1859) he had described how living things have evolved to be adapted to their environments. Knowing this, you might imagine that Darwin would have proposed that emotions had functions in our survival. Indeed many psychologists and biologists assume that this is what he did say. But he did not. His argument was both closer to common sense, and more subtle than anything that we might commonsensically believe.

Darwin began writing notes on his observations of emotions in 1838. At that time, the accepted theory was that God had given humans special facial muscles that allowed them to express uniquely human sentiments unknown to animals. A central tenet of Darwin's theory, however, was that humans are descended from other species: we are not only closer to animals than had been thought, but we ourselves are animals. Darwin gathered many kinds of observations, which would have enduring effects on the contemporary study of emotions (Darwin 1872/1998). He observed emotional expressions in nonhuman species, as well as in adult and infant humans. He was interested in both the normal and the abnormal. He enlisted the help of many people to make observations for him, including the director of a large mental asylum in the north of England. He developed new methods, realizing the importance of cross-cultural study. He was one of the first to use questionnaires: he sent a set of printed questions to missionaries and others who could observe people in other cultures, asking them to observe particular expressions. He received 36 replies. Darwin was one of the first to use photographs of naturalistic and posed expressions (such as the one at the head of this chapter) to make scientific points.

In his book on emotions, Darwin asked two broad questions that guide emotion researchers today. First, how are emotions expressed in humans and other animals? In table 1.1 we present a taxonomy of some of the expressions Darwin described.

The second question Darwin addressed is where do our emotions come from? Darwin concluded that emotional expressions derive largely from habits that in our evolutionary or individual past had once been useful. These are based on reflex-like mechanisms. Some actions occur in modern humans whether they are useful or not, and are triggered involuntarily in circumstances analogous to those that had triggered the original habits. His book is full of examples of such actions: of tears that do not function to lubricate the eyes, of laughter that seems not to assist the performance of any task, and so on.

For Darwin, emotional expressions showed the continuity of adult human behavioral mechanisms with those of lower animals and with those of infancy. Because these expressions occur in adults "though they may not . . . be of the least use," they had for Darwin a significance in evolutionary thinking rather like that of the fossils that allow us to trace the evolutionary ancestry of species. More precisely, he thought emotional expressions were like vestigial parts of our bodies. In our digestive system, for instance,

Table 1.1 Emotional expressions discussed by Darwin (1872), the bodily systems used, and the type of emotion which was expressed

Expression	Bodily system	Emotion example
Blushing	Blood vessels	Shame, modesty
Body contact	Somatic muscles	Affection
Clenching fists	Somatic muscles	Anger
Crying	Tear ducts	Sadness
Frowning	Facial muscles	Anger, frustration
Laughing	Breathing apparatus	Pleasure
Perspiration	Sweat glands	Pain
Hair standing on end	Dermal apparatus	Fear, anger
Screaming	Vocal apparatus	Pain
Shrugging	Somatic muscles	Resignation
Sneering	Facial muscles	Contempt
Trembling	Somatic muscles	Fear, anxiety

Source: Oatley (1992)

is a small, functionless organ, the appendix. Darwin proposed that this is evidence that we are descended from prehuman ancestors in whom this organ had a use. Emotional expressions have the same quality: Darwin argued that sneering, an expression in which we partially uncover the teeth on one side, is a behavioral vestige of snarling, and of preparing to bite. This preparation was functional in some distant ancestor, but is so no longer. Though we sometimes make mordant remarks, adult human beings do not now use the teeth to attack.

Darwin traced other expressions to infancy: crying, he argued, is the vestige of screaming in infancy, though in adulthood it is partly inhibited. He carefully described screaming in young babies, and gave an argument for the function of closing the eyes and the secretion of tears to help protect them when this occurred. When adults cry they still secrete tears, but he argued that tears no longer have any protective function. One of Darwin's most interesting suggestions is that patterns of adult affection, of taking those whom we love in our arms, are based on patterns of parents hugging young infants.

In Darwin's eyes, then, our emotions link us to our past, both to the past of our species and to our own infancy. In making this argument, Darwin would shape the contemporary study of emotions. He helped provide descriptions of facial expressions. He argued for the universality of expressions, an uncommon view at the time. It is a claim that has generated numerous studies, as we shall see in chapter 4. He gave a new perspective on the common question of how beneficial emotions are. It is reflected in the quotation at the head of this section. Might we be better off if we could rise above our more bestial passions, which emerged in a prehuman phase of our evolution? Although the bulk of his book is given over to examples

(a)

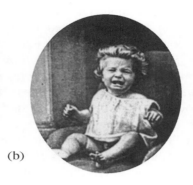
(b)

Figure 1.1 Two of Charles Darwin's photographs, sneering and crying:
(a) Plate IV No. 1; (b) Plate I No. 1.

in which emotional expressions occur whether or not they are any use,
toward the end of his book he writes:

> The movements of expression in the face and body, whatever their origin
> may have been, are in themselves of much importance for our welfare. They
> serve as the first means of communication between the mother and her infant;
> she smiles approval, and thus encourages her child on the right path, or frowns
> disapproval. We readily perceive sympathy in others by their expression
> . . . The movements of expression give vividness and energy to our spoken
> words. (Darwin, 1872/1998, p. 359)

So despite his reservations, Darwin thought that emotions have useful functions too. We return to this issue throughout the book.

William James: the bodily approach

> *. . . bodily changes follow directly the perception of the exciting fact . . . and
> feeling of the same changes as they occur, IS the emotion.*
> **James, 1890, p. 449**

In this well-known quotation from *The Principles of Psychology* (1890),
William James argued against the commonsense idea that when we feel
an emotion it impels us to a certain kind of activity – that if we were to
meet a bear in the woods we would feel frightened and run. Instead, James
thought that when we perceive the object of fear, a bear, "the exciting fact"
as he put it, then the emotion is the perception of changes of our body
as we react to that fact. When we feel frightened, James thought, what
we feel is our heart beating, our skin cold, our posture frozen, or our legs
carrying us away as fast as possible (see also Lange, 1885).

James's theory is really about the nature of emotional experience. He
stressed the way in which emotions move us bodily. We may tremble or
perspire, our heart may thump in our chest, our breathing may be taken

over by an involuntary force as we weep or laugh helplessly. The core of an emotion, James contended, is the pattern of bodily responses. This vital point about the embodied nature of emotion is captured in this idea of James: "*If we fancy some strong emotion and then try to abstract from our consciousness of it all the feelings of its bodily symptoms, we find we have nothing left behind*" (James, 1890, p. 451). This proposal of James, now over 100 years old, has guided the contemporary study of emotion in two important ways.

First, James stressed that our experience of many emotions, from fear to joy, is the set of changes of the autonomic nervous system, that part of the nervous system that supplies inner organs including the heart, the blood vessels, the stomach, and the sweat glands. James also thought that changes from movements of muscles and joints were parts of the felt bodily changes. Here James anticipates a central interest in the study of emotions: What are the distinct physiological reactions associated with the different emotions? We discuss this question in chapters 5 and 6.

Second, James proposed that emotions give "color and warmth" to experience. Without these effects of emotion, he said, everything would be pale. Colloquially we speak of "rose colored glasses" or a "jaundiced view of life" to indicate how our emotions affect our perceptions. In different parts of this book we will look at how scientists have studied this question. In particular, in chapter 10 we see that emotions guide our most important judgments, from what is right and wrong, to what is fair and just.

Sigmund Freud: the psychoanalytic approach

"*I came away from the window at once, and leant up against the wall and couldn't get my breath . . .*" (description given by Katharina, subject of one of Freud's early case histories).

Freud & Breuer, 1895

Sigmund Freud proposed that certain events, usually of a sexual kind, can be so damaging that they leave psychological scars that can affect the rest of our lives. His principal exposition was in a series of short case studies.

Consider one, the case of Katharina (Freud & Breuer, 1895, pp. 190–201). Walking in the Eastern Alps in the early 1890s Freud was approached by a young woman he called Katharina, the niece of the proprietor of the inn at which he was staying, who asked him if, as a doctor, he might help her. She described how she suffered from attacks in which she thought she would suffocate. When asked by Freud about her attacks, Katherina said: "I always see an awful face that looks at me in a dreadful way, so that I am frightened" (p. 192). She could not say whose face this was.

Freud was clear that the attacks were of anxiety. His aim in therapy was to discover how such attacks had started, and what – or whom – the feared object was. He questioned Katharina further. The attacks, she said, started some two years previously. "If you don't know," Freud said, "I'll tell you

how *I* think you got your attack . . . you must have seen or heard something that very much embarrassed you" (p. 192). "Heavens, yes!" she
replied. "That was when I caught my uncle with the girl, with Franziska,
my cousin" (p. 193). She had peeped through a window in a passage, into
a room to see her uncle lying on top of Franziska. She said: "I came away
from the window at once, and leant up against the wall and couldn't get
my breath – just what happens to me since. Everything went blank, my
eyelids were forced together and there was a hammering and buzzing in
my head" (p. 193).

Katharina maintained that the face she saw during her attacks was not
that of Franziska. It was a man's face. Was it her uncle's? She did not know.
"Why, she asked, should he have been making such a dreadful face just
then?" (p. 194). Freud agreed, but continued to question. Katharina said
that three days later she suffered from nausea and vomiting for three
days. Freud suggested she had felt disgusted when she had looked into the
room. "Yes, I'm sure I felt disgusted," she said reflectively, "but disgusted
at what?" (p. 195).

Katharina said that she had reported the incident to her aunt, who
eventually moved out with Katharina to take over the present inn, leaving
the uncle with Franziska who was by then pregnant. But, Freud says, instead
of continuing to discuss this separation, Katharina now broke off to relate
an incident from two years before these events. She had gone with her uncle
on an expedition. In the inn where they stayed he had got into bed with
her. She said she "woke up suddenly, 'feeling his body' in the bed." She
protested and went to stand by the door, ready to escape. On other occasions too, when her uncle was drunk, she had had to defend herself from
him. It was at this time she had begun to feel the pressure on her eyes and
chest, but with nothing like the strength of her current attacks.

Freud describes how, as she finished this account, "She was like someone transformed. The sulky unhappy face had grown lively, her eyes were
bright, she was lightened and exalted" (p. 197). Freud says the meaning of
the case had become clear: she had carried the two sets of experiences,
of her uncle's attempts on her, and the goings-on between her uncle and
Franziska. When she had seen her uncle on top of Franziska, her mind refused
consciously to accept the meaning. After three days' incubation, vomiting
began, an indication of her disgust. Freud gave Katharina his conclusions:
"You thought," said Freud, "now he is doing with her what he wanted
to do with me, that night and those other times." "It may well be," she replied,
"that that was what I was disgusted at, and that that was what I thought"
(p. 197).

Katharina then said the face that had persecuted her during her attacks
was now recognizable as her uncle's. It did not come from these scenes
but from the time of her uncle and aunt's divorce. He would be contorted
in rage, threatening her, saying it was all her fault.

Freud never saw Katharina again, but hoped she benefited from their conversation. In a footnote added in 1924, he wrote: "I venture after the lapse
of so many years to lift the veil of discretion and reveal the fact that Katharina

Figure 1.2 Group photograph of the conference to mark Freud's honorary degree at Clark University in 1909. In the front row Freud is fourth from the right and Jung third from the right. William James is third from the left.

was not the niece of the landlady, but her daughter. The girl fell ill, therefore, as a result of sexual attempts on the part of her own father" (p. 210).

Freud was one of the first to argue that emotions are at the core of many pathologies. Katharina would now be diagnosed as suffering from panic attacks (American Psychiatric Association, 2000). In her case we see elements of psychoanalytic therapy as it has developed since: the telling of one's life story that is found to have gaps, the filling of these gaps by "interpretations" of the therapist, and the insights of the person receiving the therapy who realizes something that had been unconscious (these issues are discussed in chapter 14). Freud's theories were critical to Richard Lazarus as he developed his theory of appraisal on the basis of goals, which we discuss in chapter 7. It was Freud's work, moreover, that prompted John Bowlby, from 1951 onward, to develop his theory of attachment – the love between an infant and its mother – and his idea that social development derives from this emotional base. We discuss this in chapter 11.

Philosophical and literary approaches

Darwin, James, and Freud laid important foundations, but they were not the first in the Western tradition to think about emotions. Philosophers have grappled with the nature of emotions, as have writers of fiction. In this section, we focus on three thinkers who influence important currents in the contemporary study of emotions.

Aristotle: the conceptual approach

... there is nothing either good or bad but thinking makes it so.
Shakespeare, Hamlet, II, 2, 1. 249–250

Aristotle, who lived from 384 to 322 BCE (Before the Common Era), offered some of the first systematic analyses of different emotions. His most fundamental insight was that emotions are connected with action. Whereas many assume that emotions happen to us outside of our control, Aristotle contended that they depend on what we believe, that they are evaluations, so we are responsible for our emotions because we are responsible for our beliefs and valuations of the world.

In his book *Rhetoric*, Aristotle had practical concerns: how do we persuade others? He offered three principles. First, a hearer is more likely to believe a good person than a bad one. Second, people are persuaded when what is said stirs their emotions. Third, people are persuaded by arguments that seem truthful. Following from the second principle, Aristotle discussed how different judgments give rise to different emotions. "Anger," he says, "may be defined as an impulse, accompanied by pain, to a conspicuous revenge for a conspicuous slight directed without justification towards what concerns oneself or towards what concerns one's friends" (1984, 1378b, 1.32). The emotion is defined cognitively, in terms of knowledge: that a slight has occurred. To be slighted is to be treated with contempt, or thwarted, or shamed.

Aristotle makes it clear that he is not interested in arousing emotions to sway people irrationally. He conceives rhetoric as a search for truth, by speaking and discussion. He says about speaking in a law court: "It is not right to pervert the judge by moving him to anger or envy or pity – one might as well warp a carpenter's rule before using it" (1984, 1354a, 1.24). He observes, however, that when speaking to persuade, you must know something about the people to whom you speak, about their values, and about the effects that speaking may have on them. When "people are feeling friendly and placable they think one sort of thing; when they are feeling angry or hostile, they think either something totally different, or the same thing with different intensity" (1377b, 1.29).

In this ancient discussion of the role of emotion in persuasion, we see the message, echoed by Shakespeare's quotation from *Hamlet* at the head of this section, that our emotional experiences are shaped by our judgments and evaluations. Think of it like this: it is a warm summer evening and you are lightly dressed, waiting in line at the theater. A light touch on your arm by the person you invited to the movie might trigger a surge of love. The very same pattern of touch from a stranger might make you feel anxious, angry, or even repelled. Our experience depends on judgment.

Solomon (2004) puts it like this: Emotions are judgments, and to understand how this occurs we can say they are subjective engagements in the world.

In *Poetics*, which is about narrative writing, mainly about tragedy, Aristotle concerned himself with other questions about emotions. Drama, said Aristotle, is about universal human action, and what can happen when well-intentioned human actions miscarry. They have effects that are unforeseen. We are human, not gods. We simply do not know enough to predict the consequences of everything we do. Nonetheless, and this is the root of human tragedy, we remain responsible for our actions.

Aristotle noticed two important effects of tragic drama. First, people are moved emotionally. As the principal character grapples with consequences that were unforeseen and uninvited, we see the somber spectacle of a person who is good being tortured by circumstances to which he or she has contributed. We are moved to feel sympathy (or pity) for this person – and to feel fear for ourselves, because in the universal appeal of these plays we know that the principal character is also ourself.

Second, we can experience what Aristotle called *katharsis* of our emotions. This term is widely mistranslated as purgation or purification, as if one goes to the theater to rid oneself of toxic emotions, or to elevate them. But as philosopher Martha Nussbaum (1986) argues, for Aristotle

Figure 1.3 The theater in classical times was an important institution. Theaters were constructed to portray action in the context of fellow citizens who sat there in full view.

katharsis meant neither purgation nor purification. It meant clarification – the clearing away of obstacles to understanding our emotions. By seeing universal predicaments of human action at the theater we may come to experience emotions of pity and fear, and understand consciously for ourselves their relation to the consequences of human action in a world that can be known only imperfectly.

So here, in the very origins of Western philosophy, we see timeless ideas about emotion that guide researchers today. We see that emotions are kinds of judgments, and we catch a glimpse of how, in the universal human pursuit of listening to and watching human stories, our own emotions are stirred. In reflection, we can come to understand why they are stirred.

René Descartes: the philosophical approach

The Passions of the Soul

book title of Descartes

René Descartes is generally regarded as the founder of modern philosophy and the scientific view of the brain. Descartes wrote in the seventeenth century in Holland, which had just blossomed from having been an obscure Spanish colony to a center of commercial and intellectual life, perhaps at that time one of the few places in Europe where bold thinkers could work and publish without persecution. Descartes focuses on the emotions in *The Passions of the Soul* (1649), the book that many think of as the basis for modern neurophysiology, with its detailed discussion of sensory and motor nerves, reflexes, and memory. As for emotions, he opens the book as follows: "There is nothing in which the defective nature of the sciences which we have received from the ancients appears more clearly than in what they have written on the passions" (p. 331).

So what new insights did Descartes offer? He claimed that six fundamental emotions – wonder, desire, joy, love, hatred, and sadness – occur in the thinking aspect of ourselves that he called the soul. At the same time they are closely connected to our bodies, for example, to our heart beating rapidly, to blushing, or to tears. Descartes differentiated emotions from other perceptions about events that happen in the outside world and perceptions that arise from events within the body, such as hunger and pain. Whereas perceptions tell us about what is important in the outside world, and bodily passions like hunger and pain tell us about important events in the body, emotions tell us what is important in our souls – as we might now say, in our real selves, our goals, our concerns, and our identities.

Having identified the origins of the emotions in our souls, Descartes then described how emotions cannot be entirely controlled by thinking, but they can be regulated by thoughts, especially thoughts which are true. So, he says:

> . . . in order to excite courage in oneself and remove fear, it is not sufficient
> to have the will to do so, but we must also apply ourselves to consider the
> reasons, the objects or examples which persuade us that the peril is not great;

that there is always more security in defense than flight; that . . . we could expect nothing but regret and shame for having fled, and so on. (Descartes, 1649, p. 352)

Like Aristotle, Descartes suggested that the emotions depend on how we evaluate events.

Descartes was also one of the first to argue that emotions serve important functions:

> . . . the utility of all the passions consists alone in their fortifying and perpetuating in the soul thoughts which it is good it should preserve, and which without that might easily be effaced from it. And again, all the harm which they can cause consists in the fact that they fortify and conserve those thoughts more than necessary, or that they fortify and conserve others on which it is not good to dwell. (ibid., p. 364)

We might reflect on how, when we love someone, our love perpetuates and extends our thoughts of this person, and when we are overanxious or depressed we dwell on issues we cannot affect. Descartes's idea, then, is that our emotions are usually functional, but can sometimes be dysfunctional – a central idea of this book.

Descartes wrote in the era that historians call the Early Modern Period. He was a contemporary of William Harvey who discovered the circulation of the blood, which formerly had been thought to be one of the four humors. Ideas of these humors derived from Greek doctors such as Hippocrates and Galen. Disease was caused by imbalance among them, and each gave rise to a distinct emotional state. Blood gives rise to hope and vigor, from it comes the term "sanguine"; phlegm gives rise to placidity, from it comes the term "phlegmatic"; yellow bile gives rise to anger, from it comes the world "choleric"; black bile gives rise to despair, from it comes the word "melancholy." Before the mid-seventeenth century it was thought that the very emanations of these humors *were* the consciousness of each kind of emotion, that we feel melancholy (for instance) from an excess of black bile that gives off the experience of sadness as a stagnant pool gives off a stench (Paster, Rowe, & Floyd-Wilson, 2004). Among those making new efforts of imagination was Descartes. His saying, "I think, therefore I am," takes us into the modern world. In the new physiology to which he contributed, emotions arise in the mind, enable our plans, and affect our bodies.

George Eliot: the literary approach

> *No life would have been possible to Dorothea which was not filled with emotion . . .*
>
> **George Eliot, Middlemarch, p. 894**

Many of the greatest insights into emotions come from novelists and poets – Virginia Woolf on the stream of consciousness, D. H. Lawrence on

Figure 1.4 William Holman Hunt's "The Hireling Shepherd." George Eliot wrote of this painting, "How little the real characteristics of the working classes are known to those who are outside them, how little their natural history has been studied . . . Even one of our greatest painters of the pre-eminently realistic school, while, in his picture 'The Hireling Shepherd,' he gave us a landscape of marvelous truthfulness, placed a pair of peasants in the foreground who were not much more real than the idyllic swans of our chimney ornaments."

emotional dynamics between women and men, J. D. Salinger on the self-consciousness of adolescence. The writing of George Eliot (pen-name of Mary Ann Evans) offers some of the most impressive ideas regarding emotional experience and its place in intimate relationships.

In 1856 she had written an essay for the *Westminster Review* entitled "The natural history of German life" (Pinney, 1963). In it she reviewed two books by von Riehl, a pioneer anthropologist, describing the life of German peasants. Her essay was a kind of manifesto for her own novels. It includes the following:

> The greatest benefit we owe to the artist, whether painter, poet or novelist, is the extension of our sympathies. Appeals founded on generalizations and statistics require a sympathy ready-made, a moral sentiment already in activity; but a picture of human life such as a great artist can give, surprises even the trivial and the selfish into that attention to what is apart from themselves, which may be called the raw material of moral sentiment . . . Art is the nearest thing to life; it is a mode of amplifying experience and extending our contact with our fellow-men beyond the bounds of our personal lot. (George Eliot, 1856, reprinted in Pinney, 1963, p. 270)

In the years 1871 to 1872, Eliot published *Middlemarch*, a novel about emotions, which portrays experience from inside the person's own consciousness. Each character has aspirations and plans, but each is affected by the unforeseeable accidents of life. George Eliot's question is this: if we are unable to foresee the outcomes of all our actions, if there is no fate or divine force guiding us toward an inevitable destiny, how should we find our way in life? Her answer is that our emotions can act as a sort of compass. They are also the principal means by which people affect each other.

In the book, Eliot contrasts Dorothea, who longs to do some good in the world, with Edward Casaubon, an elderly scholar whom she admired and married in the hope of gaining entrance to the world of learning. Dorothea is responsive to the emotional currents of her own and others' lives, whereas for all his erudition Casaubon barely recognizes his emotions at all. About a third of the way through the book, Casaubon has a heart attack in suppressed anger following an argument with Dorothea. Lydgate, the town doctor, attends and counsels Dorothea to avoid all occasions that might agitate her husband.

Some days later Lydgate makes another call and Casaubon asks him to be candid about his condition. Lydgate says that although prediction is difficult, he is at risk. Casaubon perceives that he might die, and sinks into bitterness. When Lydgate leaves, Dorothea goes into the garden with a sympathetic impulse to go at once to her husband.

> But she hesitated, fearing to offend him by obtruding herself; for her ardour, continually repulsed, served with her intense memory to heighten her dread, as thwarted energy subsides into a shudder, and she wandered slowly round the nearer clumps of trees until she saw him advancing. Then she went toward him, and might have represented a heaven-sent angel coming with a promise that the short hours remaining should yet be filled with that faithful love which clings the closer to a comprehended grief. His glance in reply to hers was so chill that she felt her timidity increased; yet turned and passed her hand through his arm.
>
> Mr Casaubon kept his hands behind him, and allowed her pliant arm to cling with difficulty against his rigid arm.
>
> There was something horrible to Dorothea in the sensation which this unresponsive hardness inflicted on her. That is a strong word, but not too strong; it is in these acts called trivialities that the seeds of joy are for ever wasted. (Eliot, 1871–1872, p. 462)

In this passage we see many of Eliot's ideas about how emotions arise and are communicated. They are what relationships are made of. They have powerful effects. We understand our own emotions differently from those of other people. We the readers are moved emotionally in ways that do indeed succeed in "extending our sympathies." Later George Eliot wrote in a letter: ". . . my writing is simply a set of experiments in life – an endeavour to see what our thought and emotion may be capable of – what stores of motive, actual or hinted as possible, give promise of a better after which we can strive" (Haight, 1985, p. 466).

Historical figure: George Eliot

George Eliot was one of the greatest English novelists. She was born Mary Ann Evans in 1819, on a farm near Coventry. Her father, Robert Evans, was a carpenter and farm manager, and her mother, Christiana Pearson, was from a yeoman family. Mary Ann learned French and German from pious teachers, and was influenced by Evangelical Christianity. At 16 she was withdrawn from school due to her mother's ill health, but by her thirties she had also learned Italian, Latin, and Greek, and had translated theological and philosophical books as well as keeping house for her father, who died when she was 30. She moved to London, calling herself Marian Evans, and became assistant editor of the *Westminster Review*. She must have been one of the few women of her time to support herself financially in such a way. She became a close friend of the philosopher and psychologist Herbert Spencer. Later she lived with George Henry Lewes until he died in 1878. Lewes was a literary critic and biologist, whose work won the esteem of Charles Darwin. Lewes was separated: his wife had left him to live with another man. Divorce was unobtainable since Lewes had tolerated the affair, so he and Marian Evans were unable to marry – a scandal to polite society. Theirs is one of the great emotional and intellectual relationships of the history of letters. They traveled, read together, commented on each other's work, discussed everything, worked on joint projects. It was Lewes who encouraged her to start writing fiction. *The Mill on the Floss* (Eliot, 1860) established her reputation, and brought financial security. Lewes was delighted at her success, even when it outstripped his own. (Biographical information from Haight, 1968.)

Brain science, psychology, sociology

Thus far we have considered how founding figures grappled with the nature of emotions. How would the scientific study of emotions emerge? During the twentieth century there would be some resistance. The currents of psychology were first of behaviorism, and then of cognitive psychology, both of which tended to ignore emotions. In the past 50 years, however, at first gradually, and then with gathering momentum, the study of emotions has come into its own in the brain sciences, in psychology, and in the social sciences.

Walter Cannon and Walter Hess: brain science

> *Most often the cat in its defense/attack reaction turns against the nearest person participating in the experiment.*
> **Hess & Brügger, 1943, p. 184**

Before the age of electronics, and the finding that the brain itself works by sending electrical signals from neuron to neuron, the main findings about brain function came from brain lesions, either made deliberately in animals, or accidentally in people. Among the pioneers of this kind of research as it affected emotions was Walter Cannon, professor of physiology at Harvard from 1906 until he retired in 1942. He argued against his Harvard colleague, William James. He starts a paper in 1927 by citing observations by commentators that James's theory is "so strongly fortified by truth and so repeatedly confirmed by experience" (p. 106) that he felt trepidation at venturing to criticize it. Cannon uses the term "trepidation" rhetorically. It is unlikely that he felt any such thing. His 1927 paper was one in a line of published criticisms he made of the James–Lange theory. His principal evidence was that if James were right, then when the viscera (from which bodily feelings were supposed by James to arise) were severed from the brain of laboratory animals, one would expect a reduction in their emotions. With this operation, however, no such reduction occurred.

Instead, as Cannon found, it was transection of neural pathways at a quite different level that had huge and striking effects on emotions. Cannon showed that when, in a laboratory cat, the cerebral cortex was severed from the lower parts (subcortical regions) of the brain, or removed altogether, the result was an animal that showed very intense emotions, for instance, anger with no provocation. The phenomenon contributed to the idea that higher regions of the brain – the cortex – act to inhibit its lower regions where emotions reside.

Accidents to people have pointed to similar conclusions. A famous case was that of Phineas Gage, foreman of a railway construction gang in Vermont. On September 13, 1848, he was about to blast a rock, which was drilled and the hole filled with gunpowder. Gage rammed the powder down with an iron rod, three and a half feet long, an inch and a quarter in diameter, weighing 13 pounds. This tamping iron must have struck up a spark, for there was an explosion. The rod entered Gage's skull just beneath the left eyebrow, exited from a hole in the top of his head, and landed 50 feet away. He bled terribly, suffered an infection of his wound, but recovered, in body though not in mind. The country doctor, John Harlow, who attended him wrote that the "balance, so to speak, between his intellectual faculties and his animal propensities seems to have been destroyed" (Harlow, 1868, p. 277). Though previously amiable, he was now impatient, irreverent, and easily moved to anger. His employers, who had regarded him as their "most efficient and capable foreman," could not give him back his job.

Antonio Damasio starts his book *Descartes' Error* (1994) with the case of Phineas Gage. Damasio's book takes Cannon's idea forward to show that the cortex, in particular the frontal region, exercises an important modulating function on human emotions. As we shall see in chapter 6, Damasio et al. (2000) have shown in brain imaging studies that the experience of human emotions derives not from the cortex, but from subcortical regions.

When electronics became available, brain researchers were no longer confined to studying the results of damage to the brain; they could stimulate the brain electrically. The results confirmed inferences that had been

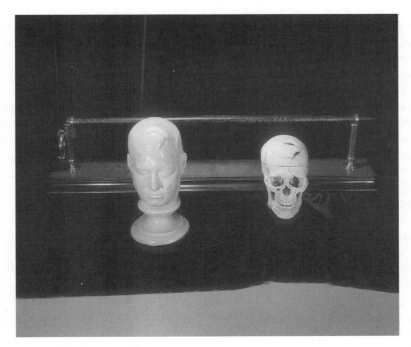

Figure 1.5 Model of Phineas Gage's head, his skull showing the exit hole made by the iron tamping rod in 1848, and the tamping rod itself.

drawn from lesions. Well-coordinated patterns of response, propensities characteristic of emotions, can be induced experimentally by electrically stimulating subcortical areas of the brain. The pioneer was the Swiss physiologist Walter Hess, working in his laboratory in Zurich.

During the 1920s Hess conceived a novel and technically demanding program of research (Hess, 1950). He developed insulated wires one-hundredth of an inch in diameter to use as electrodes, a new kind of electrical stimulation, and maps of the brain derived from thin slices of brain tissue. He implanted the electrodes into the hypothalamic regions of the brains of cats. When the cats recovered from their operations, electrical stimulation could be applied to their brains via these electrodes, as the animals moved freely around.

Hess's striking result for understanding emotions was this: When electrodes had been implanted into one region of the hypothalamus, stimulation produced the following response: the heart speeded up, the cat became alert and aroused, and if the stimulation were continued it would become angry, even ferociously attacking objects in its environment. "Most often the cat in its defense/attack reaction turns against the nearest person participating in the experiment" (Hess & Brügger, 1943, p. 184). Hess called the reaction an "affective defense reaction," and suggested that one region of the hypothalamus was specialized to organize responses of fighting or fleeing. From another region of the hypothalamus, stimulation slowed the heart and induced calmness and drowsiness. Stimulation of neighboring areas of the hypothalamus produced other well-coordinated, recognizable, emotional responses characteristic of the species. Emotions seem to depend on programs based in the brain.

So, the result of research by Cannon and Hess is that areas of the brain such as the hypothalamus and the closely associated limbic system are said to be lower, in that they were prominent in animals that emerged earlier in the course of vertebrate evolution. These regions are associated with emotions. Areas in the more recently evolved cerebral cortex may function to modulate the output of the hypothalamus and limbic system. So, if the higher centers are damaged, as occurred with Phineas Gage, this control of lower centers may no longer occur. Emotional behavior may be uncoordinated and unsocialized.

This view is consistent generally with what is known about the development of the nervous system. What are described as lower parts of the nervous system, such as the spinal cord and medulla, are concerned with simple reflexes – reflexes are characteristic of the evolutionarily oldest vertebrates. The behavior of human infants too is thought at first to be largely a set of reflexes. Layers in the middle of the brain were added next in evolution and they come next to mature in the brain of the developing individual. They include the hypothalamus and the limbic system. These are concerned with emotions, such as anger. Such patterns are seen frequently in lower mammals, and in young children not yet socialized. Finally the cortex has evolved. In human adulthood it modulates the reflex and emotional centers below it.

In 1949 Hess was awarded a Nobel Prize for Medicine and Physiology. It is an odd quirk of history that he shared the prize with Egas Moniz who had developed the operation of prefrontal leucotomy for the relief of certain psychoses. This operation causes similar effects to those that Phineas Gage performed accidentally on himself. It produces emotional blunting, which can be soothing to agitated psychotics, although it was the downfall of poor Phineas Gage.

Magda Arnold and Sylvan Tomkins: new psychological theories

> . . . emotions involve a double reference, both to the object and to the self experiencing the object.
>
> **Magda Arnold and J. Gasson, 1954**

> It is my intention to reopen issues which have long remained in disrepute in American psychology.
>
> **Sylvan Tomkins, 1962**

In the second half of the twentieth century, faintly at first, voices were heard expressing concerns that emotions had been neglected in the academy.

Among the voices were those of Magda Arnold and Sylvan Tomkins; in 1954 both published something that became influential. Arnold (with J. Gasson, 1954) proposed that emotions are based on appraising events, and Tomkins offered a theory about emotions and facial expressions.

Most researchers now assume that emotions follow appraisals of an event, a view similar to Aristotle's idea of emotions as evaluations (Nussbaum, 2001). If we know what appraisals (or evaluations) are made we can predict the emotion; if we know what the emotion is we can infer the appraisals.

Arnold and Gasson proposed that an emotion relates self to object. Unlike perception, which is about our knowledge of what is out there, or personality, which is about what each of us is like in ourselves, emotions are essentially relational. Arnold and Gasson put it like this: "An emotion . . . can be considered as the felt tendency toward an object judged suitable, or away from an object judged unsuitable" (1954, p. 294).

So appraisals involve at first attraction to, or repulsion from, some object, and they dictate whether the emotion is positive or negative. Then come further distinctions, depending on whether the object is present or not, and whether there are difficulties in acting. "Impulsive" emotions arise if there is no difficulty in attaining or avoiding an object. The "emotions of contention" arise when there are difficulties in acting. Specific emotions, Arnold and Gasson argue, arise according to these appraisals. If an object is judged suitable and if it is present, then the impulse emotion is love; if an object is judged unsuitable and is not present, then the contending emotion is fear. These ideas would be widely influential, as we shall see in chapter 7.

Like Magda Arnold, Sylvan Tomkins saw emotions as central to human life. His hypotheses were first proposed at a meeting of the International Congress of Psychology in 1954 and published in a series of complex books starting in 1962. Tomkins's central claim is that affect is the primary motivational system. Emotions are amplifiers of drives. It had long been assumed that drives, such as hunger, thirst, and sex, are the primary determinants of behavior. Not so, argued Tomkins: "This is a radical error. The intensity, the urgency, the imperiousness, the 'umph' of drives is an illusion. The illusion is created by the misidentification of the drive 'signal' with its 'amplifier.' Its amplifier is its affective response" (Tomkins, 1970, p. 101). In Tomkins's account, human action and thought reflect the interplay of motivational systems, each capable of fulfilling a certain function (eating, breathing, sex), each potentially capable of taking over the whole person. What prioritizes these systems? It is emotion. It does so by amplifying one particular drive signal, just as loudness of sound on an audio system is amplified by turning up a control to adjust its volume.

Here are two of Tomkins's illustrations. First: when, for any reason, there is some sudden obstruction to breathing, as when drowning or choking, it is not the shortness of oxygen that is obvious, it is a panicky fear that amplifies the drive signal making us struggle to breathe again. Those pilots in World War II who refused to wear oxygen masks suffered lack of oxygen, said Tomkins, but slowly. The effect was not unpleasant. The signal was not amplified, and some of these pilots died with smiles on their lips. Second: when we are sexually excited, it is not the sexual organs that become emotionally excited. It is the person who is excited, and moves toward the other person and to fulfillment. The bodily changes, for instance in the sex organs, amplify the sexual drive, making it urgent, and taking priority over other matters.

Tomkins offered arguments that would inspire the study of facial expression. He claimed that changes of facial expressions are the primary amplifiers of emotions in humans. Emotion-related changes in blood flow and muscle movements in the face direct attention to some particular need or goal. We will return to these ideas about the face in chapter 4.

Arnold, with her idea of appraisal, can be seen as focusing largely on inputs, on the perceptual side; Tomkins, with his idea of bodily feedback and priorities among drives focused on outputs, on the motor side. What they had in common was a concept of emotions as central to normal functioning, which made possible a new era of research.

Stanley Schachter and Jerome Singer, and Alice Isen: the new experimenters

> *The warm glow of success*
> **From the title of a paper by Alice Isen, 1970**

For psychology, the period from the 1950s to the 1970s was a time of renewal and expansion. Psychology became popular with undergraduates, and popular as a research discipline. The *Zeitgeist* was for experimentation. In perception and learning, as well as in social psychology, the ideal was to find some participants (animals or people), and randomly assign each either to an experimental manipulation or to a control group, in order to compare the effect of the experimental manipulation with that of the control condition. Although less frequently the objects of enquiry than memory or social persuasion at this time, emotions were also studied experimentally. Perhaps the most famous experiment on emotions in this era was performed by Stanley Schachter and Jerome Singer (1962). In their experiment, which we discuss further in chapter 5, they found that participants injected with adrenaline (also known as epinephrine), which has an arousing effect, felt and acted happily when they were put with an accomplice of the experimenter who was laughing and larking about. By comparison, participants felt and acted angrily when they were put in an insulting situation of having to answer a rudely intrusive questionnaire, and were accompanied by the experimenter's accomplice who expressed anger at this questionnaire. These effects only occurred, however, when participants were uninformed as to the physiological effects of the injection. By comparison, subjects who were given the injection and informed that it would make them feel aroused and perhaps jumpy, did not become as happy or angry as the un-informed subjects.

Schachter and Singer's theory was that emotion has two parts: a bodily physiological arousal of the kind proposed by William James, and an appraisal of the kind described by Magda Arnold. Influential though it was, the reported findings of Schachter and Singer's experiment – that emotion is actually produced by arousal plus appraisal – have not been replicated (Manstead & Wagner, 1981; Reisenzein, 1983). What has happened, however, is that there are now many demonstrations that emotions elicited in one way can be mistakenly attributed to some other aspect of a situation. One of the most engaging studies of this effect was performed by Dutton & Aron (1974). They recruited young male passers-by who were not accompanied by a female, who crossed the Capilano suspension bridge (near Vancouver, Canada). This bridge is 450 feet long, and has cables that act as low handrails. One walks across on boards suspended from steel cables. The whole bridge rocks and sways alarmingly, so one fears one will fall more than 200 feet to the rocks and rapids of the Capilano River below. The comparison group was of young men who crossed a fixed cedar bridge, further upstream, that is firm, wide, and only 10 feet above the river. At the other side of each bridge, each man was met either by a young woman or by a young man, who asked them to take part in a study she or he was conducting for a psychology class on the subject of scenic attractions. Subjects were asked to fill out a short questionnaire and part of the Thematic Apperception Test, which consists of pictures with ambiguous meanings. The picture used in this experiment was of a young woman covering her face with one hand and reaching out with the other. After completing the questions, the interviewer wrote her or his phone number on a piece of paper, gave it to the subject, and asked him to phone if he wanted to talk further. Sexual imagery in response to the ambiguous picture was significantly higher for subjects met by the female than by the male interviewer, and it was increased in the group who crossed the high suspension bridge as compared with the group who crossed the low sturdy bridge. Not only that, but many more phone calls to the female interviewer were made by men who crossed the suspension bridge than by those who crossed the low bridge.

This is one of the most imaginative studies in experimental psychology. To solve the problem of whether their results might be explained because those who crossed the high suspension bridge were more adventurous than those who crossed the low fixed bridge, Dutton and Aron included a laboratory study in their paper, in which subjects saw "an attractive female" (an accomplice of the experimenters) in a laboratory, though they did not talk to her. She was supposedly a participant like themselves in an experiment on the effects of electric shock. Each participant and the accomplice tossed a coin to find whether they would receive a painful or a non-painful shock, and each went to a separate cubicle to complete a questionnaire and do the same Thematic Apperception Test item that was used after crossing the bridges. Those participants who were more anxious in expectation of the painful shock were more attracted to the female accomplice, and had more sexual imagery to the picture in the Thematic Apperception Test, than those who expected the non-painful shock.

The effect of transferring arousal has been widely replicated. Foster et al. (1998) performed a meta-analysis of 33 experiments on the effect. A meta-analysis is an integrative review of many studies on a particular question. The idea is to find the average effect size, or magnitude of causal relationship, across a set of studies. Typically this effect size is expressed as the mean difference between experimental and control group scores expressed in terms of the standard deviation of the control group. In their meta-analysis Foster et al. found that arousal did increase sexual attraction.

In Dutton and Aron's experiment an emotion was not created, as Schachter and Singer had supposed, from non-specific arousal plus appraisal. The specific emotion of fear was first evoked by crossing a high swaying bridge; the participants who crossed it rated their fear as high. Then some of its effects transferred to amorousness.

In a different set of experiments that occurred early in the scientific study of emotions, Alice Isen has found that emotions such as happiness also have transferable effects. In one experiment (1970) she gave a test of perceptual-motor skills. Some people, randomly selected, were told that they had succeeded in this test, and as a result were made mildly happy. As compared with other subjects who had taken the same perceptual motor test but who were not told they had succeeded, they were more likely to help a stranger (an associate of the experimenter) who dropped her books.

Perhaps the most striking of Isen's experiments, however, dealt not with social responses but with cognitive effects. Isen et al. (1978) induced a mildly happy mood in people in a shopping mall by giving them a free gift. In an apparently unrelated consumer survey, these people said their cars and television sets performed better than those of control subjects who had received no gift. In subsequent research, Isen has shown that happiness has widespread effects on cognitive organization (Isen et al., 1978), which we summarize in table 1.2. It can make people more creative in problem solving, and induce them to give more unusual associations to words.

Isen's work provided some of the first evidence on how emotions affect our perception of the social world – a notion advanced by Aristotle and others. The finding that an emotion or mood experienced in one situation can affect behavior, social judgments, and the intensity of emotions in other situations is now one of the most firmly established effects in experimental social psychology (Forgas, 2000; Forgas & Laham, 2005; Martin & Clore, 2001). The effect is strongest when the person concerned does not know the source of their original mood. In chapter 7, we will consider in more depth how emotions influence social cognition. These findings have been useful in clinical psychology: for instance, the selective bringing to mind of sad incidents when in a sad mood may be important in the persistence of depression (see chapter 13).

Table 1.2 Examples of effects found by Isen and her associates in which happiness was induced. In each study comparisons were made with effects of neutral and/or negative moods

Study	Method of induction	Effect of induction
Isen, 1970	Told of skill success	Larger donation to charity, and help stranger
Isen & Levin, 1972	Given cookies	More helpful, less annoying in library
Isen et al., 1978	Free gift	Better recall of positive memories Report fewer problems with consumer goods
Isen et al., 1985	Positive word association and two other methods	More unusual word associations
Carnevale & Isen, 1986	Cartoons and gift	Integrative bargaining, less contentiousness
Isen & Geva, 1987	Bag of candy	More cautious about loss when risk is high, less cautious about loss when risk is low
Isen et al., 1987	Comedy film or candy	Better creative problem solving
Kraiger, Billings, & Isen, 1989	Watching TV bloopers	More satisfaction in performing task
Isen, 1990	"Stickers" for children	More advanced developmental levels
Isen et al., 1991	Told of anagram success	Faster clinical diagnosis, extra interest in patients

Erving Goffman and Arlie Russell Hochschild: the dramaturgical perspective

Create alarm
Slogan on an office wall of a debt-collecting agency

Erving Goffman proposed that when Shakespeare wrote "all the world's a stage" (in *As You Like It*, 1623) this was not just metaphor: we literally give dramatic presentations of ourselves to each other, and create the social reality in which we live as a kind of play. From such performances moral worlds are created, from them we derive our own selfhood, and from them others derive their sense of who we are.

Experimentation is not the only way of doing science. Goffman, a sociologist, introduced into social science the method of careful observation through a theoretical lens. His lens was his idea that life is a kind of drama, in which we take on roles. For understanding emotions, Goffman's most instructive work is perhaps the essay "Fun in games," published in his book

Encounters (1961). It is one of the most important analyses since Aristotle of the nature of happiness. It is also a reworking in social terms of Freud's *The Psychopathology of Everyday Life* (1901). It shows how emotions are constructed within specific roles, such as being with your family, or with your boss, or with a first date.

We can think of each kind of social interaction, in a shop, in the workplace, in the family, as like a game, says Goffman. When we enter it, we pass through an invisible membrane into a little world with its own rules, its own traditions, its own history. We take on the role that is afforded in that kind of interaction – in a game of tennis perhaps we serve first, in a school or university perhaps our role is to be a student. Within the membrane, we give a certain performance to sustain our role, following the outline rules or scripts that are relevant within that world. So in tennis we try to hit the ball over the net, as a student we try to learn. These performances are viewed by ourselves and others as good or bad of their kind, as correct, incorrect, or partially correct. They invite commentary from others – including suggested modifications, blame, and praise. The distinctive rules within each kind of membrane provide for moral worlds that provide the subject for much of our conversation.

Now comes Goffman's insight into emotions: as well as giving a more or less good performance we can ask how strongly engaged we are in a role. Games are fun because they invite wholehearted engagement (we discuss this further in chapter 9). By extension, we can see that happiness occurs more generally when we are engaged fully in what we are doing. But in much of life there can be inner conflict: we can follow the rules, enact the script, take part in the interaction, but not be engaged. We might prefer to be doing something else. Then occur some of the painful and unsatisfying aspects of our lives.

Arlie Hochschild was influenced by Goffman. In her work she explored the tension that may occur when the person is in conflict about the role he or she plays, when there are questions about who one is in oneself, and the performance one is giving.

Hochschild's parents were in the US Foreign Service, and she describes how at the age of 12 she found herself passing round a dish of peanuts at a diplomatic party and wondering whether the smiles of those who accepted her offerings were real. Her parents often commented on gesture: the "tight smile of the Bulgarian emissary, the averted glance of the Chinese consul, and the prolonged handshake of the French economic officer" (Hochschild, 1983, p. ix). These gestures did not just convey meaning from one person to another – they were messages between governments. Had the 12-year-old just passed peanuts to actors playing prescribed diplomatic roles? Where did the person end and the job begin? How much of emotion is not involuntary, but a dramatic performance guided by strategy and rules?

As a graduate student Hochschild sought answers to this problem: do sales people sell the product, or their personalities? She developed a theory of "feeling rules." These rules can be private and unconscious, or socially engineered in occupations that require us to influence other people's emotions and judgments.

Hochschild observed the training of Delta Airlines cabin staff, which includes learning how to act in emergencies, how to serve food, and so on. But what Hochschild described was how, in becoming a Delta stewardess, one had to learn to give a particular kind of performance. The trainee had to play a role, much as if she were an actress. The main aim is to induce a particular emotional tone in passengers: "Trainees were exhorted: to 'Really work on your smiles . . . your smile is your biggest asset' " (Hochschild, 1983, p. 105). They "were asked to think of a passenger as if he were a 'personal guest in your living room'. The workers' emotional memories of offering personal hospitality were called up and put to use, as Stanislavski would recommend" (p. 105). Both practicing particular expressions and recalling memories to aid performances are parts of the training that Stanislavski (1965) proposed for professional actors; it is now generally referred to as method acting. It is easier to give a convincing performance when one fully enters into the part.

Work that involves constructing emotions in oneself in order to induce them in others is quite widespread: Hochschild calls it emotional labor. She calculated that in 1970, 38 percent of paid jobs in the USA needed substantial emotional labor. Within the job categories that called for such labor there were roughly twice as many women as men. The purposes served are social. The job of secretary requires amiability, cheerfulness, helpfulness: its purpose includes providing pleasant emotional support for the boss. Many jobs that require emotional labor are at interfaces between companies and customers. As in the airline business, often their purpose is to sell more of the company's product.

Not all jobs requiring emotional labor are intended to induce pleasant emotions. Being a debt collector is something like the opposite of being an airline stewardess: "Create alarm" was the motto of one debt-collecting agency boss (Hochschild, 1983, p. 146).

Goffman and Hochschild offered a rather different view of emotion than the ones we considered previously. In this view, culture-related roles, values, and social obligations affect our emotions – a central theme in our treatment of culture and emotion in chapter 3.

What is an emotion? Preliminary distinctions

Thus far, we have encountered what scholars have said about emotions. They have framed many of the questions that we will try to answer in this book. They have also begun the task of understanding emotions. Descartes, for example, differentiated emotions from bodily states like hunger and pain. Sylvan Tomkins differentiated emotions from specific drives, like thirst or hunger. Let's push this effort a step further, and concentrate on two questions: What is an emotion? And how do emotions differ from related phenomena, such as moods, emotional disorders, and personality traits?

Theorists' conceptions of emotion

To start this task, let's look at theorists' definitions of emotion in table 1.3. Definitions of emotions are rather odd affairs. They tend to be offered by people in order to summarize huge amounts of research. They are not conceived as sets of necessary and sufficient conditions. All the same, there have been complaints that emotion is too heterogeneous a category to define (Mandler, 1984; Griffiths, 1997). We nonetheless believe that theorists' definitions, as seen in table 1.3, are valuable pointers. Many scholars agree that emotions serve important functions, and that they help individuals with their goals. As Barrett and Campos put it (table 1.3), they help the individual "maintain significant relationships to the environment."

What sort of functions do emotions serve? The view we explore in this book is that emotions are profoundly social. Emotions help us form attachments to offspring, to form friendships and romantic bonds, and to negotiate social hierarchies. In table 1.3, many of the "fundamental life tasks" to which Ekman refers are social, and as Lutz and White put it, they help negotiate "social relations of the self in a moral order."

Table 1.3   Proposed definitions of emotion by leading theorists

James, 1884	My thesis . . . is that the bodily changes follow directly the perception of the exciting fact, and that our feeling of the same changes as they occur is the emotion.
Arnold & Gasson, 1954	An emotion or an affect can be considered as the felt tendency towards an object judged suitable, or away from an object judged unsuitable, reinforced by specific bodily changes.
Lutz & White, 1986	Emotions are a primary idiom for defining and negotiating social relations of the self in a moral order.
Barrett & Campos, 1987	We conceive of emotions as bidirectional processes of establishing, maintaining, and/or disrupting significant relationships between an organism and the (external or internal) environment.
Tooby & Cosmides, 1990	An emotion corresponds to a distinctive system of coordination among the mechanisms that regulate each controllable biological process. That is, each emotional state manifests design features "designed" to solve particular families of adaptive problems, whereby psychological mechanisms assume unique configuration.
Lazarus, 1991	Emotions are organized psychophysiological reactions to news about ongoing relationships with the environment.
Ekman, 1992	Emotions are viewed as having evolved through their adaptive value in dealing with fundamental life-tasks. Each emotion has unique features: signal, physiology, and antecedent events. Each emotion also has characteristics in common with other emotions: rapid onset, short duration, unbidden occurrence, automatic appraisal, and coherence among responses.
Frijda & Mesquita, 1994	Emotions . . . are, first and foremost, modes of relating to the environment: states of readiness for engaging, or not engaging, in interaction with that environment.

In reading these theorists' definitions, it is clear that emotions have several components (Lang et al., 1993; Levenson, 1999). We express emotions in facial movements, posture, gesture, touch, and the voice. Emotions involve physiological responses in the body and brain. They involve specific action tendencies. We represent our experience of emotion in a language that reaches inspiring forms in poetry, music, and art. Emotions color our thoughts and enable our reasoning. These different facets will organize our chapters on communication, autonomic physiology, central nervous system physiology, and language, experience, and appraisal. We shall see that these different elements of emotions serve different functions, and together, help the individual respond adaptively to the social environment.

Putting these insights together, one may treat **emotions**, at least to start with, as *multi-component responses to challenges or opportunities that are important to the individual's goals, particularly social ones*.

Before the age of science, definitions used to be all-important for understanding. Now we know that it is more important to understand deeply how a particular process works. Think of it like this. Several hundred years ago the motions of planets were defined as circular. It was not until the understandings offered by Newton, that planetary motions depended on the forces of gravity and inertia acting at right angles to each other, that it was understood that planetary motions were better understood as ellipses. Understanding had to precede proper definition. Writing a textbook relies on a good start having been made in a field of research, and we believe a good start has been made on understanding emotions, but we have not yet reached the equivalent of the Newtonian stage. So let us regard definitions as suggestions and starting points, rather than matters to be contentious about. But let us also distinguish emotions from several other related processes, in what might be called the affective realm.

The affective realm: emotions – moods – dispositions

The English language has hundreds of words to describe how people feel. We might say that our roommate is angry, or irritated, or hostile. We might say that we ourselves are feeling sad, or blue, or depressed. Many scientists use the word "affect" to encompass phenomena that have anything to do with emotions, moods, dispositions, and preferences, though some people refer to this whole realm as that of the emotions. In figure 1.6 we show this spectrum in terms of the duration of each kind of state.

Episodes of emotion

The term "emotion" or "emotion episode" is generally used for states that last a limited amount of time. As indicated in figure 1.6, facial expressions and most bodily responses generally last for a few seconds. When researchers record states of which people are conscious and can report, by asking them to keep structured diaries of these episodes, or by getting people to remember episodes of emotions, people typically report experiences lasting between a few minutes and a few hours. Sometimes,

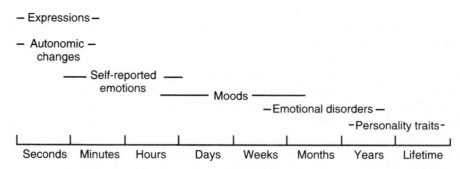

Figure 1.6 A spectrum of affective phenomena in terms of the time course of each.

however, the term "emotional" can have a wider reach, and mean the same as "affective."

Moods

The term "mood" refers to a state that typically lasts for hours, days, or weeks, sometimes as a low-intensity background. When it starts or stops may be unclear. Whereas episodes of emotion typically have an object, moods are often objectless, free-floating (Frijda, 1993a). We feel emotions about specific people and events. Philosophers call the focus of an emotional experience its "intentional object." When you are angry, you have a very clear sense of what you are angry about (e.g., your roommate's arrogance or your dad telling an embarrassing story about your first date). When you are in an irritable mood, in contrast, it is not so obvious why you feel as you do: the intentional object is not clear.

Emotional disorders

Emotional disorders such as depression and clinical anxiety states last for weeks or months, some for many years. Such disorders are now routinely assessed by research interviews, which relate them to categories in the *Diagnostic and Statistical Manual of Mental Disorders*, DSM-IV-TR (American Psychiatric Association, 2000). Thus major depression is a mood disorder that includes depressed mood, or loss of interest or pleasure in most activities, that lasts at least two weeks. It is a matter of considerable research interest to find what relation episodes of depression have to normal episodes of sadness. We will take up this issue further in chapters 12 and 13.

Personality

In a further step along the spectrum, there are terms used to describe aspects of personality that can last a lifetime. We say that people are "warm" or "sarcastic." Many aspects of temperament or personality have an emotional component: shyness implies a tendency to social anxiety, agreeableness involves a tendency to feel love and compassion. The term "trait" is used to designate any long-lasting aspect of personality. As we shall see in chapter 11, many significant aspects of personality have emotional cores, and these emotional tendencies shape the kinds of lives people lead.

Summary

This book is about understandings of emotions. It will take you on a tour of studies of far-away cultures and the inner workings of the brain. The new sciences that contribute most to our book, however, have old and influential roots. Our task in this chapter has been to provide a sampling of insights into the nature of emotions, by reviewing the claims of formative thinkers, from Aristotle to Freud, who have identified some of the abiding questions that concern us in this book. What are emotions? How do we express them? Where do our emotions come from? How are they registered in our bodies and brains? How do emotions shape our reasoning? What functions do emotions serve? How do they act as compasses in our relationships?

We charted the emergence of studies of emotion in brain science with figures such as Cannon and Hess who sought to identify specific areas of the brain associated with emotions. We described the approaches of Arnold and Tomkins, whose theories have been highly influential. We reviewed the coming of the experimentalists such as Schachter and Singer, and Isen. We saw how Goffman and Hochschild worked in the sociological tradition to show how emotions are constructed within particular roles we adopt in our social life.

Finally, we offered some preliminary definitions of emotion as functional, specific, responses that help us navigate our social environment. Emotions are briefer and more specific than moods, emotional disorders, and personality traits. In the next chapter we put these questions and claims to use as we consider evolutionary approaches to emotions.

Further reading

Two excellent comprehensive handbooks on emotions are:
Michael Lewis & Jeannette Haviland (Eds.) (2000). *Handbook of emotions, second edition*. New York: Guilford.
Richard Davidson, Klaus Scherer, & Hill Goldsmith (Eds.) (2003). *Handbook of affective sciences*. New York: Oxford University Press.

A recent and useful volume, the fourth in a series on Feelings and Emotions that started with the Wittenberg Symposium in 1927, is:
Antony Manstead, Nico Frijda, & Agneta Fischer (2004). *Feelings and emotions: The Amsterdam Symposium*. Cambridge: Cambridge University Press.

Two important books that range across diverse approaches to emotions including philosophy, psychology, sociology, narrative literature – while integrating these different approaches are:

Thomas Scheff (1997). *Emotions, the social bond, and human reality: part/whole analysis*. New York: Cambridge University Press.

Martha Nussbaum (2001). *Upheavals of thought: The intelligence of emotions*. New York: Cambridge University Press.

For a brief history of emotion research:

George Mandler (1984). *Mind and body: Psychology of emotions and stress*. New York: Norton, chapter 2 "The psychology of emotion: Past and present."

For an engaging general account of emotions and their properties:

Nico Frijda (1988). The laws of emotion. *American Psychologist, 43*, 349–358.

For discussions of unanswered questions in the study of emotion:

Paul Ekman & Richard Davidson (Eds.) (1995). *The nature of emotion*. New York: Oxford University Press.

For Darwin's classic text on expression together with a contemporary commentary:

Charles Darwin (1872/1998). *The expression of emotions in man and animals* (3rd edition, edited by Paul Ekman). New York: Oxford University Press.

Evolution of Emotions

Contents

Figure 2.0 About ten minutes before this photograph was taken these two male chimpanzees had a fight that ended in the trees. Now one extends a hand toward the other in reconciliation. Immediately after this they embraced each other and climbed down to the ground together.

In 1860, on hearing that humans are descended from apes, the wife of the Bishop of Worcester is said to have remarked: "My dear, descended from the apes! Let us hope it is not true, but if it is, let us pray that it does not become generally known" (Leakey & Lewin, 1991, p. 16). Though we are not exactly descended from present-day apes we do share common ancestors with them. The line that led to modern humans is thought to have diverged from that leading to modern chimpanzees some six million years ago. And evolution from other animals has become the central theory in biology. It also offers central insights into the nature of emotions (Dawkins, 1986; Ekman, 1992; Keltner, Haidt, & Shiota, in press).

As has often been remarked, Darwin (1859) dethroned human beings from their place as unique creations in the image of God. A piece of Darwin's evidence was the similarity of human emotional **expressions** to those of lower animals. Darwin (1872) argued that human emotional expressions have some primitive aspects. Fridlund (1994, p. 14) cites Darwin as having written, in a letter to Alfred Wallace in 1867, that in his book on emotional expression he wanted "to upset Sir C. Bell's view . . . that certain muscles have been given to man solely that he may reveal to other men his feelings." His hypothesis that emotional expressions are behavioral vestiges was described in chapter 1. Darwin wrote that "some expressions, such as the bristling of the hair under the influence of extreme terror, or the uncovering of the teeth under that of furious rage, can hardly be understood, except under the belief that man once existed in a much lower and animal-like condition" (1872, p. 12).

Darwin's specific analysis of facial expression would give birth to the modern study of emotional expression, as we shall see in chapter 4. His broader theory of **evolution** would change how scholars think about emotion. Understanding the evolutionary approach to emotion is the task of this chapter.

Elements of an evolutionary approach to emotions

The engine that drives evolution has three parts. The first of these Darwin called **superabundance**: animals and plants produce more offspring than necessary merely to reproduce themselves. The second is **variation**; each offspring is somewhat different than others, and differences are passed on by heredity. The third is **natural selection**: characteristics that allow the individual to be adapted to the environment are selected for; disadvantageous characteristics are selected against.

Selection pressures

At the core of natural selection are **selection pressures**. For humans these are features of the physical and social environment in which humans evolved, that determined whether or not individuals survived and reproduced. Some selection pressures involve threats or opportunities directly related to physical survival. To survive, the individual needs to find food and water, to stay warm but avoid extreme heat, to avoid predation and disease. Many systems such as our preferences for sweet foods and aversion to bitter foods, our thermoregulatory systems, our fight and flight responses, developed in response to these kinds of selection pressures.

Hereditary elements that Darwin was ignorant of, but that we now know as genes, are passed during reproduction from one generation to the next. Two kinds of sexual selection pressures determine who reproduces. **Intrasexual competition** occurs within a sex for access to mates. In many species there is intense and continual struggle of this kind, often most pronounced among males. Stags lock horns and engage in ritualized, at times violent, battles to find who is dominant and gains access to mates. One could argue that the status dynamics of young men – the banter, teasing, playful wrestling, and tests of strength – serve a similar function: to determine who rises in status, and who will have more access to young women. Within intrasexual competition, those traits, whether it be strength, beauty, cunning, emotional intelligence, or humor, that allow some to prevail over others are more likely to be passed on to succeeding generations.

Intersexual competition refers to the process by which one sex selects specific kinds of traits in the other sex. In humans this is seen in the preference women report for males of higher status. Social status affects the amount of resources one has (Buss, 1992), and more resources will benefit future offspring. Conversely, males seek out mates who are fertile and of optimal reproductive age. This might account for the preference men show for youth and beauty, because many of the cues of youth and beauty – full lips, youthful skin, an hourglass figure, for example – are physical signs of optimal reproductive age (Buss, 1992).

Recently evolutionary theorists have proposed that our capacity to cooperate is a powerful determinant of who reproduces and who survives (Buck, 1999; Buck, 2002; Cronin, 1991; De Waal, 1996; Eibl-Eibesfeldt, 1989; Sober & Wilson, 1998). Humans accomplish the central tasks of survival and reproduction within relationships, groups, and communities. We reproduce, raise offspring, avoid predation, gather food, and stay warm, in relationships with other people. We are more likely to succeed at these endeavors when we behave in cooperative fashion, mindful of others' needs, not just our own. As we shall see later, these kinds of social selection pressures may in part account for the evolution of moral emotions like gratitude, anger, and compassion.

Adaptation

A second important concept of evolutionary theory is **adaptation**. Adaptations are genetically based traits that allow the organism to respond well to specific selection pressures, and to survive and reproduce. In table 2.1 we list some examples of adaptations that have emerged in the course of human evolution. We hope they give you a sense of the extent

Table 2.1 Examples of adaptations

Problem/Pressure	Adaptation
Avoid eating toxins	Distaste for bitterness, pregnancy sickness
Find healthy mate	Perceive facial symmetry as beautiful
Find fertile mate	Prefer mate with youthful appearance
Protect offspring	Emotional response to baby-like cues

to which evolutionary theorists argue that humans have been designed by evolution to meet specific problems and opportunities.

Consider our dietary likes and dislikes. The typical human has 10,000 taste buds, each with 50 short hair-like structures that convert food particles to an electrochemical signal, and eventually to our experience of sweet, sour, salty, and bitter tastes. The preference for sweet tastes helps us identify foods of nutritional value, such as foods that provide Vitamin C, which humans, unlike many mammals, cannot synthesize. Plants also contain toxic compounds that deter predators. They are bitter-tasting, and pungent-smelling. When you eat a turnip or cabbage, you are getting a sub-lethal dose of such toxins. Our distaste for bitter foods helps us avoid these toxins (Rozin & Kalat, 1971). Interestingly, women are particularly sensitive to bitter tastes and smells during the first trimester of pregnancy. Sometimes they may experience such preferences as overwhelming. Profet (1992) has proposed that the morning sickness of the first three months of pregnancy may be part of a mechanism to avoid intake of certain toxins that may harm the fetus.

Consider the problem of finding a healthy and fertile mate, one with good genes, so to speak. It is disadvantageous to devote resources to the pursuit of mates who have little chance of reproduction, or who might bear unhealthy offspring. To meet these problems, the reasoning goes, humans have evolved preferences for potential mates who show signs of fertility and reproductive readiness. For example, people find symmetrical faces more attractive than asymmetrical faces. As it turns out, exposure to parasites early in development is associated with facial asymmetry, and in more extreme cases, disfiguration. Our preference for symmetry, then, guides us toward potential mates who have been raised in healthy environments.

An important determinant of whether one's genes are passed on is survival of offspring in infancy (Hrdy, 1999). Human babies are very vulnerable and not physically self-sufficient. They require tremendous care, devotion, and resources. Evolutionary theorists have argued that our responses to baby-like cues ensure that parents help their offspring reach the age of viability. The overwhelming love parents feel for their offspring, in response to baby-like features (large forehead, big eyes, small chin), their smiles, coos, and laughs, their smells, and the softness of their skin, overwhelms the many costs of raising children, and increases the chances that genes will be passed from one generation to the next.

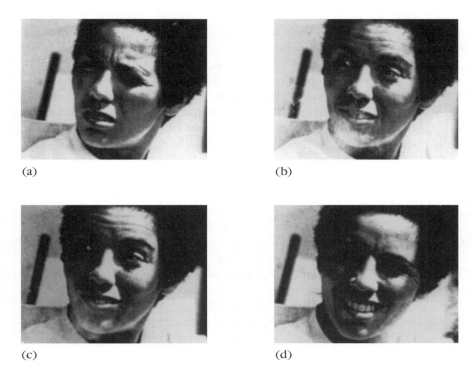

(a)　　　　　　　　　　　　　(b)

(c)　　　　　　　　　　　　　(d)

Figure 2.1 Frames from a cine film taken by H. Hass of a French woman greeting a friend with an eyebrow flash that is universal. In (a) the face is neutral, in (b) and (c) the eyebrows are raised for about one-third of a second, and in (d) a smile occurs.

There are some qualifications to what we have just said. Not all human traits or behaviors are adaptations. Many human traits, from snoring to nervous leg jiggles, serve no apparent evolutionary function, and are better thought of as byproducts. Moreover, you should not conclude that all, or even most, human traits emerged *de novo*, to meet survival- and reproduction-related problems and opportunities. Evolution is a tinkerer, and often endows old anatomical and behavioral features with new functions. A trait that acquires a new function like this is called an exaptation. Andrew (1963, 1965) uses this principle to propose how facial expressions in primates, including humans, were developed from reflexes. Many animals have a reflex in which they flatten their ears when startled, or when approaching another member of their species. Its original function was to protect the ears. But as well as being protective the pattern is easily recognized by others: if we think a dog looks friendly, part of this look is due to the flattened ears. Humans are not able to retract their ears, but raising the eyebrows seems to derive from this same movement, and Eibl-Eibesfeldt (1970) has shown, by inconspicuous filming in many different cultures, that a brief raising of the eyebrows, lasting a fraction of a second, occurs when people approach one another during greeting, and in flirting. It is probably a **human universal**.

Our final caveat pertains to genetics. Natural selection is based on genetic variation, and selects for genetically based traits that help certain individuals meet selection pressures. This does not mean to imply that human action is rigidly determined by genes. As we shall see in chapters 13 and 14, many genes only influence human behavior in relation to particular environments. Genes provide potentialities for behavior. You can think of them as providing inherited start-up programs that give us the initial bases for walking, for learning language, for emotions, and so forth, which are then elaborated and given content by experience.

Historical figure: Charles Darwin

Not everyone is fortunate enough to have a family that is both illustrious and well off: Charles Darwin was fortunate in this way. His father's father was the famous biologist Erasmus Darwin, and his mother's was Josiah Wedgwood the potter. His own father was a doctor; his mother died when he was eight. At 16 he was sent to Edinburgh University to study medicine, but he would skip classes to collect specimens of invertebrate animals along the shores of the Firth of Forth, developing his strong interest in natural history. In despair about the failure of Charles's medical studies, his father sent him to Cambridge to study theology. Again, he was not fully engaged with his courses: he was more interested in collecting beetles, and in hunting. He obtained an ordinary BA in 1831, and seemed headed for a life as a country parson with the hobby of natural history. He had not been idle at Cambridge, however. He had won the esteem of a number of scientists and, at the age of 22, he was appointed naturalist on the *Beagle*, a British Navy ship with a mission to chart coastlines in South America. On his return from this five-year voyage, with independent means, Darwin wrote up his findings. From 1837 his notebooks show him struggling to understand the change of one species into another, and his notes about emotions were prominent in this period. In 1842 and 1844 he wrote sketches of his theory of evolution by natural selection. He proceeded slowly, gathering more and more evidence, and started to write a compendious work. But in 1858 Alfred Wallace independently developed this same idea, and sent a paper on it to Darwin asking for his opinion. Greatly perturbed at the problem of priority, Darwin consulted friends who had read his own earlier sketch. They arranged that the paper by Wallace, and a hastily prepared revision by Darwin of his sketch, would be read at the same meeting of the Linnaean Society – in the absence of both authors. Neither paper attracted much attention outside a small circle, but the incident at last spurred Darwin toward publication of a book that could be appreciated by the educated public. A year later *The Origin of Species* appeared. Darwin did not stop there: his book on emotional expression is the foundation of the study of emotions, and his paper in the journal *Mind*, in which he describes observations of his son William's emotional and cognitive development, is one of the first contributions to developmental psychology. (Biographical information from Bowlby, 1991; Gruber & Barrett, 1974.)

Emotions serve functions

At the core of evolutionary analyses is the idea of function: human traits solve survival- and reproduction-related problems, and help individuals take advantage of opportunities. So this should be true of emotions. As you learned in chapter 1, this view, that emotions serve functions, was not much accepted in Western thought until recently. It was more typical to portray emotions as disruptive, and harmful influences resulting in destructive behavior, to be mastered by rational thought (Calhoun & Solomon, 1984; Dewey, 1895; Keltner & Gross, 1999). Subsequent accounts, influenced by the theory of evolution, tend to describe emotions in terms of functions in ways that increase the chances of survival and reproduction. Emotions are adaptations.

One aspect of adaptation is that emotions enable rapid **orientation** to events in the environment. Emotions, in effect, interrupt ongoing processes and direct attention to significant threats and opportunities. The individual who quickly shifts attention to a threat or an opportunity is at an advantage in survival and reproduction. People may believe emotions are irrational and disruptive for this very reason – that they disrupt our ongoing thought and reorient us. Emotions like fear and anger also shut down basic physiological processes, like eating, digestion, or sexual response.

A second general function is **organization** (see, e.g., Levenson, 1999). Emotions coordinate the cardiovascular and respiratory systems, the different muscle groups, and facial expression and experience. This coordination enables more adaptive response to events in the environment.

In terms of a more specific analysis, evolutionary theorists have sought to identify the functions of different emotions (Campos, Campos, & Barrett, 1989; Ekman, 1992; Keltner & Haidt, 1999; Levenson, 1999; Oatley & Jenkins, 1992; Tooby & Cosmides, 1990). Anger is more than just a specific family of facial expressions or patterns of neural activation; it is a set of coordinated responses that help restore just relations with others. Embarrassment is more than the blush or the pronounced desire to hide; it is a form of appeasement. Compassion is more than the lump in the throat, the feeling of expansion in the chest, and the unyielding inclination to help; it enhances the welfare of vulnerable individuals, especially when they have been harmed.

Evolutionary theorists have offered functional analyses of the different facets of emotion. Why do we experience our emotional states as powerful, and at times overwhelming (we discuss this further in chapter 7)? One answer is that emotion-related feelings are informative about specific social events or conditions that need to be acted upon (Campos et al., 1989; Clore, 1992; Damasio, 2003; Ketelaar, 2004, 2005; Ketelaar & Clore, 1997; Lerner & Keltner, 2001; Lowenstein & Lerner, 2003; Schwarz, 1990). This notion challenges the assumption that emotions have no rational basis. The hypothesis is that they reflect important functional relationships with the environment. The informative function of emotions has shed light on how emotional experiences figure in social dilemmas, in moral judgments, and in decisions on personal well-being.

What about emotion-related physiology? What of the shifts in heart rate, blood flow, respiration, swelling of the chest, muscle tension, and digestive processes that were the focus of William James's theory? The answer is that emotions are states of readiness to act (Frijda, Kuipers, & ter Schure, 1989; Levenson, 2003). The autonomic physiology associated with different emotions prepares for specific kinds of action, such as fighting or flight or soothing (Levenson, Ekman, & Friesen, 1990; Stemmler, 2003). This is, however, not true of certain physiological responses, such as the blush. Moreover, certain emotions such as contentment or amusement do not seem to have an obvious action tendency (Fredrickson, 1998).

What about communication? Emotions are communicated in facial expression, the voice, gaze, posture, and touch (Ekman, 1992; Fernald, 1992; Hertenstein, 2002; Keltner et al., 2003a; Juslin & Laukka, 2003; Klinnert et al., 1986; Öhman & Dimberg, 1978; Scherer, 1986; Scherer, Johnstone, & Klasmeyer, 2003). Researchers in this area agree that emotional communication coordinates social interactions. Emotional expressions communicate information about current emotions, intentions, and dispositions (Ekman, 1993; Fridlund, 1994; Keltner et al., 2003a). Emotional communication evokes complementary and reciprocal emotions in others that help individuals respond to significant social events (Dimberg & Öhman, 1996; Klinnert et al., 1986).

Bear in mind that not every emotion will reveal the functions it evolved to serve. In a fit of anger, you may vacuum your room until the carpet is threadbare. In a burst of love, you might drive too fast on a dangerous road. It's hard to imagine what functions might be served by these emotion-related actions. An evolutionary approach does not demand that every emotional response be explained in terms of survival and reproductive fitness. An evolutionary approach looks for the ways in which, on average, emotions brought reliable, specific benefits to individuals within the environment in which we evolved (Tooby & Cosmides, 1990).

Emotions are species-characteristic patterns of action

For the most part, when we think of an emotion, we think of something more extensive than a smile or a frown. The older term used in biology for a genetically based, extended, pattern of action is "instinct." In his famous textbook William James (1890) wrote: "Every object that excites an instinct excites an emotion as well" (vol. II, p. 442).

What does this mean? Think back to chapter 1 where we described Hess and Brügger's (1943) discovery of patterns of attack made by cats when a part of their hypothalamus was stimulated electrically. We can infer that the electrical stimulation made the cat angry. In the state of the brain evoked by the stimulation a pattern of attack – characteristic of cats – was directed at a nearby target such as the experimenter. In the older terminology this was an instinct, a pattern for which the start-up program is genetically given.

A large step was made by Lorenz (1937) who demonstrated the genetic basis of instincts by showing that, like anatomical features, they are characteristic of species. One such pattern – part of the repertoire of maternal caregiving in greylag geese – was described by Lorenz and Tinbergen (1938). If an egg gets out of a goose's nest she extends her neck toward it and stays in that position for several seconds. Next, apparently grudgingly, she gets up. With her neck still extended she approaches the egg and touches it with her beak. Then, after sliding her beak over the top of the egg, she quivers, then bends her neck and starts rolling the egg back toward her feet while backing toward the nest. She steers the egg carefully up and over the incline of the nest. This pattern occurs even in geese that have never seen it performed by other geese.

These processes have several components. The first was called by Lorenz a "fixed action pattern," although as one wag put it, this term is great so long as you realize that what it refers to is not fixed, not an action, and not a pattern. In fact it is recognizable as a pattern, and biologists now call it a **species-characteristic pattern**. It is goal-directed, not at the consciously accessible level at which, for example, you might plan to study for an exam. It involves brain-derived procedures that have been shaped by evolution. The function of egg retrieval by geese is to make the survival of goose genes more likely. When a discrepancy from the goal is perceived, "egg out of the nest," a goal-directed, plan-like set of actions brings the errant egg toward the nest until the goal state "all eggs in the nest" is reached. Species-characteristic patterns of action have also been discussed as scripts (Schank & Abelson, 1977; Tomkins, 1979). One output of our genetic makeup, then, is a repertoire of such species-characteristic outline scripts for important functions like maternal caregiving, mating, aggressive conflict.

A second component of a species-characteristic process is the perceptual pattern that triggers it, sometimes called an "innate releaser," or "sign stimulus." Even crude features are often effective. For some species-characteristic patterns an unnatural stimulus does better than a natural one, and is called a "super-normal stimulus." For instance, Tinbergen (1951) showed that oyster-catchers retrieve eggs more energetically if the eggs are much bigger than their own. They cannot manage to retrieve really big eggs, but they try unremittingly to do so. Although the cult of stardom has many aspects that have nothing to do with evolutionarily prepared patterns, the mere visual appearance of some stars and models seems to act as a super-normal stimulus for us humans. We can be attracted even though efforts we make toward such stars would be useless, and though they can mean nothing to us personally.

The third component of a species-characteristic pattern is motivational. Without this, the action pattern does not occur. In geese, egg retrieval only occurs during incubation. It does not occur after hatching.

Species-characteristic patterns are easily triggered, but less easily modified by the individual. In his book of 1872 Darwin described an experiment upon himself that nicely illustrates this point:

I put my face close to the thick glass-plate in front of a puff-adder in the Zoological Gardens, with the determination of not starting back if the snake struck at me; but, as soon as the blow was struck, my resolution went for nothing, and I jumped a yard or two backwards with astonishing rapidity. My will and reason were powerless against the imagination of a danger which had never been experienced. (Darwin, 1872/1965, p. 38)

What does it mean for empirical research to claim that emotions are species-characteristic patterns, whose start-up features are programmed by our genes? If this is true, then emotions have biological bases that include patterns of autonomic and central nervous activity, recognizable facial expressions, particular gestures, and specific vocal tones. Such aspects of emotion, furthermore, should be universal. As human-characteristic patterns, they should be found in similar forms in all cultures,. This claim about universality, as we shall see, has been generative, but it is also controversial. Emotion-related patterns of action should serve important goals, and this is part of the topic of the next section.

Origins of human emotions

Why did emotions emerge in the course of human evolution? Why do they take on the forms that they do today? Evolutionary theorists turn to a specific question (Darwin, 1872; Eibl-Eibesfeldt, 1989; Ekman, 1992; Krebs & Davies, 1993; Öhman, 1986; Plutchik, 1980; Tooby & Cosmides, 1990). They ask what are the benefits of particular emotions. An important concept is the **environment of evolutionary adaptedness**, an abstract description of the social and physical environment in which the human species evolved during the six million years since the human line branched off from the line that led to chimpanzees and bonobos.

What conditions prompted the emergence of human emotions in the environment of evolutionary adaptedness? Evolutionary theorists have relied on many kinds of evidence to answer this question. In this section we will consider three: the study of our close primate relatives, such as chimpanzees and bonobos, whose emotions are similar to our own; prehistoric evidence of human ancestors; and contemporary human societies living in ways thought to be like those of humans at the time when we first became a distinct species. These three viewpoints suggest a conclusion that is central to this book. The story of human emotions is really a story of our intensely social lives. At their core, emotions evolved to serve important social functions.

The social lives of our living primate relatives

Evidence of our relatedness to other animals is now extensive. Anatomical and behavioral correspondences provide qualitative indications, and now analyses of proteins, immunological reactions, and genetic material have allowed quantitative estimates of the degree of similarity between species

Table 2.2 Human relatedness to other primates, expressed in terms of differences in DNA and estimates of the time before the present at which divergence from human stock occurred

Humans to . . .	Chimpanzees	Gorillas	Orangutans	Gibbons	Monkeys
% unshared DNA	1.8	2.4	3.6	5.2	7.7
Millions of years since divergence	6*	7*	10	12	20

* Updated figures based on more recent estimates since Sibley and Ahlquist's figures of 4 and 5 million years, respectively, since divergence of humans from the line that led to chimpanzees, and divergence of chimpanzees and humans from the line that led to gorillas.

Source: After Sibley & Alquist (1984)

(Washburn, 1991), though the accuracy of such estimates is controversial (Marks, 1992). Closest of our animal relatives are chimpanzees and bonobos.

What then, do we learn by studies of our close relatives, the chimpanzees? Answers emerge from the work of people like Jane Goodall and Frans De Waal. Goodall (1986) and her colleagues spent many years observing 160 or so common chimpanzees in Gombe, Tanzania, an area of rugged forest, about the size and shape of Manhattan, with a shoreline on Lake Tanganyika, and with deep valleys made by streams running down to the lake. After establishing trust with the chimpanzees, Goodall and her trained observers identified the chimpanzees individually, gave them names, and could sit a few yards away from groups of them, or follow an individual for many days taking notes and photographs. Consider the following description by Goodall:

> Melissa and her daughter Gremlin have made their nests [in the trees] some 10 meters apart. Melissa's son Gimble still feeds on *msongati* pods . . . Gremlin's infant, Getty, dangles above his mother, twirling, kicking his legs, and grabbing at his toes. From time to time Gremlin reaches up, idly, tickling his groin. After a few minutes he climbs away through the branches, a tiny figure outlined against the orange-red of the evening sky. When he reaches a small branch above Melissa's nest, he suddenly drops down, plop, on her belly. With a soft laugh his grandmother holds him close and play-nibbles his neck . . . He goes back to his mother and lies beside her, suckling, one arm on her chest . . . Suddenly from the far side of the valley come the melodious pant-hoots of a single male: Evered, probably in his nest too. It is Gimble who starts the answering chorus, sitting up beside Melissa, his hand on her arm, gazing toward the adult male – one of his "heroes." (Goodall, 1986, p. 594)

With such observations, Goodall has documented many kinds of chimpanzee emotions and the situations in which they arise: apprehension at a stranger, fear at an aggressive interaction, distress when lost, annoyance at a bothersome juvenile, anger in a fight, mourning following the death of a parent, which can lead to immobility and death. Goodall has also catalogued emotional displays, including bared teeth threats, piloerection during excitement (sexual or aggressive), a pant-grunt indicating social apprehension, squeaking and screaming indicating fear, angry barks, distressed whimpers, laughter and panting that accompany the enjoyment of body contact, and pant-hoots and roars that accompany social excitement.

These expressions are bases for distinctive patterns of interaction. So, when they find a tree with a lot of fruit on it, chimpanzees pant-hoot. Others come to the spot, and they eat together with obvious enjoyment. In maternal–infant interactions, in play, and in reconciliation there is affectionate body contact, touching, stroking, and hugging. If an animal is hurt, it screams a distinctive SOS call; the effect is to summon others to its aid. When patrolling their range, groups of males are tense and alert to sounds, and they become excited when they attack an animal from outside their community.

Frans De Waal has likewise devoted over 20 years of his life to the close observations of nonhuman primates, including chimpanzees. For the most part he has studied primates in captivity, at Arnheim Zoo in the Netherlands, and more recently at the Yerkes Regional Primate Research Center at Emory University in Atlanta, Georgia. He has studied how primates reconcile following conflicts, how they share food, and how they come to the aid of other chimps in distress. The work of scientists like Goodall and De Waal reveals the profoundly social nature of our close primate relatives, and the role of emotions in social interactions.

Caregiving is common   In his studies of different primates, De Waal has catalogued remarkable acts of caregiving (1996). Chimpanzees, baboons, and macaques become intensely distressed when witnessing harm to other group members. Primates take care of vulnerable individuals. For example, monkeys, like humans, are sometimes born blind, which exposes the blind monkey to numerous dangers ranging from falling out of trees to straying from the group. De Waal observes that other monkeys in the group will take on the burden of protecting the blind monkey and helping with such activities as feeding. Caregiving is a way of life in our primate relatives.

Social life is hierarchical   Primate social life is hierarchical, in large part because hierarchies enable group members quickly and relatively peacefully to decide how to allocate resources. The so-called "alpha male," to whom all others defer, wins his position by defeating the previous holder with intimidation displays that might involve charging, pulling branches, throwing stones, and making a great din (Goodall, 1992). Occasionally there are overt fights. The alpha male usually holds his position for several years. Other males have a status in a rough hierarchy below him. Females too have a parallel hierarchy and animals of both sexes defend their position, or challenge to rise in the hierarchy, usually by angry threats sometimes backed by overt fights, which often occur after two animals at about the same level in the hierarchy have not met for an interval.

It's not just brute strength, however, that determines a chimpanzee's place in the social hierarchy. Caregiving matters as well. Consider the example of food sharing. Chimpanzees eat mainly fruit, but will hunt opportunistically for small animals such as cebus monkeys or piglets they may come across in the forest. When chimpanzees make a kill, high-ranking animals tend to get more of the food, even if they took no part in the catch (Nishida et al., 1992). Yet high status chimpanzees do not monopolize all of the foods. Social species like chimpanzees have developed sophisticated rules for sharing food (Boesch & Boesch, 1989; De Waal, 1996). In his observations of over 5,000 incidents of food sharing, De Waal found that chimps systematically shared with other chimps who had shared with them, as well as with other chimps who had groomed them earlier in the day. Chimpanzees trade and reciprocate. High ranking individuals often also spend a good part of their day breaking up the conflicts of lower status chimps.

Think of it like this: we humans live in societies in which there are huge differences of wealth and status. Though angry conflicts sometimes occur over resources (for instance in civil lawsuits), and though envy is prevalent (especially of others who are close in status to ourselves, see, e.g., Chetkovich, 2004; Moldoveanu & Nohria, 2002), for the most part we tolerate such differences without consternation.

Cooperation is prevalent   One stereotype of evolution is that it is ruthlessly competitive, a bloody, selfish survival of the fittest. De Waal and Goodall have found, however, that cooperation over food and peace-making are frequent and sophisticated. They have also documented how chimpanzees reconcile following aggressive encounters. Prior to Goodall and De Waal's work, the prevailing wisdom, first formally developed by Lorenz, was that following an aggressive encounter, the two aggressors would move away from each other as far as possible. This view might make sense, for solitary species, like the golden hamster, who flee upon attack, or territorial species, like many birds, who rely on territorial arrangements to avoid deadly conflicts. But many mammals, and in particular primates, are highly social, and need to reconcile to maintain cooperative bonds.

De Waal observed how pairs of chimps or macaques behaved after angry conflicts. He compared those behaviors with how the same pairs behaved during calmer, less strife-ridden times. He discovered that previous antagonists were actually more likely to remain in physical proximity with one another, and they would engage in ritualized reconciliation behaviors (see the photo at the head of this chapter). Sometimes the aggressor initiates reconciliation, sometimes the subordinate or defeated animal. In the latter case he or she would approach with trepidation, and engage in well-known submissive behaviors, like bare teeth displays, head bowing and bobbing, and submissive grunts. This eventually would lead to affectionate grooming, physical contact, and even embraces that would repair their social bonds (De Waal, 2000). Here is Goodall's account of a reconciliation between two chimpanzees:

Once Figan, aged about 10 years, was badly pounded by the alpha male (Goliath at the time). Screaming and tense, Figan began cautiously approaching his aggressor, who sat with his hair still bristling. Every so often, the desire to flee seemed almost to overcome the adolescent's desire for contact and he turned, as though to retreat. But each time he went on again until eventually he was crouched, flat on the ground, in front of Goliath. And there he stayed, still screaming, until Goliath, in response to his submission, began to pat him gently on the back, on and on until the screaming gradually subsided, and Figan sat up and moved away quite calmly. Such incidents are common and almost always the aggressor responds to the submissive gestures of the subordinate with a touch, a pat, or even an embrace. (Goodall, 1986, p. 144)

Sexuality is varied Across our primate relatives, sexuality varies dramatically. Chimpanzees are sexually promiscuous. Once she is sexually mature at age 15, a female chimpanzee advertises her sexual receptiveness by a large pink patch of sexual skin (the labia). During the period of sexual advertisement, typically lasting 10 days out of the 36-day menstrual cycle, the female may copulate several dozen times a day, with all or most of the adult males in her social group. Alternatively she may go off with a single male consort, away from the rest of the community. Aggression and jockeying for access to female chimpanzees are common among male chimpanzees. Mothers will raise infants more or less on their own. Males make contributions to the community, but not to individual offspring. No one knows who has fathered which infants.

Bonobos are now recognized as a separate species, one that is probably more closely related to humans than the species of common chimpanzees. They used to be called pygmy chimpanzees (De Waal & Lanting, 1997). They are less aggressive than common chimpanzees, and their social lives seem to revolve almost entirely around sex (De Waal, 1995; Kano, 1992). Bonobo females are sexually active for about five years before they become fertile. They are receptive for more than half the time in each menstrual cycle, and they are sexually inactive only from a month before giving birth to about a year after it. They copulate freely with many of the adult males in their immediate social group. Female and male homosexual relations are also common. Younger males often engage in sexual activity with older females in what might be thought of as sexual initiation play. Sexual contact amongst the bonobos is the basis of friendships, conflict reduction, and play.

Among olive baboons, by contrast, there is a different mode of organization, though it too revolves around sexual activity (Smuts, 1985). Although they are also promiscuous, females form long-lasting friendships with two or three males, involving grooming and keeping close. These friendships are marked by emotions such as jealousy that seem similar to our own. Friendships function to protect females against aggression from males (who are twice as large as they). For males advantages are of being groomed and more often accepted as mating partners.

Evidence of human ancestry

We have seen that among our living primate relatives, emotions link individuals together with bonds of social interaction: of caregiving, dominance and submissiveness, cooperative exchange, and sexual intimacy. Such features point to possible characteristics of the environment of human evolutionary adaptedness. Is anything known about early humans that might supplement this picture?

The average difference in size between modern human males and females is about 15 percent, a difference that was reached by our ancestors about 1.9 million years ago with the emergence of *Homo erectus*. In the hominid species that preceded them in our line (*Homo habilis*), males were about 50 percent bigger than females (Wrangham, 2001). Size differences between males and females are associated with a form of social organization in which males compete with each other for access to females, and are associated also with sharp social hierarchies. *Homo erectus* people had brains about 1,000 cc, which is 50 percent bigger than those of *habilis*. They had smaller arms and longer legs than *habilis*, and as Wrangham says: "For the first time [in evolution] they could be put in clothes and given hats, and they could walk down a New York street without generating too many stares" (p. 123). *Homo sapiens* (our species) with brains about 1,200 cc appeared about half a million years ago.

But the path from there involved curious accidents. Calculations of rates of mutation allow the small differences in the RNA of modern people from all over the world to be traced back to a point of convergence. All modern humans may have had a set of common ancestors, a small group of perhaps 5,000 *Homo sapiens* women who lived about 200,000 years ago in Africa (Wilson & Cann, 1992). According to this hypothesis (which is controversial), we are all descended from these African Eves. They are our direct forebears, anatomically little different from ourselves. Their descendants migrated to populate every part of the earth except Antarctica.

During the past several hundred thousand years, the earth's climate has fluctuated between warm periods such as that in which we now live and ice ages, when glaciers spread south of the Great Lakes in America and across northern Europe. Because so much water was stored as ice, during these cold periods the sea level was as much as 400 feet lower than now. Developing the technologies of clothing and shelter, probably much like those of Inuit people, the forebears of the native peoples of the Americas are thought to have crossed, during a cold period, the land bridge between what are now Siberia and Alaska, around 15,000 years ago. Also in such cold periods, Australia and New Guinea were joined, and separated by only 40 miles of sea from Asia. At some time before 60,000 years ago humans (but no other mammals) crossed the water, later to be isolated as sea levels rose again when glaciers began to melt, to live as the aboriginal hunting and gathering peoples of Australia and New Guinea (Stringer & Gamble, 1993).

The domestication of plants and animals occurred in several parts of the world some 10,000 to 12,000 years ago (Diamond, 1997). At the same time, or shortly afterward, came the invention of cities as centers of trade (Leick, 2001). In such movements the evolution of human cultures overtook the evolution of species. If we take Wilson and Cann's estimate of 200,000 years ago as the time when the common ancestor of all living human beings was alive, the 10,000 years of civilizations of the kind in which most people now live is only 5 percent of that time; this same period is less than a quarter of one percent of the time from the divergence of humans from apes.

For much of the time in which our emotional responsiveness was being shaped by natural selection, therefore, most researchers propose that our environments of evolutionary adaptedness were of extended family groupings. One possible pattern is that groups of 10 to 20 people lived closely together as scavenger-hunter-gatherers, and frequently met other such groups who shared the same range. Overall these early people would know about 150 other people (Dunbar, 1993, 2004) to many of whom they were related. Findings of flint tools (starting about two-and-a-half million years ago) show that behavioral skills were important. Preserving or making fire started about 700,000 years ago, and language perhaps 500,000 years ago. Social skills like sharing food, division of labor and exchange, and the arts of conversation, disputing, gossiping, planning, story telling, became central. All of these are human universals (for discussion see Brown, 1991; Hockett, 1973). All are cultural inventions that mark us off from other living primates. All are social. Many have an emotional basis, such as the distinctive warmth and acceptance of sharing food and the grateful cooperativeness of exchange. Other emotions may have evolved to support human activities, such the engrossment of making flint tools and other such things.

Among the first concerns of early hominid groups were the demands of raising offspring, and the need for attachments to carry out this work (Hrdy, 1999). With increasing brain size, early humans needed to be more immature at birth for the large head to pass through the birth canal. Infants had a longer period of dependency than those of apes, and required more care of parents.

Division of labor became established. Women took primary care of infants during the extended period of immaturity, and they traveled less. A critically important evolutionary step was the emergence of monogamy, which is unusual among our primate cousins, and never (except among us) associated with a mixing of the sexes in large groups without territorial boundaries. Among the changes toward monogamy, females evolved to become sexually active throughout their menstrual cycles; a male and a female could maintain exclusive sexual interest in each other. Division of labor meant that men could hunt and bring home meat, while sexual bonding enabled them to make a specific economic contribution to one female and her offspring, an arrangement that has become known as the male provisioning hypothesis (Lovejoy, 1981).

Monogamous pairing carries the advantage for the males of knowing that offspring to whom they contribute economically are their own (Lancaster & Kaplan, 1992; Lovejoy, 1981). Although the proportion of societies (like Western ones) where monogamy is official policy is only 16 percent among a total of 853 societies sampled (Van den Berghe, 1979), and although extramarital activities are not uncommon in most societies, in practice monogamy is overwhelmingly the most usual sexual pattern, amounting to a human universal. Even in societies where one male can have several wives, this pattern is practiced only by a few men who have large resources. The emotional accompaniment of the adoption of monogamy is jealousy, which tends to occur when the pair bond is threatened by an interloper (Dunbar, 2004).

The central structure of human life is the family and this too is a human universal. The human family is a group that often includes both sexes and individuals of all ages, living with a female and her offspring. In the group there is usually at least one adult male. He may be the woman's sexual partner, perhaps father of her children, but at some times and in some societies the male of the family may be a father, brother, or son. The extended family group typically includes other relatives, such as siblings, older offspring, and their sexual partners who have joined the family from other groups. (A taboo on incest, and social mechanisms for people to marry outside the family, are other human universals.) By contrast, a chimpanzee or bonobo family is a female and a group of her offspring.

Perhaps also, as we discuss in chapter 10, humans are adapted to compete with other groups similar but noticeably different from ourselves, whose ecological niches have overlapped with ours. For almost all of the six million years since the human divergence from the chimpanzee line, several other hominid species have shared the same ecological niches with our ancestors, but then became extinct. The last such species were the Neanderthals who became extinct some 28,000 years ago, perhaps because of the aggressive success of our ancestors, in a type of action we now know as genocide (Stringer & Gamble, 1993). The prehistory of war is not the angry jockeying in hierarchies within our immediate social group. It is the emotion of group-based, prejudiced contempt that is easily directed at groups of our own species, who are recognizable but may differ from us in ways that are of no more importance than living in a different place. This genocidal tendency occurs in our cousins the chimpanzees, and was first seen by Goodall (1986). A division occurred in the whole community of chimpanzees she was studying in Gombe. A small contingent, containing six adult males, formed a separate community to the south of Goodall's camp. It was with profound shock that in 1974 researchers saw gangs (this term seems appropriate) of the larger northern community start to patrol, attack, and kill members of the southern group, if they came across them either alone or in numerically weaker groups in the forest (see chapter 9).

Hunter-gathering ways of life

We can get another glimpse of the origins of human emotions by asking what is known about existing cultures of **hunter-gatherers**. In Australia and in the savannas of southern Africa the hunter-gatherer way of life has existed for several thousand years. This was the way of life of the San of the Kalahari who include the !Kung and the G/wi. (Their languages include clicks: ! designates a click made by drawing the tongue sharply away from the roof of the mouth, and / is made by drawing the tongue away from the front teeth, like the "tsk" of scolding.) Lorna Marshall and her family lived among them in the 1950s (Marshall, 1976; Thomas, 1989). In the 1960s and 1970s, Lee (1984) and other American anthropologists visited these peoples.

Until its recent erosion by Western influences, !Kung and G/wi peoples lived in a semi-desert land, and traveled over a range of several hundred square miles that they know intimately. Thomas describes the G/wi as small and lithe, living in extended families. In their travels they meet other families to whom they are related by blood or marriage. Round a fire, the G/wi scoop out shallow impressions in the ground to sleep in. The women especially are expert botanists: they gather roots and other vegetable foods from the land, and obtain fluid from tsama melons. The men hunt and shoot animals with bows and arrows tipped with a poison made from a grub. They may have to follow a shot antelope for a day before it dies. It is brought

Figure 2.2 Two groups of San camping together, under the shade of the same small tree.

back to camp, and there are complex rules about how it is divided. Nothing is wasted. The society of these people is cooperative.

It is probable that our environment of evolutionary adaptedness, the way of life of the modern *Homo sapiens* since their descent from the ancestral Eves of 200,000 years ago, was in semi-nomadic hunter-gatherer groups of 10 to 30 people living face-to-face with each other in extended families, and meeting other related groups from time to time, much like the G/wi and !Kung. Most of our emotions, then, are probably adapted to living in this kind of way; cooperating, though with division of labor, in hunting and gathering, in preparing and sharing food, in rearing and protecting children.

Summary of the environment of evolutionary adaptedness

We have learned from our primate relatives, from the fossil record of human ancestry, and from studies of modern hunter-gatherers, that emotions structure interactions in ways that enable individuals to respond to threats and opportunities. The environment of evolutionary adaptedness was defined not by being hot or cold, forest or seashore, but by its social characteristics: sexual attachments, caregiving for vulnerable offspring, cooperation amongst group members, and ever-changing hierarchies that affect the allocation of resources, just as people today are well-off or poor. As Oatley (2004c) put it, projecting backward from our current emotional patterns, the environment of evolutionary adaptedness must have been one:

> in which people were made happy by being with friends, close relatives, lovers. Just as now, our ancestors were concerned for their children, concerned that friends and loved ones liked them, upset if something, or someone, they valued was lost or taken. (pp. 28–29)

Emotions as bases of social relationships

There is an emerging consensus that, although some emotions such as fear emerged long ago in vertebrate evolution and without any necessary social significance (LeDoux, 1996), many emotions that have become important for humankind evolved as the bases of social relationships. In table 2.3 we summarize insights of theorists who have contributed to this view (Bowlby, 1971; Ekman, 1992; Izard, 1971, 1977; Keltner & Haidt, 1999, 2001; Nesse, 1990; Oatley, 1992, 2004c; Plutchik, 1991; Tooby & Cosmides, 1990).

An evolutionary approach strongly suggests that human emotions are the language of human social life. They provide the outline patterns that relate people to each other. As you can see, emotions help humans form and maintain attachments that are critical to reproduction and the raising of offspring to the age of reproduction. Romantic love helps motivate long-term commitments to romantic partners, and countervails self-interested

Table 2.3 Relations, recurring situations, and emotional responses in relation to members of the same species, other species, and inanimate objects

Relation	Recurring situation	Emotion
Attachment	Maintain contact with parents	Love of parents
Sexual contact	Reproductive possibility	Sexual desire, Love
Maintaining pair bond	Threat from interloper	Jealousy
Interruption of attachment	Separation	Distress, Anxiety
Resumption of attachment	Reunion	Relief (and maybe Anger)
Loss of attachment	Parting, Death	Sadness, Despair
Caregiving	Assisting others, including infants	Compassion, Caregiving love
Cooperation	Formation of relationships and plans	Love
Cooperation	Reciprocation, Exchange	Gratitude
Repair transgression of cooperative bond	Mistake	Guilt
Motivate other to repair	Transgression	Anger
Reduce unfairness	Unfair inequalities	Envy
Loss of relationship, failure of plans	Parting, Failure	Sadness
Other exerts power in hierarchy	Pacify aggressor, Signal lower status	Shame, Embarrassment
Reduce status of other	Other rises unfairly in status	Anger, Contempt, Envy
Endow entity with power	Other seen as greater than self	Awe
Predation	Hunting	Excitement
Being hunted	Role as prey	Fear
Group antagonism	Inter-group conflict	Cruelty, Lethal hostility
Inanimate resources	Seeking, Fnding	Enthusiasm
Avoid physical danger	Threat	Fear
Avoid contamination	Toxicity	Disgust
Explore environment	Novelty	Interest, Surprise

courses of action, such as sexual infidelity, that damage monogamous bonds. Attachment-related emotions are sensitive to threats or disruptions to our relationships. Jealousy relates to mate protection, and is triggered by cues that signal potential threats to the relationship, such as possible sexual or emotional involvement of the mate with others (Buss, 1992, 1994), and motivates possessive and threat behaviors that discourage competitors and prevent sexual opportunities for the mate (Wilson & Daly, 1996). Separation from attachment figures produces distress and anxiety, and the return of the attachment figure produces relief. Sadness follows the loss of important bonds, and helps individuals establish new bonds (Lazarus, 1991). Caregiving-related emotions, such as parental and child love and sympathy, facilitate protective relations between parent and offspring (Bowlby, 1971). We hope that in reading this chapter you have come to see cooperation as a central part of human social life. Cooperation, and the management of competition or defection, is especially central to relations among non-kin, who are not bound together by shared genetic interests (Axelrod, 1984; De Waal, 1996; Trivers, 1971).

In table 2.3 you can see that several emotions help form and maintain cooperative bonds. Love and gratitude help promote cooperative bonds like friendships (Frank, 1988; Nesse, 1990; Trivers, 1971). Weisfeld (1980) discusses how the roots of this emotion are seen among chimpanzees as they share food with a friend, in alliances, and in mutual grooming. The effect of this emotion is to set up a desire to reciprocate and cooperate in enduring relationships.

When the rules of cooperative bonds, such as reciprocity or equality, have been violated, we experience emotions that motivate the restoration of cooperation. Guilt occurs following violations of reciprocity and is expressed in apologetic, remedial behavior that motivates cooperation and reestablishes reciprocity (Keltner & Buswell, 1997; Ketelaar & Au, 2003). Anger motivates the punishment of individuals who have cheated or violated rules of reciprocity. Envy motivates individuals to derogate others whose favorable status is unjustified, thus preserving equal relations (Fiske, 1991). And forms of sadness occur when cooperative bonds have been lost. Hierarchical emotions help form and maintain status hierarchies, which provide heuristic solutions to the problems of distributing resources, such as mates, food, and social attention, and the labor required of collective endeavors (Fiske, 1991; De Waal, 1982; 1996). Embarrassment and shame appease dominant individuals and signal submissiveness (Keltner & Buswell, 1997; Miller & Leary, 1992). Eales (1992), on reviewing the large etho-logical and cross-cultural literature on this topic, has concluded that gestures of appeasement and submission are inherited universals among higher primates, including humans. They include looking downward, hunching the body, averting or lowering the gaze, immobility, and facial expressions of fear. Contempt is defined by feelings of superiority and dominance vis-à-vis inferior others. Awe tends to be associated with the experience of being in the presence of an entity greater than the self (Keltner & Haidt, 2003) and thereby endows higher status individuals with respect and authority. Some of our most influential emotions do not even have very specific names in English; in table 2.3 we have called them cruelty and lethal hostility: the emotions of war, between groups and between nations. Though we are used to thinking of war as politics by other means, the historian John Keegan (1994) has done us a favor by being blunt. He acknowledges that war is a very emotional matter, based on the human urge to kill.

Finally, there are emotions that guide human behavior in the physical world, and such tasks as avoiding predation, violence, and disease, and finding resources in the environment. There are emotions – excitement and fear –

that may be specific to responding to predators. Disgust, along with its simpler precursor distaste, helps humans choose a balanced and safe diet, avoiding dangerous toxins and disease. And more positively valenced emotions, enthusiasm and interest, help us concentrate on tasks, pursue resources, and explore the environment.

In the case of an evolutionary approach to emotion, the critical evidence will concern whether these emotions serve the functions they are thought to serve, whether they found to be universal and have biological bases, and whether they do provide the outlines of social relationships.

The evolution of language

Perhaps the most important species-characteristic of humans that distinguishes us from our nonhuman relatives is language. Robin Dunbar (1993, 2003, 2004) has observed that chimpanzees and other primates use grooming to maintain social bonds. Grooming makes up a fair amount of all social interaction, and chimpanzees spend about 20 percent of their waking time doing it. In this activity, they sit quietly and affectionately with another individual, taking turns picking through the other's hair. Dunbar's hypothesis is that laughter and conversation have replaced grooming as the glue that holds society together. So conversation is the verbal equivalent of grooming. As compared with manual grooming that can only be performed with one other at a time, we can converse with more than one person, and also while we are doing something else like preparing food or walking. The huge increase in the size of the human neocortex, in comparison with the neocortex of chimpanzees, is thought to have occurred because in our highly social lives we build and maintain mental models of 150 to 200 people whom we know, models that we elaborate in conversation. This compares with the much simpler models of up to 50 individuals in their social groups that chimpanzees have to maintain. We humans recognize others as like ourselves (Astington, 1993). We have a theory of mind: we can think about what others might be thinking and we can know some of what others know. In addition we can share intentions. These are abilities beyond anything chimpanzees can manage (Tomasello, 1999; Tomasello et al., 2005).

Conversational language evolved to substitute for manual grooming, argues Dunbar, when manual grooming of all the people with whom we need to maintain friendly relationships in a maximum group size of about 150 would have taken about 40 percent of the time, about twice as much as the allowable limit of 20 percent beyond which our ancestors would no longer have had time available for sleep and foraging. Human brains enlarged to contain mental models of people in our social group, and in addition, conversational language allowed us to discuss what these others might know, how to act in different social situations, and how to do things together. Our task in the next chapter is to understand how language and culture work to shape the biological raw materials of emotion.

Summary

We first presented the elements of evolutionary theory and its emphasis on natural selection, selection pressures, and adaptation. We then considered how evolutionary accounts make three general claims about emotion. First, emotions serve various functions, for example by orienting the individual and organizing various responses to enable adaptive response. Second, emotions are species-characteristic patterns of action; they are coordinated, script-like behaviors, with biological bases observed in different cultures. Third, emotions helped individuals meet specific selection pressures in the environment of evolutionary adaptedness, which is illuminated when one studies our close primate relatives, our human ancestors, and modern hunter-gatherer societies. We concluded our chapter with a discussion of the emerging consensus in evolutionary approaches to emotion: human emotions evolved to become the bases of social relationships, which is the most important theme of this book.

Further reading

An introduction to evolutionary theory as it affects emotions is:

Dacher Keltner, Jonathan Haidt, & Michelle Shiota (in press). Social functionalism and the evolution of emotions. In J. Simpson & D. Kenrick (Eds.), *Handbook of evolution and social psychology*. New York: Psychology Press.

For an accessible account of the social and emotional life of chimpanzees:

Frans De Waal (1996). *Good natured: The origins of right and wrong in humans and other animals*. Cambridge, MA: Harvard University Press.

For readable discussions of human evolution:

David Christian (2004). *Maps of time: An introduction to big history*. Berkeley, CA: University of California Press. Part III of this book is on human evolution and the beginnings of human history.

Robin Dunbar (2004). *The human story: A new history of mankind's evolution*. London: Faber.

CHAPTER 3

Cultural Understandings of Emotions

Contents

Figure 3.0 Two bronze figurines from the Han dynasty in China, made more than 2,000 years ago, probably representing people from alien northern tribes.

For nine months the American anthropologist Catherine Lutz lived on a tiny island in the Pacific Ocean, Ifaluk, studying the emotional lives of the 430 people who lived there (Lutz, 1988). One day, sitting with another woman, Lutz watched a five-year-old girl dancing and making silly faces, showing happiness, or *ker*. Lutz responded warmly to the little girl, whom she thought was rather cute. "Don't smile at her," said her companion, "she'll think that you're not *song*," meaning justifiably angry (p. 167). The woman was indicating that the girl was approaching the age at which she should have social intelligence, the concern for others that is so valued on Ifaluk, and that she should not show inappropriate levels of happiness, which is disapproved of on Ifaluk as showing off.

In this exchange, Lutz encountered how different the emotional lives of people on Ifaluk are from her own. On Ifaluk, the little girl should not have displayed *ker*, with its risk of misbehavior. Instead, she should have been sitting quietly, as good socially intelligent people do. One also sees differences in the nature of anger. On Ifaluk, *song*, or justifiable anger, occurs with a public breach of social rules. So *song* is not anger as we in the West tend to experience it, arising from violation of a right. It is people's social duty to express *song* if they notice anything that might disrupt social harmony. To *song*, the natural response is *metagu*, which means anxious concern for others.

The construction of emotions in the West

How, then, might we characterize our implicit theory of emotions in the West? First, we might note a distrust of emotions. If you want to disparage another person's argument, just say that person is being "emotional," meaning "irrational." The idea goes back at least to Plato (375 BCE), who thought emotions arise from the lower part of the mind and pervert reason. The distrust was brought into the modern era by Darwin (1872) who implied that, in human adults, expressions of emotions are obsolete, vestiges of our evolution from the beasts and of our development from infancy.

We in the West are not, however, very consistent, because we also think emotions are the very guarantee of authenticity, our best guide to our true selves. As Solomon (1977) has put it: "Emotions are the life force of the soul, the source of most of our values" (p. 14).

These stances toward emotion, distrust on the one hand and appreciation on the other, are constructions of Western culture. The appreciation became marked in Europe and America, during the historical era of **Romanticism**. (The era must be distinguished from the term "romantic" which is a polite synonym for sexual as in "romantic love."). In the Romantic era emotions came to be valued in personal life, in politics, in literature, and in philosophy.

It was Jean-Jacques Rousseau (1755), an impoverished citizen of Geneva, who is generally credited with the articulation of the Romantic spirit. He it was who first published the idea that religious sensibility is based on how you feel rather than on authority, or on scripture, or on arguments for the existence of God. He it was who began to attack cultivated pursuits as artificial and corrupting: he proposed instead that education should be natural, and that people's natural emotions indicate what is right – they have merely to be alive to the feelings of their conscience. His ringing phrase from the beginning of *The Social Contract* (1762), "Man is born free, and is everywhere in chains," became a rallying call for the Jacobins in the French Revolution, and such thoughts also crossed the Atlantic to help fuel the American War of Independence.

By 1800 Romanticism had become firmly part of Western culture, more or less inseparable from ideas of individual freedom. It inspired poets, novelists, dramatists, painters, and musicians, who saw it as their mission to express their emotions through art and to move readers, audiences, viewers, and listeners to emotional experiences (recall George Eliot's new social science, discussed in chapter 1, in which the experience of emotions became central). The Romantics were fascinated by the natural. Wild scenery, previously thought barbarous, began to be valued. Writers

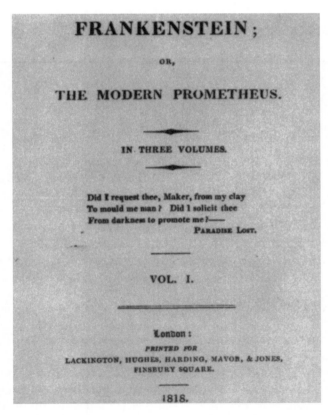

Figure 3.1 Title-page of Volume I of the first edition of *Frankenstein*, written by Mary Shelley but originally published anonymously – an early novel of the Romantic period.

began to explore the worlds of ordinary life, rather than the artificial lives of aristocrats. They explored childhood, dreams, far-away places, the exotic. Writing itself became a way of discovering inner emotional truths. Emotion, experienced and accepted, became an ideal to be cultivated.

Let us consider just one Romantic novel – by Mary Shelley, daughter of the famous feminist Mary Wollstonecraft and the social reformer William Godwin – to see themes of Romanticism in action. At the age of 16, Mary Shelley eloped with the poet Percy Bysshe Shelley. When she was 18, Mary, her husband, her step-sister Claire, Lord Byron, and another friend were on holiday during an "ungenial" summer in the Alps. Incessant rain confined them to the house for days. They read a great deal, and had long conversations on literature, philosophy, and biology. One day Byron suggested that each should write a ghost story. Retiring to bed Mary Shelley could not sleep. Prompted by a conversation about experiments in which electricity was used to stimulate muscle movements in dead creatures, there rose to her mind an image of a scientist with a powerful engine beside him, kneeling over a hideous phantasm of a man that he had put together. Her story became *Frankenstein* (1818), a Romantic novel, and one of the world's first science fiction stories.

Historical landmark: Mary Shelley's novel *Frankenstein*

The novel is about Victor Frankenstein, an idealistic scientist who discovers how to imbue dead matter with life. He collects body parts from charnel houses and constructs an artificial man, eight feet tall. He had meant him to be beautiful but "his yellow skin scarcely covered the work of the muscles and arteries" (p. 105). After years of hard work driven by the excitement of research he infuses the spark of life – then rushes from the room in disgust as the thing begins to move. In exhaustion he tries to sleep – he dreams joyfully of meeting his beloved in the street, and they kiss: with this gesture her lips "became livid with the hue of death, her features appeared to change, and I thought that I held the corpse of my dead mother in my arms" (p. 106).

With this surprisingly modern image of an incestuous abuse of nature, Frankenstein wakes. He goes upstairs again to his laboratory. The creature rises and stretches out his hand as if to detain his creator. Frankenstein again rushes from the room. When the creature's face was at rest he was ugly, but with animation he became a vision from Hell.

After two years and a long illness Frankenstein returns to his family in Geneva to find that a child, his brother, has been murdered. He glimpses his creature in the woods, and guesses that he had done the deed. A servant girl is convicted of the crime, and dies for it. When they meet, the creature declares devotion to his creator. He tells of his first meetings with humans. He took refuge in a disused hovel that leant against the wall of a peasant's cottage. Through a chink he observed the cottagers: a young woman, a youth, and a blind old man – a sister and brother with their father. When the old man smiled at the young woman with kindness and affection, the creature "felt sensations of a peculiar and overpowering nature, such as [he] had never before experienced, either from hunger or cold, warmth or food, and withdrew from the window, unable to bear these emotions" (pp. 153–4). While keeping concealed, the creature collects wood and does other tasks for the family. Painstakingly he learns their language and customs. In an emotional innocence that reflects Mary Shelley's close reading of Rousseau, he comes to feel natural love for the cottagers in their simple life. After a year he visits the blind old man when the others are out. He starts to explain that though he looks frightening he wishes them only well; he is their "good spirit" who has helped them, he desires their friendship. The old man listens – but the others return and are horrified. The youth beats the creature, who rushes off in impotent despair. Next day the family abandons their cottage. That night during a gale, the creature rages and sets fire to his hovel and to the cottage.

The creature wanders that winter in bitterness, but in the spring feels benevolence returning. He decides to find his creator. In Geneva he comes across a small boy, and approaches him thinking that the child would be too young to feel prejudice. But the child is alarmed, calls him an ogre and threatens that his father, "Monsieur Frankenstein," will punish him. The creature strangles the boy – prompted by rage at hearing the family name of the man who has been responsible for his disfigurement.

Days later the creature catches up with Frankenstein amid the majestic scenery of the Alps. He says he will always be despised by human beings. He owns that he has become wicked, but it is because emotions of kindness have turned to rage in response to the hatred directed towards him. So his creator must make another creature, a female, equally deformed, with whom he can live in sympathy. "If any being felt emotions of benevolence towards me," the creature says, "I should return them a hundred and a hundredfold . . . cut off from all the world our lives will not be happy, but they will be harmless . . ." (p. 191).

Frankenstein is horrified by his dilemma: should he risk creating another monster so that two of them could wreak havoc, or should he gratify the wish of this creature who seeks the indulgence of his creator?

In *Frankenstein* are many of the themes of Romanticism: settings amid wild scenery, the emphasis on the natural, distrust of the artificial, apprehension of humans arrogantly overstepping their boundaries. There are thought-provoking, prescient ideas about our exploitation of natural resources and the construction of ever more clever but risky technological systems (Perrow, 1984). More generally, in the Romantic movement, we see core beliefs about human nature, and about emotions as original, primordial, authentic causes of behavior, that are alive today. Emotions are powerful forces, often at odds with more deliberate, rational thought embodied in science and codified in cultural conventions.

The elements of a cultural approach to emotion

The story of Romanticism, and how it shaped our current conceptions and experience of emotion in the West, illustrates the central theme of this chapter. That theme is that values, concepts, and ideas about the self, as expressed in art forms, rituals, social practices and institutions, shape how members of particular societies experience emotion, and that these matters are not universal. Our beliefs about emotion in the West, that emotions are both irrational and also authentic aspects of the true self, are products of a particular culture: the culture of Europe and North America, which is different, for instance, from the belief systems of the people Catherine Lutz met on Ifaluk.

What does it mean to take a cultural approach to emotion? Most importantly, a cultural approach involves the assumption that emotions are constructed primarily by the processes of culture. Aspects ranging from how emotions are valued to how they are elicited are shaped by culture-specific beliefs and practices, which in turn have been affected by historical and economic forces. The more radical claim is that emotions derive from human meanings which are necessarily cultural. They are like languages or works of art. They are radically different across different cultures, so that the interest in emotions across cultures is an interest in their differences. Your experience of love, for example, might not be comparable to the experience of love of people from a different culture.

A second assumption of some cultural approaches is that emotions can be thought of as roles that people fulfill to play out culture-specific identities and relationships. You'll recall Arlie Hochschild's work in chapter 1 on the emotional role that airline stewardesses are required to perform. Averill (1985) argues that falling in love, like many emotions, acts as a temporary social role. It provides an outline script for the role of "lover" in which it is permissible for other social roles to be suspended, for instance in relation to parents, or to former loved ones. The emotion "falling in love" accomplishes a transition, from one structure of social relationships to another.

Batja Mesquita (2001), a pioneer in the study of emotion and culture, contends that cultural approaches focus on the "practice" of emotion, in contrast to the "potential" for emotion. Potential means asking whether people of different cultures, if put in an appropriate experimental situation, would be capable of showing certain universal emotional responses in terms of experience, expression, and physiology (for relevant studies, see Tsai et al., 2002; Tsai & Levenson, 1997; Tsai, Levenson, & Carstensen, 2000). The answer is probably yes. In contrast, "practice" refers to what actually happens in people's emotional lives. The day-to-day emotional experiences of people from different cultures do differ, often dramatically. For instance, some cultures value or at least permit public expressions of anger (e.g., the Ilongot chronicled by Rosaldo, 1980), while others work hard to suppress all such expressions (e.g., the Utku Inuit people described by Briggs, 1970; see chapter 9). In some cultures (such as ours in the West), shame is seen as damaging and to be avoided; in more hierarchically structured societies shame seems more valued and positive, in particular when displayed by the lower status person in an interaction (Abu-Lughod, 1986; Doi, 1973; Menon & Shweder, 1994). As Mesquita, Frijda, and Scherer (1997) observed: "people from different cultures appear to be similar in their emotion potential, especially when this potential is described at a higher level of meaning. Yet, despite the similarities in basic elements of emotional life, concrete emotional realities in different cultures may widely vary."

The self-construal approach: independent and interdependent selves

Now that we have discussed some assumptions of cultural approaches to emotion, let's consider three specific approaches that have emerged in psychology's new interest in culture (Peng, Ames, & Knowles, 2001). Consider first the two quotations below. The first is a famous passage from the Declaration of Independence of the United States:

> We hold these truths to be self-evident, that all men are created equal, that they are endowed by their Creator with certain inalienable rights, that among these are Life, Liberty, and the pursuit of Happiness.

Now consider this well-known passage from *The Analects*, a book by the great Chinese philosopher Confucius:

> A person of humanity wishing to establish his own character, also establishes the character of others.

The American Declaration of Independence and the *Analects* of Confucius have shaped the lives of billions of people. They reflect radically different ideas. The Declaration of Independence prioritized the rights and freedoms of the individual, and it protected the individual from having those rights and liberties infringed by others. Confucius emphasized the importance of knowing one's place in society, of honoring traditions and roles, and of thinking of others before the self. In Western societies, people are concerned about their individuality, about self-actualizing, about freedom, and self-expression. "The squeaky wheel gets the grease." "If you've got it, flaunt it." In Asian cultures, homilies and folk wisdom encourage a markedly different self: "The empty wagon makes the most noise." "The nail that stands up is pounded down."

In an influential way of thinking about these cultural differences, Hazel Markus, Shinobu Kitayama, Harry Triandis and others have characterized two different kinds of **self-construal** (Fiske et al., 1998; Hofstede, 1980; Markus & Kitayama, 1991, 1994; Triandis, 1989, 1994, 1995). In table 3.1 we summarize two kinds of self-construal.

Table 3.1 Two different self-construals. This table outlines the contrasting elements of the independent, individualist, self, widespread in much of Northern Europe and North America, with the interdependent self, prominent in much of Asia, Africa, and South America

The independent self	The interdependent self
I am autonomous, separate	I am connected to others
I have unique traits and preferences	I fulfill roles and duties
My behavior is caused by internal causes	My behavior is the result of the social context
Who I am is stable across contexts	My identity varies across contexts

Within the independent self-construal, the self is autonomous and separate from others. This type of self-construal is also sometimes referred to as individualism (Schimmack, Oishi, & Diener, 2005). The imperative is to assert one's distinctiveness and independence, and to define the self according to unique traits and preferences. When explaining human behavior, the focus is on internal causes, such as one's own dispositions or preferences, which are thought of as stable across time and social context.

For people with interdependent, or collectivist, self-construals, the self is fundamentally connected with other people. The imperative is to find one's status, identity, and roles within the community and other collectives – for example, families and organizations. In explaining human action the emphasis is on the social context and the situational influences on behavior. One thinks of oneself as embedded within social relationships, roles, and duties, with a self that is ever-changing, shifting, and shaped by different contexts, relationships, and roles.

So how do these culture-specific self-construals lead to cultural variation in emotions? First let us consider anger. In Japan, although it is thought appropriate between people from different social groups, for instance in the tradition of Samurai warfare in feudal Japan, Markus and Kitayama (1991) report that anger is considered highly inappropriate between relations or colleagues. By contrast, anger between Americans who know and like each other is relatively common and accepted. Averill (1982) found in Massachusetts, by means of people keeping diaries structured like questionnaires, that incidents of anger occurred about once a week. Most concerned someone the participant knew and liked (e.g., a spouse, parent, child, friend). Most (63 percent) participants said the reason for their anger was to assert authority or independence, or improve their image.

These culture-related differences may account for how Japanese and American infants respond to the anger expressions of their parents. Miyake et al. (1986) showed interesting toys to American and Japanese infants of 11 months, pairing each toy with the mother's voice expressing joy, anger, or fear. Measuring the time it took for the infants to start moving toward the toy after hearing the mother's expression, American and Japanese infants were no different in how soon they moved after the sound of their mothers' joyful or fearful voices. Cultural differences were pronounced, however, after their mothers had spoken in an angry voice: American infants started moving toward the toy an average of 18 seconds later, but Japanese infants took significantly longer, an average of 48 seconds, to start moving. Japanese babies were probably more inhibited by their mother's angry expressions because these were rare and highly negative events.

Independent and interdependent self-construals appear to be at work in culture-related differences in the evaluation of a more positive emotion. In Japan there is an emotion *amae*, for which there is no simple translation in English (Ferrari & Koyama, 2002). *Amae* is an emotion of interdependence, arising from a kind of merged togetherness, from comfort in the other person's complete acceptance. It is not that this emotion is unrecognizable in other cultures, or that it lacks universal significance. Rather, it has no approved place in adult Western life. Its original Chinese ideogram was of a breast on which the baby suckled. But as Westerners imagine this emotion, they know they ought to have grown out of it because it seems a bit infantile, a bit regressed. In Japan this is not so: this is an emotion of an accepting relationship within the family, and it is also valued as a mutual dependency between lovers.

The values approach

A second approach seeks to understand cultural differences in emotion in terms of differences in **values**, which refer to broad principles that govern our social behavior. Numerous values govern how we as members of a culture coexist in communities and accomplish tasks like allocating resources, pursuing different goals, fulfilling duties, or punishing moral violations. For example, people from different cultures attach different priorities to values like freedom, individual rights, equality, expressing thoughts and feelings, respect for authority, sexual purity, and the need to fulfill duties and obligations (e.g., Haidt, Koller, & Dias, 1993; Rozin et al., 1999; Shweder et al., 1997; Tsai, Simenova, & Watanabe, 2004). As one illustration, the anthropologist Benedict (1946) explained, in a book written in the last year of World War II and commissioned by the US Government to help understand the Japanese who were the adversaries, that to be sincere in America is to act in accord with one's innermost emotions. In Japan, the concept usually translated as sincerity, *makoto*, means something different: doing a social duty not according to inner feelings, but doing it completely, with expertise, without inner conflict.

Members of cultures that differ in the importance of specific values should experience different **elicitors** of emotions related to that value. In cultures where a particular value is prioritized, say respect for hierarchy, then one should expect emotions related to that value. So one would expect embarrassment or shame to be more readily elicited and more commonly experienced in Japan, for instance, than in America. We have already suggested that in more hierarchical cultures status- or honor-related emotions like embarrassment, shame, and pride are more common and elaborated. Now consider a rather striking observation about jealousy (Salovey, 1991; Van Sommers, 1988). Elicitors of jealousy that seem obvious in one culture do not seem to evoke jealousy in another, and these differences stem from cultural differences in sexual values. In the West, jealousy tends to be felt when the sexual attention of a primary partner turns toward someone else (Buss et al., 1992; DeSteno & Salovey, 1996; Harris, 2003; Harris & Christenfeld, 1996). As Hupka (1991) points out, in Western society monogamy, which leads to the two-parent family, is a cherished value, and a key to establishing one's adult status, economic security, housing, rearing of children, adult companionship, and sex. A sexual interloper threatens this value, and the accompanying social structure, so in Western society such a person is jealously feared and hated.

In some other, more clan-based, societies, however, the self is more interdependent, collective, extended. Cooperative effort supports everyone including the elderly, child-rearing is distributed among several people, adult companionship derives from many relatives, and monogamy is not so highly cherished. In some such societies, extramarital recreational sex is customary. Hupka (1991) discusses how when at the beginning of this century the Todas of India were visited by anthropologists, they were found to live in a society of this kind. They were not jealous when marriage partners had lovers from within their social group. Instead, Toda men did become jealous if their wives had intercourse with a non-Toda man. Interestingly Hupka says they also became distressed in a similar way if a second-born son got married before the first-born. He suggests that the core cultural value of jealousy is invoked when something highly valued, which has been hard to achieve, is threatened by an interloper. For Toda men, a great deal is invested in their first-born children, and so if this structure is threatened, distressing emotions with characteristics similar to jealousy can occur.

Heelas (1986) has proposed that in some cultures a particular emotion is recognized, has special names, and is the subject of social discussion. Such emotions are **hypercognized** (Levy, 1984). They are emphasized in the language of the culture. By contrast, certain emotions seem little noticed in some cultures; they are not conceptualized or commented upon. They are **hypocognized**. For example, in China it is important to act with honor, to fulfill one's place within a community and its many hierarchies, and to avoid losing face. Shame is an emotion that closely connects to these values. It reinforces social hierarchies, and signals respect for those in power. In China shame is hypercognized: the Chinese language has at least 113 words related to the concept of shame (Li, Wang, & Fischer, 2004). Insofar as Western culture is becoming shameless, perhaps in the West shame is on its way to being hypocognized.

The epistemological approach

Epistemologies are ways of knowing. They refer to knowledge structures and theories that guide patterns of thought, affect, and behavior in domain-specific ways (Peng, Ames, & Knowles, 2001; Peng & Nisbett, 1999). Kaiping Peng and Richard Nisbett have characterized the epistemologies of East Asians and Western Europeans (Peng & Nisbett, 1999). East Asians are guided in their knowledge and thought by a holistic, dialectical system of thought that has its roots in the great intellectual traditions of East Asia, including Confucianism, Taoism, and Buddhism. This epistemology is based on five principles: (1) change so that nothing is static; (2) contradiction, that opposites often are consistent and both true; (3) covariation, so that events are interrelated in complex fields or systems; (4) compromise, so that truth may lie in the synthesis of opposites; and (5) context, so that events occur not alone but in contexts.

In an imaginative demonstration, Peng and Nisbett (1999) tested the hypothesis that Asians should find greater meaning, and even pleasure, in contradictory ideas than Americans. They first found that Chinese proverbs involved more contradiction (e.g., "half humble is half proud") than American proverbs, which involved more one-sided, singular truths ("half a loaf is better than none"). Then Chinese and American students were presented with a set of proverbs. Chinese students found contradictory, dialectical proverbs to be more comprehensible, likeable, and usable. US students preferred the more linear proverbs.

One would expect that as compared with Americans, East Asians might experience greater **emotional complexity**: the simultaneous experience of contradictory emotions, such as happiness and sadness, compassion and contempt, or anger and love. Perhaps East Asians would be more willing to endorse multiple, even contradictory, meanings for the complex social situations and as a result, experience contradictory emotions. By contrast, Westerners might focus more on singular meanings of a situation, and experience simpler emotions.

Recent findings lend credence to this possibility. Thus, in **experience sampling** studies, in which students were beeped electronically and reported on their current emotions, as well as in laboratory studies, Chinese, Japanese, and South Korean participants were more likely than Western European students to report feeling positive and negative emotion in the particular moment (Kitayama, Markus, & Kurokawa, 2000; Schimmack, Oishi, & Diener, 2002). Western Europeans often showed negative correlations in their reports of positive and negative emotion: the more they reported of one kind of emotion, say happiness, the less they reported of its opposite, say sadness. Westerners strive to maximize positive emotion and minimize negative emotion, whereas Asians seek a balanced emotional state (Kitayama et al., 2000).

Approaches to studying cultural influences on emotion

Cross-cultural comparisons

Do cultures differ with respect to elicitors of emotions? Here researchers have given participants from different cultures emotion terms, like anger or fear, and asked them to provide situations that would produce each kind of emotion (e.g., Boucher & Brandt, 1981). Or they have provided situations and asked participants to report what emotions they might feel. Or they have given members of different cultures pictures of facial expressions of different emotions, and asked them to describe an event that would produce the emotion in the photo (Haidt & Keltner, 1999).

While there are universals in the elicitors of emotion, which we examine more closely in chapter 7, cultures have been found to differ in their emotional responses according to whether the elicitors of emotion are socially "engaging" and involve other people, or "disengaging" so that they primarily involve the self. It has been found that members of interdependent cultures such as Japanese, Surinamese, and Turkish tend to experience positive emotions (calm, elation) in socially engaging situations, for example, in informal exchanges with friends (Kitayama, Karasawa, & Mesquita, 2003; see also Mesquita, 2001). By contrast, Americans and Dutch people are more likely to experience positive emotions in relatively disengaged situations, for example in activities oriented toward personal accomplishments (see also Frijda & Mesquita, 1994; Haidt & Keltner, 1999).

A further cultural difference to emerge centers upon the notion of **display rules**, which are thought to influence how and to whom it is appropriate to express different emotions. We saw at the start of this chapter, for example, that on the Pacific island of Ifaluk it is not appropriate to express too much happiness. More generally, people can de-intensify their emotional expression, for example suppressing the urge to laugh when someone is pompous at a public meeting. People can also intensify their expression, for example smiling more appreciatively upon hearing a boss tell the same story for yet another time.

Across cultures, people vary in how they modulate their expression of emotion. For example, in many Asian cultures it is inappropriate to speak of personal accomplishments, and in these cultures individuals may de-intensify their expressions of pleasure at personal success. Among the Chewong, a small group of aboriginal hunters and shifting cultivators in Malaysia, prohibitions exist against the expression of all emotions with the exception of fear and shyness (Howell, 1981). The Chewong have explicit behavioral rules about what to do and what not to do in different circumstances. Penalties of severe bodily ills are believed to occur if rules are broken. The result is that the Chewong are emotionally inexpressive with each other. "They rarely use gestures of any kind, and their faces register little change as they speak and listen" (pp. 134–5). This raises the interesting question of whether the Chewong actually experience emotions they seem to avoid expressing.

The original demonstration of display rules is an experiment by Ekman and Friesen (Ekman, 1972; Friesen, 1972). Participants were 25 American and 25 Japanese males, each in his own country. In Phase 1 participants were alone and watched film clips of a canoe trip, a ritual circumcision, a suction-aided delivery of a baby, and nasal sinus surgery. In Phase 2 a graduate student from the participant's own society entered the room, and interviewed the participant briefly about his experience while viewing the clips. In Phase 3, the interviewer remained, sitting with his back toward the screen and facing the subject, while the very unpleasant clip of nasal surgery was replayed and the interviewer asked the participant: "Tell me how you feel right now as you look at the film." In each phase, participants' facial expressions were videotaped, although they did not know this.

The results were that when they were alone, in Phase 1, American and Japanese participants displayed similar facial expressions of fear and disgust at almost exactly the same times in the films. But in Phase 3, facing the interviewer and the screen, the Japanese participants smiled more and inhibited their negative expressions more than the Americans. When viewed in slow motion, the videotapes showed Japanese participants beginning to make a facial expression of fear or disgust, but then masking it with a polite smile. The conclusions in terms of display rules have aroused controversy, however. Fridlund (1994) is critical of the concept of display rules, and prefers the explanation that the Japanese were more polite, and tended to look more, and smile at, the interviewer rather than concentrate on the film.

Ethnographies

A further method by which we gain insights into the cultural influences upon emotion is the ethnographic approach, the method used by Lutz, with whose anecdote of the little girl who made silly faces we started this chapter. **Ethnographies** are in-depth descriptions of the social lives of a member of a particular culture. They are typically written by anthropologists who have made intensive study of the history, language, practices, customs, and rituals of a people, and who have lived amongst them, often for several years.

Rather than focusing on fairly brief emotional responses within thin slices of time, ethnographers aim to offer what the influential anthropologist Clifford Geertz (1973) has called "thick descriptions" which, in the case of emotions, concern not just what emotions occur but their settings and cultural significance. Ethnographies often focus on discourse – the means by which people use language, in its many forms, to make sense, socially, of emotional experience. Ethnographers study not just the single words people use to label their emotions, but more complex acts of communication: ritualized apologies, gossip, songs, poetry, community meetings about disruptive people, for example (Abu-Lughod & Lutz, 1990;

Lutz & White, 1986). Several influential ethnographies of the emotional lives of people of different cultures have profoundly shaped how emotion researchers think about emotion (e.g., Abu-Lughod, 1986; Briggs, 1970; Rosaldo, 1980). Let's consider Lutz's work in greater depth to give you a sense of a thick description.

Emotions on Ifaluk

Ifaluk, where Lutz did her work, is a tiny Pacific atoll about one-fifth the size of New York's Central Park. Lutz (1988) wanted to see: "if and how it was possible for people to organize their lives in such a way as to avoid the problems that seemed to me to diminish American culture, in particular its pervasive inequality of both gender and class and its violence" (p. 17). Ifaluk is a highly interdependent society. People have come to rely on each other on this island which has its highest point just a few yards above sea level and where typhoons sometimes sweep the huts away, destroy the taro gardens, and deplete fish in the lagoon.

During her first weeks on the island Lutz asked some young women who came to visit her hut: "Do you (all) want to come with me to get drinking water?" (p. 88). Their faces fell. Lutz writes that it was not until later that she realized what she had done wrong. By addressing them as "you" she had implied a separation between them and her own decision-making independent self. She writes that a more correct form, indicating an interdependent self, would be something more like: "We'll go and get water now, OK?" implying that such decisions are collective.

There are noticeable differences between social meanings of emotion in America and Ifaluk. Take the Ifaluk *ker*. Lutz translates it as "happiness/excitement." In America people believe that it is a truth self-evident that there is "a right . . . to the pursuit of happiness" (American Constitution). On Ifaluk people do not think they have any right to the pursuit of *ker*. They think they should avoid it. *Ker* is not contentment or interpersonal pleasantness, which are common on Ifaluk. A person feeling *ker* is likely to be too pleased with him- or herself. It can lead to showing off, perhaps even to rowdiness, behavior of which the Ifalukians disapprove. In interdependent cultures, certain forms of happiness can separate people from each another. They are avoided because they can lead to people not thinking enough about others. For the Ifaluk, it is better to be "*maluwelu*, gentle, calm and quiet" (p. 112).

The differences between her own and Ifalukian culture caused Lutz to make many social mistakes. One night she was frightened by a man entering the doorless hut that she had negotiated for herself. Her scream awakened her adopted family who came to see what was wrong. They were asleep a yard or two away in their communal hut, with each one's sleeping mat touching others so that no one would be lonely. The man had fled, and the family laughed hilariously when they heard Lutz had been alarmed by such an event. She said that she had been on the island long enough to know that men sometimes called on women at night for a sexual rendezvous. But she had imported the American idea that an uninvited

Figure 3.2 An Ifaluk woman smiles as she makes an impromptu head-dress for her small son. This kind of socially responsive smiling is of a lower intensity, and signals something different from *ker*, meaning "excited happiness."

visit from a man inevitably meant harm. On Ifaluk, Lutz says, although men may very occasionally seem frightening in public if drunk, so that others may fear that a disagreement might break out between them, interpersonal violence is virtually nonexistent, and rape unknown. Hence a night visitor means the very antithesis of fear. The incident became a topic of conversation. Though no one could understand why she had been frightened, Lutz sensed that her adopted mother showed some satisfaction in the story of the event because, although the anxiety that Lutz displayed was inappropriate, it was anxiety: her adopted mother thought that this meant that at last Lutz was capable of showing this valued emotion!

The most valued emotion on Ifaluk, Lutz discovered, is *fago*, translated as "compassion/love/sadness." It is the primary index of positive relationships, including those with children, relatives, and sexual partners. It is felt particularly when loved ones are in need in some way, including when they are absent, since in this absence they will be separated from those on whom they depend. It expresses the sadness that a needful state implies, and the compassion that has transmitted this sadness to the more resourceful one.

By studying the emotional lives of the Ifaluk people Lutz helped show that cultures can differ dramatically in the value they attach to particular emotions, and in the elicitors of emotion. She moved the emphasis, moreover, from thinking of emotions as brief responses toward thinking of them as complex unfolding social roles and rituals that enable individuals to situate themselves within communities.

Historical approaches

An enlightening, although infrequently used, cultural approach to emotion is the **historical method**. A hundred years from now scientists employing this method might study talk shows and soap operas, cell-phones, MTV, video games, or internet chat rooms, to glean insights into our emotional lives. For different historical periods, other kinds of documents, such as religious texts (Menon & Shweder, 1994), etiquette manuals (Elias, 1939), poems and love songs (Abu-Lughod, 1986), and popular music have been revealing of the emotional life of a culture at specific historical moments.

Consider what Stearns and Haggarty (1991) learned about the period 1850 to 1950 in their survey of 84 advice manuals for parents and popular literature aimed at children. Before 1900 three features stood out: warnings to parents about dangers of arousing fear in their children, silence on the subject of childhood fears, and boys' stories aimed at inspiring courage and acting properly despite fear. Then a change occurred: "Twentieth-century parents were told not only to avoid frightening their children as a disciplinary device but also to master their own emotions lest they give disturbing signals" (Stearns & Haggarty, 1991, p. 75). Dr Benjamin Spock (1945) in his influential manual described childhood fears as requiring careful management. Separations from toddlers arouse fears, and are to be avoided. If fears occur they should be met with patience and affection. As to boys' stories, by the 1940s the idea of acting well despite fear had disappeared, and was replaced by adventures in which tough guys felt no fear at all. In American society controlling fear has been important, first because it prevents one from being a good citizen, and latterly because it prevents one becoming an effective individual. As President Franklin Roosevelt famously put it in his 1933 inaugural address: "The only thing we have to fear is fear itself."

Consider another set of historical documents, related to the Western idea of falling in love. Here, first, is a newspaper story from the early 1950s:

On Monday Cpl. Floyd Johnson, 23, and the then Ellen Skinner, 19, total strangers, boarded a train at San Francisco and sat down across the aisle from each other. Johnson didn't cross the aisle until Wednesday, but his bride said, "I'd already made up my mind to say yes if he asked me to marry him." "We did most of the talking with our eyes," Johnson explained. Thursday the couple got off the train in Omaha with plans to be married. Because they would need to have the consent of the bride's parents if they were married in Nebraska, they crossed the river to Council Bluffs, Iowa, where they were married Friday. (Cited in Burgess & Wallin, 1953)

More than 30 years after the events recounted in the newspaper, Averill (1985) showed the story to a sample of American adults: 40 percent of them said they had had experiences conforming to the ideal embodied in the story. Another 40 percent said their experiences of love definitely did not conform to it, basing their responses on an unfavorable attitude to this ideal plus any single departure they had felt from it. In responding in this way, they too indicated that they were influenced by this ideal.

Averill argues that love of this kind has features that are distinctive to Western culture. Certainly, passionate sexual love occurs worldwide. It is experienced as joyful and energizing. It is enacted in courtship, and it includes a biological core, including increased levels of phenylalanine in the brain (Diamond, 2003; Liebowitz, 1983). To investigate its universality, Jankowiak and Fischer (1992) surveyed ethnographies of 166 societies, asking whether the writer, typically an anthropologist, made a distinction between love and lust and noted the presence of at least one of the following attributes of love occurring within the first two years of a couple meeting, irrespective of whether they married or not: (a) personal anguish or longing, (b) love songs and the like, (c) elopement due to mutual affection, (d) indigenous accounts of passionate love, or (e) the anthropologist's affirmation that love occurred. In 147 of the 166 cultures (88.5 percent) there was evidence of this kind of passionate, sexual love.

The point that Averill (1985) makes, however, is that the Western ideal of love, eagerly taken up by Hollywood, enacted 50 years ago by Floyd Johnson and Ellen Skinner, and still very much alive today, is not just the same old worldwide story. It has features that are distinctive to the West, which started their development in medieval Europe.

The germ of the idea was courtly love, created in Provence in the eleventh century, and elaborated in many medieval documents. The word "courtly" originally meant occurring at a royal court; the later meaning of "courtship" is derived from it. The idea was that a nobleman might fall in love with a lady and become her knight. Courtly love had to occur outside marriage. The lady was at first seen at a distance, and was unattainable. The knight had to offer his service, do whatever she might wish, however dangerous or however trifling, and worship her. Although the knight had to be a paragon of Christian virtue, the very idea of worshiping a lady gave the extra frisson of bordering on blasphemy.

For several hundred years courtly love was the subject of some of Europe's greatest poetry. Prototypical was the story of Lancelot and his love for Guinevere, the queen and wife of King Arthur at his court in Camelot –

told by the French poet Chrétien De Troyes in *The Knight of the Cart* (Chrétien De Troyes, 1180).

Later came the *Romance of the Rose* (De Lorris & De Meun, 1237–77). The first part, written by Guillaume De Lorris, is an extraordinary psychological allegory, in which the lovers are represented as a set of emotions and psychological characteristics, each of which is a distinct actor in the drama. The poem begins with the lover, a young man, falling asleep and dreaming. As interpreted by C. S. Lewis (1936), the reader experiences the story through the young man's eyes. He strolls by the river of life, then enters the beautiful garden of courtly love, and sees a lady there. As the wooing proceeds, his consciousness is represented by the appearance in turn of distinct characters, Hope, Sweet Thought, Reason, and so on. The lady also does not appear as a whole. She too is a cast of characters: Bielacoil (meaning "fair welcome" from the Provençal *belh aculhir*) is something like the lady's conversational self, pleasant and friendly, and it is, of course, via this aspect that the young man must first approach. Then there is Franchise (the lady's sense of aristocratic status), and Pity. But then also there are others: Danger, Fear, Shame. When the young man sounds a false note, Bielacoil disappears for hours, and only Fear or one of these others is present. Then, in addition, there is Jealousy, and the god of Love, not permanent characteristics of either the young man or the lady but able, in a somewhat unpredictable way, to take over either of them. As the young

Figure 3.3 The origin of the culturally distinctive version of romantic love that occurs in the West is traced from courtly love in medieval Europe. The most famous book depicting this was *Roman de la Rose*, for which this was an illuminated illustration from about 1500 depicting the garden of courtly love.

man reaches towards the Rose in the center of the garden, it is the god of Love who fires arrows at him, and makes him Love's servant.

One might argue that some elements in this pattern occur elsewhere. So, for instance in the Bible, Jacob is devoted to Rachel for a long period before they can unite. Nonetheless, the Western idea of being in love involves elements that do seem to be distinctive. Falling in love (in the Western way) happens suddenly, unexpectedly, involuntarily. In the full pattern devotion becomes a kind of worship. It unfolds as a script (Schank & Abelson, 1977; see also Frijda, 1988). Some 400 years ago it was described rather exactly in another historical document: *Romeo and Juliet*, by William Shakespeare (1623). Here is the script, in Schank and Abelson's sense (Oatley, 2004b): Two people must be open to the experience. Each sees the other, a stranger, and is attracted. Looks pass between them, words are not necessary. Then there is an interval of separation during which fantasies build. Then there is a meeting at which there is confirmation that the fantasies are mutual. Ping: one is in love! The state includes devotion. Shakespeare has Romeo show this by touching Juliet and saying in his very first words to her:

> If I profane with my unworthiest hand
> This holy shrine, the gentle sin is this,
> My lips, two blushing pilgrims, ready stand
> To smooth that rough touch with a tender kiss.
> (Romeo and Juliet, *1, 5, 90-4*)

The state of being in love includes the other within the idea of the self (Aron, Aron, & Allen, 1989; Aron et al., 1991; Aron & Aron, 1997; Rusbult, 1980, 1983). It becomes a temporary role that enables people to overcome difficulties, and to relinquish all previous commitments and relationships. What made the story of Floyd Johnson and Ellen Skinner so newsworthy is that it fits this pattern so perfectly.

Averill (1985) argues that without such cultural elaboration, we would not experience love as we do today. La Rochefoucauld (1665) said: "Some people would never have fallen in love if they had never heard of love" (Maxim 136). Averill and Nunley (1992) go further: they doubt whether anyone would fall in love if they had not heard of it.

Integrating evolutionary and cultural approaches to emotion

In chapter 1, we raised enduring questions about the nature of emotion. In exploring evolutionary and cultural approaches to emotion in this and the previous chapter, we have begun to answer some of those questions. While it is tempting to highlight differences between evolutionary and cultural approaches to emotion, it is just as important to recognize their convergences. Both approaches start from the assumption that emotions

Table 3.2 A comparison of evolutionary and cultural approaches

Question of interest	Evolutionary approach	Cultural approach
What is an emotion?	Biological processes	Language, beliefs, roles
Are emotions universal?	Yes	Possibly not
What are the origins of emotions?	Environment of evolutionary adaptedness	Practices, institutions, values
Functions	Individual: Action readiness	Reify intentions and values
	Dyadic: Social coordination	Reify roles, identities, and ideologies

contribute solutions to basic problems of social living. Both assume that emotions help humans form attachments, take care of offspring, fold into hierarchies, and maintain long-term friendships. The central theme of this book is squarely at the heart of the two approaches.

Evolutionary and cultural approaches both assume that emotions serve important functions. The two approaches focus on different kinds of functions, but both assume emotions are functional and adaptive. Gone is the view that emotions are dysfunctional, maladaptive, and pernicious to social life.

There are numerous differences however, as one sees in table 3.2. A first concerns the simplest question: What is an emotion? For evolutionary theorists, emotions are universal, hard-wired affect programs that solve ancient, recurrent threats to survival and occurrences of opportunity (Ekman, 1992; Lazarus, 1991; Plutchik, 1980; Tomkins, 1984; Tooby & Cosmides, 1990). Emotions, from this perspective, are species-characteristic patterns of action, derived from natural selection. For cultural theorists, the core of an emotional experience is found in words, in metaphors, in concepts that permeate the conscious experience of emotions. Emotions are discourse processes, and they are roles that we fulfill within relationships. For these theorists, some elements of emotion may be universal, but what is most striking are pronounced cultural differences in emotion that are socially learned in the process of social discourse, according to culturally specific concerns about identity, morality, and social structure (Averill, 1985; Lutz & White, 1986; Mesquita, 2003; Shweder & Haidt, 2000).

Cultural theorists often push cultural specificity one step further. They sometimes contend that the experience of different emotions is not really comparable across cultures. The argument is, for instance, that *fago* is distinctive to Ifaluk. It can be hinted at by describing how it arises, and indicated by a composite of English terms (compassion/love/sadness), but you cannot experience the Ifaluk emotion *fago* unless you are a member of that society. Similarly, as Averill (1985) argues, you could not experience falling in love, with its mixture of sexual attraction, devotion, the feeling of altruism, and the making of lifelong commitment, unless you have been enculturated in the West.

On the question of where emotions come from, we hope you now have a sense of how the two approaches each answer this question. Evolutionary theorists locate the emergence of emotions in our phylogenetic history, identifying emotions in nonhuman primates, and see them as adaptations to problems or opportunities that are specific to the environment of evolutionary adaptedness. Cultural theorists locate the origins of emotions within the history of cultural developments. They trace the origins of emotions to the emergence of new institutions, values, technologies, cultural narratives, social practices, and the like.

So why do we have emotions? Evolutionary theorists tend to concentrate on how emotions serve functions for the species by way of species-characteristic mechanisms possessed by individuals. At the individual level of analysis, emotions prepare the individual for action in his or her best interest (e.g., Frijda et al., 1989; Levenson, 1999). At the dyadic level of analysis, the focus is on communication and coordination of emotion through facial, vocal, and postural channels (Ekman, 1992; Keltner et al., 2003; Juslin & Laukka, 2003; Dimberg & Öhman, 1996; Scherer, 1986; Scherer, Johnstone, & Klasmeyer, 2003). At this level, emotions communicate information about current emotions, intentions, and dispositions, to help accomplish mutuality or conflict and coordinated responses to problems and opportunities in the environment.

Cultural theorists tend to focus on another level of analysis: on how emotions serve functions for groups and societies. They see emotions as helping define values and enabling group members to negotiate roles (e.g., Clark, 1990; Collins, 1990). The ritualized experience of shame, for example, signals the individual's place within group hierarchies and reinforces certain roles and values. At this cultural level of analysis, emotions help individuals achieve identities, and they help reify, or fortify, cultural ideologies and power structures, regarding gender roles, for example (e.g., Hochschild, 1990; Lutz, 1990).

Let us conclude our integration of the evolutionary and cultural approaches to emotion by considering how researchers working within the two traditions would approach one emotion: embarrassment. Researchers guided by an evolutionary approach would seek to document the biological bases of embarrassment – the blush and its characteristic nonverbal display, for example – and how these aspects of embarrassment are universal, and can even be seen in the rudimentary appeasement displays of nonhuman primates and other species (Keltner & Buswell, 1997). This approach would claim that embarrassment informs the individual of transgressions to avoid, that it signals to others a sense of remorse for the transgression, thus evoking forgiveness, and in these ways prompts reconciliation following conflict and social transgressions (Keltner & Buswell, 1997; Miller & Leary, 1992).

From a cultural approach, what's interesting about embarrassment is how it is represented in words, how it is valued, how it is associated with important values, like deference, modesty, and submissiveness. Researchers working from a cultural approach would seek to document how the meaning, value, and elicitors of embarrassment vary dramatically across cultures, according to cultures' self-construals, or values, or epistemologies. Cultural theorists would seek to identify the origins of a culture's specific version of embarrassment within that culture's social history. In ancient Japan, for instance, embarrassment was hypercognized. In *The Tale of Genji* (Shikibu, *c*.1000), which is thought to be the world's first full-length novel, written 1,000 years ago by Murasaki Shikibu a lady in the Emperor's court in what is now Kyoto, we see that embarrassment can occur simply by being in the presence of a higher ranking individual. (You might get a glimmer of this kind of emotion if you have ever felt shy in the presence of an important person.) Here are some glimpses from that distant culture. When the youthful Prince Genji visits the house of his former nurse who is ill, the nurse speaks to Genji fondly and tearfully. Her children are "acutely embarrassed . . . before so unbecoming a show of emotion in Genji's presence" (p. 57). They would not have been embarrassed if their mother had spoken to them in this way. It is Genji's rank that causes their embarrassment. Later in the same chapter Genji stays the night with a lover, Yugao, who is of lower social status than he. She wakes in the morning, in her humble house, to the sound of her uncouth neighbors calling out to each other. In the West one might be annoyed at such a din, or worried that it might wake the sleeping loved one. Not so for Yugao: she is "deeply embarrassed by this chatter and clatter all around them of people rising and preparing to go about their pitiful tasks" (p. 63). Had they awoken in a royal palace there would have been nothing pitiful. All would have been appropriate to Genji's high status. In theorizing about the functions of embarrassment, a cultural approach would suggest that it serves important functions for particular groups in particular societies. It communicates the individual's position within a group, and conveys commitments to cultural mores and standards. We believe that to understand emotions fully in social life, we need the wisdom of both theoretical perspectives.

Summary

How do we explain cultural differences in emotion? To answer this question, we first considered how emotions in the West themselves are products of a particular culture known as Romanticism, which prioritized the emotions in social life. We then outlined the basic assumptions of a cultural approach to emotions: emotions are shaped by dynamic cultural processes, they can be thought of as roles, and insights into the cultural influences upon emotion are gleaned when we focus on emotional practice, that is, how emotions are experienced in day-to-day living. Having outlined the basic assumptions of cultural approaches to emotion, we considered three specific approaches to cultural variation in emotion. One approach traces culture-related differences in emotion back to differences in self-construal, a second to cultural differences in values, and a third back to differences in culture-specific epistemologies, or ways of knowing. We then reviewed how to study cultural influences on emotion. We looked at cross-cultural comparisons of emotions, rich descriptions of culture known as ethnographies, and historical approaches. As we reviewed these different conceptual and methodological approaches to culture, we saw that cultures vary in the value they attach to different emotions, in emotion display rules, in the elicitors and language of emotion, and the complexity of emotional experience. We concluded our chapter by integrating evolutionary and cultural approaches to emotion.

Further reading

If you do not like the idea of reading Mary Shelley's *Frankenstein*, perhaps you would prefer the most famous European romantic novella of the eighteenth century, a semi-autobiographical piece by the scientist-novelist-playwright:

Johann von Goethe (1774). *The sorrows of young Werther* (translated by M. Hulse). Harmondsworth: Penguin (1989).

A book based on living for nine months on a tiny Pacific island – one of the classics of emotional life and customs:

Catherine Lutz (1988). *Unnatural emotions: Everyday sentiments on a Micronesian atoll and their challenge to Western theory*. Chicago: University of Chicago Press.

For a superb treatment of how emotions like embarrassment and shame help members of a culture fulfill social roles and values, and how emotions permeate social practices, like poems and articles of clothing, read:

Lila Abu-Lughod (1986). *Veiled sentiments*. Berkeley: University of California Press.

An excellent recent review is found in:

Batja Mesquita (2003). Emotions as dynamic cultural phenomena. In R. J. Davidson, K. R. Scherer, & H. H. Goldsmith (Eds.). *Handbook of affective sciences* (pp. 871–90). Oxford University Press.

PART II

Elements of Emotions

Communication of Emotions

...there is a kind of universal language, consisting of expressions of the face and eyes, gestures and tones of voice, which can show whether a person means to ask for something and get it, or refuse it and have nothing to do with it.

Augustine, Confessions, 1–8

Contents

Figure 4.0 Chimpanzees communicate emotions in many ways, including touch, as in this activity called grooming, by which they maintain their affectionate relationships.

The next time you leave a classroom, take a look at the students standing around and talking, perhaps hashing over an inspired lecture they just heard or planning the weekend. You're likely to see some people flirting. If you look closely enough, you may conclude that everyone is flirting, almost all of the time.

To document how people flirt, Givens (1983) and Perper (1985) studiously spent hundreds of hours in singles bars, laboriously writing down the patterns of nonverbal behaviors shown by women and men. They homed in on those that predicted whether women and men would pursue a romantic encounter. What they discovered was a layered and varied language by which women and men negotiate romantic inclinations. In the initial attention-getting phase, men roll their shoulders and raise their arms with exaggerated gestures that allow them to show off potential signs of their social status – their well-developed arms or flashy watches. At the same time, women smile coyly, they look askance, they flick their hair, and walk with arched back and swaying hips. In the recognition phase, women and men gaze intently at each other, they express interest with raised eyebrows, sing-song voice, melodious laughter, and subtle lip puckers. Then women and men explore their interest in each other with provocative brushes of the arm, pats on the shoulder, or not so accidental bumps against one another, looking for subtle signs of delight or disgust. Finally, in the keeping-time phase, the potential partners mirror each other's glances, laughter, gaze, and posture, to assess their interest in one another.

In most social interactions, like flirting, people express emotions. The communication of emotion is central to play, grieving, arguing, soothing, status negotiation, persuasion, and socialization. People express emotions with facial actions, with their voice, with touch, with posture (Weisfeld & Beresford, 1982), and with their gait (Montepare, Goldstein, & Clausen, 1987). The communication of emotion occurs in different channels, many of which were recognized by Darwin, in his pioneering study of emotional expression, discussed in chapter 1. We list some of these forms of expression in table 1.1.

Five kinds of nonverbal behavior

Words such as "smile," "laugh," "gaze," and "touch" seem simple enough, but they can refer to many classes of nonverbal behavior, with different and often contrasting emotional connotations. Take the word "smile." There have been heated debates about what smiles mean, and the extent to which they necessarily accompany the experience of positive emotion (e.g., Frank, Ekman, & Friesen, 1993; Fernandez-Dols & Ruiz-Belda, 1995, 1997; Fridlund, 1992; Kraut & Johnston, 1979). The answer, in part, is that there are many different smiles, with different meanings. We smile to be polite, to hide inappropriate feelings of disgust or disapproval, to express romantic attraction, to signal weakness, to pretend that we are following what another person is saying, to name a few of the many kinds of smiles.

Figure 4.1 "Flirtation," by the Hungarian painter Miklós Barabás, showing characteristic elements: the man shows direct interest with body and head oriented toward the woman; the woman shows classic coyness, with head and gaze cast away.

Often single words like "smile" fail adequately to describe the language of **nonverbal communication**.

To help clarify the study of emotional communication, Paul Ekman and Wallace Friesen (1969) organized the language of nonverbal behavior into five categories. First is the category of *emblems*: nonverbal gestures that directly translate to words. Well-known examples for English speakers include the peace sign, the rubbing of one forefinger with the other to say "shame on you," and in the late 1960s, the raised, clenched fist for Black

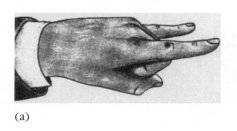

(a)

(b)

Figure 4.2 Two coarse gestures of contempt: (a) seen in Italy and Spain, but not in northern Europe; (b) seen in Britain, but not in southern Europe. Such gestures are based on learned conventions like words (from Morris et al., 1979).

Power. Researchers have analyzed over 800 emblems throughout the world. No doubt there are many more.

Emblems vary in their meaning across cultures. For instance, the gesture of extending the index finger and little finger of one hand toward someone (see figure 4.2) indicates contempt in Italy and Spain, but it is largely unknown in Britain and Scandinavia. In Britain the equivalent gesture is raising the first and second fingers of one hand with the palm facing towards the sender, and it is largely unknown elsewhere. In America the equivalent gesture is raising the middle finger, and in Australia it is raising the thumb. All four gestures have comparable meanings as insults with a coarse sexual connotation, but except for being made with fingers they share few morphological features. They are like a word in four different languages. Politicians wanting to show a common touch and believing in the universality of such gestures sometimes get them wrong: so there are news photographs of US President George H. W. Bush raising his thumb on his state visit to Australia in the early 1990s, evidently intending a sign meaning "OK," but seen quite differently by Australians.

A second category of nonverbal behaviors is the *illustrator*, a nonverbal gesture that accompanies our speech, and often makes it vivid and visual. We make hand gestures most of the time when we speak – spend a few minutes observing. McNeill (e.g., 2000) has shown that these gestures slightly precede the corresponding words we say. We also make facial gestures, but we do not just raise our eyebrows when uttering important phrases, we nod our head, and move our torso to show empathy. When Bill Clinton was President of the United States, a signature illustrator of his was a fist with a partially exposed thumb. Perhaps there was a bit of emblematic meaning to this gesture as well; perhaps he hoped to signify that he was optimistic (the thumb pointing upwards) and strong (the clenched fist).

Regulators are nonverbal behaviors that we use to coordinate conversation. People look and point at and orient their bodies toward people whom they want to start speaking. They look and turn their bodies away from those they wish would stop speaking. It is a remarkable feat of human social life that people can carry on civil conversations in groups without explicitly designating who is to speak and who is not. They do so, in large part, thanks to the use of regulators.

A fourth kind of nonverbal behavior is the *self-adaptor*, which refers to nervous behaviors people engage in with no seeming intention, as if simply to release nervous energy. People touch their necks, tug at their hair, jiggle their legs, and stroke their chins. Finally, there are nonverbal expressions or displays of emotion: signals in the face, voice, body, and touch that convey emotion.

Facial expressions of emotion

How can we differentiate emotional expressions from other kinds of non-verbal behavior? What distinguishes, for example, an exhilarated laugh from a laugh that nervously fills the gaps in a conversation? How do smiles of enjoyment differ from smiles that actually accompany pain and suffering, for example, when someone receives a painful injection but smiles? How does a sincere expression of anger at being slighted differ from a mock expression of anger, in which someone dramatically enacts the expression of anger, but in actuality feels little emotion?

The markers of emotional expressions   Several characteristics have been identified that differentiate emotional expressions from other nonverbal behavior (e.g., Frank et al., 1993). Most of these criteria have been established in the study of facial expression, although we expect some of these criteria to apply to other kinds of emotional communication as well. First, expressions of emotion tend to be fairly brief, typically lasting between 1 and 10 seconds (Bachorowski & Owren, 2001; Bachorowski, Smoski, & Owren, 2001; Ekman, 1993). A smile accompanying enjoyment will typically start and stop within a span of ten seconds. A polite smile that does not accompany the experience of emotion might be exceptionally brief, lasting a quarter of a second, or it might endure for some time, for instance when someone smiles politely through the entire course of an unpleasant dinner party.

Second, facial expressions of emotion involve involuntary muscle actions that people cannot produce when they feel like it, and cannot suppress, even when instructed to do so (Dimberg, Thunberg, & Grunedal, 2002; Kappas, Bherer, & Thériault, 2000). The facial expression of anger, for example, involves the action of the muscle that tightens around the mouth, which most people cannot produce voluntarily. The facial expression of sympathy involves two muscle actions in the upper part of the face that produce oblique eyebrows, which cannot be produced by most people voluntarily (Eisenberg et al., 1989). Feigned expressions of anger, therefore, would lack the muscle tightening around the mouth; feigned expressions of sympathy would lack the oblique eyebrows. These involuntary actions that accompany emotional expressions have a different neuroanatomical basis than voluntary facial actions such as the furrowed brow or lip press (Rinn, 1984). This suggests that affective displays, as opposed to mock or feigned expressions, are reliable indicators of the individual's feeling (Frank, 1988). We suspect you can think of many occasions when it really mattered to you that a person's expression of emotion – for example of love or sympathy or anger – was indeed sincere.

Third, emotional expressions should have their parallels, or homologues, in the displays of other species. If emotions derive from our evolutionary heritage, then certain elements of human affective displays should be seen in other species.

Studies of the universality of facial expressions

Darwin (1872) proposed three principles to explain why emotional expressions have the appearance that they do. First, according to the *principle of serviceable habits*, expressive behaviors that have led to rewards will re-occur in the future. For example, the furrowed brow, which protects the eyes from blows, and exposed teeth, which signal imminent attack, are beneficial in aggressive encounters, and therefore they occur when you're angry. Second, the *principle of antithesis* holds that opposing states will be associated with opposing expressions. For example, strength and confidence are expressed by expanding the chest and shoulders whereas weakness and uncertainty are expressed by the opposite, a shoulder shrug. This principle is probably at play in the properties of expressions of embarrassment and pride, which we will discuss later. Third, the *principle of nervous discharge* states that excess, undirected energy is released in random expressions, such as face touches, leg jiggles, and the like.

In his book on expression, Darwin advanced his claim that facial expressions of emotion, as part of our evolutionary heritage, are human universals and – as we discussed in chapter 1 – he marshaled several kinds of evidence. Sylvan Tomkins, Paul Ekman, and Carroll Izard carefully read this work of Darwin's, and distilled his observations into two simple hypotheses (Ekman, Sorenson, & Friesen, 1969; Izard, 1971; Tomkins, 1962, 1963). First the **encoding hypothesis**: if emotions are universal, the experience of different emotions should be associated with the same distinct facial expressions in every society, worldwide. Second, the **decoding hypothesis**: if there are universal emotions, people of different cultures should interpret these expressions in the same ways. These hypotheses could be tested with facial expressions, vocal expressions, and with touch.

Ekman and Friesen initially took over 3,000 photos of different people as they expressed six different emotions, anger, disgust, fear, happiness (a big smile), sadness, and surprise, according to Darwin's descriptions of the muscle configurations. Ekman, Sorenson, and Friesen then took the most easily identified examples of each emotion, and presented these photos to individuals in Japan, Brazil, Argentina, Chile, and the United States. Participants in these five cultures were asked to select from six emotion

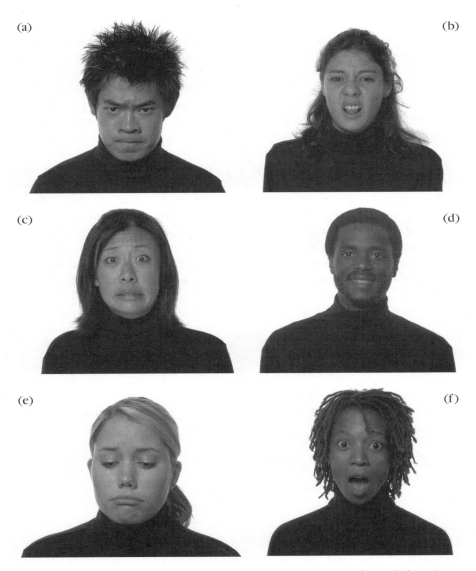

Figure 4.3 Six different emotions: (a) anger, (b) disgust, (c) fear, (d) happiness, (e) sadness, and (f) surprise. These photos are similar to those described by Darwin, to those used by Ekman and Friesen in their universality studies, and to those used in many other studies of facial expression.

terms the one that best matched the feeling the person was showing in each photo. Across the five cultures, participants achieved accuracy rates between 80 and 90 percent for the six emotions (Ekman, Sorenson, & Friesen, 1969). In these studies, chance guessing, by randomly selecting one term out of six that actually matched the emotion in the photo, would produce accuracy rates of 16.6 percent. Critics, however, noted a problem: participants in Japan, Brazil, Argentina, and Chile had all seen American media, and so were not really representative of isolated and distinct cultures. They might have become familiar with American culture by watching TV and film actors.

To meet this challenge, Ekman and Friesen needed to find a culture that had little or no exposure to Western media or to Westerners. This proved a difficult challenge. To meet it, Ekman went to Papua, New Guinea, and for six months lived with a people of the Fore (pronounced "Foray") language group who lived in Stone Age conditions. The Fore who participated in Ekman's study had seen no movies or magazines, they did not speak English or pidgin (a combination of English and a native language), and they had had minimal exposure to Westerners.

In this study, Ekman relied on a judgment paradigm known as the Dashiell method (Ekman & Friesen, 1971), in which he devised an emotion-appropriate story for each of the six emotions. For example, the sadness story was: "the person's child had died, and he felt sad." He then presented photos of three different expressions along with a story that matched one of the expressions, and asked participants to match the story to one of the three expressions (chance guessing would have yielded identification rates of 33 percent). In another task, he videotaped Fore participants as they

Table 4.1 Accuracy rates for participants from New Guinea and the USA in judging photographs of six emotions. For the Fore judges (the first two columns), chance guessing would yield accuracy rates of 33%. For the US college student judges, chance guessing would yield accuracy rates of 16.6%

	The Fore of New Guinea		US college students
	Judging Ekman and Friesen's photos		Judging emotional expressions posed by the Fore
	Adults	Children	
Anger	84	90	51
Disgust	81	85	46
Fear	80	93	18
Happiness	92	92	73
Sadness	79	91	68
Surprise	68	98	27

Source: Adapted from Ekman (1972)

displayed facial expressions they would show in response to the emotion-specific story. Ekman videotaped these posed expressions and presented unedited clips of these expressions to college students in the US, who selected from six emotion terms the one that best matched the Fore's pose in each clip (chance guessing would yield identification rates of 16.6 percent).

The results from these two studies largely confirmed Darwin's earlier ideas about the universality of emotional expression. The Fore participants achieved accuracy rates between 80 and 90 percent in identifying the six emotions portrayed in Ekman and Friesen's photos. This was even true of children, suggesting that the ability to judge emotions from facial expression occurs early in development. US college students correctly interpreted the posed expressions of the Fore, with the exception of fear and surprise.

There have been dozens of similar studies since this one, and they consistently find that people from cultures that differ in their religion, political structure, economic development, and self-construals agree in how they label the photos that depict anger, disgust, fear, happiness, sadness, and surprise (Ekman, 1984, 1993; Elfenbein & Ambady, 2002, 2003; Izard, 1971, 1994). The implication is that recognition of the six facial expressions used in these studies is a universal, evolved parts of human nature (Brown, 1991).

Critiques of the studies of universal facial expressions

There have been several **critiques** of the hypothesis of universal facial expressions (e.g., Fridlund, 1992; Russell, 1994). First is the *gradient critique*. According to the universality hypothesis, facial expressions that are universal should be produced in much the same way, and be equally recognizable in all cultures. But the results show gradients between the recognition of some expressions that are well recognized universally, like happiness, and other expressions such as those of fear, surprise, and disgust, which are less well recognized by people in cultures remote from those of the person portraying the expression.

Second is the *forced choice* critique. In Ekman and Friesen's study, and many other judgment studies, participants were forced to label the expressions using terms the researchers provided, namely, anger, disgust, fear, happiness, sadness, and surprise, or their translations. Might participants label the faces in different fashion if allowed to use their own words? Might they label a smile "gratitude" or "reverence" or "amae/pleasurable dependence" (see chapter 3) rather than "happiness," or might they label it with some concept that does not map onto Western conceptions?

The best way to address this important critique is simple: simply gather participants' own descriptions of photos of facial expressions of emotion, and ascertain whether there is universality in their free response data. Haidt and Keltner (1999) did this in the United States and India. Participants were asked to label photos of 14 different expressions, including the Ekman expressions, in their own words. Haidt and Keltner reported evidence that tended to support the *gradient critique*. They found a gradient of recognition (of the kind that Russell had pointed out) in which some expressions were more recognizable than others. They also reported evidence to counter the *forced choice critique*. When coded, the freely produced labels revealed that participants from these strikingly different cultures used similar concepts in labeling facial expressions of anger, disgust, fear, happiness, sadness, surprise, and embarrassment (see also Izard, 1971).

The *forced choice* critique maintains that the response format of the Ekman and Friesen study may have yielded the robust accuracy rates by allowing participants to make educated guesses about expressions they may not have known how to label (Fridlund, 1992; Russell, 1994). That is, in forced choice judgments, a participant can label a face correctly by a process of elimination ("that face {a disgust face} doesn't look like sadness, or anger or fear, and it clearly isn't happiness, or surprise, so it must be disgust"). Here again the critique has been put to the test. In one study, participants were presented with the usual facial expressions and terms, but they were also given options such as "none of the above," or they were given additional response options (Frank & Stennett, 2001). These techniques, which made guessing strategies less likely, did not reduce agreement in judging facial expression. There is, however, room for disagreement. In this field researchers have looked at the same data, and some have seen strong evidence for universality, while others have seen only modest evidence.

A third critique is in terms of *ecological validity*: perhaps expressions portrayed in Ekman's studies are not the kinds of expressions that people routinely judge in their daily lives. The expressions are highly stylized and exaggerated, often made by actors or others who are adept at moving their facial muscles. This raises the question of whether everyday expressions of anger, disgust, fear, and sadness would look like the expressions in the Ekman and Friesen photos. Perhaps more importantly, this critique asks whether more subtle expressions of emotion, perhaps more typical of everyday emotional expression, would be so reliably judged (Wagner, MacDonald, & Manstead, 1986).

Most of the research on recognition of facial expressions has, for convenience, used static pictures. Recently, Ambadar, Schooler, and Cohn (2005) have shown that people are better at recognizing emotional expressions from dynamic displays, that is to say video clips, which of course come closer to real-life conditions. Some of the conclusions we have reviewed above might change if and when moving video faces are used more in research on expression.

Discovering new facial displays of emotions

We have seen that anger, disgust, fear, happiness, sadness, and surprise may have universal facial expressions. Have **other expressions** with properties of universality been newly discovered? The answer is yes. Contempt has been added to the list. It is expressed by an asymmetrical tightening of the lip corners or sneer, and conveys a moral disapproval of another

(Matsumoto & Ekman, 2004). Laughter involving the contraction of the muscle surrounding the eyes also appears to be a signal of a distinct emotion, namely exhilaration (Ruch, 1993).

Think for a moment of your own emotional interactions. Have you seen facial displays of emotion other than those that Ekman, Friesen, and Izard studied 30 years ago? Can you tell whether your romantic partner is or is not jealous by studying his or her face? Can you detect a friend's guilt at having forgotten your birthday? How about love or gratitude, emotions crucial to romantic bonds and friendships?

To document emotional expressions beyond the six originally used by Ekman, plus contempt and exhilaration, one needs to show that the experience of a specific emotion correlates with a unique pattern of facial actions (encoding evidence). Then one needs to show that others perceive that display as a sign of the target emotion, preferably in different cultures (decoding evidence). And finally, it is important for evolutionary claims to show that other species show similar expressive behaviors in contexts that resemble those of the emotion of interest. There have been recent studies guided by these principles. They suggest that there are distinct nonverbal signals for embarrassment, shame, pride, love, desire, and sympathy.

Embarrassment   As we briefly noted in chapter 2, embarrassment is thought of by many as an appeasement-related emotion, which signals the individual's lower status, in particular after transgressions, so as to bring about social reconciliation (Keltner & Buswell, 1997; Miller & Leary, 1992). Darwin had many things to say about the self-conscious emotions, but largely focused his analysis on the blush.

How might one elicit the experience of embarrassment in the lab, to document its accompanying affective display? Researchers have resorted to rather mischievous means. To these ends students have sucked on a pacifier in front of friends or modeled different bathing suits for an experimenter. Young children have been lavished with excessive praise by different experimenters avidly snapping photographs of the slightly confused child. In perhaps the most mortifying test, participants had to sing Barry Manilow's song "Feelings" using dramatic hand gestures and then watch a videotape of their performance with a group of other students.

To characterize the nonverbal actions of embarrassment, Keltner (1995) chose a task in which participants' heads would be relatively stationary, so that their facial actions could be coded in frame-by-frame analyses. So he had participants complete the following embarrassing task. They had to follow muscle-by-muscle instructions, given by a rather stern experimenter, to achieve a difficult and odd-looking facial expression, as they were being videotaped. The instructions were:

Raise your eyebrows.
Close one eye.
Pucker your lips.
Puff out your cheeks.

Typically, after a 15-second struggle, participants achieved the expression. They then were asked to hold the expression for 10 seconds, and then were told to rest. Performing this task resembles a common elicitor of embarrassment – loss of physical poise and composure in front of others (Miller, 1992; Miller & Tangney, 1994). For those participants who spontaneously reported experiencing embarrassment, Keltner coded the 10 seconds of behavior that occurred immediately after the participant was asked to rest.

Careful frame-by-frame analysis uncovered a fleeting but highly coordinated 2- to 3-second affective display, the components of which are presented in figure 4.3 (see also Edelmann & Hampson, 1979, 1981; Harris, 2001). First, the embarrassed individual's eyes went down, within .75 seconds. Then the individual turned his head to the side, typically leftward, and down within the next .5 seconds. As this head movement occurred, the individual smiled a smile that lasted about two seconds. At the onset and offset of this smile were other facial actions in the mouth, such as lip sucks, lip presses, lip puckers. And while the person's head was down and to the left a few curious actions occurred: the person looked up two to three times with furtive glances, and often touched his or her face. Like other expressions, this pattern of actions unfolded in this same order, in a coordinated and reliable way within a period of 5 seconds. It had the fluid, gradual onset and offset times of an involuntary expression. It did not have characteristics of feigned expressions which, like polite smiles, can come on the face in milliseconds, or remain for hours (Frank et al., 1993).

Is there decoding evidence to show that observers can readily identify this display as embarrassment? In one study, participants were presented with 2- to 3-second long video-clips of the embarrassment displays along with spontaneous displays of other emotions, including disgust, anger, shame, amusement, and fear. Using a forced choice method, they had to label each expression (Keltner, 1995). They reliably judged the displays as communicating embarrassment.

One might wonder whether observers can judge embarrassment from its static cues – the downward gaze and head movement, the controlled smile – in the absence of dynamic cues contained in the unfolding display of embarrassment represented in figure 4.4. Or, perhaps embarrassment is a different kind of display, one that is only decoded when the observer can watch it unfold over time. To address this question, and to see whether the display of embarrassment may be universal, people from a small town in India were presented with static photos of the embarrassment display and allowed to interpret the expression with their own words (Haidt & Keltner, 1999). They too labeled the display as embarrassment, and readily differentiated between this display and that of shame, which is signaled by downward head movements and gaze aversion (Keltner & Harker, 1998).

Do other species show similar, embarrassment-like behavior? Keltner and Buswell (1997) analyzed approximately three dozen studies of appeasement displays of other species to answer this question. In appeasement interactions, one individual, typically a subordinate, relies on certain signals to pacify and reduce the aggressive tendencies of another individual, often a dominant individual in the social hierarchy (De Waal, 1989). Human embarrassment displays do resemble the appeasement displays of other species. Let's take it behavior by behavior, in the Darwinian fashion, to understand the deeper significance of the elements of the embarrassment display.

First, there is gaze aversion. This is a classic cut-off behavior many species rely on to appease others. Many primates turn their heads away to interrupt escalating aggression. Extended eye contact signals the opposite: the intent to escalate. What about the head movements down? Various species, including pigs, rabbits, blue-footed boobies, pigeons, doves, and loons, use head movements down, head turns, and head bobs to appease. These head movements reduce the size of the body, signaling submissiveness. As for the embarrassed smile, it is more than a simple smile; it has accompanying smile controls that include lip presses, no doubt a sign of inhibition, as well as lip puckers. This kind of controlled smile is a common signal of appeasement in certain nonhuman primates. The face touch may be the most mysterious element of embarrassment. Several primates cover their faces when appeasing, as do rabbits. The elements of embarrassment, then, are routinely seen in the appeasement displays of other species.

Displays of positive emotion   You might have been struck by the fact that Ekman and Friesen only studied one positive display – the smile. Are there displays associated with other positive emotions? From the perspective we have developed in this book – that emotions help coordinate significant social interactions – one could readily argue that several positive emotions are likely to have distinctive displays. Might love have a display that is critical to romantic exchanges? And if shame has a display, what about pride?

As to love, Robert Frank (1988) has argued that it serves a vital commitment function, signaling devotion and commitment to potential romantic partners. This analysis may strike a chord with you, reminding you of how carefully you scrutinize a potential partner's nonverbal displays to discern their romantic intentions. It also suggests that humans may have evolved displays that inform others of their romantic inclinations. Guided by this commitment-based analysis, Gonzaga et al. (2001) have studied the nonverbal displays of romantic partners as they experienced love and desire while talking to each other on a first date. They found that the momentary experience of love is expressed in a coherent pattern of smiling, mutual gaze, affiliative hand gestures, open posture, and forward leans. In contrast, desire is signaled in a variety of lip-related actions, including lip licks, wipes, and tongue protrusions.

As to pride, Jessica Tracy and Rick Robins have hypothesized it to be signaled by nonverbal actions that signal the opposite of weakness, which is signaled by postural constriction and reduction of physical size. For pride, then, one would expect expansive posture, head movements up and back. Tracy and Robins (2004) photographed people displaying postural expansion as well as a backward head tilt and a slight smile, and observers reliably judged these displays as pride.

Finally, what about sympathy, or compassion – the feeling of concern for enhancing the welfare of someone who is in need or suffering? In a series of studies, Nancy Eisenberg and her colleagues have carefully coded the facial actions of people who are witnessing someone suffer and who are inclined to help (Eisenberg et al., 1989). They have found that the experience of sympathy is correlated with a distinct display, namely oblique eyebrows and concerned gaze. She also has found that this display is associated with increased helping behavior, and that this display is different from a display of distress.

Taken together, there is evidence that eight facial expressions of emotion, the six original ones investigated by Ekman and his colleagues, plus contempt and exhilaration, at least in prototypical forms, are universal (Ekman, Friesen, & Ellsworth, 1982; Ekman, 1994; Elfenbein & Ambady, 2002, 2003; Mesquita & Frijda, 1992). There is still controversy in the field, however. Russell and his colleagues (Russell & Ferandez Dols, 1997; Russell, Bachorowski, & Fernandez-Dols, 2003) favor what they call minimum universality, in which the evidence is strong that some expressions such as the smile of happiness are recognized worldwide, while for other expressions the evidence is less strong. Some recently investigated expressions – of embarrassment, shame, pride, love, desire, and sympathy – also have characteristic features of evolved displays. Whether they are universal remains a question for the future, but preliminary evidence indicates that they may be.

Facial expression and the coordination of social interaction

Another line of research has uncovered how facial expressions of emotion **coordinate social interactions**. Groundbreaking studies by people like Arne Öhman and Ulf Dimberg, and conceptual analyses of facial expression by Alan Fridlund and others, have suggested that facial expressions of emotion are more than just signals of internal states. Facial expressions coordinate social interactions through their informative, evocative, and incentive functions (Keltner & Kring, 1998).

The informative function is that emotional experience and expression are sources of information about the social world. Emotion displays indicate the sender's emotions, intentions, and relationship with the target (Ekman, 1993; Fridlund, 1992). They convey information about the environment external to the relationship as well, allowing individuals to coordinate their responses to outside opportunities or threats (e.g., Klinnert et al., 1986; Sorce et al., 1985).

Emotion displays have evocative functions, eliciting complementary or matching emotions from relationship partners (Eibl-Eibesfeldt, 1989; Keltner & Kring, 1998). For example, photographed facial displays of anger enhance fear conditioning in observers, even when the photographs are not consciously perceived (Öhman & Dimberg, 1978; Esteves, Dimberg, & Öhman, 1994). Several studies have also shown that expressions of distress evoke compassion or sympathy in observers (e.g., Eisenberg et al., 1989).

As to incentives, displays invite desired social behavior. Displays of positive emotion are often used by parents to reward behaviors in children, thus increasing the probability of those behaviors in the future (e.g., Tronick, 1989). Laughter from interaction partners also rewards desirable social behavior in adults (Owren & Bachorowski, 2001).

Cultural variation in facial expressions of emotions

If you have traveled abroad, you may have been struck by how similar emotional expression is in different cultures. Stroll in a *zocolo* (square) in rural Mexico or market place in Thailand or wait at a bus stop in Nigeria and you're likely to be impressed by the many similarities in emotional expression across cultures. You'll see children smiling and laughing as they play. Courting adolescents might show familiar coy expressions. People arguing might furrow their brows or sneer in obvious disdain in recognizable ways. The studies that we have reviewed thus far capture this universality of emotional expression.

At the same time, there is **cultural variation**: emotional expression seems to vary dramatically across cultures. Early cultural researchers argued that cultures vary profoundly in how they express emotion, a view that found support in various observations. Briggs (1970) found that the Inuit who live in the Canadian Arctic (colloquially referred to as Eskimos) do not express anger. Seventeenth-century Japanese wives of Samurai soldiers were alleged to smile upon receipt of the news that their husbands had died nobly in battle. Along these lines, Birdwhistell (1970) concluded: "There are probably no universal symbols of emotional state . . . We can expect them [emotional expressions] to be learned and patterned according to the particular structure of particular societies" (p. 126). So how do variations occur in different cultures?

Cultural variation in facial behavior   Researchers have identified two ways that members of different cultures vary in their emotional expression.

First, cultures develop culture-specific **ritualized displays** of emotion, which are stylized ways of expressing particular emotions. Recall that each emotional display that we have studied has numerous actions involved in it. The anger expression, for example, involves the furrowed brow, the glare, the lip tighten, and the lip press as prototypical actions. We saw that the embarrassment display involves gaze down, head turns and movements down, a controlled smile, and face touches. The idea with ritualized displays is that cultures might take elements of an emotion display and elaborate upon it, dramatize it, make it more stereotypical and exaggerated, to express an emotion. Throughout much of Southeast Asia, the tongue bite and shoulder

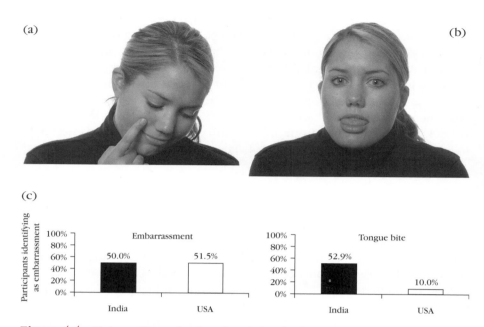

Figure 4.4 Universality and cultural variation in the meaning of the embarrassment display. People in the United States and India agree in their judgments of a prototypical embarrassment display, but only people in India recognize the ritualized tongue bite as a display of embarrassment (Source: Haidt & Keltner, 1999).

shrug is a ritualized display of embarrassment. It involves exaggerated versions of two elements of the embarrassment display: inhibitory muscle actions around the mouth (the tongue bite), and constricted, size-reducing posture (the shoulder shrug). This display might only signal embarrassment in Southeast Asian cultures. To explore this possibility, Haidt and Keltner presented participants with two expressions of embarrassment, which are shown in figure 4.4, along with the rates at which members identified the two expressions as embarrassment (Haidt & Keltner, 1999). As you can see, members of both cultures interpreted the prototypical expression to the left as embarrassment. Indian participants also readily perceived the expressions that included the tongue bite as embarrassment. In contrast, US college students were bewildered by this expression, and achieved little consensus in identifying the emotion communicated by the display.

Second, members of different cultures can vary in how they **regulate** their expressive behavior according to culture-specific display rules. Recall in chapter 3 we discussed Ekman and Friesen's early study of display rules. In more recent work, David Matsumoto and colleagues (Matsumoto et al., 1997) studied the emotional responses of people from individualistic and collectivistic cultures. The participants in the study were unobtrusively videotaped as they watched emotionally evocative film clips, first alone, and then in the presence of an experimenter. Both individualists and collectivists reported experiencing the same emotions in response to the clips, and they showed very similar facial expressions. When in the presence of the experimenter, however, the collectivists attenuated their negative expressions and more often masked them with smiles, much as in the Ekman and Friesen study of display rules discussed in chapter 3, and they also muted their expression of positive emotion. In related research, Matsumoto and colleagues (Matsumoto et al., 1998) have created the Display Rule Assessment Inventory, which assesses participants' tendencies to regulate several different emotions across many social contexts. They have found that Americans report being less likely to control their emotions compared to people in Japan, South Korea, and Russia. They also found that women exerted more control over the expression of anger, contempt, and disgust, whereas men exerted more control over fear and surprise.

Cultural variation in the interpretation of facial expressions of emotion   Dozens of studies have uncovered how members of different cultures vary in their **interpretation** of facial expressions of emotion. Let's look at three fairly robust differences. First, there appear to be interesting differences in the accuracy with which members of different cultures interpret the Ekman and Friesen photographs of facial expressions (e.g., Matsumoto, 1990; Russell, 1991a). Matsumoto and colleagues have found that Americans were better at recognizing anger, disgust, fear, and sadness than the Japanese, but accuracy rates did not differ for happiness or surprise (Biehl et al., 1997; Matsumoto, 2002; Matsumoto et al., 2002; Matsumoto et al., 1999).

What might account for this culture-related difference in judgmental accuracy? Matsumoto (1989) and Schimmack (1996) have both found that individuals from more individualistic, independent cultures are more accurate judges of facial expressions of emotion. Why might this be? One possibility is that greater emotional expression may be encouraged in individualistic cultures, and members of these cultures may therefore have greater practice in judging emotional expressions, and as a result show greater accuracy when presented with photos of emotional expressions.

A second culture-related difference in the interpretation of facial expression is in how appropriate members of different cultures believe emotional expressions are vis-à-vis different targets. Early work by Matsumoto (1990) found, for example, that Americans rated negative emotions as more appropriate than the Japanese did when expressed toward in-group members, consistent with individualistic values of the expression of the true self around intimates. The Japanese, in contrast, rated the expression of negative emotion as more appropriate than Americans when directed toward out-group members, consistent with the interdependent, collectivist emphasis on in-group harmony.

Thirdly, individuals from different cultures differ in the emotional intensity that they attribute to facial expressions of emotion (Matsumoto & Ekman, 1989). In several studies it has been found that Japanese participants attribute less intense emotion than Americans to all facial expressions of emotion posed by Caucasian and Japanese individuals, except expressions of disgust (Matsumoto & Ekman, 1989; Biehl et al., 1997; Matsumoto, 1990; Matsumoto et al., 2002; Matsumoto et al., 1999). Why might these differences occur? Matsumoto et al. (1999) compared American and Japanese judgments of the intensity of the outward display and of the inner experience. The Japanese assumed that the display and inner experience of emotion were the same. The Americans, in contrast, indicated that the external display of emotion was more intense than the inner experience, consistent with the emphasis in the United States on expressing feelings.

Vocal communication of emotions

Very few species rely as extensively as humans on the voice. Some scientists have speculated that the complexity and sophistication of human **vocalization** – talking, along with our capacity for play and the degree to which we care for infants, are what set humans apart from our closest primate relatives, and what may account for the emergence of the enormous frontal lobes in the human brain (MacLean, 1993; Porges, 1998; Dunbar, 2003). In this section, we will examine how humans communicate emotion in the voice.

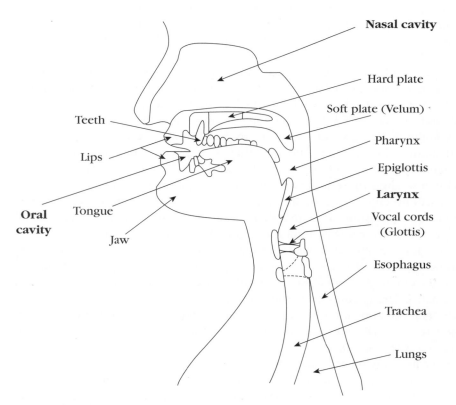

Figure 4.5 Anatomy of the vocal apparatus.

The nature and measurement of vocal communication

Vocal communication requires that muscles squeeze the lungs to move air through the larynx. This air is then given vibratory patterns through contractions of muscles of the vocal folds of the larynx. A deep, low pitched voice is the product of slow vibrations in the vocal folds (or chords); a high pitched voice is the product of rapidly vibrating vocal folds. These sounds are given additional acoustic qualities, known as resonance and articulation, by the throat and mouth and tongue, by the openness of the nasal passage, by tension in the lips, and the placement of the teeth. The patterns of sound waves so produced can then be perceived by others as morphemes and phonemes, the basic units of spoken language.

Researchers who study the acoustics of speech rely on complex measurement devices to capture over twenty different properties of speech (e.g., Bachorowski, 1999; Juslin & Laukka, 2003; Scherer, 1986). Electronic and computer instrumentation allows the gathering of information about speech rate and fluency, including number of syllables per second, syllable duration, and number and duration of pauses. Other measures reflect the changing vibration frequencies of the vocal folds, as well as their variability and range.

Researchers can also rely on the perceived acoustic properties of speech, and this is the approach that has been taken in the studies we review here. Researchers have focused on the perceived pitch of speech, ranging from low to high, which reflects the vibration of the vocal folds. They take note of the perceived tempo, loudness, and rhythm of speech. They also derive measures of perceived variability of pitch: the extent to which an individual speaks in many different pitches, or in a uniform pitch across time.

Examples of vocal communication: teasing and laughter

One problem with the idea of emotional expression is that it implies something within that is let out. But what about more deliberate emotional communication? Consider teasing (Keltner et al., 2001), in which one person playfully provokes another, typically commenting on some unusual and potentially undesirable act or attribute. There are many forms of teasing, from the lifelong nickname to the tickle in the ribs. One kind is the sarcastic comment, in which the teaser states one thing, but in a tone of voice that implies the opposite. In commenting on a friend's disastrous haircut, a person might say "your hair looks fabulous." The tease is in how the words are delivered. Teasers rely on several acoustic markers to communicate that they don't mean what their words say: they utter words with unusual tempos (e.g., unusually slow or fast), clipped vowels, drawn-out syllables, and nasal-rich sarcastic tones, to communicate the opposite of what is said. Speech patterns carry a great deal of information.

Or consider the case of laughter, one of the most frequent and subtly complex kinds of vocal communication, which may have been part of the human communicative repertoire for several million years (Bachorowski & Owen, 2001; Provine, 1992, 1993; Provine & Fischer, 1989). It probably preceded language in its evolutionary emergence (Dunbar, 2004). It was and is a primary means for enabling closeness with others. Next time you're in a conversation with a group of friends, listen carefully and you will discover a world of laughter. There are laughs that reflect tension, anxiety, contempt, anger, sarcasm, embarrassment and modesty, and sexual desire. Many laughs seem to involve little emotion at all. People laugh to fill the empty gaps in conversations, to signal that they are paying attention and understanding what the speaker is saying, or to encourage the speaker to continue.

To bring some order to this complex realm of communication, Jo-Anne Bachorowski and her colleagues have mapped acoustic characteristics of different laughs and their functions (Bachorowski & Owren, 2001; Bachorowski, Smoski, & Owren, 2001; Smoski & Bachorowski, 2003). They have analyzed thousands of laughs gathered as participants responded to amusing film clips or engaged in amusing tasks together. There are cackles, hisses, breathy pants, snorts, and grunts, and voiced or songlike laughs, which include vowel-like sounds and pitch modulation. Women more frequently produce voiced laughs, whereas men often laugh with snorts and grunts (Bachorowski & Owren, 2001). People find voiced laughs more attractive, because, Bachorowski and Owren reason, they have direct effects upon the listeners' emotions, and because they signal or remind the listener of positive experiences. Smoski and Bachorowski (2003) have found that friends are likely to engage in antiphonal laughter, in which the two individuals overlap in their bouts of laughter. Laughter, then, is a sign of friendship, and even intimacy. A common reason that women give for being with a long-term male sexual partner is: "He makes me laugh."

The communication of emotions with the voice

Let us now think about how emotional states might alter speech in discernible ways. Klaus Scherer has argued that several emotion-related physiological changes alter pitch, tempo, and loudness of speech (Scherer, 1986). For example, when in an anxious state, the muscles around the lungs are likely to be tense and restrict the amount of air flow that moves through the larynx. In a state of physiological arousal, our vocal chords are likely to be tense, producing less variability in pitch. We are likely to have less saliva in the mouth, and the shape of our lips will tighten. All of these changes will influence speech patterning. The same is likely to be true for other emotions that have different physiological effects (see chapter 5).

To study whether people can communicate emotions with the voice, researchers have asked people, often trained actors, to express different emotions in the voice while reading nonsense syllables or relatively neutral passages of text (Banse & Scherer, 1996; Juslin & Laukka, 2003; Klasmeyer

& Sendlmeier, 1999; Wallbott & Scherer, 1986). These vocal expressions are then presented to listeners, who select from a series of options to identify the term that best matches the emotion conveyed in the speech output. In one early study, Van Bezooijen, Van Otto, and Heenan (1983) had four male and four female native speakers of Dutch say the words *twee maanden zwanger* (meaning "two months' pregnant") in a neutral voice and in voices expressing nine emotions (disgust, surprise, shame, interest, joy, fear, contempt, sadness, and anger). Audio recordings of the phrases were then played to Dutch subjects, and to subjects in Taiwan and Japan who were unfamiliar with Dutch and had little contact with any Western language.

In a recent reviews of 60 studies of this kind, Juslin and Laukka (2003) concluded that hearers can judge five different emotions in the voice – anger, fear, happiness, sadness, and tenderness – with accuracy rates that approach 70 percent, well above chance, and roughly comparable to the accuracy rates observed in facial judgment studies (see also Scherer, Johnstone, & Klasmeyer, 2003). Judgments are best when hearers listen to members of their own culture; their judgments are not quite as accurate for members of other cultures. Some emotions, such as disgust, are not easily communicated by tone of voice.

Is there evidence for continuity of human emotional vocalization with that of nonhuman species? Certainly, vocal communication is quite sophisticated in apes and monkeys. For example, Cheyney and Seyfarth (1990) describe how vervet monkeys have three main predators, and an avoidant action appropriate to each kind. When an eagle appears a monkey hides in the undergrowth, when a leopard is seen the monkey climbs a tree, if there is a snake the monkey rears on its hind legs and looks downward. If any monkey sees a predator, he or she makes one of three species-characteristic alarm calls appropriate to the predator. The signal is heard by monkeys nearby, evokes the specific kind of fear in them, and induces them to take the appropriate evasive action.

In a recent review of animal vocal communication, Snowdon (2003) has documented several nonhuman vocalizations that resemble those of humans. Several species have high pitched, unmodulated alarm calls with abrupt onset and offset times that resemble human fear vocalizations. Macaque infants will utter coos when separated from their mothers, sounds that resemble those that human infants make when separated from their mothers. Macaques also emit "girns," which are purr-like vocalizations that occur in the context of affiliation, and these may have their parallels in humans being affectionate with one other. Macaques in Sri Lanka utter a food call when they discover a source of ripe fruit, which may resemble as yet unstudied human vocalizations that occur when we are approaching or consuming resources. Dominant primates often emit threat vocalizations that most likely have similar properties to those of human anger. And chimpanzees emit calls when copulating – the male soft, short panting calls, the female long, loud screams – that have parallels in humans.

Figure 4.6 Three different kinds of fearful response by vervet monkeys to three kinds of predator.

Communication of emotions by touch

Touch is the most developed sensory modality at birth, and contributes to cognitive and socio-emotional development throughout infancy and child-hood (Field, 2001; Hertenstein, 2002; Stack, 2001). In most cultures that have been studied, adults touch in specific ways when flirting, expressing power, soothing, playing, and maintaining proximity between child and caregiver (Eibl-Eibesfeldt, 1989; Henley, 1973; Hertenstein et al., 2005).

Four functions of touch

Touch serves several functions that are emotion based. More specifically, it is widely used to cultivate and maintain relationships. In nonhuman primates, **grooming**, in which two individuals sit quietly and comfortably together, sorting through each other's fur, and removing twigs and para-sites, is an activity that takes up large amounts of time: 20 percent of their total time in the case of chimpanzees (De Waal, 1989; Dunbar, 1996). It is the primary means whereby nonhuman primates maintain affectionate relationships with each other. Within this relationship-maintaining idea, a number of distinct sub-functions can be discerned.

The first is that the right kind of touch soothes. For example, in one study, 30 human infants were observed in the course of a painful heel lance pro-cedure, in which the infants' heels were cut by doctors (Gray, Watt, & Blass, 2000). In one condition, infants were held by their mothers in whole body, skin-to-skin contact. In the other condition, infants received the procedure while being swaddled in a crib. The infants who were touched during the procedure cried 82 percent less than the comparison infants, they grimaced 65 percent less, and they had lower heart-rate during the procedure. The right kind of touches soothes, and seems to reduce pain. In nonhuman primates, grooming reduces heart rate and displacement activities related to stress, such as striking others (Aureli, Preston, & De Waal, 1999). Rat pups who are handled extensively by their mothers show reduced activity of the hypothalamic, pituitary adrenal axis, which is involved in stress responses, and reduced corticosterone, a stress-related hormone, both immediately and when they are mature (Francis & Meaney, 1999; Levine & Stanton, 1984; Meaney, 2001).

A second function of touch is to signal safety. This insight emerged first within the **attachment** literature, where theorists observed that a primary need of infants is to know whether the environment is safe. To make this kind of judgment, they gather information from their parent's touch (Main, 1990). In one illustrative study, Anisfeld and colleagues compared the attachment styles of infants who were carried in soft infant carriers that put them in close physical contact with their parents with infants who were more likely to be carried in harder infant seats (Anisfeld et al., 1990; see also Main, 1990; Main & Stadtman, 1981; Weiss et al., 2000). Infants who were carried next to their parents' bodies were more likely to be later judged as securely attached, and confident when exploring the environment.

A third function of touch is that it reinforces reciprocity. Chimpanzees use touch as a reward, and as a means of asking for favors. For example, De Waal (1996) has found that chimps are more likely to share food with other chimps who groomed them earlier in the day. The same appears to be true of humans: the act of touching produces compliance, sharing, and cooperation. In one study, participants were asked to sign a petition in support of a particular issue of importance locally (Willis & Hamm, 1980). Those participants who were touched when asked to sign were much more likely to comply (81 percent) than participants who were not touched during the request (55 percent).

A final function of touch is to provide pleasure. Touch is a primary reinforcer, a basic reward. The simple touch of the arm with a soft velvety cloth activates the region of the prefrontal cortex that is involved in the processing of rewards such as pleasurable tastes and smells (Berridge, 2003; Rolls, 2000). This reward function of touch may account for a rather sad observation regarding touch and marriage. One study found that couples who were married for more than one year, and perhaps past the period of romantic passion, touched each other less often than couples married less than one year or who were just dating (Willis & Briggs, 1992). In another study, happily married partners were found to touch more than less happily married partners (Beier & Sternberg, 1977). Touch, as a source of reward, may be a good place to look to discern the satisfaction of a romantic bond.

Communicating emotions with touch

The relational importance of touch and its several functions raises the question of whether touch can communicate different emotions. This question may have been at the heart of William James's observation that "Touch is the alpha and omega of affection" (James, 1890). The question motivated a recent study by Hertenstein, Keltner, and Apps (2005) in which an encoder (or toucher) and decoder (or touchee) sat at a table. They were separated by an opaque black curtain, which prevented communication other than touch. The encoder was given a list of twelve emotion words in a random sequence and asked to make contact with the decoder's arm from elbow to the hand to signal each emotion, using any form of touch. The decoder could not see any part of the touch because his or her arm was positioned on the encoder's side of the curtain. After each action of touching, the decoder selected from 13 response options the term that best described what the person was communicating. The dependent measure of interest, represented in table 4.2, was the proportion of participants selecting each response option on each occasion. You may see that people can reliably communicate certain of the well-studied emotions – anger, disgust, fear – with a brief one- or two-second touch of another's forearm. The same is true of several prosocial emotions, namely love, gratitude, and sympathy, consistent with claims regarding the soothing, compliance, and reward

Table 4.2 Percentages of verbal labels offered to describe communications of emotions by touch: participants touched another person on the forearm for a second or two, in an attempt to communicate 12 different emotions

Encoded emotion (target)	Percentage of labels correctly identifying target emotion	Second most commonly chosen emotion	Percentage of labels of second emotion chosen
Well-studied emotions			
Anger	57	Disgust	15
Disgust	63	Anger	10
Fear	51	Anger	14
Sadness	16	Sympathy	35
Surprise	24	Fear	17
Happiness	30	Gratitude	21
Self-conscious emotions			
Embarrassment	18	Disgust	16
Envy	21	Disgust	12
Pride	18	Gratitude	25
Prosocial emotions			
Love	51	Sympathy	28
Gratitude	55	Sympathy	16
Sympathy	57	Love	17

functions of touch. These findings also make contact with claims about the evolutionary origins of cooperation and altruism, which presuppose that signals which reward cooperation and help identify cooperative individuals make altruism more likely to occur (Frank, 1988). The communication of love, gratitude, and sympathy through touch is likely to reward altruistic actions and serve as indicators of the individual's cooperative intent.

Communication of emotion in art

In the experience of some of your emotions you may feel drawn to **artistic expression**. In a state of despair or longing, you might feel inclined to write a story, play the piano, or paint abstract patterns. When euphoric about a new loved-one, you might write poetry or songs, or find cinematic images rising in your mind. Art is a kind of communication. Unlike a smile or a grumble, however, which are ephemeral, art tends to persist in time and often it travels beyond the place of its inception (Oatley, 2003). Unlike saucepans and bicycles which are made primarily to be useful, works of art are often thought of primarily as expressions of emotion that attain cultural significance. Unlike the other expressions we have discussed in this chapter, there is no question that works of art are human species-characteristic patterns. They are quintessentially cultural. Art differs widely from society to society, from the epics of ancient Babylon, to the bronzes of Benin, to the jazz of New Orleans. But art did evolve. It started to appear in the human archaeological record between about 50,000 and 30,000 years ago when, as Mithen (1996, 2001) puts it, signs began to emerge of the uniquely human cognitive ability for metaphor and imagination. A metaphor points to something both immediate and imagined, so when Hamlet said, "Denmark's a prison," Denmark was present and immediate. The prison was that of his imagination. Unlike useful objects, which are what they are, objects of art both are what they are and they are something else. A cave painting (the oldest known is 31,000 years old) is both a set of marks on a wall and it is a mammoth. A stone is both a stone and a figurine. Human burial indicates that someone is both dead and alive in another place or another form about which stories may be told. Such artistic products – paintings, carvings, stories – have emotional significance.

The Romantic hypothesis and four kinds of evidence

As we learned in chapter 3, a central theme of the intellectual and historical movement of Romanticism is that emotions are explored and clarified by expression. In expressing our emotions in art, we come to understand their deeper and more specific facets. This is the Romantic hypothesis (Oatley, 2003) and we rely on it to organize our treatment of emotional expression in art.

Artists themselves often understand their art as a mode of expressing and understanding emotions. The poet William Wordsworth said this about poetry:

> Poetry is the spontaneous overflow of powerful feelings: it takes its origin from emotion recollected in tranquility: the emotion is contemplated till by a species of reaction the tranquility disappears, and an emotion, kindred to that which was before the subject of contemplation, is gradually produced and does itself actually exist in the mind. (Wordsworth, 1802, p. 611)

The position was put succinctly by Martha Graham, the great dancer and choreographer: "The difference between the artist and the non-artist is not the greater capacity for feeling. The secret is that the artist can objectify, can make apparent the feelings we all have" (cit. Gardner, 1993, p. 298).

What we will call the Romantic hypothesis translates to four statements about the communication of emotion in art. The first is that sometimes we experience emotions that we do not fully understand. Our emotions often have deeper meanings, themes or motifs, and personal insights that are not immediately accessible to the conscious mind. This gives rise to the need to express our emotions in art.

Is there evidence that emotions often are unclear? Oatley and Duncan (1992) found that the proportion of everyday emotion incidents recorded in structured diaries that had some aspect that participants did not understand varied between 5 and 25 percent in different samples. According to Oatley and Johnson-Laird (1987), many emotional experiences have an inchoate quality. It is on the foundation of such unarticulated emotions that artistic expression can build more specific understandings. In this sense art provides examples and understandings of such building, of aspects of our lives (our emotions) that are most important to us, which therefore demand the most effort after understanding.

A second claim that derives from the Romantic hypothesis is that emotions inspire creative expression. They tend to occur when expectations are not met, or when plans meet vicissitudes, when we have no ready answer to some pressing concern. Thus they often demand a creative response (Averill & Nunley, 1992). Art is a creative activity of expressing, and thereby understanding, such emotions in their depth and particularity. The quotations, cited above, from William Wordsworth and Martha Graham lend credence to this notion – that our complex emotions can inspire artistic expression. To investigate this idea further, Csikszentmihalyi (1996) and his students interviewed 91 exceptionally creative people, including many artists. One of the themes that emerged is indeed that creative expression arises out of emotional experience. Here, for instance, is an excerpt from Hilde Domin, a leading German poet, in her seventies at the time of the interview. In her poetry, she says:

> [The emotion] gets fulfilled, I guess. You know what was in you, and you can look at it now. And it is a kind of catalyst . . . You are freed for a time from the emotion. And the next reader will take the place of the author, isn't it so? If he identifies with the writing he will become, in his turn, the author. (Csikszentmihalyi, 1996, p. 245)

A third proposition that flows from the Romantic hypothesis is that artistic expression should often take on the form of emotion, and have the dynamic and thematic properties of an emotion. For example, if you take to painting while enraged in the aftermath of a bitter breakup, your painting might have emotional tones of your rage and despair. Fiction that you write about a tragic childhood might center upon themes of loss and longing.

Music seems to offer evidence of this third proposition. Gabrielsson and Juslin (2001) and Juslin and Laukka (2003) have argued that the voice and music share many expressive properties. Music, therefore, should express emotion much as the voice does, with acoustic features that the performer can control, such as tempo, loudness, timbre, and pitch. This may account for how instruments such as the violin, cello, organ, the slide guitar, and saxophone can resemble the human voice. In the words of the famous composer Richard Wagner, "the oldest, truest, most beautiful organ of music, the origin to which alone our music owes its being, is the human voice." The influential philosopher Susan Langer arrived at a similar conclusion: "Because the forms of human feeling are much more congruent with musical forms than with forms of language, music can *reveal* the nature of feelings with a detail and truth that language cannot approach" (1957, p. 235).

In a recent analysis of the cues that people use to infer emotion from the voice and music, Juslin and Laukka (2003) found support for the claim that emotion is communicated in the voice and in music with similar acoustic parameters. They found that tempo, loudness, and pitch were used by listeners of vocal communication and music alike to infer that anger, sadness, happiness, and tenderness were being communicated.

A final prediction inspired by the Romantic hypothesis is that readers or spectators of art should readily perceive the emotion communicated. If the artist draws upon emotion to create art, and that art has properties of emotional communication, then we as spectators should be able to detect the emotions the artist expressed. People certainly respond emotionally to the emotional content of art (e.g., Lipps, 1962). We experience the emotions of protagonists in novels or films based on human action (Tan, 1996). Empathetically we feel the weight of the roof bearing down on the heads of the caryatids in the Erechtheion on the Acropolis of Athens. We soar toward the heavens in the vaulted space of a great cathedral. In an imaginative study of empathic responses to art, Kreitler and Kreitler (1972) unobtrusively observed 90 randomly selected visitors to an exhibition of sculpture, choosing 15 visitors who viewed each of six figural sculptures. They used a notation system to document all the spectators' bodily movements, and found that 84 percent of the spectators "displayed overt imitatory movements during their inspection of the statues" (p. 275).

How accurate are we in recognizing the emotion communicated with art? This question has been studied in the domain of music. Gabrielsson and Juslin (2003) and Juslin and Laukka (2003) have reviewed the relevant studies in which a performer was asked to sing a brief melody with no words and attempt to communicate specific emotions. The listener was then asked, in a forced choice paradigm, to choose the word from a list of words that best matches the emotion conveyed in the performance. Performers were asked to convey anger, fear, happiness, sadness, joy, and on occasion tenderness or love. Across over a dozen studies of this kind, listeners on average achieved accuracy rates of about 70 percent, which is comparable to the accuracy with which we perceive emotion in the face and voice.

Aesthetic emotions in the Natyasastra

Are there benefits to understanding and feeling the emotions expressed by artists in their art? As you will recall from chapter 1, the benefits of appreciating art were at the very center of Aristotle's idea of *katharsis*. He reasoned that drama expresses many of the universal predicaments and conditions of humanity. In drama, people suffer, they face mortal danger, they fall in love, they encounter infidelity, they strive for difficult goals. In viewing dramatic expressions of emotion, the spectator arrives at a clearer understanding of his or her own emotions. Freud arrived at this kind of view in his writings about literary and visual arts. He thought that art is a forum less distressing than neurotic symptoms, more public than dreams, and more substantial than jokes, but serving some of the same purposes of expressing aspects of inner emotional conflicts in disguised forms that allow some satisfaction of expression while avoiding censure. Freud's (1904/1985) early paper on identification with characters on the stage is thought provoking:

> Being present as an interested spectator at a spectacle or play does for adults what play does for children . . . The spectator is a person who experiences too little, who feels that he is a "poor wretch for whom nothing of import-ance can happen," who has long been obliged to damp down, or rather displace, his ambition to stand in his own person at the hub of world affairs; he longs to feel and to act and to arrange things according to his desires – in short, to be a hero. And the playwright and actor enable him to do this by allowing him to identify himself with a hero. (pp. 121–2)

One of the most sophisticated treatments of the emotions and insights of art is found in a Hindu-Indian treatise, the Natyasastra, attributed to Bharata from around the second century BC (Bharata Muni, 200 BC). In this text, there are specific descriptions of how actors and dancers are to express emotions in performance. Hejmadi, Davidson, and Rozin (2000) presented participants in India and the United States with videotapes of Hejmadi's own renditions in dance of ten different emotions (she performed as a dancer in India for twenty years). The performances largely involved face and hand movements for ten different emotions: anger, disgust, fear, heroism, humor, love, peace, sadness, lajya (embarrassment/shyness/modesty), and wonder. Each videoclip lasted between 4 and 10 seconds. Remarkably, in both forced choice and free response exercises, observers were well above chance, achiev-ing accuracy rates between 61 and 69 percent, in judging the ten emotions communicated with dance and gesture.

In the Natyasastra, Bharata also discusses the theory of **_rasas_**, which are distinct aesthetic emotions. They have recently been discussed in Western theories of emotions (Oatley, 2004c; Shweder & Haidt, 2000). Each *rasa* corresponds to an everyday emotion. But the idea of the ancient theorists was that in a *rasa* one would be able to experience and understand more clearly, without – as they put it – being blinded by our usual thick crust of egoism. In Indian texts on *rasas* the usual mapping is between everyday emotions and *rasas*. Pursuing our interest in communication in this chap-ter, we have taken a slight liberty with this tradition in table 4.3, in which we list emotions as enacted by an actor, the Sanscrit name of the cor-responding *rasa*, and its approximate translation to indicate what would be experienced by the spectator. Seeing an actor suffering and sorrowful, for example, produces an aesthetic emotion of compassion, though because it is an aesthetic emotion it also includes the pleasure of understanding and insight. Seeing a performer persevere against all odds – a frequent theme in stories – inspires a heroic feeling in the spectator. A recent move-ment in Western theater has been to train actors in the theory of *rasas*

Table 4.3 Emotions as performed by actors, *rasas*, and English translations of them as aesthetic emotions that spectators may experience

Performer's emotion	Rasa	Spectator's emotion
Sexual passion	*srngara*	Love
Amusement	*hasya*	Amusement
Sorrow	*karuna*	Compassion
Anger	*raudra*	Anger
Fear	*bhayanaka*	Terror
Perseverance	*vira*	Heroism
Disgust	*bibhatsa*	Loathing
Wonder	*adbhuta*	Awe
Calmness	*santa*	Serenity

(Schechner, 2001). You may also like to observe that each emotional theme in table 4.3 corresponds to a particular genre (love story, comedy, tragedy, etc.)

Summary

In this chapter we examined the communication of emotion by the face, voice, and touch, as well as in art. We began by breaking down the realm of nonverbal behavior into five categories: emblems, illustrators, regulators, adaptors, and affective displays. We considered how affective displays, such as smiles of enjoyment, differ from non-emotional expressions, like polite smiles, in terms of their duration, and their incorporation of involuntary actions. With this as background, we then considered the different ways that humans communicate emotion. We reviewed the studies of the universality of facial expression of emotion, as well as studies of cultural variation in emotional expression and in the interpretation of facial expressions. We considered how vocal communication permeates communicative acts like teasing and laughter, and how people communicate emotion in the voice. We then turned to a less well-studied channel of emotional communication: touch. From the first moments of life, touch functions to soothe, to signal safety, to gain compliance, and as a reward, and recent evidence suggests that humans can communicate several different emotions with brief touches to the arm, including love, gratitude, and sympathy. Finally, we considered how emotion is communicated in art, exploring this question from the perspective of Romanticism. This perspective suggests four propositions: we often experience emotions we don't fully understand, these emotions motivate us to creative exploration of their meaning, artistic expression often takes on themes and qualities of other expressive channels such as the voice, and observers can readily judge emotions from artistic objects. We concluded our discussion of the communication of emotion in art by reviewing what an ancient Indian, the Natyasastra, described about how emotion is expressed in dance and drama, and the nature of aesthetic emotion.

Further reading

For Ekman's view of facial expression of emotion:
Paul Ekman (1993). Facial expression and emotion. *American Psychologist, 48,* 384–392.

And for a more recent review of this topic:
Dacher Keltner, Paul Ekman, Gian Gonzaga, & Jennifer Beer (2003). Facial expression of emotion. *Handbook of affective sciences* (pp. 415–432). R. Davidson, K. Scherer, & H. Goldsmith (Eds.). London, England: Oxford University Press.

For a broad discussion of the evolution of communication in humans and other species, read:
Marc Hauser (1996). *The evolution of communication.* Cambridge, MA: MIT Press.

For a review of what is known about how emotion is communicated with the voice and music:
Patrik Juslin & Petri Laukka (2003). Communication of emotions in vocal expression and music performance: Different channels, same code? *Psychological Bulletin, 129,* 770–814.

Bodily Changes and Emotion

CHAPTER *5*

A cold sweat covers me, and trembling seizes me all over.
Sappho (c.580 BC, trans. Page, 1955, p. 20)

Contents

Figure 5.0   Bernini: St. Teresa. Of this sculpture Gombrich (1972, p. 345) says that Bernini has "carried us to a pitch of emotion which artists had so far shunned."

In 1884 William James turned the field of research on emotions on its head. Most writers until that time had argued that the experience of an emotion follows the perception of an emotionally exciting event. Emotional experience, in turn, generates emotion-related bodily changes. Within this formulation, emotion originates in the mind. James altered this sequence, locating the origins of emotional experience in the body. His would prove to be a controversial but lasting thesis. He contended that an emotionally exciting fact provokes bodily responses, which in turn lead to the experience of emotion. "My thesis," he said, "is that the bodily changes follow directly the perception of the exciting fact, and that our feeling of the same changes as they occur is the emotion" (p. 13).

There is no doubt that bodily changes such as sweats, trembling, heart flutters, blushes and flushes, tensed muscles, and tears do invade our experience of emotion. Poets have known this for more than 2,500 years. Yet James's claim is more provocative. It is that every emotion, from anger to sympathy to the rapturous delight of hearing a favorite musician, involves a distinct "bodily reverberation" detected by the **autonomic nervous system** and by neural signals from the workings of our muscles.

How did James arrive at this view? Largely through thought experiments. One of the most famous was the following: What would be left of fear or love or embarrassment, or any emotion if you took away the physiological sensations such as the heart palpitations, trembling, muscle tensions, feelings of warmth or coldness in the skin, churning of the stomach? James argued that you would be left with a purely intellectual state. Emotion would be absent.

James's rather counterintuitive analysis points to five questions. The first may be the simplest conceptually, but the most difficult empirically. Is there emotion-specific activation in the autonomic nervous system? A second question concerns action. Do bodily changes of heart rate, breathing, and the like support specific kinds of action such as fight or flight? A third is: to what extent is the experience of emotion based on activation of the autonomic nervous system? Fourth: do bodily changes produce the experience of emotion? Fifth: is the body really the primary organ of emotional experience?

All five of these questions inspired by James's analysis over 100 years ago require an understanding of the autonomic nervous system. To evaluate the plausibility of the claims, let's look at this system, to see how it might relate to emotion.

Historical figure: William James

William James was born in 1842, eldest of five talented children. William's father, a dreamer, a bit of a crank, a man of leisure with independent means, had inherited from his own Irish immigrant father a large house in New York, where William was born. William's mother

Mary was the practical one of the family. His brother Henry, born in 1843, became one of the world's great novelists, while his only sister Alice, as talented as her brothers, was not able to overcome the barriers to women in that period, and declined into invalidism. The family led an affectionate but chaotic life, with a pot-pourri of educational experiences for the children, including a procession of governesses and tutors, long stays in Europe, and periods in private experimental schools. At the age of 18, William studied art for a year, then took up chemistry. Two years later he changed to medicine, gaining an MD degree in 1869. He obtained an instructor's post in physiology at Harvard in 1872. In 1878, a turning point occurred: he met Alice Gibbens, who introduced a degree of organization into his life, shared his interests, and helped him concentrate his energies. From then on his hypochondria, which had been disabling, decreased. In 1885 James became Professor of Philosophy. He was the principal founder of American psychology, as well as a considerable influence on the philosophical school of Pragmatism, whose adherents included John Dewey. James was an amiable, tolerant, widely read man, with a gift for thoughtful literary expression. His *Principles of Psychology* is regarded still as the best textbook that psychology has had; besides this book his theory of emotions is the work for which he is best known.

The autonomic nervous system

Neural signals from the cortex communicate with the limbic system and the hypothalamus, which we will describe in the next chapter. These brain regions send signals through clusters of neurons of the autonomic nervous system to the target organs, glands, muscles, and blood vessels. These structures, in turn, send signals back via the autonomic nervous system to the hypothalamus, limbic system, and cortex.

The autonomic nervous system The autonomic nervous system's most general function is to maintain the internal condition of the body, to enable adaptive response to varying environmental events. The **parasympathetic** branch helps with restorative processes, reducing heart rate and blood pressure and increasing digestive processes. The **sympathetic** branch increases heart rate, blood pressure, and cardiac output and shuts down digestive processes, to help the individual to engage in physically demanding actions.

The autonomic nervous system maintains the inner environment of the body, to enable the individual's adaptive response to varying external environmental events. It does this in several ways. It controls processes such as digestion, body fluids, blood flow, and temperature. The autonomic nervous system is also closely associated with various behaviors with direct relevance to emotion, including defensive behavior, sexual behavior, and aggression.

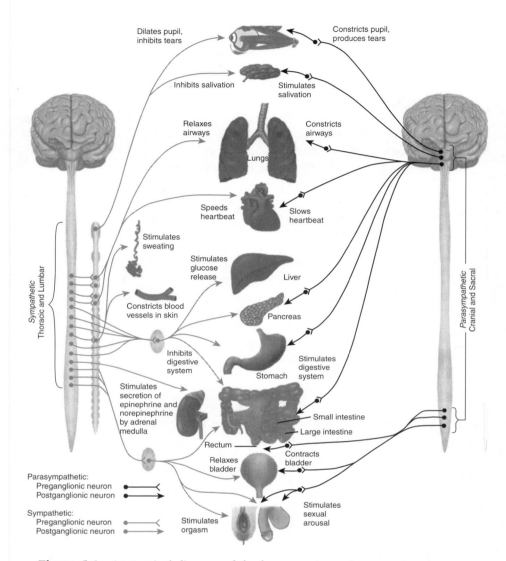

Figure 5.1 Anatomical diagram of the human autonomic nervous system.

The autonomic nervous system's two branches originate in different parts of the spinal cord and that are controlled by different neurotransmitters. You may see a diagram of the system as figure 5.1, and in table 5.1, we represent the different effects of the parasympathetic and sympathetic branches of the autonomic nervous system. As you can see, the effects of these two branches are far-reaching, and related to several different functions.

The parasympathetic and sympathetic branches

The parasympathetic autonomic nervous system incorporates nerves that originate in two different parts of the spinal cord: the vagus nerve, at the

Table 5.1 Effects of the activation of the parasympathetic and sympathetic branches of the autonomic nervous systems

Organ	Activation of parasympathetic nerves	Activation of sympathetic nerves
Heart muscle	decrease of heart rate	increase of heart rate
Blood vessels: arteries	decrease of contractility	increase of contractility
Trunk, limbs	0	vasoconstriction
Skin of face	vasodilation	vasoconstriction
Visceral domain	0	vasoconstriction
Skeletal muscle	0	vasoconstriction
Erectile tissue	vasodilation	vasoconstriction
Cranium	0	vasoconstriction
Blood vessels: veins	0	vasoconstriction
Gastrointestinal tract		
Circular muscle	increased motility	decreased motility
Sphincters	relaxation	contraction
Urinary bladder	contraction	relaxation
Reproductive organs		
Seminal vesicles	0	contraction
Vas deferens	0	contraction
Uterus	0	contraction
Pupil	constriction	dilation
Tracheo-bronchial muscles	contraction	relaxation
Piloerector muscles	0	contraction
Salivary glands	strong secretion	weak secretion
Lachrymal glands (tears)	secretion	0
Sweat glands	0	secretion
Digestive glands	secretion	decreased secretion
Metabolism		
Liver	0	glycogenolysis
Fat cells	0	free fatty acids in blood
Pancreas	secretion of insulin	decreased secretion of insulin
Adrenal Medulla	0	secretion of adrenaline, noradrenaline
Lymphoid tissue	0	depression of activity (e.g., of natural killer cells)

Source: Adapted from Janig (2003)

top of the spinal cord, and in the sacral region near the bottom of the spinal cord. The parasympathetic system decreases heart rate and blood pressure. In a few places it facilitates blood flow by dilating certain arteries. It increases blood flow to erectile tissue in the penis and clitoris, and thus is essential to the sexual response. It increases digestive processes by moving digested food through the gastrointestinal tract. The parasympathetic system also constricts the pupil and bronchioles. It stimulates the secretion of various fluids throughout the body, including those in the digestive glands, salivation, and tears.

The sympathetic system involves over a dozen different neural pathways originating at several sites on the spinal cord, and most typically acts in the opposite way from the parasympathetic system. It increases heart rate, blood pressure, and cardiac output. It produces vasoconstriction in most veins and arteries. It shuts down digestive processes, which is why it is often harder to eat when experiencing great stress. It is associated with contractions in the reproductive organs that are part of orgasm. The sympathetic system leads to the contraction of the piloerector muscles that surround the hairs on the arms, neck and back, which helps with thermoregulation, and may be part of certain emotional responses that involve goose-bumps. And it increases many processes that provide energy for the body, including glycogenolysis and the freeing of fatty acids in the blood stream. At the same time the sympathetic system reduces activity of natural killer cells, which are involved in immune responses. This may account for chronic stress producing poor health outcomes. For these reasons, many have argued that the sympathetic system helps prepare the body for **fight or flight** responses.

Psychologists measure the activity of the autonomic nervous system in several ways. They measure heart rate. They assess the sweat response, which goes by the name of the galvanic skin response. They measure vasoconstriction in the arteries and veins. They measure blood flow to different parts of the body. They measure finger and facial temperature, which reflects changes in blood flow and vasodilation.

In inspecting table 5.1, one finds two kinds of potential support for James's claims regarding **autonomic specificity** and emotion. A first is that there are over a dozen distinct autonomic pathways that activate different regions of the body, so different emotions could potentially be involved with distinct pathways in the autonomic nervous system (Janig, 2003). A second kind of support is that one can imagine many different ways in which components of the autonomic system could combine, including heart rate, blood flow to the skin (e.g., blushing), sweating, production of tears, stomach activity, and breathing. Such patterns could plausibly account for the diversity of emotional experience. For 100 years, however, a much different view of the autonomic nervous system and emotion has prevailed, in part thanks to the critiques of Walter Cannon.

Cannon's critique of autonomic specificity

Walter Cannon was a student of William James at Harvard University, and apparently was unconvinced by James's arguments about emotion. As we described in chapter 1, Cannon (1927, 1929) argued against James's theory. He proposed instead that bodily changes are produced by the brain, and that they are similar during different emotions such as anger and fear.

He proposed that quite different emotions involved exactly the same general activation of the sympathetic nervous system. This so-called **arousal response** includes release of the hormone adrenaline. The effects of this sympathetic-adrenal response are a shift of bodily resources to prepare for action, including what have been known as the three Fs: fight, flight, and sexual behavior.

Cannon criticized James's autonomic specificity thesis by arguing, first, that the responses of the autonomic nervous system, the changes in heart rate, breathing, sweat responses, and so on, are too diffuse and nonspecific to account for the distinct varieties of emotional experience. Heart rate, for example, increases or decreases a few beats in response to stimuli. There might be slight increases or decreases in salivation or sweating. These kinds of changes do not carry enough distinct meaning to account for the many distinctions people make in their emotional experience – differences, for example, between gratitude, reverence, compassion, pity, love, devotion, desire, and pride. The specificity and nuance of different emotions, Cannon contended, was to be found not in the body, but in the brain.

A second criticism was that autonomic responses are too slow to account for the rapidity with which we experience emotion, or move from one emotion to another. The autonomic nervous system typically produces measurable responses within 15 to 30 seconds after the perceived stimulus (Janig, 2003). But people's emotional experiences can occur more quickly. The blush peaks at about 15 seconds after the embarrassing event (Shearn et al., 1990). Think back to the last time you felt acute embarrassment, in some social situation. You probably experienced feelings of embarrassment more rapidly than 15 to 30 seconds after the embarrassing event. Cannon contended that the experience of emotion arises more quickly than autonomic activity.

A third criticism was that the main actions of the autonomic nervous system, which James contended were specific to emotion, actually occur in a variety of other states, such as fevers, cold exposure, or asphyxia. If the research were done, Cannon implied, one might find that love and fevers have the same autonomic patterning. This is an intriguing possibility (and it might conform to your own view of love as a form of illness), but it does not support a strong version of James's hypothesis that each emotion is associated with a distinct autonomic pattern.

Finally, Cannon questioned whether our sensitivity to change in the autonomic nervous system is refined enough to result in the many emotional states we experience. If you look at table 5.1, many of the autonomic responses may be part of your emotional experience: heart rate increases, sweaty palms, vasoconstriction in the veins of your arms or legs, blushing, or activity in your intestines or reproductive organs. Yet Cannon argued that for the most part we are insensitive to autonomic sensations. They are simply too inaccessible or dull to give rise to emotional experience. Cannon noted, for example, that people actually feel little when their intestines are cut or burned. More recent studies have found that people are only moderately attuned to their heart rate activity (Roberts & Pennebaker, 1995) or to other bodily responses (Katkin, 1985; Katkin, Blascovich, &

Figure 5.2 Autonomic changes related to emotions, such as heart rate and galvanic skin response, are measured using electronic apparatus, and can also be used for such purposes as lie-detector tests and biofeedback.

Godband, 1981; Rimé, Philippot, & Cisamolo, 1990). Even if the autonomic nervous system generated emotion-specific responses, it is not clear that they would translate to distinct emotional experiences.

A two-factor theory of emotion

In light of Cannon's criticisms, in 1962 Stanley Schachter and Jerome Singer (1962) proposed a **two-factor theory** of emotion that would help shift the emphasis from bodily responses to how people construe emotional situations as the source of different emotional experiences. One important component of an emotional experience within Schachter and Singer's theory is undifferentiated physiological arousal. Clearly, Schachter and

Singer were convinced by Cannon's critiques of physiological specificity. They assumed that a single type of general arousal is associated with very different emotions. You will remember, from chapter 1, how Schachter and Singer produced general arousal in their participants by injecting them with adrenaline. You'll remember too that they kept some participants uninformed of the injection's physiological effects and gave other participants information of such effects. Then they put them in a social situation in which an experimenter's accomplice was either angry or euphoric. Those who were injected with adrenaline, who did not know its physiological effects, became happy if the experimenter's accomplice was euphoric, and angry if the experimenter's accomplice was angry at the rude questionnaire that both the participant and the accomplice had to complete.

Notwithstanding the fact that the experiment of Schachter and Singer (1962) has not been replicated in full (Manstead & Wagner, 1981; Reizensein, 1983), the theory has had two lasting influences upon the field of emotion. First, because it became so well known, the theory added to the interest in **appraisal** of the kind that Arnold and Gasson (1954) had proposed (see chapter 1). The second influence was the finding that has been replicated, that when physiological arousal or an anxiety state does not have an obvious source, people do tend to label and experience their arousal according to what is happening in the current situation. For example, if you drink too many cappuccinos, then later on an outing with a new group of friends you might attribute your heightened arousal to the charm and wit of your friends. Or you might arrive at the home of a first date where you are grilled by imposing parents who are rumored to have been involved with the CIA. In tension and anticipation, you fall madly in love as your date descends the stairs. (This at least, perhaps with a slight tendency to generalize, would be predicted from the heightened sexual attraction found by Dutton and Aron, 1974, in their experiment that we described in chapter 1, on the men who crossed the alarming Capliano suspension bridge and were met on the other side by a female interviewer.) In such examples, people experience specific emotions – excitement or love – as a result of attributing heightened arousal or anxiety to what is happening in their immediate social environment.

This idea of **misattribution** of arousal has been pursued in many experiments exploring how arousal from one source (e.g., difficulties at work) can be attributed to some other, salient source in the environment (tensions over housework at home). One major finding is that participants who engage in arousing physical exercise have greater emotional responses to stimuli presented a few moments later when participants think their arousal has subsided (Zillmann, 1988, 1989). Thus, people who have just taken physical exercise find cartoons funnier and erotica more arousing (Zillmann, 1978). The general finding, then, which has been replicated many times, is that arousal, sometimes purely physiological, and sometimes from certain emotions such as anxiety, can transfer to other situations and have effects on our emotional experience of the social world (see also Zillmann & Vorderer, 2000).

Evidence for autonomic specificity in emotion

In part due to the influence of Schachter and Singer's work, for nearly two decades researchers in the field of emotion tended to assume that there was little physiological specificity to the different emotions, that all emotions were associated with elevated sympathetic arousal. This would change, in part, due to a discovery by Paul Ekman, who inadvertently noticed something in his studies of facial expression that suggested greater specificity to emotion. Ekman and his collaborator Wallace Friesen developed a coding system that allowed them to identify facial muscle actions of the face (Ekman & Friesen, 1978, 1984; Ekman & Rosenberg, 1997). To develop this system, Ekman and Friesen spent thousands of hours moving their facial muscles, taking careful notes about how these movements created new creases, wrinkles, dimples, bulges, and changes to the appearance of the face.

In doing this work Ekman noticed that moving his facial muscles seemed to change how he felt. When he furrowed the brow his heart rate seemed to increase and his blood pressure to rise. When he wrinkled the nose and stuck out the tongue, as one does during intense disgust, his heart rate seemed to slow down. Might moving facial muscles into emotion configurations produce specific autonomic activity? This would be in keeping with William James's idea that specific bodily responses give rise to specific emotional experiences.

To answer this question, Robert Levenson, Paul Ekman, and Wallace Friesen (1990; see also Ekman, Levenson, & Friesen, 1983) conducted the following study employing the **directed facial action** task. They had participants follow muscle-by-muscle instructions to configure their faces into the six different expressions of the emotions that Ekman had studied in his cross-cultural judgment studies. For example, for one expression participants were instructed to:

1.   Wrinkle your nose.
2.   Raise your upper lip.
3.   Open your mouth and stick out your tongue.

In this case the emotion portrayed is disgust, but the participants did not know what emotion they were portraying. Once participants had made the pose in a fashion that conformed to the required specific emotional expression (which at times took some coaching), they held the expression for 10 seconds. As they held the pose, measures of autonomic activity were gathered and then compared to a neutral baseline. Table 5.2 presents results from one study using the directed facial action task.

Let's put these results in the context of the claims about physiological specificity. At the time, there were really two hypotheses inspired by Cannon about the non-specificity of emotion-related changes in the autonomic nervous system (Levenson et al., 1990). The first was that all emotions involve

Table 5.2 Emotion-related changes in autonomic physiology observed in the directed facial action task

	Anger	Fear	Sad	Disgust	Smile	Surprise
Heart rate (BPM)	5.0	5.5	4.2	.70	2.4	.20
Finger temperature	.20	−.05	.07	.07	.01	.01
Galvanic skin response	.41	.58	.43	.52	.07	.07
Muscle activity	−.01	.01	−.01	.01	.01	.00

Source: Adapted from Levenson et al. (1990)

elevated sympathetic response. The second was that the negative emotions – anger, disgust, fear, and sadness in this study – all involve increased sympathetic arousal, whereas positive emotions involve reduced arousal. The results challenge the two predictions of the kind that Cannon made. Had William James heard about these results, he might well have experienced the mildly elevated heart rate of happiness.

The main results of Ekman, Levenson, and Friesen's studies were of differences among negative emotions. First, large increases of heart rate occurred for fear, anger, and sadness, but almost none for disgust. Second, galvanic skin response (the measure of sweat activity) was found to be greater for fear and disgust than for anger and sadness. Third, finger temperature was greater for anger than fear, suggesting that in anger blood flows freely to the hands (perhaps to aid in combat), whereas with fear blood remains near the chest to support flight-related locomotion. This is most likely due to vasoconstriction in the veins of the chest and arm being more pronounced in fear than anger. Thus, four negative emotions differ on certain measures of autonomic activity, suggesting that a one-arousal-fits-all model of autonomic activity is inadequate (although see Cacioppo et al., 1993 for critique).

In more refined analyses, Levenson and colleagues asked whether sharper physiological distinctions were observed in certain conditions. When participants produced better versions of the facial expressions, as judged by experts, and when they themselves reported experiencing the target emotion (say disgust when the disgust expression was posed), they were more likely to show: (a) reduced heart rate for disgust; (b) increased galvanic skin response for fear and disgust; and (c) increased finger temperature for anger compared to fear. This lends further credence to the idea that once an emotion is activated, it is associated with some distinct physiological responses.

To the extent that these autonomic responses are part of the evolved components of emotion, one would expect these differences in physiology to be observed in different cultures. To answer this question, Levenson and Ekman packed their physiological equipment to conduct a similar directed facial action study with the Minangkabau, a matrilineal, Muslim people in West Sumatra, Indonesia (Levenson et al., 1992). For the most part, they observed similar emotion-specific physiological distinctions produced by the directed facial action task, suggesting that these distinctions may be universal. Subsequent studies have replicated these emotion-specific autonomic patterns in elderly adults, although interestingly, in general, elderly adults (aged 65 and above) show attenuated autonomic responses (Levenson et al., 1991).

In a different approach, Stemmler (1989) had 42 female students who were led to experience emotions through three real-life inductions, while their physiological reactions were recorded. One was of fear. Participants listened to the terrifying ending of the story "The Fall of the House of Usher" by Edgar Allan Poe accompanied by scary music and then – unexpectedly – all the lights went off for one minute. One was of anger. Participants were required to solve insoluble anagrams, and were told brusquely to shout "I don't know" louder, because the sound equipment was not working well. One was of happiness. They were told all the recordings had been successful, that there was a short rest, and that the payment for taking part in the experiment had been increased. There were also two emotional imagery inductions, in which participants were asked to recall an episode of fear and an episode of anger. For the real-life inductions, some bodily measures (such as skin conductance and head temperature) did discriminate between fear, anger, and happiness. Some other measures found to discriminate in other studies (such as heart rate) did not. In the imagery conditions, none of the bodily measures discriminated among the emotions.

The blush

One autonomic response that seems different from others is the blush. This response has long been fascinating to novelists (especially during the Victorian era), poets, adolescents (many of whom would give up all future earnings to blush less often), and people who are courting. The great American satirist Mark Twain observed that "humans are the only species who blush, and the only one that needs to." As it turns out, Twain was not entirely correct: some nonhuman primates show reddening in the face, perhaps as an appeasement gesture (Hauser, 1996). So what is the blush? And is it an emotion-specific autonomic response?

In his chapter on the blush in his book *The Expression of the Emotions in Man and Animals*, Darwin observed that the blush is associated with several states, including modesty, embarrassment, shyness, and shame. Darwin offered a rather odd theoretical account: he argued that the blush is the product of self-focused attention. He said that when we direct our attention to any part of the body, physiological activity is stimulated in that region so that when, in shyness or embarrassment we think of our face as an object of attention, blood flows to that region. In one story passed on to Darwin by a doctor, as this man gradually opened the blouse of a female patient, button by button, incrementally baring her neck and upper chest, a blush extended to the newly exposed areas of her body.

More recently, Mark Leary and his colleagues have carefully analyzed situations that produce the blush. They have discerned the more specific elicitors of the blush and proposed a more specific cause: negative, self-focused attention (Leary et al., 1992). We don't blush when we receive attention from others, or when we think of what others think of us. Rather, we blush when we are the objects and recipients of **undesirable social attention**, that is, attention that is potentially damaging to our self-concept, in particular in the eyes of others.

So how is the blush related to emotion? People commonly report that they blush during embarrassment; some 21 percent of Spanish participants (Edelmann, 1990) report blushing, as do 92 percent of American students (Miller & Tangney, 1994). Furthermore, the blush may be fairly specific to embarrassment: in one study people rarely reported blushing during shame or guilt (Miller & Tangney, 1994).

The blush involves the spontaneous reddening of the face, ears, neck, and upper chest produced by increases in blood volume in the subcutaneous capillaries in those regions (Cutlip & Leary, 1993; Leary et al., 1992). By contrast, a more generalized flush is a nonsocial response that often is associated with physical exertion, temperature changes, or alcohol consumption (Leary et al., 1992).

Is the blush distinct from the autonomic response of other emotions? One candidate with which one might make comparison is the autonomic response of fear. The experience of blushing often is associated with certain fears, most notably social anxiety. And we learned that fear is defined by elevated heart rate and other indicators of sympathetic response, such as vasoconstriction. In a study that compared the blush to anxiety-related physiology, participants' cheek blood flow and temperature, finger temperature, and galvanic skin response were recorded in two conditions. In a standard embarrassment condition, the participant and four confederates of the experimenter watched a videotape of the participant previously singing "The Star Spangled Banner." In a condition that elicited heightened fear, the participant and confederates watched the frightening shower scene from Alfred Hitchcock's movie *Psycho* (Shearn et al., 1990). Participants' cheek blood flow, cheek skin temperature, and finger skin conductance increased more while they and others watched themselves singing than while they watched the frightening film clip. These autonomic correlates of the blush have been replicated (Shearn et al., 1992). Interestingly, measures of cheek coloration and temperature were uncorrelated while participants watched themselves singing but were correlated as they watched the frightening film clip. Researchers have argued that these different patterns of correlations indicate that the autonomic controls of blushing and feeling fearful may involve distinct neural pathways and cortical regions (Leary et al., 1992; Shearn et al., 1990).

In a second study of embarrassment-related physiology, participants' heart rate and skin conductance were monitored while they anticipated doing an embarrassing task, namely suck on a pacifier (Buck & Parke, 1972). In this study, and in subsequent research (Leary, Rejeski, & Britt, 1990; Leary et al., 1994), embarrassment was associated with reduced heart rate, which may be the product of inhibited sympathetic and increased parasympathetic nervous system activity. The heart rate deceleration of embarrassment is distinct from the elevated heart rate of amusement (Ruch, 1993), and of fear and sadness (Levenson et al., 1990). Here is another way in which emotion involves distinct autonomic patterning (see also Gross, Fredrickson, & Levenson, 1994; Levenson, 2003; Porges, 1995; Stemmler, 1989, 2003).

Parasympathetic response and social connection

What about positive emotions? Here the story of autonomic specificity is less developed, but promising. Laughter, for example, is associated with exhalation, and shifts in respiration and heart rate (Ruch, 1993). Smiling tends to reduce stress-related heart rate acceleration, allowing the individual to return to a calmer state (e.g., Fredrickson & Levenson, 1998), no doubt of benefit to the individual. Are there other ways that positive emotion may activate fairly specific autonomic responses?

One candidate emerges in the creative theorizing of Steven Porges (1995, 1998). Based on comparisons of the autonomic nervous systems of different species, from fish to humans, Porges has made a case for three stages in the evolution of the autonomic nervous system. A first stage produced the **dorsal vagal complex**, which is present in all species. It regulates digestive processes, and it produces the immobilization response seen in many reptiles and fish when attacked by predators. Next to emerge in evolution was the sympathetic nervous system that controlled fight and flight behavior. The last portion of the autonomic nervous system to evolve, and only in mammals, is the **ventral vagal complex**. It is controlled by the tenth cranial nerve, known as the vagus nerve. As Porges points out, this affects several behaviors critical to social interaction and attachment, such as facial muscle actions and vocalizations. The ventral vagal complex also influences cardiac output in ways that allows the individual to rapidly adapt to changing social circumstances, and in particular, in ways that allows the individual to be calm around others.

Researchers measure vagal tone by looking at the patterns of heart rate, then filtering out respiratory and sympathetic influences on heart rate, thus yielding an index of parasympathetic influence upon heart rate (Berntson, Cacioppo, & Quigley, 1993). Inspired by Porges' claims, there is an emerging empirical consensus that vagal influences upon the parasympathetic nervous system may be associated with social engagement and altruistic emotions like love and compassion. This would be consistent with Porges' claims that the ventral vagal complex influences processes – vocalizations, facial behavior, and adaptability in cardiac output – that help in soothing, attachment, and connection.

Recent research has linked increased parasympathetic activity to compassion-related emotional responses. In a video induction study, participants were shown either a depiction of a person helping a homeless man or an amusing film (Oveis, Sherman, & Haidt, 2004). Both films produced increased physiological activity, but only participants who witnessed compassion displayed increased vagal tone. Similarly, Eisenberg et al. (1989) found that individuals who reported an intention to help a suffering woman experienced a heart rate deceleration while learning about the woman's plight. In a recent study, participants were shown slides that evoked compassion (e.g., images of babies crying) and pride (pictures of inspiring symbols of their University) (Oveis, Horberg, & Keltner, 2005). Only the compassion slides triggered elevated parasympathetic activity, suggesting that vagal tone is not involved in all positive emotions, but perhaps only those involved in pro-social response.

Emotional experience with reduced bodily input

Thus far we have seen that there is some degree of autonomic specificity for emotions. Another way to evaluate James's specificity hypothesis is to ask whether the experience of emotion derives from bodily sensations as he implied. Our experience of fear, for example, should correlate with accelerations in heart rate, and vasoconstriction that produces the cold hands and feet. Our experience of love, by contrast, or sympathy, should correlate with increased vagal tone (see Eisenberg et al., 1989 for relevant data).

This notion was in part advocated by the influential theorist Sylvan Tomkins (1962), who argued that the experience of emotion closely tracks emotion-specific bodily responses:

> Affects are sets of muscle and glandular responses located in the face and also widely distributed through the body, which generate sensory feedback which is either inherently "acceptable" or "unacceptable." These organized sets of responses are triggered at subcortical centers where specific "programs" for each distinct affect are stored. These programs are innately endowed and have been genetically inherited. They are capable of simultaneously capturing such widely distributed organs as the face, the heart, and the endocrines and imposing on them a specific pattern of correlated responses. (pp. 243–244)

In one of his thought experiments, James asked what emotional experience would be like if all bodily response and sensation was removed from that experience? What would your experience be like, for example, if some pharmacological agent blocked your experience of anger-related bodily changes? Although no studies have resorted to this kind of manipulation, the study of special populations sheds some light on the question of what happens to emotion in the relative absence of bodily sensation.

Consider the work of Hohmann (1966). He interviewed 25 adult men who had suffered **spinal injuries**. They had lost all sensation, including bodily sensation, below the injury. The subjects had all completed high school, and none had psychiatric problems. Hohmann conducted the interviews, and says that the fact that he was himself paraplegic allowed him to establish rapport. He asked the men about sexual feelings, fear, anger, grief, sentimentality, and overall emotionality. Most of the men reported decreases in sexual feeling since their injury. Those with injuries at the neck level reported large decreases: before injury, one single 29-year-old described his previous feelings in sexual encounters: "a hot, tense feeling all over my body," but said that since the injury "it doesn't do anything for me" (p. 148). A 33-year-old was typical of paraplegic men with injuries in the lower back: "I believe the pressure I feel for sex is just a bit less. It's hard to tell because now I'm married, and of course the emotional part of it is greater because I want to please my wife, and that makes it confusing to try and say what my own feelings inside myself are. I used to be always on the hunt, maybe to make a conquest and reassure myself. All told there seems to be less tension and pressure for sex" (p. 149). Hohmann also found decreased feelings of fear. One man had his injury at the high chest level. One day he was fishing on a lake when a storm came up and a log punctured his boat. He said: "I knew I was sinking, and I was afraid all right, but somehow I didn't have that feeling of trapped panic that I know I would have had before" (p. 150).

One subject talking of anger said: "Now I don't get a feeling of physical animation . . . Sometimes I get angry when I see some injustice. I yell and cuss and raise hell because if you don't do it sometimes I've learned that people will take advantage of you, but it just doesn't have the heat in it. It's a mental kind of anger" (p. 151).

Along with such decreases in sexual feelings, fear, and anger, most subjects reported an increase in feelings that Hohmann called sentimentality, feeling tearful and choked up on occasions such as partings. Of course, as you read Hohmann's descriptions, you should be concerned about certain confounds in the study. (Confounds are variables other than those at the focus of the study that might produce the results obtained.) What is the effect of disablement itself on people's reactions to emotion-inducing events? What is the effect of simply getting older – the time lapse since the injury ranged from 2 to 17 years with a mean of 10 years? Were Hohmann's results affected by the subjects' or the interviewer's beliefs of the dependence of emotions on the body?

None of these questions is easy to answer, but a replication of Hohmann's study was carried out by Bermond et al. (1991). They conducted interviews with 37 people who had suffered spinal injuries during the previous one to nine years (mean of 4.5 years). The interviewers were carefully trained. To avoid bias they were told that both peripheral and central theories of emotion are valid.

Participants were asked separately about the intensities of physiological disturbances and about the subjective intensities of the emotional experiences.

They were asked to remember two experiences of fear that were similar in what caused them and in their importance for the participant, one from before and one from after the injury: 23 participants could remember a pair of such incidents. Contrary to James's prediction, they reported subjective experiences of fear following the injury as significantly increased. They found that purely physiological disturbance in the post-injury emotion had diminished, as would be predicted by the autonomic damage caused by the injury, and that the extent of this was correlated with loss of sensory input. But this did not have a noticeable effect in decreasing the experience of emotions.

Participants were also asked to remember two similar incidents of anger, one before and one since their injury: 32 could remember such incidents. For these responses there was a slight increase in the subjective experience of anger, but no change in the remembered bodily experience of anger.

Bermond et al. also asked their participants to rate fear, anger, grief, sentimentality, and joyfulness, on scales indicating increases and decreases since their injury. Neither in the whole group, nor in the 14 participants with injuries in the neck region and hence the greatest sensory loss, was there any general decrease in rated emotional intensity. Most participants reported no change on most scales, though some reported some increases in intensity since their injury.

Hohmann's participants often spoke of intense mental emotions while saying that the bodily aspect had decreased, and because of this Bermond et al. point out that their own results may therefore not be as discrepant from Hohmann's as they seem. How people experience emotions may depend on how they interpret them, on the extent to which they believe emotion to be affected by body sensations. We have to remember that both studies are based on memory. But if the memories are accurate, the results of the more recent and systematic study seem, at least, to make difficulties for James's hypothesis, that emotional experience depends crucially on responses in autonomic physiology.

Action and emotion

In the history of research on the relation of bodily processes to emotion, autonomic effects have been a principal focus. But as Andalmann and Zajonc (1989) point out, though in their theories of emotion Lange (1885) concentrated on autonomic effects, James (1884) did not exclude feedback from muscles, joints, and skin. Feedback from actions might be particularly important in understanding bodily bases of emotion because different emotions are certainly associated with different kinds of action. In love we gently caress the beloved, while in anger we might hit someone. So how might we think of the relation of action to emotion?

As we learned in the discussion of the autonomic nervous system, one primary function autonomic responses serve is to support different kinds of action, like fight, flight, defensive behavior, sexual response, and soothing

Table 5.3 Examples of action readiness items

Dimension	Action readiness item
Antagonistic	I wanted to oppose, to assault, hurt, or insult
Approach	I wanted to approach, make contact
Avoidance	I wanted to have nothing to do with someone or something, to be bothered by it as little as possible, to stay away
Exuberant	I wanted to move, be exuberant, sing, jump, undertake things
Helplessness	I wanted to do something, but I did not know what; I was helpless
In command	I stood above the situation; I felt I was in command; I held the ropes
Inhibition	I felt inhibited, paralyzed, or frozen
Rest	I felt at rest, thought everything was OK, felt no need to do anything

Source: Adapted from Frijda et al. (1989)

(Janig, 2003; Stemmler, 2003). As well as autonomic responses, patterns of action give rise to bodily changes of the kind that William James thought would produce emotions. Nico Frijda has argued that **action readiness** supported by autonomic activity is the core of an emotion (Frijda, 1986, 1988). Emotions, for Frijda, are about preparing the individual for different courses of action in response to events in the environment. At the core of emotions are tendencies to approach goals, to soothe, to aggress, to submit, and so on.

To explore this action readiness perspective, Frijda, Kuipers, and ter Schure (1989) started with 32 names of emotions (e.g., happiness, sadness, anger, etc.) and asked student participants to remember episodes of emotion corresponding to each of these names. For each remembered episode each participant was asked to check a seven-point scale of intensity for each of 19 dimensions of appraisal (similar to those given in the section on appraisal). Then the same incident was rated for each of 29 dimensions of action readiness. Table 5.3 lists a selection of the action readiness dimensions, and the items to test for them, which were to be rated from "not at all" to "very strongly."

Frijda, Kuipers, and ter Schure (1989) found that patterns of their 29 items of action readiness correctly predicted 46 percent of the names of the emotions about which the subjects had been asked. This percentage would no doubt have been higher had some of the emotion names not been synonyms (for instance, sadness, sorrow, upset). By comparison, the success of predicting emotions from the appraisal items was similar but slightly lower (43 percent). Profiles of action readiness are, therefore, at least as good in characterizing emotions as profiles of appraisal. Moreover, appraisals were meaningfully related to states of action readiness. Looking at individual groups of emotions, therefore, meaningful patterns emerge. For instance, positive emotions (such as pride, relief, enthusiasm) all show "pleasant" and "self-agency" as appraisals, and "exuberant" as the state of action readiness. Anger and rage involved "unpleasant" and "other-agency" as appraisals, and "antagonistic" action readiness.

In another study, students from 27 nations provided self-reports on emotional incidents. Wallbott and Scherer (1986) found actions specific to emotions, and that differences between responses as a function of the different countries of the respondents were small: "moving toward" was associated with joy, "moving against" was associated with anger, and "moving away" was associated with all negative emotions.

As well as such individual actions, societies also provide culturally specific rituals for communal action on important emotional occasions. Funerals allow a bereaved person to express grief, to withdraw from the usual actions of life, to receive support and recognition from relatives and friends. Celebrations provide socially scripted occasions for rejoicing. And, as several writers have remarked, the rhetoric and music that accompany such rituals have a quality of arousing and sustaining the appropriate emotions in groups of people acting in concert, a quality often referred to when described in societies other than our own as "magic" (Collingwood, 1938).

These culturally specific rituals for communal action appear to be recognizable to others. Sogon and Masutani (1989) filmed four Japanese actors (two male and two female) from behind, so that viewers of the films could not see their faces. The filmed actions depicted a range of emotions (joy, surprise, fear, sadness, disgust, anger, contempt) and three "affective-cognitive structures" (affection, anticipation, acceptance), with the actors performing from scripts they were given. American and Japanese subjects watched the filmed scenes, and chose from a list of words the one that best corresponded to each scene. Recognition was 52 percent for Americans and 57 percent for Japanese. Some patterns – fear, sadness, disgust – were well recognized by both groups. Some patterns, such as slumping shoulders and slowly sitting in sadness, may be universal. Others, such as the low bow to authority, can indicate fear but it is certainly affected by culture. Bowing is a conventionalized form of greeting and parting in Japan.

Emotions, then, mark the junctures in our actions. Something has happened that is important to us. Emotions are the processes that allow us to focus on any problem that has arisen, and to change course if necessary, by making ready a new course of action.

Eliciting emotion by bodily action

Although Ekman and his colleagues experimented with having people pose specific facial expressions, their focus was on the autonomic responses that were produced. They did find some evidence of inducing emotional experience by these maneuvers, but what happens when the focus is on experience? Does making distinct bodily changes produce distinct emotional experiences?

Zajonc, Murphy, and Inglehart (1989) proposed that some facial expressions have emotional effects by constricting flow through blood vessels in the face. In turn, these constrictions affect blood flow through parts of the brain, which then produce temperature changes that are experienced as positive or negative. In particular, facial muscle actions that allow air to flow to the brain cool the brain, which is experienced as a positive emotion. To test these notions, Zajonc et al. performed experiments to show that merely contracting certain muscles had these effects. German speakers read four 200-word short stories, two of which had a high frequency of the vowel "ü" and two of which had none of these vowels. The German "ü" sounds like the French "u" as in "*sur*," and is somewhat like the English "oo." It requires vigorous action of the muscles round the mouth, protruding the lips, rather in the opposite way to smiling. Reading the two "ü" stories subjects (as compared with reading the two "no-ü" stories) gave rise to an increase of facial temperature, and also a dislike of the "ü" stories, although all four stories were similar. In another experiment, subjects simply pronouncing the vowel "ü," as well as other vowels, liked the other vowels more. It would seem that producing the ü sound has effects upon brain temperature that alter affective state.

Other studies illustrate how moving emotion-relevant muscles induces an affective experience. In another unobtrusive manipulation Strack, Martin, and Stepper (1988) found that getting subjects to hold a pen in the mouth, thus making the muscle movements characteristic of a smile without the subjects realizing it, gave rise to judgments of cartoons as funnier than for subjects not contracting these muscles. Larsen, Kasimatis, and Frey (1992) induced subjects to draw their eyebrows together in a way that mimicked those of a sad face. They found that subjects' judgments of pictures indicated greater sadness, although they did not know that their eyebrow pose had implied sadness. And Berkowitz and his colleagues (see Berkowitz, 2003) have shown that simply making people raise their arms horizontally for three minutes, which induces pain and irritation, can make them act more aggressively toward others.

So there is suggestive evidence that facial and bodily changes can cause or intensify emotions, though the intensity of these emotions remains low. As Zajonc et al. (1989) have said: "We would not expect someone who has just learned that he has cancer to turn his grief to joy by the mere contraction of the zygomatic muscle" (p. 412).

The somatic marker hypothesis

The final contribution to the understanding of the role of bodily response in emotion comes from studies of patients with damage to a region of the frontal lobes known as the ventromedial frontal cortex. Remember Phineas Gage (discussed in chapter 1), the railroad construction foreman whose frontal lobes were damaged when an iron bar was shot through them by an accidental explosion, and who became unable to organize his life. Hanna Damasio and colleagues (1994), using computer methods with Gage's skull, determined that the region of his brain that was destroyed was the lower middle part of the frontal lobes. Antonio Damasio (1994) and his colleagues have now studied many patients with this kind of brain damage and have noticed that, like Phineas Gage, their emotions seem blunted. Along with the emotional deficit, frontally damaged patients have great difficulties in planning ordinary life: they make disastrous social decisions such as associating with the wrong kinds of people, while dithering endlessly over issues that are inconsequential. They also show many deficits in the social moral realm, which has led some to conclude that they suffer from "pseudo-psychopathy" or "acquired sociopathy." Patients with damage to the ventromedial frontal cortex show inappropriate manners and a lack of concern for the well-being of others (Stuss & Benson, 1984).

Why would damage to the ventromedial frontal cortex produce this pattern of behaviors? And how does this all relate to emotion-related bodily reactions? Antonio Damasio (1994) proposes the **somatic marker** hypothesis. For patients with damaged ventromedial frontal cortex, the deficits in emotions, planning, and a concern for others have a common cause. Emotions are necessary because when we plan our lives, we rely on our emotions to guide our decision making. Rather than examining every option, some possibilities are emotionally blocked off. We do not even consider decisions that would be socially punishing. Some other directions are emotionally attractive, so we search more extensively for solutions in those directions. Damasio proposes that it was this socioemotional guidance system that was affected in the brains of the original Phineas Gage and of the modern Phineas Gages he has studied.

For Damasio, the guidance system is the body itself: emotional events are experienced as bodily reactions, somatic markers as he calls them. These markers can be learned so that in thinking of possible decisions, any outcome of a kind that has previously been bad for you "you experience as an unpleasant gut feeling" (1994, p. 173). Automatically, based on conditioned avoidance, you then tend not to make decisions leading to this kind of punishing event. Similarly you tend to be attracted to events that have been associated with reward. Our emotions, then, guide our decision making (see chapter 10). When we damage the ventromedial frontal cortex, we no longer have access to these somatic markers. Our decision making in many realms suffers, and life starts to be lived without the wisdom of the body, so to speak.

What is the evidence for the somatic marker hypothesis? First of all, compared to control participants, patients with damage to the ventromedial frontal cortex showed little galvanic skin response to emotionally evocative slides, such as nudes or scenes of mutilation (Tranel, 1994; Tranel & Damasio, 1994). Importantly, the group with ventromedial frontal damage did show elevated galvanic skin response to other kinds of stimuli, such as a loud noise or taking a deep breath. Their particular deficit, it would seem, is in responding emotionally to emotionally evocative stimuli.

In a well-known gambling paradigm, the group with ventromedial frontal damage showed an inability to stay away from high risk gambles (Bechara et al., 1997). In these studies, patient groups and controls were allowed to choose from four different decks of cards. Two of the decks were risky: they offered the chance of a big win but when chosen repeatedly led to a loss of money. The other decks represented the safe, reasonable route: they offered the chance of a smaller win, but when chosen repeatedly led to a small gain. Typical control participants eventually developed a heightened galvanic skin response (generated by the sympathetic nervous system) to the risky decks as they chose from those decks, and eventually avoided those risky choices. In contrast, the group of patients with ventromedial frontal damage showed no such sympathetic system response to the risky deck, and as a result more often chose the risky cards and lost money. Normal participants started to choose advantageously even before they could consciously articulate the best strategy. By contrast, patients continued to choose disadvantageously even after they consciously realized the best strategy. Without the wisdom of emotion-related bodily responses, patients with ventromedial frontal damage make self-destructive decisions, and more generally, have many difficulties in being effective members of society.

Summary

William James argued that emotional experience is related to emotion-specific bodily responses, especially those in the autonomic nervous system. To consider this perspective, we first reviewed the functions of the two branches of the autonomic nervous system. The parasympathetic branch slows the body down, restores the body's resources, and may be involved in social connection. The sympathetic branch increases cardiac output to facilitate metabolically demanding actions like fight or flight behavior. With this knowledge as background, we considered questions raised by James's proposals. First, we asked whether there are distinct autonomic responses associated with emotion. Recent studies suggest that there are: emotions like anger, disgust, fear, embarrassment, and love and compassion are associated with different autonomic responses. We next asked what emotional experience would be like in the absence of autonomic response. With diminution of autonomic response following spinal cord injuries, emotional experience was found be diminished in one study, but not in another. We then looked at studies of emotion-specific action, which suggest that at the core of an emotion is a tendency toward a specific kind of action. Complementing this work, we turned to a prediction that engaging in bodily actions can generate the experience of emotion. Several studies show that moving facial muscles and bodily posture influences emotional experience. Finally, we discussed a specific clinical group with damage to the frontal lobes that is postulated to prevent them from using bodily responses in making decisions. Consistent with the somatic marker hypothesis, we saw that these patients have trouble avoiding self-destructive decisions and engaging in social interactions, perhaps because they have little access to emotion specific physiological responses.

Further reading

This book, written for a non-specialist readership to explore William James's question "What is an emotion?", became a best-seller:
Antonio Damasio (1994). _Descartes' error_. New York: Putnam.

For a review of the autonomic nervous system, and emotion-relevant findings, read:
Gerhard Stemmler (2003). Methodological considerations in the psychophysiological study of emotion. In R. J. Davidson, K. R. Scherer, & H. H. Goldsmith (Eds.), _Handbook of affective sciences_ (pp. 225–55). New York: Oxford University Press.

Some of the most robust findings concerning physiological specificity are described by:
Robert Levenson, Paul Ekman, & Wallace Friesen (1990). Voluntary facial action generates emotion-specific autonomic nervous system activity. _Psychophysiology_, _27_(4), 363–84.

For a superb treatment of the blush, read:
Mark Leary et al. (1992). Social blushing. _Psychological Bulletin_, _112_, 446–60.

Emotions and the Brain

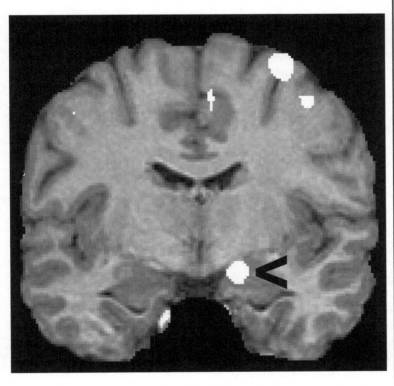

Figure 6.0   Image from a functional Magnetic Resonance Imaging (fMRI) study by Leah Somerville and Bill Kelley: coronal slice through the brain showing greater blood oxygen level dependent response in the right amygdala (the white region indicated by the black arrow) when participants viewed faces previously associated with emotional information, in contrast to faces previously associated with neutral information.

CHAPTER 6

Whatever may be our opinion as to the relation between "mind" and "matter," our observation only extends to thought and emotion as connected with . . . central organs of the nervous system . . . made up a vast number of little starlike bodies embedded in fine granular matter, connected with each other by ray-like branches in the form of pellucid threads.

Oliver Wendell-Holmes, Pages from an old volume of life (1863, cit. Panksepp, 1998)

Contents

In his book *Awakenings* (1973) Oliver Sacks describes treatment of the survivors of the sleeping sickness (*encephalitis lethargica*), a disease that started in Europe in the winter of 1916–17 and spread throughout the world. It continued for more than 10 years, and affected five million people. It was caused by a virus that attacked the striatal regions of the brain. Victims fell into a suspended state: "they were as insubstantial as ghosts, as passive as zombies" (Sacks, p. 32), sitting motionless and speechless all day, observing but doing nothing. A few remained alive in hospitals for up to 50 years. In 1969, a precursor of the transmitter substance dopamine was discovered that became the drug L-Dopa. With its administration, some transmitter functions in the striatal system were restored: Sacks described how, with L-Dopa, people in suspended animation experienced awakenings. They began to act spontaneously and schedule their daily activities.

With this restoration not only did there arise emotions of joy and excitement with emergence from decades of lethargy, but the drug gave rise to excitements, mood swings, and other emotional effects. Neural messages started to traverse long-dormant nerve pathways. In the case of the patient Frances D., Sacks writes, there occurred:

> . . . certain violent appetites and passions, and certain obsessive ideas and images – [that] could not be dismissed by her as "purely physical" or "completely alien" to her "real self" but on the contrary were felt to be in some sense releases or exposures or confessions of very deep and ancient parts of herself . . . prehistoric and perhaps prehuman landscapes whose features were at once utterly strange to her, yet mysteriously familiar. (p. 77)

Such emotions, passions, and appetites, sexual and otherwise, were common with the administration of L-Dopa in the cases Sacks describes. One may suppose that the effects occurred because the neural activity caused by the drug in the severely damaged striatal regions was not exactly the same as the activity of normal coordinated functions, and as well as restoring partial function to the damaged striatal region gusts of nerve impulses were sent to the nearby limbic system where experiences of emotions arise.

This story of the treatment of patients with sleeping sickness illustrates how brain regions and neurotransmitters are intimately involved in emotion. Understanding this is the task of this chapter.

How do brain mechanisms of emotion work?

The human brain has about 100,000,000,000 neurons; typically each may have perhaps 10,000 synapses, some as many as 150,000 (Kandel, Schwartz, & Jessell, 1991). Imagine making sense of how the brain works. Neuroanatomists have mapped the brain, and traced pathways. In a development that has excited much interest, the anatomical methods of **neuroimaging** have become widely used. In these, a machine monitors biochemical events in a series of conceptual slices through a person's brain, while a computer takes this information and constructs visual images of the brain to show which regions have been metabolically most active. These methods are non-invasive. They include Positron Emission Tomography (PET) and functional Magnetic Resonance Imaging (fMRI) in which movie pictures are constructed to show brain activity changing over time in the course, for instance, of different emotional states. As well as using these methods, some neuroscientists have studied emotional effects of accidental damage to the brain, while others have made lesions deliberately in the brains of animals for experimental purposes. Neurophysiologists have stimulated parts of the brain electrically, and with pharmacologically active substances that affect the chemical mechanisms of neurons, applied either generally as drugs or locally to small regions of the brain. They have then related these effects to knowledge of biochemistry and cell biology. Other neurophysiologists have recorded the electrical activity of single neurons or groups of neurons. That is it: anatomy, lesions, stimulation, pharmacology, electrical recording.

With these methods researchers have begun to explore the functions of regions of the brain, which we portray in figure 6.1. The hindbrain includes regions that control basic physiological processes: the medulla regulates cardiovascular activity, the pons controls human sleep, the cerebellum is involved in controlling motor movement. The so-called forebrain includes

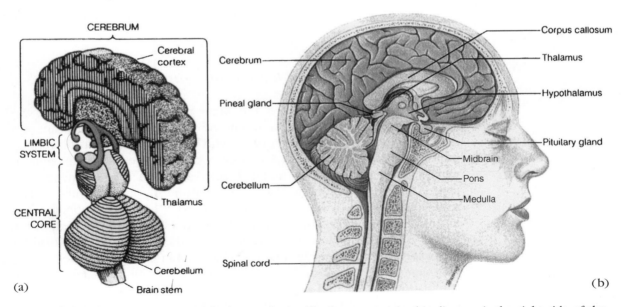

Figure 6.1 (a) Exploded view of the human brain. The largest part in this diagram is the right side of the cortex; the left side is not shown. The frontal lobes are at the left of this diagram. This diagram also shows the limbic system, on both sides. The hypothalamus (not shown) lies in front of and below the thalamus. (b) Diagram of the human brain as it would be seen if sliced in the midline. Here the hypothalamus and pituitary gland to which it connects can be seen, but the main parts of the limbic system cannot because they lie to each side of the midline.

the thalamus which is involved in integrating sensory information, the hippocampus which is critical for memory processes, and the hypothalamus which regulates important biological functions like eating, sexual behavior, aggression, and bodily temperature. The forebrain also includes the limbic system – with structures involved in emotions like the **amygdala** – and the cortex which most sets the human brain apart from that of other species. Its growth of the cortex in the human species is closely associated with our abilities to lead complex social lives (Dunbar, 2003). We know, also, that frontal lobes of the cortex are involved in planning and intentional action, as well in as emotion regulation.

Over 350 years ago, Descartes (1649) proposed that sensory stimuli pulled little strings that ran inside the sensory nerves to open valves which would let fluids from a central reservoir in the brain run down tubes (the motor nerves) to inflate muscles (see figure 7.0). This, he thought, was the mechanism underlying the human reflex. We now know that nerve messages are carried not by strings and hydraulics but by electric and chemical signals. Nevertheless, Descartes's analysis of the reflex – as involving events (stimuli) that excite sensory receptors, which send messages along the sensory nerves to the brain, which in turn send signals to motor nerves to work the muscles – remains a principal framework today. Emotions, however, are more than reflexes. We need additional concepts to understand the brain mechanisms of emotion. We need to understand how actions and experience are shaped by the individual's goals and appraisals, and we need to understand how human plan-like patterns of action that are characteristic of the species influence these responses.

Early research on brain lesions and stimulation

The first substantial theory of the brain mechanisms of emotion was proposed by Cannon (whom we discussed in chapter 1). Work in Cannon's laboratory particularly by Bard (1928) who was Cannon's graduate student, indicated that cats deprived of their cortex (see figure 6.2) were liable to make sudden, inappropriate, and ill-directed attacks. The phenomenon was called "sham rage" (Cannon, 1931). If fed artificially and carefully tended, these cats could live for a long time, but would show few spontaneous movements except this angry sham rage (Bard & Rioch, 1937). Such observations prompted Cannon to propose that the cortex usually **inhibits** this expression. As we described in chapter 1, Hess and Brügger (1943) complemented the research on lesions with experiments using electrical stimulation that elicited angry behavior not from the thalamus, as Cannon had supposed, but from the hypothalamus which lies just below it.

Cannon and Bard's formulation was really the continuation of the nineteenth-century hypothesis of the nervous system proposed by Hughlings-Jackson (1959). In this view lower levels of the brain (the hind brain) are reflex pathways related to simple functions like posture and movement. At the next level are more recently evolved structures, including those of

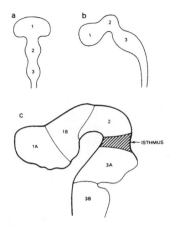

Figure 6.2 MacLean's diagrams of the development of the brain in the human embryo. The upper diagrams (a and b, from the back and side respectively) represent the parts of the brain as they appear at four weeks, with the forebrain (1), midbrain (2), and hindbrain (3). In the lower diagram (c, shortly thereafter) the forebrain begins to differentiate into 1A, the telencephalon (which includes the neocortex, the limbic system, and the striatal region), and the diencephalon 1B (which includes the hypothalamus).

emotions. At the highest and most recently evolved level, the cortex controls all levels below it. According to this argument, children abound with uncontrolled emotion until their cortex develops sufficiently to inhibit their lower functions. Similarly, brain trauma (as with poor Phineas Gage) leads to the diminished activity of the higher regions of the brain, thus releasing the lower ones from inhibition.

The limbic system

A more recent theory, with some affinity to the idea of levels, has been offered by MacLean (1990, 1993). His theory found inspiration in a speculative paper of Papez (1937) who argued that sensory impulses from the body and outside world reach the thalamus and split into three main pathways. One goes to the striatal region, the stream of movement. One goes to the neocortex, the stream of thought. One goes to the limbic system with its many connections to the hypothalamus, the stream of feeling. Evidence for this last claim included observations that the rabies virus attacks the limbic system, and that rabies patients sometimes experience extreme terror. Also, tumors in the limbic area sometimes cause a loss of feeling and of memory.

Inspired by Papez's analysis, MacLean proposed that the human forebrain includes three distinct systems, each of which developed in a distinct phase of vertebrate evolution, with each system fulfilling new functions related to its species-characteristic repertoire. Apart from the hypothalamus, the

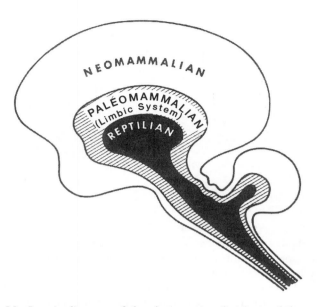

Figure 6.3 MacLean's diagram of the three major divisions of the telencephalon (the larger part of the forebrain). Evolutionarily the oldest part of the telencephalon is the reptilian brain (including the striatal region). Next is the part of the brain that evolved newly in the earliest mammals, the paleomammalian limbic system which includes the amygdala and septum. Next is the neocortex, which MacLean calls "neomammalian."

earliest and most basic part of the forebrain is called the striatal region. This area became enlarged with the evolution of reptiles, argues MacLean, and it provides the basis for all animal behavior evolved from this stock. It is devoted to scheduling and generating basic behaviors, including: preparation and establishment of a home site, marking and patrolling of territory, formalized fighting in defense of territory, foraging, hunting, hoarding, forming social groups including hierarchies, greeting, grooming, mating, flocking, and migration. When striatal areas are damaged in humans, for example as a result of a hereditary disease called Huntingdon's chorea, patients become unable to organize daily activities; they tend to sit and do nothing, though they happily partake in activities planned for them. The striatal region was also damaged in the patients who suffered *encephalitis lethargica* with whom we started this chapter.

MacLean (1993) next asked: "What do mammals do that reptiles do not?" His answer: maternal caregiving with infant attachment, vocal signaling, and play, all of which were served, according to MacLean, by a second part of the forebrain, the limbic system. Reptiles do interact with one other, but they hatch from eggs and start life on their own. In many reptile species, infants have to escape as soon as they hatch to avoid being eaten by parents. Though some species form aggregations, for the most part reptile lives are solitary. By contrast, every mammal is born in close association with another, and broadly speaking mammals are **social creatures**.

Huntingdon's chorea = hereditary disease

The limbic system has close connections with the hypothalamus (MacLean, 1949), which not only controls the autonomic nervous system (see chapter 5) but via the pituitary gland, which is an extension of it, controls also the body's hormonal system. As mammals diverged from reptiles in the course of evolution, the limbic system developed, according to MacLean (1993), to enable mammals' increasing sociality.

MacLean's interests in the limbic system stemmed from several sources. The first was a paper by Klüver and Bucy (1937), who described effects of an operation to remove large parts of the limbic system in wild monkeys housed in a laboratory. The wild monkeys in this study were normally aggressive, but with this operation they became docile. They were also completely indiscriminate and approached everything without fear. It is now known that this syndrome only occurs if an area called the amygdala is removed or damaged (Weiskrantz, 1956). A second relevant discovery was of self-stimulation that showed "pleasure centers" in the brain. These were first described by Olds and Milner (1954) in experiments where rats were neither hungry nor thirsty but, with placements of electrode tips into the septal parts of their limbic systems, they would press a lever repeatedly for up to four hours a day to deliver stimulation to themselves. Olds (1955) reported that with 35 out of 41 electrode sites within the limbic system, rewarding effects were obtained, but such effects were seldom obtained with electrodes in other placements.

Stimulation of the septal region of the limbic system induces a tendency to approach. Glickman and his colleagues (Glickman & Schiff, 1967; Vaccarino, Schiff, & Glickman, 1989) argued that the pleasurable or unpleasurable qualities associated with the activation regions of the limbic system (as revealed by self-stimulation) depend on whether the action is generally to approach, or to withdraw. In other words, if the mood produced by some kinds of electrical stimulation is based on approach, it is a mood of encouragement and it facilitates curiosity and exploration. Patterns based on withdrawal involve different areas of the limbic system, and the species-characteristic actions here include avoidance and escape from painful encounters, freezing or flight from predators, and rejection of anything that tastes or smells bad.

A further window into the emotion-related functions of the limbic system is provided by people who suffer from temporal lobe epilepsy (Gibbs, Gibbs, & Fuster, 1948). In epilepsy, nerve cells in a region of the brain all start firing together in a self-sustaining pattern, a kind of electrical storm that spreads to involve a progressively larger area. These discharges can last from a few seconds to a few minutes, and the sufferer may lose consciousness. In temporal lobe epilepsy (which can be caused by brain damage, viruses, and other means) discharges are contained within the limbic region, which implies the region is physiologically separate. Epileptic attacks in this area are preceded by auras, subjective states that often include strong emotions. The Russian novelist Dostoevsky, who suffered from epilepsy, wrote of the aura of his attacks: "a feeling of happiness such as it is quite impossible to imagine in a normal state and which other people have no idea of . . . entirely in harmony with myself and with the whole world" (Dostoevsky, 1955, p. 8). The feelings are also sometimes associated with a motor automatism, for instance Gowers (1881) described a 20-year-old woman for whom: "each slight seizure was followed by a paroxysm of kissing." In other cases people have displayed "pugilistic behavior, with the arms flailing somewhat like those of a fighting chimpanzee" (MacLean, 1993, p. 79). Some people who suffer from this kind of epilepsy become less interested in sex but more socially aggressive (Bear, 1979). About the emotions associated with temporal lobe epilepsy, MacLean says: "*Significantly, these feelings are free-floating, being completely unattached to any particular thing, situation, or idea*" (p. 79, emphasis in original). He lists six kinds of emotions that occur in this way: desire, fear, anger, dejection (sadness), gratulant feelings (of happiness, insight, or achievement), and feelings of affection.

Part of MacLean's hypothesis has been adopted and extended by Jaak Panksepp (1998, 2001, 2005). Let us call it the MacLean–Panksepp conjecture. It is that experience of emotions is generated in the limbic system, and that each distinct emotion type is based on a particular system of limbic brain circuitry. For each emotion, its circuitry creates a readiness for a set of species-characteristic brain processes and behaviors, somewhat appropriate to the event that triggered them. It is in these processes that the experience of a particular emotion arises, and the experience – of happiness, anger, fear, and so on – is something we share with other animals. According to this conjecture, these are the original forms of consciousness. Each is associated with an urge to engage in a particular kind of action – to be encouraged in what we were doing, to escape, to fight, and so on. Each is adapted to circumstances that have recurred during mammalian evolution: making progress, danger, confrontation, and so on.

Panksepp has said that Descartes might properly have announced not: "I think therefore I am," but "I feel therefore I am" (1998, p. 309). But as Darwin proposed, more than 200 years after Descartes, we know that however close this "I" seems to human individuality, we are also kin to other mammals. Newer parts of the brain and new developments of culture did not replace these fundamental circuits of emotional readiness and experience, they augmented them. Language, in particular, has enhanced our modes of emotional relatedness. All the same, we can still find ourselves caught up in emotional effects that seem to have – as with the feelings of Sacks's patient Frances D. – marks of the primitive, in systems that that are, as it were, closed and impenetrable to cognitive modification. To get the sense of this, Panksepp invites you to imagine yourself one night in a dark alley, threatened by a crazed drug addict with a knife, desperate to obtain some of your monetary resources to fix his pharmacologically induced craving. You are terrified, your heart pounds, but you manage to keep the mugger at bay by screaming, flailing your arms, and throwing gravel at him. Now he is angry, and vows to get not just your money but you. By luck some police officers notice the commotion. They save you and take the man away, but not before he shouts "I'll get you next time." As Panksepp puts it:

You are filled with dread and lingering horror . . . Months later you are still prone to recount the incident . . . you avoid going out at night, particularly alone. Only a fool would deny that the memory of your emotional experience continues to control your behavior for some time to come. (1998, p. 15)

To investigate the importance of the limbic system for the experience of emotions, Damasio et al. (2000) asked participants to recall and re-experience incidents of sadness, happiness, anger, and fear. The researchers checked that participants did indeed experience each of these emotions, and they measured changes of heart rate and galvanic skin response associated with the experiential changes. Using positron emission tomography, they found that brain regions in which activation increased when people relived specific emotions were almost all sub-cortical. They occurred especially in the limbic system. By contrast, neural activity in the cortex tended to decrease when emotions were experienced.

The amygdala as an emotional computer

In an important development in the study of emotion, Joseph LeDoux (1993, 1996) has argued that the idea of the limbic system which MacLean derived from Papez's circuit is vague because some of its functions can be more specifically localized to the amygdala. LeDoux has argued, indeed, that the amygdala is the central emotional computer for the brain: it is the **appraisal** mechanism for emotions. The evidence includes the following. The amygdala has connections to the right places to fulfill this role. It receives inputs from regions of the cortex concerned with visual recognition of objects and from regions concerned with recognition of sounds. The amygdala also has close connections with the hypothalamus, which from the work of Hess onward has been known to be concerned with emotional behavior. Rewarding self-stimulation can be demonstrated in the amygdala (Kane, Coulombe, & Miliaressis, 1991), and components of emotional behavior and autonomic responses can be elicited by electrical stimulation in this region (Hilton & Zbrozyna, 1963).

A distinctive part of LeDoux's hypothesis is that as well as inputs from the visual and auditory cortex, the amygdala receives visual and auditory inputs directly via the thalamus – not via routes that result in the recognition of objects or events. Experiments by LeDoux and his colleagues (e.g., LeDoux et al., 1990; LeDoux, 1993; LaBar & LeDoux, 2003) use Pavlovian conditioning, which is considered a basic mechanism of learning about the emotional significance of events that signal something pleasant or unpleasant. The standard arrangement involves two stimuli. One is called the conditioned stimulus – the one whose significance will be learned – perhaps a flashing light or an auditory tone. Before the experiment it has no significance other than being noticeable. The unconditioned stimulus has biological significance – something rewarding like delivery of meat powder into the mouth of a hungry dog as in Pavlov's original experiments (Pavlov, 1927), or something nasty like an electric shock. What is learned in Pavlovian conditioning is an emotion about what signals the important event: readiness for something pleasant (happy anticipation), or for something unpleasant (fear or anxiety). Such emotional effects are expressed in species-typical actions, for example a dog wagging its tail and salivating when it sees its meal being prepared, or the same dog freezing, slinking, cringing, struggling to escape, when threatened. In primates emotional conditioning can occur purely by observation: monkeys not originally frightened of snakes, observing another monkey reacting fearfully toward a snake, then become themselves permanently frightened of snakes (Mineka & Cook, 1993). Emotional conditioning for negative stimuli is quick to be learned and slow to extinguish – one of the reasons why anxiety can be such a severe and long-lasting clinical disorder.

LeDoux and his collaborators have found that with conditioned stimuli of simple auditory tones or flashing lights, and with an unconditioned stimulus of an electric shock to the feet, rats will learn an association so long as the amygdala and the thalamus are present. This learning occurs even if the cortex has been removed. LeDoux interprets this as meaning that the amygdala can receive sensory information that has not been processed by the cortex. Based on the simplest features of stimuli, such as intensity, emotional learning can occur. Based on this work, LeDoux has proposed that the amygdala is the core of a central network of emotional processing.

LeDoux's work is seen as important by emotion researchers because it seems possible that in it neuroscience has met psychology. The amygdala defined by neuroanatomy and physiology meets the function of emotional appraisal defined by psychology (see chapters 1 and 7). The amygdala seems to be a site of what we will describe in the next chapter as primary appraisal: the automatic evaluation of events in relation to goals and concerns. In particular it seems to be responsible for assigning emotional significance to events that signal dangers and threats, and possibly to emotionally significant events of other kinds (see also Aggleton, 2000; Emery & Amaral, 2000). Several recent imaging studies of humans lend further credence this idea (Baxter & Murray, 2002; Gottfried, O'Doherty, & Dolan, 2003). The amygdala (along with some other brain regions) has been found to increase activation in response to emotionally evocative stimuli. For example, it increases in activation when people watch sad film clips (Levesque et al., 2003) or erotic film clips (Beauregard, Levesque, & Bourgoin, 2001), when they watch disturbing slides (Lane et al., 1997; Phan et al., 2004), and when they experience unpleasant tastes and odors (Zald, 2003; Zald et al., 1998). The perception of fear faces activates regions in the left amygdala (Breiter et al., 1996; Phillips et al., 1997), even when the presentation of the fear face is masked by the presentation of an immediately ensuing neutral expression (Whalen et al., 1998). The perception of sad faces activates the left amygdala and right temporal lobe (Blair et al., 1999).

Using functional magnetic resonance imaging Hart et al. (2000) asked young Black and White men to view photographs of Black and White faces, and to say if each face were male or female. All participants showed increased activation of the amygdala as they did this task, but with repeated viewing, activation of the amygdala in Black people to Black faces decreased, as did that of White people to White faces. Activation to faces of the ethnic group to which participants did not belong, however, stayed high. So unfamiliar faces can be threatening. But whereas faces that are visibly those of members of one's own ethnic group become less threatening with time, those of another group may remain threatening.

Several studies also suggest a role of increased amygdala activation in depression (Davidson et al., 2003b). Some studies find that depressives suffering from bipoloar disorders have enlarged amygdalas (Altshuler et al., 1998; Strakowski et al., 1999). Other studies find that at a resting baseline, depressives show elevated activation in the amygdala compared to control participants (Drevets et al., 1992; Ho et al., 1996; Nofzinger et al., 1999). Still other studies find that depressives show elevated amygdala activation compared to controls in response to emotionally evocative stimuli such as fearful faces (Yurgelun-Todd et al., 2000).

Amygdala activation also appears to predict whether people will recall emotionally evocative stimuli. For example, Turhan Canli et al. (1999) presented participants with slides evocative of positive emotion (for example, pictures of ice cream) and negative emotion (for example, pictures of guns or gore), and recorded brain activation in response to the slides. They later asked participants to try to recall the slides they had seen. Memory for the negative slides was correlated with activation in the amygdala and the insula (see also Hamman et al., 1999).

Despite evidence of its involvement in appraisal, the amygdala seems not to be involved in the **experience** of emotions. Anderson and Phelps (2002) measured the experience of affect in patients with damage to the amygdala, and in normal control participants. Over a 30-day period no differences were found between patients and normal participants in self-reported positive or negative affect. Anderson and Phelps (2000) had also found that damage to the amygdala did not impair patients' expression of emotions.

Panksepp (e.g., 2001) argues that there is good evidence in humans that the amygdala is involved in the evaluation of potentially fear-inducing events, and possibly of events with other kinds of emotional significance. But studies such as that of Damasio et al. (2000) and of Anderson and Phelps (2002) indicate that experience of fear and other emotions seems to be a function either of other parts of the limbic system or of the whole limbic system acting together.

Prefrontal cortex, emotion, and emotion regulation

According to MacLean (1993), after the emergence of the striatum and the limbic system, the third large step in the evolution of the human brain was the neocortex, which, MacLean asserts, is distinctive to higher mammals. The neocortex (often referred to as the cortex) reaches its largest development in human beings: in us about 80 percent of the whole brain is taken up by it. The cortex (meaning "outer layer") of the brain is between 0.06 and 0.12 inches thick, but it is deeply folded. If spread out flat it would have an area of about 310 square inches. In humans the cortex is greatly enlarged compared to that of our closest animal relations. The frontal lobes of the human cortex have shown the largest increase in size relative to those of other animals. It was this area, remember, that was damaged in Phineas Gage (discussed in chapter 1). The frontal lobes have close connections with the limbic system, and as we shall see, play an important role in the regulation of emotion.

As mentioned above, from early on in the study of the brain, scientists have assumed that the cortex inhibits more "primitive" behaviors served by the lower regions. This view has also guided recent studies of the role of the cortex in emotion, in which the frontal lobes have been seen as centers of regulation or executive control (Gazzaniga, Ivry, & Mangun, 2002). The prefrontal cortex includes three areas of interest: the orbitofrontal region, the dorsolateral prefrontal region, and the anterior cingulate and medial frontal regions. Regions of the prefrontal cortex have dense reciprocal connections to the amygdala and the nucleus accumbens, which are centrally involved in valence, wanting and liking (Oenguer & Price, 2000; Rolls, 2000). In general, numerous studies suggest that the prefrontal corex, in particular the orbitofrontal cortex, is centrally involved in the representation of goals (Miller & Cohen, 2001), rewards (Rolls, 1997, 1999; Rolls & Baylis, 1994; Rolls et al., 1994; O'Doherty et al., 2001), and approach- and withdrawal-related tendencies (Davidson & Irwin, 1999; Davidson et al., 2000).

Two kinds of evidence suggest that the prefrontal cortex is important to the **regulation** of emotion (see chapter 8 for further disussion). First, patients with damage to the orbitfrontal cortex, who have normal language, memory, and sensory processes, have problems regulating their emotional behavior, that is, they have difficulties showing emotional reactions that are appropriate to the social context. Orbitofrontal patients have been observed to greet strangers by kissing on the cheek and hugging (e.g., Rolls et al., 1994), to engage in uncontrolled and tasteless social behavior such as inappropriate joking (Stuss & Benson, 1984), and to disclose to a stranger in inappropriately intimate fashion (Beer, 2002). Orbitofrontal patients have also been shown to show inappropriate self-conscious emotion, which is intimately involved in the regulation of social behavior (Beer et al., 2003). Specifically, after teasing a stranger in an inappropriate fashion, some felt a great deal of pride, whereas comparison participants reported embarrassment. This poor emotional regulation seen in orbitofrontal patients has in part been attributed to the difficulties they have empathizing with others and judging others' emotions (Blair & Cipolotti, 2000).

Second, imaging studies have begun to show that regions of the prefrontal cortex are activated when people try to inhibit emotional responses to evocative stimuli (e.g., Beauregard, Levesque, & Bourgoin, 2001; Levesque et al., 2003). In one such study, Kevin Ochsner and his colleagues had 15 females view 114 photos, two-thirds of which were evocative of negative emotion, and one-third of which were relatively neutral in content (Ochsner et al., 2002). For the negative photos, on half of the trials participants were asked to reappraise the photo so that it would "no longer elicit a negative response." This reappraisal condition led to greater activation in the dorsal and ventral regions of the left lateral prefrontal cortex and the dorsal medial prefrontal cortex.

Lateralization effects and emotions

In humans, information from the outside world crosses over to the opposite side of the brain. So if you look directly at something vertical such as the edge of a door, then information about the world to the right of that edge is relayed via the thalamus to the visual regions at the rear of the cortex on the left side, while information about things to the left of it are similarly relayed to the right side. In a comparable way the neural pathways of action are crossed. So if you reach out with your right hand, this action is controlled from the left side of the cortex. If a person has a stroke (a blood clot that blocks a brain artery or a hemorrhage due to a blood vessel bursting) on the left side he or she often becomes paralyzed somewhere on the right side of the body, and often has some loss of language. With right-sided brain damage a person often becomes paralysed somewhere on the left side of the body, but will not be impaired in language. Such a person may, however, be unable to recognize emotions of other people.

The right side of the cortex has been found to be more closely associated with the processing of emotional events (Berridge, 2003; Cacioppo & Gardner, 1999). As well as the findings that patients with damage to the right side of the cortex often have difficulty in recognizing facial expressions of emotion, there are three kinds of evidence for this (Etcoff, 1989).

First, normal people shown faces which have the upcurved lips of a smile on one side of the face and the downcurved lips of sadness on the other side tend to interpret the expression in terms of the part relayed to the right side of the brain. Look at figure 6.4. One face looks happier than the other, probably because one side of the brain is relatively more important than the other in processing emotional expressions.

Second, Strauss and Moscovitch (1981) have found that when pictures of faces are flashed quickly onto a screen, recognition of emotional expressions is better for faces in the left visual field (relayed to the right cortex). The difference is not large, though it is more pronounced for difficult discriminations. So again here is evidence of a superiority of the right side of the cortex in recognizing emotional expressions.

Etcoff et al. (1992) have tested the ability to detect lying and its relation to hemispheric lateralization. In their experiment, patients with damage to their left cortex were significantly better than those with damage on the right, and than normal people, in detecting whether people were lying or telling the truth on videotape. Etcoff et al. explained this by saying that subjects who attend to language were more likely to be misled by words,

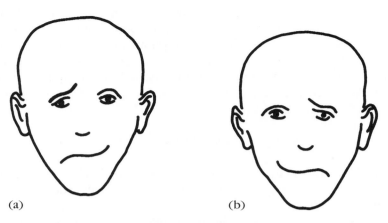

(a)   (b)

Figure 6.4   Chimeric faces. These caricatures have expressions of happiness on one side and sadness on the other. Look at the nose of each face in turn to see which face looks happier and which sadder. If you are right-handed, you are likely to see (b) as happier than (a). The probable explanation is that more of the left side of any picture or visual scene is processed by the right side of your brain where recognition of emotional expression is thought primarily to occur in right-handed people.

while subjects with poor language ability, but whose sensitivity to facial expressions of emotion was intact, relied on facial clues.

As Etcoff (1989) points out, **right-brain superiority** in recognizing facial expressions of emotion is separate from recognizing the person to whom the face belongs. Etcoff also reviews recognition of emotion by tone of voice and other nonverbal aspects of speech. These abilities are separable from visual recognition of emotions, as well as from processing verbal meanings with emotional significance. Moreover, lesions in a region of the right frontal area can affect emotional aspects of the production of speech and gestures (Ross, 1984). As Etcoff points out, it is not that the right hemisphere globally processes everything emotional. Rather, there are specific mechanisms for recognizing and producing emotional expressions that have greater representation in the right cortex for right-handed people.

Taking a more global view, Tucker and Frederick (1989) have argued that the right side of the cortex has closer connections to the amygdala, develops earlier during infancy, and is generally attuned for emotional processing, perhaps especially in activities that involve relations with others. By contrast, the left cortex is specialized for processing which is verbal, symbolic, and analytical. One problem for us human beings is to integrate these two kinds of processing, given the indications that they are somewhat separate. One indication of separateness, found by Lois Bloom (1989), is that babies who made more emotional expressions started to talk later than those who made fewer. When the babies she studied started speaking around the age of 13 months, their emotional expression as they spoke was neutral; emotional and verbal expressions were statistically independent of each other. Only by around 19 months were the infants able to say a word and at the same time express an emotion in a coordinated way.

We have reviewed evidence that experience of emotions is associated primarily with sub-cortical activation (Damasio et al., 2000) but there are also cortical effects. For experience (cortically represented towards the front of the brain) there is no overall right-sided superiority for emotional events as compared with nonemotional ones. Instead at least some mechanisms concerned with the experience and expression of positive emotions are situated on the left side, and those for negative emotions are on the right. Several kinds of evidence have been gathered (Davidson et al., 2003). With negative emotional episodes there is more activation on the right side of the cortex; for positive episodes there is more activation on the left. For example, in one study, Davidson et al. (1990) had subjects individually watch four short film clips. Two amusing films were of animals playing. Two grue-some ones were training films for nurses, one showing a burn victim and the other an amputation. While each subject watched, electroencephalo-gram (EEG) recordings were made from four positions on each side of the scalp, and facial expressions were videotaped. Expressions of happiness (indicated by smiles) and disgust (indicated by wrinkling of the nose) were found. While the subjects were making happy expressions there was a significant average increase of activation in the left frontal region of the cortex as compared with the right frontal region. When expressing disgust there was greater right-sided activation in the frontal region. For each subject the experimenters calculated an index of asymmetry of frontal activation. Every subject showed more activation on the right for episodes in which their faces had showed disgust as compared with episodes in which they had showed happiness.

Davidson (1992a) has reviewed a number of other studies from his laboratory, including one of adults playing a video-type game in which they either gained monetary rewards or suffered monetary punishments for actions, and one in which 10-month-old infants were approached either by their mother or by a stranger. In both studies similar patterns were found in the EEG: positive emotions were accompanied by more left-sided activation in the frontal region and negative emotions by more right-frontal activation. Subsequent studies have found that people showed greater activation in the left hemisphere in response to sweet tastes (Lane et al., 1997), and that people who are prone to experience frequent positive emotions showed greater activation in the left hemisphere (Sutton & Davidson, 1997).

The explanation Davidson offers is this: the frontal region of the brain is specialized for intention, self-regulation, and planning. In most people, moreover, approach to something often involves using the right hand to reach out, and this is controlled by the left side of the brain; positive emotions like happiness involve approach tendencies. Negative emotions such as disgust and fear are associated with withdrawal, and activation is controlled in the right frontal and temporal regions. In left-handed people one would expect the activation patterns to occur on the opposite sides, but too few studies have been made on left-handed people.

Davidson's studies are correlational; experimental confirmation of the lateralization of emotional experience has been found by Schiff and Lamon (1989, 1994). They found that having people contract the muscles of the left side of their face, or having them squeeze a rubber ball in their left hand as hard as they could for four periods of 45 seconds interspersed with 10-second pauses, induced negative emotions, principally sadness. Contracting facial or hand muscles on the right produced emotions that were more positive, and sometimes assertive. In these inductions nothing explicit or verbal was said concerning emotions, so different emotional effects were independent of subjects' conscious knowledge. Schiff and Lamon asked subjects to tell stories about ambiguous pictures from the Thematic Apperception Test (Bellak, 1986) that are known to be sensitive to mood. Independent raters, who did not know which kind of induction the subject had received, counted the number of emotionally positive, negative, and neutral propositions in the transcribed stories that the subjects told. Following contractions of the left side of the face or the muscles of the left hand (presumably involving activation of the right side of the brain), subjects wrote stories with significantly more emotionally negative propositions. With contractions on the right side, there were fewer negative propositions. More informally, Schiff and Lamon report on what people said spontaneously. One subject after the contractions said:

> Left hand contraction: "I felt teary in my eyes. It felt like being a sulking child."
> Right hand contraction: "I felt aggression, anger towards my brother. Lots of determination." (Schiff & Lamon, 1994, p. 253)

What about longer-term episodes, moods, temperaments, psychiatric syndromes? Patients who have suffered left-sided strokes that damage the frontal regions have a high probability of becoming clinically depressed, while symptoms of mania are more common when a stroke damages the right frontal region (Starkstein & Robinson, 1991). Henriques and Davidson (1991) have found that patients who are depressed (without brain damage) have less activation in the left frontal regions than nondepressed people.

Genetically based asymmetries of function have been called by Davidson (1993) **affective styles**; he describes a study performed with Kagan and others (Davidson, 1992a). At 31 months of age 386 children were tested in pairs with their mothers during 25-minute sessions in a large playroom with toys that included a play tunnel. Ten minutes after starting the session, an experimenter came in with a remote-controlled robot that moved toward each child and spoke. After three minutes the robot said it had to take a nap, and it was removed. Twenty minutes after starting, a stranger came into the room with a tray of interesting-looking toys, invited the children to play with them, and left three minutes later. From these sessions three groups of children were selected. In an inhibited group the children (a) spent more than 9.5 minutes of the 25-minute session near their mothers, (b) did not touch a toy, (c) did not speak until more than

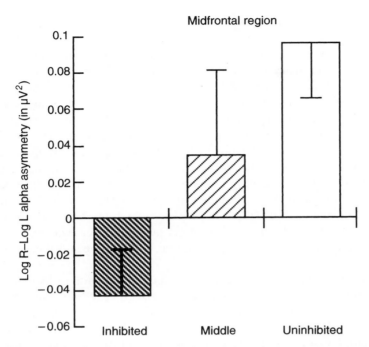

Figure 6.5 Mean scores at age 38 months on an index indicating relatively more EEG activation on the left as compared to the right hemisphere of children who at age 31 months had been classified as inhibited, middle, or uninhibited in a 25-minute play session (from Davidson, 1992a).

three minutes after the start, (d) did not approach the robot, (e) did not approach the stranger, and (f) did not enter the play tunnel.

Then there was an uninhibited group. These children spent less than 30 seconds near their mother and did all the other activities (b to f) readily. There was a middle group of children who fell in between on these measures. Twenty-eight children were selected for each group, approximately balanced by sex. Seven months later, these children were tested for their resting EEG patterns. As can be seen from figure 6.5, there was a substantial difference. The inhibited children had much higher right-sided activation, the uninhibited much less. Children of the middle group were in between.

Results on lateralization of positive and negative emotions in the human cortex agree with the Glickman and Schiff's theory (1967) that some species-typical actions include approach and are positively toned and pleasurable. By contrast, patterns of withdrawal are negatively toned. Anatomically the mechanisms of approach and avoidance are separate in the limbic system. In humans this separate grouping of approach-related and withdrawal-related brain mechanisms is continued on different sides of the cortex, and is associated with positive and negative emotional experience (Davidson et al., 2003b).

Mirror neurons and empathy

A discovery that is currently causing a stir in the community of neuro-scientists comes from recording the electrical activity of single neurons. In this way, Giacomo Rizzolatti et al. (1996) discovered in the pre-motor cortex of monkeys' brains, neurons that they called **mirror neurons**, which fired either when an intended action by another individual was perceived by the monkey or when the same action was carried out by the monkey itself. These neurons also occur in humans, as indicated by neuroimaging studies. What is exciting about the study of such effects for understanding emotions is that new developments have occurred that link these kinds of neurons to empathy. So, although it has been fascinating to find, in brain research, mechanisms of emotions like fear, which must have been common to mammalian brains for many millions of years, it is even more exciting that now mechanisms are being found that underlie the social bases of some of our emotions.

Wicker et al. (2003), for example, found, in a paradigm like that which defined mirror neurons, that the area of the brain called the insula was activated both when a human participant saw someone else's facial expression of disgust and when the participant experienced disgust. Singer et al. (2004) investigated a similar idea. Each volunteer sat in the same laboratory room as a loved one. The volunteer had brain states measured by functional imaging, and either received a painful shock or a signal that his or her loved one received a shock. Whereas some brain regions were activated only when the participants received the shock, others including the anterior insula and the rostral anterior cingulate cortex were activated both when the participant received a shock and when the signal was given that his or her loved one received the shock. The authors conclude that part of the pain network is associated with the emotional aspects of pain, and that this can be activated equally either when something happens to oneself or to someone with whom one empathizes.

Gallese, Keysers, and Rizzolatti (2004) say that these neural mechanisms: "allow us to directly understand the meaning of the actions and emotions of others by internally replicating . . . them without any explicit reflective mediation" (p. 396). They call these mechanisms simulation systems. Thus, not only have neural processes been identified for understanding other people's actions in terms of intentions that we ourselves might have, but also for empathetically understanding other people's emotions in a comparable way.

Neurochemicals and the emotions

The most important discovery yet made about the nervous system was that nerve fibers work by electricity. This was Galvani's finding, part of Mary Shelley's inspiration in writing *Frankenstein* (Tropp, 1976). The next most momentous event was finding that chemicals are the messages from neuron to neuron. This was discovered when Otto Loewi was conducting experiments of electrically stimulating the vagus nerve of a frog; this stimulation slowed down its heart (Brazier, 1959). If during stimulation Loewi bathed the frog's heart in fluid, and then applied this fluid to the heart of a second frog, this second frog's heart slowed down too. He inferred that some chemical substance was released into the fluid by the nerve endings of the first frog, and was then responsible for slowing down the heart of the second. The substance was acetyl choline. Subsequently more than 50 substances have been discovered that are released by nerve cells and have effects on other nerve cells, or on glands or muscles. Various distinctions have been made: one is that some neurochemicals have small molecules that diffuse rapidly, while others (more recently discovered) have larger molecules made up of short chains of amino acids. They are like small fragments of protein, and they are called peptides.

Neurochemicals can be thought of in three functional families, which overlap with each other. The first family is of transmitter substances released into the synapses of nerve cells. There are a limited number of such substances. Most have small molecules. As well as acetyl choline they include nor-adrenaline, dopamine, serotonin, and gamma-amino butyric acid. Some simple amino acids act as transmitter substances, most importantly glutamine, a chemical (in the form of monosodium glutamate) that is often used as a taste enhancer. Transmitter substances are released by nerve impulses from the end of a neuron's axon. They diffuse rapidly across the tiny synaptic gaps between cells to activate or inhibit the receiving neuron or muscle fiber.

Secondly, there are hormones: substances carried in the blood to affect organs that are sensitive to them. They take longer to act than transmitter substances, and their effects tend to endure for long periods of time. They include both small molecules like adrenaline and cortisol, and also peptides. The principal gland that controls most hormonal systems is the pituitary, which is joined to, and largely controlled by, the hypothalamus. Other glands remote from the brain also release hormones that have effects on the body, and in some cases also on nerve cells in the hypothalamus.

Thirdly, there is a group of substances that are neuromodulators. Many of them are peptides. Neuromodulators do not themselves excite or inhibit other neurons in the way that transmitter substances do. Instead, they change the effectiveness of transmitter substances. Their significance is only beginning to be guessed at, but endogenous opiates (chemically similar to addictive drugs like opium and heroin) modulate the pain system, and other peptides (such as cholecystokinin) have important emotional effects. Some peptides are transmitters, but when they act as neuromodulators they are released by some neurons, and diffuse some distance to affect many thousands of nearby neurons.

Reasons why chemical effects in the brain are so important for understanding emotions are, first, that separate emotional systems seem to employ specific **chemical messengers**, so systems are distinguished not only anatomically but also chemically (e.g., Panksepp, 1998). Secondly, there is an effect of this arrangement that has been useful for researchers and clinicians: some chemicals introduced into the body by mouth or injection diffuse via the bloodstream throughout the whole body, including the cerebro-spinal fluid that bathes the nerve cells. Because different brain systems use different chemical messengers, each drug affects some systems more than others. This is the basis for all drugs that have effects on emotions, moods, arousal, and other psychological states. For instance, a drug may induce fear (as in a bad trip, one of the lesser risks of certain recreational drugs), another may reduce fear (as is intended for tranquillizers, also called anti-anxiety drugs), another may induce happiness (a high), and yet another may reduce feelings of despair (as antidepressants are designed to do).

Serotonin and serotonin reuptake inhibitors

The transmitter substance that has been, perhaps, most in the news during the past 10 years or so is serotonin. It is known that low levels of serotonin are related to clinical states of depression. Also, low levels of serotonin are often found in people with histories of arson and violent crime. Serotonin is newsworthy because drugs that increase its concentration in synapses – selective serotonin-reuptake inhibitors like Prozac (chemical name, fluoxetine) – became a new class of antidepressants. Drugs of this kind have been called designer drugs, because they are being developed not just for people with psychiatric problems but to take the edge off of everyday anxieties and disappointments, to help social confidence, to enhance mood generally, increase enthusiasm for life, and enhance a sense of well-being (Kramer, 1993), though they are not without their dangers (Healy, 2004). If you want to meditate on the general availability of feel-good drugs you might like Aldous Huxley's (1932) novel *Brave New World*, in which a super-version of this kind of drug is imagined as having become central to society.

Despite the idea of designer drugs, it was not known until recently what effect serotonin reuptake inhibitors might have in people who had no psychiatric problems. Brian Knutson et al. (1998) therefore tested the effects of such drugs on such volunteers. In a double blind trial – an experiment in which neither participants nor members of the research team who administered the drugs or conducted assessments knew which treatment was administered – a serotonin reuptake inhibitor was given to some volunteers and a placebo to others. All participants completed personality tests, and played a cooperative game in pairs. The game involved assembling the pieces of a puzzle, and each participant who had been given the drug was paired with one who had been given the placebo. The results were that, as compared with those given the placebo, those who had been given serotonin reuptake inhibitor had decreased indices of hostility and negative affect as measured by personality tests. They also showed more cooperation and affiliation as they played the puzzle game.

In another test of the effects of serotonin reuptake inhibitors using the technology of positron emission tomography (PET), Helen Mayberg et al.

(1999) asked normal women volunteers to write two pieces of autobiography about events that made them sad. After a test session to see that reading and thinking about the sad pieces of writing did indeed make them sad, the participants again read and thought about what they had written while regional blood flow was measured by PET scanning. The areas where brain activation was substantially increased during sadness as compared with neutral moods were in an area of the limbic system called the subgenual cingulate. The main areas of decreased activity were in the prefrontal cortex. These results were compared with those of different participants who were depressed and were given a therapeutic course of six weeks of serotonin reuptake inhibitor drug. The depressed participants whose symptoms and mood improved showed increased activity in the prefrontal cortex, and a decreased activity in the subgenual cingulate region. That is to say, they showed the reverse of the limbic and cortical changes induced by sadness.

Drugs that affect mood do not alter the outside world. They have no effect on achievements, disappointments, or adversities. Neither do they work via the processes of thought. They are wordless, concept free. The drugs that are currently of great interest for the treatment of emotional disorders work on the brain mechanisms in the limbic system that orchestrate the repertoires of readiness, generate the experiences, and set up the social-interactive styles and scripts of emotions.

Peptide effects on fear

To illustrate the role of peptides we will describe some work on panic attacks, which are sudden onsets of fear that usually last 15 to 30 minutes, only rarely for an hour or more (American Psychiatric Association, 2000). Unlike phobias, which are fears of some recognizable object or situation, a panic is unexpected and occurs without it being clear what caused it. It typically includes intense apprehension and bodily symptoms such as shortness of breath, dizziness, or the heart beating rapidly. Bradwejn et al. (Bradwejn, 1993; Harro, Vasar, & Bradwejn, 1993) have found that a peptide called cholecystokinin induces panic attacks, without any external cause. Like many other peptides this one seems to work by modulating effects of transmitters. In its most active form it has four amino acids, with this structure:

Trp-Met-Asp-Phe-NH$_2$

The main elements in this structure (Trp, Met, etc.) are single amino acids. Injections of 50 mg of cholecystokinin have been found reliably to induce panic attacks, even in people who do not suffer clinically from such attacks (Eser et al., 2005). Symptoms of the injection include a strong panicky fear, sometimes with such bodily changes as dizziness, and sometimes with a sense of depersonalization. Symptoms of fear have also been found in monkeys and rats with injections of cholecystokinin. Moreover, when the activity of the human brain was studied by positron emission tomography and magnetic resonance imaging, increases in blood flow in the limbic system were found with the administration of this substance.

Researchers on pharmacology set criteria for recognition of a specific action of a neurochemical. In inducing fear, they require for a substance like cholecystokinin that:

- it reliably produces fear or panic;
- patients recognize the symptoms as like those of their usual panic attacks;
- patients susceptible to such attacks have greater sensitivity to the neurochemical than those who are not susceptible;
- there is a dose-response relationship so that a placebo produces no effect and larger doses of the drug give rise to more symptoms in a greater proportion of subjects;
- effects occur in double-blind studies in which neither subject nor experimenter knows whether an injection is drug or placebo;
- effects are neutralized or reduced by agents known to antagonize the effect of the specific neurochemical at sites on the nerve cells;
- effects are not reduced by agents that antagonize other systems.

Cholecystokinin has passed these tests. It may be responsible for spreading the effects of fear through the brain, with processes of particular importance being localized in the limbic system. It is not a chemical that could have any clinical use. "Tranquillizer" is the generic name for drugs that do the opposite, that is to say, that lessen fear and anxiety. They range from alcohol, to Valium, and to newly developed pharmaceuticals.

The nucleus accumbens, dopamine, and the opiates

Let's look at another well-studied area of the brain and its role in emotion, especially in the distinction between wanting and liking. The nucleus accumbens lies at the front of sub-cortical forebrain. It is rich in dopamine and opioid neurotransmitter pathways, and has long been thought central to the experience of positive affect (Panksepp, 1998; Rolls, 1999; Phillips et al., 1992). For example, there is elevated activation in the nucleus accumbens and dopamine release in response to pleasurable food (Schultz, Dayan, & Montague, 1997), the opportunity for sex (Fiorino, Coury, & Phillips, 1997), and conditioned neutral stimuli that have been repeatedly paired with food, sex, or rewarding drugs (Di Ciano, Blaha, & Phillips, 1998). Dopamine cells even fire in response to the anticipation of reward (Bowman et al., 1996; Schultz et al., 1997).

In light of this evidence, you might conclude that the nucleus accumbens and dopamine are central to the experience of pleasure. Work by Kent Berridge and colleagues offers a more subtle picture. They have found that activation of opioid receptors, but not dopamine receptors, enhances the value of the taste of sucrose, as measured by behavioral reactions in rats to sweet tastes (Berridge, 2000; Pecina & Berridge, 2000). This research has led Berridge to distinguish between wanting and liking. Wanting is the motivated, goal-oriented, approach to rewards, including exploration, affiliation, aggression, sexual behavior, food hoarding, and nursing. It involves dopamine release and activation in the nucleus accumbens (see also, Depue & Collins, 1999; Panksepp, 1986). Lesions to the nucleus accumbens reduce the motivation to work for reward (Caine & Koob, 1993). By contrast, liking involves consummatory processes and the enjoyment of rewards. Central to liking are the opiates, which are released by lactation, nursing, sexual activity, maternal social interaction, and touch (Insel, 1992; Keverne, 1996; Matheson & Bernstein, 2000; Nelson & Panksepp, 1998; Silk et al., 2003a). In contrast to dopamine, opiates produce a state of pleasant calmness and quiescence (Wyvell & Berridge, 2000).

Let's now put these notions to use in understanding attachment processes, which are important to mammalian sociality and a source of several emotions. In a recent theoretical synthesis, Richard Depue and Jeannine Morrone-Strupinsky (2005, in press) have offered the following analysis of affiliative bonding, which prioritizes the roles of dopamine and the opiates. They propose that distal affiliative cues like smiles and gestures serve as incentive stimuli, they motivate approach-related tendencies served by dopamine release. These cues trigger dopamine, which promotes actions that bring individuals into close proximity with one another. As one illustration, dopamine is activated in heterosexual males by viewing attractive female faces (Breiter et al., 2001; Aharon et al., 2001).

Once in proximity, affiliative behaviors like touch and soothing vocalizations elicit the release of opiates. The opiates, in turn, bring about the powerful feelings of warmth, calmness, and intimacy. For example, when the opiates are blocked in juvenile rats, they spend less time with their mothers after separation (Agmo et al., 1997). Human females given naltrexone, which blocks opiate release, spend more time alone, less time with friends, and enjoy interactions less (Jamner et al., 1998).

Oxytocin

The mammalian hormone, oxytocin, is a peptide of nine amino acids. It is produced in the hypothalamus, and released into both brain and blood stream. Receptors for this peptide are found in the olfactory system, limbic-hypothalamic system, brainstem, and regions of the spinal cord that regulate the autonomic nervous system, especially the parasympathetic branch (Uvnas-Moberg, 1994). Oxytocin is involved in lactation, maternal bonding, and sexual interaction (Carter, 1992). In the most general sense, oxytocin promotes bonding behavior possibly by reducing anxiety (Carter & Altemus, 1997; Taylor et al., 2000) and making social contact and affiliation pleasant (Panksepp, 1998). For several reasons, oxytocin is thought to be a biological substrate of love (Carter, 1998; Insel, 1993). One should not think, however, that an injection of this substance would induce love. It is not the juice of the "little western flower" that Puck dripped into the eyes of sleeping people in Shakespeare's (1623) *A Midsummer Night's Dream* (2, 1, 166), to make them fall in love with whomever they saw when they awoke. Substances such as oxytocin produce biases, and work in conjunction with all the other processes of the mind.

First, comparisons between prairie voles who display pair-bonding, and the closely related montane voles, who do not pair-bond, have revealed differences in the location of oxytocin receptors in the brains of each species (Carter, 1998; Insel, Young, & Wang, 1997). Moreover, in the prairie vole injections of oxytocin directly into specific areas of the brain have been found to increase preferences for a single partner over other partners, while injections of oxytocin antagonists decreased single partner preference (Williams et al., 1994). In other studies of voles it has been found that mating stimulated oxytocin release (Carter, 1992) and that blocking the activity of oxytocin prevented maternal behavior (Pederson, 1997; Insel & Harbaugh, 1989). Prosocial behavior was found to increase, and aggression to decrease, when female prairie voles were given oxytocin (Witt, Carter, & Walton, 1990). Male and female prairie voles increase their social contact after oxytocin treatment (Witt, Winslow, & Insel, 1992).

Studies of other species have shown similar bonding functions of oxytocin. In primates, injections of oxytocin have led to increases in the frequency of touching and watching infants, and decreases in agonistic yawns and facial threats (Holman & Goy, 1995). Separation distress calls in isolated domestic chicks have been found to decrease after oxytocin treatment (Panksepp, Nelson, & Bekkedal, 1997). Oxytocin injections have caused ewes to become attached to unfamiliar lambs (Keverne, Nelson, & Martel, 1997). Rat pups show preferences for odors of mothers, except when pretreated with oxytocin antagonists (Nelson & Panksepp, 1996).

In humans, the evidence is less specific, but suggestive. In studies of lactating women, it has been found that oxytocin reduces activity of the hypothalamic–pituitary axis (Carter & Altemus, 1997; Uvnas-Moberg, 1997, 1998). Massage leads to increased oxytocin release in the bloodstream (Turner et al., 1999, 2002). And oxytocin has been found to be released during sexual activity (Carmichael et al., 1987; Murphy et al., 1987).

To explore whether oxytocin release relates to human emotion, Gonzaga et al. (2005) had female participants (who on average have seven times the rate of circulating oxytocin as men) recall a time of intense feelings of **warmth** toward another person. The researchers coded the participants' nonverbal displays of love, including warm smiles, open posture and open-handed gestures, and desire, including lip licks and puckers (see chapter 4). Consistent with the claim that oxytocin may motivate devoted, monogamous sentiments, oxytocin release correlated significantly with the occurrence of displays of love, but not with those of desire. In addition oxytocin is involved in **trust**. Kosfeld et al. (2005) found in an experimental study that intranasal administration of oxytocin increased people's willingness to accept interpersonal risks arising from economic exchanges with others. The implication is that in ordinary interactions, certain appraisals of the other person promote trust and activate specific neural networks, and that this activation includes release of oxytocin.

Integration of neurochemical and anatomical information in emotional behavior

As Panksepp (1993, 1998) has proposed, it is likely that mammalian brains contain a small number of emotional mechanisms or circuits, and that these circuits are common to many species. Each system has its own distinctive brain organization, and when activated each gives rise to a pattern of emotion-relevant action which provides a script that is characteristic for each species. So there are likely to be systems for anger, fear, attachment, maternal nurturance, warmth, anticipatory eagerness, play, and sexuality. Each system is somewhat localized anatomically, so that it is differentially susceptible to lesions and stimulation. Moreover, each system employs its own transmitter substances, neuromodulators, and in some cases hormones, so that it is also differentially affected by neurochemical manipulations such as drugs.

Summary

In this chapter we explored the regions of the brain involved in emotion. We reviewed current understandings of how the brain works, and how different regions of the brain serve different functions. We considered different methods for the study of the brain, ranging from studies of patients with brain damage to the imaging of brain regional activity as humans respond to different stimuli, and the effects of psychoactive drugs. We saw that a small portion of the limbic system, the amygdala, is probably involved in assigning, at an unconscious level, emotional significance to stimuli, and that the experience of emotion is probably dependent on the whole limbic system. Patients with damage to the prefrontal cortex have pronounced problems with emotion regulation, shown for instance by imaging studies in which the prefrontal cortex is found to be active as people try to alter their feelings. In terms of cortical mechanisms, the right cortex has been found to be more involved with emotional experience than the left. The new discoveries of mirror neurons and the application of neuroimaging methods have suggested a neural basis of empathy. Transmitter substances, hormones, and neuromodulators all produce effects on emotions. Among these are effects that are useful, such as those that relieve depression. Specific neurochemicals affect particular emotions, for instance the peptide cholecystokinin produces fear. We saw that a region known as the nucleus accumbens, rich in dopamine networks, motivates the approach to rewards, or the subjective state of wanting, whereas opiates are involved in how stimuli are liked. We reviewed a recent theory that makes the claim that neurotransmitters are central to attachment processes. Oxytocin may be part of the biological basis of love, devotion, and trust.

Further reading

An excellent and wide-ranging introduction to affective neuroscience:
Jaak Panksepp (1998). *Affective neuroscience: The foundations of human and animal emotions*. New York: Oxford University Press.

The best paper we know linking evolution of emotions to brain anatomy is:
Kent Berridge (2003). Comparing the emotional brains of humans and other animals. In R. J. Davidson, K. Scherer, & H. H. Goldsmith (Eds.), *Handbook of affective science* (pp. 25–51). New York: Oxford University Press.

For the most recent summary of LeDoux's influential work, see:
Kevin LaBar & Joseph LeDoux (2003). Emotional learning circuits in animals and humans. In R. J. Davidson, K. Scherer, & H. H. Goldsmith (Eds.), *Handbook of affective sciences* (pp. 52–65). New York, Oxford University Press.

For a wide-ranging and thoughtful review of emotion and cortical lateralization:
Richard Davidson (1998). Affective style and affective disorders: Perspectives from affective neuroscience. *Cognition and Emotion, 12*(3), 307–30.

Appraisal, Knowledge, and Experience

CHAPTER 7

Herein too may be felt the power-lessness of mere Logic... to resolve these problems which lie nearer to our hearts.

George Boole, 1854, An Investigation of the Laws of Thought, p. 416

Contents

Figure 7.0 Diagram from Descartes's book *Traité de l'homme*. In Descartes's scheme, the soul – which was moved by emotions – was able to open valves to let vital fluids from the reservoir (labeled F) into the tubes to work the muscles and produce actions.

In 1961, a patient with epilepsy – a kind of electrical storm in the brain – had an operation to separate the left side of the cortex from the right, and hence to stop the spread of epileptic disturbances since no other treatment had been effective. This procedure is called a **split brain** operation, and in it the corpus callosum, a large bundle of nerve fibers that connects the left and right sides of the cortex, is severed (Gazzaniga, 1985), A number of such operations have been performed, and they do reduce or eliminate certain kinds of epileptic disturbance. Despite the left and right cortices being no longer in communication, the patient's IQ, personality, language, and ability to engage in meaningful interactions are not diminished. Twenty years after the first split brain operation Roger Sperry was awarded a Nobel Prize for his research with these patients, which showed in a striking new way the different functions of left and right hemispheres.

The experiments depended on the fact that if a picture or text is presented to the right side of the visual field, it is processed by the left hemisphere. When anything is shown in the left visual field, it is processed by the right hemisphere. But with the split brain the two hemispheres do not communicate, and each remains ignorant of what the other has seen. Research indicates that the right hemisphere responds more readily to the emotional content of stimuli (Borod, 1992), whereas the left is more ready to interpret experience in terms of language (Gazzaniga, Ivry, & Mangun, 2002).

Here is an example from Michael Gazzaniga (1988) who worked with Sperry. He showed a frightening film about fire safety to the left visual field of a woman split-brain patient. Because the images were not accessible to the "interpretive center" in the left hemisphere of her brain, she was not conscious of having seen the film. Gazzaniga then interviewed the patient, as follows.

M.G. (Michael Gazzaniga): What did you see?

V.P. (Patient): I don't really know what I saw. I think just a white flash.

M.G.: Were there people in it?

V.P.: I don't think so. Maybe just some trees, red trees like in the fall.

M.G.: Did it make you feel any emotion?

V.P.: I don't really know why but I'm kind of scared. I feel jumpy. I think maybe I don't like this room, or maybe it's you. You're getting me nervous.

The patient seems to feel fear. Her right hemisphere has processed the emotional content of the film about fire safety, triggering anxiety and agitation. She takes part in the interview by using her linguistically competent left hemisphere; with it she does not consciously know why she feels as she does, presumably because the fearful stimulus has been processed only in the right cortex, and been communicated to the unsplit subcortical regions which are essential to emotional experience. When asked by Gazzaniga to explain her feelings, the patient starts working on the problem: She draws upon her anxious feelings together with the knowledge of her narratizing left hemisphere, and offers a story about how Gazzaniga was making her feel nervous.

In this chapter we discuss these two kinds of process. The first is unconscious, and automatic. It is something like the reflex, which is illustrated in the opening picture for this chapter, from Descartes's book *Traité de l'homme*. In this chapter we will call it **primary appraisal**. The second is potentially conscious, and thought-like, and it gives rise to specific emotions. We will call it **secondary appraisal**.

Appraisal and emotion

In the past three chapters we have devoted attention to answering the question William James posed: "What is an emotion?" We have examined emotion-specific facial expressions, vocal cues, autonomic responses, and central nervous system activity. But what is it that gives rise to our moods and emotions? The consensus in the field is that for events to prompt emotions, they must be evaluated, or appraised, in relation to the individual's goals.

Historical background and definitions

As we explained in chapter 1, the concept of evaluation of events in relation to an individual's purposes goes back 2,400 years, to Aristotle. He was followed by philosophers such as Epicurus and Chrysippus who took the idea of evaluation and applied it to the question of how the damaging effects of emotions could be avoided in the course of living a good life. These and other philosophers in the schools of Epicurean and Stoic ethical philosophy, which have had a huge influence on Western thought, were – if one may put it like this – the first thoroughgoing Western emotion researchers. One of the most interesting analyses to emerge from this work was made by Chrysippus who distinguished between what he called first movements of emotions, which are automatic, and second movements which are mental, and which involve judgment and decision. Chrysippus thought that one cannot avoid the first movements, they are made simply by the body. But since the second movements involve thought, they are more, as these philosophers said, "up to us." The second movements of bad emotions such as giving in to angry revenge, or to greedy selfishness, later became in Christian thinking the seven deadly sins (Oatley, 2004c; Sorabji, 2000). The idea of first and second movements maps exactly onto the idea of **primary and secondary appraisals**, which provides the framework for this chapter.

Aristotelian and Stoic ideas were discussed by Magda Arnold and J. A. Gasson (1954; their analyses are described in chapter 1). They reintroduced the idea of emotion as evaluation, known as appraisal in modern psychology, where it has become a central concept for understanding emotions. An important figure in its development was Richard Lazarus, who spent the early part of his career studying stress, a condition in which personal challenges exceed the individual's capacities and resources (see, e.g., Lazarus, 1991). Stress produces vigilant attention and heightened activity in the sympathetic branch of the autonomic nervous system. In the short term, it is an adaptive process, helping people respond to threats, dangers, and likely punishments with quick, energetic efficiency. In the long term, chronic stress produced by enduring sources of tension such as pressures at work, turbulent periods during marriages, or financial problems that deprive one of basic necessities, is dangerous. Chronic stress can lead to heart disease, cancer, and even cell death in the hippocampus and memory loss (Sapolsky, 1994). Social threats, for example in being the target of prejudice or discrimination, can lead to health problems as well (Blascovich & Mendes, 2000; Blascovich et al., 2001).

The concept of stress is intuitively appealing and has been the focus of hundreds of studies. Yet Lazarus raised a problem: there seem to be many different kinds of stress. The stress associated with humiliation is different from the stress associated with losing a spouse to death or dealing with a life-threatening disease like cancer, or even the stress of positive events like starting a new career or having a child. How is one to account for this? Lazarus's answer was the emotions. Each different kind of stress promotes a particular kind of emotion, by means of a specific appraisal processes.

Here is how Lazarus defines an appraisal approach to emotion:

> This approach to emotion contains two basic themes: First, emotion is a response to evaluative judgments or meaning; second, these judgments are about ongoing relationships with the environment, namely how one is doing in the agenda of living and whether the encounter of the environment is one of harm or benefit.

What is critical in this definition, first of all, is evaluation. Agreeing with Aristotle, and with Arnold and Gasson, Lazarus proposed that appraisals involve judgments of how good or bad an event is. A second theme is that appraisals concern the individual's goals and aspirations, and how he or she is interacting with the environment. Emotions, then, have a critical place in psychology: they refer both to events in the world and to the person's concerns. They relate the outer world and the inner self.

A related approach has been offered by Stein, Trabasso, and Liwag (1994). They propose that the appraisals that give rise to emotions also involve beliefs, inferences, and plans. These aspects of emotion-related appraisal unfold, in Stein and colleagues' view, as follows:

1. An event, usually unexpected, is perceived that changes the status of a valued goal.
2. Beliefs are often challenged; this can cause bodily changes and expressions to occur.

3. Plans are formed about what to do about the event to reinstate or modify the goal, and the likely results of the plans are considered.

These stages are captured in the questions: "What happened? What can I do about it, and what might then happen next?"

Stein et al. (1994) give an example of a five-year-old, Amy. Her kindergarten teacher had just told the class that she had a paint set for each child, and that after painting pictures for Parents' Night the children could take their paint sets home. When the children had been given their paint sets, Stein et al.'s research assistant noticed Amy looking apprehensive. She asked why. Amy said: "I'm jittery. I'm not sure why she wants to give me the paints. So do I have to paint all of the time at home? I really don't want to do this. I didn't think teachers made you paint at home. I don't like painting that much. Why does she want me to paint at home?"

Here we see that Amy has a goal which has been violated (1): she doesn't want to paint. The idea of being given something to do at home violates a belief about what teachers do (2). The conversation continues with Amy's plans (3).

Research assistant: What will you do, Amy?

Amy: I don't want to take the paints home. I want to know why I have to do this.

Research assistant: Well Amy, what are you going to do about this?

Amy: I'll take the paints home, but when I get home, I'll ask my Mom why I have to do this.

Two weeks later the research assistant talked casually to Amy. She was still worried about the paints. She said she had used them only once. But she has not told the teacher, fearing that the teacher might be mad at her.

Stein et al. (1994) propose that how a person sees an event – the frame they use, which depends on the person's goals and values – will determine how the event is perceived, what emotions are elicited, and even what is remembered. This is consistent with Lazarus's treatment of appraisal. The same event might lead to much different emotions in different people. Notice that the processes leading to these specific emotions are thoughts or thought-like processes, of the kind we are calling secondary appraisals.

Automatic appraisals of good and bad

Into our lives come events that affect us profoundly. You arrive at college and meet your roommate, who instantly fills you with a reassuring sense of comfort and familiarity. While searching for an apartment to rent, most strike you as impersonal and cold, until you find one that feels like home. What are the appraisal processes that give rise to these fast, immediate, reactions?

As one answer to this question, Robert Zajonc (1980) has proposed that we process stimuli through several different appraisal systems. One system provides an immediate, unconscious evaluation of whether the stimulus is good or bad (LeDoux, 1993; Mischel & Shoda, 1995). This system gives rise to what we are calling primary appraisals, automatic emotional reactions to events and objects in the environment, which motivate rapid approach or avoidance responses. These primary appraisals correspond to what Chrysippus (discussed above) called the first movements of emotions. As you have learned in chapter 6, the system that makes these appraisals probably involves the amygdala. This first appraisal system appears to give rise to our core feelings of positivity or negativity (Russell, 2003). Other systems – which we are calling secondary, and which Chrysippus called second movements – provide more deliberate, conscious, complex assessments in terms of such matters as what caused the event and what to do about it.

To study the automatic evaluations, Sheila Murphy and Robert Zajonc (1993) presented participants with photos of people smiling or displaying facial anger. In a "suboptimal" subliminal condition, participants viewed these photos for four milliseconds. Subsequent recognition tests revealed that these participants had no idea whether they had seen a happy or angry face, establishing that the faces had indeed been processed unconsciously. In an "optimal" condition participants viewed the same faces for one second, and were clearly aware of which faces they had viewed. After viewing the faces, all participants then viewed Chinese ideographs and rated how much they liked those ideographs.

To the extent that there is a separate appraisal system that unconsciously evaluates the affective meaning of stimuli, one would expect the suboptimally presented faces to influence participants' ratings of the Chinese ideographs. The initial positive or negative feelings induced by the photos of the faces should color participants' evaluations of the ideographs. This is exactly what Murphy and Zajonc found. As you can see in figure 7.1, for the suboptimally presented faces, smiling faces led participants to express greater liking for the Chinese ideographs that followed them, and angry faces to prompt less liking for the ideographs that followed them, even though participants could not tell the experimenter what faces they had seen. No such priming effects emerged with the optimally presented faces. When we are consciously aware of emotionally charged stimuli, they are less likely to sway our judgments of other stimuli (Clore, Gasper, & Garvin, 2001; Gasper & Clore, 2000).

Is there evidence that automatic appraisals generate emotional experience as well as affecting preferences? As you will recall from chapter 1, this notion, that how our unconscious perceives the environment triggers powerful, and often inexplicable emotional reactions, was a cornerstone of Freud's analysis of emotional conflict. Ulf Dimberg and Arne Öhman (1996) suggest that there are such effects. They first presented participants with photos of a smiling face or an angry face for extremely brief periods of

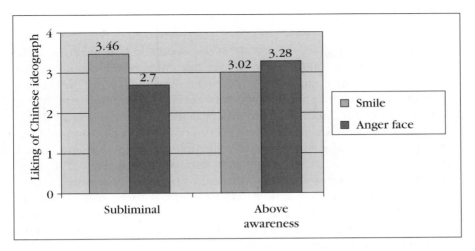

Figure 7.1 Unconscious appraisal. To explore whether evaluations can be produced unconsciously, Shelia Murphy and Robert Zajonc presented participants with slides of a smiling face or an angry face, either at suboptimal (subliminal) or optimal (above awareness) levels, and then had participants rate how much they liked Chinese ideographs. People liked the Chinese ideographs more after they have first been presented with a subliminally presented smile, suggesting that that smile had activated positive feeling at an unconscious level. When presented with a smiling face long enough to be consciously aware of it, the smile did not lead participants to evaluate the Chinese ideographs more positively (Source: Murphy & Zajonc, 1993).

time. These photos were then masked, that is to say immediately followed, by other photos that prevented the possibility of consciously perceiving the original face. Again, participants were not aware of having seen the angry or happy face, but these suboptimally presented facial expressions did influence the individual's emotions; they prompted participants to smile or to furrow their brow and show lowered or elevated physiological arousal associated with threat or danger, depending on whether the suboptimally presented face had been respectively smiling or angry (see also Dimberg, Thunberg, & Elmehed, 2000; Whalen et al., 1998). In other work, Öhman and Soares (1994) presented photos of snakes to people with snake phobias below their awareness, and found that these photos generated a galvanic skin response and negative emotion.

These studies suggest that there is a primary appraisal process that is automatic, fast, and primitive in the sense that it gives rise to an immediate feeling of good or bad, or positivity or negativity. Before we turn to the more specific appraisal processes that gives rise to different kinds of positive and negative emotions, let's digress a bit, and ask which might be more potent: negative or positive evaluations?

Is the bad stronger than the good?

The research on automatic appraisals of the good and bad qualities of the stimulus raises an intriguing question: Are our initial positive and negative evaluations of stimuli comparable? Or is one stronger and more potent than the other? Reviews by Shelley Taylor (1991), John Cacioppo and Wendy Gardner (1999), Roy Baumeister and his colleagues (Baumeister et al., 2001), and Paul Rozin and Edward Royzman (2001) offered a conclusive, and perhaps unsettling answer: our negative evaluations appear to be more potent than our positive evaluations. The bad is stronger than the good. It would make evolutionary sense for the individual to be more responsive to pain than to pleasure, to danger rather than to safety. Without such a bias, the chances of survival would seem to be diminished. This would suggest, more generally, that our negative emotions might seem more intense, or more readily elicited, and harder to regulate.

Numerous studies lead to the conclusion that the bad is stronger than the good. Negative stimuli, such as startling, frightening sounds or disgusting smells, trigger more rapid, stronger physiological responses than positive stimuli, such as pleasing sounds or delicious tastes. In various experiments, the loss of $10 is experienced as more painful than the pleasure one experiences in gaining $10. Negative trauma, such as the death of a loved one or sexual abuse, can change the individual for a lifetime. It is hard to think of analogous positive life events that alter life in such profound and enduring ways. Or consider Paul Rozin's ideas about contamination, the process by which one disgusting object endows another object with its vile essence through simple contact (Rozin & Fallon, 1987). Brief contact with a cockroach will spoil a delicious meal (the negative stimulus contaminates the positive stimulus). The inverse – making a pile of cockroaches delicious by touching it with your favorite food, say chocolate – is unimaginable (Rozin & Royzman, 2001).

To address whether negative evaluations are more potent than positive evaluations, Tiffany Ito, John Cacioppo, and their colleagues presented participants with positively toned or valenced pictures – for example, photographs of pizza or chocolate ice cream – and negatively valenced slides – for example, photographs of a mutilated face or of a dead cat (Ito et al., 1998). They recorded participants' electrocortical activity on the scalp, focusing on one region of brain activity that is associated with evaluative responses. Ito and colleagues discovered a clear negativity bias in evaluation: the negative stimuli generated greater brain activity than the positive or neutral slides. It seems, alas, that the bad is indeed stronger than the good.

Appraisal theories and distinct emotions

Thus far we have seen that people respond with unconscious or automatic evaluations of events, evaluations that are centered on simple good–bad assessments (Feldman-Barrett & Russell, 1999). These automatic evaluations are likely to form a central core to our experience of moods and emotions (Russell, 2003). Although goodness and badness are no doubt funda-mental properties of our reactions to objects, such things as ice cream, an exhilarating walk in the woods, and an enjoyable novel are all equally good in many people's eyes, yet these experiences differ in many ways. Much more is needed to account for the complexity of emotional experience. In particular, what is needed is a more precise theory of the specific appraisal processes that elicit different emotions, such as anger, guilt, gratitude, and love. Enquiry into this area takes us beyond automatic primary appraisals to more sophisticated secondary appraisals. Modern research on appraisal has tended to be in two families: that of **discrete approaches** that emphas-izes that unique appraisals give rise to different emotions; and **dimensional approaches**, which focus on the many components of appraisals that relate to different emotions.

Discrete approaches to appraisal

In his theory of discrete emotions, Richard Lazarus proposed that there are two stages to the appraisal process (1991). In his version of the primary appraisal stage, which we represent in figure 7.2, the individual appraises the event in terms of its relevance to goals. First, the individual evaluates whether the event is relevant to personal goals or not. If so, an emotion is elicited; if not, no emotion ensues. Then the individual appraises ongoing events in terms of the extent to which the event is congruent or incongruent with the person's goals. Goal congruent events elicit positive events, and goal incongruent events produce negative emotions. Finally, the individual appraises the event in terms of its relevance to more specific goals, or issues for the ego. Events can concern moral values, for example to be kind to others or to honor the golden rule. Events might bear upon issues of the self and identity, for example whether one is excelling in areas that are central to self-definition, such as academics, artistic performance, or charity work. Events can pertain to important ideas, for example that societies should be fair and just. And in light of how much emotion is triggered by events that happen to other people, events might implicate other people's goals, and their well-being.

An approach to discrete emotions related to Lazarus's is that of Oatley and Johnson-Laird (1987, 1996). They postulate appraisals with two com-ponents, as we have been discussing. First there is an appraisal of an event in relation to goals that is automatic and unconscious. It corresponds to the automatic and nonverbal process mentioned in relation to Gazzaniga's patient discussed at the beginning of the chapter. In this account the auto-matic process is in terms of basic emotions (such as happiness, sadness, anger, fear, and disgust). According to Oatley and Johnson-Laird, each of these basic emotions has the function of setting the brain into a mode adapted to deal with a recurring situation (respectively: progress with a goal, loss,

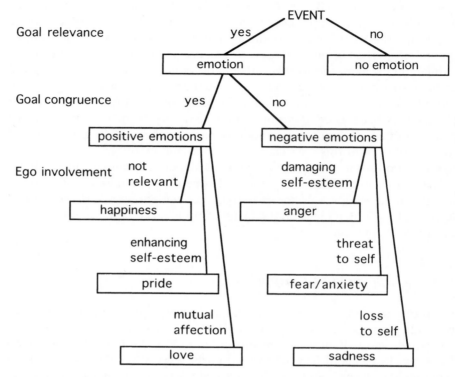

Figure 7.2 Decision tree of primary appraisals based on three features (goal relevance, goal congruence, and ego involvement), plus the kinds of emotions that can occur with these appraisals, derived from Lazarus (1991). Further differentiation among emotions occurs in secondary appraisals.

frustration by another, threat, and toxicity). Notice that in this account the primary appraisal is not just of positive or negative, but of a small number of basic emotions. Remember Gazzaniga's patient did not say she experienced something negative: she said she felt "kind of scared." Each mode is a state of **readiness** (cf. Frijda, 1986) with a distinct phenomenological tone, but no necessary verbal meaning. The effect is a bit like having several kinds of bell or alarm in your house, say a door bell, a telephone bell, a smoke detector, a burglar alarm. If one goes off you are alerted to something potentially important of a particular kind, and your readiness changes accordingly, but initially you do not know what the event was that caused the bell or alarm to sound. For that you need to investigate. Similarly, an emotion starts, but its verbal meaning is supplied by a secondary process that occurs more in awareness, in which you make a mental model of the event, what caused it, and how to act in relation to it.

In the secondary appraisal stage as proposed by Lazarus, the individual considers a causal attribution for the event, how to respond to the event, and future consequences of different courses of action. The result of these processes is what Lazarus calls the **core relational theme** of the emotion.

Table 7.1   Core relational themes of different emotions

Anger	A demeaning offense against me and mine
Anxiety	Facing uncertain, existential threat
Fright	Facing an immediate, concrete, and overwhelming physical danger
Guilt	Having transgressed a moral imperative
Shame	Having failed to live up to an ego-ideal
Sadness	Having experienced an irrevocable loss
Envy	Wanting what someone else has
Jealousy	Resenting a third party for loss or threat to another's affection
Disgust	Taking in or being too close to an indigestible object or idea
Happiness	Making reasonable progress toward the realization of a goal
Pride	Enhancement of one's ego-identity by taking credit for a valued object or achievement, either our own or that of someone or group with whom we identify
Relief	A distressing goal-incongruent condition that has changed for the better or gone away
Hope	Fearing the worst but yearning for better
Love	Desiring or participating in affection, usually but not necessarily reciprocated
Compassion	Being moved by another's suffering and wanting to help

Source: Adapted from Lazarus (1991)

The core-relational theme is the essential meaning for each emotion. In table 7.1 we present Lazarus's analysis of several emotions.

You can think about these core relational themes as summaries of the different classes of events that elicit emotion. In evolutionary terms, the core relational themes map onto the problems and opportunities to which people respond with emotions, the slights (anger), dangers (fear), moral transgressions (guilt), losses (sadness), and sufferings of others (compassion), for example, that have been critical to human survival, reproduction, and cooperative group living. You can also think about these core relational themes as the language of our emotional experience: they capture the themes and issues that organize our emotional experience.

Dimensional approaches to appraisal

Can you think of any aspects of emotional experience that approaches to discrete emotions do not adequately explain? Are there specific emotions they fail to address? Are there properties of your emotional life that do not readily follow from the approach of discrete emotions?

Phoebe Ellsworth (e.g., 1991) has highlighted two reasons why we need to think about emotion-related appraisal from another perspective, which has come to be called dimensional. The first has to do with the similarities between emotions. Approaches to emotions as discrete, such as those of Lazarus, highlight the differences between emotions in terms of their eliciting appraisals. The kinds of events that produce anger no doubt differ from those that produce fear, or sadness, or shame. Yet many emotions are similar in fundamental ways. Anger and fear, for example, at their core feel similar: they feel unpleasant and arousing. The same could be said, for example, about gratitude and love, which both feel quite pleasant and are marked by a feeling of devotion for others. An appraisal theory, Ellsworth contends, needs to account for the interesting similarities across emotions, as well as their differences.

A second gap, in approaches to emotions as discrete, according to Ellsworth, is their inability to account for transitions between emotions. Very often in our emotional experience we move from one emotion to another, we shift from anger to guilt quite rapidly, or sadness to hope, or, hopefully not often, love to anger. It is not transparent how Lazarus's discrete model of appraisal would account for these rapid transitions between emotions, which presumably make up such an important part of our daily emotional life.

In light of these and other conceptual interests, Phoebe Ellsworth and Craig Smith (1985, 1988) have developed a theory of appraisal that can account for interesting similarities among the emotions, as well as the many differences (for comparable accounts see Frijda, 1986; Ortony, Clore, & Collins, 1988; Roseman, 1984; Scherer, 1988; Weiner, 1986). To arrive at their theory, Smith and Ellsworth reviewed numerous studies of the semantic content of emotions, like those of Ira Roseman and his colleagues, and from this review derived eight different dimensions of meaning that capture the appraisal processes that lead to various emotions. These dimensions are presented in table 7.2. Think of these dimensions as the basic units of the meaning ascribed to events in your life. They have to do with how positive or negative the event is, who is responsible for it, whether it is fair, how much energy is required, to what extent does the stimulus require intense attention, how certain things seem, and so on.

To document the patterns of appraisal associated with the different emotions, Smith and Ellsworth had 16 participants imagine experiencing

Table 7.2 Dimensions of appraisal

1. Attention: Degree to which you focus on and think about the stimulus
2. Certainty: Degree to which you are certain about what is going to happen
3. Control-coping: Extent to which you have control over outcomes in the environment
4. Pleasantness: Degree that the event is positive or negative
5. Perceived obstacle: Extent to which the pursuit of your goals is blocked
6. Responsibility: Extent to which other people, you, and situational factors are responsible for events
7. Legitimacy: Extent to which the event is fair and deserved or unfair and undeserved
8. Anticipated effort: Extent to which you must expend energy to respond to the event

Source: Adapted from Smith & Ellsworth (1985)

15 different emotions. After this, participants then rated the original emotional experience on the eight dimensions presented in table 7.2. Each emotion was found to be defined by a fairly distinct pattern of appraisal. For example, interest is associated with appraisals of elevated pleasantness, the desire to attend, the sense that situational factors are producing events, the perceived need to expend effort, moderate certainty about future outcomes, together with little sense of perceived obstacle or illegitimacy of events. Hope is associated with appraisals of elevated attention and effort and situational agency, moderate pleasantness, and little certainty or sense of perceived obstacle or illegitimacy. Happiness is the emotion that is pleasant, associated with low effort, high certainty, and high attention.

A second important result found by Smith and Ellsworth was that certain dimensions stood out in their ability to differentiate among related emotions. They found that a combination of control and responsibility, which they called "agency," was the critical dimension that differentiated three negative emotions: anger, sadness, and guilt. When we blame others, we become angry, when we attribute similar events to general circumstances or fate, we become sad, when we attribute events to ourselves, we become guilty. Agency was also an important dimension to differentiate certain positive emotions. The same positive event attributed to the self is a source of pride, but when attributed to others is a source of gratitude.

This importance of causality in emotion-related appraisal is likewise seen in the work of Weiner and Graham (1989). They found that some distinct emotions depend on **attributions**, the explanations of the causes of events that people give. They describe how children between the ages of 5 and 11 were given vignettes and asked to decide what emotion would occur. One was this:

> This is a story about a boy named Chris. Chris's teacher gave a spelling test and he got all the words right. Chris received an "A" on the test. (Weiner & Graham, 1989, p. 407)

If the children were told that Chris had studied all the words the night before (implying that the cause of his success was his own action) they tended to say that he would feel pride, but if the cause was that the teacher gave an easy text (a cause external to Chris), then the children, especially the older ones, thought Chris would not feel pride. Comparable results were found with guilt: if an event that caused damage could have been controlled, the children thought the person causing it would feel guilt, but if it was an accident, the older children thought the person would not feel guilt.

This finding, that agency or causal attributions differentiate various emotions, has an important implication: the same negative event may happen to you (perhaps you don't do as well on an exam as you had hoped) but which emotion you experience will depend on how you appraise the causes. Attribute the event to yourself and you're likely to feel guilt. Attribute it to others and you'll feel anger. Attribute it to circumstantial factors and you'll be more likely to experience sadness.

Critiques of appraisal research and new methods for studying appraisal

Think for a moment about the Smith and Ellsworth study, which is something of a classic in the study of appraisal, or about the studies of Weiner and Graham on attribution and emotion. Are you skeptical about these retrospective, self-report studies? About how they studied appraisal? In the Smith and Ellsworth study, people relived an emotional experience from their past, and then reported on the appraisals that produced the emotion. Is this really a study of appraisal as we have defined it in this chapter?

Several critiques have been levied against this kind of retrospective, self-report study of appraisal (e.g., Parkinson & Manstead, 1992; Parkinson, Fischer, & Manstead, 2004). First, the evidence from studies like that of Smith and Ellsworth is not causal. That is, they did not document how appraisals cause emotion; instead, it is more fair to say that their evidence reveals how when one thinks about an emotional experience, such appraisal patterns come to mind.

Second, there is reason to doubt whether the kinds of conscious assessments of appraisal that Smith and Ellsworth gathered actually correspond to the more spontaneous, rapid, even unconscious appraisals that produce emotion. Perhaps it is more fair to say that Smith and Ellsworth studied people's theories about the causes of their emotions, rather than the actual causes of emotion. Indeed as Parkinson, Fischer, and Manstead point out, such appraisal seems to be part of the language in which people discuss emotions with their confidants, and in the changing appraisals of such discussions emotions can change. Nonetheless, the appraisal dimensions proposed by Smith and Ellsworth and others have shed important light on how people construct their emotional experiences.

There are several other methods for studying appraisal that are less subject to the biases of retrospective, self-report methods. One approach is to rely on **diary studies**, in which people report on their daily emotional experiences in diary-like entries. One of the first to do this was Joanna Field (1934), who wanted to see what it was in her life that made her happy. Here are some of her thoughts after falling in love, thinking about the man she would marry. "June 8th. I want us to travel together, exploring, seeing how other people live . . . sleeping at country inns, sailing boats, tramping dusty roads together . . ." (p. 48). Here the thoughts take the form of plans of activities in a shared life of new experiences with the loved one.

In anxiety the thoughts are quite different. Here is Joanna Field again:

> Oughtn't we to ask those people to tea? That's best, say, "Do you ever have time for a cup of tea? Will you come in any day?" Say we are free all the week, let them choose, will the maid answer the door? will she be too busy? what shall we give them? go into town and buy a cake? will they expect it? Can't afford these extras, but bread and jam won't do, what does one give people for tea . . . ? (p. 114)

In this anxious little train of thought, Field wonders how to approach some people who are wealthier than she, rehearsing different forms of invitation, worrying about how she would feel if she calls and a maid tells her that the person she wants to see is too busy. Recent uses of the method of having subjects keep emotion diaries have yielded many examples. Oatley and Duncan (1992) report a 20-year-old woman, Abigail, who had had an angry argument with her boyfriend about preferences for different kinds of music. The argument lasted two and a half hours, but intrusive thoughts continued for three days, and kept her from sleeping for three nights. She said: "I just couldn't get through to him." Her thoughts included: "Is this going too far? If it goes too far, it [the relationship with the boyfriend] would end." Memories came to mind: the argument "reminded her of an ex-boyfriend" and made her "wonder if it [the relationship] was worth it" (p. 275).

A second new approach is to identify appraisals as they occur, and ascertain whether emotion-specific appraisals relate to other measures of emotional response. For example, one might code appraisal-related themes, such as uncertainty or loss, or dimensions, such as responsibility or effort, in individuals' spontaneous speech, and ask whether those appraisals relate to measures of experience, or expression or physiology. In one such study, Bonanno and Keltner (2004) coded the narratives of people who, six months prior, had experienced the death of their romantic partner. These narratives were complex, moving accounts of participants' lives with their partner, how they had met and fallen and love and often raised families, and ultimately how their partner had died. The narratives included numerous references to loss, an appraisal theme related to sadness, and injustice, an appraisal theme at the heart of the experience of anger. These researchers coded spontaneous references to these two appraisal themes and related them to other measures of emotion gathered during the interview. They found that appraisals of loss correlated with facial expressions and self-reports of sadness but not anger, and that appraisals of injustice correlated with facial expressions and self-reports of anger but not sadness.

Cultural variation in appraisal

Our preceding discussion may have left you wondering about cultural variation in appraisal processes. Examples of cultural variation in appraisal abound (e.g., Russell, 1991). Consider the work of Rick Shweder and his colleagues on culture and moral judgment (Shweder et al., 1997). They conducted interviews to explore people's ideas about the kinds of events that they found morally repugnant, and the source of anger and disgust. In Hindu India, they found that people are angered by several events that would tend not to elicit much emotion in European cultures. These include the following: when a child cuts his hair after the death of his father, when a woman eats with her husband's elder brother, when a husband cooks for his wife or massages her legs, and when upper-caste individuals come into physical contact with lower-caste individuals.

Certain studies, however, point to a surprising degree of universality in the elicitors of emotion. Boucher and Brandt (1981) asked young Americans and Malaysians to describe events that made them feel emotions such as fear, disgust, and joy. From this collection of situations, a subset of those generated by Americans and Malaysians were presented to new participants from each culture, who were asked to identify which emotion would be elicited by these situations. Members of both cultures were in agreement in judging which emotions would be elicited by different events and, remarkably, each group was just as accurate in predicting emotions that would be elicited by the situations listed by the other group as for their own. This implied great commonality in the triggers for emotions across very different cultures (see Mesquita & Frijda, 1992). Other researchers have also concluded that the appraisals that elicit emotions are quite similar across cultures as well (Mauro, Sato, & Tucker, 1992; Mesquita & Ellsworth, 2001; Scherer, 1997).

How, then, do cultures differ in the events that elicit emotion? Think back to our discussion of individualist, independent cultures and collectivist, interdependent cultures in chapter 3. In light of this framework, one might expect solitary and social experiences to have different meaning for members of individualist and collectivist cultures. Or consider the simple situation of being alone. Middle-class Europeans are likely to appraise being alone in positive terms, and experience contentedness. By contrast, Utku Inuit people as studied by Briggs (1970), or the people of Ifaluk as studied by Lutz (1988), as well as numerous other interdependent peoples, appraise being alone in terms of isolation, which elicits feelings of sadness (Mesquita & Ellsworth, 2001; Mesquita & Markus, 2004).

Being dependent upon others also appears to generate different appraisals and emotions across cultures. For example, among the Awlad'Ali, a nomadic tribe in Egypt, being in the presence of powerful others is the source of shame, or *hasham*, because such situations are reminders of one's dependence on others (Abu-Lughod, 1986). In contrast, it is reported that the Japanese experience a pleasurable emotion known as *amae* within relations between people of greater and lesser power (Lebra, 1983). This is a comforting sense of dependence the less powerful person feels vis-à-vis the more powerful person, which permits the less powerful person to engage in passive or helpless behavior in the satisfying knowledge that it will be accepted.

Knowledge of emotion

Bermard Rimé and his colleagues have found using diary methods that people have a powerful tendency to **confide** their emotional experiences in others (Rimé et al., 1991, 1998). They call this social sharing, and it occurs even for emotions such as guilt and shame that might not reflect flatteringly upon the person doing the sharing. When we share our emotions with others, we necessarily are relying upon our knowledge of emotions. We use specific words, concepts, categories, and narratives to understand our emotions and convey our experiences to others.

Emotion words

An important component of emotion knowledge is our vocabulary of emotion words, or **emotion lexicon**. In English there are thousands of words that people use to describe emotional experience. Relevant studies reveal four different properties of emotion words.

First, applying a label to an emotional experience helps identify the **intentional object** of an experience: what the emotion is specifically about (Ben Ze'ev & Oatley, 1996). (The philosophical term intention means a mental state of "aboutness." So thinking, knowing, and usually feeling, are intentional in this sense, and an intentional object is what a particular mental state is about.) Emotion words direct us to the focus of the experience (Ben Ze'ev, 2000). For example, in the midst of a lively exchange at a party, you might suddenly realize you are jealous. Applying this word to your ongoing experience is likely to sharpen the focus of your experience, and guide you to attend to specific events: perhaps your partner is smiling flirtatiously at your best friend. The experience may also evoke past experiences of a similar theme, perhaps with this current partner. Emotion words, then, appear to shape diffuse experiences into more specific emotional experiences.

Second, many emotion words have a metaphorical content. **Metaphors** are concepts that people use to describe other concepts that are typically more abstract or hard to describe. For example, in English we say metaphorically "this party is a blast," to provide a vivid image – the blast of a bomb – to characterize the more complex features of a party. We say that "justice is blind" to characterize one concrete (and hoped for) property of an abstract process like justice: that it be applied similarly to all, independently of their means or identities.

In their study of metaphor, George Lakoff, Mark Johnson, and Zoltán Kövesces have argued that there are five metaphors that speakers of English frequently use to describe emotional experience (Kövesces, 2003; Lakoff & Johnson, 1980). First, emotions are *natural forces*. We speak of being swept away by our emotions, as if they are waves. We talk about feelings of hope or despair that ebb and flow like the tides. We refer to a highly emotional child as stormy. Second, emotions are *opponents*. We struggle, often unsuccessfully, with our desire, grief, and frustration. We fight off the urge to cry. Third, emotions are *diseases*. We say that we are sick with love or envy. We can be insane with jealousy or grief. Fourth, we conceptualize our emotions as fluids in containers. We simmer with rage. We feel as if we are bursting with joy. And finally, at times we refer to emotions as animals, or living objects. People are expressing love are "lovey-dovey."

We speak of nurturing a child's love or interest, otherwise it may wither and die.

Where do these interesting metaphors of emotion come from? Johnson and Lakoff speculate that the metaphors we use to describe our emotions arise from our own experience and observation. For example, certain physiological properties of emotion, such as the elevated blood pressure associated with emotions like anger, might give rise to the metaphor of emotion as a fluid in a container. We look out into the natural world and see other species courting, which gives rise to metaphors of our own experience of love.

Thirdly, our emotion lexicon has structure. It is organized at different levels and into categories. In one important study on the structure of the emotion lexicon, Shaver et al. (1987) gave participants 135 emotion terms written on cards, and asked them to sort those words into as many or few categories as they deemed appropriate. Based on how participants sorted these words, Shaver et al. captured people's organization of emotion knowledge, at least for these Western participants. What this task revealed, according to Shaver and colleagues, is that there are three levels to our emotion knowledge.

At the broadest or superordinate level of emotion knowledge is a basic distinction between positive and negative, or good and bad. This seems to fit well with how people appraise the goodness and badness of stimuli immediately and automatically.

At the next level, which is known as the basic level of knowledge, are six emotion concepts: love, joy, surprise, anger, sadness, fear. From what is known from cognitive psychology, one might expect these terms to be those that people most frequently use to describe their emotional experience. It is interesting to note as well that many of these terms correspond to the emotions that appear to have universal facial expressions. This same list of emotions replicates (with slight variations) in analyses of other languages (Romney, Moore, & Rusch, 1997).

Below each of the basic emotion terms are many more specific states. This is known as the subordinate level of emotion knowledge. These are likely to be states that in fundamental ways share properties of the basic emotion concept above them, and that are in important ways similar to one another. For example, below the basic emotion concept "love" is: love, compassion, lust, longing. Below the concept "happiness" is: amusement, enthusiasm, pleasure, pride, hope, enthrallment, relief. Below "sadness" is agony, depression, disappointment, guilt, embarrassment, pity.

Emotion words do, however, vary dramatically across cultures. Because of this, Wierzbicka (1999), who speaks many languages, has been critical of attempts to infer universal categories of emotion from intuitions by members of English-speaking cultures. She proposes, instead, universal concepts of emotions based on the following kind of analysis (somewhat abbreviated). Happiness: (a) X was happy because X thought something, (b) X thought: "some good things happened to me," (c) X thought "I wanted things like this to happen," (d) X thought: "I don't want anything else now."

One type of variation among cultures occurs, as we discussed in chapter 3. We spoke of how certain cultures hypercognize specific emotions, that is, they have rich vocabularies of experience related to certain emotions, presumably because the emotion plays a central role in the culture. To explore how cultures vary in their language of emotion, James Russell read hundreds of ethnographies written by anthropologists who had lived in different cultures and were familiar with the language and life of that culture (Russell, 1991). After observing that almost all languages have terms for anger, fear, happiness, sadness, and disgust, Russell paints a fascinating picture of how cultures vary in the language of emotion.

Cultures vary in the *number of words* that represent emotion. Researchers have identified 2,000 emotion-related words in English, 750 in Taiwanese, 58 in Ifaluk of Polynesia, and 8 in the Chewong of Malaysia.

Cultures vary in which states they represent with emotion terms. In the Gifjingali language of the Aborigines of Australia, fear and shame are captured by the same word, *gurakadj.* The distinction between shame and embarrassment is not made by the Japanese, Tahitians, Indonesians, or Newars of Nepal. There are states represented by a single word in other languages that are not represented by single English terms. For example, in Czech one finds *litost*, which means the sudden realization of life's tragic circumstances. In German there is the well-known word *Schadenfreude*, pleasure in seeing the failure or suffering of another person.

Finally, cultures vary according to whether they hypercognize an emotion, that is, represent it with numerous words and concepts. For example, in Tahiti there are 46 separate terms that refer to anger. It has been claimed that in the United States, guilt and love are hypercognized. It seems probable that, with hypercognized emotions, people may be more likely to experience the emotion, and to experience many shadings of that emotion.

So emotion words and concepts affect emotional experience. In thinking about the emotion lexicon, the question arises as to how far it corresponds to features of emotional experience. For example, do members of one culture who have many more words for a certain kind of emotion than do members of another culture have experiences that are somehow different? Interesting questions of this kind await empirical attention.

Concepts of emotion as prototypes

How do we categorize emotions? Are there necessary and sufficient features of the concept of emotion, or of specific emotions? For some concepts we can fairly easily give a correct definition with necessary and sufficient features – so "a grandmother" is "a mother of a person who is a parent." For most concepts exact definition is difficult or impossible because the natural world is not so neatly divided into categories, and for many objects we just do not know enough. So when you say "tree," you mean that kind of thing called "tree" of which we all know typical examples but about which, if need be, those scientists in the Botany Department could tell us more.

Thus language and thought have the wonderful property of allowing people to talk and be understood quite well even when we do not know very much. To do this we rely on thinking with **prototypes** that the hearer can summon into mind (Putnam, 1975). A prototype is good example of objects in a category, so a prototypical bird is a robin. It possesses features that we most typically associate with the category of bird. It flies, is of medium size, sings, builds nests, and so on. When invoking prototypes to explain things, we can specify modifications if need be. Although our prototype for tree might include the concept "large," we can modify it and say: "It is a tiny tree that has been grown in a pot and pruned to keep it small."

In several studies Fehr and Russell (1984) have made the persuasive case that people think about emotions in terms of prototypes. More specifically, people's everyday prototype of an emotion is something like a **script**, which refers to a characteristic outline of a sequence of events. Russell (1991b) has contrasted this kind of approach with approaches such as that of Johnson-Laird and Oatley (1989) who have offered a semantic analysis of the English lexicon in terms of primary emotions and their derivatives. Russell suggested that although in science we need to understand defining characteristics of emotions, perhaps in a manner such as that of semantic analysis, in ordinary life we think with prototypical examples of emotions with no sharp boundaries dividing off good from less good examples,

For example, in one of the first studies systematically to explore prototypical scripts for different emotions, Shaver et al. (1987) had participants write about the causes, thoughts, feelings, actions, and signs of several different emotions. They coded these narratives and identified the features of the emotion prototypes (namely, those features that occurred in at least 20 percent of participants' descriptions). This approach yielded prototypes for different emotions. For example, the prototype for sadness is listed in table 7.3.

By this narrative methodology, participants offer scripts, or as De Sousa (1987) calls them, **paradigm scenarios**, of different emotions (see also De Sousa, 2004). The idea has been useful for researchers in differentiating various emotions. For example, there has been a good deal of confusion regarding how the self-conscious emotions, namely embarrassment, shame, and guilt, might differ from one another. Researchers using these narrative methods have sought to identify the distinct prototypes of the self-conscious emotions, including embarrassment, shame, and guilt (Keltner & Buswell,

Table 7.3 A prototype of sadness

Causes:	Death, loss, not getting what one wants
Feelings:	Helpless, tired, run down, slow
Expression:	Drooping posture, say sad things, crying, tears
Thoughts:	Blaming, criticizing self, irritable,
Actions:	Negative talk to others, take action, suppressing negative feelings

Source: Adapted from Shaver et al. (1987)

1996; Miller, 1992; Miller & Tangney, 1994; Parrott & Smith, 1991; Tangney et al., 1996). Embarrassment most typically follows violations of social conventions that increase social exposure (e.g., after pratfalls or a loss of body control). Shame tends to follow the failure to live up to expectations, either one's own or those of significant others, that define the "core self," "ego ideal," or character. Guilt appears to follow transgressions of moral rules that govern behavior towards others (Tangney, 1992). The common antecedents of guilt, therefore, include lying, cheating, stealing, infidelity, and neglecting personal duties (Keltner & Buswell, 1996; Tangney, 1992; Tangney et al., 1996).

There are several interesting implications of taking a prototype perspective to emotion knowledge. First, it assumes that are no sharp boundaries between emotion categories. For example, there is going to be overlap in people's representations of sadness and anger, for example, or fear and guilt. Second, a prototype approach helps account for the varieties of experiences that are represented by one category of emotion. For example, there are numerous varieties of anger: some involving blame, others that are accidental, some directed at others, other experiences directed at the self, some experiences of high intensity (like rage), others more modest (like irritation). A prototype perspective suggests that within each emotion category, there are better examples of an emotion, which possess the prototypical features of an emotion, such as those that we presented for sadness. Then there will be many variations of that emotion that have fewer of those features, or other features as well.

Categorical properties of emotion knowledge

In other ways it appears that we do think about emotion, or facets of emotion, in terms of **categories** with distinct boundaries between one another. An important demonstration of this was provided by Etcoff and Magee (1992). They argued that if there were basic emotions, then facial expressions would be recognized in categories. All happy faces would be sorted into one category, angry ones into another, and so forth. Perception of these expressions should be comparable to certain phenomena in the perception of speech. What distinguishes a spoken "b" from "p" in words like "bit" and "pit" is the time between the mouth opening and the onset of sound made by the larynx, called "voicing onset time." People are bad at making discriminations of voicing onset time on either side of the b–p boundary, but they are excellent at discriminations across this boundary, indicating that time differences of a few milliseconds are sorted into functional categories to define "b" and "p." Etcoff and Magee did an experiment on faces: they created several series of faces ranging between pairs of states: happy to neutral, happy to sad, angry to disgusted, and so forth. To do this they traced faces from expressions of six basic emotions and a neutral face in photographs taken by Ekman and Friesen (1975) and used the caricature-generating computer program of Brennan (1985). For each pair

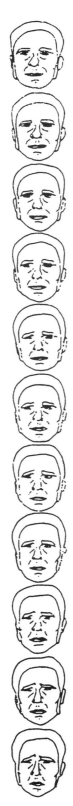

of states they created 11-point scales with exactly equal increments of transition. You can see the series of 11 faces from happiness to sadness in figure 7.3. They found that for these series there were abrupt shifts in discriminability between the faces, indicating a boundary between, for instance, happy and sad, angry and disgusted, and so forth. On either side of the boundary, people were not good at telling the difference between, for instance, the second and fourth faces in such series, but across the boundary, for instance between the fourth and sixth faces in the series, they were good. This experiment implies that functional categories of basic emotions affect discriminability of facial expressions.

In a similar vein, Conway and Bekerian (1987) provided evidence that emotional knowledge is organized into groups corresponding to basic emotions: love/joy/happiness; misery/grief/sadness; anger/hate/jealousy; and fear/terror/panic. They found that, as compared with priming with an unrelated word, priming with any emotion term within one of these basic groups produced faster reaction times in a lexical decision task. In another study Conway (1990) found that when people were asked to generate an image in response to an emotion word, more than 60 percent of the images were of specific incidents that had occurred at a particular time in their life that had emotional significance for them. By contrast, other kinds of words had different effects. Images generated in response to self-referring personality traits were derived from lifetime experience but were not identifiable with any particular incident. Images generated in response to abstract words were semantic: they indicated pieces of knowledge which were not related to specific experiences. Conway suggests, therefore, that when we remember particular incidents many of them are indexed in memory under specific kinds of emotion. According to the idea of emotion modes, preferential access to the emotion-indexed set of memories of incidents occurs when we are in that same emotional state. The function of this mechanism, we believe, is to bring to mind incidents comparable to the one that started the current emotion, to provide examples of how we have dealt with that kind of problem in the past, as well as a sense of continuity of our own actions in situations that produce a specific kind of emotion.

Experience

Thus far in this chapter, we have avoided one of the most difficult issues in the field: how to measure emotional experience. How do researchers capture fleeting experiences of emotions like fear, love, or compassion? And what determines the subjective feeling state associated with different emotions? In this last section of this chapter, we shall provide preliminary answers to these difficult questions.

Figure 7.3 (*Left*) Series of faces in equal increments from happy to sad (from Etcoff & Magee, 1992).

Measurement of experience

In one approach to the study of emotional experience, Green, Goldman, and Salovey (1993) surveyed the different approaches to the assessment of positive and negative moods. One method is to construct **adjective checklists**, using items of the following kind:

cheerful	blue
contented	depressed
happy	downhearted
pleased	gloomy
satisfied	sad
warmhearted	unhappy

The principle is to make up sets of adjectives that are synonyms of the moods in which you are interested (in the above cases happy and sad, or positive and negative). Then scramble all the adjectives and ask the subject to check any that apply to him or her. You count one point for each adjective from each set.

A second method is to offer statements like: "I am feeling sad and dispirited." Then ask people to indicate agreement on a scale – a common five-point scale is "strongly agree, agree, not sure, disagree, strongly disagree." Alternatively you can make up a scale indicating the extent to which each statement "Describes me."

A third method is to use a scale like the following:

Circle a number on the scale below to indicate how sad you feel.

Not at all 0-1-2-3-4-5-6-7-8-9-10 The most intense I have felt in my life

The ends of this kind of scale are marked with verbal expressions called anchor points, with which the subject can compare his or her current experience.

There are now a number of self-report scales of these kinds that measure the tendencies to experience global positive and negative moods (Watson, Clark, & Tellegen, 1988), the tendency to express specific emotions like anger (Spielberger, 1996), shame and guilt (Tangney, 1990), embarrassment (Miller, 1995), fear (Spielberger, 1983), and gratitude (McCullough, Tsang, & Emmons, 2004). Researchers have also become quite inventive in using these kinds of measures to measure emotional experience in contexts in which people are actually experiencing emotion. This is a significant development, for it allows researchers to measure a purer form of emotional experience that is less filtered through memory biases. They do so by means of experience sampling techniques. Participants are given Palm pilot computers or pagers, and beeped at random times during the day, at which time they provide information about their current feelings (Bolger, Davis, & Refaeli, 2003; Feldman-Barrett & Barrett, 2001).

A well-regarded proposal about how to conceptualize the experience of emotion has been by Lambie and Marcel (2002). As we have discussed in this chapter, they started with the fact that some aspects of emotions occur automatically and unconsciously, while others have a quality of conscious understanding and thinking. They make several distinctions, among which is a primary appraisal of the kind we have discussed, which has unconscious elements and takes the form of a readiness for certain kinds of action together with a distinctive phenomenology, and a secondary appraisal that is accompanied by awareness, and which includes direction of attention and action. Frijda (2005) adds to Lambie and Marcel's proposal by emphasizing how emotional experience contributes to the sense of self and of social coherence.

Specific emotions and core affect

What are the fundamental elements of emotional experience? Reizensein (1992a) has pointed out that historically attempts to answer this question have taken two forms. In one form, experience of certain basic emotions that include happiness, sadness, anger, and fear, is taken as being irreducible. This, for instance, is the position of Oatley and Johnson-Laird (1987). The idea is supported by diary studies such as those of Oatley & Duncan (1984), and by findings that there seem to be a small number of emotions or moods that can occur in a **free-floating** form without any relation to external events, for instance the emotional auras of certain kinds of epileptic seizure (MacLean, 1993), or the experience that Gazzaniga's (1988) split brain patient had of being scared. The basic emotions cannot be reduced to lower level components, although they can be labeled superordinately as pleasant or unpleasant.

In the second form, Reizensein says that experience of emotions has sometimes been derived from more primitive elements that are not themselves emotions. So, for instance, Feldman-Barrett and Russell (1999) and Russell (2003) have proposed valence and arousal as the two underlying components of emotional experience. Russell refers to valence and arousal together as **core affect**. Valence, or pleasantness, or good/bad, is something people can readily report. The element of arousal, or activation, is a bit more problematic (we discussed some of the problems in chapter 5), but here Feldman-Barrett et al. (2004) have found, by combining self-report experience sampling with continuous autonomic measurement, that people can often report on their arousal, though some are more aware of it than others. Our feelings of valence plus arousal, the reasoning goes, reflect the most fundamental and continuing assessments of how the individual is doing in the world. The claim is that when experienced in more global terms, core affect is felt as more diffuse moods ("I feel unenthusiastic" or "I feel energetic").

In the case either of certain emotions themselves as the primitives of experience, or of pleasantness and arousal as the primitives, we can say that such experience arises as a primary appraisal, which is not necessarily conscious.

With specific emotions as primitives, the approach to distinct emotions is that an emotion or mood might be either one of the basic states, or it might be a complex emotion derived from one or more basic emotions, combined elements derived from secondary appraisals such as the cause and/or object of the emotion. For the idea of core affect, Russell (2003) offers one speculation for deriving specific emotions that resembles Schachter and Singer's two-factor theory of emotion that we discussed in chapter 5. He contends that we rely on our emotion knowledge to place specific attributions upon our core affect, in particular when our core affect is intense and influenced by sudden events. When we do this we experience more distinct emotions.

In either case, there is consensus that after primary appraisal comes a stage of secondary appraisal in which we construct a good deal of our emotional experience, some of which is idiosyncratic, some influenced by our family upbringing, and some by our culture.

In addition, there is evidence that other emotion-related responses feed into our emotional experience. Numerous studies find that our facial expressions of emotion correlate modestly with specific emotional experiences (Hess, Banse, & Kappas, 1995; Keltner & Bonanno, 1997; Matsumoto, 1987; Rosenberg & Ekman, 1994; Ruch, 1993). Select studies reveal that certain measures of autonomic nervous system likewise correlate with emotional experience (e.g., Eisenberg et al., 1989). Among the most recent studies of this problem is that of Mauss et al. (2005) who found good coherence of facial expression and experiential measures during emotional responding, but low coherence with physiological measures. One possibility for understanding findings of low coherence among emotion measures is that how the brain registers the specific inputs from facial muscle actions and the activity of the autonomic nervous system shapes the primitives of emotional experience into more specific emotional experiences. This kind of possibility remains one of the more mysterious aspects of the study of emotion. Much more thought will be given to the nature of emotional experience.

Summary

In this chapter we examined how emotions arise and how we represent and experience them. We defined appraisal in terms of evaluations of events vis-à-vis the individual's goals. We studied primary automatic appraisals, and how the mind appears unconsciously to evaluate objects in terms of the appropriateness of an event to a goal. We compared discrete and dimensional approaches to appraisal, and how secondary appraisal varies across different cultures. We then turned to the topic of emotion knowledge: how people understand their emotions with words, concepts, and categories. We considered the nature of emotion words, how they help focus emotional experience, as well as their metaphorical content and their variation across cultures. We looked at studies that reveal that people think of their emotions in terms of prototypes or scripts, which highlight the most typical features of an emotion episode. And we also surveyed studies of face perception and emotion knowledge that suggest that there are distinct boundaries in people's representation of emotions as well. In our final section, we looked at the nature of emotional experience. We surveyed approaches to its measurement, and we considered whether basic emotions themselves, or components such as valence and arousal, might be the primitives of emotional experience. We concluded with a brief discussion of how multiple influences bear on emotional experience.

Further reading

For a cognitive account of emotions, their nature, and their implications for life and health, see the long and scholarly book:
Richard Lazarus (1991). *Emotion and adaptation*. New York: Oxford University Press.

Alternatively, a more popular book with the same themes is:
Richard Lazarus & Bernice Lazarus (1994). *Passion and reason: Making sense of our emotions*. New York: Oxford University Press.

For an excellent review of emotion, language, and metaphor, read:
Zoltán Kövesces (2003). *Metaphor and emotion*. Cambridge: Cambridge University Press.

For an account of the prototype approach to emotion concepts, comparing it with necessary and sufficient conditions, see:
James Russell (1991). In defense of a prototype approach to emotion concepts. *Journal of Personality and Social Psychology, 60*, 37–47.

PART III

Emotions and Social Life

Development of Emotions in Childhood

...for all the time of our infancy and child-hood, our senses were joint-friends in such sort with our Passions, that whatsoever was hurt-full to the one was enemy to the other...

Thomas Wright, The Passions of the Minde in Generall *(1604)*

Contents

Figure 8.0 This picture of a four-year-old girl was taken after her father had photographed her sister in her confirmation dress: finally this little girl jumped forward and shouted: "I want to have my picture taken too." The picture shows a characteristic angry expression (eyebrows raised, square mouth) and posture with fists clenched.

The emergence of emotions

Emotion is the first language of us all. Within seconds of birth, the human baby makes its first emotional communication – a cry. According to MacLean (1993), vocal sounds during evolution were momentous. They signaled the beginnings of a new kind of adaptation as mammal-like reptiles started to become mammals, and as social cooperation began to emerge among vertebrates. Understanding the development of emotions includes understanding how biologically based expressions (Papousek, Jürgens, & Papousek, 1992) enable infant and parent to communicate, and how such expressions take on the forms of culture and individuality.

In this chapter we focus on childhood. We continue with themes of emotional development across the life-span in chapters 9 and 11. In this and the following chapters we use the term "caregiver" to indicate any parental figure. We write of mothers more than fathers because most of the research on interaction with infants has been done with mothers, although this is now starting to change.

Emotions in the first year of life

Emotional development is social development. Although at birth the baby might well be described as a small bundle of reflexes, by the end of the first year, she or he is clearly a social being, with sociality organized around emotions. A good introduction to infant development, including emotions and social life, is by Slater and Lewis (2002); see also Bremner and Slater (2004). Kopp and Neufeld (2003) trace the patterns of research on infant emotions from the 1930s to recent times, and they include the roles of emotions in social life.

An important way of thinking about emotions is that there is a small set of primary emotions, as we discussed in chapters 4 and 7. The idea of discrete emotions derives from Tomkins's (1962) proposal that each emotion comes as an innate package with its own neural program. Emotional expressions, then, are outward, and visible signs of inner programs. In terms of child development, although in the few days after birth there is not much differentiation, the idea is that as development proceeds specific emotions are expressed in forms that are recognizable to others. Among the best-known proponents of this view are Izard (e.g., Abe & Izard, 1999; Izard, 1991; Izard et al., 2002), Magai and McFadden (1995), and Michael Lewis (2002). Babies' expressions have been appealing from a research perspective because of the link to work on adult facial expressions (see, e.g., Keltner et al., 2003a).

The facial expression of disgust has been seen in newborns in response to sour tastes, and Steiner et al. (2001) have shown that the expressions that human infants make to sour tastes are similar to those of other primates. Although crying obviously also occurs in very young infants, expressions of distinct emotions other than disgust are hard to distinguish in the first

Figure 8.1 Photographs of babies showing emotional expressions: (a) a positive or happy expression, (b) a negative expression.

few days of life. By the time babies are two months old, adults are good at seeing expressions of happiness in their faces (Emde et al., 1985). There are two schemes for analyzing babies' facial expressions: Izard's MAX (Izard, 1979) with its later modification AFFEX (Izard, Dougherty, & Hembree, 1983), and Oster's Baby-FACS (see, e.g., Oster, 2003) an adaptation for infants of Ekman and Friesen's (1978) coding scheme for adult expressions, FACS. Infant smiles can be rated as indicating happiness by experts trained in one of these schemes (Abe, Beetham, & Izard, 2002; Oster, Hegley, & Nagel, 1992). Although the youngest babies do occasionally seem to give off smiles, at first these are probably not social. Similar smiles are made frequently by babies during sleep (Messinger, 2002). Social smiles do not emerge until after the first month or two (Sroufe, 1978). In the second month smiles begin to occur with gentle stroking, and by the third month they occur frequently in interaction with a caregiver (Malatesta et al., 1989a), a situation that we can infer is associated with happiness.

By the time children are three months old they smile in response to the same kinds of events that make older children and adults happy – attention, invitations to play, and other pleasurable social encounters. Lewis, Alessandri, and Sullivan (1990) have also shown that smiling occurs when infants master skills. They placed babies in an infant seat and attached a string to their arms. For babies in one condition, pulling the string turned on a short period of music: infants of two, four, six, and eight months soon learned to start the music by pulling the string. They showed higher levels of interest and smiling than those for whom the music came on irrespective of their string pulling. As in adults, mastery of a skill made the children happy.

One function of infants' smiles is to make adults interested and happy. Malatesta and Haviland (1982) found that when infants showed interest in playing with their parents, the parents' expressions of interest also increased. Huebner and Izard (1988) showed pictures of infants' facial expressions to mothers: the mothers said the expression of positive emotion or of interest would make them feel good, that they would talk, play, and interact with the baby, and show love. So, even before infants can direct expressions at specific people, their smiles function to draw adults into affectionate interactions.

Evidence for the early expression of distinct negative emotions is more problematic. With negative emotions, some researchers accept that if a facial expression meets coding criteria then a specific emotion is inferred. Thus, researchers using Izard's MAX coding system have seen expressions of anger, sadness, and pain-distress in three-month-olds (Malatesta et al., 1986; Izard, Hembree, & Huebner, 1987). Other researchers such as Oster et al. (1992) have argued that babies' negative expressions show only undifferentiated distress, whereas others such as Izard and Malatesta (1987) have argued that expressions of fear, anger, and sadness can be seen from early on.

A more exacting criterion is that discrete emotions should only be inferred if a specific facial expression is made in the context of an appropriate elicitor. Remember that in the experiment by Lewis et al. (1990) one group of babies turned on music for a short period by pulling a string attached to their arm. Two-month-old babies in this condition showed more anger and fussiness when their string-pulling no longer turned the music on, than when they could turn the music on. Anger is what we would expect in response to frustration and this is what was seen. In a more recent study using this technique (the babies' arm actions turned on music and made a colored picture of a happy baby appear for three seconds), Sullivan and Lewis (2003) studied three different kinds of frustration: loss of the stimulation (extinction), reduction in contingent stimulation (partial reinforcement), and loss of stimulus control (noncontingency). For all these conditions four- to five-month-old babies increased their arm movements and showed anger expressions, but not sadness, as coded by MAX.

Hiatt, Campos, and Emde (1979) tested the relation of emotional expressions to specific elicitors by presenting 10- to 12-month-old babies with six eliciting conditions. The hypotheses were that either playing peekaboo or allowing the child to play with a toy would elicit happiness; confronting a visual cliff (see figure 8.2) or seeing the approach of a stranger would elicit fear; seeing an object vanish (by means of a tachistoscope and mirror), or a piece of mild conjuring, where a toy was hidden and replaced by another, would elicit surprise. Components of infants' facial expressions were coded

Figure 8.2 The visual cliff: visually the baby sees a steep drop, but thick plate glass supports the infant safely when he or she moves onto it, for instance towards the mother when she calls to him or her.

using features described by Ekman and Friesen (1978). To conclude that discrete emotions exist two criteria were to be met:

- the predicted expression should occur more often than any non-predicted expression in response to the specific elicitor, for instance an expression of fear must occur more often than surprise in response to the visual cliff and to approach of the stranger;
- the predicted expression must be displayed more often in its appropriate eliciting circumstances than in non-predicted eliciting circumstances, for instance the fear expression must occur more in response to the visual cliff and the approach of a stranger than in response to the vanishing object or to the substitution of a toy.

Hiatt et al. (1979) found that babies did express happiness: both criteria were met. Fear met the criteria least well. Stimuli intended to elicit fear provoked a wide range of expressions, and significantly more non-predicted expressions than expressions of fear. For the situations designed to elicit surprise, the predicted expressions were seen more frequently than non-predicted ones, but surprise was elicited just as often by elicitors hypo-thesized to elicit fear and happiness.

In a follow-up study of surprise by members of Campos's and Camras's group, Camras et al. (2002) found that surprising events were greeted by prototypical surprise expressions in only 30.5 percent of a group of American, Japanese, and Chinese infants of 11 months of age, as compared with 32 percent during a baseline condition in which no surprising event happened. The surprising event was, however, frequently greeted by a bodily stilling (in 72 percent of the babies as compared with 12 percent at baseline). Scherer, Zentner, and Stern (2004) were also unable to find prototypical surprise reactions in children between 5 and 14 months old.

In babies who are less than a year old, happy smiling occurs in response to playful games like peek-a-boo, and anger in response to frustration (Lewis, 2002). Certainly other expressions occur, but it is less clear that they always occur in specific eliciting conditions (Bennett, Bendersky, & Lewis, 2002), or that such expressions are fully related to discrete emotion programs. Izard (2004) has, however, recently said that he accepts there is flexibility in the programs of discrete emotions, and agrees with some of the points made by dynamic systems theorists to whose work we now turn.

Dynamic systems

There is increasing interest by researchers in the idea that although distinct emotions may be recognizable later in life, such expressions may not appear fully formed at first so that sometimes just partial expressions occur, and sometimes expressions seem inappropriate. Some naturalistic data illustrate this. Camras (1992) made video recordings of her daughter Justine's facial expressions in the first year of her life. She also kept careful notes about the circumstances in which each expression occurred. Using Izard's AFFEX coding scheme Camras found that Justine showed expressions of disgust, fear, distress-pain, and anger in her first months. Her expressions often did not occur with expected elicitors, however. For instance, Justine showed the fear expression when she was protesting being fed. Although it is possible that she was feeling frightened, her mother thought that this was unlikely given the circumstances. She showed a sadness expression when eating a sour vitamin. Why should this event cause sadness? Camras provides many such observations of episodes when the eliciting circumstances do not seem to be compatible with the child's emotional expression.

Some researchers argue that infants' negative emotions are only of undif-ferentiated distress (Oster et al., 1992) but at different levels of intensity. Camras (1992) has elaborated this view: most negative expressions of infants can be coded as distress-pain, as anger, or as blends of discrete expressions. When making negative expressions infants often contract their *orbicularis oculi* muscles and close their eyes. According to AFFEX the only difference between codings of expressions of distress-pain and anger is that in anger the eyes are open. In young infants negative expressions certainly occur, but at different intensities: at high intensity the expression is coded by AFFEX as distress-pain, at slightly lower intensity as anger, and at low or waning intensity as sadness.

To elaborate this kind of idea researchers such as Alan Fogel and his group (Fogel et al., 1992), Linda Camras (1992, 2000), Carlson, Sroufe, and Egeland (2004), and Marc Lewis and his colleagues (e.g., Lewis & Douglas, 1998; Lewis & Granic, 2000; M. D. Lewis, 2005) have proposed that emotions develop as dynamic, **self-organizing systems**. According to this idea neurophysiological programs do not come genetically specified as ready-assembled packages. Such packages do occur, but they are constructed during early life from lower-level genetically derived components, which are formed into distinct structures by interaction among the components, and by interaction of babies with other people.

The theory of dynamic systems is related to chaos theory (Gleick, 1988). You will have heard the idea, from this theory, that a butterfly that flaps its wings in Brazil might be the beginning of a tornado in Texas. The idea of chaos is that the same butterfly making the same wing flap in the same place a few minutes later would not set off a tornado. Think of it like this. According to nineteenth-century thinkers, science was often conceptualized in terms of atoms as billiard-balls. If it were possible to know the positions and velocities of every atom in the universe, the argument went, it would be possible to predict exactly what would happen this time tomorrow. Chaos theory starts from the idea that this is not true. An observation of a butterfly flapping its wings in the Amazon does not allow exact prediction of a storm in Sweden. Some systems, which include the weather, do not work by billiard-ball determinism. They are self-organizing. The idea of a self-organizing system is that certain kinds of interactions among parts of a system maintain their relationship and overall form because the forces of internal coherence are stronger than those that might impinge on the system from outside. Unlike a system of billiard balls, future behavior is not fully predictable from knowing the system's starting point. Let us take another weather phenomenon: hurricanes. From the middle of the summer onward, hurricanes form in the Atlantic and move toward the Caribbean. Although they start by atoms and molecules behaving in a billiard-ball manner, for instance air molecules rise when the air is heated, once a hurricane starts, it assumes the distinctive self-maintaining form of winds blowing round an area of low pressure, which resists many of the forces that might tend to affect it. Many biological systems have self-organizing properties, and there are mathematical theories of such systems. In a comparable way, the dynamic systems theorists of psychology say, the systems of components that have their expressions as smiles, frowns, and distinctive emotional interactions, is not made up of billiard-ball-like interactions of parts. It is dynamic, self-organizing, resistant to disruption. Unlike hurricanes, many different forms can occur. Some of these forms become recognizable as emotional expressions. Dynamic systems theory does not so much make specific predictions as offer a point of view in which behavior does not occur in response to specific external causes, but is constrained largely by the inner organization of the system. Offered instead of predictions are a set of metaphors, most notably that of the attractor state, an organization to which a system will gravitate, however it starts. Thus a cheerful person's attractor states will be emotions of happiness; a person who is suspicious of the world will head toward an attractor state of fear and anger. Further discussion of attractor states for emotions occurs in chapter 11.

Dynamic systems theory has certain affinities to theories discussed in chapter 4, that emotions are made up from components. But there is a difference: in componential theories of adult emotions of the kind suggested by Ortony and Turner (1990), components occur together because they are elicited by features of the environment that occur together. In Fogel's developmental view the components that will affect emotions do become neurophysiologically linked together, but they did not start that way. The components constrain each other within a whole self-organizing system. Izard (e.g., 2004) now agrees that self-organization, as postulated by dynamic systems theorists, may be important in early development of discrete emotions.

Fogel et al. (1992) propose that in interactions of such systems with the social world, further interdependencies occur. The whole system of person-with-other becomes self-organizing, and emotions occur as modes of interaction among components, and between individuals and external events. Such modes have distinctive time courses, for instance the rise and fall of an episode of laughing has been studied in close detail (e.g., Hsu & Fogel, 2003). Fogel et al.'s hypothesis has three principles: (a) emotions are based on self-organizing dynamic systems; (b) these depend on continuously evolving sequences of action in particular environments, rather than on internal programs; (c) categories of emotions are constructed from gradients of timing and intensity of vocal, gestural, and other features. According to this proposal, emotions emerge, and they derive from the interactions of lower-level processes that are not themselves emotions.

Before leaving this question, think for a moment about the function of emotions in the lives of infants. A baby's smile makes a caregiver happy and interested, as if the baby's happiness were directly communicated. A baby's expressions of negative emotions signal that something is not right. A parent is then prompted to pick the baby up, give comfort, offer food, and consider a range of other reasons for the distress. In the first year, before the baby is mobile, there may be no point in a caregiver discriminating more than positive and negative emotions. Instead, the parent pays attention to the context to make sense of the baby's signals: How many hours since the baby was fed (Richards & Bernal, 1972)? Has the baby been hit by her sister? Has a stranger come into the room? Has she rolled onto a sharp toy? Only when the baby starts to move around and function at a distance from the caregiver would finer discrimination among negative emotions become important.

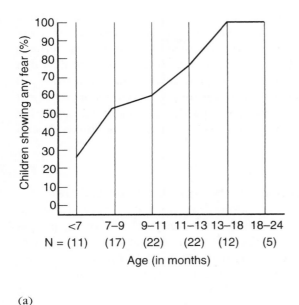

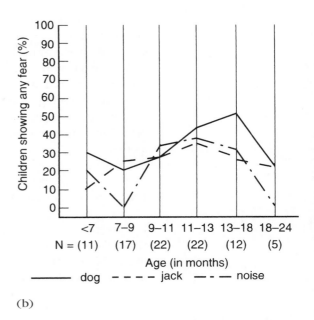

(a)   (b)

Figure 8.3 Percentages of children showing fear of the visual cliff (left-hand graph) and of dogs, noises, and a jack-in-the-box (right-hand graph) as a function of age (Scarr & Salapatek, 1970).

Developmental changes in elicitation of emotion

As well as changes in children's capacities to signal different emotions with increasing age, there are marked changes in the kinds of events that elicit emotions. Scarr and Salapatek (1970) exposed infants between two months and two years to strangers, a visual cliff, a jack-in-the-box, a moving toy dog, loud noises, and someone wearing a mask. Few children under seven months showed marked expressions of fear/distress to any of these stimuli. With increasing age up to two years, children showed more fearful avoidance of the visual cliff, and more fear of strangers and masks. Their fear of loud or sudden movements, and of unfamiliar toys, showed a different pattern: for these fear began around seven months, reached a peak at the end of the first year and then declined in intensity (see figure 8.3).

Later in childhood further developments occur. Preschoolers are often frightened by imaginary themes: monsters, ghosts, frightening dreams. In the early school years fears surrounding bodily injury and physical danger start to occur (Bauer, 1976).

In adolescence, social concerns become the predominant causes of fear and anxiety (Bamber, 1979). Using experience sampling methods (as discussed in chapter 7), Larson et al. (2002) studied the reports of 220 young people over two one-week periods. They confirmed the common idea that adolescence is a time of increased negative emotions. There was increasing negativity of emotional experience from Grade 5 to Grade 9. It was associated with reduced self-esteem (i.e., social fears). As the participants got older, their negative emotional experience became more closely associated with stressful life events (a topic we treat in chapter 12), perhaps reflecting growing fears and depression about such events, from which younger children are often shielded. The good news is that from Grade 10 onward, an average growth of positivity was found in adolescent emotional experience. Adolescence, of course, is also the period of life at which sexual love first comes to be important: well known for its downs as well as ups.

Infants' perceptions and parents' special expressions

Let us now consider how infants perceive emotions in other people (Pascalis & Slater, 2003). One method for studying the issue has been to use **habituation**, based on the finding that infants look at patterns that are new to them for longer than patterns that are familiar. If infants are presented with a picture of a happy face they look at it for a long time, then turn away. If presented with another happy face they tend to look more briefly because the expression is not new. But if they are now presented with a sad face, they tend to look at it for a long time, as this expression is new. From working carefully with this methodology we can tell what discriminations infants can make about emotional expressions.

An important review of the extensive research in this area is by Arlene Walker-Andrews (1997). Infants do recognize emotionally significant expressions from parents and others from the age of a few months, but the expressions that can be recognized usually involve both visual and acoustic aspects. First, infants learn that certain communications do have emotional significance. Then there is a process of progressive differentiation so that, later, particular expressions of the voice or of the face can be discriminated (see also, Montague & Walker-Andrews, 2002).

Infants tend first to recognize emotional expressions from their parents' voices. Fernald (1989) has shown that parents often use a different voice in talking to infants than they do when talking to adults. Infants pay more attention to this special voice of **motherese** and show more positive emotion during it. From five months they can discriminate affective messages indicating approval or prohibition, either in their parents' language, or in a language their parents do not speak. Infants showed more positive affect to approvals, and more negative affect to prohibitions (Fernald, 1993). Mothers' singing may be yet more engaging. Nakota and Trehub (2004) found that six-month-old infants who saw an image of their mother and heard her voice looked longer at the mother's image when she was singing than when she was talking. They also moved less, which implied they were more strongly engaged. The authors suggest that music – in lullabies and other songs – may enhance emotional coordination between mothers and infants.

Less studied than motherese are the special facial expressions that have been found by Chong et al. (2003) to be made by both English-speaking

Figure 8.4 Three distinctive visual expressions equivalent to motherese, made by two Chinese-speaking and two English-speaking mothers to their infants (Chong et al., 2003).

and Chinese-speaking mothers to their children. Three are prominent. One involves puckered lips of the kind one would make when saying "ooooh." One is a kind of mock surprise with raised eyebrows. One is a kind of exaggerated smile, but accompanied by raised brows. These affectionate and exaggerated facial expressions seem to have some of the same functions as motherese – to engage the infant.

By seven months babies can match facial and vocal expressions. Walker-Andrews (1986) presented five- and seven-month-old infants with filmed expressions of happiness and anger, and recorded the voices that went with them. In the film the mouth of the person was obscured so the infant could not match mouth movements with the voice. By seven months of age babies spent longer looking at the film clips of visual expressions that matched the sounds than at expressions that did not match, but at five months of age infants could not make this discrimination.

It may be that **imitation**, which babies show from the first few hours of life, has emotional effects for them. Melzoff (1993) has demonstrated these abilities. He has also suggested that the internal feedback of facial actions when infants mimic adult emotional expressions could evoke emotions in the child. This could occur because there are discrete neural programs of emotions which start up when any part is activated. Alternatively it could occur because making a particular expression contributes to a particular mode within a dynamic self-organizing system. In either case this could mean that babies' imitative expressions are important in sharing affective states with caregivers (Stern, 1985; Trevarthen, 1979).

By one year of age, skills have developed that allow infants to take part in complex interactions. Preschool children were found by Widen and Russell

(2003) to have only a modest ability to offer emotion labels for photographs. Happy, angry, and sad emerged early, in that order, and scared, surprised, and disgusted emerged later, but without being readily accessible. By school age, children are good at recognizing emotions in other people. Battaglia et al. (2004) found a 72 percent correct identification of pictures of emotional expressions by children in Grades 2 and 3. Although they found no differences in recognition between boys and girls, they did find that shy children made more misidentifications of anger than did non-shy children.

Attachment

The psychological aspect of the concept "mammal" – an animal that is live-born and is suckled by its mother – is attachment. As well as being able to drink their mother's milk, infant mammals must stay close by. They become fearful when separated, and their cries summon the mother.

It was John Bowlby who realized that the species-characteristic pattern of **attachment** is central to human emotional development. In a book that derived from his study of children separated from their parents during World War II, he wrote: "What is believed to be essential for mental health is that the infant and young child should experience a warm, intimate and continuous relationship with [his or her] mother (or permanent mother substitute) in which both find satisfaction and enjoyment" (Bowlby, 1951).

Momentously, in Bowlby's conception, love is an emotion, but not just something in the mind or body of an individual. It is the foundational relationship of infancy, and it forms a template for intimate relationships for the rest of life. Bowlby thought that love in the early years was as important for emotional development as proper nutrition is for physical development. Without it, he thought, a person was in danger of growing up into an affectionless sociopath.

Mary Ainsworth worked with Bowlby on attachment in London, then moved to Uganda and there undertook a naturalistic study of babies and mothers in a culture different from her own (Ainsworth, 1967). She discerned a set of behavior patterns that young children showed when they were with their mothers, but did not show with anyone else (see table 8.1).

When the mother is present there is a sense of security, and a distinctive set of actions occurs. When she is absent quite different actions occur. So, in widely different cultures attachment patterns can be seen. They serve the vital function of keeping the mother nearby, able and willing to protect the infant from any and all threats (Bowlby, 1971).

In 1935 Konrad Lorenz had described an instinctive pattern. Baby goslings follow, then stay close to, almost any object that moves around and makes sounds. The process is called imprinting. Lorenz proposed that there is a critical period – in goslings about two days – during which a biological mechanism is set to recognize characteristics of the mother: but objects acceptable to this mechanism are not closely specified. If no real mother appears, characteristics of the first crudely plausible moving

Table 8.1   Ainsworth's (1967) list of attachment behaviors

1. Differential crying (i.e., with mother as compared with others)
2. Differential smiling
3. Differential vocalization
4. Crying when the mother leaves
5. Following the mother
6. Visual motor orientation towards the mother
7. Greeting through smiling, crowing and general excitement
8. Lifting arms in greeting the mother
9. Clapping hands in greeting the mother
10. Scrambling over the mother
11. Burying the face in the mother's lap
12. Approach to the mother through locomotion
13. Embracing, hugging, kissing the mother (not seen in Ugandan infants but observed frequently by infants in Western societies)
14. Exploration away from the mother as a secure base
15. Flight to the mother as a haven of safety
16. Clinging to the mother

object that appears are learned instead. In Lorenz's studies this object was often himself. The effects are irreversible; geese imprinted in this way do not recognize other geese, but make social signals to whatever they have been imprinted on. When Robert Hinde and Julian Huxley introduced Bowlby to the idea of imprinting and to the works of Lorenz and Tinbergen, Bowlby quickly realized that in ethology and Darwinian evolution theory lay the key: "attachment theory's main structure emerged whole in this first flash of insight and gave coherence to all that followed" (Ainsworth, 1992). Attachment has become the most important single theme in the emotional development of children.

In a series of experiments that became famous, Harlow (1959) demonstrated in monkeys that attachment to a parent figure was based on a need for comfort. Harlow separated infant monkeys from their mothers within 12 hours of birth and supplied two artificial mothers made so that the baby monkeys could cling to them. One was made of wire topped with a schematic head. The other was made similarly but its wire frame was covered with terry cloth and it had a different-shaped head.

In Harlow's first experiment four baby monkeys got their milk from a bottle attached to the wire mother, and four others got milk from the cloth mother. During the first 5.5 months of their lives all eight monkeys spent an average of 14 to 18 hours per day clinging to their cloth mother. Even when milk was obtained entirely from the wire mother, infants spent less than an average of two hours a day on her. Preference of all the infants for the cloth mother was a measure of a primary motivation. Another was shown when a mechanical toy teddy bear beating a drum was introduced to the cage. The infant monkeys were terrified and rushed to the cloth mother

Figure 8.5 A baby monkey in Harlow's experiment clings in terror to the cloth mother when a large toy insect is introduced into the room. Even if the baby monkey has obtained all its nourishment from the wire mother, it only uses the cloth mother for comforting anxiety.

(see figure 8.5) irrespective of which they had obtained their milk from. When the baby monkeys were placed in an unfamiliar room they tended to cower and hide in a corner. With the cloth mother in the room they were not frightened, but clung to her, then used her as a base for explorations.

In his 1959 article Harlow drew conclusions that now seem strange. He wrote: "All our experience, in fact, indicates that our cloth-covered mother surrogate is an eminently satisfactory mother . . . available 24 hours a day . . . she possesses infinite patience, never scolding her baby or biting it in anger. In these respects we regard her as superior to a living monkey mother" (p. 94). Not until later was it realized that monkeys reared with surrogate mothers were damaged for life in almost every way, emotionally, socially, and intellectually.

Kraemer (1992) summarized the effects of baby monkeys reared with artificial mothers. They do not eat or drink normally. They stare into space, show repetitive and stereotyped behavior like body rocking. They bite their own limbs, alternating this with self-clasping. They are poorer in many cognitive tasks. Most of all they act in socially inappropriate ways. They make mutually exclusive expressions of fear and threat at the same time. They alternate between reclusiveness and aggressively attacking other monkeys from adult males to juveniles. They are sexually incompetent, male mounting and female presenting are disrupted, and if a female is artificially impregnated she will ignore, maim, or kill her infant. Damaging effects are most marked in monkeys who are reared with an artificial mother in their first six months of life. Monkeys who have been reared in this way, and then have some experience of peers who will cling to them, groom with them, etc., recover some aspects of normal social functioning (Suomi, 1999; Suomi & Harlow, 1972). As Kraemer points out, what is at issue in attachment is not just survival, but building an inner model of interactions with another individual. Without such an individual, no such inner model is built. Although monkeys who were maternally deprived but had "therapy" with peers seemed to be rehabilitated in many of their day-to-day interactions, these rehabilitated monkeys remained abnormal in reacting to stress, or conflict. They have persisting neurobiological defects in brain transmitter metabolism and in the anatomy of some nerve cells (Kraemer, 1997).

The socio-emotional building-potential of attachment is innate. It is a species-characteristic process. It is like a set of building bricks, such that growing up with reliable caregivers allows these bricks to be assembled into meaningful and useful structures. Running the genetic program without social interaction, as happened to the monkeys raised as social isolates with artificial mothers, is like dumping the bricks in a heap on the ground. Even then some, though not all the bricks, can be later assembled into more meaningful patterns with care and persistence. But these do not reinstate the processes that were missed. Rather, alternative pathways are developed to enable some of the goals of social interaction to be met. Despite this, vulnerabilities to stress remain.

The principal emotion of attachment is anxiety, and a cry to the caregiver brings her close, in her protective role. Separation from a caregiver, then, causes an intense, noisy, and fearful distress. Separation distress begins in the second half of the first year, reaches a peak between 15 and 18 months, and then declines, so that by three years of age very distressed reactions to separation become rare. Children raised in orphanages who do not develop an attachment relationship with a particular caregiver seem not to have separation anxiety. They are seen as indiscriminately friendly (O'Connor et al., 2003).

Cooperative action and the goal corrected partnership

As well as studies of imprinting, Bowlby was also impressed by ethologists' descriptions of genetically based patterns such as that of egg retrieval by the greylag goose, which we described in chapter 2, as goal directed. In attachment, the goal state for mother and baby is to be close to each other. If the mother moves away, this is a stimulus for the baby to cry, and the crying is effective in getting her back, achieving the goal. Bowlby (1971) proposed a version of this idea he called "the goal corrected partnership," which enables **cooperation** between two individuals that allows them to achieve mutual goals. Bowlby was concerned with how goal corrected partnerships came about between parents and children, but also saw this as the basis of cooperative relationships throughout life. Early in life infants know little about their parents' goals, but with increasing cognitive maturity and through repeated interactions, the child develops a model of the other person's desires and intentions, allowing for a partnership in which parents and children collaborate in the fulfillment of each others' goals. We discuss the work on attachment further in a subsequent chapter; here our concern is with the important changes in cognitive development that allow for the development and elaboration of cooperative action.

An important set of studies on this topic has been conducted by Grazyna Kochanska and her colleagues. For instance Kochanska and Aksan (2004) have shown that there is a developmental progression of mutual responsiveness between children and their parents. Between the children's ages of 7 and 15 months, children increased the frequency of their attempts to influence their parents, and this included a marked increase in the number of overtures with positive emotional overtones. Parents were more responsive to positive than to negative overtures. Over this same period, as their children grew from 7 to 15 months – evidently aware of their children's growing autonomy – parents decreased the frequency of their attempts to influence their children.

Construction of the child's relationship with others

Emotions show that an interaction is going well or that adjustments need to be made. Als, Tronick, and Brazelton (1980) give details of finely tuned interaction between mother and infant. The mother plays with her baby, and gears her own responses to each shift in the baby's emotional state. To start with the mother engages the baby with motherese, making big shifts in intonational pattern that capture the baby's attention (Fernald, 1989). She moves close to the baby and nuzzles her. Stimulation gradually increases as the mother touches the baby and speaks. The mother is sensitive to the baby's level of arousal so that when the baby fusses, she withdraws a bit, then tries again more slowly. Stern (1985) has made similar findings, that when a baby smiles, the parent very often mirrors the happy expression but in a different way, for instance with her or his voice: "Ooooh. That's a nice smile." Field (1994) suggests that the caregiver helps regulate arousal, by reading a baby's signals, keeping in time with them, and altering the environment to maintain the best level of stimulation for the baby. This keeping-in-time is called attunement.

The role of emotion in regulating interactions between mothers and young babies has also been demonstrated experimentally by Cohn and Tronick (1983) who examined what happened when mothers showed no emotions to their babies (see Figure 8.6). Twelve baby girls and twelve baby boys took part. The mother sat face to face with her infant who sat in an infant seat. In one condition (called flat affect) mothers were asked to direct their gaze at their infant, speak in a flat uninteresting monotone, keep their face expressionless, minimize body movement, and not touch their infant. This was contrasted with three-minute periods of the mother acting normally. Babies were videotaped. When mothers demonstrated flat affect, infants

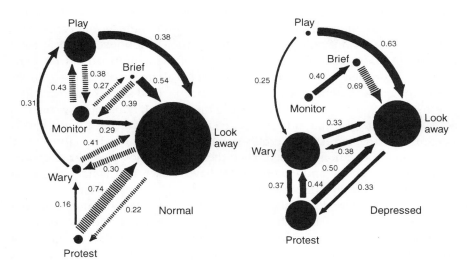

Figure 8.6 State transition diagrams for infants when their mothers were (a) in a normal condition and (b) when depressed. The proportion of time spent in a state is indicated by the size of circles representing that state. The thickness of arrows represents the conditional probabilities, with numerical values shown next to them. Striped arrows indicate conditional probabilities with $p < 0.05$ (Cohn & Tronick, 1983).

showed more wary expressions, made more protests and showed positive expressions that were briefer, were much more disorganized, and were more likely to enter a negative state. During normal interactions infants were likely to cycle between play, brief positive expressions, and monitoring. Once this positive cycle had started they were less likely to enter a negative state. There have now been many studies of babies' reactions when the mother is asked to keep her face still, and remain unresponsive to the baby: the still-face paradigm (e.g., Moore & Calkins, 2004; Striano, 2004; Lewis & Ramsay, 2005). Without the ongoing engagement by the mother the baby becomes sad and distressed, and well-being suffers.

So although it has been hard to demonstrate unequivocally how well babies can discriminate specific adult emotional expressions, it is more clear that adult emotions do function to regulate interaction. Serrano, Iglesias, and Loeches (1995) found that when four- to six-month-old babies saw pictures of happy adult faces, they themselves became behaviorally more positive, whereas when they saw angry faces their behavior became more negative. Infants' expressions of happiness signal that their goals are being achieved; negative expressions signal that the interaction is not going well for them. Tronick, Cohn, and Shea (1986) call this the mutual regulation model; emotional messages are exchanged so that each partner achieves his or her own goals in coordination with those of the other. (It may be that mutual regulation is a better concept than self-regulation of emotions, since as Campos, Frankel, and Camras, 2004, point out, the processes that are said to regulate emotions are the same as those that generate them, and are largely interpersonal.) Emotions are communications: the infant signals to the parent, the parent signals to the infant, each alters behavior accordingly.

In the first year not only do babies change their emotional signals as their relationships develop, but they acquire skills of using information from caregivers to alter their own actions, for instance if there is something ambiguous in the environment. These skills have been called **social referencing**. For instance, Sorce et al. (1985) exposed one-year-old babies to a visual cliff adjusted to a height that did not evoke clear avoidance, and found that 74 percent of babies crossed the cliff when mothers showed a happy facial expression, though none crossed when their mother showed a fearful expression. Campos, Thein, and Owen (2003) have shown that facial expression alone can powerfully affect whether a child will cross the visual cliff.

Mumme and Fernald (2003) have shown that 12-month-olds, but not 10-month-olds, will change their behavior in response to adults' televised emotional displays. Vaish and Striano (2004), however, have found that vocal cues – expressions of emotion in the mother's voice – may be more important than visual cues in social referencing.

In a variation on the social referencing idea by Hertenstein and Campos (2004), 11-month-old and 14-month-old babies saw a yellow toy bird and a blue toy animal come down from the ceiling on strings. Initially both toys had neutral effects on babies. In the experiment, the mother sat quietly to one side. The toys descended from the ceiling and arrived on a table in front of the baby, but out of reach. As the toys arrived, the experimenter, who faced the baby, pointed at one of them. For half the babies he made a joyful facial expression and said "ahhhh." For the other half he made a disgust expression as he pointed and said "euuuh." The toys were then retracted into the ceiling. There was then a repeat of the procedure, in which the positions of the two toys were exchanged, but the experimenter made the same emotion expressions to the same toy. The babies then returned to their mothers to play for an hour. When they came back into the laboratory the toys again descended in front of them, but this time within reach. The 14-month-olds took four times as long to reach toward the toy at which the experimenter had shown disgust as compared to the one at which joy had been shown (17.8 as compared with 4.1 seconds). The younger babies (11 months) were found to have been unaffected by the experimenter's expressions, but in a second experiment on 11-month-olds with a delay of three minutes rather than an hour, these babies took twice as long to reach toward the toy to which a disgust expression had been made as to the one at which a joyful expression had been made. Positive emotional expressions by adults toward objects on which they intend to act seem generally to assist infants in recognizing actions that are intended (Phillips, Wellman, & Spelke, 2002).

Infants older than ten months, as compared with six- to nine-month-olds, are more likely to look at a parent's face for emotional information than at other parts of the body, and it is only the older babies who look at a parent before taking action with respect to an ambiguous elicitor (Walden & Ogan, 1988). Thus from the end of the first year babies begin to alter their own behavior on the basis of their parents' appraisals and emotions, and this influences how they themselves appraise and react to the world.

Differentiation between self and others

The ability to form a partnership relies on the ability to differentiate self from others. Developmentalists have argued that such differentiation is only rudimentary during the first year (Stern, 1985). Remember too, as we discussed in chapter 3, that in some cultures distinctions between self and other are minimized as compared to Western individualistic societies. During the second year, differentiation between self and other becomes more established. At this point we see the emergence of emotions of empathy and embarrassment.

Newborn babies respond to the cries of other infants by crying themselves. Some have argued that this early indication of emotion contagion is an important precursor of later empathy, but others argue that the response may be more like a reflex, with the baby confusing another person's cry with their own. As early as six months, however, babies show much clearer interest in others' emotions, by leaning toward a peer who shows distress, by touching, and so forth (Eisenberg, 1992, 2000).

Between 12 and 24 months children respond to another's distress by comforting, bringing a parent, offering an object (Zahn-Waxler et al., 1992). They do react with concern – but they tend to offer comfort in the way that they themselves like to be comforted. When Hannah (the daughter of KO and JJ) was 14 months old, another baby was crying in our apartment. Hannah had some shoes that she particularly liked. When she heard the baby crying she walked over, watched her for a moment, then tried to offer her own shoe to the baby. Young children do perceive distress and feel motivated to do something about it. But they offer comfort in the way that they like to be comforted, rather than being able to know what the other person might find comforting.

By the time children are three years old, the ways they offer comfort are more appropriate to the needs of the other person. For instance, children comfort a child in distress by fetching the mother of the crying child. Also, as children get older, they are more likely to respond with concern to distress that they have not caused (Zahn-Waxler et al., 1992). This shows the older child's increasing ability both to think about the event from the other's point of view and to start, perhaps, experiencing guilt.

We can see the crucial role of the child's sense of herself or himself in **empathy**. Hoffman (2000) has argued that although empathy has limitations it is essential to prosocial behavior, kindness, caring, and justice. When we see that another person is sad or angry in response to our actions, we usually feel some motivation to modify our behavior and reassess our own actions. And, from early in life experiencing emotions that are similar to those of someone else provides us with a stepping-stone to the other's internal world. With increasing cognitive capacity our ability to understand

Table 8.2 Numbers of children who showed embarrassment as a function of whether they recognized themselves from the rouge-on-the-nose test

	Showed self-recognition	Did not show self-recognition
Showed embarrassment	19	5
Showed no embarrassment	7	13

Source: From Lewis et al. (1989)

that world becomes more complex and allows for more appropriate responses to the other person. For several hundred years **compassion**, or as we now tend to say, empathy and sympathy, have been thought of as the very foundation of society (Smith, 1759; Staines, 2004).

Other complex emotions are intimately tied to the child's dawning recognition of self. Embarrassment, for instance, relies on the development of the differentiation of self, which comes with cognitive maturity. Lewis et al. (1989) compared the ability of children to feel embarrassment with their ability to feel fear, arguing that fear is a simpler emotion, not reliant on self-recognition. To test reactions to fear they introduced a stranger. They tested self-recognition by putting children in front of a mirror, having surreptitiously placed some rouge on their noses. The children who recognized that the reflection was of themselves showed this by touching their own noses. To test for embarrassment the researchers did such things as over-complimenting the child, and asking him or her to dance. The researchers' prediction was that though all the children would show fear, only those who recognized themselves in the mirror would be able to experience embarrassment.

The relationship between self-recognition and embarrassment can be seen in table 8.2. Children were much more likely to experience embarrassment when they could recognize themselves in a mirror. But there was no significant relationship between self-recognition and showing fear. The conclusion is that embarrassment is experienced mainly when a sense of self has developed. In a subsequent study, Lewis and Ramsay (2002) have shown two different kinds of embarrassment, one involving negative evaluation of self, and one simply resulting from non-evaluative self-exposure. Shame and embarrassment that involved negative self-evaluation were more stressful, as indicated by higher cortisol responses.

The self, however, is not just an isolated object: the very **concept of self** is social. It would be better described as self-in-relation-to-other. The self is that aspect of our character that lets us know how to interact with others. In studies of empathy we see something of its development: the self-with-other-in-distress. In studies of embarrassment, the embarrassed self is the self with too much attention from others. In Western societies the ideal self is not a Robinson Crusoe self cut off from society. As we have described in chapter 3, Westerners tend to conceive themselves not as isolated but as self-reliant, not dependent. In Asiatic and other "we-based" or interdependent societies, the ideal self tends to be thought of as connected to others and embedded within myriad relationships (Markus & Kitayama, 1991).

The language of emotions in cooperative action

Naturalistic studies have shown how children learn emotion words and what they know about emotions. Bretherton et al. (1986) have written a comprehensive review. Dunn (2004) says that it is notable that children have the "ability and propensity to talk about and reflect on emotions as soon as they begin to use language" (p. 307). Children start talking about internal states around 18 months, and the proportion of time they spend talking about emotions gradually increases with age. Dunn and her colleagues (see e.g., Dunn, 2003 for a review) have recorded talk of feeling states between mothers, children, and their siblings in their homes.

Learning to discuss emotional experiences has several important consequences for cooperative action. The most common early function of talking about emotions is simply to comment (Dunn, 1987). But by the time children were three, Dunn et al. (1991) found that half of the conversations about emotions were about the causes of the feelings, and they show the complexity of children's knowledge. For instance, 28-month-old children understand common relational antecedents of distress: "You sad mommy. What did daddy do?" as well as how an emotion of one person can affect actions of another: "I cry, lady pick me up and hold me" (Bretherton et al., 1986). Here, rather than just comment, emotion talk can become part of the negotiation of relationships. Between the ages of three and seven Hughes and Dunn (2002) have shown in a longitudinal study that children become more competent in talking about negative emotions, including themes of loss in relation to sadness, and of control in relation to anger.

Mothers markedly increase their talk about internal states to children between 13 and 28 months old, presumably responding to their children's grasp of such matters. By the time children are 28 months, 60 percent of their mothers' speech to them involves references to internal states (Beeghly, Bretherton, & Mervis, 1986). Through their talk, parents implicitly teach children how to represent their internal states, how emotions function between people, how they are expressed, controlled, and so forth. Jenkins et al. (2003) have shown not only that parents fit their talk of mental states to the age of their children, but that more talk of emotional and other mental states by family members at one point in time (when children were two and four years old) predicted more talk of emotions and mental states by children one and two years later. Dunn (2000, 2004) has proposed that children's awareness and discussion of feeling states precede and lay foundations for their (implicit) theories of other people's minds.

By learning to talk about emotions and their causes children move well beyond the simple communication system that facial expression and voice tone allow. Language about emotions enables the development of shared meanings about internal states (Stern, 1985). A new degree of relatedness is possible. The child can talk about a feeling, give their version of its cause, refer back to emotions, alter their understanding of them. And, crucially, instead of a model based only on the child's experience, parents can offer their understandings to be put together with those of the child. Similarly, parents can understand an event from their child's perspective. The shared meanings that are created become part of that relationship and its shared history. Dunn and Brown (1991) provide wonderful examples; here is a conversation in which a 21-month-old child initiates a conversation with his mother about an event that happened at breakfast (p. 97).

Child: Eat my Weetabix. Eat my Weetabix [breakfast cereal]. Crying.

Mother: Crying weren't you? We had quite a battle. "One more mouthful, Michael." And what did you do? You spat it out!

Child: (Pretends to cry).

They go over the event with the child referring to the emotion – "Crying" – and then doing a reenactment. The mother learns that the child has been thinking about the event, and the child learns why his mother thought it had happened. Maybe he is apologizing, maybe he is trying to find out whether she is still angry with him, maybe he is wondering about what next breakfast time will be like. They have shared an experience together and are in the process of constructing a shared representation of that experience that gives each of them a better model of the other. Simple empathic experiences link people together; with language shared meanings become possible, facilitating the process of cooperative action. Katz and Gottman (1997) have shown that parents who listen empathetically to their children's emotions, and who coach children in **meta-emotion**, for instance by helping them talk about difficult emotional matters, buffer these children from deleterious consequences of marital conflict.

Emotions in play and games

Children spend a great deal of their time at play. In adulthood, games, sports, and perhaps entertainment more generally, seem to be extensions of the play of early childhood. In infants, playing peek-a-boo and playing with toys have been shown to elicit smiles of happiness (Hiatt, Campos, & Emde, 1979), and play more generally as the continuation of such activities, is meant to be fun. Children like to play, and although it is possible to see sad children, or children in angry conflict with each other, there is a characteristic sound of a school playground at recess. It is the sound of laughter and excitement.

The prototype of play is rough and tumble (Panksepp, 1998; Pellegrini, 2002, 2003), which can be seen in most young mammals, often at first with parents, but then more frequently with siblings and peers. The kind of explanation offered for this, and indeed other kinds of play, is that it enables practice of social skills, perhaps particularly relating to aggression and dominance, in a safe way (Smith, 1982). Symbolic play, sometimes called pretend play, seems to be an extension. It depends on the imagination (Harris, 2000), and also often involves trying out roles, and the use of objects as props (Pellegrini & Bjorkland, 2004).

Why do we expect to have fun in playing and in games? The best introduction, we believe, comes from Erving Goffman's (1961) essay "Fun in games." Goffman proposes that a game is a model, or a microcosm of, some aspect of the social world, and we enter into it in order to take part in a particular kind of interaction. Rough and tumble is play fighting, not usually dangerous and often with the pleasurable properties of touching and body contact. Hide-and-seek is mock deception and detection. Chess is a symbolic version of medieval warfare in which peasant soldiers plod forward square by square while the aristocrats dash anywhere they like with ease and élan. Monopoly is a model of commercial competition in which no one's family is thrown destitute onto the street. Despite their symbolic nature, however, what Goffman correctly points out is that games offer a cast of roles and the opportunity of **interpersonal engagement**. All play, and perhaps as Winnicott (1971) suggests, all human cultural pursuits, retain that original connection to another person that was established in our first interactions with a caregiver. A game may be artificial, but the engagement is real. It is engagement with the other that makes a game fun. As soon as the engagement flags, so does interest, and we stop enjoying ourselves.

Children's understanding of emotions as mental states

Between two and three years of age comes a great growth of language, including emotion terms and the ability to communicate with others about emotions. From this point forward, as we have discussed above, it is clear that children think about what causes emotions, consider how they are caused, and so on. They construct, as we might say, their own theories about emotions.

Adult understanding of emotions makes implicit reference to people's desires: "He wanted that car so he was angry when he couldn't have it," or beliefs: "He was surprised when he saw her because he thought that she had left." It has been argued that children under four are not capable of such representations. Consequently, their ideas of emotions are more behavioral than mentalistic (Harris & Saarni, 1989). The argument goes that young children are more likely to describe emotions as facial expressions or behavior rather than as internal feelings, and as caused by external situations rather than being provoked by mental entities such as what a person wanted or believed. At the age of three, the daughter of two of us (KO & JJ) provided an example after being reprimanded. Her face crumpled and she started to cry. After a moment she burst out with: "See what you've done to my face." We could say that her theory of emotions at that time was: "What someone shows IS what they feel."

Yet there are now also many examples that indicate that children as young as two or three can talk about emotions in ways that look convincingly mentalistic, as if they understand that internal mental states drive their actions. Wellman (1995) reports on an intensive study of the language of five children starting when they were two years old. He asked whether children have the concept that one kind of situation elicits only one kind of emotion, and argued that if children understand that situations elicit different kinds of emotional reactions in different people, then they have some conception of emotion as an internal mental state. He found that between two and three years of age children speak about the same object eliciting different emotions in different people:

Adam (age 3): Shaving. I don't like shaving cream . . .

Mother: You don't like shaving cream.

Adam: No. Daddy like shaving cream. Daddy like shaving cream. Mommy wipe it off.

By three to four years old children give plausible reasons for experiencing emotions in which they make reference to the goal states (or desires) of other people. Stein and Levine (1989) read three- to six-year-old children stories in which the goals and consequent outcomes varied for different protagonists: in one story a child wanted something and got it. In another the child wanted something but did not get it. In yet another the child did not want something but got it. If children understand that specific emotions are a consequence of having a goal (i.e., a mental state drives the experience of the emotion rather than the outcome), then we would expect children to predict negative and positive emotions on the basis of the protagonist's goal. Three-year-olds were able to do this, and they were also able to generate explanations involving reference to the protagonists' goals for why the protagonist would feel as he or she did. Further evidence for preschool children explaining the causes of emotion with reference to mental states comes from Harris et al. (1989) who found that four-year-olds were able to predict story characters' emotions on the basis of the characters' desires. In both of these studies age made a difference: as children got older more of them made predictions that took into account the goals of the protagonist.

In naturalistic circumstances, preschool children frequently explain the emotions of other children by making reference to the desires and beliefs of the other child. In a study by Fabes et al. (1991), observers noted details of incidents of emotion in three-, four-, and five-year-olds, at a nursery school. A child who was the closest to each incident, but not involved in it, was asked what emotion had occurred and what had caused it. These children made external attributions by referring to behavior such as "He's mad because she took his toy." To be rated as providing an internal explanation a child had to make explicit reference to an internal or psychological state, such as: "She's sad because she misses her mom," or "She's mad because she thought it was her turn." The majority (55 percent) of explanations of negative emotions given by three-year-olds were external, but 45 percent were internal – mainly involving explanations around a child's goal not being met. Negative emotions received more internal explanations than did positive ones. So preschool children start to think about the internal worlds of other people. If emotions are communications in a social world it makes sense that negative emotions and intense emotions provoke thoughts of the other's inner states: they signal a need for attention, a possibility that a participant's behavior needs changing in some shared activity.

These developments in understanding the causes of emotion are early indications of the child's **theory of mind**: understanding that their own mental states are distinctive and may change, and that others have mental states that can be different from their own (Astington, 1993; Harris & Saarni, 1989). By the age of four, children become good at explaining people's actions in terms of these people's own mental states, including desires and emotions (Lagattuta, Wellman, & Flavell, 1997; Wellman & Lagattuta, 2004).

This development in children's ability to represent other people's mental states is an important development for cooperative partnerships. When children can conceptualize other people's desires, goals, and beliefs, they can negotiate plans in the world knowing what the other person wants and believes. Cooperation provides a good context for understanding the other. Astington and Jenkins (1995) found that children with a fuller understanding of how beliefs can affect behavior showed more joint planning during make-believe play with other children. According to Tomasello et al. (2005) it is this ability to know that others are like ourselves, and to construct mutual plans, that most distinctly separates us from our chimpanzee cousins.

Emotional competence

Carolyn Saarni (1999) has provided a useful schema of emotional competence in children. She proposes eight basic skills, as follows:

1. Awareness of one's emotional state, including the possibility that one is experiencing multiple emotions.
2. Ability to discern and understand others' emotions using situational and expressive cues.
3. Ability to use the vocabulary of emotion and expression terms.
4. Capacity for empathetic and sympathetic involvement in others' emotional experiences.
5. Ability to realize that inner emotional state need not correspond to outer expression.
6. Capacity for adaptive coping with distressing emotions by self-regulation.

7. Awareness that the structure or nature of relationships is in large part defined by how emotions are communicated within the relationship, such as by emotional immediacy or genuineness, and by emotional reciprocity.
8. Capacity for emotional self-efficacy: the individual views him- or herself as able to accept emotional experience.

These skills derive from the abilities that we discuss in this chapter, and indeed in the whole of this book. The move that Saarni makes follows that of Salovey and Mayer (1990) and Mayer, Salovey, and Caruso (2004): to conceptualize research results about people's emotional abilities as skills, and to ask how well can one recognize one's own emotions, recognize the emotions of others, manage or regulate one's emotions, and so on. Salovey and Mayer argued that skills of this kind can be thought of as **emotional intelligence** (see also Goleman, 1995). Saarni's additional move here was to argue that such skills comprise emotional competence, that they are learned in childhood, and that they form the bases of **socialization** (see also Gottman, 1998). Perhaps most importantly for Saarni's argument, there is evidence that emotional competence predicts both current and future social competence (Denham et al., 2003). We have discussed the abilities represented by skills 1, 2, 3, and 4 earlier in this chapter. Skill number 6, self-regulation, is discussed in chapter 11, on individual differences. In this section we discuss Saarni's skills numbers 5, 7, and 8.

Inner and outer emotions

Saarni's skill number 5 involves recognizing that emotions are in part mental, and that there are questions of the appropriateness of certain emotions to certain social situations. As adults, we recognize a difference between what we feel inside and what we express and how we act. We might decide not to express open anger, for instance, if it would have negative consequences. Sometimes we even try to show one emotion although we feel another one inside. We do these things both for ourselves and for others, for instance to maintain positive interactions with people who are important to us. Sometimes we feel extremely sad about an event but instead of allowing ourselves to think about it, we make ourselves think about something else. When can children make distinctions between showing and feeling something, and how might controlling emotions help them in carrying out cooperative plans?

Harter and Buddin (1987) showed that between the ages of four and twelve children became more competent at recognizing that they might feel ambivalence, the experience of two conflicting emotions at once. Conscious modulation of emotion, or substitution of one emotion for another, begins in the early school years. Harris et al. (1986) read stories to children aged four, six, and ten years, about child characters who felt a certain way but for whom an unwelcome consequence would follow if they expressed a certain emotion. Children were asked how the character really felt and what feelings they would show. For instance, "Diana wants to go outside but she has a tummy ache. She knows that if she tells her mom that she has a tummy ache her mom will say that she can't go out. She tries to hide the way she feels so that her mom will let her go outside." The child is then asked: "How did Diana feel when she had a tummy ache? How did Diana try to look on her face when she had a tummy ache?" Six-year-olds consistently made a distinction between what a child felt and what they showed. This distinction was just beginning in four-year-olds in relation to hiding negative feelings but not positive ones. Although four-year-olds understood that real and apparent emotion need not correspond, they showed a less systematic understanding of this issue than the older children.

What children think about stories such as those read to them by Harris and his colleagues, and what they can do to modulate their emotions in everyday life may be different. Saarni (1984) arranged an event in which she thought children would modulate their emotions in response to social pressure. In the first session six- and ten-year-old children received an age-appropriate present following the performance of an unimportant task. In the second session their present was a baby toy. Would the children show their disappointment at receiving a baby toy? Their expressions were video-recorded, and coded as negative, positive, or transitional (defined as suggesting uncertainty or tension). Differences between the expressions following the age-appropriate gift and of the baby toy were calculated. Children's ability to mask disappointment increased with age, although this skill was seen to a limited extent in six-year-olds. Girls did more masking of their emotional expressions than boys did (see also Terwogt et al., 1986).

Conscious awareness of controlling emotions in a wide range of circumstances is unlikely to emerge before about the age of six. This corresponds to the finding, discussed in chapter 3, that parents in many cultures expect children to behave – more or less – according to the social standards of adult society by this age (Briggs, 1970; Lutz, 1988).

Being able to mask emotions may help cooperation in a social world in which everyone has multiple goals. Sometimes our own goals conflict with one another and we may need to prioritize one goal rather than another. A child feels disappointed to receive an inappropriate present, but knows that showing disappointment will hurt another person. When children begin to understand this process in themselves and others, they are drawing on a more elaborate – actually a better – model of understanding other people, and indeed following the work of Gross and John (2003, which will be discussed further in chapter 11) we would say that what is involved in the really competent adolescent or adult is concentrating on the relationship with the person involved rather than, for instance, on one's own concerns. Skills in constructing such models equip people for negotiating complex situations in which the goals of another person are understood to be multiple, sometimes contradictory, sometimes obscured. A difficult aspect of masking emotions is that as we distance ourselves from our experience, our emotions can become obscure to ourselves, a process that we discuss in chapter 14.

Emotions and relationships, emotions and selfhood

The final two skills that Saarni (1999) proposes are indeed the subject matter of our whole book: the fundamental importance of emotions in relationships, and emotions as foundations of selfhood.

Saarni says her seventh skill, of emotional communication, integrates the previous six skills with awareness that emotions depend on the nature of a relationship. She illustrates this with an incident in a 12-year-old child who looks angrily at her friend, and says: "You took my library book and lost it. I can't believe you'd do that" (p. 250). When the friend apologizes and promises to replace it, the girl is gentle and says she knows the friend didn't mean to lose it. But if the 12-year-old spoke of the library book to someone who was not a friend, she might be met with the response: "Oh look at her have a temper tantrum. I'm so scared I might just pee in my pants" (p. 250), and a fight develops.

Among the empirical research on the effects of relationships on the emotions of children and adolescents is that of Keller et al. (2004). They asked children between the ages of three and ten about the emotions of someone who had been cheating. They found that the relationship between the participant and the person who had been cheating affected what emotions were attributed to the cheating person. In a similar way, Whitesell and Harter (1996) presented to 96 children between the ages of 11 and 15 brief stories of an anger-inducing action. The action that was thought about was imagined to be either that of a best friend (as nominated by the child) or of a classmate who was not a close friend. In the story the friend or the classmate called the participant "stupid," and said "some other mean things" (p. 1348). Whitesell and Harter varied other features that are known to affect anger, such as provocation for the incident, intent, and apology, but these dimensions had less effect than the relationship. Preadolescents and adolescents would be more hurt, angry, and sad, if mean things were said by a best friend than by someone who was not close, and they were also more concerned with implications for the relationship. With an acquaintance, blame was more direct, and self-centered concerns prevailed, because an important relationship was not threatened.

Other effects of relationship have been found by Stein and Albro (2001). They showed that children become good at arguing from the age of three or four, but during arguments, neither they nor adults (such as parents) are especially good at understanding the emotional state of the other. Moreover, neither parents nor children are good at resolving conflicts when they are angry. Stein and Albro did, however, find that when sadness occurred in a conflict – perhaps related to their greater concern for the relationship than for winning an argument – resolution became more likely. Levine, Stein, and Liwag (1999) also found that conflict of goals also made it less likely that children would agree with their parents about memories of an emotional event that had occurred to them.

So, relationships affect emotions, both our own and those we imagine others are having, but what of the effect of emotions on relationships? As early as two years old, children use more sad expressions than expressions of other kinds to elicit support from their mothers (Buss & Kiel, 2004). By adolescence, people are skilled at expressing different kinds of emotions in different relationships. What may not necessarily be recognized by the end of adolescence is that emotions expressed in a relationship actually shape those relationships. Thus Gottman et al. (1998) have found that in newlywed couples the main factor to predict happiness or breakup is the ratio of positive to negative emotions expressed (see also, Gottman & Notarius, 2000). Before Gottman's research this was not generally known. Now emotional communication has become a major factor in marital therapy (Gottman, 2002). The work of Kochanska and Aksan (2004) has shown a comparable effect of the importance of positive interactions in mutual responsiveness between parents and children.

A particularly upsetting effect of an opposite kind has been shown by Kim et al. (2001) in a nine-year longitudinal study. They found that reciprocal patterns of negative emotion between adolescents and their parents carried over, in an adverse way, into adult relationships with partners. By contrast, Neff and Harter (2003) found that mutuality with parents tended to be associated with good outcomes including mutuality with friends and romantic partners. So knowing results of these kinds suggest ways in which we might seek to improve our skills and competencies.

What of Saarni's skill number 8, which she calls emotional self-efficacy, which is an aspect of identity? The term self-efficacy was coined by Bandura, who has recently written about it in relation to the development of affective self-regulation (Bandura et al., 2003). Useful for understanding the issues, also, is Harter's (1999) book on the construction of the self. How should we think about this? At least since the work of Erikson (1959) it has been recognized that a principal preoccupation of adolescence is with identity. With the onset of sexuality, the growing importance of the peer group, and progressive distancing from parents, adolescents experiment with roles and identities.

During childhood and adolescence, some people construct what Winnicott (1965) has called a false self, a defensive structure that functions to hide the true self but which lacks creativity and feelings. Winnicott describes one patient in psychoanalysis with him. She was a middle-aged woman who had a very successful false self system, but she also had "the feeling all her life that she had not started to exist" (p. 142). This is the extreme. Further toward health are false selves that defend the true self, or seek for conditions in which the true self may one day come into its own, or selves built mainly on identifications with others. Harter et al. (1996) conducted a study of the degrees of false-self organization, and its relation to the normal adolescent experimentation with identity, in 549 middle- and high-school students. They found that in this phase, adolescents do indeed adopt roles that are different from what might be called their true selves. Some adolescents were aware that they did this, and discussed these roles in terms of experimentation; they had the best knowledge of their true selves, the most optimistic hope for the future, and the most positive emotions. An intermediate group adopted roles that were different from their true selves out of a desire to please others. By contrast, some children, who experienced low social support from parents or peers, felt their true selves were devalued in the eyes of others. Their false-self system predominated. They had the least knowledge of their real selves, the least hope for the future, and the most negative emotions. Corroborating this kind of finding from another perspective, Pomeranz and Rudolph (2003) have found in a longitudinal study of 9- to 13-year-old children that emotional distress produced decrements in their views of themselves and of their competence.

Saarni's eighth skill in its positive sense is an acceptance of our emotions as appropriate in relation to our understanding of our identities, and constitutes a balance between individuality and society.

Summary

In the first part of this chapter, we discussed how emotions are central to how parents and children relate, and to how they develop their relationships. Through emotional expressions parents and children come to learn about each others' desires and beliefs. Children's own experience of emotions signal what is working or not working for them in an interaction. Even babies alter their behavior in response to another person's negative and positive emotional expressions. We learned that the emotional communication system starts simply, as children signal negative states such as distress, and positive states by smiling and eye contact. Differentiation of emotional expressions (e.g., of happiness, fear, anger) and targeting such expressions to specific people develop during the first year. Similarly, during the first year infants come to discriminate different emotions in adults. We discussed how attachment is a central theme in socio-emotional development. It is the system whereby infant and caregiver remain close, so that the caregiver can protect the infant. Babies and caregivers develop a dance together in which the emotions of one are treated by the other as communications. Emotions orient children to constructing models of the internal worlds of others. We learned how the emergence of talk about emotion allows for the development of shared meanings around emotional experience. Such shared meanings become part of the fabric of relationships. Meta-cognitive skills allow for elaborated models of other people, in play and in ordinary life. Without elaborated models of other people, joint cooperation would be more difficult. Finally we discussed how we can think of emotional development as the attainment a set of skills that comprise competence in understanding emotions of self and others. These skills are the foundations for living in the social world.

Further reading

The best general introduction we know to the development of emotions is:
Paul Harris (1989). *Children and emotion: The development of psychological understanding*. Oxford: Blackwell.

For an excellent account of infants' abilities to recognize emotions in others:
Arlene Walker-Andrews (1997). Infants' perception of expressive behaviors: Differentiation of multimodal information. *Psychological Bulletin*, *121*, 437–456.

On the significance of children's emotions and their understanding in social interaction:
Judy Dunn (2003). Emotional development in early childhood: A social relationship perspective. In R. J. Davidson, K. R. Scherer, & H. H. Goldsmith (Eds.), *Handbook of affective sciences* (pp. 332–346). New York: Oxford University Press.

A good summary of the development of emotions that involve the self:
Michael Lewis (1995). Self-conscious emotions. *American Scientist*, *83* (Jan.-Feb.), 68–78.

Emotions in Social Relationships

Contents

Figure 9.0 Auguste Renoir, "Dance at Bougival," 1882–83. This painting was used to illustrate a story, by Lhote, about an artist seeking to persuade a young woman to model for him. In the painting we see the man thrusting his face eagerly toward the young woman, and grasping her possessively. We also notice from her ring that she is married. Keeping her polite social smile, she turns away. (Compare figure 4.1.)

Social goals and social emotions

...I came to myself as if out of a great sickness. There was something strange in my sensations, something indescribably new and, from its very novelty, incredibly sweet. I felt younger, lighter, happier in body; within I was conscious of a heady recklessness... a dissolution of the bonds of obligation, an unknown but not an innocent freedom of the soul...

...This familiar that I called forth out of my own soul, and sent forth to do his good pleasure was a being inherently malign and villainous, his every act and thought centered on self, drinking pleasure with a bestial avidity from any degree of torture of another; relentless like a man of stone.

(pp. 83, 86)

These passages are from Robert Louis Stevenson's (1886) *Dr Jekyll and Mr Hyde*. According to this story, human beings are mixtures of good and evil. Dr Jekyll has discovered a potion to fractionate out the purely evil part, called Mr Hyde, and what we read are his first sensations as he comes into being. The evil is liberation from "the bonds of obligation." He is purely selfish and, as one might imagine, it is not long before he commits a cruel murder.

This notion, that humans are a mixture of good and evil, still guides accounts of human nature. For many theorists, there are two fundamental dimensions to human social life that provide, as it were, two coordinates like North–South and East–West, that locate us in interpersonal geography. The sociologist Kemper traces back these dimensions to the Greek philosopher Empedocles (Wright, 1981), who called them "love" and "strife"; modern sociologists tend to call strife power. Freud saw life in terms of sexuality and death, humankind's creative and destructive tendencies. More recently theorists speak of cooperation, affiliation, and prosocial behavior on the one hand, and competition, dominance, and antisocial behavior on the other.

The two aspects have been found in studies of child development where they are called "love" and "control" (Sroufe, 1978), in anthropology where Triandis (1972) has called them "intimacy" and "superordination-subordination," in semantic analyses such as those of Osgood, May, and Miron (1975) where they emerge as evaluation (goodness) and potency, and in many other studies of social interaction (Kemper, 1978; Moskowitz, 1994).

Certain emotions, like love, compassion, and gratitude, are underpinnings of cooperative behavior. They enable humans' extraordinary sociality and our daily acts of benevolence. Despite conflict, primates, rather like social insects, have found modes of life in which cooperation and interdependency are advantageous in reproducing the genes of individuals and those to whom they are closely related. In this chapter, as well as explaining how modes of behavior promote reproduction of genes, we need to explain what induces individuals to act socially. This is the realm of emotions like love and compassion. In an essential way, what sets primates, especially humans, apart from other species is the capacity for kindness (Buck, 2002; De Waal, 1996; Keltner, 2004). In Tibetan Buddhism, monks have for thousands of years practiced the cultivation of the compassionate side to their nature. The conviction is that when the mind is rid of desire, one discovers the compassionate core of human nature. In the words of the 14th Dalai Lama: At the most fundamental level our nature is compassionate, and cooperation, not conflict, lies at the heart of the basic principles that govern our human existence.

At the same time, in the history of Western thought anger, aggression, and revenge have been seen as unavoidable aspects of human character. The Stoics saw anger as the emotion that was most essential to master. For Buddhists, anger is a destructive emotion. The human species' capacity to destroy its own members in political repression, ethnic hostility, war, and genocide, is one of the deepest and most enduringly problematic aspects of human nature.

Historical figure: Konrad Lorenz

The foremost figure in modern ethology was Konrad Lorenz. Born in Vienna in 1903, he died in 1989. Throughout his life he kept a menagerie of animals, and he is remembered for the geese who followed him about. In the 1920s and 1930s he had no paid post and his father supported him until he married Greta Gebhardt, a physician, in 1927 – then she supported him! He finally obtained a professorship, but only held the job for a year when war broke out and he was drafted into the army as a doctor. He was in a Russian prisoner of war camp for four years where he kept himself healthy by eating insects and spiders. After the war, he was again without a job. In 1955 the Max Planck organization enabled him to set up an Institute at Seewiesen in Bavaria, and in 1973, with Niko Tinbergen and Karl von Frisch, he received a Nobel Prize.

When Hitler came to power, Lorenz went along with the Nazis. In 1940 he wrote a shocking article in which he proposed that people who had been overdomesticated should be eliminated as an act of public health. He regretted this appalling lapse for the rest of his life. But his theory that aggression was a "big drive," that "resembles a horse . . . which must have daily exercise to keep down its superfluous energy" (Lorenz, 1967, p. 77) made him an enemy of those who saw such arguments as justifying human militarism. While no one can excuse Lorenz's links with Nazism, one may note that after the war many of his friends believed his involvement to have been misjudgment rather than commitment. These friends included Tinbergen, who was sent to detention camp by the Nazis for protesting the dismissal of three Jewish faculty members from the University of Leiden where he worked. (Biographical information from Bateson, 1990)

The ethologist Lorenz (1967) argued that aggression is an innate drive like hunger, and that human culture is in peril: aggression threatens to run out of control because technology and bureaucracy hold back humans from reconciliation and peace-making. Ardrey (1966) speculated, in a similar vein, about a "territorial imperative": that we are programmed for aggression in defense of territories ranging from a seat on the bus to a nation. The drift of such writing was that beneath the clothes of civilization there lurks a killer ape liable to burst out in irrational violence (see Fox, 1991 for critique). In this chapter, we consider the emotions that promote cooperation and those that promote aggression, and this task is guided by thinking about three kinds of social motivations.

Three kinds of social motivation: attachment, affiliation, and assertion

We discussed in chapter 4 how emotions most typically arise with evaluations of events in relation to goals. If, as we propose in this chapter and indeed in this book, human emotions are primarily social, we can ask: What are our social goals and concerns? We propose that three are important (Jenkins & Oatley, 1996; Goldberg, Grusec, & Jenkins, 1999; Jenkins & Ball, 2000; Oatley, 2004c). One is attachment, which we introduced in the previous chapter. Its function is primarily that of protection and care for the immature infant. The infant and caregiver cooperate to allow the infant to thrive in an environment that contains dangers. A second kind of social motivation often accompanies it. We call this affiliaton, and it is often described in the research literature as warmth. Colloquially we might call it **affection**. It contributes to parenting, and more generally it draws individuals together even when they are not genetically related. This motivation may be seen in action in the mutual grooming of chimpanzees. In humans it is the core of kindness, of friendship, and also of long-term sexual bonding that we call romantic love. The third kind of social motivation is assertion, power as described by the sociologists. We human beings create hierarchies in many of the things we do, in the academy, in sports, in politics, in music. Each, it seems, must have its Number 1, the top person, with others arranged below. Assertion is the motivation to rise in the social hierarchy, and to resist challenges from those who would diminish us. It is the motivation of competition, and of conflict.

We can think of social emotions as managing social goals, and as moving us in a three-dimensional space of the three primary social motivations, as shown in figure 9.1. Typical positive emotions associated with the presence of an attachment figure are trust, comfort, and reassurance, while loss of such a figure produces anxiety and distress. Typical positive emotions associated with affiliation are affection, warmth, and liking, whereas loss of someone to whom one felt affection produces sadness and grieving. The typical emotion of assertion is anger: to win or maintain status, whereas loss of status is accompanied by shame or embarrasssment and other emotions of deference. These three dimensions are not the only social motivations, and some goals, such as curiosity and self-preservation in the face of physical dangers, are not social at all. Nonetheless, these three social

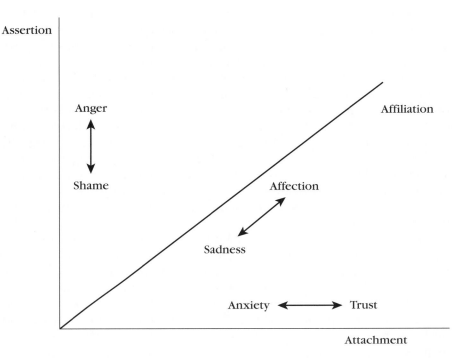

Figure 9.1 Jenkins and Oatley's schema of three principal social motivations, attachment, affiliation, and assertion, as orthogonal dimensions, with emotions represented by lines with arrows at each end as movements in this three-dimensional space.

motivations are sufficiently pervasive across contexts and cultures and sufficiently important in human life that they deserve to be emphasized. In contrast, moreover, to the predominance of negative emotions in relation to positive, and to the finding that the bad is often stronger than the good (which we discussed in chapter 4), is it significant that as far as human societies are concerned there are two principal social motivations that are cooperative, and only one that is competitive?

Attachment and its separation from affiliation

Bowlby's (1971) conceptualization of attachment was that its function is essentially protective. The human infant is so vulnerable that it would not survive without an adult caregiver, typically a mother, who is preoccupied with protecting it from threats of predators and members of its own species, as well as from threats of the physical envioronment.

Even with this protection, early childhood remains the most vulnerable period of life. The attachment system keeps the mother close by or ready to be summoned by crying. Bowby's idea of the secure base, of the mother's presence from which exploration can be made when the baby starts to move about, follows this same conception. The functioning of the mother as a secure base continues into adolescence (Allen et al., 2003). We can imagine that trust, of the kind emphasized by attachment theorists as well as theorists of stages of emotional development (e.g., Erikson, 1950, 1959), is really confidence that one is, and can continue to be, safe.

At the same time there is a great deal more to parental love than protecting a child and providing a secure base. Thus the idea has emerged of maternal sensitivity to the infant's needs. For instance, Ainsworth et al. (1978) observed mothers interacting with their babies. Mothers were rated on behaviors such as: appropriately interpreting the infants' signals, behaving in an accepting way toward the infant, respecting the baby's autonomy, being accessible to the baby, and being tender. Scores on these ratings were associated with infant security. So Ainsworth et al. hypothesized that infants developed their sense of trust from parents being sensitive and responsive.

Subsequent studies have not found such robust relations between maternal sensitivity ratings and attachment (Goldsmith & Alansky, 1987). Grossmann et al. (1985), for instance, found that mothers who were more sensitive during their babies' first year had infants who were more securely attached at the end of the year, although this relationship was not found at all measurement points during the year. Atkinson et al. (2005) have found further evidence of dissociation between maternal sensitivity and attachment security.

What is going on? In their review of relevant studies, Goldberg et al. (1999) conclude that alongside the protective functions of attachment there is another function that is separable but equally important, the system of affiliation, warmth, and affection. This includes senstivity. Affiliation and warmth are fundamentally important in human development, but they involve different processes than of protection (MacDonald, 1992). For example, Fox and Davidson (1987) found that babies seeing their mothers approaching with open arms showed joy and an activation of the left side of the cortex. The system activated here is part of afflilation. By contrast, distress on separation from a caregiver involved not so much a reduction of such activation, but changes in a separate system, on the right side of the cortex. MacDonald (1992) also points out that although attachment occurs among all primates, only some species form affectional bonds based on warmth.

Human caregivers in some societies can be strong in attachment although not particularly warm to their infants. In fact, the society in Uganda in which Ainsworth (1967) first discerned the set of infant attachment behavior patterns (described in chapter 8) was of this kind. Ainsworth found that hugging and kissing between infants and mothers was, for instance, not very common in Uganda, whereas it is more common in America. Ainsworth concluded that although American mothers were warmer, their responsiveness to children's distress was less than the Ugandan mothers.

In light of these kinds of observations, MacDonald (1992) and Goldberg et al. (1999) hypothesized that the separate systems of attachment and affiliative warmth can be differently prioritized in different cultures. The system of affiliation and warmth is built on positive reward, and it is closely associated with the system of touch that we reviewed in chapter 4. We touch and hug those to whom we feel affectionate. When chimpanzees spend 20 percent of their time grooming, it is their affiliative system that is at work. It creates and maintains relationships of affection that are characteristic of apes, and even more characteristic of humans. Clark and Finkel (2005) have written about affiliation in terms of what they call communal relating (caring) as opposed to relating in terms of exchange such as "I'll do this for you if you do that for me," which have a more commercial quality. People express more emotions in relationships that are communal, i.e., caring, relationships.

Emotions as social

Emotions are social in several different ways. First, just as with individual goals, emotions are evaluations, or appraisals, of events that affect different kinds of social goals. People are anxious if an attachment figure is inexplicably absent. People are happy when they see a friend. To see this, watch people meeting each other at an airport or train station. People are angry if their status is threatened. Second, as Parkinson (1996) and Parkinson, Fischer, and Manstead (2004) point out, emotions are not solely determined by appraisals of events. In the discussions that occur of almost every substantial emotion (Rimé et al., 1998), emotions are reappraised, so that the emotions become amalgams of what started them and the social negotiations they have occasioned. Moreover, if one is (say) angry, that emotion might have just as much to do with maintaining a position one has staked out in such discussions as it has to do with what started it. Third, and most importantly, emotions create social relationships. A smile is not just a smile. It is an invitation to a cooperative relationship. An angry expression is a declaration of conflict. Such emotions are not just states of readiness. They are, as Aubé and Senteni (1996) have put it, **commitments**. We commit ourselves, for a time at least, to the relationship for which the emotion sets the frame (Oatley, 2004c). In addition, Clark, Fitness, and Brissette (2004) argue that emotions signal our goals, and others can then be responsive to them.

One of the interesting features of the three kinds of social motivation that we have proposed – attachment, affiliation, and assertion – is that they do not just coexist; in human society they need actively to be combined. Sexual love, as we shall discuss in the next section, does best with a strong combination of attachment and affiliation. Effective parenting needs all three social motivations: attachment to ensure a child's world is safe, affiliation to surround the child with affection, and assertion to ensure, as Finkenauer, Engels, and Baumeister (2005) point out, effective control and monitoring. Let us therefore explore social motivations and the emotions with which they are associated within three relational contexts (e.g., Fiske, 1992): intimate relations between family and friends, within groups, and between groups.

Emotions within intimate relationships

Early attachment as a template for later love

In long-term love two people cooperate to accomplish together what they could not do alone. The result is what Bowlby has called an **affectional bond**:

> Affectional bonds and subjective states of strong emotion tend to go together, as every novelist and playwright knows. Thus, many of the most intense of all human emotions arise during the formation, the maintenance, the disruption, and the renewal of affectional bonds – which, for that reason, are sometimes called emotional bonds. In terms of subjective experience, the formation of a bond is described as falling in love, maintaining a bond as loving someone, and losing a partner as grieving over someone. (Bowlby, 1979, p. 69)

Bowlby's idea was that the attachment relationship of infancy creates a template for later intimate relationships. Try this little experiment on yourself. Think about patterns of attachment that we discussed in chapter 8, and look back to table 8.1 where 16 such patterns discovered by Ainsworth are listed, for instance infants smiling more, vocalizing more, and so on with mothers than with anyone else. Now imagine that instead of being patterns that infants show with their mothers, these are descriptions of interaction between two adult lovers. Do the patterns fit? Do lovers show differential smiling and vocalization with each other, do they follow each other, gaze at each other, do they show distress at separation? If they do, might this confirm Bowlby's hypothesis that adult love is formed on a template of the infant attachment relationship. Intimations of the idea were first put by Darwin (1872), who supposed that the infant pattern of holding and being held is elaborated in adult caressing. To this idea Freud added the romantic notion that adult love is the return to the Eden of blissful merging with one's original love, with one's mother. Adult romantic love and sexuality, according to this, is an elaboration upon universal, evolved, behavioral patterns of earlier life.

Phillip Shaver's recent research agenda has been based on this idea (e.g., Hazan & Shaver, 1987). Shaver, Hazan, and Bradshaw (1988) propose that adult love depends on three systems: attachment, caregiving of infants by parents, and the sexual relating of reproduction. They argue that attachment and caregiving both carry forward experiences from infancy to adult relating. We have discussed some aspects of attachment, so let us look more closely at caregiving.

Maternal caregiving and affiliative warmth

The principal researcher in the area of maternal caregiving is Alison Fleming (see, e.g., Fleming et al., 2002), who studies both laboratory animals and humans. In rats, mothers show three distinctive kinds of maternal behavior toward their infants. (a) When infant rats suckle, the mothers assume a crouching posture over them. (b) If infants get out of the nest, they make ultrasonic squeaks (Knutson, Burgdorf, & Pankseep, 2002) and mothers retrieve them. Retrieval (but not other kinds of maternal behavior) is dependent on the nucleus accumbens (Li & Fleming, 2003). (c) Mothers lick their infants, particularly on and around the ano-genital region.

Enabling infants to suck is a characteristic of all mammals, so the pattern arose with the first mammals, 70 million years ago. Retrieving is also a typical species-characteristic pattern. Indeed it is homologous to egg-retrieval by the greylag goose, which we discussed in chapter 2. It too, therefore, is evolutionarily old. Retrieval is equivalent, in human mothers, to the attachment function of responding to the babies' cries, picking them up, and keeping them safe. In infant rats, being licked and stimulated in a tactile way, is essential for health and proper development. It switches on various neural and hormonal systems. In rat mothers it is a more elaborate pattern, and more variable, than suckling and retrieving. It requires mother rats to be attracted to their infants, and it can be dissociated from suckling and retrieving. Michael Meaney's group (Weaver et al., 2004) has shown that the experience of baby rats who were licked more and nursed more by their mothers (as compared with those who were licked less and nursed less) made a difference in DNA methylation at a gene promotor region in the hippocampus. Experience of being licked and nursed more was found to affect gene expression, which in turn had a calming effect on responses to stress of the offspring in their adulthood. This is a new finding of gene–environment interaction, of how although environmental experience does not affect genes as such, it can alter genes' expression.

Maternal licking in the rat species finds its equivalent in humans in cuddling, kissing, stroking, and other forms of physical contact. Again, in humans, it is thought that this has influences on neurobiological development. As Fleming and her group have shown, this physical touching is dependent, both in rats and humans, on the mother herself having experienced bodily contact when she was an infant: that is, intergenerational transmission of mothering depends on experience. So, as Fleming's group has shown (Krpan et al., 2005), women who have themselves not had much in the way of mothering tend, when they become mothers, to be much more instrumental in their caregiving behaviors (changing diapers, adjusting clothes, and such like). By comparison, mothers who received more affection when they were infants spend more time cuddling and kissing their babies. Human mothers can raise children perfectly successfully without being particularly affectionate to them, but their children's ability to show affection in their later life, and perhaps their interest in affection, depends on having been objects of affection to their parents.

In parenthood the mother, and ideally the father too, fall in love with their specific infant. This love will sustain them through the life-upheavals that child rearing demands. They will develop what Winnicott (1958) called "primary maternal preoccupation," which sustains the devotion they need for the baby to flourish. Klaus and Kennell (1976) described a process of the mother becoming bonded to her baby by bodily contact during the first days after delivery. They recommended this body contact as part of early infant care. Klaus and Kennell's work led to changes in the organization of hospital maternity care, although their findings of widespread benefits to children's health and development with early maternal bonding have not all been replicated in subsequent studies (Svejda, Campos, & Emde, 1980; Svejda, Pannabecker, & Emde, 1982). For instance, Klaus and Kennell's emphasis on an early critical period for bonding was overstated. Parents who, for whatever reason, are unable to have close contact with their babies in the first few days do become perfectly good and loving parents, and their babies thrive just as well. Most tellingly, adoptive parents who have not had early contact make just as good and loving mothers and fathers as biological parents (Tizard & Hodges, 1978).

Early contact may, however, help mothers and fathers become bonded to infants. Fathers who were present at the birth of children (Peterson, Mehl, & Leiderman, 1979) showed more intense attachment to their infants early on. As well as skin-to-skin contact, releaser patterns such as the babies' smiles easily elicit gazing and "oohah" sounds from adults, emotions like filial love and sympathy, and facilitate the growth of loving relationships. But bonding to a child can involve a wide range of processes, not just early sensory cues (Corter & Fleming, 1990; Fleming & Corter, 1995).

So caregiving is itself an amalgam of elements, one of which is based in what we have identified as the affiliative-warmth system. Let us, however, follow Shaver, Hazan, and Bradshaw and now ask how the mating system gets involved in the amalgam that supports sexual love.

Affiliation and sexual relating

If you see dogs copulating, they are intent for a few seconds, then they disengage. The whole thing is perfunctory. By contrast, sexual love in humans is elaborate. In evolutionary terms it is likely that the elaboration started with the joining of the affliative-warmth system to the reproductive one, according to what has become known as the **male provisioning hypothesis** (Lovejoy, 1981). Lovejoy argued that the critical evolutionary moves occurred when humans started to walk upright, when with the formation of specialized feet infants could no longer cling to their mothers as ape babies do, so that mothers must devote more resources to tending them. At the same time, males started to make a contribution to the rearing of specific infants. The moves were accompanied by movement from the promiscuity characteristic of apes to the formation of long-lasting sexual relationships between specific females and specific males, often called pair bonding, which is rare elsewhere in the primate world. With pair bonding, a male has a good chance of knowing that the child to whose upbringing he contributes bears his genes. In return for her exclusive sexual attention – so the idea goes – the female acquires from the male additional resources to contribute to child rearing, while she (more hampered in childcare than chimpanzee mothers) can move around less during her offspring's infancy. Evolutionary pressures have therefore led women to choose males on the basis of their predicted investment in parenting, rather than (as in some species) from indicators of genetic prowess. Since women make the main investment in bringing up children, it is thought that (as discussed in chapter 2) the genetic aspect of male preference in mate selection is based on indications of a woman's abilities to rear children and readiness to reproduce (Buss, 1992; Fisher, 1992; for critique, see Eagly & Wood, 1999).

Human infancy is so long, so demanding, and so fraught with physical difficulty that it strains the resources of a single caregiver. The human family – a woman, her offspring, and (typically) a male partner – are bound together by emotions of affection. The demands of raising offspring, and group living more generally, often require cooperation with non-kin as well (Hrdy, 1999), and have given rise to forms of affection that are the basis of friendships.

Principles of sexual love

The human experiences of loving and of being loved are thought by many to be what give life its principal meaning, and are much celebrated in fictional literature. Here for instance is Laura Esquivel in the novel *Like Water for Chocolate*:

> My Grandmother had a very interesting theory; she said that each of us is born with a box of matches inside us but we can't strike them all by ourselves . . . the oxygen would come from the breath of the person you love; the candle could be any kind of food, music, caress, word, or sound that engenders the explosion that lights one of the matches. For a moment we are dazzled by the intense emotion. A pleasant warmth grows within us . . . Each person has to discover what will set off these explosions in order to live, since the combustion that occurs when one of them is ignited is what nourishes the soul. (Esquivel, 1992, chapter 6)

For most people in Western society love is what is most important in life. As Freedman (1978) found in his survey of 100,000 Americans who responded to a magazine questionnaire, it was not wealth, not power, not youth, not health – but love in marriage that the respondents thought was the good that they most closely identified with happiness.

Human beings have a species-characteristic repertoire of actions such as caressing, smiling, cooing, caressing, and kissing, based on their early relationships with caregivers. Of course, there is much more to intimate love than these patterns. We differ from most of our mammalian relations in that important people in our lives do not just fulfill roles – infant, sexual partner, parent – we become unique individuals intertwined in our identities and life narratives. But even the idea of individuality has an evolutionary history. By the stage at which apes evolved, so too had individuality.

Goodall (1986) found that an infant chimpanzee who at the age of six had lost its mother, though able to forage for itself, would pine and die. It was a particular, irreplaceable relationship with that individual which was lost. So too it is with us. Our parents are not just caregivers, but our particular mothers or fathers, parts of our life story. Our children are not just offspring, they are individuals. And when it comes to sexual partners, there is the longing for that special someone, a particular individual. Contented romantic partners, for example, tend to idealize and mythologize their loved ones, attributing rare virtues to them that set them apart from others (Murray & Holmes, 1993, 1997).

Perhaps among us human beings there is an element of repetition, and of hope of being able to regain the closeness of our first relationship, in someone who seems familiar – as if we had always known them. The taboos against incest and the social processes of exogamy that promote mating between unrelated adults are human universals. It is for this reason that children raised in kibbutzim tend not to enter into sexual relationships with those with whom they grew up with in the same kibbutz. As Bateson (1983) has said, and this may be the most we can say about the characteristics of people with whom we fall in love: we tend to choose as a mate someone similar to people we know, but not too similar!

Our love of unique others makes us uniquely vulnerable. Falling in love hinges on being dependent, committed in spite of possible exploitation, and merging the self with the loved one (Aron et al., 1991; Rusbult, 1980, 1983). When that special person becomes ill, or dies, or does not turn out to be quite as expected, part of the self is lost. This kind of issue is problematic not just in the West but in other societies in which personal choice is the basis for marriage or its equivalent, for example in a matrilineal society in Melanesia (Macintyre, 1986).

What then is meant by "love"? How do we accomplish the transition from the urgent, fantasy-based, erotic state of being in love – passionate love as it is called by Hatfield and Rapson (2002) – to the state of permanent loving and caring for the other (Djikic & Oatley, 2004)? How does love change as we maintain a state of cooperative affection during the greater part of adult life when offspring are raised? Jung (1925) wrote about the psychological repercussions of withdrawing the fantasies on which being in love is based, and of the changing roles that occur as the life span is traversed. In terms of emotions, several forms of love, as we noted earlier, help with these transitions: love that is centered upon caregiving, affection, friendship, and eroticism (Aron & Aron, 1998; Berscheid, 1988; Diamond, 2003).

Several studies have differentiated sexual desire from romantic love (Chojnacki & Walsh, 1990; R. J. Sternberg, 1997; Whitley, 1993). For example, people often nominate love as a prototypical emotion, and sexual desire is believed to overlap only modestly with the content of love (Fehr & Russell, 1984; Fehr & Russell, 1991; Shaver et al., 1987). In another study, participants were asked to exclude emotion terms that did not belong in the category of love (Fehr & Russell, 1991). Few participants excluded the words caring (8 percent), and affection (27 percent), but many participants excluded the words desire (59 percent), infatuation (82 percent), and lust (87 percent). The people participants say they love only partially overlap with those for whom they say they feel sexual desire (Myers & Berscheid, 1997).

These studies suggest that whereas some facets of sexuality are served by an intense emotion we might call sexual desire, other facets such as enduring commitment one feels are guided by emotions of romantic love (see chapter 3). These two states have different nonverbal displays (see chapter 4), which incorporate many of the affiliative–affectionate behaviors seen between parent and child (kissing, smiling, hugging, touch). Only romantic, or sexual, love, it seems, is associated with the release of oxytocin, which itself promotes devotion and monogamy (see chapter 6).

Anger and contempt in marriage

Not all intimate life is lovely. With divorce rates in many industrialized nations hovering near 50 percent, and with levels of marital dissatisfaction also very high (Myers, 2000), it is essential to ask about sources of marital distress. At this point the social motivations of assertion, which we illustrate as the vertical coordinate in figure 9.1, enters intimate relations.

In a series of studies over 20 years, Gottman and Levenson have studied married partners engaged in conversations for 15 minutes about an issue of conflict between them, for example unsatisfying sex, the husband's inability to get better-paying work, or their child's academic difficulties. Participants also engage in other non-conflictual conversations about the events of the day and about something pleasant in the relationship. Gottman and Levenson then code the interactions for several emotional behaviors.

In one long-term study that started in 1983, Gottman and Levenson followed the marriages of 79 couples from Bloomington, Indiana. They have identified what they call "the Four Horsemen of the Apocalypse" – negative behaviors most damaging to relationships. First is *criticism*. Those partners who are more critical, who continually find fault with their partners have less satisfying marriages. The next two predictors of dissatisfaction and divorce are defensiveness and stonewalling (resisting dealing with problems): when romantic partners are unable to talk freely about their difficulties without being defensive, they are in trouble. The fourth is contempt for the partner. In their study, Gottman and Levenson used measures of the four toxic behaviors (criticism, defensiveness, stonewalling, and contempt), gathered from the 15-minute conversation about a conflict, to predict who would stay together and who would be divorced 14 years later. Remarkably, they predicted who would stay married and who would divorce with 93 percent accuracy (Gottman & Levenson, 2000).

Here we see the benefits of thinking in precise terms about emotions in relationships, and about different negative emotions. Among the emotions, contempt is most toxic to relationships. Anger, on the other hand, while distressing in the moment, can bring about beneficial change. The benefits

Figure 9.2 Anger may be an important part of intimate relationships. It is typically less destructive in relationships than is contempt.

of anger were discovered in empirical work by James Averill (1982). He distributed structured diaries to 80 randomly chosen married people and 80 single university students, asking them to record an incident of anger. He also distributed somewhat different diaries to 80 more students asking them to record incidents in which they were a target for someone else's anger. He proposed that anger has a quality of the speech act of promising. To be angry with someone involves a commitment to seeing an argument through to some end. Indeed as Aubé and Senteni (1996) have pointed out, all social emotions have an element of commitment. They are commitments to specific kinds of relating.

Most of Averill's participants who reported feeling angry (66 percent) reported an incident of anger once or twice a week, usually elicited in interactions with people the participant knew and liked: parents, children, spouses, or friends. Approximately two-thirds of angry people felt their anger as negative, and targets mostly felt even worse. But despite this, 62 percent of angry people and 70 percent of targets rated the episode of anger as beneficial. Usually anger functions in long-term relationships to allow the participants to readjust something in that relationship. So anger usually starts with a sense of being wronged, and ends with both partners making some adjustment, and coming to a reconciliation and new understanding (see also Jenkins, Smith, & Graham, 1989).

In terms of social motivation, it is clear that even when we join with another person in a mutual goal that includes living together, sharing resources, and having children, we do not abandon all our individualistic concerns. These concerns express themselves in emotions such as anger. Anger is a bid to increase one's status, or maintain it. Shame is the social emotion of being diminished. So important is maintaining one's sense of oneself, that Scheff (1997) calls shame the master emotion. Despite its import-ance, it is not much discussed in conversation. It is hypocognized because in Western society it is too shameful to talk about.

Anger and resolution can be thought of as an emotional response to something that has gone wrong in a relationship, where one has been disregarded, exploited, taken for granted, or slighted. Resolution is the readjustment of the relationship in response to this anger, and our ability to bring about such reconciliations is part of our primate heritage (De Waal, 2000). One can think of the four toxic factors in intimate relationships as unfair maneuvers that usurp the place of anger and resolution. Criticism, particularly repeated criticism, is the attempt to reduce the other in one's own eyes and in that person's eyes too. Defensiveness and stonewalling are maneuvers that block the commitment to carry the matter through until the problem is resolved. Contempt is denial of the other person's right to take part in the relationship at all.

Friendship and gratitude

We have spoken of love for offspring and sexual partners. Yet people feel love, often profound, for non-kin, for lifelong friends, and for friends in the immediate moment. In friendships, children learn their generation's morals and values. In friendships, young adults sort out the difficulties of family and romantic life.

From an evolutionary perspective, friendships present something of a conundrum: they require cooperation with non-kin. In evolutionary terms it seems problematic for the individual to devote resources to another individual, whose own success brings no benefit to the benefactor's genes. As an answer to this puzzle, Trivers (1971) offered an influential analysis of the basis of friendships, and he focused his claims on reciprocity and gratitude. He proposed that cooperative alliances like friendships have emerged in human evolution, and are successful in our more immediate lives, to the extent that there is reciprocal giving and affection. He further argued, along with evolutionary theorists like Randolph Nesse (1990), that emotions such as love and gratitude promote cooperative, affectionate alliances between friends. Ross Buck (1999, 2002) and Buck and Ginsberg (1997) have extended this idea with what they call the communicative gene hypothesis. Although genes are inherently selfish, they survive and continue from generation to generation only in the context of other genes.

Therefore, genes evidently relate to each other, either in the same cell or in cells of other organisms. Gene lines that survive because of their communication with genes in other organisms of the same species, therefore, could theoretically provide a basis for prosocial emotions of altruism and empathy, as well as the emotions of other social arrangements that we discuss in this chapter like attachment and monogamous sexual relating.

Michael McCullough, Robert Emmons, and their colleagues have taken the analysis of gratitude a step further. They contend that gratitude is a glue of cooperative social living amongst non-kin; it is a moral emotion (McCullough et al., 2001). How so? First, gratitude serves as a barometer; it helps us keep track of what friends are generous, and which friends are not. It is much like the grooming between nonhuman primates; our feelings of gratitude track, the argument goes, who are cooperative non-kin. Second, gratitude motivates altruistic, affectionate behavior. It is one of the emotions of affiliation. Gratitude leads people to be more likely to reciprocate acts of generosity. And finally, the expression of gratitude acts as a reward; it reinforces affectionate, cooperative behavior. One might think of the kind of touching of another person to express gratitude (see chapter 4) as inherently rewarding in this fashion. To cite another example, waitresses who express their gratitude by writing "thank you" on restaurant bills receive substantially larger tips than those who do not (McCullough et al., 2001).

Emotions of assertion within groups

The most characteristic emotion of assertion is anger, and Leonard Berkowitz (1989) has become well known for his argument that any aversive event – pain, hunger, fatigue, humiliation, anxiety, insults – will elicit aggression when it produces anger, because anger is associated with thoughts about a perpetrator's responsibility, and feelings of injustice and revenge. Once activated, this constellation of thoughts, feelings, and physiological reactions promotes aggression – in which we seek to raise onself and lower someone else in status. In empirical demonstrations, Berkowitz has shown that people who experience pain brought about by holding their arms horizontally for six minutes were more critical of another person (Berkowitz, 1990). In another study, Berkowitz, Cochran, and Embree (1981) found that female participants were more likely to punish and less likely to reward another participant when their arms were immersed in painfully cold water (6 degrees C; 43 degrees F), than when their arms were in water at room temperature (18 degrees C; 65 degrees F) (see figure 9.3). This kind of reaction may not be very rational, but in our social species, it is indicative that when something aversive happens, it is immediately transferred into the social domain. It is interesting in this regard, that participants in Berkwitz, Cochran, and Embree's experiment reduced punishment when they knew it would hurt the other person.

In social mammals and birds, dominance hierarchies are common (Eibl-Eibesfeldt, 1970). In primates, including monkeys (Cheyney & Seyfarth, 1990)

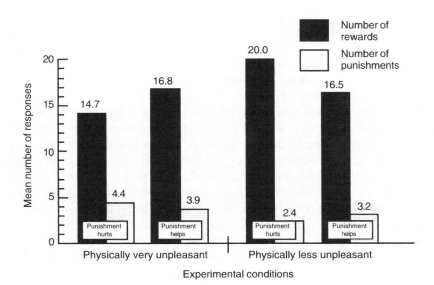

Figure 9.3 Mean numbers of rewards and punishments given to others by women who were in pain (physically very unpleasant condition) or not in pain (physically less unpleasant condition) (Berkowitz et al., 1993).

and apes (De Waal, 1982; Goodall, 1986), hierarchies have been described in detail. Positions within hierarchies, as well as alliances with relatives and others, persist through time, and govern access to resources, such as food and sexual partners (Mason & Mendoza, 1993).

Emotionally these hierarchies are negotiated by threatening displays of anger and complementary displays of deference, or by actual fights that have a winner and a loser. Although Lorenz thought of aggression only as a single movement: to attack someone else, it is clear that more typically there are two phases, aggression and reconciliation. After a fight or scuffle chimpanzees almost always reconcile (De Waal, 2000). In bonobos, this is initiated by the original aggressor on 61 percent of occasions, and in common chimpanzees on 44 percent of occasions (Visalberghi & Sonetti, 1994). Even high ranking and powerful males need allies. To defeat someone in a fight and leave it at that would produce a long-term opponent, who could muster support from elsewhere and become a threat. Alliances and relationships, then, are essential to the life of many primates. So we should see the typical aggressive sequence as (a) a phase of aggression, (b) a readjustment or acknowledgement of dominance position or resolution of some other issue, then (c) a reconciliation on the basis of the readjustment. As Visalberghi and Sonetti put it: in terms of either a species or an individual "aggression would be fatal if mechanisms to restore positive interactions were not present as well" (p. 66). Without reconciliation, cooperative relations would suffer dramatically, and perhaps not be possible.

The species-characteristic mechanisms on which dominance is based may indeed be seeds of emotional dynamics that establish social hierarchies amongst humans. Sociologists have long claimed that people who rise in social hierarchies have a certain charisma (Weber, 1947) or emotional energy (Collins, 1990). Moldoveanu and Nohria (2002) have shown how, in organizations, despite all the explicit talk being of rationality, decision making, and so on, competitive social motivations, including envy, are the more important influences.

Recent experimental work highlights in more specific fashion how emotions like anger establish positions of power, and emotions like embarrassment or shame are associated with low status positions in social hierarchies (for review, see Keltner, Gruenfeld, & Anderson, 2003). For example, Larissa Tiedens and her colleagues have found that people assume that high power people respond to difficulties with anger (Tiedens, 2000), and in another study, participants attributed more elevated status to an individual who displays anger (Tiedens, 2001; see also Keltner, Young, & Buswell, 1997; Knutson, 1996). In recent work, Timothy Ketelaar has actually found that the same individual displaying anger in the face is assumed to be larger physically than when displaying a submissive emotion like embarrassment (Ketelaar, 2005).

Or consider the results of a study of teasing, a common means by which people playfully, and at times destructively, use emotion to negotiate social status (Keltner et al., 2001). In the study, fraternity members teased each other by making up nicknames and embarrassing stories about each other in foursomes comprised of two low and two high power members (Keltner et al., 1998). The individual's power was defined according to his position in the fraternity. As you can see in table 9.1, high power members tended to display smiles of pleasure, anger, and contempt, emotions associated with high power. In contrast, the low power members were more likely to show submissive emotions like fear and pain (see also Öhman, 1986).

Cross-cultural variations in the management of anger

A fascinating aspect of the cross-cultural study of emotions is to see how different societies regard anger. Some view it as destructive and to be avoided. One such culture is the Utku, an Inuit group living near the Arctic Circle. Briggs (1970) has written about the 17 months during 1963 to 1965 she spent living with her adoptive family, a couple and their children. The community consisted of 35 people in eight families. They lived mainly on fish, and they trapped foxes which they exchanged for industrial goods at Gjoa Haven, a trading post 150 miles away. In winter they lived in an igloo village; in summer families dispersed to different camping sites and lived in tents.

What seemed most remarkable to Briggs was that Utku adults did not express anger interpersonally, and they did not use anger or threats in child rearing. Young children were treated with indulgence and were never scolded. By contrast, the Utku were alarmed by Briggs's propensity for anger. During her stay, she did sometimes become angry with the cold and physical

Table 9.1 In groups of four, high power (HP) and low power (LP) fraternity members teased one another. During these interactions, high power individuals were more likely to smile with delight, and to show facial displays of anger and contempt, especially when being challenged by a low power member. Low power fraternity members, in contrast, were more likely to show displays of fear and pain

	High power (HP)		Low power (LP)	
	Teasing LP	Teased by LP	Teasing HP	Teased by HP
Duchenne smiles	83.3	95.8	56.5	95.8
Facial anger	8.3	25.0	0.0	0.0
Facial contempt	4.2	16.7	0.0	0.0
Facial fear	0.0	0.0	16.7	8.3
Facial pain	4.2	4.2	12.3	25.0

Note: Duchenne smiles involve the action of the *zygomatic* major muscle, which pulls the lip corners up, and the *orbicularis oculi* muscle surrounding the eye, and are closely tied to the experience of positive emotion.

hardship, and at such events as children constantly wanting her supplies of raisins. Then, in the summer toward the end of her stay, there was a pivotal occasion. Some Canadian vacationers had come north from the city, had borrowed one of the two canoes owned by the Utku families, and had carelessly damaged it. The Utku response to this, as to all such events, was calm and smiling acceptance. Then the vacationers wanted to borrow the other canoe! Briggs confronted them angrily, on behalf of her adopted family who lived so precariously and with so few possessions, all of which were needed for survival. The result was that the Utku found it subsequently very hard to have anything to do with Briggs: a person who could be angry in such an alien way. (In case any reader might think that Briggs is especially prone to anger, one of us, KO, who has met her, can vouch that by Euro-American standards she is charming and amiable.)

In contrast with the lives of the Inuit, Chagnon (1968) went to stay for 19 months on three visits, between 1964 and 1968, with a group called the Yanomamö who live by hunting and growing vegetables in the forests of southern Venezuela and northern Brazil. The Yanomamö conceive of themselves as a fierce people. They live in chronic warfare and shifting alliances between neighboring villages. Individual aggression is common, as is collective aggression when groups of men go on raiding parties to other villages intending to kill at least one man on each raid, and to abduct women if possible. Chagnon recorded that during the time of his fieldwork, one of the villages in which he lived was raided approximately 25 times (p. 2). He estimated that among the Yanomamö, while "54% of all adult deaths were due to malaria and other infectious diseases . . . 24% of adult males die in warfare" (p. 20).

Children are brought up to be fierce in their interactions with each other. Eibl-Eibesfeldt (1979, p. 157) describes how he filmed an incident in which a small Yanomamö girl was instructed by her mother on how to hit and bite her brother in retaliation for some wrong. In his stay with the Yanomamö, Chagnon describes how he had to find fierce ways of dealing with angry threats such as "Don't point your camera at me or I'll hit you" (p. 8). He became more skilled at angrily rebuffing such approaches, and at retaliating when his supplies were stolen.

The Yanomamö live in huts, each occupied by a family, and grouped together in villages. The smallest size of village was about 40 people. Chagnon estimates that this minimum size is set by needing to raise at least 15 adult males for a raiding party. The largest villages were about 250 people, and maximum size seemed to be set by disputes becoming so frequent that the village divides in two, with one party going off to start a new village elsewhere. Although only men take part in raiding and organized fighting, anger and fights are frequent among women too.

Distinctive among the Yanomamö are several forms of dueling. The least destructive is chest pounding, in which one man stands while his antagonist delivers "a tremendous wallop with his fist to the man's left pectoral muscle, putting all his weight into the blow" (p. 114), raising a severe welt, causing the recipient to cough up blood for several days afterward. After one or several blows have been struck, roles are reversed and the hitter receives as many blows as he has delivered. Another common set-piece is to fight with clubs eight to ten feet long, rather like double-size pool cues. The adversaries take turns striking each other over the head with the thick end. Chagnon describes individual club fights starting within a village, for instance over a wife caught in a liaison with another man. As soon as blood begins to flow, these fights often enlarge to involve all the male members of a village getting their clubs, and joining in on one side or the other. "The tops of most men's heads are covered with long ugly scars of which their bearers are immensely proud" (p. 119).

There have been, and are still, many societies in which anger plays a predominant role, because the self must be asserted against others. One mode, which seems to recur throughout history and across cultures, is male-dominated, aggression-based, power and revenge. This is the pattern among the Yanomamö, but it is common, and much celebrated elsewhere. We see it in Homer's *Iliad*, in Aeschylus and the classical Greek playwrights' themes of cycles of family revenge, in Viking sagas (Miller, 1994), in medieval European stories of valiant knights, and in the history of industrialized warfare in modern times. However dressed up by epic tradition, or by talk of chivalry and courage, the elements are surprisingly similar: rival males fight against each other, with the spectacle and even the story of a fight creating high interest and excitement. Fighting occurs mainly in groups, but also individually. Campaigns are justified by vengeance for wrongs of others. Shifting alliances are based on economic necessity or military weakness. Some individuals emerge as heroes, their exploits marking them out. The resources they gain are displayed conspicuously (Veblen, 1899), and others admire rather than envy. Despite our primate heritage of reconciliation, it is not difficult to feel that such aggressive violence will, in the end, be our undoing. As the poet W. B. Yeats put it, meditating on the orgies of destruction known as World War I:

> Things fall apart; the centre cannot hold;
> Mere anarchy is loosed upon the world,
> The blood dimmed tide is loosed . . .

The role of anger in aggressive societies is that it fires people to perform deeds of which they would be otherwise incapable. Again and again, narrative accounts of aggressive exploits go to lengths to explain how anger creates courage and justifies slaughter. So, in the _Iliad_, Achilles reenters the war with Troy after his long sulk, in vengeful rage because his close friend Patroclos was killed (Homer, _c_.850 BCE). Erec, in Chrétien De Troyes's medieval story of Erec and Enide (Chrétien De Troyes, 1180), goes out looking for fights because his wife has shamed him by saying that people think he has become soft, and devoted himself to the pleasures of love. Chagnon (1968), in his account of the Yanomamö, describes Damowa, the head and fiercest man of Monou-teri village. He and his men set out in anger to raid Patanowa-teri village because its men had managed to recapture five of seven women Damowa's raiders had abducted. In the inevitable return raid, Damowa was ambushed while he was in his village garden with two of his wives and a child. He was shot with arrows and killed. Next his brother affirmed solidarity with allies, and organized the necessary return raid.

Fighting fueled by anger, in our species as in certain other mammalian species, functions at least in part as the lever of individual power to control resources, including the resources of access to females who in aggressive societies typically have a rank inferior to that of men. It suspends fear and reduces consideration for other people. But as with passionate love, contradictions are evident. Anyone from a nonviolent society reading the violent history of Europe and America would be appalled, uncomprehending.

Vengeance is a frequent accompaniment of anger. Yet from a functional point of view it seems puzzling. As Frijda (1994) points out, it does nothing to right the wrong that was suffered, it is often harmful to the individual who wreaks revenge, and it is immoderate, often far exceeding the original offence. What seems to be going on is that as an emotion vengefulness is highly social: it seeks to restore a balance of power, and the threat of it can deter. As Axelrod (1984) has shown, tit-for-tat is a highly successful social strategy – it is not clear whether in some conflictual situations there is a better one – and this may be how it evolved. Moreover, if one is humiliated, then to take revenge means at least that the other does not enjoy the fruits of his or her act. And if revenge requires plans that extend over months or years, it may be because the social inequity was too flagrant. At the same time, cycles of revenge have often been seen as fatal to the social order. The Biblical law "an eye for an eye" is not the expression of cruelty, but a restraint on it. The world's great playwrights, including Aeschylus and Shakespeare, have returned again and again to patterns of vengeance that are destructive, and to the possibilities of replacing them with societal processes. Peaceable life in Western societies has included the control of feuding in which cycles of revenge and counter revenge, of triumph and shame, constantly escalate. Instead, righting of wrongs is given to supra-personal agencies, the police and the courts.

Cultural codes

Often in response to anger, the target also gets angry, in a symmetrical way. But a pattern that is complementary to anger is fear. Öhman (1986) has shown that although one pattern of fear evolved from escaping from predators, social fear is a separate pattern: a response in deference to social anger. In societies which are very hierarchical, or where power is frequently asserted, those who are not powerful need to be wary.

Shweder (1990) has proposed that all societies are based on one of three ethical codes, though as we describe these you will see traces of the other codes in the one with which you are most familiar. In much of the West the code is of autonomy and individual rights. Its emotion is anger at moral trespass, resulting in social readjustment as individuals establish their rights against any who infringe them. Its social enactment is the law suit. Not far beneath this, barely concealed, is the morality of the dominance hierarchy, where individuals acquire and defend position and resources, while others tolerate the inequities that result. A quite different kind of society is based on an ethics of divinity, on the idea of the self as a spiritual entity that has to be protected against contamination, from food and other pollutants. In such societies, as Rozin, Haidt, and McCauley (1993) show, the emotion at the center is disgust. Yet other kinds of societies are based on an ethics of duty, and for these Rozin et al. suggest that twin emotions of contempt and honor are at the center, as actions of the self as well as of other people are appraised and commented upon in terms of what is proper and what is improper.

Gender relations

The biological term for being female or male is sex. We derive it from our genes. But the term for one's female or male social role is gender, and it is a pervasive theme in life. Whereas in many societies, past and present, women spent most of their time with women, and men with men, gender has perhaps become more pressing in the modern Western world, because women and men now interact more than in former times.

As compared with men, women are thought of as more emotionally express-ive, and more emotionally sensitive, more interested in emotions. This is a

stereotype but it is important because it represents a folk theory, and hence an expectation about how women and men will behave. As Stephanie Shields (2002) has explained, it also represents a set of normative standards of appropriateness that affect how people do indeed behave. Although some people find the restricting assignment to gender roles unsatisfactory, children are almost always socialized into one or the other gender role, and usually in adulthood they maintain that role.

As Agneta Fischer and Tony Manstead (2000) explain, stereotypically female emotions include happiness and fear, the emotions of affiliation and sub-missiveness, while stereotypically male emotions include anger and other emotions of dominance (see also Fischer, 2000). Confirming this, Hess, Adams, and Kleck (2005) found in three experiments that women were expected to be less dominant and to smile more, while men were expected to be more dominant and to frown more. When emotions have been observed, expected differences between women and men have been found. For instance, in their review of evidence in this field, Brody and Hall (2000) conclude that while women have been found to show warmth, happiness, shame, and fear more frequently and more intensely than did men, men's expressions have been found to show more pride, loneliness, and contempt, which are consistent with male roles of maintaining high status, individualism, and independence. The size of the gender effects in observational studies has, however, often not been found to be as large as would be expected from the stereotypes of the social roles.

Both in terms of the stereotypes and empirical results, if you have an emotion to confide, you would probably be better doing it with a woman, regardless of your own gender. Women are on average more empathetic, more able to offer better social support. So the female role meshes with prioritization of social goals of nurturance and affiliation. As Fischer and Manstead (2000) say: "Caring requires emotional commitment, sensitivity to others, and the ability to help others deal with negative feelings" (p. 75). But as they point out, however admirable these attributes are, they are also associated with low status.

We might expect that gender and power affect intimate relationships, and this is so. In their research on factors that predict marital breakdown (discussed above), Gottman and Levenson (2000) have found that two of the maneuvers they describe as toxic – defensiveness and stonewalling – are especially destructive when performed by men. By contrast, contempt is especially predictive of marital dissatisfaction and divorce when it is expressed by women.

In humans, anger is not as closely tied to asserting and defending hierarchical positions as among other primates, though at least one recent and widely popular analysis has it that Western men relate to each other primarily by locating themselves in dominance hierarchies (Tannen, 1991), even when overt aggression does not occur.

Imbalances in power and respect that are related to gender do vary in different cultures. Leakey and Lewin (1991) point out that male dominance and a corresponding lower position of women is somewhat associated with the proportion of food acquired by hunting. Where hunting is important men tend to occupy a higher rank associated with providing the group with meat and with joyful celebrations that occur with a catch. When humans hunt for a living it is usually men who do it. The Chambri (Gewertz, 1981) are a near exception; for them fishing is an important part of life, and it's women who do it. An implication of these kinds of conclusions is that as patterns of labor change with modernization, patterns of power, and their emotional accompaniments are likely to change too.

Emotions between groups

In 1949 Muzafer Sherif and Carolyn Sherif (1953) performed an experiment on the formation and interaction of human groups. They invited boys aged 11 to 12 to go on what was for them a standard summer camp in the country. The boys were were white, healthy, well adjusted, from stable lower-middle-class homes, and all had around average intelligence (a mean IQ of 105). The main data gathering was by participant observers who were graduate students, but who appeared to the boys as camp counselors. Muzafer Sherif himself took the role of caretaker; this enabled him also to observe, and to ask the boys occasional naive questions. Activities were arranged to be interesting; the boys plunged into them without suspecting that they were being observed. In Phase 1 all 24 boys, who had not previously known each other, were housed together for three days. All activities occurred on a basis of personal interest and choice. The boys quickly formed friendships, and chose buddies.

In Phase 2 (five days), two evenly matched groups were formed, taking care to separate best friends. Each group now had its own cabin to sleep in. The pain of separation was assuaged by each group going on a separate hike and camp-out, which the boys found exciting. In this phase, kitchen duties, games, and all other activities were done in the separate groups, and all rewards were on a group basis. Each group quickly developed its own culture. In each a leader emerged and rough hierarchies formed with structures that were remarkably similar to those described by Goodall (1986) among chimpanzees. The boys chose names for their groups, "Bulldogs" and "Red Devils," developed insignia, established territories, customs, and nicknames.

The leader of the Bulldogs rose to his position "by his greater contribution to the planning and execution of common activities and by regulating and integrating the tasks and roles of the group members" (p. 252), including those for quite complicated activities such as improving the bunkhouse, building a latrine, and creating a secret swimming place. That is to say that, unlike among the chimpanzees, he became the alpha of the group without the use of threats. He praised others for their work, gave support, showed concern for other members including those of low rank in the group. Only once was he seen to threaten a group member (verbally, p. 262), though punishments included removing stones from the swimming place. These were seen as "fair." The Bulldogs' solidarity occurred by collaborating on joint goals that all wanted to achieve. Although the focus of the study was not on emotions as such, the account of affection among the Bulldogs is striking.

Although the Red Devils also achieved group cohesion, their style contrasted. They had greater distance between the more and less popular boys, the leader was cliquish, favoring his lieutenants. He "sometimes enforced his decisions by threats or actual physical encounters" (p. 259), and used "roughing up" as punishment. Despite this, he remained the "acknowledged leader and had great prestige within the group" (p. 259).

Each group achieved stability, and the predominant tone was one of interpersonal harmony, without competition with the other group. Bonding to the group and among its individuals was high. The choices of friends that had been made in Phase 1 were revised, and at the end of Phase 2 about 90 percent of the friendships were within the group.

So, it seems, groups can function primarily on the basis of affection and shared activities, as with bonobos' interest in sex or with the Bulldogs' interest in organizing joint plans for agreed goals of the group. They can also function on the basis of dominance, as with chimpanzees, or as the Red Devils did on occasion.

Intergroup conflict

Both humans and chimpanzees are adapted to cooperating together in smallish groups: they do this in food gathering, in rearing young, in hunting, and in fighting. It seems to be an aspect of humankind's remarkable capacity for emotional bonding within cooperative groups that others outside these groups can become targets for hostility (cf. Sober & Wilson, 1998).

Perhaps the most extraordinary of Goodall's (1986) observations on the chimpanzees of Gombe occurred when she recognized the formation of a new community, when the original one divided. The smaller contingent, which had tended to range south of Goodall's camp, had six adult males. Though the two sub-communities met occasionally, for example to get fruit at Goodall's camp, and though some inter-individual contacts were sometimes friendly, in general the two groups were tense on meeting. They started to avoid each other. Finally southern males stopped visiting the camp. In 1974 violent episodes began. Northern males, who would patrol their borders, started to make incursions into the southern range. On one of these a group, consisting of six adult males, an adolescent male, and a female, came across a southern male on his own. He tried to flee but was caught by the northern males. While one held him, the other males beat him with fists for about 10 minutes, and one bit him several times. When they left him he was severely wounded, and although his body was never found, he was presumed to have died from his injuries. One by one all the other adult animals of the southern group, including a female, were killed in like manner. Adolescent females from the southern group joined the northern group.

The attacks clearly were meant to kill: they lasted longer than those within a community, and included biting and tearing flesh of the kind seen when eating animals of other species. Attacks were not caused by victims being strangers. Some had previously been friends of some of the attackers.

Attacks were only made by roving gangs of northern males on individuals or on numerically weaker groups in the southern community. So, annihilating the southern community seemed not predominantly territorial. Hostilities seemed to have more to do with the southerners becoming an **out-group**. They became "them," no longer "us."

The emotional preference for "us," and hostility to "them," is indeed a candidate for a biologically inherited human universal. This can be seen in several lines of research. Tajfel's studies have been discussed widely (Tajfel & Turner, 1979). They consist of assigning people, such as schoolchildren, to groups randomly (that is to say meaninglessly) and then showing that people give preference to other members of the group of which they had been told they were members (the in-group) even when they did not know who was in that group or who was in the out-group, and even when their actions and preferences had no effect on themselves.

We described above Phases 1 and 2 of Sherif's studies of within-group relations of boys at a summer camp (Sherif, 1956; Sherif & Sherif, 1953). In Phase 3 the investigators studied relations between groups. They arranged a tournament of competitions between the two groups, the Bulldogs and the Red Devils, including tug-of-war, football, and baseball, with cumulating points and coveted prizes of camping knives for every member of the group that got the most points. Success of one group would mean failure for the other. At this point – though not before – boys started to make distinctions between "us" and "them." Accusations and name-calling began between the groups. Fights between members of one group and the other started to occur. Frustration increased angry attitudes and actions towards the out-group. A proud, self-glorifying attitude arose. Each group believed itself to be strong and fearless. Each individual believed himself to possess all the strengths of the whole group. While an affectionate, inter-reliant attitude was present within the in-group, the out-group was seen to have very negative qualities.

More recently, Diane Mackie and Eliot Smith and their colleagues have offered an account of what factors account for the emergence of aggressive anger and contempt between groups, so richly documented in Sherif's work (Mackie et al., 2000; Mackie, Devos, & E. R. Smith, 2000; Mackie & Smith, 2002; E. R. Smith, 1993; see also Dumont et al., 2003; Yzerbyt et al., 2003). They have found that anger directed at the out-group is more likely when group members individually feel that their group is strong vis-à-vis the out-group, and when the members are strongly identified with the group. Once again, dominance and assertiveness, this time between groups, give rise to emotions like anger.

We described above how a solution to the problem of interpersonal feuding has been to devolve such feuds to an authority such as the police. But what if the police behave in an us-and-them way? In his book, *Blink* (2005),

Malcolm Gladwell discusses how police officers are more liable to behave inappropriately when in groups than when alone, and also when emotionally over-aroused by occasions such as high-speed car chases. The widely publicized beating in 1991 of Rodney King, a black man, by a group of police officers in Los Angeles, happened after a high-speed car chase.

It is partly because police in groups tend not to think as well as they ought that some US police departments now have officers patrolling singly, and some have banned high-speed chases. But what can be done more generally about inter-group hostility? Sherif explored one solution in the summer camp study. One summer, with one pair of groups, he tried arranging for everyone to share a meal together. But one group arrived before the other and ate most of the food. The other group was furious: a fight occurred and the meal had to be abandoned. The method the investigators finally hit upon was not meeting together but cooperating on **joint projects**. One such was when the investigators arranged that the water supply to the camp was cut off. The boys had to search for the problem in the long pipeline coming into the camp, and then repair it. They could only do this by both groups cooperating. Another was when the boys were hungry and the investigators arranged that the truck, which was to go to town to get food, would not start. The boys used a rope – one that had been used in the tug-of-war competitions, to pull together to start the truck. Hostility did not cease immediately, but after a number of such co-operative activities it was much reduced (see figure 9.4).

Another solution is **forgiveness**, which has its roots in the reconciliation processes nonhuman primates so routinely engage in to maintain

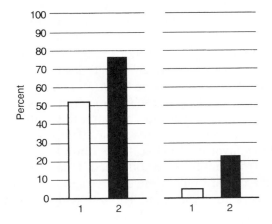

Figure 9.4 Hostility toward an out-group in Sherif's study. On the left the open histogram shows the proportion of boys in group 1 who thought that *all* (rather than some or none) in group 2 were cheaters, sneaks, and so forth, while the solid histogram shows the proportion of group 2 who thought that all members of group 1 were cheaters, sneaks, and so forth. On the right are comparable histograms after harmony had been restored by cooperative activities.

peaceful communities. Forgiveness has been a central aim of cultures in the wake of devastating group conflict. In South Africa after the end of apartheid, the Truth and Reconciliation Commission set out to bring white perpetrators of violence face to face with their black victims, with the intention of promoting forgiveness. A similar approach has been pursued following the genocide in Rwanda, in which 800,000 Tutsis were massacred by their Hutu compatriots.

The scientific study of forgiveness suggests that such procedures may be worth the many difficulties. Forgiveness involves the release of negative feelings and increased compassion and empathy toward the perpetrator of injustice (McCullough, 2000; McCullough, Sandage, & Worthington, 1997; Worthington, 1998). Forgiveness appears to have salutary effects. In one study participants were asked to imagine a grudge they held against someone (whom they had not forgiven) or forgiving someone who had harmed them (Witvliet, Ludwig, & Vander Laan, 2001). Participants who imagined being harmed unjustly but who also forgave showed lower blood pressure, less stress-related heart rate increase and skin conductance response in the hands, and reduced brow furrowing associated with anger (see also Lawler et al., 2003). In a study of actual harm, Snyder and Heinze (2005) found that among people who had been sexually or physically abused in childhood, forgiveness, particularly of the self and of the situation, was able to lessen both hostility and psychiatric symptoms of the survivors.

Violence between societies

When whole societies are disrupted, as has occurred when traditional societies have been invaded by industrial ones, violence has often become widespread. In the Americas, for instance, the cultures of native peoples, including hunter-gatherer groups, the alliance of independent nations of the Iroquois League, the city-based states of Mexico, Guatemala, and Peru, and many other kinds of society, were almost all destroyed (Wright, 1992).

On May 15, 1521, after the Aztec chief Montezuma had formally, and tearfully, signed papers making himself a subject of King Charles V of Spain, acquiescing to the invaders' demands, and after the Spaniards had ransacked his family's treasures, a group of Aztec nobles had asked permission to hold a spring festival that involved dancing. The Spanish leader Cortez had agreed, on condition that the nobles were unarmed. One of Cortez's lieutenants, Alvarado, took the opportunity of the unwary gathering to stage a massacre of the Aztec officers and noblemen. The following is from an account by an Aztec, written down by a Spanish missionary:

> They [the Spaniards] appeared suddenly [at the festival] in battle array . . . quickly they surrounded the dancers; then they rushed among the drums. They hacked at the drummer and cut off both his hands; they chopped off his head and it fell away. Then they ran the people through with iron spears, and slashed at them with iron swords. Some they cut open from behind and these fell to the ground with their intestines hanging out . . . The

blood . . . ran like water, like slimy water, the stench of blood filled the air, and the entrails seemed to slither along by themselves. (Wright, 1992, p. 40)

Such scenes have been enacted time and again when societies have clashed. On the opposite side of the world, Dentan describes how the Semai became involved in a war with Communist troops in Malaya. People had thought the Semai would never make soldiers because they were such a nonviolent society, but when some of their people were killed then, outside the context of their culture, their behavior was different. One typical Semai veteran said: "We killed, killed, killed. The Malays would stop and go through people's pockets and take their watches and money, we did not think of taking watches and money. We thought only of killing" (Dentan, 1968, p. 59).

The relation of aggression to anger is not well understood. On the one hand, cycles of revenge occur in many societies, and are certainly associated with anger. But violent events such as these seem to go beyond anger to an appalling capacity of people in our species, usually acting in groups, to treat people of other cultures as **nonhuman**.

Disgust and contempt

Probably the best way to begin to understand these phenomena is to think not just in terms of anger, though this may also be involved, but in terms of the emotions of disgust and contempt. Though primarily taking impersonal objects, disgust can also be felt toward people. Here, for instance, is a description of the result of the Aztecs under Montezuma offering a gift of precious works of art in gold and other materials, hoping to buy off the aggression of Cortez and the Spaniard invaders:

The Spaniards faces grinned: they were delighted, they were overjoyed. They snatched up the gold like monkeys . . . They were swollen with greed; they were ravenous; they hungered for that gold like wild pigs . . . They babbled in a barbarous language; everything they said was in a savage tongue. (Wright, 1992, p. 26)

The Aztecs, from whose eye-witness reports this is taken, observed the Spaniards' behavior with disgust, seeing those alien others as behaving not as people but as animals. As Rozin, Haidt, and McCauley (1993) have shown, disgust, though originally derived from taste, often extends from protecting the body from disease, to protection against contamination of all kinds, to anything that might harm our soul, or the social order.

If the Aztecs were disgusted in the above account, what are we modern people to say? Instead of the politeness with which a gift is received from an equal within a culture, the Spaniards behaved with contempt. Not just in the eyes of the Aztecs, but also in the eyes of us moderns, their behavior was appalling. To have in our emotional repertoire the possibilities of such contempt toward members of our own species is a taint we humans share.

Though in some ways similar to disgust, contempt is, however, separate. It is the emotion of rejection of members of out-groups. The term most often used in this context is prejudice. To see opponents as non-people is often a critical move in warlike relations. It allows them to be massacred, tortured, enslaved, without a thought. Hitler's Nazis were able to convince themselves that Jews, homosexuals, gypsies, and other minority groups were non-people who could be annihilated. In accounts of concentration camps aggressive cruelty often occurred, but the main killer was contemptuous indifference, the treatment of people as non-people, as things (Levi, 1958).

When different societies meet, a typical repertoire of emotions is elicited: first is an anxious distrust, perhaps hostility, perhaps a tentative friendliness. One can read about such reactions in the early European meetings with the native inhabitants of the Americas (Wright, 1992), in Captain Cook's meetings with native peoples of the Pacific, or in modern meetings with the few remaining groups previously untroubled by inter-cultural contact (Nance, 1975). What happens next is more problematic.

Wright makes the point in describing the European conquest of the Americas that both the Spaniards and the Aztecs were fierce and warlike peoples. The Europeans, however, had a secret weapon. To the New World they carried European infections and diseases such as measles, influenza, smallpox, cholera, and malaria which Chagnon describes as now responsible for a high proportion of adult deaths among the Yanomamö. The invaders had developed resistance to these diseases. Native peoples of the Americas had none because the diseases had not existed there. In 1492 when Columbus landed in the New World, there were perhaps 100 million people living in the Americas, about a fifth of the world's population at the time. By 1600 disease had reduced the native population to perhaps 10 million (Wright, 1992, p. 14). To grasp the scale of this, imagine that half the people you know, previously in good health, were to die within the next few years, including your parents, children, the knowledgeable, those in responsible positions. This aspect of the European invasion of the Americas is a tragedy.

Deaths from sickness were not at first deliberate, but infection was later used by Europeans as a means of killing native people. Wright (1992) informs us that: "Lord Jeffrey Amhurst secured his place in history [in 1763] as the inventor of modern germ warfare with this notorious command, 'Infect the Indians with sheets upon which smallpox patients have been lying, or by any other means which may serve to exterminate this cursed race'" (p. 136). The term tragedy is not adequate for this and other deliberate aspects of the European conquest, forwarded principally by its firearms and iron-based technology, and characterized by its utter disregard of human standards of behavior. In reading about this, we feel as we do when we read of the deliberate destruction of six million civilians by the Nazis because they were members of an out-group.

The emotions of war may be yet more complex: sometimes impelled by material greed, very often fueled by angry revenge, almost invariably insu-lated from compassion for those who are contemptuously killed, almost always fostered by close bonding within a male group which cultivates its traditions and heroes. In these ways warriors down the ages and across cultures have experienced their own emotional excitements. It may be, as Keegan (1994) says in what has been regarded as the best history of warfare yet written (one that includes anthropological evidence), that: "War is almost as old as man himself, and reaches into the most secret places of the human heart, places where self dissolves rational purpose, where pride reigns, where emotion is paramount, where instinct is king" (p. 3).

The **warrior mentality** is part of the human repertoire, but to be expressed it needs to be culturally cultivated, and cultures change. So, as Keegan points out, in medieval times the Vikings were universally feared round the coasts of Northern Europe, their name a synonym for ruthless aggression. Now Scandinavians are known for peaceable neutrality and tolerance. Canadians were among the fiercest fighters of World War II; now the Canadian army is known for its peacekeeping role. A convincing aspect of Keegan's history is the evidence he gives that warfare is a cultural form that can and does wither when social arrangements no longer support it. Its roots, however, are not so much political as emotional. When these roots are watered by loyalties to an ethnic, religious, or other cultural group, and by emotions of revenge, or shame for humiliations, the warlike mentality quickly arises again in all its destructive force.

But if emotions are to some extent universal, then as well as separating people they can build links. Just as empathy becomes an emotional foundation of children's sense of morality toward other children, emotional empathy for other people and other cultures can provide a foundation for an intercultural morality. If there were no universals of emotions, there would be no basis for concerted world action on anything, no human sympathy for the oppressed, no outrage against tyranny, no passion for justice, no concern for protecting or sharing the world's limited resources.

Summary

In this chapter we propose that emotions structure social relationships, and they are commitments to these relationships. We saw that there are three primary social goals or motivations: attachment, affiliation, and assertion. We considered how romantic relationships depend on attachment, on caregiving which has an affiliative core, and erotic attraction. In evolutionary terms, attachment and affiliation form the childhood bases for the co-operative arrangements of families and societies, on which the human adaptation depends. Human societies are also widely dominated by status hierarchies. Anger, within a society, is typically an emotion of trying to improve one's status or to maintain it, and it is typically followed by reconciliation in which some aspect of the relationship is renegotiated. Although some interdependent societies avoid anger, in individualistic societies anger functions to enable assertion of the self in conflictual situations. In contrast to anger, the emotion of contempt is of rejection of someone or some group from society, and it amounts to treating others as non-people. Though anger and contempt both share a repertoire of aggressive action, there are reasons for distinguishing them. Among societies, contempt enables out-groups to be denied human rights.

Further reading

For an excellent recent review, by leading scholars, of research on emotions in social life:
Larissa Tiedens and Colin Leach (Eds.) (2004). *The social life of emotions.* New York: Cambridge University Press.

Among the several interesting books recently published on love, one with a number of useful articles is:
Robert Sternberg & Michael Barnes (Eds.) (1988). *The psychology of love.* New Haven, CT: Yale University Press.

Among the best single author works on love is a book by an anthropologist:
Helen Fisher (1992). *Anatomy of love.* New York: Norton.

The best general book on anger, in our view, is:
Carol Tavris (1982). *Anger: The misunderstood emotion.* New York: Simon & Schuster.

For the emotions of war one could scarcely do better than:
John Keegan (1994). *A history of warfare.* New York: Vintage.

CHAPTER 10

The heart has its reasons of which reason knows nothing.
Blaise Pascal, Pensées, iv

Emotions and Cognition

Figure 10.0 Reason, advised by Divine Grace, holds the Passions, Feare, Despaire, Choler, and others in chains. The caption starts: "Passions araing'd by Reason here you see / As she's Advis'd by Grace Divine . . ." From Senault (1671).

Contents

On July 2, 1860 Eadweard Muybridge, a founding figure in photography, boarded a stagecoach for St. Louis, where he was to catch a train and then make his way to Europe to buy rare books for his San Francisco bookstore. In Northeastern Texas the driver of the stagecoach lost control of the horses, and the coach careened down a mountainside. In the crash, Muybridge was thrown headfirst into a tree. Miraculously he survived, and although he suffered serious brain damage, he made the trip to England, where he spent six vague years recuperating.

Muybridge returned to California in 1866, but he was not the same man. His photography had an eerily risky and often obsessive quality. He would take thousands of photographs of animals in motion, and uncover certain principles of movement. He took hundreds of photos of himself, often naked, with his characteristic furrowed brow, glaring into the camera.

In 1872 Muybridge married Flora Shallcross Stone, 21 years his junior. Not long after the wedding, while Muybridge was away on assignment, Flora had an affair with a dashing young man, Harry Larkyns, and from this assignation had a baby. At an acquaintance's house, Muybridge saw a photo of the baby he thought was his, and casually looked to the back of the photo. On it were written the words "Little Harry." The acquaintance confirmed Muybridge's suspicion that the baby was not his.

Muybridge went to the ranch in Calistoga, California where Larkyns worked. He found Larkyns amongst some friends. Muybridge greeted him by stating in a matter of fact way: "I am Muybridge, and this is a message from my wife." He raised a Smith & Wesson No. 2 six shooter, shot, and killed Larkyns.

At Muybridge's highly publicized trial, witnesses spoke of how different he seemed upon his return from England. Silas Selleck, a friend and fellow photographer observed: "After his return from Europe he was very eccentric, and so very unlike his way before going." M. Gray noted that before the accident Muybridge was "much less irritable than after his return; was much more careless in dress after his return." J. G. Easland testified that after the accident Muybridge had "certain eccentricities of speech, manner, and action."

Muybridge had damaged his orbitofrontal cortex. In chapters 1 and 5, we have referred to Damasio's work with people who have suffered the same kind of damage, which has had effects on their emotions and social lives. Here we extend that line of thought. Without a functioning orbitofrontal cortex and the information that an array of social emotions provide, people lack judgment. We might say they become no longer **rational**. They do not appreciate or abide by morals, norms, and conventions. If most of us are admixtures of Dr Jekyll and Mr Hyde (Stevenson, 1886), people with this kind of brain damage can be tilted toward Mr Hyde, and engage in impulsive and immoral acts. We see Eadweard Muybridge's shooting of Larkyns as driven by jealousy, and we can understand that jealousy. In his case, however, this emotion became a compulsion, unaffected by other emotions: love for the child he had thought was his son who was innocent of the events that upset Muybridge, compassion for his victim, fear of the consequences for himself. To be functioning members of society, our emotions need to be in working order in relation to each other, so that they may guide our reasoning and action wisely.

One of the most striking qualities of emotions is how they influence our reasoning. The philosopher Jean Paul Sartre referred to this as **magical transformation** by the emotions of how we see the world. This is reflected in the many aphorisms that capture the effects of emotion upon cognition: we see the world through "jaundiced eyes" or "rose colored glasses." When angry, afraid, euphoric, or in love, we construe the world in different lights. We are aware of different themes, or events. We recall different experiences from our past. We envision different futures. It is as if each emotion is accompanied by its own lens through which we view and construct the world.

In this chapter we will examine how emotions influence cognition. To set the stage, let us consider one of the oldest questions in philosophy: Are emotions rational?

Historical perspectives on the interplay between passion and reason

In the Western philosophical tradition, there has tended to be suspicion of the emotions, and the position taken by the famous ethical philosophers of the third century BCE, the Epicureans and Stoics, was that to lead a good life, emotions should be extirpated altogether (Nussbaum, 1994). If Epicureans or Stoics heard about Muybridge's jealousy, they would say: "There you are, see?" Drawing on these same intuitions, many philosophers have assumed that the emotions are lower, less sophisticated, more primitive ways of perceiving the world, especially when juxtaposed with loftier forms of reason (Haidt, 2001). The implication is that human society is better off when the more primitive passions are reigned in by rational thought. The rare exception was someone like the eighteenth-century moral philosopher David Hume, who contended in a famous statement that "Reason is and ought to be the slave of passion."

What do we mean when we ask whether emotions can be rational? A first meaning has to do with whether the emotions are based on substantive beliefs. That is, do the beliefs and appraisals supporting our emotions correspond to actual events in the world? Although we often experience emotions in response to imaginary or fictitious occurrences, most often our emotions meet this criterion of rationality. The literature on emotion-related appraisal (see chapter 7) suggests that emotions are often the product of rather complex beliefs about real events in the world.

A second meaning of rationality concerns whether emotions help individuals function effectively in the social world. We think of rational human beings as those who navigate their environment effectively. Delusional beliefs of grandiosity or persecution, for example, are irrational in this sense. They make it more difficult for the individual to be effective, functioning members of society. A central assumption of this book is that emotions in many contexts are rational in that they help individuals respond adaptively to the environment. This is not true all the time, as we shall see in chapters 12 and 13, but many, if not most, occurrences of emotion help people respond adaptively.

A third meaning is particularly relevant to this chapter. Do emotions guide cognitive processes like perception, attention, memory, and judgment in principled, organized, and constructive ways? Or do they interfere and disrupt cognitive processes? Certainly extreme levels of emotion can get the better of our rational thought. For example, extreme anger may prevent us from perceiving the cooperative gestures of an ideological opponent or romantic partner. Yet, 25 years of research – the focus of this chapter – generally suggest that emotions have principled, systematic effects upon cognitive processes, and that emotions lead to reasonable judgments of the world (Clore & Parrott, 1991; Clore, Gasper, & Garvin, 2001; Forgas, 1995, 2003; Gasper & Clore, 1998; Isen, 1987). Emotions structure perception, direct attention, give preferential access to certain memories, and bias judgment in ways that help the individual respond to the environment in ways that we recognize as valuable aspects of our humanity.

Emotions as prioritizers of thoughts, goals, and actions

The notion that emotions guide cognitive processes in rational, adaptive fashion emerged within a movement known as cognitive science, which matured in the 1960s, and included among its methods the construction of mind-like processes in computers. The question for this kind of activity is: if one had to design a mind, what problems would have to be faced, what principles embodied, what considerations included, not just for humans, but for any intelligent being?

In an influential paper, Simon (1967) argued that emotions would be necessary in any intelligent being; a human, a Martian, or – if we were ever able to create it – an intelligent computer. Emotions, Simon continued, are a solution to a general problem: they set priorities among the many different goals that impinge upon individuals at any moment in time (see also Tomkins, 1995).

This need for some sort of interrupt and prioritization mechanism necessarily emerges in complex organisms like humans (De Sousa, 1987; Oatley, 1992). In very simple animals behavior is controlled by reflexes. Take the behavior of the female tick as an example (Von Uexküll, 1934). After mating, she climbs a tree and hangs at the end of a lower twig. When she detects a particular stimulus – the smell of butyric acid – she lets go. Because tiny quantities of butyric acid are released into the air by mammals, letting go the branch in response to this stimulus gives a fair probability of falling onto the back of a passing mammal, such as a deer browsing beneath the branch on which the tick is hanging. If the tick lands on a mammal's back, another stimulus comes to control behavior: warm temperature causes the tick to climb through the fur toward the warmth. When she reaches the mammal's skin, another stimulus triggers burrowing into it, to suck the mammal's blood, which will be necessary for laying her eggs. In the simple world of the female tick, the perceptual system is tuned to just a few kinds of event. And in the tick's world there is no hint of emotionality.

Now imagine a different kind of being at the other end of the scale of complexity, one vastly more intelligent than ourselves, perhaps a god. A god is often conceived of as omniscient and omnipotent or, as a cognitive scientist might say, having a perfect model of the universe and no limitations of resources. Such a being could predict the results of its every action even in a complex universe. Again there is no place for emotions. Everything would be known, everything anticipated.

We humans and other mammals are somewhere in between ticks and gods. Our world is complex and we act with purposes. But our actions sometimes produce effects we did not anticipate. We have limitations of resources and knowledge. Sometimes we need encouragement to continue what we were doing. Sometimes we are better to switch goals and change plans. For us human beings events occur – small successes, losses, frustrations, threats – for which we have no ready prepared response, no skill or habit that works properly, not enough knowledge to be certain what to do next. And when such events occur, emotions signal them. They do not tell us exactly what to do next. We typically do not know enough. What they do is prompt us, create an urge and a readiness, to act in a way that on average, during the course of evolution and assisted by our own development, has been better either than simply acting randomly or than becoming lost in thought trying to calculate the best possible action.

This notion that emotions signal conflict, and redirect the individual's action, was a focus of classical Greek dramas, of some of Aristotle's work, and much of Freud's. What was new in the era of cognitive science was the idea of just how important emotions (or something like them) are, not just for human beings but for any complex intelligent system that has several motives and which operates in a complex world. Emotions guide action in a world that is always imperfectly known, and can never be fully controlled. It is not so much that emotions are irrational, rather that when we have no fully rational solution because we do not know enough, they offer bridges toward rationality.

In elaborating this view of emotions, Oatley and Johnson-Laird (1987, 1996) have proposed that emotions involve two different kinds of signaling in the nervous system, which we have discussed in chapter 7. One kind is a signal that occurs automatically and derives from what in chapter 7 we called primary appraisal. In evolutionary terms it is old, simple, and it does not carry specific information about objects in the environment. We can call it **organizational**, because it rather simply sets the brain into a particular mode of organization, or readiness, along with an urge to act in line with this readiness, specific to the particular basic emotion (happiness, sadness, fear, etc.). It has the phenomenological feeling tone of one of these emotions but no other content. Such an emotion-related signal can have many sources, both inside the body and outside in the environment (Izard, 1993). It is a quick, automatic, "guess" about the kind of thing to do next (e.g., Sebeok & Umiker-Sebeok, 1983). It is significant that phenomena of emotional priming, in which stimuli are shown subliminally (discussed in chapter 7) operate at this automatic, unconscious, level (Murphy & Zajonc, 1993; Winkielman, Zajonc, & Schwarz, 1997), and are resistant to attributional interventions.

The second kind of signal derives from what, in chapter 7, we call secondary appraisal. It is **informational**. The information it carries enables us to make mental models of the events and their possible causes and implications. On the basis of these two kinds of signal we act in accordance both with how we feel and with what we know.

Normally the organizational and informational signals occur together to produce an emotional feeling with a consciously known cause and object, in a way that help the individual respond to emergent opportunities and challenges in the environment. But the two kinds of signal can be dissociated, as we discussed in relation to split-brain patients in chapter 7. According to Oatley and Johnson-Laird (1996), the dissociation accounts for why we can sometimes have emotions with no objects, and how we can have psychoactive drugs such as tranquillizers and antidepressants that change our emotional state without doing anything whatever to the events of the world. It is also how we can know some things in the world without caring about them. Figure 10.1 is a diagram of the two kinds of signal.

To illustrate the organizational and informational aspects of an emotion, consider fear as it spreads through the brain and body. In humans, the organizational part interrupts ongoing action. It makes ready physiological mechanisms and a repertoire of actions for flight or for defensive fight, and urges us toward this kind of action. It directs attention to the environment for any sign of danger or safety, and it induces checking of the results of actions just completed. In this mode, we can think of the brain as having been simplified, and resources marshaled, to respond to danger. The emotion signal has a control function of turning on this mode. In this account emotions are like actions, they induce changes. Moods are based on the same organizational signals, but they maintain the brain in a certain mode despite events that might tend to switch it into some other mode. The informational part of fear is about the thing we are frightened of. And as we know, sometimes this thing can be quite insubstantial.

Three perspectives on the effects of emotions on cognitive functioning

In more specific terms, how do emotions guide thought processes? In what specific ways, for example, does fear shift your perception and judgment and enable you to flee or avoid danger?

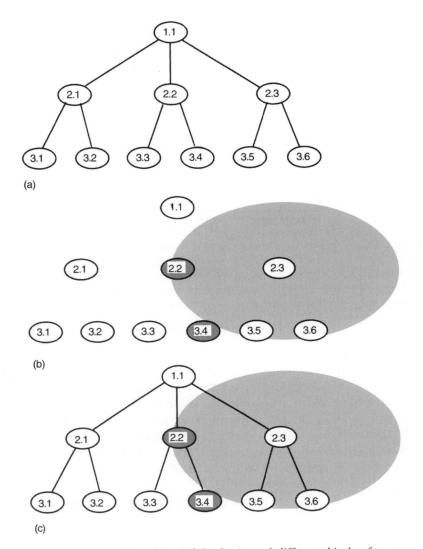

Figure 10.1 Diagram of modules of the brain and different kinds of messages passing among them (to illustrate Oatley & Johnson-Laird's (1987) theory). In (a) the signals are informational, and travel along particular pathways. In (b) is depicted the emotion control signal spreading diffusely from one module (2.3), turning some other modules on and some off, thereby setting the system into a distinctive mode. Normally (c) these two kinds of signals occur together.

Emotion congruence

One view of how moods and emotions influence cognition was articulated by Gordon Bower, an influential memory researcher. According to his perspective, moods and emotions are associative networks in the mind (Bower, 1981; Mayer et al., 1992). In memory, there are pathways devoted

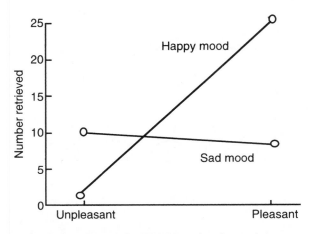

Figure 10.2 A result from Bower's (1981) study of people's memories from before the age of 15. The figure shows the number of items recalled by participants when a happy or sad mood was induced by hypnosis. In a happy mood they remembered many more memories they classified as pleasant. In a sad mood they recalled slightly more unpleasant memories.

to each emotion, in which past experiences, images, related concepts, labels, and interpretations of sensations are all interconnected in a semantic network. When you experience an emotion, all of the associations of that emotion become more accessible and available for use in different judgments. For example, if you are reacquainted with a person in whom you once had a romantic interest and feel renewed attraction to that person, the past experiences, related concepts, images, and beliefs related to feelings of attraction and desire will more readily come to mind, guiding your interpretation of the current event.

According to Bower's emotion congruence account, we should be better able to learn material that is **congruent** with our current emotion, because that material is more extensively integrated into active memory structures, and more easily retrieved at the time of recall. In one test of this hypothesis, participants were hypnotized to feel happy or sad; they then read a brief story about two college students, one doing really well, the other poorly (Bower, Gilligan, & Monteiro, 1981). In a memory test the next day, the participants who were happy when reading the story remembered more facts about the student doing well, whereas the sad participants remembered more about the student doing poorly.

Bower's hypothesis stimulated much research. In its original form, the hypothesis has not been supported; for instance, sometimes memories that are incongruent with mood may be recalled better than those that are congruent (Parrott & Spackman, 2000). Eich and Macaulay (2000) sum up the conclusions of research on this issue as follows. Mood-dependent effects do occur in memory and other cognitive functions, but not in terms of a mechanism that affects all processes of perception and memory in the same way, as Bower proposed. Effects depend on the tasks that participants perform, on the moods that are induced, and on who the participants are. So as Eich, Macaulay, and Ryan (1994) put it:

> Two individuals – one happy, the other sad – are shown say, a *rose* and asked to identify and describe what they see. Both individuals are apt to say much the same thing and to encode the *rose* event in the same manner. After all, and with all due respect to Gertrude Stein, a rose, is a rose is a rose . . . memory for the rose event will probably not appear to be mood dependent under these circumstances. Now imagine a different situation. Instead of identifying and describing the rose the subjects are asked to recall a specific episode, from any time in their personal past, that the object calls to mind. (p. 213)

Under these circumstances, Eich and his colleagues have found that mood effects do occur.

Perhaps the best known modification of Bower's proposal is the Affect Infusion Model of Joseph Forgas (Forgas, 1995, 2000; Forgas & Laham, 2005). According to this model, emotions infuse into a cognitive task, and influence memory and judgment depending on the extent to which the task depends on complex and constructive processing, or on matters that depart from prototypes. In one of Forgas's studies, for example, participants were induced to experience different moods and then asked to make judgments about images of couples who were either matched (and hence prototypical) on physical attractiveness and race, partially matched, or mismatched. Mood affected participants' judgments more with the images of mismatched couples, than for partially matched or completely matched couples. Forgas says that his model is parsimonious and responsive to experimental data on the effects of mood on cognitive processes.

Feelings as information

A second approach to the effects of emotion upon cognition is the perspective of **feelings as information** (Clore, 1992; Clore & Gasper, 2000; Clore & Parrott, 1991; Martin & Clore, 2001; Schwarz, 1990; Schwarz & Clore, 1983). This perspective assumes that emotions themselves are informative when we make judgments. This account rests on two assumptions. The first is that emotions provide us with a rapid signal triggered by something in our environment. For example, anger signals that a state of injustice exists and needs to be changed. A second assumption is that many of the judgments that we make are often too complex to review all the relevant evidence. For instance, a comprehensive answer to the question of how satisfied you are with your political leader might lead you to think about current environmental policy, the state of health care, unemployment and inflation rates, what is being done about global warming, and whether the leader is living up to his or her numerous campaign promises. Given this complexity of so many important judgments, we often rely on a simpler assessment based on our current feelings, asking ourselves "How do I currently feel about this person?" Another way to put this is that only very seldom can human beings act with full rationality. Seldom can we fully think through all the relevant evidence and principles for sorting out that evidence and arriving at a justified position. Emotions are **heuristics**, guesses that work better than chance a lot of the time (Polya, 1957), short cuts to making judgments or taking action.

To test this feelings-as-information perspective, Schwarz and Clore (1983) studied the powerful effects that bright sunny days and gloomy overcast days have on the emotional lives of people in the Midwestern United States. They telephoned people in Illinois either on a cloudy or sunny day and asked participants "all things considered, how satisfied or dissatisfied are you with your life as a whole these days?" In one condition participants simply rated their life satisfaction. In a second condition, before being asked about life satisfaction, participants were asked: "How's the weather down there?" Schwarz and Clore predicted that only those participants who had not been asked about the weather would use their current feelings as heuristics, or short-cut strategies for making the complex judgment of how satisfied they were: those who were called on a sunny day would report greater life satisfaction than participants who were called on a gloomy day. Participants who were asked about the weather, Schwarz and Clore reasoned, would no longer consider their current feelings (perhaps affected by the weather) as relevant to their judgments of life satisfaction. As you can see from figure 10.3, the results of this study confirm Schwarz and Clore's claim that people will use their emotions as heuristics in making judgments, except when they attribute those feelings to a specific source. Once again,

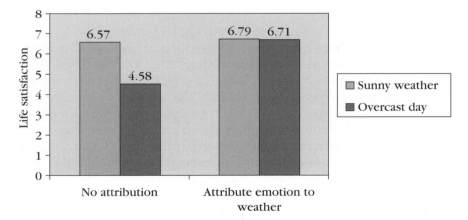

Figure 10.3 Results from Schwarz & Clore (1983). People are more satisfied with their life on sunny as opposed to rainy, overcast days, except when they are explicitly asked to think about the weather. This study indicates how we use our current feelings to make judgments of various kinds.

however, as with the effects of mood congruence, the effects are not uniform. They depend strongly on the nature of the task being performed, that is to say on the context (Martin, 2000).

Processing style

A third perspective on the effects of emotions and moods on cognition is processing style. Different emotions promote different **processing styles**. This perspective would suggest that when you feel guilty or angry, grateful or enthusiastic, for example, that you are engaging in qualitatively different forms of reasoning, of considering and weighing evidence, and drawing conclusions. A general conclusion is that positive mood facilitates use of already existing knowledge structures, such as heuristics and stereotypes, whereas negative moods, in particular sadness, facilitate more **analytical** thought and careful attention to situational details (Bless et al., 1996; Bless, Mackie, & Schwarz, 1992; Bless, Schwarz, & Wieland, 1996; Bodenhausen, Kramer, & Süsser, 1994; Fiedler, 2001; Forgas, 1998; Lambert et al., 1997). There are differences among negative emotions. If people feel sad they are less likely to rely on stereotypes than if they feel angry, when they make social judgments of others (Bodenhausen, Sheppard, & Kramer, 1994). Stereotypes are automatic, effort-saving tools for judging others, and they are more likely to be used when one is experiencing moods and emotions that make one less systematic, such as happiness or anger.

Research on processing style was, as we discussed in chapter 1, started by Alice Isen (1987, 1993). She suggested that happiness prompts people to think in ways that are flexible and creative. She induced positive emotion in simple ways, by giving participants candy, for example, or having them watch a pleasurable film clip, or having them find a dime in a public telephone. In one of Isen's demonstrations (Isen et al., 1987) participants were made happy, or left in their previous emotional state, by watching a funny or a neutral film. They were given a problem: to use only a box of tacks, a book of matches, and a candle, and fix the candle to a cork-board wall so that it could be lit. The tacks were not long enough, and the candle was too friable, to tack the candle directly to the cork-board. The solution was to empty out all the tacks, and pin part of the box to the wall as a holder for the candle. After watching the neutral film 20 percent or fewer people found this solution in 10 minutes, but in one experiment 75 percent, and in another 58 percent, of participants who had watched the funny film solved this problem in 10 minutes. The happy mood seems to enable the imagination to explore further, with fewer constraints and assumptions. The size of the effect of happiness on promoting correct solutions in the candle task is about the same as that of pouring all the tacks out of the box onto the table, so that the box itself does not appear just as a container (without any mood manipulation).

Other studies by Isen and her colleagues further reveal how happiness makes cognitive organization more flexible, and produces more unusual associations (reviewed in Isen, 1987, 1993). Happiness has been found to prompt people to aim for higher goals (Hom & Arbuckle, 1988), as well as to continue in what they are doing, and to resist change to some other state. When given one word (for example, "carpet") and asked to generate a related word, people feeling happy generated more novel associations (for example, "fresh" or "texture") than people in a neutral state. People feeling happy categorized objects in more inclusive ways, rating fringe members of categories (for example, "cane" or "purse" as an example of clothing) as better members of that category than people in a neutral state, whose categories were more narrowly defined.

Why might positive moods prompt us to think in more flexible, creative ways? In an important theory, Barbara Fredrickson (e.g., Fredrickson, 1998, 2003; Fredrickson & Branigan, 2005) has argued that the overarching function of positive emotions is to **broaden and build** our resources. Positive emotions broaden our thought repertoires, they enable more creative and flexible thought, to aid the individual in forming important bonds and exploring the environment. Thus, the creativity associated with positive emotion, that Isen has consistently documented, builds schemas and intellectual resources by enhancing our perspective taking, our novel ideas, and our learning. Positive emotions also help us build interpersonal resources, by motivating us to approach others, to cooperate, to express affection, and to build bonds. These kinds of findings strongly suggest that we would be well advised not to look upon happiness and pleasure so skeptically, or consider happiness a luxury. Instead, happiness appears to be a well-spring of complex, integrative, creative thought that is essential to learning, insight, and healthy bonds.

Effects of moods and emotions on cognitive functioning

In this chapter we ask whether moods and emotions are rational, whether they influence cognitive processes in systematic and adaptive fashion. Let's now review specific cognitive processes that are influenced by emotions and moods. As we do, we ask you to be the judge of whether emotions indeed are rational, and how the findings conform to the claims of the three accounts just given – congruence, feelings-as-information, and processing style – of the influences of moods and emotions on perception, attention, memory, thinking, and judgment.

Perceptual effects

Do moods and emotions influence events that we perceive? Experience suggests so. You may have gone to a family gathering or a student get-together and had your perception of the event shaped by your feelings. When feeling blue, you might have been more attuned to all that has been lost, the unfulfilled hopes of others, and perhaps the minor tragedies that hover behind many gatherings. In a euphoric or exhilarated mood, the same event might strike you entirely differently, as full of conviviality and promise.

Are we more tuned to perceiving things that are congruent with our mood? Two important experiments by Niedenthal and Setterlund (1994) suggest that this is so, that happiness and sadness have emotion-congruent effects upon selective perception. Niedenthal and Setterlund induced happy and sad moods by giving their participants earphones and playing music throughout the experimental session. To put people in a happy mood they played pieces such as the allegro from Mozart's *Eine Kleine Nacht Musik*, and parts of Vivaldi's Concerto in C Major. To induce sadness they played pieces such as *Adagietto* by Mahler, and the adagio from the Piano Concerto No. 2 in C Minor by Rachmaninov. The task subjects performed was standard in experimental psychology: a lexical decision task. Strings of letters were flashed on a screen: some were words, some were non-words (strings of letters that do not appear in the dictionary but that can be pronounced in English, like "blatkin"). Subjects were asked to work as quickly as possible to press one button if the letters formed a word, another if it was a non-word. Words were from five categories: happy words such as "delight," positive words but unrelated to happiness such as "calm," sad words like "weep," negative words unrelated to sadness like "injury," and neutral words like "habit."

Niedenthal and Setterlund found that the music did indeed put people into happy or sad moods. Consistent with the thesis of emotion-congruence, when in a happy mood participants were quicker at identifying happy than sad words. When sad, they were quicker at identifying sad than happy words. But the effects of happy and sad moods did not extend to the positive or negative words that were unrelated to the specific emotions of happiness or sadness.

This work makes an impressive point: our current moods and feelings lead us to selectively perceive emotion-congruent objects and events. This in part helps explain why emotions and moods can persist: because built into our experience is a tendency to perceive emotion-congruent objects and events, thus prolonging our experience. These findings also fit the claim that moods and emotions can redirect perception to objects and events that are relevant to current feelings (Niedenthal & Halberstadt, 2000), most likely to guide adaptive action.

Attentional qualities of emotions

William James, in his textbook of psychology (1890, vol. 1, p. 402) wrote: "My experience is what I agree to attend to." It is also what we attend to even when we do not consciously agree to it. Emotions affect attention. The effects range from largely unconscious processes of filtering incoming information to conscious preoccupation of the kind that we have when we worry.

The most fully researched effects of emotions on attention concern anxiety: it is clear that anxiety narrows attention (Mathews & MacLeod, 1994; Mineka, Rafaeli, & Yovel, 2003). When people are fearful or anxious they focus mainly on what they are afraid of, or on safety from this thing, and they disregard almost everything else.

Many effects of anxiety on attention can be demonstrated in the laboratory. Mathews and others (Broadbent & Broadbent, 1988; Mathews, 1993) have used a method in which two words are flashed, one above the other, on a screen, then these are replaced by a dot. One of the words is threatening like "failure" or "disease." The other is neutral, like "table." Subjects are instructed that when the dot appears they should press a button. Some subjects are anxious, as indicated by a scale of trait anxiety; others do not have an anxiety trait. When the dot appears in the position where the threat word was, anxious people have a shorter reaction time to its appearance than non-anxious people. When the dot appears in the position of the neutral word, there is no difference between the anxious and the non-anxious people. The explanation offered by Mathews is that reaction time is shorter when the dot appears in the position of the word that the subject was actively attending to. Anxious subjects are much more likely to be looking at the threat word rather than the neutral one. This kind of finding has been replicated with clinically anxious patients as well as with people with an anxious trait of personality.

Or consider results obtained in studies using the dichotic listening task, which requires that participants listen to different messages that are fed into the right ear and the left ear. When in a state of fear, participants are particularly likely to have their attention drawn away from the message they are supposed to be tracking in one ear to words presented in the other ear when the words presented to the other ear are threatening, such as "death," or "blood" (Mathews & MacLeod, 1994).

A similar kind of experiment is based on the so-called emotional **Stroop test**. Stroop (1935) found that if subjects were asked to look at words such as "red," "yellow," "blue," that were printed in different colors, and to name the color of the *print* for each word, they were slowed down when the color of the print and the color word were different – they were slower if the word "red" were printed in blue ink and they therefore had to say "blue," than if it were printed in red ink and they therefore had to say "red." The meaning of the word involuntarily captures attention, distracting subjects from naming the ink color. This idea of the emotional Stroop test is that words are shown that are neutral or that have emotional significance, to see if people are slowed down in naming the colors in which words with emotional significance are printed.

Foa et al. (1991) found that people who had been the victims of rape were slowed down in naming the print-colors of words that were related to rape. People who had coped with their trauma better showed less interference. Mathews (1993) summarizes the conclusions of the many experiments that have been conducted with this technique: the slowing of color naming is greatest with words that correspond to the subjects' greatest anxiety. Thus people who have a social phobia are slowed by words about confidence, people with eating disorders are slowed by words for food, and so forth. Mathews and Klug (1993) found that the words did not have to be threatening to produce this effect: the issue was whether they were emotionally significant. If the emotional words included such terms as "confident" or "healthy" then people who were socially anxious or were anxious about disease would be slowed in naming color-printed positive words, but only when these positive concepts were related to their own specific anxiety. Subjects who were anxious were slower than control subjects in naming the colors of those words that were related to their specific anxieties, whether these words were positive or negative.

A number of explanations have been put forward for these effects of anxiety upon attention. The most straightforward is that when people are fearful – either because of some immediate fear, or because they are suffering from an anxiety state that makes them fearful for much of the time – their nervous system is switched into a particular mode of processing. Mathews, Yiend, and Lawrence (2004) have shown that in this mode, regions of the brain known to be associated with fear are activated, and that diverting attention is only partly effective in decreasing this activation. The fear/anxiety mode is one in which attention is narrowed, and directed to cues in the environment about threat and safety. It is even more specifically tuned for cues related to particular objects of a person's anxiety. For instance, people who believe themselves vulnerable to cancer are induced to worry whenever they experience symptoms, including very un-cancer-like bodily symptoms, that remind them of their vulnerability (Easterling & Leventhal, 1989).

In the normal course of events the mechanism of fear and anxiety has no doubt been invaluable for our survival but, it seems, it can get switched on almost permanently, occupying people's cognitive resources, making the world a frightening place, undermining confidence, and preventing the sufferers from concentrating on much else. We will discuss this further in chapter 13. More generally, we would expect emotions to direct attention to the core aspects or themes of their own state. While most of the research has been done on fear and anxiety, we would expect analogous results for other emotions like anger or sadness. Anger might direct attention to unjust, blameworthy actions. Disgust is likely to direct attention to noxious elements.

Emotions and memory

In an essay on autobiography, Russian novelist Esther Salaman (1982) recounts the following emotionally laden memory:

> I have a memory of being bitten by a dog when I was three. I have always remembered this. I am standing outside the closed front door when suddenly I see a big dog bounding towards me, his broken rope trailing on the left;

there is no snow or mud, the season is late spring . . . The moment that came back after fifty years was this: the dog has knocked me over, and I am actually turning my head away and burying my face in the earth while the dog is searching between my petticoats and the long black stockings on my left leg for bare flesh to dig his teeth into. It is like a picture in slow motion. Today I am writing only a memory of a memory, but at the time it came back to me I actually was that child of three; the "then" was "now," and time stood still. (Salaman, 1982, p. 56)

Salaman discusses other such incidents from her own life, and from other writers including De Quincey, Martineau, and Proust, memories that arise involuntarily, often after many years, and that are imbued with powerful emotion. This example brings into focus the two themes of this section on emotions and memory: first, that we seem to remember emotional events particularly well; and second, and somewhat paradoxically, our current emotions and moods influence what we recall. To understand the effect of emotions on memory, we need first to say something about how memory in general works, and to do so, we shall rely on the groundbreaking work of Bartlett (1932).

Bartlett gave people meaningful material such as pictures or stories to remember, then asked them to reproduce it as exactly as possible, both immediately after being presented with it, and at intervals up to several years later – see box below.

Historical landmark: Bartlett's study of remembering

Bartlett (1932) had people read an American Indian folk story, collected by Franz Boas. The story starts like this:

One night two young men from Egulac went down to the river to hunt seals, and while they were there it became foggy and calm. Then they heard war-cries, and they thought: "Maybe this is a war party." They escaped to the shore, and hid behind a log. Now canoes came up, and they heard the noise of paddles, and saw one canoe coming up to them. There were five men in the canoe, and they said:

"What do you think? We wish to take you along. We are going up the river to make war on the people."

One of the young men said: "I have no arrows."

"Arrows are in the canoe," they said.

"I will not go along. I might be killed. My relatives do not know where I have gone. But you," he said, turning to the other, "may go with them."

So one of the young men went . . .

There follow 11 lines about how the young man who went took part in a fight in which he was shot but did not feel sick, and thinks "Oh, they are ghosts." The story ends like this, after his return home:

> He told it all, and then he became quiet. When the sun rose he fell down. Something black came out of his mouth. His face became contorted. The people jumped up and cried.
> He was dead.

After reading the story through twice, people were asked to reproduce it.

Here is a reproduction by Bartlett's participant P, who had been asked to reproduce the story several times in the first months after reading it, but had then not thought of it for two and a half years:

> Some warriors went to wage war against the ghosts. They fought all day and one of their number was wounded.
> They returned home in the evening, bearing their sick comrade. As the day drew to a close, he became rapidly worse and the villagers came round him. At sunset he sighed: something black come out of his mouth. He was dead.

In this version much is lost – such as the whole introductory sequence about the two young men going hunting for seals – and also much is changed. In the remembered story the man dies at sunset rather than sunrise. But the single striking detail "something black came out of his mouth" is preserved here, as it was in most of the reproductions that Bartlett reported.

Bartlett concluded that when we remember a verbal account the words are never exact. What we perceive is assimilated into our own structure of meaning, which Bartlett called a **schema**, which includes a great deal of general knowledge. Then when a recall is asked for, the participant takes a few significant remembered details and a general emotional attitude to the story, and from the schema constructs what the story must have been. So style becomes the participant's style, details such as "to hunt seals" become "fishing," and things happen in ways appropriate to the culture of the person remembering, such as dying in the evening rather than at sunrise.

As Bartlett said, remembering "is an imaginative reconstruction, built out of the relation of our [emotional] attitude towards a whole active mass of organized past reactions or experience, and to a little outstanding detail . . . It is thus hardly ever really exact . . . and it is not at all important that it should be" (1932, p. 213).

In some cases it is important to be exact, for example when giving evidence in a court of law. So here is the issue for research on emotions: do intense emotions increase or decrease the accuracy of what is remembered?

A bias for recalling emotionally evocative events

One general conclusion to be drawn from the study of emotions and memory is that we are better able to recall past events if those events are emotionally arousing. Several studies reveal that people are better able to recall emotionally arousing material compared to relatively neutral material (Bradley, 1994; Christianson, 1992; Heurer & Reisberg, 1992; Levine & Burgess, 1997; Levine & Pizarro, 2004; Ochsner, 2000). This is true, for example, in the recall of emotionally evocative slides compared to neutral slides, and emotionally evocative faces as compared to neutral faces.

Wagenaar (1986) recorded an event from his own life every day for four years. He made up standard forms, and for each event he wrote whom it concerned, what it was, where it happened, and when. He also described a critical detail about each event, and he rated the event on three scales: salience (how frequently events such as this occurred, from every day to once in a lifetime), emotional involvement, and pleasantness. A colleague transcribed all the events into typewritten booklets, so that on recall he could be given one, two, three, and then all four, of the recall cues (who, what, where, when) in order. His task was to recall all the other cues, and when all four cues had been given, also to recall the critical detail. If he were unsuccessful in all these the event was scored as completely forgotten. Over a period of five years, the numbers of events forgotten were about 20 percent. Wagenaar found that in general events characterized by **emotional involvement** were remembered better than uninvolving ones, and pleasant events were recalled better than unpleasant events (see figure 10.4). This result was predicted by Freud: we do protect ourselves somewhat from unpleasant thoughts.

Emotional involvement and eyewitness testimony

The theme encountered in the last section – that emotionally involving events are memorable – is relevant to studies of eyewitness testimony. To understand how, consider the following question: What if you are an eyewitness to a crime? How would your memory for that event be affected? Psychologists know from Bartlett's (1932) principles (discussed above), and from specific research (Loftus & Doyle, 1987), that eyewitness testimony usually has mistakes. Neither certainty nor vividness guarantee that "remembered" details are correct. In Britain the Devlin Report (of an official committee set up to examine cases of wrongful conviction for crimes) recommended that it is not reliable to convict someone on the basis of eyewitness testimony unless the circumstances are exceptional or the testimony is corroborated by evidence of some other kind.

There has now been a large amount of research on memory for stressful events (Christianson, 1992). Here is an influential study. Five months after a thief had held up a gun shop in a suburb of Vancouver, Yuille and Cutshall (1986) were able to re-interview 13 witnesses, previously interviewed by

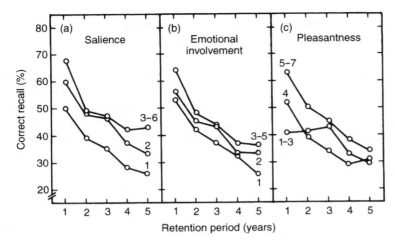

Figure 10.4 Results of Wagenaar's study of his own autobiographical memory. In each panel the percentage of events correctly recalled when all the cues were given is shown as a function of one of three variables over five years. In (a) the variable is salience; the graph marked 3–6 indicates events of the kind that happen once a month to once in a lifetime, 2 indicates the kind that happen once a week, and 1 indicates the kind that happen once a day. In (b) the variable of emotional involvement is shown by a graph marked 3–5 for moderately to extremely involving, one marked 2 indicating little involvement, and one marked 1 meaning no involvement. In (c), the variable of pleasantness, the graph marked 5–7 means pleasant to extremely pleasant, 4 means neutral, and 1–3 means unpleasant to extremely unpleasant.

the police, about the event. The thief had tied up the owner of the shop, and left with money and several guns. The owner had freed himself, taken a revolver, and gone out to take the thief's car number. The thief had not yet departed and, in full view of several people, he shot the shop owner twice. After a pause the shop owner fired all six rounds of his revolver at the thief, who died. The shop owner recovered. Because the thief was dead, and there were no legal complications, Yuille and Cutshall were able to gain access to police files, to reconstruct events from the rather complete forensic evidence of the event, including police photographs, and from the testimony of the witnesses where they corroborated each other. Yuille and Cutshall made up a list of details of actions, of people present, and of objects.

In their research interview, Yuille and Cutshall found that witnesses who had contact with the store owner or the thief rated themselves as very stressed by this event, and said they had difficulty sleeping for several nights after it, though other less involved witnesses were not so stressed. Witnesses were fairly accurate about the event, including incidental details such as the color of the thief's car and of the blanket that was used to cover his body. And consistent with findings from the previous section, at the police interview the stressed witnesses correctly remembered 93.36 percent of the details, and at the research interview five months later 88.24 percent of details. The accuracy of the less stressed individuals was lower: approximately 75 percent in both the police interview and the later research interview. So for emotionally involving events it seems likely that accuracy is increased.

Such events are also subject to the processes of reconstruction that Bartlett discussed. Pynoos and Nader (1989) interviewed children who attended a school where a sniper had "shot repeated rounds of ammunition at children on an elementary school playground" (p. 236) from an apartment opposite the school in Los Angeles on February 24, 1984. One passer-by and one child were killed, and 13 other children and a playground attendant were wounded. In the accounts of 113 children who were interviewed between 6 and 16 weeks afterwards, characteristic distortions occurred. Children who had been wounded tended to have emotionally distanced themselves from the event, and five did not even mention their minor gunshot injuries when interviewed. By contrast, children who were not at school that day, or who were on their way home, tended to place themselves nearer to the events.

Naturalistic studies do not allow full corroboration of an actual event, so such studies are supplemented by laboratory experiments. Christianson and Loftus (1991) report five experiments in which 397 students in Sweden and the USA watched a set of 15 color slides of what a person might see leaving home and walking to work. In each slide there was a central detail, and a peripheral detail. There were three versions of the critical eighth slide – shown in figure 10.5. In a neutral version the central detail was a woman cycling along the road just in front of a car. In an unusual version a woman was walking in the road in front of a car carrying a bicycle upside down. In an emotional version a woman was lying at the side of the road evidently injured and bleeding, near an upturned bicycle and just in front of a car. In each case the woman's coat was either blue or beige. In all versions the peripheral detail was a Volvo 242 car in the distance, which was either white or orange. Christianson and Loftus found that subjects who saw the

Figure 10.5 The three versions of the critical eighth slide in the sequence used by Christianson and Loftus: scene (a) is neutral, (b) unusual, and (c) emotionally shocking.

emotional version of the eighth slide remembered the central details of the woman and the color of her coat better than those who saw the neutral version. By contrast, the peripheral detail for the emotional version was remembered less well than that of the neutral slide. The unusual version of the eighth slide was meant to control for the fact that emotional events are typically unusual: but as compared with the emotional version, subjects did not remember either its central or the peripheral details very well.

Overall we can conclude that, both in real life and in the laboratory, emotionally salient material is remembered better than neutral material. If an event is important and unusual, the condition is set both for an emotion and for distinctive recall. And if the event is subject to being thought about often, or if traumatic flashbacks occur as they can do with severely traumatic events (American Psychiatric Association, 1994, p. 424), then the event itself will remain more salient in memory. The question of whether there is some special form of repressed memory is controversial: many researchers do not discount the possibility but are skeptical (Hardt & Rutter, 2004; Loftus & Ketcham, 1994).

Effects of moods and emotions upon remembering

Acts of memory are constructive processes, and likely to be influenced by the individual's current state or condition. Here is a laboratory demonstration in which effects of selective attention and memory on social judgment were examined. Baron (1987) brought pairs of people of the same sex together for a study in forming impressions. In fact, while one member of each pair was a student participant, the other was an accomplice of the experimenter. The student participant was, apparently randomly, chosen from the two to be an interviewer in a practice interview for a job as a management trainee, while the accomplice was chosen as interviewee. While the accomplice was (supposedly) studying the interview questions, the experimenter made the student participant happy or sad by giving them problems to solve, and telling them either that they had done much better than others, or had performed at an average level, or had done much worse than others.

In the interview the interviewer had to ask a prearranged set of six questions; the interviewee gave the same prearranged, but mixed, answers to the questions. One question was: "What are your most important traits?" In reply the interviewee would mention three positive traits, saying: "I'm ambitious and reliable. Also I'm pretty friendly." He or she would also mention three negative traits: "On the minus side, some of my friends tell me I'm pretty stubborn and I know I'm impatient. Also, I'm pretty disorganized." After the interview the interviewer rated the interviewee on job-related and personal dimensions. When happy they tended to rate the interviewee more positively, and were more likely to say they would hire him or her, but when despondent they tended to rate the interviewee negatively, and said they would probably not hire the person (these effects were more marked for male than female interviewers). Baron also

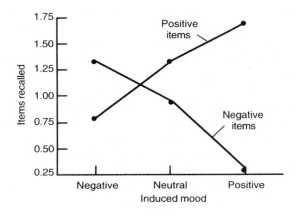

Figure 10.6 Mean number of positive and negative items mentioned in an interview by interviewers who were in a happy or sad mood (Baron, 1987).

asked the interviewers to recall the things that the interviewees had said about themselves, presumably the base for their judgments. You can see the result in figure 10.6. Interviewers who had been made happy recalled significantly more positive things the interviewee had said and fewer negative things; those who had been made sad recalled more negative things and fewer positive things. According to the mood-congruent memory hypothesis, positive decisions about hiring would be influenced by more positive things being recalled by the happy interviewers, and negative decisions by more negative things being remembered.

The phenomenon of mood-congruent memory has, however, been found not to be as robust or wide-ranging as was at first assumed. As we discussed above in relation to Bower's original formulation, effects are highly dependent on context (Eich & Macaulay, 2000). Stronger effects occur when remembering real incidents of emotional significance in a person's life, than (for instance) when remembering lists of words.

A second question is how current feelings influence our recollection of past events. Some researchers have done the difficult work of gathering people's reactions to particular events, and then assessing their memories of that event at some later time. In one study Linda Levine (1997) gathered responses to Ross Perot's withdrawal and then re-entrance into the 1992 US presidential race. She asked Perot supporters how angry, sad, and hopeful they felt when he withdrew from the race in July of 1992. Four months later, in November, she asked those same participants to try to recall their feelings from July. In general, people were fairly accurate in recalling the extent to which they felt angry, sad, and hopeful. Levine also studied whether different kinds of Perot supporters were prone to misremember their initial emotions reported in July depending on how they felt about Perot in November. Perot loyalists, who remained loyal to Perot all along, even after his withdrawal, underestimated how sad they felt upon his withdrawal. In contrast, supporters who initially gave up on Perot but then returned to his camp underestimated how angry they had been when he originally announced his withdrawal. Though there is a background of accuracy, current emotions do also shape how we recall the past (Levine & Pizzaro, 2004; Levine & Safer, 2002).

In a study of bereavement, Safer, Bonanno, and Field (2001) asked individuals how much grief they were suffering six months after the death of their spouse. Five years later they again asked participants to report on their grief, and to try to recall how much grief they reported suffering at six months post-loss. Participants' memories of their past grief were more highly correlated with their current grief, five years after the death of their spouses, than with the actual grief they reported six months after the death.

The tendency for current feelings to bias our recall of past emotions is seen in other realms as well. For example, Feldman-Barrett (1997) found that highly neurotic individuals, who are prone to negative emotion (see chapter 11), overestimate the intensity of the negative emotions they reported earlier. McFarland and Ross (1987) had participants rate their feelings for a dating partner initially and then two months later. Participants who had become more attached to their partner recalled more positive initial evaluations of their partner, a memory that fit with their current romantic feelings. Participants who became less attracted to their partner recalled initial feelings that were more negative.

Effects of moods and emotions on judgment

Effects on evaluative judgments   Gerald Clore, a central figure in the study of emotion and judgment, made a striking remark in a paper in 1992: "The most reliable phenomenon in the cognition-emotion domain is the effect of mood on evaluative judgment" (Clore, 1992, p. 134). He was referring to evidence that shows that when in a positive or negative emotional state, those feelings are likely to color your evaluative judgments of events and objects as good or bad, even when the objects being judged have no relation to the cause of the emotion.

In fact, current positive and negative moods have been shown to influence a striking array of judgments (Forgas, 1995). This includes evaluations of consumer items (Isend, Shalker, Clark, & Karp, 1978), political leaders (Forgas & Moylan, 1987; Keltner, Lock, & Audrain, 1993), general life circumstances (Schwarz & Clore, 1983), and fundamental evaluations of losses and gains (Ketelaar, 2004, 2005). When in a positive emotional state, we evaluate objects and events in a more positive light. When in a negative emotional state, we evaluate the very same events and objects in a more negative light.

Consider an illustrative study by Forgas and Moylan (1987). They interviewed nearly 1,000 people leaving movie theaters after seeing a movie that had been previously classified as happy, sad, or aggressive, in emotional tone. In the interviews, subjects were asked about political figures, future events, crime, and their own life satisfaction. People who had seen the sad movie offered more negative evaluations of these things than people who had seen the happy movie. This occurred even though the movie had no semantic relationship to what they were judging, and in spite of the fact that the source of their current feelings – the movie – was pure fiction.

Effects on judgments of the future   Do our current moods and emotions affect our judgments of the future? Indeed they do. First of all, negative moods lead people to view the future pessimistically, whereas positive moods lead people to look at the future in more optimistic fashion. In a study to document this, Johnson and Tversky (1983) had participants read newspaper accounts about the death of a young man, which induced a negative mood. People in a negative mood judged negative life events in the future, like contracting a disease, to be more likely than people feeling a positive mood. Our current moods shape our vision of our future.

More recent studies have uncovered more nuanced effects of specific emotions upon judgments of the future. It would seem that different emotions are associated with more specific strains of **pessimism or optimism**. For example, Keltner, Ellsworth, and Edwards (1993) asked whether people feeling angry or sad would judge different events to be more likely in their future. They reasoned that angry people, attuned to the blameworthy actions of others, would judge unfair acts caused by others to be frequent in the future. In contrast, sad people, attuned to situational causes of negative outcomes, should judge negative life events caused by situational factors as more likely.

To test this hypothesis, they asked angry or sad participants to estimate the likelihood of different events, some of which were caused by other people (a pilot's error causes a friend to die in a plane crash) and some caused by situational factors (icy roads cause a car accident). Consistent with expectation, angry people judged the negative life events caused by other people to be more likely than sad people, who judged the events caused by situational factors to be more likely.

In similarly motivated work, DeSteno and colleagues (2000) asked people feeling anger or sadness to estimate the likelihood of "sad" events (of the 60,000 orphans in Romania, how many will be malnourished) and "angry" or unfair events (of the 20,000 violent criminals put on trial in the upcoming year, how many will be set free because of legal technicalities). As you can see in figure 10.7, angry participants judged the anger-inducing events to be more likely, whereas sad participants judged the sad-inducing events to be more likely. In similar work, fearful individuals have been shown to have heightened estimates that risky, dangerous events will be part of their future (Lerner & Keltner, 2001).

While negative moods make us more pessimistic about the future in general, increasing our sense that unfortunate events will happen to us, specific emotions result in more specific forms of pessimism. In this study, you can see that sadness led people to judge tragic, sad events to be more likely, whereas anger led people to judge unfair events to be more likely.

Taken together, these studies reveal that negative and positive moods make people more pessimistic or optimistic, respectively. And there appear to

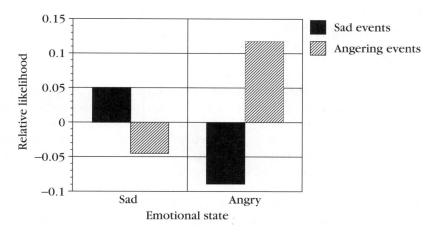

Figure 10.7 Estimates of likelihood of saddening events and angering events made by participants who were induced to feel either sad (left-hand side of diagram) or angry (right-hand side of diagram) (from De Steno et al., 2000).

be more subtle kinds of pessimism associated with more specific negative emotions like anger, sadness, or fear.

Effects on causal judgments   Another domain of interest is that of causal judgment. Causal judgments, or attributions, of behavior figure prominently in legal judgments, for example in determining a sentence for a convicted criminal. They figure prominently in whether we forgive loved ones or not. They are a central activity of the social mind, as it seeks to understand the world. And several studies suggest that causal judgments likewise shift dramatically according to our current moods and emotions.

First of all, there appears to be a general attributional bias produced by negative and positive moods. Thus, Forgas (1994) induced people to feel a positive or negative mood by having them read a sad or humorous literary passage. Participants then recalled one experience with a romantic partner that was pleasant, and one that was laden with conflict and difficulty. Forgas coded the different attributions offered for these events, and in these codes, observed a now familiar pattern in the perceptions of people feeling negative or positive moods. Specifically, people feeling the negative mood attributed the positive romantic experience to situational factors and they blamed themselves for the romantic conflict. Happy people, in contrast, took personal credit for the positive romantic experience and blamed the conflict on circumstantial factors.

In other research, more specific emotional states have been found to have fairly distinct influences upon causal attributions. In a number of studies, it has been found that anger leads people to blame others for various actions, and to be acutely sensitive to unfair actions, whereas sadness leads people to attribute events to impersonal, situational causes (Feigeson, Park, & Salovey,

2001; Keltner, Ellsworth, & Edwards, 1993; Lerner, Goldberg, & Tetlock, 1998; Quigley & Tedeschi, 1996).

Persuasion

In chapter 1, we described how Aristotle was interested in the problem of how emotions figure in the process of persuasion. One of his central claims was that people are persuaded by messages that stir their emotions. As we shall now see, the relevant research offers a slightly more complex message about emotion and **persuasion**, but one that is in keeping with Aristotle's general emphasis on emotion. How are we to think about emotional influences in persuasion?

One way is suggested by research on why people change their minds under the influence of persuasion. Chaiken, Lieberman, and Eagly (1989) described two kinds of processing of arguments. One is systematic; the person carefully attends to the validity of the argument itself. The other involves short cuts; it is superficial, more careless, and involves responses to less essential aspects of the communication, for instance to the personality or reputation of who is presenting the argument, rather than to the validity of the argument itself. Petty and Cacioppo (1986) argue that people in good moods follow the short-cut route, and people in a neutral or negative mood tend to process arguments more systematically.

Worth and Mackie (1987) performed an experiment in which they measured (near the beginning and end of an experimental session) student subjects' ratings of agreement or disagreement with a proposal about controlling acid rain. After the first rating subjects took part in an apparently unrelated procedure that they thought was about risk taking. In fact the experimenters used this to put half the subjects into a good mood by allowing them to win $1, while the other half neither won anything nor knew there was anything to win. Then subjects were asked to evaluate a short speech about controlling acid rain, given at a student conference. Half the subjects had a speech that contained arguments that had previously been judged to be weak, and the other half had a passage with arguments previously judged to be strong. Then in a further split, half the students were told that the speech they read was made by an expert (an environmental studies major), and half were told the speech they read had been made by a non-expert (a mathematics major).

Figure 10.8 shows the results of Worth and Mackie's study. Look first at the top graph, when no mood was induced (the neutral condition). Subjects changed their attitude toward the proposal about acid rain by nearly 1.5 points (on a nine-point scale) after reading the strong arguments, but they changed their attitude by only about half a point when they read the weak arguments. By contrast, when in a happy mood from having just won $1, they changed their attitude the same amount in response to both strong and weak arguments.

What were the people in the happy mood doing? The lower graph of figure 10.8 gives an indication. Whether the speech was said to have been

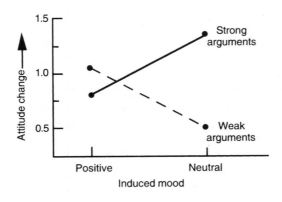

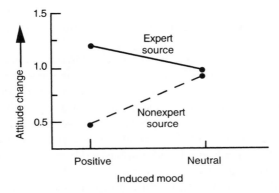

Figure 10.8 Attitude change toward agreeing with a proposal to control the effects of acid rain in happy and neutral moods, in response to strong and weak arguments, by experts and nonexperts (Mackie & Worth, 1987).

given by an expert or nonexpert had no influence on the attitude change of people in the neutral mood. But people in a happy mood were more persuaded by the supposed expert than by the nonexpert.

Two years later, Mackie and Worth (1989) published a similar study although, presumably because of inflation, positive mood was now induced by subjects being given $2 rather than $1. When subjects were given a limited time to read the arguments for the proposal, the attitudes of those in a neutral mood shifted significantly more toward the proposal after reading the passage of strong as compared with weak arguments. But in a positive mood, attitude change was just as great with the weak as with the strong arguments, in fact slightly greater. With unlimited time, however, the happy subjects performed like those in a neutral mood. Mackie and Worth propose that this effect is attentional; perhaps the happy people were preoccupied with feeling good about having won $2 unexpectedly, and were therefore less inclined to concentrate on the arguments. When allowed as long as they wanted to read the arguments, those in the happy mood were less persuaded by the weak arguments.

So under at least some circumstances, how we feel can change our judgments for reasons quite irrelevant to the problem in hand: in Mackie and Worth's experiments mood was induced by a small gift of money which had nothing whatever to do with acid rain. We can imagine that this effect, if general, would give a handy formula to advertisers in magazines and television – perhaps one they already know without psychological experiments – if you can induce a happy mood and not give people too much time to think, you can incline a person favorably toward your product, independently of its merit or usefulness.

Recent research by DeSteno et al. (2004) points to another relation between emotion and persuasion. This work suggests that messages are more effective to the extent that they match the emotional state of the listener. If a politician is running for office and trying to mobilize an angry group of supporters, it would appear to be most effective to frame the communication in more anger-related terms, centering upon injustice and blame.

To test this notion, DeSteno et al. induced participants to feel either sadness or anger by reading hypothetical newspaper stories that elicited one of the two emotions. Participants were then presented with one of two persuasive messages about raising taxes (not a popular message for most Americans). One of the messages was sadness-framed, and emphasized how increasing taxes would help special needs infants and the elderly. The other message was anger-framed, and emphasized how increasing taxes would keep criminals from getting off on legal technicalities and would prevent aggravating traffic jams. As you might anticipate, sad people changed their attitudes more toward raising taxes when presented with the sadness-framed message, whereas angry people changed their attitudes more when given the anger-framed message.

Emotions and moral judgment

We began this chapter with the tragic story of Eadweard Muybridge, and how the damage he sustained to his orbitofrontal cortex altered his emotions and the ability to live a moral life. The more general conclusion is that emotions, when they are properly functioning, act as guides to **moral judgment**. This certainly would be in keeping with a central theme of this book: that emotions are bases for our social life.

This view of moral judgment has not been a widely accepted one in philosophy and psychology. More prevalent has been the view that moral judgment is guided by complex cognitive processes like perspective taking, cost–benefit analyses, and considerations of rights and duties. More recently, however, researchers have argued that emotions act as social-moral intuitions (Haidt, 2001; McCullough et al., 2001). According to this perspective, fast, automatic, involuntary experiences of specific emotions provide gut feelings about right and wrong, virtue, and punishment, without the need for elaborate calculation at the conscious level (Batson, Engel, &

Fridell, 1999; Campos et al., 1989; Greene & Haidt, 2002; Haidt, 2003; Rozin, Haidt, & McCauley, 2000).

Jonathan Haidt has made the case for four categories of moral emotions, which appear rapidly and effortlessly in consciousness and are emotional in nature (Greene & Haidt, 2002; Haidt, 2003). *Harm-related* emotions like sympathy and concern motivate prosocial responding to people who suffer or are vulnerable (Batson & Shaw, 1991; Eisenberg et al., 1989). *Self-critical* emotions, like shame, embarrassment, and guilt, arise when we have violated moral codes or ideas about virtue and character, and they motivate moral behavior (Baumeister, Stillwell, & Heatherton, 1994; Higgins, 1987; Keltner & Anderson, 2000; Keltner & Buswell, 1997; Tangney et al., 1996). *Other praising* emotions, most notably gratitude and "elevation" or awe, signal our approval of others' moral virtues (Haidt, 2003; Keltner & Haidt, 2003; McCullough et al., 2001). And *other condemning* emotions, such as anger, disgust, or contempt, underlie our condemnation of others' immoral actions (Lerner, Goldberg, & Tetlock, 1998).

Haidt further proposes that slow, effortful, and controlled reasoning processes are a second influence on our moral judgment (2001). Recall that we have argued in chapter 7, and earlier in this chapter, for a primary, automatic, appraisal process and a slower, more reasoning-based and deliberate secondary appraisal. When we encounter morally relevant events, we contemplate the evidence, we consider logical and ethical principles, and we debate the consequences of different actions. Our emotional intuitions feed into these more deliberate cognitive processes.

Let's conclude our chapter on emotion and cognition by looking at a recent study that illustrates how these two systems are at play in moral judgment, and likely to involve different central nervous system structures (Greene et al., 2001). Participants judged the appropriateness of different moral and non-moral dilemmas. Some of the moral dilemmas were impersonal. For example, in the "trolley dilemma" the participant imagines a runaway trolley headed for five people who will be killed if it proceeds on its present course. The only way to save them is to hit a switch that will turn the trolley onto an alternate set of tracks. But there is a person on that track, so the trolley will kill one person instead of five. The participant is asked whether it is appropriate to hit that switch and save five lives. Most answer yes with only a little hesitation.

Other dilemmas were more evocative of emotion. For example, in the "footbridge dilemma," again five people's lives are threatened by a trolley, but in this case the participant is asked to imagine standing next to a very heavy stranger on a footbridge over the trolley tracks. Pushing the stranger off the bridge and onto the tracks would kill the stranger, but his dead body would cause the train to veer off its course and thus would save the lives of the five other individuals. Is it appropriate to push the stranger off the footbridge? It's the same two options as in the trolley dilemma – one death or five deaths – but in the footbridge dilemma the action is highly personal: the participant must imagine using his or her own hands to push the stranger to his gruesome death.

While participants responded to dilemmas of this sort, functional magnetic resonance imaging techniques ascertained which parts of the participant's brain were active. The personal, emotionally evocative moral dilemmas activated regions of the brain that are involved in emotion: the medial frontal gyrus, the posterior cingulate gyrus, and the angular gyrus. The impersonal moral dilemmas and the non-moral dilemmas activated brain regions associated with working memory, regions centrally involved in more deliberative reasoning. The speculative conclusion from this study is that some of our emotional moral intuitions arise in fairly specific parts of the brain that differ from the regions that are activated during more complex cognitive processes involved in moral judgments and, perhaps, even more provocatively (Marcus, 2002), that processes that we value in public life such as justice and democracy would be impossible without the emotions.

Summary

We centered this chapter on the question: What is the relationship between emotion and reason? We began this chapter by defining rationality and making the case that emotions are usually rational, in that they guide cognition in systematic ways that enable the individual to respond to the environment, when perfect rationality is impossible, for instance because of insufficient knowledge. This view is in keeping with a central premise of this book: that emotions serve important social functions, helping the individual navigate complex and changing social relationships. We then considered three theoretical perspectives: that moods and emotions exert emotion congruent effects upon cognition, that emotions are themselves informative, and that different moods or emotions lead to different styles of reasoning. With these theories at hand, we reviewed specific effects of moods and emotions upon cognition. We examined how emotions lead people to more readily perceive emotion-congruent stimuli. We considered the attentional effects of emotion, focusing on how anxiety narrows attention onto threatening stimuli. We looked at memory, uncovering two conclusions: we more readily recall emotionally evocative, unique events, and at the same time, our current emotions bias our recall of the past. We reviewed effects of moods and emotions upon evaluative judgments, judgments of the future, and causal attribution. We concluded by discussing a new theory of emotion and moral judgment that is consistent with the approach taken to emotion in this chapter and in this book, that emotions act as moral intuitions, guiding our judgments of right and wrong in the social world.

Further reading

An excellent introduction to the philosophy of emotions, providing a basis for understanding the sense in which emotions are rational rather than irrational:
Ronald De Sousa (1987). *The rationality of emotions*. Cambridge, MA: MIT Press.

A useful review of experimental work on the effects of mood on memory and attention, including some of the clinical implications of the phenomena:
Andrew Mathews (1993). Biases in emotional processing. *The Psychologist, 6*, 493–9.

A fine theoretical treatment of effects of mood on social judgments:
Joseph Forgas (1995). Mood and judgment: The affect infusion model (AIM). *Psychological Bulletin, 117*, 39–66.

For an excellent statement regarding the role of emotion in moral judgment:
Jonathan Haidt (2001). The emotional dog and its rational tail: A social intuitionist approach to moral judgment. *Psychological Review, 108*, 814–34.

Emotions and the Individual

PART IV

CHAPTER 11

Individual Differences and Personality

A child forsaken, waking suddenly,
Whose gaze afeared on all things
  round doth rove
And seeth only that it cannot see
The meeting eyes of love.
                              George Eliot

Contents

Figure 11.0 A mother picks up her child after an absence. Notice the child clasping the mother and pushing away the baby-sitter.

Introduction

As Charles Darwin was preparing to submit a first article on his theory of evolution, his tenth and last child, his beloved baby Charles, fell ill of scarlet fever. He died, and cast the Darwin family into grief and despair. Darwin and his wife Emma had had the closest attachment to baby Charles, whom Darwin wrote had a "remarkably sweet, placid, and joyful disposition." Darwin believed that emotional tendencies were at the heart of people's characters, personalities, and disorders. It is in part, for this reason, that Darwin collected photos of the emotional expressions of patients in insane asylums, and it is in part for this reason that Darwin made many observations about the emotional tendencies of his ten children, the most poignant of which was evident in his writings about baby Charles.

In this chapter, we explore individual differences in emotion. Although emotions have universal aspects, based in our need to communicate with others, different emotions are experienced and displayed differently by different individuals. Some children are cheerful and contented much of the time, and they continue in the same kind of way as adults. Others are easily frustrated and grumpy. Yet others are habitually sad, or fearful. Such individual differences in emotions are central to personality. How do we understand them?

Emotion regulation

Every parent knows that crying lasts longer and is more intense in infants than in toddlers. Temper tantrums are most common in the second year. They decline in frequency and intensity subsequently (Goodenough, 1931). And, though we may think that physical aggression is greatest in adolescence and early adulthood, this is not so. It reaches its peak between 24 and 42 months of age and declines steadily thereafter (Tremblay, 2004). With crying, tantrums, and physical aggression, there are individual differences in how children regulate these expressions as they grow older. Calkins, Dedmon, and Gill (2002) studied six-month-olds and concluded that the extent to which they regulate their emotions in response to frustration constitutes an important basis of individual differences. In this section we extend this idea, and will see that people differ both in their success at managing emotions in ways appropriate to the social situation and the means they use to accomplish this management and regulation.

Children's ability to use language influences how they regulate their emotions. When they learn to speak they can talk about what distresses or angers them, rather than communicating only through expressions and actions (Kopp, 1992). Being able to talk about emotional issues may have an important impact on children's relationships with parents, as children start to "argue rather than resort to physical violence, to wait rather than wail, to contain their impatience rather than explode in tantrums" (Dunn

& Brown, 1991, p. 89). Mobility has an important effect: when infants begin to move and can start to satisfy some of their own desires, their need for an intense signaling system lessens (Campos, Kermoian, & Zumbahlen, 1992).

One view is that regulation starts with the **modulation** of the expression of emotion. In children, this is initially fostered by the caregiver, and gradually becomes internalized by the child. Kopp (1989), for instance, has argued that the regulatory function begins with the parent soothing the child. Crying has an insistent effect on parents, and they try to lessen it, modulating the emotion by picking the infant up, soothing, rocking, and so forth. Gradually the infant becomes able to soothe himself or herself.

Cicchetti, Ganiban, and Barnett (1991) described stages of emotion regulation. Failure at one stage has implications for subsequent stages. In the first months the task is to achieve stability in functioning. When the infant becomes too distressed, he or she learns to regain stability by signaling distress and by being comforted by the parent. With neurological development and repeated interactions, the child learns during the first year to inhibit certain expressions and soothe the self. At the end of the first year, attachment to a close, emotionally available caregiver becomes the central issue. Mental representations are formed of interactions with the caregiver, of when, where, and how she or he is available. So both child and caregiver regulate their emotions according to what can be expected from the other. The next phase is the development of the self system, and of self-regulation. At this point children begin to develop a notion of an autonomous self. They start to think about events, to find different ways of interpreting them, to calm themselves with thought. They learn gradually to become more independent in regulating their emotions, but supportive people remain vital to emotional equilibrium.

So what is emotion regulation? Some researchers have used it to refer to individual differences in intensity, frequency, and duration of emotions. So, for instance when a goal is blocked, one person may shout and behave angrily for several minutes, while another may feel mildly inconvenienced, look momentarily angry, and then forget about it. Another meaning of emotion regulation concerns the balance of emotions displayed by the individual (Cassidy, 1994). For instance, one person may show a propensity to anger rather than sadness, or may show few emotions.

Emotion regulation is also used to refer to the processes involved in modifying emotional reactions: the coping processes that lessen or augment the intensity of experience (Gross, 2002). If you are sitting in a traffic jam on the way to catch an airplane, you might try various means to feel less anxious: turn on the radio, think that you can always get on another plane, take deep breaths and try to relax. Regulatory processes affect every stage of the emotion process: appraisal of the event, evaluation of the context, the suppression of urges, as well as the selection and control of various kinds of expression and action (Frijda, 1986; Gross, 2002). Thompson (1994) has defined emotion regulation as "the extrinsic and intrinsic processes responsible for monitoring, evaluating, and modifying emotional reactions, especially their intensive and temporal features, to accomplish one's goals"

(p. 27). As an example of such a process, Rothbart, Ziaie, and O'Boyle (1992) have shown that some infants regulate arousal by shifting attention away from objects or people that are causing a high level of arousal. Individual differences in regulation are visible throughout childhood. For instance, Rydell, Berlin, and Bohlin (2003) found that children's emotionality and their skills of emotion regulation in the year before entering school predicted both prosocial behavior, and behavior problems in the early school years.

Emotion regulation is essential to socialization, since parental guidance involves encouraging some activities of offspring, and applying disciplinary measures to others. Feldman and Klein (2003) found that children who were able to regulate their emotions were those who had experienced warm parental control. As compared with children whose socialization was less successful, these children achieved a self-regulated compliance with mothers, fathers, and other caregivers.

One way to approach the problem of regulation is suggested by James Gross and his collaborators (e.g., Gross & John, 2003; John & Gross, 2004). In one study by this group (Butler et al., 2003) women viewed an unpleasant film clip. Each then met with another woman she did not know. Some women who had viewed the clip were asked to suppress their emotions by not expressing them. Others were asked simply to respond naturally. Yet others were asked to reappraise the experience by thinking of their current situation. Women who were asked to suppress, and the women they met, were found to have increased blood pressure, as compared with those who responded naturally, and those who reappraised. Suppression also reduced rapport: emotional responsiveness is important for communication. It made the people to whom the women spoke less willing to take part in a friendship. In other words, successful regulation is not accomplished by suppression. Shifting attention and **reappraisal** are the keys, and they are often accomplished by concentrating on what one is doing, for instance concentrating on the person one is talking to, or on the task in hand. John and Gross (2004) found that individuals differed in the means they used to regulate emotions. Individuals who aimed at suppression were not only less successful at regulation than those who reappraised, but less healthy. In terms of childhood regulation, socialization, and responsiveness to parental discipline, reappraisal means the child being able to hold the relationship with the parent as a high-level goal, even when other things may seem tempting. This helps to explain why firm but warm parenting is so important.

The theme of regulation continues into adolescence. For instance, Silk, Steinberg, and Morris (2003b) used the method of experience sampling (discussed in chapter 4), and found that adolescents between the ages of 12 and 15 who gave reports of greater intensity, greater lability, and less effective regulation, of their emotions over a week were more liable to depression and problem behavior. We continue our discussion of the perplexing question of how one may control one's emotions in chapter 14.

Issues of emotion regulation continue into later life. Carstenson, Fung, and Charles (2003) argue that as people get older their motivation increases to derive emotional meaning from life, rather than to expand emotional horizons. Lawton (2001) has reported that although responsiveness of the autonomic nervous system (discussed in chapter 5) decreases with age, experiential changes in emotion do not decline as people get older. Instead, despite social losses and health changes that occur with aging, people seem to increase their skills of emotion regulation as they age.

The implicit notion, common to the various approaches to emotion regulation, is that everyone has certain emotions, and that there are optimal levels at which these emotions are experienced and expressed. Dysregulation is what happens to individuals who cannot manage their emotions or accommodate to the current social situation. It is often used as a synonym for emotional disorder (Garber & Dodge, 1991), which we discuss in chapters 12 and 13.

Attachment

The "Strange Situation" and styles of attachment

Attachment theory, discussed in chapters 8 and 9, is perhaps the most developed and influential framework for thinking about how parent–child relations shape enduring patterns of emotionality (Shaver & Mikilincer, 2002; Mikulincer & Shaver, 2005). Emotions function as signals: the infant cries, and signals fear and a need for protection; this brings the parent closer. Bowlby (1971) saw attachment as an evolutionarily derived aspect of the parent–child relationship that is activated when the infant experiences a threat. If the baby expects the caregiver will be there to provide protection, the baby feels secure to explore the world, and learn new skills.

Research was advanced by Mary Ainsworth, who made attachment simultaneously a subject for experiments and for the identification of individual differences. She developed a test of infants' responses to a situation that was strange to them – the **Strange Situation** test – based on observations of infants' emotional reactions to brief separations from, and reunions with, their caregivers.

Using this test, Ainsworth et al. (1978) identified three distinct **attachment styles**. "Securely attached" infants are distressed when caregivers leave, but when their caregivers return they seek them, and can be comforted. There are then two styles of insecure attachment. "Ambivalently attached" infants want to be near caregivers upon their return, but at the same time will not be comforted, and show a great deal of angry and resistant behavior. "Avoidantly attached" infants make no effort to interact when their caregivers return.

Subsequently another style was added to these three by Main and Solomon (1986). It is called the disoriented/disorganized style, and it is seen in children who respond to parents in the Strange Situation with disorientation and contradictory behaviors. Main and Solomon (1990) found it in 13 percent of infants in a middle-class population. It was found in

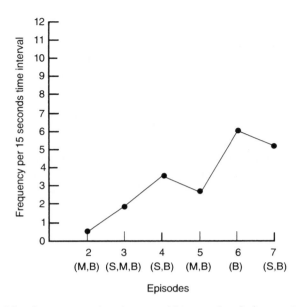

Figure 11.1 The frequency of crying per 15 seconds of observation, in different episodes of the "Strange Situation" test (Ainsworth & Bell, 1970). Along the x-axis are the episodes as follows: (Key: M = Mother present, B = Baby present, S = Stranger present) 2. Mother sits quietly with Baby; 3. Stranger enters and sits quietly, at the end of this episode Mother leaves unobtrusively; 4. Stranger tries to interact with Baby; 5. Mother returns and Stranger leaves unobtrusively, then at the end of the episode Mother leaves saying "bye-bye"; 6. Baby alone; 7. Stranger returns to interact with baby.

54 percent of infants of low-income mothers suffering from depression (Lyons-Ruth et al., 1990) and in 82 percent of abused children (Carlson et al., 1989).

Each attachment style has a specific pattern of emotionality, a bias, associated with it. Secure infants show both positive and negative emotions, as well as neutrality. Ambivalent infants show more negative emotions such as anger, and avoidant infants show fewer emotions of all kinds (Goldberg, MacKay, & Rochester, 1994). These emotional styles may reflect the child's history of interacting with caregivers (Cassidy, 1994). Secure babies demonstrate a range of negative and positive emotions, it is argued, because their parents have been responsive to all their emotional expressions. And indeed, Goldberg, Mackay, and Rochester (1994) found that, when mothers returned to their babies in the Strange Situation, the mothers of secure infants responded with behaviors such as distractions, prohibitions, and encouragement to a wider range of emotions than mothers of ambivalent or avoidant babies. By contrast, ambivalently attached infants may have been responded to only inconsistently, so that they have developed a strategy of noisy expression of negative emotions in an effort to get parents to respond to them; Goldberg, Mackay, and Rochester found that mothers of ambivalent babies were most responsive to negative affect, and were least responsive to positive affect. Avoidant babies are thought to have experienced repeated rejections; Goldberg, Mackay, and Rochester found that mothers of these babies were the least responsive to their babies' negative emotions. So it is thought that although avoidant babies feel negative emotions, these babies have adopted a strategy of infrequently showing them. Consistent with this claim, one study found that avoidant babies showed fewer facial and vocal displays of emotion during the Strange Situation than secure babies, they had similar levels of heart rate during the test, but higher cortisol levels after it (Spangler & Grossmann, 1993).

Studies carried out in English-speaking countries with middle-class subjects have generally found that about 65 percent of infants show secure attachment in the Strange Situation test, as compared with 15 percent who are ambivalent, and 20 percent who are avoidant. In other countries these proportions are different. In Israel, Sagi et al. (1985) found that a very high proportion of babies showed the ambivalent style in the Strange Situation: with marked distress on separation, and anger and sadness when the mother returned. In Germany, the Grossmanns and their colleagues (1985) found that nearly half of the babies were avoidant: they showed little emotional reaction to either the mother leaving or the mother returning. In Germany as compared with the USA, parents were less encouraging of close bodily contact and more encouraging of independence as soon as the child became mobile. In Japan, Miyake, Chen, and Campos (1985) found no avoidant babies. These differences have many potential sources. Children in different cultures are likely to vary in how frequently they experience separation from parents, so the separation and reunion procedure varies from being terrifying to being commonplace. Also possible is that some cultures may value early independence, whereas others discourage it. Another possibility is that in some cultures the expression of fear and sadness is encouraged, but in other societies it is discouraged, leading to different emotions being expressed during the Strange Situation procedure.

Internal working models of attachment

Early emotional interactions with caregivers, Bowlby hypothesized, lead children to build an **internal working model** of relationships. It is a mental model, or set of beliefs, of what to expect in an intimate relationship. Can the other person be trusted? Can one expect comfort and love from others? Such a model is preverbal, it is formed before the child learns language, but if it could be spelled out in words, the model of a secure child would be something like "When I am in danger, I can trust my parent to protect me." For an avoidant child it would be something like: "When I am in danger, be wary, rely only on myself." So, it is thought, such internal models form the basis of a persisting emotional bias. They start in early relationships with caregivers, they are somewhat resistant to change, and they affect all later intimate relationships (Bowlby, 1988; Mikulincer & Shaver, 2005). The striking idea conceived by Bowlby (and before him by Freud) is that each intimate relationship leaves an imprint. It becomes an element in the construction of selfhood, a template of how to understand and act in intimate relationships subsequently.

If internal working models are important, and if they do influence later relationships, we would expect the experiences of childhood to influence parenting when individuals become adults and have babies of their own. In early work in this area, George, Kaplan, and Main (1985) developed the Adult Attachment Interview to examine how people think about their early attachment relationships: people are asked about their relationship with their parents when they were children, and also in the present. The interview covers what they remembered doing when they were upset in childhood, whether they were ever rejected, and so forth. On the basis of this interview, adults are classified into secure/autonomous, preoccupied, or dismissing, and these categories are thought respectively to derive from secure, ambivalent, and avoidant attachment in infancy. Autonomous adults are those who talk about their childhood experiences with objectivity and balance. They give a coherent account of difficulties in their childhood, experiences that may have been good or bad. Adults are rated as preoccupied when they give incoherent accounts of their experiences and still seem overwhelmed by their memories of their often traumatic childhood. Dismissing adults give a very distanced account of their childhood, characterized by inability to recall events, by idealization or by over-rationalization, with little show of emotion.

So how do adults with these different styles affect the attachment styles of their own babies? To answer this question Fonagy, Steele, and Steele (1991) assessed women on the Adult Attachment Interview during their pregnancy, then measured the attachment style of their babies at age one in the Strange Situation test: 75 percent of the secure/autonomous women had securely attached one-year-olds, and 73 percent of preoccupied or dismissing women had insecurely attached one-year-olds (ambivalent or avoidant). This evidence tells us that adults do have relational styles that are measurable, and that something of these styles is passed on from generation to generation (see also Van Ijzendoorn, 1992).

A critical test of the idea that attachment forms a template for subsequent intimate relationships would be to measure attachment styles of children at age one, and then use the Adult Attachment Interview to measure the **continuity** of styles of relating into adulthood. In 2000, Everett Waters and colleagues published three studies using this method (Waters, Hamilton, & Weinfield, 2000).

In the first study, Waters et al. (2000) followed up 60 white middle-class people who had been classified in the Strange Situation as infants and were given an adult attachment interview at the age of 21. Seventy-two percent of participants maintained their style of secure versus insecure attachment. Was anything associated with switching into a different attachment style? The answer was yes: a negative life event such as loss of a parent, parental divorce, parental physical or psychiatric illness, and physical or sexual abuse of the child. The second study, by Hamilton (2000), was of 30 children in a project on family lifestyle. Of the 30 children 12 were from conventional families in which the parents were married, and 18 from unconventional families that had either a single parent, or unmarried parents, or parents who were living in a commune, or who were living in a loosely affiliated group of non-related people. Despite lower income and higher turnover of people in the families with unconventional lifestyles, both the initial attachment classifications and the continuity of attachment style of these children were similar to those of the conventional families. Overall 77 percent of participants in this study maintained their secure versus insecure status. The third study was of 57 children from backgrounds of poverty with high developmental risk. In this cohort, Weinfield, Sroufe, and Egeland (2000) did not find continuity of attachment style from age one to age 21. They did, however, find that this group had high rates of negative life events – child maltreatment, depression in mothers, and family malfunctioning in early adolescence – and that these events seemed to be major influences in changes from secure to insecure attachment styles.

In another study Grossmann et al. (2002) found less strong evidence of continuities in Germany than did Waters et al. in America. They measured: attachment style by the Strange Situation (as well as home observation variables) in infancy, separation anxiety at age six, and attachment as indicated by the Adult Attachment Interview at age 16. In a sample of 38 people who were followed up to age 21 or 22, security of relationships at that age was predicted by the attachment measure at 6 years and by the interview at 16, but not by the Strange Situation or other measures in infancy. Nor did attachment styles in the Strange Situation at age one predict Adult Attachment Interview styles at age 16.

Evidence of continuity in young adults has been offered by Treboux, Crowell, and Waters (2004) who gave the Adult Attachment Interview to members of 157 couples three months before they were married, and 15 months after they were married. They found that 78 percent of participants retained their attachment classification (secure, preoccupied, dismissing) from the measurements before and after marriage, and that change was related to experience in the marital relationship and/or to life events.

So although continuities of attachment styles do occur in quite striking ways, they do not imply that internal working models of relating are rigid in programming behavior. Life events, such as severe relational problems, can affect such models. And even individuals who have experienced early attachment failures can recover from them, to build satisfactory attachment relationships later in their lives, as we shall see in the next chapter.

Influences on attachment

According to Bowlby's evolutionary approach, the attachment system is based on babies' expressions of fear and distress which keep the mother close to the baby, and summon her to the baby's aid. Ainsworth et al. (1978) visited the homes of mothers and their babies every three weeks during the first year. Among other observations, they noted how rapidly mothers responded to their babies crying. Mothers who responded to their babies rapidly and consistently were more likely to have babies who were classified as secure in the Strange Situation at one year.

The striking finding about influences on attachment is that whereas the attachment system is universal, the style of attachment that each individual acquires comes from parenting. This has been shown in a behavioral genetic study of 157 twins by Bokhorst et al. (2003). They found that although genetics had a large influence on temperament (see below), there was almost no influence of genetics on style of attachment (secure, ambivalent, avoidant) as measured by the Strange Situation test. Instead, some 52 percent of the variance was attributed to shared environment, that is to say the conditions in the family that were experienced by all the children in the family, and 48 percent to unshared environment, that is to say conditions of particular relationships of parents with individual children. Bokhorst et al. also found no evidence of a genetic influence on the disorganized attachment style. Reactive disorders of attachment are associated with childhood maltreatment (Zeanah & Fox, 2004). One implication is that style of attachment, represented in mental models of relating, is passed on from parent to child. In their review of the evidence for this phenomenon Van Ijzendoorn and Bakermans-Kranenberg (1997) say that intergenerational transmission of attachment style is an established fact. Support for this statement comes from a meta-analysis of interventions to improve the sensitivity of parenting by Bakermans-Kranenberg, van Ijzendoorn, and Juffer (2003) in which it was found that such interventions were effective in promoting secure attachment style in infants. The intergenerational transmission of attachment may be compared with the intergenerational transmission of mothering abilities, also little influenced by genetics but based on experience of being mothered during childhood (Fleming et al., 2002), that we discussed in chapter 9.

Effects of attachment

Children classified as securely attached at age one have been found, later in their preschool years, to have better relationships with other children (Sroufe et al., 1984), to be more sociable and communicative with adults (Lutkenhaus, Grossmann, & Grossmann, 1985; Main, Kaplan, & Cassidy, 1985), to have better problem-solving skills, and to be more compliant (Londerville & Main, 1981; Matas, Arend, & Sroufe, 1978). Attachment styles have also been found to exert influences upon adults' intimate relationships (Collins & Feeney, 2000; Feeney & Collins, 2001; Fraley & Shaver, 1998; Rholes, Simpson, & Orina, 1999; Simpson, Ickes, & Grich, 1999; Simpson, Rholes, & Phillips, 1996).

Several studies suggest, in addition, that securely attached individuals are more contented (for example, Cooper, Shaver, & Collins, 1998; Shaver & Brennan, 1992). Moreover, DeOliveira, Moran, and Pederson (2005) found that mothers who were securely attached according to the Adult Attachment Interview had a much more flexible and adaptable mindset towards their own and their toddlers' emotions than mothers who were insecurely attached. And further studies have uncovered certain general life problems associated with an anxious attachment style (Mikulincer & Shaver, 2003). Anxiously attached individuals were found more likely to interpret life events in pessimistic, threatening fashion, which may increase chances of depression.

In an imaginative study, Fraley and Shaver (1998) surreptitiously observed romantic partners as they said good-bye in airports. Afterwards, they had them fill out an attachment questionnaire. Those who sought less physical contact and engaged in fewer embraces and less hand-holding as they departed from one another were more likely to be avoidant. In other studies, secure individuals were found more likely to report that their partners and friends were more forthcoming in offering support than were anxious and avoidant individuals (Florian, Mikulincer, & Bucholtz, 1995). The securely attached also tended to interpret their partners' criticism or insensitivity in a charitable fashion (Collins, 1996).

Warmth and the socialization of emotions

In chapter 9, we presented evidence that alongside the system of attachment is another system, which we called affiliative, based on warmth and affection. In a range of studies, parental warmth and affection – not just influences on attachment – have been found to influence many aspects of a child's development. Parental warmth and affection influence childhood friendships, social skills, and many other aspects of children's later emotional well-being (Maccoby & Martin, 1983; Steelman et al., 2002). O'Connor et al. (2001b) found that parental warmth predicted success of children's friendships at school, in both biological and adoptive families. Belsky and Fearon (2004) found that whereas secure infants tend to have the best outcomes in terms of social competency, infants classified as insecure who have warm and sensitive mothers had better outcomes than those who were secure but who had insensitive mothers.

Kochanska et al. (2004) have studied the mutuality of child–parent interactions that emphasized mutual responsiveness. In a warm atmosphere, not only is the mother responsive, but so is the child. A mutual responsiveness develops (Kochanska & Aksan, 2004; Kochanska et al., 2005). In terms of individual differences, the responsive child is one who can switch her or his goals to mutual ones shared with parents. Kochanska et al. (2004) have shown that children brought up in their first year with warm positive parenting by their mothers are able to accept the mother's socialization agenda, and that this acceptance has an important influence on the development of conscience and moral conduct at the age of four and a half (see also Rothbart et al., 2003). Belsky et al. (2005) found that children observed since the age of three, who were further observed when they themselves became parents of three-year-olds, showed an intergenerational effect of warm parenting.

Closely related to the idea of mutuality is "synchronization," which is typically captured with more fine-grained measures than the global ratings of attunement used to capture maternal sensitivity. Isabella, Belsky, and Von Eye (1989) separated mothers into two categories. The mothers who were synchronized kept in tune and in time with their babies: when the babies vocalized they did too, when the babies wanted to gaze at the mother's face the mother gazed back, when the baby wanted to explore, the mother assisted this, and so on. The interactions of the pair were reciprocal and mutually rewarding. By contrast, non-synchronized mothers would vocalize or try to stimulate their babies when the babies were asleep or being quiet, and they would sometimes remain quiet and unresponsive when the babies vocalized. Isabella, Belsky, and Von Eye found that mothers who kept more closely in time with their one-month-olds and three-month-olds during interactions with them had babies who were more likely to be securely attached at one year.

Learning to speak about emotions

Among the processes that are important in the patterns of emotional expression that individuals develop, consider the role of language. Through emotion language, parents and other caregivers structure a world that will contribute to the emotional experience of children. Parents do this in several ways. One way is to talk to children about the kinds of events that evoke emotions. For instance, a father says to his daughter who is recoiling at the sight of a big dog: "You don't need to be scared of him." On another occasion she wanders into the cycle path, and a bicyclist narrowly misses her. Her father rushes to her and says, "That's dangerous! You really frightened me." Such emotional communications teach children about what events appropriately elicit emotions in their community, inducting the child into the cultural rules of emotional expression. Emotion talk also structures the child's own internal experience, and lets the child know about the internal experience of others.

Consider for instance when a mother talks about why she is angry. She makes clear her motivations and intentions; the child can construct a model of what makes the mother angry and why. When a mother does not explain herself, the child's information is less complete, and more likely to be incorrect. Zahn-Waxler, Radke-Yarrow, and King (1979) found that parental explanations and reasoning (delivered at intense emotional levels) were associated with increased displays of empathy in children. When children were given better information about internal states of others through language, they were better able to respond with understanding and concern to others.

We can see effects of certain kinds of extreme family experience on emotion talk from work by Cicchetti and Beeghly (1987). They compared talk about mental and other internal states of a group of maltreated children with that of a group of children of similar socioeconomic background who had not been maltreated. Toddlers who had been maltreated used fewer words for bodily states such as hunger and thirst, and for negative emotions, such as hatred, anger, disgust. Presumably, children who have been maltreated had either not much opportunity to discuss internal states or were frightened to do so because of negative consequences.

Effects of modeling

Any time a parent enacts some behavior, drying the dishes or speaking angrily to the cat, for example, this person acts as a **model** for children who are then more likely to perform the same kinds of behavior, and this process is thought to be very important in passing on messages about what emotions to display, and how. Families differ in the type and frequency of emotions that are displayed to their children. Malatesta and Haviland (1982) found that most mothers display negative emotions to their infants only rather rarely. In six-minute periods of mother–baby interaction, mothers showed an average of 21 enjoyment expressions to babies, 0.5 sadness expressions, and 0.2 anger expressions. These mothers showed their children 100 times more enjoyment than anger and 40 times more enjoyment than sadness. As their children got older, parents displayed more negative emotions to their babies, but these expressions still remained very infrequent. Jenkins (2000) has provided evidence for what she calls an anger organization in some children. Children exposed to many instances of anger between their parents also became angry, and showed more frequent anger, more deviant anger, and more angry taunting, than children who were not exposed to angry conflicts between their parents (see also Jenkins et al., 1995; Jenkins & Oatley, 2000).

Over time individual infants become more similar to their mothers in terms of their expressions of emotion (Malatesta & Haviland, 1982). If their own mothers' expressions include more anger than those of other mothers, then by six months the infants too show more anger than do other infants. If their mothers display more happiness, then by six months the infants show more happiness. The way that children can produce the same emotions as people they observe has also been called emotion contagion (Hatfield, Cacioppo, & Rapson, 1994).

Responding to some emotions but not others

As babies develop language, they learn many different ways of communicating about internal states. As they see their infants having more flexible ways of expressing their needs, parents change the ways in which they respond to their children's emotions. One way of doing this is to pay attention to acceptable modes of expression, and to ignore other modes of expression. Brooks-Gunn and Lewis (1982) found that mothers responded more to crying in their babies' first six months than in their second year.

But as their children reached a year, and then two years, parents increased their responding to their child's vocalizations and efforts to speak. Such behavior says to the children: "I'll pay attention to you when you talk to me, but not just when you cry." They also found that mothers responded less to the crying of boys than to the crying of girls. We see that even by two years old mothers are inducting their children into a culture in which it is less acceptable to cry to achieve goals, and less acceptable for boys to show sadness than girls (see also Fivush, 1989).

Dunn, Bretherton, and Munn (1987) provide other evidence showing how parents change the way in which they respond to emotions as children get older. They found that mothers' references to feeling states following a child's distress decreased as the child aged from 18 to 24 months, presumably to de-emphasize negative emotions (see also Kochanska & Aksan, 2004). Martini, Root, and Jenkins (2004) found that in middle income families mothers were more likely to control their own angry responses to their children's anger, whereas in lower income families mothers tended to suppress their non-angry responses to their children's anger, perhaps because they had a greater belief in firmness in parenting.

We might think from our discussion about attachment and **parental responsiveness** that the best thing for parents to do as soon as a child is distressed is to respond immediately and sympathetically. Indeed, we discussed one study that did find that mothers of secure infants responded to a wider range of infant's emotions than mothers of insecure babies (Goldberg, Mackay, & Rochester, 1994). But as we see from the way that parents selectively attend to emotions, it is clear that parents' goals are more complex than simply protecting or comforting children, particularly as children get older. Imagine for instance a three-year-old who whines whenever another child reaches over to play with his toy. The likelihood is that a parent watching this may comfort, but will also explain about the need to share. If the whining and refusal to share escalate, the parent may use assertion: "You won't be able to play with those toys if you are going to whine like that." As infants become toddlers, parents make complex evaluations about how distressed their child is, what the context of their expression is, how important the situation is in teaching a long-term lesson, and so forth (Dix, 1991).

In studies of the outcomes of parental responses to children's emotions, two kinds of outcomes are typically investigated: the frequency of expression of certain negative emotions (e.g., anger) and whether children are liked by their peers (social competence). Roberts and Strayer (1987) examined parental responsiveness to emotion in three- to five-year-old children. They found that most parents responded to children with firmness, but also helped the children with what had caused the distress, thereby communicating that they understood the child's goal. A medium level of parental responsiveness was associated with higher levels of social competence in children; however, a high level of responsiveness was not. Some parents were too responsive to negative emotions; these parents had children who were less competent in their interactions with others. Other work also points to the delicate balancing act that parents need to achieve when responding to their children's emotions. Eisenberg and Fabes (1994) found that parents who were higher on trying to control or minimize their children's display of negative emotion, by, for instance, telling a child to go to another room when he or she started to cry, had children who showed less anger in their peer group. However, these investigators found that being more sympathetic and comforting when children showed negative emotions was also associated with children showing less anger in their peer group. In a more recent study, Valiente et al. (2004) found that mothers' reports of their own negative emotions predicted their children's negative emotionality when watching a distressing film.

It may be that when children get older, responding sympathetically to their negative emotion displays without also giving some coaching on a way of communicating anger or distress that is developmentally, socially, and culturally acceptable, may reinforce the negative emotion expression. Snyder and Patterson (1986) have found that certain kinds of parental responses to anger can reinforce it, thereby increasing the chances that children will respond angrily on other occasions. Patterson (1982; Patterson et al., 1998) observed that when children are aggressive, other people in the family tend to withdraw or lessen their demands, thus giving the child what he or she wants, and providing a reward for a display of aggression. Rewarding aggression in this way is associated with increased aggression, and in some families with criminal offending by the children.

What influences on the parents might contribute to how they respond to their children? One factor may be how the parents have dealt with emotional issues in their own lives. Earlier in this chapter we talked about how parents and children show concordance in their attachment styles. Perhaps one of the mechanisms contributing to this concordance is that parents train emotional styles that are acceptable to them. One way to investigate this is to ask parents about their own views about the expression of anger and sadness. Hooven, Gottman, and Katz (1995) have called this **meta-emotion** – what people think about feelings. They interviewed parents about meta-emotion when their children were aged five. They found that at the age of eight the children of parents who were both aware of their own sadness and anger, and coached their children in the meaning of such emotions and how to deal with them, showed less evidence of stress, showed less negative emotion in play with their friends, better achievement at school, and fewer behavior problems.

It would seem, then, that there is no single best formula for how to respond to children's emotions, and no single best mode of emotional expression that a child can show. Instead, it seems that parental behaviors that encourage children to consider their emotional expressions in the context of their interactions will be most effective. Beyond infancy, this will not always mean being sympathetic and responsive. Sometimes it will mean ignoring a child's whining, or angry demands. Sometimes firmness requires the assertion of power to impress upon a child that his or her mode of expression is unacceptable to others.

We have considered the impact of parental responsiveness to children's emotions. What about how other significant people in children's lives react to their emotions? Less is known about this area of emotion socialization. Strayer (1980) observed four- and five-year-olds playing and documented how children's emotional expressions were responded to by their peers. During interactions children most frequently showed happiness (34 percent), then sadness (30 percent), then anger (22 percent), and least commonly hurt (13 percent). For the most part their companions just let these expressions pass. Hurt was most often ignored, followed by anger, then sadness, then happiness; so the emotions that were most often displayed were also those that were most often responded to by other children. Children gave more empathic responses to happy expressions than to all other emotions combined, and fewer in response to anger than to all other emotions combined. When emotions were responded to, the responses were different for different emotions: happy displays usually met with happiness, sad displays usually met with an attempt to share an activity or a toy, angry expression most often met with verbal or physical acknowledgement like moving out of the way, and hurt expressions met with reassurance or a question such as "Are you OK?" So different emotions are responded to very differently by children.

It is important to note that these reactions change with the age of the child. For instance, Denham (1986) found when she observed two- to three-year-old children that they were more responsive to other children's anger than they were to their sadness, a quite different result from that found by Strayer. It may be that as children get older they get better at responding to lower intensity emotions (like sadness) in other people. In any case, such differential responding probably affects children's expressions of emotion with their peers. Children learn what results when they are angry, when they are sad, and so forth within the context of their age group. Those children who are socially integrated alter their own expressions accordingly.

How cultures affect the development of emotionality

Let us situate the influences of family members and peers upon the child's emotions within a cultural framework. Families exist within societies and are influenced by patterns of emotion within that society. As we have seen in chapters 3 and 9, among the Yanomamö anger and aggression are valued. Children and adults who are not fierce find it hard to exist in this society and the upbringing is designed to foster aggression (Eibl-Eibesfeldt, 1979). Patterson (1985) arrived at a similar claim about children's aggression in coercive families. When others are hostile, to protect oneself one also must use escalating angry aggression. In a quite different kind of society, Briggs (1970) described her observations of an indulgent style of early upbringing in an Inuit family: by the age of six Inuit children show little or no anger (see also Briggs, 2000). In yet other cultures upbringing is designed to make children tough, and show low levels of fear or sadness. Thus Harkness and Super (1985) described the Kipsigis, in a small community in Kenya. When a child aged two cries, the mother waits for the child to come to her. She comforts the child but also quickly offers distraction. With the first sign of calming, the child is returned to the care of siblings. These children are socialized to disregard any internal experience of sadness and pain. At adolescence girls will undergo clitoridectomy and boys circumcision as rites of passage into adult life. During these painful procedures they must not cry, or else they bring disgrace onto themselves and their family with very unfortunate consequences.

These cultural beliefs about emotions and their display have profound influences on emotionality in children. For example, different cultures have very different rates of certain kinds of emotional disorders in childhood. In Thailand (Weisz et al., 1987), children who are referred to clinics are low on disorders based on anger – involving aggression, hostility, stealing, and lying – when compared with children in the USA. Thai children live in a Buddhist culture in which a high value is placed on peacefulness and deference in order to avoid disturbing others. But the Thai children showed higher rates of problems with fearfulness, anxiety, and psychosomatic symptoms than their US counterparts.

Emotion schemas: bridges from childhood to adult relationships

Children develop schemas, or mental models, about emotions within relationships. These schemas are representations of self-and-other in relation to how emotions unfold, to what emotions are appropriate, and to what they mean (Mitchell, 1988). These schemas are likely to guide us in our interactions through the course of life (e.g., Baldwin, 1992).

Stern (1994) has described how we develop a variety of schemas of "being with another person" based on our early experiences. At the core of such schemas is a representation of our goals in interaction. The baby wants something to happen, and looks to the parent to join in with him or her to fulfill this goal. The goal, and the emotions associated with it, unfold over time, and lead to different representations of what it is like to "be" with another person. Stern describes how a baby might interact with a mother who is depressed. First the baby invites the mother to play, by being animated, trying to elicit a response. But the depressed mother fails to attune. In another attempt to be with the mother, the baby takes on and shares the mother's depressed mood. The baby moves from being animated to being sad, and joins in the mother's sad emotions. Next, the baby may also look to herself or himself, rather than to the mother, for engagement and arousal, while still experiencing the distanced mother in the background. Perhaps then, the mother starts to feel stronger; she may force herself to engage with her baby. The baby experiences her as more animated, but slightly out of tune because the interaction is a forced one. Now another kind of schema may emerge, from this false interaction: a "false self" with a "false mother." Stern postulates that these are all "schemas of being with" that, as the child gets older, are then experienced with other people. From childhood, and from subsequent relationships, we carry forward with us emotional schemas of how to take part in interactions, based on the kinds of relating we have experienced.

Temperament

From the very first hours of life children show marked individual differences in their emotions. Some babies are placid and easily calmed when upset. Others are more passionate; they become upset easily and intensely. Some babies enjoy social interaction and engage with other people easily. Others become distressed when people try to play with them; they attempt to withdraw. Such differences are called "temperament."

Whereas attachment categories and modes of socialization are influenced primarily by the family environment, temperament has a large heritable (genetic) component. It is an aspect of behavior that is constitutional, stable over time and across situations, and it has a neurophysiological basis (Goldsmith, 1993, 2003).

Biases of emotion at the core of temperament

Joseph Campos et al. (1983) have argued that emotion is at the core of temperament, that we can define temperamental types in terms of the propensity to experience and express different emotions. In making this claim, Campos and colleagues show how temperamental dimensions, proposed by principal temperament theorists, map onto different emotions (see table 11.1).

How do researchers measure temperament? Most typically they do so by having parents rate their children on how quickly they are roused to anger, or the amount of fear that they show in certain situations. Alternatively, research observations of temperament involve the kinds of emotional expression children show during an assessment period.

Stability of temperament

One of the criteria of temperament is stability over time. Stability over six months and one year is fairly high, particularly when parental reports are used to assess temperament. Rothbart (1986) reported correlations between parents' ratings of smiling/laughter, fear, and distress to limitations, taken at six and nine months of $r = 0.48$, 0.37, and 0.51 respectively. Worobey and Blajda (1989) reported on correlations between two months and one year of 0.46 for positive reactivity and 0.50 for negative reactivity (irritability). Continuities spanning many years have also been found. Chess and Thomas (1990) assessed a group of people as adults who had ratings of temperament made

Table 11.1 Mapping of dimensions of temperament onto aspects of emotions, for two well-known schemes of temperament: Buss and Plomin's (1975) with four dimensions, and Rothbart's (1981) with six dimensions

Dimensions of temperament	Aspects of emotion into which each dimension maps
Buss & Plomin (1975)	
Emotionality	Fear, anger, and distress
Activity	General arousal of the motor system
Sociability	Interest and positive emotions expressed towards people
Impulsivity	Time taken to express emotion or activity
Rothbart (1981)	
Activity	General arousal of the motor system
Smiling and laughter	Happiness or pleasure
Fear	Fear
Distress to limitations	Anger
Soothability	Recovery time from negative emotions when soothed
Persistence	Duration of interest

Source: Adapted from Campos et al. (1983)

each year in their first five years. Measures of easy versus difficult temperament in years three, four, and five showed the following correlations with the same measure in adulthood: $r = 0.31$, $r = 0.37$, $r = 0.15$.

Even using measures of emotionality that are only based on how frequently children show certain facial expressions of emotion, continuities across time are evident. Hyson and Izard (1985) videotaped children during brief separations from their mother during Ainsworth's "Strange Situation" procedure at 13 months and 18 months, and their facial expressions were coded in a precise fashion. Continuity across the interval between the two tests was extremely high for expressions of interest ($r = 0.90$), for anger ($r = 0.61$), and for total negative expressions ($r = 0.90$), but sadness had low continuity. Comparable results were found using Michael Lewis's procedure of having infants pull a string attached to their arm to turn on music; Sullivan, Lewis, and Alessandri (1992) compared effects of the same conditions at two-month intervals for infants of two to eight months old. High continuity was found in the frequencies of expressions of anger, interest, joy, and surprise, but low continuities were found for sadness and fear.

Another demonstration of the stability of individual differences in emotionality is found in the work of Malatesta et al. (1989a). Babies' facial expressions were coded while their mothers played with them and again on reunion after a brief period of separation. Between 7 and 22 months of age infants showed continuity of negative expressions of anger ($r = 0.32$) and sadness ($r = 0.37$). Continuity was not found for positive expressions, perhaps because these were more responsive to the moment-by-moment flow of interaction.

Shyness is another dimension of temperament. Very shy children have a high stable heart rate, and greater sympathetic reactivity, suggesting a lower threshold for limbic-hypothalamic arousal to unexpected changes in the environment, and these physiological measures also show continuity over time (Kagan, 1982). Davidson and Fox (1989) were able to predict how much babies would cry when separated from their parent from greater electroencephalogram (EEG) activation of the right, as compared with the left, side of the cortex during a baseline period. Kagan, Reznick, and Snidman (1988) followed up children from two to seven years of age who were extremely inhibited at age two: these were children who, in response to unfamiliar adults and children, clung to their mothers, stopped speaking, and did not interact with the unfamiliar person for a long time. About 7 percent of an unselected sample of two-year-olds were classified in this way. At age seven, ratings of behavioral inhibition were again made. Behavior was coded as the children were observed entering a situation with ten other same-aged, same-sex children. Frequency of spontaneous comments, and periods of standing apart were measured. Continuities were only evident in that small group of children who were found to be extremely shy at age two, not in the total sample of children, but at age seven these extremely shy children approached other children less, and were less talkative with the researchers. Continuities in shy behavior have also been found by Rubin (1993) who followed up socially inhibited children from the age of four until mid-adolescence. Preschool ratings of shyness did not predict social behavior at age 14, but ratings of shyness at seven predicted loneliness ($r = 0.50$) and lack of integration with the peer group ($r = 0.40$) at age 14 (see also Putnam & Stifter, 2005).

So using both parental ratings and facial expressions, it has been found that children have some characteristic styles of emotionality. Some biases that can be observed in infancy persist as typical emotional patterns during childhood and later in life.

Genetic basis of temperament

Most theorists argue that temperament is partly inherited (Buss & Plomin, 1984; Plomin & Caspi, 1998) and **twin studies** have been carried out to estimate the size of this influence. Identical, or monozygotic (MZ), twins who share all their genes, and non-identical, or dizygotic (DZ), twins who on average share half their genes, have been compared on parental ratings of temperament, and in some studies on observers' ratings made in a laboratory. Other designs to investigate genetic effects have involved comparing natural and adopted siblings with one another.

There is evidence for genetic effects on the main dimensions of temperament (Campos et al., 1983; Plomin & Caspi, 1998), although estimates of heritability vary depending on whether the measure is based on observation or parental report, the design of the study, and the dimension of temperament being assessed. In an investigation by Emde et al. (1992), two hundred pairs of 14-month-old twins, half monozygotic and half dizygotic, were studied. Some measures of emotionality and temperament of the children were assessed by parental report, some by independent observers, and some by both. Genetic influence was evident for behavioral inhibition (as measured by observation), and for the very similar construct of shyness (as measured by both parental report and observation). Parental reports of temperament and negative emotion also indicated genetic effects. There was, however, no evidence for genetic effects from observational measures of negative and positive emotion, overall mood, or frustration.

A recent summary from twin studies may be seen in table 11.2 from Goldsmith (2003) in which correlations between members of twin pairs (monozygotic and dizygotic) were measured on a number of temperament scales. A genetic influence is indicated where correlations between scores are higher for monozygotic than for dizygotic twins, and the size of the genetic influence is measured by a difference in these correlations. An example of a high genetic effect may be seen in the fourth line of table 11.2, where you will see that monozygotic twins showed a high correlation between their scores on Interest/Persistence on the Goldsmith Questionnaire, while dizygotic twins showed a low correlation. Where the R-values are similar for monozygotic and dizygotic twins, e.g., Pleasure on the Goldsmith Questionnaire, on the third line of table 11.2, this indicates a low genetic influence.

In summary, twin studies indicate that genetic influences play a role in children's emotionality, although the effects are not the same across all measures of temperament. Studies of adoption, in which emotional characteristics of parents and their biological and adopted children have been made, have shown less evidence of the heritability of emotional styles (Plomin, 1988).

Table 11.2 R-values (age- and sex-controlled correlations) for monozygotic and dizygotic twins on selected temperament scales

	Monozygotic R	Dizygotic R
Goldsmith's *Toddler Behavior Assessment Questionnaire*		
Social fearfulness	.50	.40
Anger proneness	.72	.55
Pleasure	.69	.64
Interest/Persistence	.81	.26
Rothbart's *Children's Behavior Questionnaire* (Factor scales)		
Negative affect	.69	.28
Surgency (positive affect)	.60	.11
Effortful control	.61	.25

Source: From Goldsmith (2003)

Temperament and parenting

Along with hereditary factors, individual differences in infant emotionality are also affected by parenting. Belsky, Fish, and Isabella (1991) examined changes in infants' negative and positive emotionality between three and nine months as a function of family dynamics. As compared with children who remained low in negative emotionality, children who changed from low to high negative emotionality had fathers who were less affectively oriented toward others, who were less positive about their marriages before their infants were born, and who were more discrepant with their wives in the amount of involvement they had with the baby. As compared to infants who remained high in negative emotionality, those who changed from high to low negative emotionality had mothers who were high in self-esteem, who experienced less negativity in their marriages, and who showed more harmonious, complementary, and responsive interaction with their infants. Stability and change in infants' emotionality over time were therefore affected by the emotional tone of the family environment.

Bowlby (1971) and Hinde (1976) have argued that the developing emotional relationship between parent and child is a reciprocal process: just as the baby has to fit in with the parents, the parents must fit in with the baby's temperament. It is a fact of life for parents that some infants are more difficult than others; some stretch adaptive abilities of parents to their limits. It has seemed likely to researchers that parents would respond differently to babies who have different temperaments. One might expect parents to withdraw more from infants with irritable temperaments, to protect themselves from feelings of helplessness and disappointment. Crockenberg (1986) reviewed research findings, and concluded that there is only modest support for this hypothesis. In some studies mothers were found to withdraw more from temperamentally difficult children (Peters-Martin & Wachs, 1984), but in others mothers were more involved when infants were temperamentally difficult (Bates et al., 1982).

Parents who are struggling with their difficult babies can welcome the acknowledgment from a clinician that they have a baby who would stretch the caregiving capacity of any parent. The concept of temperament can make all the difference to some parents who are seeking help for themselves and their babies. It can help them to renew their efforts to cope with the at times trying idiosyncrasies of their baby.

Overall we can say that both genetically influenced temperamental effects of infants, and also effects of parents as they support their children, are important in how children grow up. For instance, Kim-Cohen et al. (2004) found in a study of 1,116 twin pairs that both genetic and environmental effects affected resilience in the face of environmental deprivation. The positive genetic influences pertained to the outgoing temperament of the child. Positive environmental influences included parental warmth and the provision of stimulating activities.

Affective biases, adult personality, and the course of life

So far in this chapter we have sought to understand the origins of individual differences in emotionality. We have seen that emotional patterns become established within the attachment dynamics between parent and child, that parental warmth is important for socialization, and that inherited temperament contributes a good deal to the emotional character of the individual. What are the implications of such childhood differences in emotionality for adulthood? To what extent does your past account for your present personality and emotional life?

In light of the kinds of findings we have reviewed thus far, theorists like Carol Magai (formerly Carol Malatesta) have proposed that individual differences in emotion can be thought of as organizational structures that are at the core of adult personality, and that they affect the individual's ongoing interactions with others (Magai & McFadden, 1996; Rosenberg, 1998). Such affective biases shape how people routinely feel, how they construe life events, and how they act within the environment across the lifespan. Specific emotions like love or fear may come to predominate in how the individual responds to important social circumstances. These specific modes or **biases** may be molded by repetitive kinds of interactions, and develop a continuity through time. This idea that early established emotional biases shape adult personality and emotionality translates to several predictions, which we now examine.

Patterns of childhood emotionality that extend to adult life

Would we expect children who are angry and easily frustrated to become hostile adults? Would we expect inhibited, fearful children such as those profiled in Jerome Kagan's work on childhood temperament to develop into timid adults? Avshalom Caspi and his colleagues have provided remarkable evidence to answer "Yes" to these questions.

After an initial assessment at age eight of children who were either ill-tempered or shy, Caspi, Elder, and Bem (1987, 1988) followed up these people 30 years later. They found that those who were often angry and had temper outbursts at age eight were more likely to be ill-tempered as adults. Ill-tempered boys were less likely to stay in school and as men had a more erratic work life. This led them to have lower occupational status and more downward mobility than their even-tempered counterparts. Effects of ill-temperedness in women were evident in their home lives. They married below their social class expectations, divorced more often, expressed less satisfaction in marital relationships, and were perceived by their husbands and children as more ill-tempered in parenting than women who were even-tempered at age eight. Here we see the pervasive effects on individual differences in anger that carry across the lifespan.

Figure 11.2 Most three- to five-year-olds are shy with strangers: notice this child clinging to her mother and looking apprehensive. Extreme shyness in childhood can continue into adulthood.

Of those who had been shy as children the males were slower to marry, become fathers, and establish a stable career, than the non-shy. Their slowness to enter the workforce was in turn related to how much they subsequently achieved in their jobs and to how stable their jobs were. By contrast, girls who had been shy continued to be shy as adults but with less deleterious consequences. They were not slower to marry or have children, but they did spend less time in the workforce. They were married to men who achieved higher career status, maybe because shy women were prepared to stay at home and make fewer domestic demands on their spouses.

Emotion is central to adult personality dimensions and traits

The studies of Caspi and his colleagues suggest that at least some people's emotional dispositions identified in childhood are evident in their adult personalities. Adult personality has usually been measured by questionnaire tests of people's responsiveness to situations, to see which of people's attitudes, proclivities, and tendencies cluster together, and persist through time. The consensus of personality theorists has been to recognize the so-called "**big five**" **personality factors** (John, 1990; John & Srivastava, 1999; McCrae, 1992; Ozer & Reise, 1994). These dimensions are Neuroticism (including traits of anxiety, hostility, and depression),

Extraversion (including warmth, gregariousness, and tendencies to positive emotions), Openness (to fantasy, esthetics, feelings, ideas), Agreeableness (including trust, straightforwardness, and compliance), and Conscientiousness (including achievement striving, self-discipline, and dutifulness).

Prompted by claims that positive and negative affect are basic dimensions of personality, temperament, and mood (Goldsmith, 1993; Watson & Tellegen, 1985), there have been several studies in which relations have been studied between the big five personality dimensions and: self-reports of mood (Costa & McCrae, 1996); emotions in daily situations (Emmons & Diener, 1986); emotions associated with hypothetical events (Larsen & Ketelaar, 1991); and the predisposition to experience emotional states (Watson & Clark, 1992). Across these studies, Extraversion has been found to correlate with increased self-reports of positive affect. The effect is so strong that some consider positive emotionality to be at the very core of Extraversion. Agreeableness has also been found consistently to correlate with self-reports of increased positive affect. By contrast, Neuroticism has been found to correlate strongly with self-reports of increased negative affect (Allik & Realo, 1997; Emmons & Diener, 1985, 1986; Gross, Sutton, & Ketelaar, 1998; Larsen & Ketelaar, 1991; Pavot, Diener, & Fujita, 1990; Tellegen, 1985; Watson & Clark, 1992; Watson et al., 1992).

Individual differences in emotionality not only are central to adult personality traits, they shape people's satisfaction in their relationships and with life in general. Individuals prone to positive affect tend to be more socially engaged with others (Watson, 1988; Watson et al., 1992) and are more likely to be in a romantic relationship (Berry & Willingham, 1997). Agreeableness predicts lower levels of divorce in males (Kelly & Conley, 1987), and congeniality relates to marital stability and satisfaction in females (Bentler & Newcomb, 1978).

How might such results be explained? Hans Eysenck has argued that Neuroticism is associated with a hypersensitive limbic system (Eysenck, 1990). Eysenck's hypothesis is that highly neurotic individuals have limbic systems that readily acquire fear-related associations. As a consequence, they are prone to elevated negative emotion, and in particular, fear. Extraversion, Eysenck proposes, is associated with elevated activation in a different part of the nervous system: the reticular activating system, which regulates arousal levels. Extraverts, Eysenck claims, are people who are generally under-aroused. To maintain their ideal level, they seek excitement from social interaction and external stimulation. Introverts already have quite enough inner arousal. They try to ensure this does not get added to by external factors, so they tend to prefer quietness and self-organized activities.

Individual differences in emotion shape how we construe the world

One of the lasting insights of the study of individual differences is that people actively construe situations in idiosyncratic ways (Caspi & Bem, 1987).

Thus, one might imagine that the highly extraverted individual engages in such a full social life because he or she interprets social occasions as opportunities for fun and rewarding contact. The introvert, in contrast, is likely to construe the same situation in terms of threat, awkwardness, and likely unease. This has been confirmed. For example, highly anxious individuals perceive more threat and risk in the world and their future, whereas anger-prone individuals perceive less risk and threat (Lerner & Keltner, 2001). Other studies have found that angry individuals see greater hostile intent in the ambiguous actions of others (e.g., Rosenberg, 1998). In a particularly imaginative study, Bolger and Schilling (1991) had participants keep track in daily diary entries of the conflicts in their lives. They found that as compared with non-neurotic people, highly neurotic individuals, prone to negative emotion, were inclined to interpret interactions with close others as more laden with the potential for conflict and distress, and they responded in a more adversarial and problematic fashion.

Let's put these findings in the context of what we discussed earlier in this chapter. As children develop, they form specific attachments with caregivers, and are socialized by those around them, in ways that influence their disposition to experience specific emotions. These individual differences in emotionality exert powerful influences upon important judgments, for example of how risky some aspect of the environment is, or how trustworthy or affectionate a romantic partner is.

Emotional dispositions shape the course of life

Thus far we have seen that individual differences in emotionality will lead people to react emotionally and to interpret situations in a selective fashion. Across the life-course, individuals will create certain motifs, themes, and relationship patterns that reveal the particular facets of that person's identity. Individual differences in emotion should shape the course that life takes (Malatesta, 1990).

In one test of this formulation, Harker and Keltner (2001) asked whether measures of **positive emotionality**, derived from coding the intensity of women's smiles in their college yearbook photos, would predict various life outcomes over the next 30 years. The predictions derived from Fredrickson's (1998) Broaden and Build theory of positive emotion discussed in chapter 9. In support of this theory, positive emotional expression in the yearbook related positively to the personality traits of affiliation and competence, which reflect good interpersonal and cognitive skills respectively, and negatively with negative emotionality, in both young and middle adulthood (see table 11.3). Positive emotional expression also predicted increases in competence and decreases in negative emotionality between ages 21 and 27 and again from ages 43 to 52. Over time, women who expressed more positive emotion in their yearbook photographs became more organized, mentally focused, and achievement oriented, and less susceptible to repeated and prolonged experiences of negative affect.

Table 11.3 Correlation coefficients between positive emotionality as assessed by the magnitude of the smile shown in a yearbook photograph at age 20, and negative emotionality, affiliation, competence, personal well-being, and marital well-being, over the next 30 years

Measure	Positive emotionality
Negative emotionality	
Age 21	$-.37^{**}$
Age 27	$-.21^{*}$
Age 43	$-.21^{*}$
Age 52	$-.27^{**}$
Affiliation	
Age 21	$.33^{*}$
Age 43	$.18^{\dagger}$
Competence	
Age 27	$.19^{\dagger}$
Age 43	$.20^{*}$
Age 52	$.29^{**}$
Personal well-being	
Age 21	$.20^{*}$
Age 27	$.25^{*}$
Age 43	$.18^{\dagger}$
Age 52	$.28^{**}$
Marital well-being	
Age 52	$.20^{*}$

Note: $** = p < .01$, $* = p < .05$, $\dagger = p < .10$.
Source: Harker & Keltner (2001)

Turning to the quality of the spousal relationship, women who displayed more positive emotion in their yearbook pictures were more likely to be married by age 27 and more likely to have satisfying marriages 30 years later. Positive emotional expression in the yearbook also predicted high scores on measures of well-being at ages 21, 27, 43, and 52. Across young and middle adulthood, women likely to express positive emotions experienced fewer psychological and physical difficulties, had better relations with others, and generally felt more satisfied with their lives. Importantly, almost all of these findings remained significant when the researchers controlled for the physical attractiveness of the woman and her tendency to offer socially desirable responses.

Among the exciting developments of understanding how emotionality from an early age affects the formation of character is the recent book by Carol Magai and Jeannette Haviland-Jones (2002). They combined the theory of styles of attachment (discussed earlier in this chapter), Tomkins's theory of scripts (see chapter 8) and the theory of dynamic systems (see chapter 8). In their book they have done nothing less than to reformulate the psychological bases of **biography**. They studied three men: Carl

Rogers, founder of client-centered counseling and therapy, Albert Ellis, founder of rational-emotive therapy, and Fritz Perls, founder of Gestalt therapy. Magai and Haviland analyzed, for emotional themes and content, these men's autobiographical writings and also three scholarly books by each, and their habitual facial expressions. The facial expressions could be analyzed because these three men had appeared in the earliest movie made to demonstrate psychotherapy (Shostrom, 1966). Each in turn worked for a half-hour session with a client, Gloria.

Here is part of Magai and Haviland-Jones's emotion-based biography of Carl Rogers. Rogers was fourth of six children, and the baby of the family for five years. At the age of 22 he graduated from university and two months later began a long, and for the most part happy, marriage with a woman he had known in adolescence. In his autobiography he wrote: "As a person I see myself as fundamentally positive in my approach to life; somewhat of a lone wolf in my professional activities, socially rather shy, but enjoying close relationships" (C. R. Rogers, 1972). His wife wrote that as a teenager he had been "shy, sensitive, and unsocial" (H. E. Rogers, 1965). Many people found him a gentle person, remarkably devoid of anger. At the same time some professional colleagues found him "an irritant of monumental proportions" (Magai & Haviland-Jones, p. 57). During his academic career he moved to new positions several times, probably to escape interpersonal conflicts that had arisen in professional relationships.

These are conventional materials of biography. What binds them together, in a manner not previously offered by other biographical approaches (including psychoanalysis), are the continuities of emotionality based in attachment theory, script theory, and dynamic systems theory. As Magai and Haviland-Jones put it:

> . . . it appears that Rogers's primary attachment relationship was secure . . . Yet, his interactions with other social partners could be fractious . . . Rogers could also be painfully shy, and yet he was drawn to people and even did group encounter therapies. He often made others the center of his existence. He was also often in conflict with others, but he was not a particularly "angry" or hostile man. (p. 57)

Magai and Haviland-Jones see Rogers as having developed a script of longing for close relationships of the kind he had lost in the attachment relation with his mother, but the script also contained a great deal of shame, which had been induced frequently by his mother, always ready to recognize shortcomings as he grew older. In the family in which he was raised emotions were not valued, and anger was not tolerated. Rogers's emotional organization can be thought of (in terms of dynamic systems theory) as a large attractor area of interpersonal warmth and interest, with areas of shame repellors within it, and a very large region growing out of it (derived from family culture) by which anger is to be avoided.

In his filmed interview with Gloria, we see Rogers relating to her with attention and warmth. His dominant facial expression is interest, with eyebrows slightly slanted upwards towards the middle of his brow to suggest empathetic sadness. It is an invitation into a relationship that includes talk of intimate matters. Gloria accepts it, and thereby escapes the shame of her own self-criticism. Toward the end of the session she told him that she felt able to talk to him as she would like to have talked to her father, though that had never been possible. Rogers replied that to him she seemed like a pretty nice daughter.

Magai and Haviland-Jones draw attention to a moment when Rogers spoke to the camera to sum up after the session, after the interview with Gloria. He said: "When I'm able to enter into a relationship, and I feel it was true in this instance . . ." With the last few words his voice rose. Magai and Haviland-Jones say:

> He was being spontaneous here and the excitement and proud pleasure mounted. At the height of this juncture, the configuration of his face changed into a more open and unguarded one, and at this point we see the only "pure" prototypic interest expression (brows raised and arched) of the whole film. Furthermore, what happened next is even more revealing. The raised brow lasted only a flicker of a second before the muscles controlling the outer brow were drawn into play to pull the outer corners down, thus creating the sad brow with the oblique configuration. (p. 90)

The authors write:

> A person's face is not just the locus of both fleeting and sustained emotional reactions but also an historical document, revealing lifelong patterns of emotional expression and inhibition . . . and the dynamic interplay between historical events and learning experiences. (p. 89)

Summary

We discussed how individual differences in emotionality have several sources: the ways in which people regulate emotions, the effects of close relationships, and a genetic patterning. Three styles of attachment have been recognized: secure, ambivalent, and avoidant. We discussed evidence that some aspects of these styles continue from age one to adulthood, and can be transmitted from parents to their offspring. But other aspects of parental caregiving are also very important, particularly warmth and affection. We learned that parents shape the emotionality of their children in various ways, by language, by modeling particular emotional patterns, and by responding to some emotions rather than others. Temperament is a strong influence on continuity of emotional style, and is usually thought of in terms of a genetic bias toward one or another form of emotionality. We have seen that there is evidence from studies of angry and shy children that some of these biases persist from early to later childhood, and even into adulthood. In adulthood, researchers tend to agree that central personality traits, most notably Neuroticism, Extraversion, and Agreeableness, at their core involve individual differences in emotionality. Styles of emotionality become habitual, and this can even be seen when people, of whom photographs and films have been taken, are followed up years later. At least to some extent emotionality is character. We have seen that an understanding of the ways in which emotion-based character develops has led to an important new way of writing biography.

Further reading

A classic which is still stimulating in its thoughtful and wide-ranging treatment of fundamental issues of emotions in our human condition:
John Bowlby (1971). *Attachment and loss, Volume 1. Attachment*. London: Hogarth Press (reprinted by Penguin, 1978).

Perhaps the best book on the emotional and interpersonal life of the very young:
Daniel Stern (1985). *The interpersonal world of the infant*. New York: Basic Books.

The argument for emotional schemas of social interaction, with a review of how this idea has been approached from different perspectives:
Mark Baldwin (1992). Relational schemas and the processing of social information. *Psychological Bulletin, 112*, 461–84.

On the emotions as the bases of life span development and of biography:
C. Magai & J. Haviland-Jones (2002). *The hidden genius of emotion: Lifespan transformations of personality*. New York: Cambridge University Press.

Emotions and Mental Health in Childhood

> ... we are obliged to pay as much attention in our case histories to the purely human and social circumstances of our patients as to the somatic data and symptoms of the disorder. Above all, our interest will be directed towards their family circumstances.
>
> **Sigmund Freud (1905, p. 47)**

Contents

Figure 12.0   In childhood boys are more prone than girls to psychiatric disorder, and the most worrying kinds of disorder are based on anger and aggression, which can cast a long shadow over their lives.

Emotions and disorders

Disorders of emotional life in childhood and adolescence are states in which young people are no longer able successfully to cope, or in which they are getting into serious trouble. Much of this area is concerned with extremes of emotions: with intense and long-lasting states of anxiety, of depression, or of anger. Our aim in this chapter is to discuss the disorders of emotional life of young people, and to understand the relationship between normal emotions and these disorders. Disorders are not just extreme emotions. There are differences between a child or adolescent who is depressed and one who is very sad.

The case of Peter

To get a sense of how emotions and emotional disorders overlap we describe a boy with **conduct disorder**. He is a composite of several boys that have been seen in the course of clinical work and research interviews by one of us (JJ). We have developed this composite to maintain anonymity and to illustrate the range of issues in the child and his family that we discuss in the rest of the chapter.

Peter, aged 11, lived in an apartment with one older sister, one younger sister, and his parents. He was often in trouble at school and recently he was suspended for several days, because he had been in a fight with another child. A teacher intervened and he picked up a chair and threw it at her. He screamed and swore at her, and only stopped being aggressive when he was restrained by two adults who came into the classroom. This outburst was worse than previous ones, but for the last year the Principal had been complaining to Peter's parents that he was defiant, rude, verbally aggressive, and truanting. His behavior was similar at home. Whenever his mother asked him to do anything he refused, screamed at her, and occasionally raised his fist to her. He fought frequently with both his sisters and recently his youngest sister had complained that he had twisted her arm and it had remained sore for several days. Peter's mother found money missing from her purse several times the last few months, although Peter denied taking it. She felt she had lost control of her son. Peter's father had ignored his behavior recently, because the last time he had disciplined Peter he had become enraged and hit the boy harder than he had intended. The family was frightened to come to the clinic. By the time they were seen, Peter had been showing significant disturbance for more than 18 months.

Peter is very angry. Whenever his parents speak to him he replies in a hostile tone. But he also describes feelings of sadness and loneliness. At times he is frightened, particularly recently when he was suspended and his parents were furious with him.

Classifying childhood disorders

Many boys and a smaller number of girls show patterns similar to Peter's. The field concerned with such matters is that of clinical psychology of childhood and adolescence. It may be approached via useful books such as Carr (1999), Cummings, Davies, and Campbell (2000), and Rutter and Taylor (2002). Mental health workers have developed classification systems for clusters of disordered behavior. The main system is that of psychiatric diagnosis, usually by means of an interview. Diagnoses are descriptions of patterns of behavior. Among diagnostic symptoms of an anxiety state might be "excessive or unrealistic worry about future events." To make a diagnosis criteria are used by which behavior, experiences, and/or emotions are judged. The importance of diagnosis is that someone who fulfills defined criteria for a defined period is usually, though not always, impaired in their functioning (Pickles, Rowe, & Simonoff, 2001). The study of such abnormal functioning is sometimes known as psychopathology. For children reaching these criteria, family and school relationships have often become extremely strained, and the child's symptoms may have made normal life impossible. Such children may benefit from the help of a mental health professional.

The main scheme used to diagnose psychiatric problems of adults and children in North America is the *Diagnostic and Statistical Manual of Mental Disorders.* Current is the *Fourth edition, Text Revision* generally known as *DSM-IV-TR* (American Psychiatric Association, 2000). Another widely used scheme of diagnosis is the *International Classification of Diseases, Tenth Revision, Clinical Modification, ICD-10-CM* (World Health Organization, 2003), which includes psychiatric disorders. These schemes have similar criteria for diagnosing disorder. They are based on a medical model and focus on individuals rather than their contexts.

Another way of conceptualizing emotional disorders, often preferred by psychologists, is to accept that there are no sharp distinctions between having and not having a disorder. There is a continuum. The method of **assessment**, here, typically involves checklists of symptoms or behavior patterns, and sometimes questionnaires, which a parent or teacher completes for a particular child. At older ages the children themselves complete the checklists or questionnaires. Checklists and questionnaires provide continuous measures (Achenbach et al., 1991). Clusters of behaviors (similar to what psychiatrists call syndromes) are identified. In middle childhood two kinds of emotional disorder become important: externalizing disorders defined by anger, hostility, aggression, stealing, and lying, and internalizing disorders, which include anxiety and depression with tendencies to withdraw. In adolescence, these disorders can continue while, in addition, other kinds of disorder may also occur such as drug abuse and eating disorders. Designations of children as disturbed are made statistically to include the extreme 5 or 10 percent of a population. Though agreement of continuous measures with discrete psychiatric diagnoses is far from perfect (Jenson et al., 1988), conclusions about factors that cause emotional disorders are similar using either method of assessment.

How are emotions involved in children's disorders?

The two principal emotion-based externalizing disorders of childhood are called oppositional defiant disorder and conduct disorder. The criterion for oppositional defiant disorder (according to *DSM-IV-TR*, American Psychiatric Association, 2000) is that over a six-month period the child frequently displays four or more of the following behaviors that lead to an impairment of social or school life:

- loses temper
- argues with adults
- defies or refuses adult requests or rules
- deliberately does things that will annoy other people
- blames others for his or her own mistakes
- is touchy or easily annoyed by others
- is angry and resentful
- is spiteful or vindictive.

The criteria for conduct disorder are similar, but they include more seriously antisocial behavior such as truanting (missing school) before age 13, stealing, firesetting, sexual assault, physical fights, physical cruelty to people or animals, and use of weapons. Peter, whose case we gave at the beginning of the chapter, would be diagnosed as having a conduct disorder. Although some of the criteria for oppositional defiant disorder and conduct disorder are actions, you can see from the list of symptoms that the disorders are based around a frequent presence of anger and perhaps contempt.

As to internalizing disorders, the two main types are anxiety and depression. Anxiety disorders are fears that are abnormal in intensity, duration, and how they are elicited. One disabling syndrome is overanxious disorder, in which there is excessive or unrealistic anxiety or worry, with marked tension, for at least six months across a range of areas: future events, feelings of incompetence, self-consciousness, concerns about previous performance. Separation anxiety disorder is a different pattern, defined as excessive anxiety for at least two weeks about separation from the child's main attachment figures: worry about harm befalling them, refusal to go to school or go to sleep because of separation, and suchlike.

In a major depressive episode a child feels either very low in mood or has no interest in anything for at least two weeks, and this must be different from how the child has previously felt. For a diagnosis the child must also have four other symptoms such as weight changes, sleep disturbance, fatigue, feelings of worthlessness, inability to concentrate, and recurrent thoughts of death or suicide.

So emotions are central to how we define certain types of disorder in childhood. Not included in diagnostic criteria, however, are understandings of how the different levels of emotional experience relate to one another. In chapter 1 we described a continuum of emotional experience and expression. At one end are emotional expressions lasting for seconds, and emotional episodes lasting for minutes or hours. Near the other end are disorders like depression or conduct disorder, in which prolonged emotional states drastically affect life over a long period, and personality traits that can last a lifetime. Both emotional disorders and personality traits are based on aggregates of behavior and experience, so the level of description is different from that of emotions.

What is disordered?

There are several hypotheses about the relationship between emotion and disorder. These do not necessarily exclude each other.

Predominance of one emotion system   Probably the most common view of disorders of emotion in childhood is that, as Tomkins (1962, 1963) has argued, one emotion becomes prominent. It dominates other possible experiences, so depressed people experience more sadness than other emotions, or experience sadness more often than other people. Tomkins gives an example of a child separated from her parents when taken into hospital (Tomkins, 1979). This event elicits great fear and sadness. Memories of it, including who was there and how it happened, are incorporated into a mental schema. Subsequent events that have any similarity to the initial eliciting circumstances then trigger the same emotions, magnifying and amplifying them. So whenever this girl is separated from her parents, memories of her previous separation are re-evoked. A man with a white coat reminds her of a doctor at the hospital, and again she is afraid. So painful emotions are elicited by a broader range of events than for other children. According to this idea, a disorder would be a balance among emotions which, instead of being responsive to what happened in the world, is biased towards pre-established patterns of certain kinds, for instance patterns of angry emotions in an externalizing disorder, or sad and fearful emotions in an internalizing disorder (Jenkins & Oatley, 1998, 2000).

In chapter 11 we discussed personality in terms of emotional biases – based on appraisal biases – and this idea has been much researched as a way of thinking about disorders (Arsenio & Lemerise, 2004). In a study by Dodge and Coie (1987), for instance, aggressive and non-aggressive children were read vignettes or shown videotapes in which something negative happened – one child bumped into another or one child refused to let another child play – then they were asked to say whether the perpetrator was being deliberately mean. The aggressive children were more likely to say that the perpetrator was being intentionally hostile. A meta-analysis (De Castro et al., 2002) has shown that this kind of bias of appraisal is substantial, and has been frequently found among aggressive children. Another appraisal pattern is the depressogenic attribution style. As compared with the non-depressed, depressed children are more likely to make attributions for negative events that are stable (it will always be this way), internal (it is my fault), and global (all situations will be like this) (Bodiford et al., 1988).

Another version of emotional predominance is in terms of children's goals (Jenkins & Greenbaum, 1999). In terms of temperament, boys are more likely than girls to think that aggression enhances self-esteem (Slaby & Guerra, 1988) and this may contribute to gender differences, in which males are more frequently aggressive than females. In externalizing disorders, this predominance of goals seems to be exaggerated, so that children with externalizing disorders have been found to value gaining control over another child (a social goal of assertion) more than cooperation (a social goal of affiliation), and to value aggressive solutions more positively than their non-aggressive counterparts (Boldizar, Perry, & Perry, 1989).

Inappropriate emotional responses Another view about what becomes disordered is that children with a disorder react to events with deviant emotional responses: laughing when someone else is distressed, crying when nothing has happened, being angry when someone makes a friendly gesture. Their emotional responses are unsettling and other people find it hard to make sense of them. In this view it is not that children necessarily show more of one emotion than another, but that elicitation of certain emotions seems unusual. For instance, a child of 11 might be shy of strangers in the same way that a child of two is, whereas most children have grown out of this kind of shyness. Another child may be callous and unemotional, a trait that is seen as unusual, and is associated with externalizing disorders (Oxford, Cavell & Hughes, 2003).

Dysregulation In chapter 11 we discussed regulation of emotions. This concept provides for a third general way of thinking about disorders: that in a disorder, emotions are not properly regulated. They are inappropriate to the social context (Cole, Martin, & Dennis, 2004; Frick & Morris, 2004; Silk, Steinberg, & Morris, 2003b). Cole et al. (1996) induced negative moods in preschoolers: some children were inexpressive, some children's expressions were modulated, other children were highly expressive. Both the inexpressive children and the highly expressive children had more externalizing symptoms, both as preschoolers and at follow-up in their first year at school. Shields and Ciccetti (2001) proposed that emotion dysregulation underlies both bullying and being victimized by bullies among children who have been physically or sexually abused.

Rothbart, Ellis, and Posner (2004) think of regulation of emotions as a dimension of temperament, based on the effort to direct attention, and this relates to the processes of regulation that we discussed in chapter 11. In this vein, Eisenberg et al. (2005) relate dysregulation to lack of effortful control, so that children with externalizing disorders, but not internalizing disorders, are impulsive, and low in effortful regulation of their emotions.

Prevalence of disorders in childhood

In understanding emotional disorders some of the important findings have come from **psychiatric epidemiology**. Epidemiology is the study of how many people show a particular disorder in the population, statistically relating the disorder to factors in people's lives. Two kinds of statistic are important. Prevalence is the proportion of a population suffering from some disorder over a particular time period. Incidence is the number of new onsets of a particular disorder in a given time.

The first major study in children's psychiatric epidemiology was by Rutter, Tizard, and Whitmore (1970): the Isle of Wight study. Parents or guardians of all the 10-year-old children living on the Isle of Wight, an island off the south coast of England, were contacted. Children were first screened by asking their parents and teachers to complete questionnaires about their behavior and emotions, including the child showing very low mood, and being frequently aggressive with siblings or peers. Children who had many problems were then interviewed to see whether a psychiatric diagnosis was to be made. Some children who showed few problems on the questionnaire were also interviewed. Many estimates of the prevalence of psychiatric disorders among children in Western societies have been made subsequently. Though figures differ widely depending on the methods used, and whether degree of handicap that a disorder imposes is taken into account, a review of published studies yielded median rates of psychiatric disorder in childhood as 8 percent for preschoolers, 12 percent for preadolescents, and 15 percent for adolescents (Roberts, Attkisson, & Rosenblatt, 1998).

Epidemiological methods were a breakthrough in understanding origins of disorder, and they have helped plan services for children. Psychological instruments (for instance interviews) assessing the presence of disorder have been developed for use with parents, teachers, and children (Edelbrock & Costello, 1988; Rutter, Tuma, & Lann, 1988). In these, the criteria for disorders have been defined so that two people interviewing the same child, or the same parent about the child on separate occasions, agree about whether or not the child has a disorder.

Diagnoses differ, however, according to whether the informant is a parent, a teacher, or the child. Children are more closely in touch with fears and anxieties than parents, and report more of them; parents are more in touch with externalizing behaviors than children, and report more of them (Achenbach & Edelbrock, 1984). The reliability of children as respondents increases with age, suggesting that some of the discrepancy in reporting is simply because young children are cognitively immature (Edelbrock et al., 1985).

Externalizing disorders

Younger children show more externalizing behaviors, such as aggressive behavior, screaming, cruelty to animals, than internalizing behaviors such as sadness, anxiety, and withdrawal. Achenbach et al. (1991) surveyed parents of 2,500 children between 4 and 16 years of age, drawn from different communities across the United States and making up a representative sample. Each parent completed a questionnaire about one child, and children in the community sample were matched with a group of children receiving treatment in clinics. The questionnaire had 215 items of behavior, and parents scored the frequency with which their child showed each one. The items were based on the behaviors and emotional states commonly used in assessing psychiatric disorder. Examples were: "screams a lot," "shy or timid," "teases other children," "swears," "physically attacks people."

The same patterns are seen using measures of psychiatric disorder based on criteria based on *DSM-IV* (American Psychiatric Association, 2000). Oppositional defiant disorder is most common in early childhood, but conduct disorder becomes more common later (Offord et al., 1987). This may reflect an increased opportunity for seriously antisocial behavior as children grow older, for example greater access to weapons and increased knowledge of how to cause harm. Overall, however, as Bongers et al. (2004) showed, aggression, property violations, and opposition gradually decrease from age 4 to age 8, whereas status violations (swearing, truancy, running away from home, drug and alcohol abuse) increase with age.

Boys show more externalizing disorders of all kinds than girls throughout childhood (Achenbach et al., 1991; Bongers et al., 2004), and different levels of aggression are evident by the age of two (Prior et al., 1993). From an early naturalistic study on aggression in children, Goodenough (1931) reported that angry outbursts in children decline sharply in the second year. For girls, however, the decline is much sharper than it is for boys. Angry outbursts continue to decline as childhood progresses, though the rate in boys continues higher (Tremblay, 1999). Different rates of aggressive behavior in males and females have been found in many cultures, and in other primate species. As to diagnosable externalizing disorders, boys show much greater prevalence than girls (Anderson et al., 1987). Graham (1979) estimated a 3:1 ratio of boys to girls in prevalence of conduct disorder and this kind of ratio has been confirmed in more recent studies (Bird, Canino, & Rubio-Stipec, 1988; Fleming, Boyle, & Offord, 1993; Maughan et al., 2004).

Anxiety disorders

The prevalence of anxiety generally increases with age during childhood (Achenbach et al., 1991). Richman et al. (1982) found a nine-fold increase in maternal reports of children's worrying from three to eight years. Between middle childhood and adolescence the prevalence of diagnosable anxiety disorders remains fairly constant (McGee et al., 1990), or may even drop a little with age (Velez, Johnson, & Cohen, 1989). The forms that anxiety disorders take, however, change with age (Bernstein & Borchardt, 1991). Separation anxiety disorder is more common in early childhood, but overanxious disorder affecting many aspects of life is more common in adolescence (Kashani & Orvaschel, 1988).

Girls are more likely than boys to show single symptoms of anxiety (Achenbach et al., 1991) and to show anxiety disorders (Anderson et al., 1987; Costello, 1989). This sex difference is consistently found but relatively slight. It is not uncommon for a child to show two different types of anxiety disorder (Last et al., 1992). Often anxiety occurs with depression: Anderson et al. (1987) found that 17 percent of preadolescents with anxiety disorder were also depressed; by adolescence Kashani and Orvaschel (1990) found that this figure had risen to 69 percent.

Depressive disorders

Both normal low mood and depression become more common as children get older (Angold, 1988). Larson et al. (2002) used experience sampling to ask preadolescents and adolescents to rate their moods through the day. Adolescents' emotions were no more variable than younger children's but the adolescents were found to have generally lower mood. In a population study of preadolescents and adolescents in Germany, Esser, Schmidt, and Woerner (1990) found a similar phenomenon: 11 percent of eight-year-olds reported depressed mood or had it reported by parents, compared to 30 percent of 13-year-olds. For diagnosable depression, findings are also similar. Rates of depressive disorders increase dramatically in adolescence (Costello, 1989; Weissman, Gammon, & John, 1987a; Ford, Goodman, & Meltzer, 2004), with some studies showing as much as a tenfold increase between childhood and adolescence (Rutter et al., 1976).

In childhood, boys and girls are about equally likely to suffer from depression. By late adolescence, as Cyranowsky et al. (2000) have shown, females become almost twice as likely as males to be depressed. But this is not the case for boys, whose level of reported symptoms remains constant from earlier childhood through adolescence.

Reasons for girls' and boys' differences in rates of disorder are not fully understood, but socialization (discussed in chapter 8) is likely to play a role. Parents may be more allowing of expressions of fear and sadness in their girls, and of anger in their boys (Golombok & Fivush, 1994). Genetic factors, however, probably play the major role (discussed below).

Historical figures: John Bowlby and Michael Rutter

A renaissance of research on emotions began in the wake of World War II, when John Bowlby formulated his theory of attachment, discussed in previous chapters. With this idea, emotions became principal forces in psychology and psychiatry. Starting with

Bowlby's understandings of separations of children from their parents in wartime, people came to understand how love between adult caregivers and children developed into the cooperative activities on which family life and all culture are founded. Without love or, worse, with physically or emotionally abusive relationships, constructive adult life is made difficult, sometimes impossible. Certainly from the time of the Romantic movement in the eighteenth century, this idea was present, but it took Bowlby to ask what the processes were, and how they worked. Michael Rutter was of a younger generation but like Bowlby he trained in medicine. A book he published early in his career, *Maternal Deprivation Reassessed* (1972), was a critique of Bowlby's idea that growing up without a mother or reliable mother substitute would result in a person becoming an affectionless sociopath. Rutter argued that Bowlby's case was overstated, but his work was nevertheless stimulated by Bowlby's book. Rutter laid foundations for empirical child psychiatry. This work included (with George Brown, e.g., Brown & Rutter, 1966) working out how to interview families to understand their emotional characteristics, and undertaking the first large epidemiological study of childhood disorders (Rutter, Tizard, & Whitmore, 1970). Rutter started, systematically, to define the risks to child mental health. He is still a principal force in the field, and was knighted in the UK for his services to child psychiatry to become Sir Michael Rutter.

The stress-diathesis hypothesis

Imagine a brother and sister whose parents died when they were very young. Why is it that – as often happens – one sibling might suffer an emotional disorder related to the loss, while the other might not? The stress-diathesis hypothesis is a general idea about how such differences in outcome can occur (Davidson & Neale, 2001). A stress is something that occurs in the environment, like being orphaned. A **diathesis** is a predisposition, or vulnerability, to disorder that is inherent in the child, perhaps genetic. Perhaps surprisingly, neither stresses on their own (even when they are severe) nor vulnerability on its own causes disorder. But in combination, a stress occurring to a child with a particular diathesis can cause a disorder. In statistics this is known as an interaction effect.

Historically, what was discovered first, by researchers like Michael Rutter, was that environmental stresses could provoke disorders. Subsequently, genetic and other diatheses have been investigated. Most recently, research has concentrated on the interaction between stresses and diatheses. We too will start with stresses.

Risks

The most famous opening sentence of a novel is the one that starts *Anna Karenina:* "All happy families are alike; each unhappy family is unhappy in its own way" (Tolstoy, 1877). Was Tolstoy right? One of the big contributions to understanding families has come from the study of just how they are unhappy, how they cause distress to all their members, and cause psychiatric symptoms in some. In the area of disorders of childhood and adolescence, the several kinds of unhappiness have been understood in terms of risks.

Risks in the environment are stresses that increase the likelihood that a child will develop a disorder (Rutter, 2005). They are not rigid causes. They have been found in epidemiological studies to increase the probability of disorder, just as smoking has been found to increase the probability of lung cancer. Not every smoker, indeed not even a majority of smokers, will get the disease, but smoking certainly makes it more likely. So what are the environmental risks to disorders of emotions in childhood? To introduce them let us return to Peter, the boy whose case we described at the beginning of the chapter, and think about the factors that may have contributed to his problems. Peter's father was an unskilled worker who was made redundant from several jobs. His parents had no savings and, although periods of unemployment were relatively short, the family was very stressed during these periods. When she had her third child Peter's mother could no longer cope, became depressed, and considered leaving the family. The parents' relationship became more and more angry, so that by the time Peter was seven, loud shouting fights were common between the parents. On one occasion Peter's father left home for a month, but he returned because he was concerned about the children. Peter's relationship with both his parents was difficult. When his mother asked him to do anything he yelled at her not to bother him. She screamed back at him, but she would then leave it because it was not worth the fight. Peter's father said that he was sometimes so mad that he hit Peter hard without meaning to. Peter's sisters were always closer to each other than to him. They excluded him from their play so he often felt lonely and left out.

This kind of situation is not unusual for a child with a disorder. Not just one, but many things have gone wrong. Peter's parents had financial struggles, demands of a family, and difficulties in their relationship. Peter was exposed to extremes of emotional expression, including parents being very angry with one another and with him. Because it was so hard to get Peter to do anything, his parents became inconsistent, and did not follow through with their attempts to control or monitor him. Here, already, are seeds of a tragic life. Peter has few boundaries, and no positive relationships with anyone. Let us now describe some empirical data on risks of disorder.

Conflict between parents   Children exposed to serious and prolonged conflict between their parents are at increased risk of developing externalizing disorders (Grych & Fincham, 1992). Such children, particularly boys, show aggression and anger to parents and to other children. One of the important mechanisms is exposure to overt hostility – parents angrily shouting at one another. Jenkins and Smith (1991) examined three aspects of poor marital relationships: frequency and severity of angry arguments, disagreement over child-rearing issues, and periods of silent tension. It was frequency and severity of angry arguments that were associated with an increase in children's disorders. Open and severe quarrelling was also associated with more parenting problems, such as monitoring children less, and being overly critical of them.

In the early days of trying to explain why children become delinquent, parental divorce was thought to be the culprit. But externalizing problems in children occur before parents separate, and are related to parental conflict before divorce (Block, Block, & Gjerde, 1986; Cherlin et al., 1991). Similarly, children's disorders after their parents divorce have been found to be most strongly associated with continuing parental conflict (Emery, 1988).

Epidemiological studies are correlational. Can risks associated with adult conflict be investigated in experiments? Cummings (1987) arranged for pairs of children to play together and, while they were playing, to see two adults whom they did not know conversing in a friendly way, and then later having an angry verbal argument. Children increased their aggressive behavior after the adult argument, as can be seen in figure 12.1. Exposure

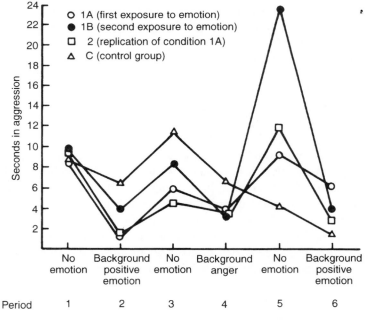

Figure 12.1 Mean number of seconds of aggression between two children who witnessed an angry adult argument in the study by Cummings (1987). In period Number 5, the children who were exposed to adult anger show increased amounts of aggression, and this is especially so for the children who were exposed to adult anger for a second time. In contrast, the control group, who have not been exposed to adult anger, show a declining level of aggression.

to the anger of strangers may have quite different significance to being exposed to the anger of one's parents. Nevertheless, adding experimental results to epidemiological findings suggests that angry emotions between adults can cause children to be aggressive themselves.

Witnessing negative expressions of emotion may increase the risk of children developing externalizing behavior in several ways (Emery, Fincham, & Cummings, 1992). Through modeling, children may learn from their parents that anger is the way to deal with conflict. Children may become aroused by anger, and their behavior may be influenced by this increased arousal. Seeing negative emotion expressed between parents may alter children's expectations about relationships such that they interpret neutral behavior of other people in a negative light (Jenkins et al., 1995). These are direct effects of marital disharmony. Indirect effects of parental conflict on childhood disturbance also occur, because relationships between each parent and the child often suffer (Fauber & Long, 1992).

Parents' psychiatric problems Epidemiological studies have repeatedly shown that psychiatric problems in a parent increase risk of disorder in the child (Bird et al., 1988; Richman et al., 1982). Often children show a similar type of disorder to that shown by parents. For instance, parental depression is more strongly related to internalizing disorders than to externalizing ones (Dowdney & Coyne, 1990; Williams et al., 1990). Hammen et al. (1990) found that when children of depressed parents showed a disorder, this disorder too was likely to include depression. Nomura et al. (2002) found in a ten-year follow-up that parental depression was associated with children's depressive and anxiety disorders. Moreover, when parents had anxiety disorders children were likely themselves to show anxiety symptoms (Rosenbaum et al., 1988). Children who lived with parents with antisocial disorders (including aggression) were more likely to show externalizing disorders than other types of disorder (Huesmann et al., 1984; Rutter & Giller, 1983; Wickramaratne & Weissman, 1998).

In interaction children learn how to respond to the emotions of depressed caregivers. As we explained in chapter 11, children construct schemas of their own and their caregivers' emotions. Field et al. (1988) compared interactions of babies with depressed mothers and babies with non-depressed mothers. Babies were videotaped playing with their mothers and then with a stranger. The stranger did not know whether the babies had a depressed mother or not. With their own depressed mothers, babies showed more gaze aversion and were more negative generally. The behavior of the infants carried into the interaction with the stranger (perhaps because of the babies' own experience, perhaps because they were temperamentally more withdrawn). The stranger was less active, made fewer vocalizations, and played less with infants of depressed mothers than with babies of non-depressed mothers. So, already in the first three months of their lives, infants show patterns of responding that they carry into new interactions.

Such interactions may lead babies to feel untrusting of their caregivers, and this may disturb the attachment relationship. Children with depressed

Figure 12.2 Depression is relatively common in mothers of young children, and there is increased risk of their children also becoming depressed before the end of their adolescence.

mothers have been found to be more likely to develop insecure attachments (Lyons-Ruth, Alpern, & Repacholi, 1993; Radke-Yarrow et al., 1985).

The child also learns about the effect of emotions on interactions, from watching their depressed parent interact with other members of the family. Hops et al. (1987) observed patterns of interactions in families in which the mother was depressed. They found that the mothers' depressed moods resulted in the suppression of fathers' and children's aggression towards the mothers. The mothers' moods therefore won the mother a respite from anger of other family members. When the fathers and children were angry at the mother, this temporarily suppressed her depressed mood. What do children learn about emotions from this kind of experience? They learn that being sad stops others' anger, and that getting angry activates other people. Another interesting finding emerged: when fathers suppressed their anger to their wives, they became more angry with their children. So children may also learn that people do not necessarily express the emotion they feel toward the person whom it concerns.

Another consequence of living in a family with a depressed parent may be that children are exposed to negative appraisals of the world, which they use subsequently in their own appraisals. Zahn-Waxler and Kochanska (1990) found that depressed mothers were more likely to say things that induced guilt and anxiety in their children, and to express feelings of disappointment than did non-depressed mothers. Garber et al. (1991) found that depressed mothers were more critical of their children than non-depressed mothers. Negative evaluations of the child by parents may encourage the development of appraisal patterns: attributing negative events to the inadequacies of the self. So in ways such as these, children develop emotional reactions that become habitual, and are compiled into emotion schemas. Though these may be adaptive in their home environment, these schemas continue forward in life, and into other settings. In the case of antisocial patterns, for instance, Patterson et al. (1991) suggest that children learn them at home, and then take them to school.

Attachment failures   Style of attachment – secure, avoidant, ambivalent – of the kind described by Ainsworth, Blehar, and Walters (1978), discussed in chapter 11, has not been found consistently to impose risks or benefits for disorders of emotion (Fagot & Kavanagh, 1990; Goldberg, 2000). These styles are styles of interaction, not problems or disorders. Only the fourth category of disoriented/disorganized attachment, developed subsequently to Ainsworth et al.'s work by Main and Solomon (1986, as discussed in chapter 11) has been found to predict subsequent disorders. Lyons-Ruth et al. (1993) followed up a group of children from 18 months to five years; these children were exposed to multiple risks including poverty, maltreatment, a history of maternal psychiatric illness, etc. Of these children, 71 percent who had significant levels of hostility at age five had been classified as disorganized at 18 months, and only 12 percent had been classified as secure. The question, then, is really whether the disoriented/disorganized style is best thought of as a style of attachment (like secure or avoidant), or whether really it is a reflection of deeper disturbances.

In his early formulations, Bowlby (1951) proposed that children who, between the ages of six months and three years, did not form a primary attachment relationship that was continuous with at least one particular person, usually a mother, would be permanently unable to form good relationships in adulthood. This idea has led to much research on children from orphanages where the possibilities of an affectionate and lasting relationship with a particular caregiver are small. Orphanages were, of course, set up to care for children who otherwise would have been uncared for. But they were set up long before Bowlby proposed his theory of attachment. They care for material needs. Many people, who work shifts, look after the children, and the turnover of staff is usually high. Orphanages, then, constitute a strong test of Bowlby's hypothesis. In an important study of this question, girls who had been **institutionalized** were followed up into adulthood when they were interviewed and observed interacting with their own children (Quinton & Rutter, 1988; Quinton, Rutter, & Liddle, 1984). As adults, 33 percent of ex-institutionalized women were found to have a handicapping psychiatric disorder in their adult life, compared with 5 percent of non-institutionalized women. Clearly, being without a primary attachment figure in early childhood does put people at risk. When they became mothers they had significant problems. They tended to be insensitive, low in warmth, harsh with their children, and showed inconsistent or ineffective control. Some, however, who had poor early experiences functioned well as parents. They were differentiated from the others by having a supportive spouse in whom they could confide and count on for help. Attachment failures in childhood do have deleterious effects on mental health and the ability to relate to others, but this study implied that those who found love later in life seemed to show a remarkable ability to recover from their early institutional experiences.

In 1989, soon after the downfall of the Ceausescu regime in Romania, the world became aware of thousands of Romanian children in orphanages that were, in terms of opportunities for attachment, as bad as, or worse than, orphanages elsewhere. Soon after the revolution, Kaler and Freeman (1994) made cognitive and social assessments on 25 Romanian orphanage children between two and four years old. None functioned at their expected age level, and 20 of the 25 functioned cognitively at less than half their chronological age. In her extensive review of research on adoption from orphanages, MacLean (2003) describes two groups of Romanian orphans who were followed up by psychologists. One group of 46 children had spent between 8 and 53 months in an orphanage; they were adopted to Canada, and compared with a group of Canadian children living with birth parents matched on demographic variables. Another group of 165 children, who were adopted to England, were compared with group of 52 English adoptees. After adoption, children's intellectual development started to improve. From the age of 9.5 and up, most children adopted to Canada after the age of two were in the normal range (mean 1Q of 89). Those adopted before the age of two did better (mean IQ of 99), while the comparison group of Canadian children did better still (mean IQ of 109). The English sample showed similar results. So adoption had a powerfully positive effect on children who, had they stayed in orphanages, would most likely have grown up very impaired. What about emotional and social characteristics? Here, the English group gives the fullest picture (see, e.g., O'Connor et al., 2003): the longer the period of institutionalization, the worse the effects. Romanian orphans did form attachments with their adoptive parents, but as compared with the non-institutionalized English adoptees, they were more likely to show (a) indiscriminate friendliness as compared with children's usual wariness of strangers, (b) more abnormal patterns of attachment to adoptive parents, and (c) more externalizing symptoms (see also Ellis, Fisher, & Zaharie, 2004). As MacLean (2003) points out, however, the striking thing about these children in the context of Bowlby's theory of attachment, and in the context of what we know can go wrong with severe neglect or maltreatment during childhood, is how adoption seems to have compensated for many of the ill effects of a baleful early experience of institutionalization.

Differences in the quality of relationship between parent and child

Hostility and criticism by parents to their children have consistently been identified as causes of disturbance, particularly of externalizing disorders (Olweus, 1980; Patterson, 1982; Stubbe et al., 1993). For instance, Richman et al. (1982) interviewed families when children were three and eight years old. We discussed warmth in chapters 8 and 9. In Richman et al.'s study, warmth and criticism were rated on the basis of the mother's tone of voice and content during a two-hour interview when she talked about her children. As compared with children who did not have any psychiatric disturbance, three-year-olds who had a disturbance were four times more likely to have a mother who was critical of them, three-and-a-half times more likely to have a mother low in warmth toward them, and three times more likely to have a mother who hit them. Patterns with fathers were similar. Caspi et al. (2004) found in a sample of 565 five-year-old monozygotic twin pairs that those members of each pair who were the recipients of more emotional negativity and less warmth from their mothers had more antisocial behavior problems. Maternal factors were also important in a study by Gilliom and Shaw (2004), who found that children who were not fearful and were subjected to high maternal control had high externalizing trajectories.

Perhaps surprisingly, Boyle et al. (2004) found, in a study of 11,512 children and adolescents in a Canadian national longitudinal survey of children and youth, that a different kind of process than the one identified by Caspi et al. (2004) also occurred. In families in which children were treated very differently – a state known as **differential parenting** – and particularly where mothers were hostile and negative toward certain children, externalizing problems were increased not just for those children who were treated most harshly, but for the whole family (Jenkins, Rasbahh, & O'Connor, 2003; O'Connor et al., 2001a). So other siblings also came to be at risk for externalizing problems. The idea common to many parents that, however different their children, all should be treated equally has an empirical justification.

Physical abuse of children results in wide-ranging developmental, cognitive, emotional, and social consequences (Cicchetti, 1990). Children are particularly likely to develop externalizing disorders and problems around aggression (Simons et al., 1991). Internalizing symptoms such as depression have also been reported (Sternberg et al., 1993).

Children in abusive homes develop hostile appraisals of other people's actions. Dodge et al. (1990) investigated children in the general population. Six months before the children entered school their parents were interviewed about the frequency and severity with which they gave physical punishment to their children. On entering school, the children's aggression with peers was assessed by sociometric interviews in which all children in the class were asked to nominate children who were mean and fought a lot. Frequency and severity of physical punishment in the home were associated with more aggression toward peers in school. Children were also asked to make attributions of intent about neutral stimuli. Children who had been subjected to high levels of physical punishment were more likely to attribute hostile intent to other children's neutral actions than non-abused children. Their cognitive appraisals of the intentions of others partially explained the relationship between the children's home experience and levels of aggression with peers. Thus, as a result of living in an abusive home children were more likely to see their peers as having hostile intentions toward them and consequently to respond aggressively.

Lack of warmth and positive affect in the parent–child relationship is also associated with increased disorder in children. Pettit and Bates (1989) carried out home observations of parent–child interaction when babies were 6, 13, and 24 months old. Mothers were rated on the positive affect that they showed toward their children: **affectionate contact** (6 months), affectionate teaching (13 months), and verbal stimulation (24 months). When children were four years old, symptoms were assessed. Lower levels of positive maternal affect in the first two years predicted internalizing and externalizing problems when the children were four years old. In this study, lack of positive maternal affect was a stronger predictor of children's problems than was the presence of negative affect. In chapter 8 we emphasized play as an important and positive component of children's lives. Frances Gardner et al. (2003) have found, in a naturalistic observational study, that in a group of toddlers who were showing externalizing problems, those whose mothers contributed a positive and warm emotional atmosphere, and who played more with them showed significant improvements in their externalizing problems.

Poverty   Having very little money raises the prevalence of psychiatric disorder (Costello, 1989; Patterson & Albers, 2001). Reporting on a general population sample of children in Ontario, Boyle (1991) found that the prevalence of disorder amongst children whose parents earned over $50,000 per year (in 1983) was 14 percent. Among children whose parents earned below $10,000 per year it was 35 percent. How does this risk work? Having little money means having few resources. In chapter 9 we discussed the socio-emotional goal of assertion, to raise oneself in the social hierarchy. In Western societies, poverty, also known as low socioeconomic status, means being low in the hierarchy, so levels of stress are higher (Rutter et al., 1975). This in turn is related to a higher frequency of expressions of negative emotion toward children (Radke-Yarrow, Richters, & Wilson, 1988), to higher rates of differential parenting (Jenkins, Rasbash, & O'Connor, 2003), to rates of parental psychiatric and personality disorder, and to marital disharmony. But poverty may also have a direct effect on the development of problems: particularly externalizing ones. Children in families with little money may feel blocked in their goals; via the media and in other ways they are exposed to objects, activities, attainments, available to others, but not to them.

Combinations of risks

In the case of Peter, discussed above, several stresses occurred together. His mother was depressed for a time, his parents were in conflict, and there was little money. Rutter (1979) describes six family factors that put children at increased risk of child disorders. We have discussed four: parental depression, parental marital disharmony or separation, institutionalization or removal of a child by a statutory authority, and poverty – the factors best understood in terms of the involvement of emotions. We have not discussed Rutter's two other factors: large family size and parental criminality. The first of these may operate, like poverty, by scarcity of valued resources including access to parents, hence increasing the frequency and intensity of negative emotions. The second may be associated with more negative parenting practices such as increased hostility to children, as well as poorer supervision of them (Patterson, 1986). Rutter et al. (1975) found that in urban, as compared with rural, areas twice as many children had disorders, largely because of the increased presence of the six risk factors mentioned above.

Look at figure 12.3. Children with one of these six risks do as well as those with none. But with each additional risk the chances of a child suffering a disorder rise sharply. Two stressors rather than one increase a child's risk of developing psychopathology four-fold. Three stressors, such as Peter had, increase the risk 20 times. So, here is the principal finding for risk factors in children. With increasing numbers of risks the probability of disorder rises exponentially.

As well as the family, or in unfortunate cases lack of family, one must also consider wider **contexts** (Ford, Goodman, & Meltzer, 2004; Greenberg et al., 1999), each of which has been shown potentially to work as a stressor even when other factors have been controlled for. Such contexts include out-of-home childcare and school (e.g., Ritchie & Howe, 2003;

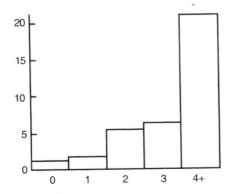

Figure 12.3 Effects of risk factors on developing a psychiatric disorder in children (Rutter, 1979): children with one risk factor are no more likely to develop a disorder than those with none, but with each added risk factor the prevalence of psychiatric disorder multiplies.

Mortimore et al., 1988), relating with peers (e.g., Dodge et al., 2003; Lacourse et al., 2003; Moffitt et al., 2002), and the neighborhood (e.g., Boyle & Lipman, 2002; Guerra, Huessman, & Spindler, 2003). In each of these contexts processes that are important for development such as affection and encouragement may be present or, when certain kinds of adverse socialization or rejection occur, act as stresses.

Bi-directional effects

Most of the data we have presented so far are correlational: associations between measures of environments and rates of disorder. We have discussed them as if parents' marital conflicts, or harsh parental actions, promote children's disorder, and they do. But could children's emotions or negative behavior provoke marital discord, or invoke harsher parenting? The answer is yes.

Children who are more difficult make their parents more angry. In turn this is likely to make children's behavior more difficult (Lytton, 1990). Patterson (1982) has described **mutually coercive** patterns in aggressive homes. In response to an aggressive action by a child, a parent responds with an escalated aggressive action, which then provokes further aggression by the child, and so forth. Similarly, Jenkins et al. (2005b) have found that predicting one and two years ahead, marital conflict between parents predicted subsequent child behavior problems, and child behavior problems predicted increases in subsequent marital conflict.

Emotions mediate relationships. Within sequences of emotional communications, attributing an emotional expression solely to an individual is generally inadequate. For instance, the more an adolescent refuses to talk with a parent, the more frustrated this parent may feel, and as the parent becomes more angry, the less the adolescent feels like talking.

Protective factors

Just as stresses combine with each other to increase risk, other factors counteract risks, and make things better (Rutter, 1992). Think about Peter again. Why did he show disturbance, while his sisters, growing up in the same family, did not? Peter's sisters had the protective factors of relationships with each other, and they each had a better relationship with their mother.

What factors have been identified in children's lives that protect them from disorder? Children in highly stressful circumstances have fewer problems if they have siblings to whom they are close (Jenkins, 1992), if they have grandparents who are very involved with them (Werner & Smith, 1982), or if they have experiences of achievement at school (Gerard & Buehler, 2004; Quinton et al., 1984). Such factors can make the difference between enabling the child to function well despite stress, and succumbing to the effects of stress by developing a disorder. Jenkins and Smith (1990) interviewed

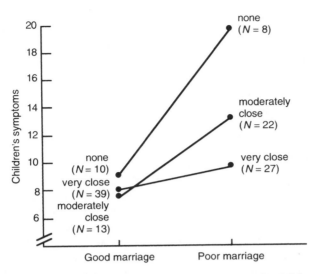

Figure 12.4 The mean number of psychiatric symptoms in children whose parents had good or conflictual marriages, as a function of whether the child has a good relationship with an adult outside the family. Children with no such relationship were most at risk (Jenkins & Smith, 1990).

parents and children from homes in which there was a high level of conflict between parents, and also interviewed children in a matched sample of families where parental conflict was low. You may see in figure 12.4 that children in conflictual homes who had a close relationship with an adult outside the family (usually a grandparent) had lower levels of disorder than children without such a relationship. The presence of a grandparent did not affect the probability of disorder among children who did not experience stress. This suggests that grandparents can sometimes compensate for problems in a child's environment. Criss et al. (2002) visited 585 families who had children in kindergarten and assessed low socioeconomic status, parental conflict, and harsh parental discipline, as three family risks. As possible protective factors, children's peer acceptance and positive friendships in kindergarten and Grade 1 were measured. Externalizing disorders were measured by means of teachers' ratings in Grade 2. The findings were that peer acceptance moderated the effects of all three risks (low socioeconomic status, parental conflict, harsh discipline), and friendship moderated the effects of harsh discipline. Children who were subjected to high levels of family risk, but who were high on peer relationships, did not have externalizing disorders. These effects were not specific as to gender or ethnicity.

Parents, too, can have substantial protective effects. El Sheikh and Elmore-Staton (2004) found, in a sample of children subjected to the risk of high conflict between the parents, that whereas conflict between a parent and child potentiated risk, a secure attachment to a parent ameliorated it. Similarly, Kim-Cohen et al. (2004) found maternal warmth to be protective. Galambos, Barker, and Almeida (2003) found that parents who exercised firm behavioral control over their adolescent offspring were able to halt upward trajectories of externalizing disorder, and to counteract negative influences of deviant peers. There is also evidence that abilities of self-control by adolescents are protective against risks of becoming a substance abuser (Wills & Dishion, 2004), and that in the presence of risk personal, cognitive and emotional resources are protective against future criminality (Stattin, Romelsjo, & Stenbacka, 1997).

Effects of genes

The current understanding of children's disorders of emotional life is that there are constitutional differences among children, which set up diatheses (vulnerabilities) to particular kinds of environmental stress. Some important diatheses are genetic. One principal genetic effect is whether you are female or male: maleness is a clear diathesis for externalizing disorders. Genetic diatheses are the continuation of temperament as discussed in chapter 11. Peter, with whom we started the chapter, was not only male but had a problematic temperament; he was difficult to soothe, never able to wait for anything. The mothers of such children find them hard to cope with, and thus make it harder for any satisfying mutual relationship to grow.

Quantitative genetics (in which rates of heritability are estimated) have been used to investigate how large are contributions to disorder of genes and of different environmental risks. As we explained in chapter 11, a favored method is to compare frequencies of disorder between monozygotic twins (who share all their genes) and dizygotic twins (who, on average, share 50 percent of their genes). The genetic component (diathesis) for depressive and anxiety symptoms in children has generally been found to be between 20 and 40 percent (Rutter et al., 1999). Twin studies also yield estimates of environmental effects. Where the concordances (probabilities that both twins have a disorder) between monozygotic and dizygotic twins are both similar and high for some disorder, it can be inferred that shared environmental experience (for instance, parents' marital conflict) has had a strong effect. Where concordance rates are similar and low for both MZ and DZ twins, then it likely that non-shared factors were important, for instance one child being physically abused more than another. As an example, a study by O'Connor et al. (1998), of the co-occurrence of antisocial behavior with depression during adolescence in 720 monozygotic twins, dizygotic twins, full siblings, half-siblings, and unrelated siblings living in the same families, found 45 percent of the co-occurrence of antisocial behavior and depression could be attributed to genetics, with 30 percent of the variance attributed to shared environmental effects, and 25 percent to non-shared environmental effects. Raine (2002) has reviewed studies of interaction between biological and social factors, and found that the presence of both kinds of factor exponentially increases the risk of antisocial and violent behavior. But a distinction should be made between different kinds of antisocial behavior (Eley, Lichtenstein, & Stevenson, 1999). Eley,

Lichtenstein, and Moffitt (2003) studied over 1,000 twin pairs, and found that antisocial behavior that was aggressive was affected primarily by genes and had high continuity, whereas non-aggressive antisocial behavior had much lower continuity and was affected by both genes and shared environmental influences.

Genes are not the only diatheses. Vulnerabilities to emotional disorder can be set up in children before birth by their mothers' drinking (Sood et al., 2001), smoking (Fergusson, 2002; Wakschlag et al., 2002), and malnutrition (Liu et al., 2004). In addition, brain damage, which sometimes is obvious and sometimes less obvious, may occur at or around birth. This can also add to vulnerability. Some factors that may not seem emotional, but that nonetheless are also diatheses for emotional life, are developmental delays and cognitive impairments. Children with lower IQ (Anderson et al., 1987; Rutter et al., 1970), language delay (Richman et al., 1982), and mild cognitive impairments associated with premature birth (Minde et al., 1989) are more likely to develop emotional disorders during childhood.

Specific genes, maltreatment, and externalizing disorder

With the accomplishment of the Human Genome Project research has entered a new era. The move is sometimes described as from quantitative genetics (as with twin studies) to **molecular genetics** (Plomin & McGuffin, 2003). One of most striking and important recent studies has involved the identification of a specific gene that has effects on aggressive violence in interaction with the childhood stress of physical abuse. The research was undertaken as part of the Dunedin birth cohort described above. Caspi et al. (2002) tested each cohort member for different forms of the Mono-Amine Oxidase-A (MAOA) gene, which promotes an enzyme that deactivates a set of amine-based transmitter substances. One form of the gene – the low MAOA gene – is much less efficient in promoting the enzyme. Whereas females have two X chromosomes, males have an X chromosome and a much shorter Y chromosome. In women, genes on one X chromosome can be moderated by genes on their other X chromosome, but in males most of the genes on the X chromosome receive no moderating influence. The MAOA gene is sex-linked, because it is located on the X chromosome in a position in which the Y chromosome has no moderating influence. So if a male has a low MAOA gene on his X chromosome, its effects will occur in the individual, whereas if a female has this gene on one of her X chromosomes, its effects will be much reduced. In addition to genetic testing, each member of the Dunedin cohort was assessed as to a history of being physically abused between the ages of 3 and 11. Cohort members were categorized as not maltreated (64 percent), probably maltreated (28 percent), and severely maltreated (8 percent).

Just 13 boys in the cohort both had the low MAOA gene and had been severely maltreated. Of these, 11 boys (85 percent) met *DSM-IV* diagnostic criteria for conduct disorder between the ages of 10 and 18. In comparison, only 22 percent of the boys who had the low MAOA gene but who had not been maltreated met the DSM criteria for conduct disorder. The males who had the low MAOA gene who had been maltreated (probably or severely) were 12 percent of the male cohort. By the age of 26 they had been responsible for 44 percent of the total cohort's convictions for violent crime. These boys grew up to show a far higher rate of aggressive violence than the boys who had been maltreated but had the high MAOA gene.

What about the girls in the cohort? Of the 481 females only 2 percent received any convictions for violence, a rate that was too small for statistical analysis. Caspi et al. did, however, find that those with the low MAOA gene on either of their X chromosomes were more likely to be delinquent during adolescence than those with only high MAOA genes. Although the presence of this gene acted in the same kind of way in girls as it did in boys, the influence of a low MAOA gene on one X chromosome setting up a vulnerability to maltreatment was **moderated** by the high MAOA gene on the other X chromosome, which conferred substantial protection against potential harmful effects.

With the new genetic technology, then, it has been shown that neither a stress (physical abuse in childhood) nor a genetic vulnerability on its own causes a disorder. But when environment interacts with a specific genetic vulnerability, disorder can occur. Putting this another way, though being abused in childhood is clearly horrible, most children are able to compensate for it in one way or another. Those who have suffered the abuse who are genetically susceptible are far more likely to travel the road of continuing aggression and criminal convictions.

Perhaps the most important fact about violent acts is that men are much more likely to commit them than women. For instance, Daly and Wilson (1997) give rates for different countries of homicides for same-sex killings in which killer and victim were unrelated. Although the overall rate of homicide differs very widely from country to country, a similar ratio is maintained: about 40 times more men kill men than women kill women. For the first time, with Caspi et al.'s (2002) study a specific diathesis (low MAOA gene) has been shown to have large effects in relation to an environmental stressor (physical maltreatment in childhood), which begins, at last, to make sense of this huge sex difference in angry and violent aggression, one of its least understood features.

Continuity of disorders

Properly speaking, we should conceptualize risks discussed above – parental conflict, poverty, and so forth – as risks for a new onset of disorder. There is another kind of risk: the risk of continuity or recurrence. A principal risk for a disorder in childhood, adolescence, or adulthood is the continuation of an existing disorder, or having had a version of a disorder previously. Such creatures of habit are we, that risks of continuity become stronger as a person gets older. Moreover, risks that start a disorder, such as poverty, or family conflict, or parental psychiatric disorder, often persist, and thus maintain disorders. We can think of continuities of disorders as extreme kinds of persisting individual differences, of the kind we discussed in chapter 11.

Continuities of disorders over time are high. In a general population sample Richman et al. (1982) found that 60 percent of children with a disorder when they were three had a disorder at eight. The highest continuities have been found in externalizing problems (Verhulst, Koot, & Berden, 1990; Bongers et al., 2004). In analyses of data from six centers in three countries, Broidy et al. (2003) found that continuities of aggression are high for boys, and that the principal effect is due to a small group of boys (less than 10 percent) who are aggressive early in life, who remain so, and who often become violent offenders, while other groups are either never very aggressive or show declining rates of aggression with age. It has been thought by some that physical aggression gives way to more indirect aggression, such as verbal aggression and social exclusion, as children get older. Vaillancourt et al. (2003) found, however, in a study of 3,089 children between the ages of four and eleven, that this was not so. Children were consistent in the type of aggression they used over time, physical or indirect.

Stability in aggression is almost as high as the stability of IQ (Olweus, 1979). Huesman et al. (1984) carried out a follow-up over 22 years. Boys and girls who were nominated by their peers at age eight as particularly aggressive were also the most aggressive 30-year-old men and women. They had more criminal convictions, were aggressive toward their children, and were more abusive to spouses. As Rutter, Giller, and Hagell (1998) discuss in their comprehensive book, once a style of aggressive and/or antisocial behavior has developed it tends to continue over time.

The high continuity of **antisocial behavior** has recently been illuminated by Moffitt and her colleagues (Moffitt & Caspi, 2001; Moffitt et al., 2002). Some antisocial males, whom they call life-course-persistent, were relatively rare. At an early age they had difficult temperament and were exposed to risks associated with externalizing disorders. The other group, whom Moffitt et al. call adolescence-limited delinquents, were relatively common and near normal in their characteristics. Moffitt's hypothesis was that as this group reached adulthood, the social skills acquired during childhood, and turning points such as marriage, would return them to normal trajectories. The distinction between the two groups was similar to findings of longitudinal studies in six other countries (e.g., Patterson et al., 1998). In Moffitt et al.'s (2002) study, the life-course-persistent antisocial males of the Dunedin sample (discussed above) were 10 percent of the male cohort. At 15 to 18 they continued the externalizing disorders of early childhood. They had weak bonds with family, antisocial personality, impulsivity, and callousness. They had convictions for violent crimes, and their behavior came to include victimization of partners and children. By contrast, the adolescence-limited males, who were 26 percent of the male cohort, became delinquent largely because of association with delinquent peers. They tended to endorse unconventional values, and their crimes were largely non-violent. Aguilar et al. (2000) found in an American sample that adolescent-onset individuals were not, however, free of other problems: they were more likely to have internalizing disorders than normal adolescents. Though the original theory proposed that delinquency of this group would not extend into adulthood, Moffitt et al. found in the males of the Dunedin sample that at age 26, they continued to be more impulsive, to have more problems with mental health and substance abuse, and to have more financial problems and property offences, than normal males in the sample.

In general, continuities for internalizing disorders have been found to be less marked than those for externalizing problems (Esser, 1990; Offord et al., 1992). Between 70 and 75 percent of children with diagnoses of internalizing disorder when first interviewed were free of disorder at follow-up. The lower estimates of continuity may, however, be due in part to the fact that depressive and anxiety disorders are more episodic.

Continuities do not occur solely from causes within the person (Lewis, 1990). The environment that causes a disorder often maintains it. For example, Richman et al. (1982), who investigated continuities in families with three-year-olds, drawn from the general population, found that half the mothers who were depressed when the children in the sample were three were still depressed when children were eight. In the same kind of way, 60 percent of parents who were found to have conflictual marriages when the children were three still had conflictual marriages when the children were eight. They found, too, that if relationships in the family were positive when the children were three, they were likely still to be positive five years later. Kim et al. (2003) have shown how stressful life events in adolescents tended to cause internalizing and externalizing disorders, and these disorders then tended to generate further stressful events. Moreover, some disorders maintain themselves by means of social effects. We have already mentioned how this happens with the frustrating social exclusion caused by aggression. But internalizing behavior can also be maintained in a comparable way. Gazelle and Rudolph (2004) found that anxious solitary children decreased their depression when they were more accepted socially, whereas those who were excluded remained anxious and socially avoidant.

We started this chapter with Peter, who began life with a difficult temperament which his family was unable to counteract, and continued as an aggressive person. With the continuity of antisocial behavior in mind, here is another vignette from a person more extreme than Peter. This time the vignette is not from a composite. The case, described by Power and Dalgleish (1997), is of a man who was seen at the Maudsley Psychiatric Hospital in London, England, and who was the subject of a BBC documentary.

[He] was a man with a violent history. He had several criminal convictions for bodily harm and can recount times when he has nearly killed people in uncontrollable rages. At the time that [he] came into contact with mental health services he would only rarely leave his home and then he would be accompanied by several bodyguards – not to protect him from others, but to protect others from him. (Power & Dalgleish, p. 340)

This man, who lives in a society devoted to civil values, has a disorder of anger and contempt. Many societies maintain male warrior castes (as we described in chapter 11), and if one reads ancient epics, one reads of people whose rages made them heroes. Perhaps in some periods of human evolution, in some periods of history, and in some kinds of society today, such traits have been advantageous. We might wonder, however, whether the usefulness of such traits to the human race might now be passing.

Therapy and prevention

There is a large field of clinical practice with children and adolescents aimed at alleviating disorders, and at helping parents. Treatments are discussed in textbooks and handbooks (e.g., Carr, 1999; Kazdin, 2004; Ollendick, 2004: Rutter & Taylor, 2002). Many of the treatment options used for adults, such as behavior therapy, cognitive behavioral therapy, and psychoanalytic therapy (to be discussed in chapter 14), are used with children and adolescents. Perhaps the most important difference is that with younger people, the family typically also needs to be treated, and indeed there is an important branch of therapy called family therapy (see, e.g., Minuchin, Rosman, & Baker, 1978).

Since we have emphasized externalizing disorders, let us discuss one treatment program for juvenile offenders described by Chamberlain and Reid (1998). The study was of 79 boys, 12 to 17 years old, with histories of serious offending (average of 14 previous criminal referrals and 76 days' detention in the previous year), who had been mandated by courts to out-of-home care. Approximately half the boys were assigned to group care in a state-run residential facility for delinquent boys that included individual therapy for the boys and family therapy for the parents. The other half were assigned to multidimensional foster care that was given by foster parents chosen for their ability to nurture, who were, in addition, given 20 hours of training in behavioral management. The boys received individual behavior therapy on non-aggressive methods of self-expression and problem solving. They had to attend school, and teachers signed off daily on attendance, attitude, and homework. Consequences of loss of privileges occurred for even minor rule infractions, but they were applied in a non-angry way. Since it has been found by Dishion, McCord, and Poulin (1999) that boys of this kind are particularly affected by deviant peers, who encourage more delinquency, substance use, and violence, contact with peers with known violent histories was forbidden. Families of origin to which the boys were expected to return were also given therapy. Results were that the multidimensional foster care was more successful in reducing antisocial behavior than group care. For the fostered boys there was a significantly lower rate of criminal referral in the 12 months following treatment, less absconding, fewer days spent locked up, and 60 percent less time in state training schools. The foster program was extraordinarily labor-intensive, with care occurring on an individual basis 24 hours per day, and case workers being on call 24 hours a day. It is one of the few programs to have shown any success with young offenders.

A principal issue for children and adolescents is **prevention**. A distinguished child psychiatrist, Paul Steinhauer (e.g., 1991) said that when he first started work it was as if he were standing by a river and saw hundreds of children being swept by the current, some struggling, some drowning. As a clinician, he tried to pull them out, but it occurred to him that he should travel up the river to see why the children were falling in, and help prevent it.

The idea is a good one, but accomplishments have been modest. As Rutter (2002) has pointed out, during the past 50 years children's physical health in the West has improved substantially. Over the same period there has been no such improvement in children's emotional health. Indeed there are indications that during this time disorders of behavior and emotions have become worse, with a range of possible causes that you will not find it hard to speculate about.

Efforts toward prevention of disorders must deal not just with the individual but with the contexts in which that individual lives: contexts that will have contributed to the onset of disorder, and then maintained it. Take aggressive children, for instance. Although some such children compensate by forming gangs and other alternative organizations, they tend to be socially excluded at school, because they quickly acquire a reputation for aggression. Other children find them aversive, treat them warily, and avoid them. So although there are programs of therapy for angry and violent children, even if such programs are successful, when these children return to the same school where they are known and unpopular, they are still regarded warily and avoided. This sets off once more the pattern of frustration, anger, and aggression. One solution, a difficult one, would be an effective program of therapy and a change of school. But it takes an extraordinarily short time for a person to acquire a reputation, and a role. Coie and Kupersmidt (1983) arranged 40-minute play sessions for ten-year-old boys, once a week for six weeks. The boys were put in groups of four who either knew each other because they were in the same class at school, or who did not know each other because they were from different schools. Coie and Kupersmidt had obtained sociometric data from the classmates of each of the boys. Each group of four was assigned one member who was popular and seen as a leader, one who was seen as average, one who was seen as aggressive and was socially rejected, and one who was seen as shy and socially ignored. In the play sessions of those who had previously known each other, the boys maintained their previous popularity and status. In the sessions of the boys who had not known each other their status was far more fluid at first, but by the end of their third session boys who had been seen as popular at school had become popular in the group, while those who had been rejected or unpopular at school had become rejected or unpopular. So, in two hours of interaction, roles were established, reputations formed. Once a person's reputation in any group is established, it is difficult to change.

Efforts toward prevention, then, from as early in life as possible, are extraordinarily important, not just because of the human misery that occurs when people suffer disorders that impair their lives, but even in very crude terms because of the economic cost to society. Think of it like this: 2,166,260 people were in prisons in the USA in the middle of 2003, with an average cost of $21,400 for each person per year (Bruner, 2003), and with the prison population continuing to rise. That comes to a total of more than $46 billion per year, despite there being no evidence that increased rates of imprisonment reduce rates of crime. Perhaps one should consider that many people in prison are those with high continuities for aggression (discussed above), so that the rest of society is free of their influence. But what if some proportion of that cost were spent alleviating known risks of externalizing disorders?

What is being done by way of prevention? Izard (2002) and Izard et al. (2002) have argued for preventive intervention programs based on research-based understandings of emotions in development, their effects, and their role in disorders. We can use again the set of widening contexts: family, school, neighborhood. One principle that has emerged is that without thinking across these contexts, interventions are unlikely to be successful.

Interventions that include the family, and that are made early, have the most evidence for effectiveness. Olds et al. (1998) have reported a 15-year follow-up of a randomized controlled trial of at-risk families based on visits by nurses during the time mothers were pregnant (average 9 visits) and during the period between birth and the child's second birthday (average 23 visits). At age 15, children of the mothers who were visited in this way, as compared with children from control families, had fewer externalizing and serious antisocial behaviors, as measured by their own self-reports, by teachers' reports, and by criminal records. Olds (2002) has described how this program is now being replicated.

Another important program, based in schools, is that of Olweus and his colleagues (e.g., Olweus, 1993; Olweus, Limber, & Mihalic, 1999) to prevent **bullying**. It started in Bergen, Norway, and has been taken up in other European countries and in North America. Bullying always involves a power imbalance. It is repeated peer physical abuse and humiliation. In one study using unobtrusive video recording of school playgrounds by O'Connell, Pepler, and Craig (1999), when bullying was seen by adolescents, about 54 percent supported it by simply watching, 21 percent joined in on the bully's side, and 25 percent aided the victim. Bullies are common among antisocial offenders: at age 24, 35 to 40 percent of former bullies (as compared with 10 percent of non-bullies) had three or more criminal convictions. In talks that he gives, Olweus sometimes says that preventing bullying is an important component of democracy. The bullying prevention program involves most of the adult members of a school, who become enthusiastically involved. The program requires adults to act with warmth to the children, but also to set firm limits to unacceptable behavior, to apply non-violent consequences for breaking rules, to act as authorities and positive role models. Children in the school stop thinking that they should connive at bullying they see, and instead think that they should report it to adults. In terms of the social motivations that we discussed in chapter 9, whereas bullies use assertion for their own psychological purposes, adults can be assertive in a non-hostile way, and at the same time act with warmth (affiliation) and humor to enlarge the attachment goal of safety, and to promote fairness. In Bergen, this program reduced bullying by 50 percent, and elsewhere to a somewhat lesser extent.

An important principle is to base policy and interventions on evidence rather than on the convictions of those who already know what should be done irrespective of evidence. Too much goes on that reminds one of public health measures 150 years ago, when people knew without having to worry about evidence that disease was spread by filth and foul air – miasmas – and who sought to counteract infection by such measures as building rooms with high ceilings. In fact, infection was found by empirical research to be spread by germs, and was to be counteracted by clean drinking water and by washing one's hands. Epidemics of disorders of emotions in society are more difficult to solve, and they depend on more factors in several contexts, but the problems are just as urgent.

Summary

In this chapter we reviewed how emotional disorders in childhood and adolescence are conceptualized as two kinds: externalizing disorders characterized by anger and contempt, and internalizing disorders characterized by sadness (in depression) and by fear (in anxiety states). Externalizing disorders are most frequently shown by boys, depression about equally by boys and girls, and anxiety states slightly more frequently by girls. We learned about the hypothesis of stress and diathesis: that environmental stresses combine with constitutional vulnerabilities to produce disorders. We found that seven principal stresses, or risks for childhood psychopathology, have been identified: conflict between parents, parental depression or other psychiatric problems, child neglect, physical abuse and other such features of parents' relationships with their children, poor socioeconomic circumstances, large family size, and parental criminality. One of these stresses on its own does not increase a child's risk of disorder, but two together increase it by a factor of four, three together by a factor of 20. We also learned that some factors in children's lives can be protective against disorder. These include having at least one close relationship, most usually with a parent, but perhaps with a sibling, grandmother, or friend, and being able to do well in some aspect of school life. We discussed how modern genetics has begun to show that specific genes combine with specific environmental stressors, such as being physically maltreated in childhood, to predispose to violent disorders. Some disorders, especially externalizing disorders, have high continuity, and extend into adulthood, often because the factors that caused the disorders continue, and maintain it. We concluded the chapter by arguing that prevention of disorders of emotion and behavior in childhood is important, but that it is still not far advanced.

Further reading

Child and adolescent clinical psychology has a useful handbook:
Alan Carr (1999). *The handbook of child and adolescent clinical psychology: A contextual approach*. London: Routledge.

A comprehensive review article on the effects of orphanages and adoption is:
Kim Maclean (2003). The impact of institutionalization on child development. *Development and Psychopathology, 15*, 853–84.

One of the first studies of child disorders of emotions to be based on the Human Genome Project, and one that will be of lasting importance:
Avshalom Caspi, Joseph McClay, Terrie Moffitt, et al. (2002). Role of genotype in the cycle of violence in maltreated children. *Science, 297*, 851–4.

On the importance of empirically based interventions:
Tom Dishion, Jean McCord, & François Poulin (1999). When interventions harm: Peer groups and problem behavior. *American Psychologist, 54*, 755–64.

Emotions and Mental Health in Adulthood

CHAPTER *13*

...human misery has awakened, stood before you, and today demands its proper place.

Jean Jourès (1897) cited by Kleinman (1988, p. 53)

Contents

Figure 13.0 One of the striking results of psychiatric epidemiology is that the prevalence of depression is nearly twice as high in women as in men.

Psychiatric disorders: symptoms and prevalence

Into the lives of many people come periods of extreme emotion: hopeless depression or immobilizing anxiety. When such states reach levels at which the person can no longer do ordinary things such as go to work or look after children, they are referred to as emotional disorders. Our objective in this chapter is to concentrate on these disorders, rather than to cover the whole of abnormal psychology, psychopathology as it is sometimes called, or psychiatry (the medical term for this field). For a psychological approach you might turn to Davidson and Neale (2001), and perhaps a book of case studies such as that of Oltmanns (2003), and for a psychiatric approach to Hales, Yudovsky, and Talbott (1999). In terms of psychiatry, the depressive and anxiety disorders we discuss here are together the most common non-psychotic psychiatric conditions. In this chapter we aim to make sense of some of the roles emotions play in depression and anxiety states. In addition we include sections on emotional influences on relapses of schizophrenia, and on the occurrence of psychosomatic disorders.

Depression, sometimes called affective disorder, is intense sadness: a despair that can be painfully persecuting and drains all meaning from life. From a neuroscience perspective, Davidson et al. (2003b) identify diminution of pleasurable goal achievement as a principal emotional component of depression. In the English-speaking world, depression is most frequently diagnosed in relation to criteria set out in the American Psychiatric Association's (2000) *DSM-IV-TR*. A major depressive episode is diagnosed when for at least two weeks the sufferer is unbearably sad or depressed, or has lost pleasure in nearly all activities, along with at least four other symptoms that include: being unable to sleep, being slowed down in one's actions, lack of energy to do ordinary things, inability to concentrate, feelings of worthlessness or guilt, and thoughts or plans of suicide.

Anxiety disorders come in several forms (described below), all of which involve overwhelming fears together with more protracted moods of disabling anxiety, often avoidance of what is most especially feared, and often a loss of personal confidence. When someone has a nervous breakdown, usually he or she suffers a major depressive episode with or without an accompanying anxiety disorder. In an emotional disorder, aspects of one's emotions tend to become more difficult to understand than normal (Oatley & Duncan, 1992; Thoits, 1985).

Psychiatric epidemiology

How common are emotional disorders in ordinary populations? To answer this question we turn to psychiatric epidemiology: the statistical study of how frequently disorders occur, which we have already introduced in chapter 12. The epidemiologist is a detective who finds out why some people suffer disorders, while others do not.

One might think that modern medicine owes its success to the discovery of drugs like antibiotics, and from advances such as surgery without germs but with anesthetics. But history shows that infectious diseases were receding before these innovations. Really, the advances that were most important in improving health were the epidemiological discoveries of how people caught infectious diseases, and the reduction of infection by providing clean water and removing sewage from towns (Cartwright, 1977). Similarly in psychiatry, the discovery of drugs for disorders has been important, but more important will be prevention (Dozois & Dobson, 2004; Munoz, Mrazek, & Haggerty, 1995).

Psychiatric epidemiology was slow to take its place alongside the epidemiology of physical medicine, mainly because it was at first difficult to agree on criteria for **diagnosis** of disorders, and because reliable psychological assessments had not been developed. Just as for the psychiatric epidemiology of childhood discussed in chapter 12, there are now suitable classification schemes and interviews to make diagnoses for both research and clinical purposes. Populations have been studied to find how common mental health problems are. Kessler et al. (1994) used a research interview to make diagnoses according to *DSM-III-R* criteria, and to determine risks in 48 states of the USA. Interviews were carried out with 8,098 people between the ages of 15 and 54, with a response rate of 82.6 percent.

Among the striking findings of this and of similar studies such as that of Robins and Regier (1991) was that depression and anxiety states were nearly twice as common in women as in men. So in Kessler et al.'s study, as you can see from table 13.1, 21 percent of adult women have had an episode of major depression at some time in their life, as compared with 13 percent of men.

Depression is recognized by the World Health Organization as the single most important chronic condition in the middle years of life, in terms of its economic impact, for instance in employment, and the impairment of relationships (Murray & Lopez, 1996). In Kessler et al.'s (1994) study, women were also much more likely (30.5 percent) than men (19 percent) to have had one of the five kinds of anxiety disorder diagnosed in the study.

As explained in chapter 12, percentages of people suffering from a diagnosed disorder over a specific time are called prevalences. By contrast with the higher prevalence for women of depression and anxiety, Kessler et al. (1994) found that 35 percent of men, but only half that percentage of women, had a disorder of alcohol or drug abuse or dependence at some time in their life. Men also had a higher prevalence (6 percent) of antisocial personality disorder – a frequent sequel of childhood conduct disorder – as compared with women (1 percent). Although, as we discussed in chapter 9, **gender differences** occur in normal emotions, they are small in comparison to the gender differences in prevalence of disorders (Nolen-Hoeskema, 2002), which continue trends seen in childhood (see chapter 12), where boys are much more likely than girls to show externalizing disorders, and girls somewhat more likely than boys to have internalizing

Table 13.1 Lifetime prevalences (in percentages) of psychiatric conditions in males and females in the 48 contiguous states of the USA, using the Composite International Diagnostic Interview from which DSM-III-R diagnoses were made

Disorder	Male	Female	Total
Affective (depression-related) disorder			
Major depressive episode	12.7	21.3	17.1
Manic episode	1.6	1.7	1.6
Dysthymia	4.8	8.0	6.4
Any affective disorder	*14.7*	*23.9*	*19.3*
Anxiety disorders			
Panic disorder	2.0	5.0	3.5
Agoraphobia without panics	3.5	7.0	5.3
Social phobia	11.1	15.5	13.3
Simple phobia	6.7	15.7	11.3
Generalized anxiety disorder	3.6	6.6	5.1
Any anxiety disorder	*19.2*	*30.5*	*24.9*
Other disorders			
Alcohol or drug abuse or dependence	35.4	17.9	26.6
Antisocial personality	5.8	1.2	3.5
Non-affective psychosis (e.g., schizophrenia)	0.6	0.8	0.7
Any psychiatric disorder	*48.7*	*47.3*	*48.0*

Source: From Kessler et al. (1994)

disorders. Although there is no gender difference in prevalence of depression in childhood, in adolescence the difference becomes large and stays so (Cyranowsky et al., 2000). Notice too, from table 13.2, that there are differences in prevalence as a function of income. People who had few material resources more frequently had a disorder.

In the Epidemiologic Catchment Area study (Robins & Regier, 1991), 20,000 people were interviewed in New Haven, Eastern Baltimore, St. Louis, Durham, and Los Angeles. This study showed patterns that were broadly similar to those found by Kessler et al. and Robins and Regier, though with some differences that probably depended on the interviews.

Cultural factors play an important part in emotional disorders (Kleinman, 1988). Tsai and Chentsova-Dutton (2002) reviewed a number of studies and found that the prevalence of depression in Western countries is far higher than in Eastern countries such as Taiwan and Korea. Some risk factors seem common to different societies, however. For instance, Patel et al. (1999) found that in India, Zimbabwe, Chile, and Brazil, being female, being poor, and having little education were associated with depression, just as in Western industrialized societies.

Some differences in prevalence may reflect roles and resources open to people in different societies. But other kinds of difference occur too.

Table 13.2 Relative lifetime prevalences of psychiatric disorders as a function of sex and income. In each section of the table one group is assigned a rate of 1.00. For other groups within the section rates are expressed as multiples of this. For instance, in the first section, the rate for any affective disorder in women is 1.82 times that for men

	Any affective disorder	Any anxiety disorder	Any alcohol or drug disorder	Any disorder	Any three or more disorders
Sex					
Male	1.00	1.00	1.00	1.00	1.00
Female	1.82*	1.85*	0.40*	0.95	1.24*
Income					
$0–19,000	1.56*	2.00*	1.27*	1.49*	2.46*
$20,000–34,000	1.19	1.52*	1.06	1.21	1.71*
$35,000–69,000	1.16	1.48*	1.06	1.21	1.55*
$70,000 or more	1.00	1.00	1.00	1.00	1.00

Note: In each group of figures an asterisk indicates a prevalence for which there was a significant difference ($p < 0.05$) from the prevalence with the standard value of 1.00.
Source: From Kessler et al. (1994)

Figure 13.1 Poverty is a fundamental cause of depression, which has hopelessness at its core.

The World Health Organization (1983) studied depression in Switzerland, Canada, Japan, and Iran, using the same diagnostic instrument. A core cluster of symptoms occurred in all four countries: sadness, joylessness, anxiety, and lack of energy. Other symptoms, however, varied in frequency. For instance, in Iran 57 percent of patients reported bodily symptoms, whereas only 27 percent of patients in Canada did so. Similarly, Weissman et al. (1996) compared epidemiological results from ten countries and found that insomnia, loss of energy, difficulty concentrating, and thoughts of suicide occurred in both Western and Asian countries. But other symptoms, such as poor appetite and feelings of worthlessness or guilt, were not common to all countries.

Differences in prevalence, such as those due to gender and poverty, are clues the epidemiological detective starts with. Some of these differences are far larger than most of those that psychologists usually consider. But the evidence is **correlational**. For instance, epidemiological evidence does not tell us whether poverty makes depression more likely, or whether being depressed makes it harder to hold a job. Next steps include starting with the clues of prevalence and then becoming more precise about what emotional disorders are and what causes them.

Different kinds of depression and anxiety

The most usual form of depression is the depressive episode, usually described as a major depressive disorder. As described above, it is characterized by a symptom of least two weeks of either depressed mood, or lack of pleasure in daily activities, plus four or more other symptoms as described above (i.e., five symptoms in all). Minor depression can be classified as having two to four symptoms in all. In a more detailed study of data from Kessler et al.'s (1994) survey, Kessler et al. (1997) found that the numbers of people who suffered during their lifetime from minor depression were 10.0 percent of the adult population, major depression with five or six symptoms altogether were 8.3 percent, and more severe major depression with seven to nine symptoms were 7.5 percent. They proposed that these conditions are progressively more severe forms of the same underlying condition.

An important distinction is between major depressive episodes and **bi-polar disorder**, sometimes called manic-depressive disorder, in which depression has been preceded or followed by at least one period of mania (Johnson & Kizer, 2002). Mania is the disorder of happiness, exhilaration, and pride. In it people are extremely happy, expansive, optimistic. Their self-esteem is inflated, and they sometimes become grandiose. They can work for long periods, need almost no sleep, and take unbounded pleasure in everything they do. As novelist Tom Wolfe said, in relation to an episode of hypomania (somewhat milder than full mania) that he experienced: "If I could only bottle that feeling . . . It was heaven on earth" (McGrath, 2004,

p. 38). Wolfe thought he was very good company during this period, and people in such states can often be charming. But with more severe mania, people can do alarming things such as run up huge debts that they can never repay. One of us remembers being in a car with someone who, in a manic episode, drove at 60 miles an hour the wrong way down a one-way street in the middle of town, laughing about how ludicrous social conventions were. Only rarely is the mood sustained. Usually – and this is what happened to Wolfe – after a few weeks there comes a plunge into depression. A first-hand account of bipolar disorder was written by Kay Jamison (1995), a professor of psychiatry, whose earlier (1993) book on manic depression and creativity gained wide attention. Bipolar disorder is relatively rare, with a prevalence of about 1 percent and no gender difference. Genetics are discussed below, but at this point one can note that genetic risk for bi-polar disorder, measured in terms of heritability of some 80 percent, is higher than for major depressive episodes (Craddock & Jones, 1999; McGuffin & Sargeant, 1991).

Anxiety disorders take several forms (*DSM-IV-TR*, American Psychiatric Association, 2000). They include unexpected panic attacks with sudden terror or dread, often with bodily symptoms such as racing heart, dizziness, shortness of breath. The panic attack is a clear example of an emotion that is difficult to understand: people may have no idea why it occurs. Anxiety disorders include also **phobias**, which are almost irresistible urges to avoid certain places, things, or activities. One of the most disabling of such disorders is agoraphobia: a fear and avoidance of being away from home (Fyer, Mannuza, & Coplan, 1996; Mathews, Gelder, & Johnson, 1981). As you may see from table 13.1, the lifetime prevalence of the condition without panics is 5.5 percent, and with panics the prevalence is higher. Often it starts when a person's life is in a precarious state. Then perhaps in the supermarket (*agora* is the Greek for market), the person has a panic attack and rushes home where she or he feels calmer. Now a powerful learning script has been established: Away from home there has been unbearable fear, back at home is calm and safety, with a strongly conditioned anxiety about repeating the experience (Bouton, Mineka, & Barlow, 2001). Some agoraphobics fear mainly being in places which they cannot leave without embarrassment. But particularly if there are further panic attacks the sufferer may find it progressively more difficult to go out at all except perhaps with a partner (an attachment figure). People with agoraphobia tend to find that the area in which they feel safe on their own becomes much reduced. It can be just their own home. It can be just the bedroom. Often they lose all social confidence, and as they isolate themselves from the world, confidence drains yet further. The restriction of life in agoraphobia can be treated successfully, for instance by cognitive-behavioral therapy (see chapter 14). With treatment people can go out again, get a job, visit friends, but they tend to remain anxious people. Their accomplishment in therapy is usually to be better able to tolerate their anxiety. Whereas phobias for specific objects or activities such as spiders or flying are common, they are troublesome rather than disabling. A phobia of social interaction, social phobia, can, however, be severely disabling. It is even more common than agoraphobia, with a lifetime prevalence of 13.3 percent. Generalized anxiety disorder is defined in terms of at least six months of disabling and persistent anxiety or worry, and this condition has a lifetime prevalence of 5.1 percent.

A second group of anxiety disorders is of **obsessions and compulsions** (Jenike, 1996). Obsessions are intrusive anxious thoughts such as those of being contaminated by germs. The thoughts occur repeatedly, and the person cannot stop them even though he or she might know them to be irrational. Obsessions are repeated actions or rituals such as washing one's hands many times a day, or checking and rechecking that certain things have been done, like turning the stove off. Performing the action temporarily diminishes anxiety, but only temporarily. It is possible that the disorder is a defect in the emotional knowledge that a security-motivated action has been completed (Szechtman & Woody, 2004). In severe cases, many hours a day can be spent performing compulsive actions. The lifetime prevalence of obsessive-compulsive disorder has been estimated at between 2 and 3 percent.

Anxiety disorders include **post-traumatic stress disorder**, which involves intense anxiety, disturbed sleep, flashbacks in which a traumatic event is remembered and repeatedly re-experienced, together with avoidance of anything that might remind one of it (McNally et al., 1990; McNally, 2003). Traumas of the kind that can provoke this disorder occur in war (Grinker & Spiegel, 1945) when people have been in danger of their own lives and when companions have been killed and maimed. The Vietnam War brought this syndrome into public consciousness in the USA (see, e.g., Shay, 1995). Its repercussions on veterans include increased antisocial behavior, mediated by post-traumatic stress disorder, of those who have been in combat (Barrett et al., 1996). But the syndrome can also result from natural and industrial disasters such as hurricanes (Ironson et al., 1997), as well as from criminal assaults such as rape (Burnam et al., 1988). Brewin, Dalgleish, and Joseph (1996) define a trauma as anything that radically violates one's basic assumptions, conscious or unconscious, about the world, especially when the assumptions are overturned by a violent event. Such assumptions might be that the world is by and large a safe place, that one can achieve one's life goals, that people including oneself will behave in reasonable and decent ways. Brewin et al. conclude that the chaotic nature of post-traumatic flashbacks and intense phobic anxiety can best be explained in terms of two kinds of memory systems, one of which is verbal and subject to the making of meaningful sense of experience. The other is automatically triggered by aspects of situations, external or internal. The working of this system is not closely coupled to the verbal system, and its processes are far less voluntary. The traumas are represented in memory in both ways, which are repeatedly activated, but they do not necessarily correspond to each other. The confusion adds to the intense fears that are experienced.

Historical landmark: Kraepelin's textbook of psychiatry

Psychiatry is the branch of medicine that deals with psychological illnesses. The specialty can be thought of as beginning in earnest in 1899 with the publication by Emil Kraepelin of the second edition of his textbook of psychiatry. In it he divided psychiatric illnesses into 13 categories, each with criteria for diagnosis. *The Diagnostic and Statistical Manual of Mental Disorders* of the American Psychiatric Association (2000) is the direct descendent of Kraepelin's book.

Two classifications in Kraepelin's 1899 book attracted attention: one was manic-depressive psychosis, the other was the psychosis called dementia praecox (dementia that occurs early in life rather than toward its end) which came later to be called schizophrenia. Kraepelin's idea was that although they had some characteristics of physical illness, these psychoses were not caused by any recognizable physical condition, such as an infection or brain damage (or, nowadays we might add, recreational drug). In both these types of psychosis, the patient is deluded. Their thoughts, which seem bizarre to others, are compelling to the sufferer. Of the two, manic-depressive psychosis was seen as less severe, because patients often recovered. Dementia praecox (schizophrenia) was thought to last indefinitely. It included emotional flattening, often with classic symptoms of madness such as hallucinations and delusions that some malign power was controlling the person's body and mind.

Stress and diathesis in the causation of disorders

Probably the most widespread general understanding of emotional disorders and other psychiatric conditions is in terms of the stress-diathesis hypothesis (Davidson & Neale, 2001; Monroe & Simons, 1991). In chapter 12 we discussed this hypothesis in relation to children's disorders. The hypothesis is that a disorder is most typically caused by a stress, an adversity in the immediate environment, in the presence of one or more predisposing factors, called diatheses, which are inherent in the person. Examples of stresses are a marital separation, or the death of someone close. Among diatheses are genetic factors and experiences in early life.

Many emotional disorders would not happen if a stress did not occur. For the most part, at least for the first occurrence of an emotional disorder, the initiating stress is severe. For psychotic disorders such as schizophrenia, less severe stresses can be triggers and seem to work by being occasions for a psychotic breakdown in which the diathesis is stronger.

Stresses: life events and difficulties

One of the most important studies on why people develop disorders of depression and anxiety was done by George Brown and Tirril Harris

(1978). They interviewed 458 adult women in London, England, and found that in the previous year, 37 of them (8 percent) had suffered an onset of depression (some with anxiety) at a level that was disabling, equivalent to major depressive disorder now defined by DSM-IV-TR (American Psychiatric Association, 2000). A further 9 percent of the women had a disabling psychiatric problem at the case level for more than a year (totaling 17 percent with a disorder during the year before interview).

In Brown and Harris's study, 89 percent of women with an onset of depression had a severe **life event or difficulty** shortly before their breakdown. By contrast, of women who did not have any disorder at the case level, only 30 percent had suffered a severe event or difficulty in the year before interview. Severe events included bereavement, marital separation, and job loss. Difficulties were long-lasting problems such as having to cope with a violent husband or looking after a demanding and chronically sick relative.

Brown and Harris developed a new method that gave stronger predictions than had previously been possible of who would get depressed. The method was a semi-structured interview, the Life Events and Difficulties Schedule, which replaced the checklists of recent changes such as the originally popular version by Holmes and Rahe (1967). In this checklist, respondents checked if they had been divorced, moved house, taken a vacation, etc. The original checklist was improved in second-generation instruments (Dohrenwend et al., 1990), and scores were used to predict depression, but such checklists are far less accurate than the Life Events and Difficulties Interview Schedule (McQuaid et al., 2000; Thoits, 1995). Using the interview schedule people are asked about 40 areas of life: employment, finances, housing, children, relationships, etc. Interviews are audio recorded, and each stressful event or difficulty is written up, with its date recorded, so that its temporal relation to any onset of depression can be found (not possible with checklist methods). The description of the event is later read to the members of a research team who make a rating of the degree of long-term threat (lasting more than a week) that this event or difficulty would cause in a woman living in the described circumstances. Ratings of long-term severity of an event or difficulty are made by people (the research team) who live in the same society. At the same time these ratings pass the tests of being reliable, because levels of severity are anchored over time by comparing them with previous ratings made by the research team over the years. The ratings are unbiased since the raters do not know the woman's diagnosis. They also are not dependent on the woman's own assessment of how distressing she found any event, which, of course, might be affected by how depressed she was.

People become depressed when extreme adversities occur. Here is the case of Mrs Trent, one of the women in Brown and Harris's study.

Mrs Trent (not her real name) had three small children and was married to a van driver. Her apartment had two rooms and a kitchen. A year before the interview she had occasional migraine headaches, but she felt quite herself. Her third child was born eight months before the interview. Around that time her husband lost his job. She didn't worry too much, and he got another job quickly. But after two weeks he was fired from that job too, without explanation. Seven weeks later her worries had become so severe that she felt tense all the time, she felt miserable, did not sleep well and became irritable with the children. She found it difficult to do the housework, became unable to concentrate, and her appetite declined. In the next two months these symptoms worsened. She would often cry all day. She got some sleeping pills from her doctor. Her relationship with her husband deteriorated. She lost all interest in sex and thought her marriage finished. Three times she packed and walked out but returned because of the children. She felt self-deprecatory, felt she could not cope, and thought that she might end it all. By three weeks before the interview things had started to get better. She still tended to brood, though her concentration was now good enough for her to watch television which distracted her. Her sexual relationship with her husband had returned, and indeed was better than before. She had been depressed for five and a half months. She had not consulted her doctor about depression, but about her migraines. It was for these, she said, that the sleeping pills had been prescribed. She thought it would have been wrong to bother her doctor about feeling depressed, since this was clearly related to her financial and marital worries (paraphrased from Brown & Harris, 1978, pp. 28–30).

In this case the severely threatening event was her husband's second occasion of being fired, which left the family without income. Low mood, sleep disturbances, loss of weight, lack of concentration, self-deprecation, loss of interest in sex, and suicidal thoughts were symptoms of major depression. In Brown and Harris's method Mrs Trent's marital difficulty was not counted as an event that could have caused the depression because it could easily have been caused by it. Other researchers, too, have distinguished between events that a person could have brought on themselves and those that were beyond their control. Shrout (1989) found that clinic patients suffering from depression were three times more likely than people in a non-depressed community sample to have suffered a negative and uncontrollable event. So depression is not necessarily irrational. It involves sadness and hopelessness, brought on by events that have serious implications for our lives and our sense of ourselves. Since the early work of Brown and Harris, the association of depression with severe social adversity, particularly for the first onset of depression, has been well established (Brown & Moran, 1998; Kessler, 1997; Monroe & Hadjiyannakis, 2002).

An event that can cause depression is most typically a **loss** of a role that is highly valued (Oatley & Bolton, 1985). Using life event interviews, Hammen et al. (1989) found that people who valued their relationships became depressed when a social loss or social disruption occurred. This kind of loss is often related to the social motivations of attachment, and perhaps of affiliation. By comparison, those to whom autonomy and work were most important were more likely to become depressed when a failure in achievement occurred, related to the more assertive social motivations.

What, in general, are the kinds of events that cause depressive and anxiety breakdowns? They are events that cause strong negative emotions: the sad emotions of loss, the painful emotions of humiliation, the desperate emotions of not being able to escape from intolerable situations, the anxious emotions of danger (Brown, Harris, & Hepworth, 1995). Kendler et al. (2003) have produced the following categories of event that have been found to produce emotional disorders:

- loss: events such as deaths of loved ones, losses of means of livelihood,
- humiliation: events such as separations in which there has been infidelity, or the delinquency of a child, rapes, put-downs and public humiliations by loved ones and persons in authority that threaten core roles,
- entrapment, in which a person is stuck in an adverse situation with no way out,
- danger, the likelihood of future loss, or of an event that has yet to realize its full potential.

The appearance of humiliation in the above list indicates that depression may be related (at least in part) to the social motivation of assertion in pursuit of status that we discussed in chapter 9 (Gilbert, 1998, 2000).

Episodes of anxiety can also be caused by negative events (Monroe & Wade, 1988). In one study of a community sample, 2,902 men and women were interviewed using standardized measures to diagnose generalized anxiety and to assess life events occurring over the previous year (Blazer, Hughes, & George, 1987). Severe negative events were associated with a threefold increase of anxiety disorder in both men and women. Lesser events were associated with an eightfold increase of generalized anxiety disorder in men, but this relationship was not found in women.

Are anxiety and depression caused by the same kinds of event? Finlay-Jones (1989), using Brown and Harris's method, interviewed women attending a general practice: 85 percent of cases of anxiety, 82 percent of cases with depression, and 93 percent of cases with mixed anxiety and depression had suffered a severe life event as compared with 34 percent of those who were not suffering from any emotional disorder. Some events were future directed, involving **danger**: receiving a diagnosis of a cancer, unwanted pregnancy, threat of eviction from home. Anxiety disorders were most often precipitated by such danger events. By contrast, depressive disorders were most often precipitated by events that were losses. These findings fit what we have learned about links between appraisals of loss and uncertainty with experiences (respectively) of sadness and fear (chapter 7). People who suffered from both depression and anxiety typically experienced events involving both loss and danger.

It is clear that most episodes of major depression and some types of anxiety occur when things go severely wrong in people's lives, and have serious long-term consequences. Like episodes of normal emotion, most emotional disorders are responses to events and circumstances. They let us know what is most important to us. When Mrs Trent's husband lost his job, she experienced feelings of defeat, and of dread about not being able to live adequately or to provide for her family.

Relation between emotions and emotional disorders

The way that severe life events elicit depression and anxiety is similar to how lesser events elicit negative emotions. But there is a difference. Short-term negative emotions and moods are usually caused by events that are setbacks to our projects and concerns. We experience the emotion, and usually we deal with its implications. Severe events are those that threaten fundamental life roles, and we cannot deal with them. They destroy hope of any way forward. Imagine losing something fundamental to your life, to which you have given your best energies and hopes: an important relationship perhaps, or your place at university, or your expectation of a career. Losses of this kind are the types of events that cause depression, and when they occur they can drain all meaning from life (see figure 13.2). This is when the despair of depression can set in, and in its depths no way forward seems possible. Negative emotions – sadness, anger, fear – become long lasting, and most importantly they become **disabling**. Mrs Trent experienced loss of her family's income, and perhaps her faith in her husband, hence her hope for her family, and indeed for the life which she had made. She became unable to do things that had been most important to her, such as care for her children.

How are clinical depression and anxiety states related to normal sadness and fear (Flack & Laird, 1999; Kring & Werner, 2004; Power & Dalgleish, 1997)? We discussed in chapter 6 the work of Mayberg et al. (1999), which showed that the same brain regions involved in depression are also involved in normal sadness. So although depression is not just sadness, the emotion or mood state of sadness is typically involved. As to anxiety, there is no question that anxiety disorders are kinds of fear. The main questions are why these fears can be entirely out of proportion to what the person seems to be frightened of (Öhman, 2000), and can be elicited by neutral or ambiguous stimuli (McNally, 1999). Some people with anxiety disorders have fears that have no clear objects. They are intense but free-floating. One approach to understanding anxiety that reaches clinical levels has been offered by Öhman and Mineka (2001) who say this happens, at least in part, because fear is elicited by appraisals carried out by dedicated neural networks that involve the amygdala (as discussed in chapters 6 and 7). So a state of fear can occur, which is overwhelming, disabling, and at the same time impermeable to cognitive influence.

Why the human condition is subject to such disabling states remains a challenge for theories of emotions. Reflect, though, that we live in very different ways now than we did in our environments of evolutionary adaptedness; depression may, moreover, help people pull back or disengage from ongoing plans and commitments that have been lost, perhaps prompting

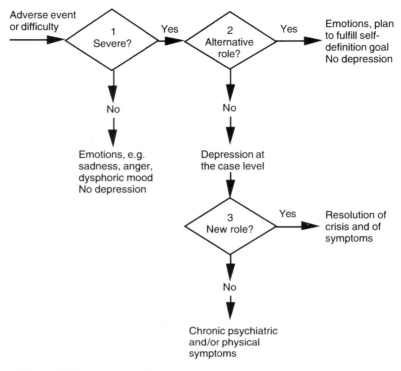

Figure 13.2 Differentiation of normal emotions from depressive breakdowns (Oatley, 1988).

new goals, or new roles (Nesse, 2000; Oatley, 1992). In the next sections we explore how, and for whom, hope becomes lost, and how it can be regained.

Diatheses: vulnerability factors

The conclusion that depression is associated with severe life events or difficulties is now widely accepted. Yet not everyone who experiences serious adversity suffers a breakdown. What is the difference between responding with a negative emotion and responding with a disabling emotional disorder of depression and/or anxiety? What makes one person more vulnerable than another to a breakdown?

Genetic biases   In chapter 11 we discussed evidence that individuals' patterns of emotionality are genetically influenced. This is also true for emotional disorders. Some people are genetically at higher risk than others for depression and anxiety (Kendler et al., 1986), For instance, Kendler et al. (1993b) examined 938 twins from a population registry at one point (Time 1) and then a year later (Time 2). At Time 1 concordance for monozygotic twins was 27 percent (i.e., in 27 percent of twins both members who had the same genes had the disorder) and for dizygotic twins (who shared 50 percent of their genes) concordance was 17 percent. The difference was slightly greater at Time 2 (28.9 vs. 15.4 percent). These concordances imply a moderate genetic risk, and somewhat stronger non-shared environmental factors, such as the stressful life events discussed above. A meta-analysis of published studies by Sullivan, Neale, and Kendler (2000) have confirmed the presence of genetic biases for major depression. Genetic biases also exist for anxiety disorders (Hamm, Vaitl, & Lang, 1990; Scherer et al., 2000). A high genetic sensitivity of a mechanism that associates certain cues to schemas of danger may explain why some people are generally more fearful than others, independently of whether they have experienced serious danger in their lives.

One way in which a genetic influence on depression could work is in terms of positive or negative bias of social confidence and dominance (as we discussed in chapter 9), mediated in part by brain mechanisms that use the transmitter substance serotonin. Many new antidepressant drugs, including Prozac, work to increase the availability of this substance. Genetic influences on depression do not, however, only operate on biases that affect depression as such. Plomin et al. (1990b) examined life events in a twin population. They found that monozygotic twins were more similar to each other than dizygotic twins in the number of adverse life events experienced during their lifetime. Kendler et al. (1993a) examined life events over the previous year in monozygotic and dizygotic twin pairs, and found that frequencies of life events were more highly correlated in monozygotic than in dizygotic pairs, with genetic effects accounting for about 20 percent of their variance. One explanation is that genetic influences on personality affect the occurrence of life events. Impulsivity, for instance, may raise the rate of severe events. Plomin and Bergeman (1991) have reviewed studies that show how variables thought to be environmental (like life events) may be influenced by genetics so that some people bring more severe events and difficulties upon themselves. It is also easy to see that some people may be predisposed to forming more problematic relation-ships than others.

One of most striking and important recent studies in this area has involved the identification of a specific human gene that affects depression in conjunction with adverse life events. Caspi et al. (2003) examined a sample of 1,032 people (52 percent male, 48 percent female) who were members of the Dunedin Multidisciplinary Health and Development Study, in New Zealand, discussed in chapter 12. These people had been followed up at approximately two-year intervals from age three to age 26. They were tested for the presence of the 5-HTT transporter gene, which acts to promote the transmitter substance serotonin. They were also assessed for stressful life events between their 21st and 26th birthdays.

The 5-HTT transporter gene occurs in two forms. One form is short (s) and the other is long (l). The long form is more efficient at promoting serotonin. In the sample 17 percent of the people had two shorts (s/s), 51 percent a short and a long (s/l), and 31 percent two longs (l/l). People who had the short form of the gene combined with a long (s/l) and, to an even greater extent, those with two shorts (s/s), who suffered an adverse life event in their twenties, were more likely to become depressed than those with two long forms (l/l) who suffered an adverse life event. The inference is that a genetically influenced low serotonin production is a vulnerability factor for the impact of life event stress on depression. The presence of the short form of the gene had no influence on depression in the absence of stressful life events.

It is thought that there are 25,000 to 30,000 human genes in all. Caspi et al.'s study comes at the beginning of the new millennium, and at the beginning of the era of **genomics**: the understanding of specific genes that have been individually recognized in the Human Genome Project. For a time, researchers who studied the effect of social influences on depression and those who studied genetics seemed to be at odds. Caspi et al.'s study shows that genes are not destiny. Genetic and social effects work together. The 5-HTT gene acts as a bias in relation to life experience and, as we have discussed in previous chapters, this may be a general pattern of how genes work to affect personality, emotionality, and vulnerabilities to emotional disorder.

Previous episodes of depression Brown and Moran (1994) have shown that for people with repeated episodes of depression, their first episode has usually been caused by a severe life event or difficulty. Subsequent episodes can, however, occur without an obvious severe life event or difficulty. Coyne and Whiffen (1995) argue that the weight of evidence indicates that depression is a recurrent, episodic disorder that usually starts in a person's twenties. A previous episode of depression makes a person more vulnerable to further episodes. To explain this, a **kindling hypothesis** has been proposed, of the brain becoming sensitized by each episode of depression. Segal, Williams, Teasdale, and Gemar (1996) described this in terms of mental patterns becoming established as habits, so that after each episode future activation is made more likely by progressively less stressful events. Moreover, detectable anatomical changes have been found in brain imaging studies to occur in depression, particularly in the anterior cingulate and prefrontal cortex (Harrison, 2002), and these may be related to kindling. Kendler, Thornton, and Gardner (2000) studied the results of four interviews over nine years with female twin pairs (some 2,000 women in all). They found that the first episode of depression was typically caused by a severe life event or difficulty, but that with further episodes of depression the association with adversity became less marked. These same authors (Kendler, Thornton, & Gardner, 2001) then considered genetic factors, and found that the kindling effect was most marked for those at low genetic risk. By contrast, those at high genetic risk frequently experienced a first depression without severe adversity. Kendler et al. proposed that these highly vulnerable people could be thought of as "prekindled." There are therefore two pathways to experiencing depression in the absence of major life stressors. One is high genetic risk. The other is several previous episodes of depression in a life of substantial adversity.

Early experience   A person who loses a parent in childhood, particularly a mother, is more likely than a person who has not lost their mother to develop depression in later life (Brown & Harris, 1978). Originally it was thought that it was loss of the attachment figure that left the individual vulnerable. It now seems that it is not this loss as such, but the lack of parental care that is likely to follow such a loss, which has the negative effect. Women who suffered **neglect** during childhood, or who experienced physical or sexual abuse, are at increased risk of both depression and anxiety as adults (Brewin, Andrews, & Gotlib, 1993; Brown & Harris, 1993).

In part, poor care in childhood tends to make people put themselves into situations of higher risk for life events. So Quinton, Rutter, and Liddle (1984, discussed in chapter 12) found that girls raised in institutions had earlier pregnancies, poorer sexual relationships, and became less competent parents than normal (see also Fleming et al., 2002, discussed in chapter 9). In other studies too, women vulnerable to depression have been found to bring more life events upon themselves; so Hammen (1991) found that women who have a history of major depression experience more life events even when not depressed, than women without a history of depression. Most such events were interpersonal, such as conflicts with a spouse or with children.

The vulnerability of early neglect may consist, in part, of damage to people's sense of themselves as being valuable and worthy of love. Negative emotion schemas of self-in-relationship can increase people's risk of depression by increasing the chances of circumstances that turn out badly. People who have experienced lack of care may have yearnings for love, which prompt them toward hasty or early marriages. With hasty choices, the risk of such relationships being punitive is increased. This can confirm expectations of defeat and loss, which become part of the self-deprecating pattern of depression.

Whitbeck et al. (1992) found that when parents are depressed they are more likely to be rejecting of their children. The children are then more likely to develop difficulties, contributing further to rejection by parents. Sadly, these cycles of vulnerability within relationships are transgenerational. In chapter 12 we reviewed evidence that children were more likely to be depressed when they were in families with a depressed parent. Based on their own experience of the parent–child relationship, such children form schemas about themselves in relationships that they carry with them into their own adulthood. Moreover, the first episode of depression has been found to be associated in women with risks such as having witnessed family violence and having a parent with a psychiatric disorder (Daley, Hammen, & Rao, 2000).

A recent study of the kinds of childhood adversities that predict adult depression has been carried out by Wainwright and Surtees (2002), on a sample of 3,941 people in Norfolk, England. Respondents made self-reports of episodes of depression that reached the criteria for DSM-IV major depression. They were also asked about eight types of adversity before the age of 17 of the kind that had been identified in the literature as potentially harmful to adult mental health and that could easily be reported by respondents. Five of these were: separation from mother for a year or more, a hospital stay of at least two weeks, parental unemployment, parental alcohol or drug abuse, being sent away from home. None of these five predicted current adult depression and lifetime depression, but the following three did: parental divorce, experience of an event so frightening that it was thought about for years afterwards, and physical abuse by someone close. The effect was more marked for women than for men.

Attributional style   A well-known clinical theory of cognitive vulnerability (Beck, 1983; Beck & Emery, 1985) identifies irrational thought patterns, carried over from childhood, as associated with depression and anxiety. In these patterns, thinking is overgeneralized and exaggerated. It is often set off by attending to events with negative connotations while events with positive connotations are not noticed. It involves jumping arbitrarily to conclusions. Events tend to be seen as personal even when they are not. Attributional versions of the theory of learned helplessness (Abramson, Metalsky, & Alloy, 1989; Abramson, Seligman, & Teasdale, 1978), which has become known as the hopelessness theory, also propose that styles of thinking predispose to depression. The idea is that people become depressed if an event occurs over which they have no control when they see the event (a) as having occurred for internal reasons, because of the self rather than anything external, (b) as global, happening in all situations rather than being local to just the current circumstance, and (c) as stable, that is to say permanent rather than temporary. Coyne and Gotlib (1983) have shown that Beck's theory and theories of attributional style (hopelessness) are very similar in their formulations and predictions.

Coyne (1994) had cautioned against drawing conclusions about depression from the use of mood scales rather than full diagnoses of clinical depression. A study that respected this caution by using full DSM diagnoses (American Psychiatric Association, 2000) was performed by Alloy et al. (2000) at Temple University and the University of Wisconsin. In this study, college students were assessed for high or low cognitive risk for depression, and followed up with self-reports and interviews every six weeks for two and a half years, and then every four months for a further three years. The students at high cognitive risk were found retrospectively to have a greater lifetime incidence of minor depression and major depression. In terms of prospective results, those at high cognitive risk were found to have a higher rate of first onset of minor depression, major depression, and hopelessness, than those in the low cognitive risk group. In a further paper on this study Hankin et al. (2004) confirmed that negative cognitive style in interaction with negative events did predict future depression, but not anxiety. They also found that Beck's theory and the hopelessness theory largely overlapped in their ability to predict depression.

Appraisal-based thinking   A new approach to the study of thinking style as a vulnerability factor, especially interesting to researchers on emotions because it is based on appraisals as described in chapter 7, comes from a research group who used narrative analysis to predict patterns of coping in people whose loved ones had died. Stein et al. (1997) followed up 30 people who were not infected with Human Immunodeficiency Virus (HIV) but whose partners had died of AIDS from this virus. The subjects were interviewed two and four weeks after their loss, and then one year later. In the two earlier interviews, they were asked to talk about their previous partners, their experience of loss, what had happened at the time of their partners' death, and what helped them to cope. Appraisals were defined as evaluations of people, places, events, actions, or outcomes that affected the status of their goals and well-being. Positive appraisals included talking about beneficial aspects of their relationship, or about how subjects felt they had been good caregivers. Negative appraisals included statements about fear of the future, and regrets about the quality of the relationship with partners. The proportion of positive appraisals made in the narrative shortly after bereavement was a strong predictor of positive morale ($r = 0.63$) as well as self-reported depressive symptomatology ($r = -0.51$) one year later. Positive appraisals remained significant predictors of well-being at one year even after controlling for well-being or depression in the first month.

Social support   Close relationships have a large effect on whether people develop major depression in response to adversities. Having an intimate relationship is protective. There has been a substantial amount of work demonstrating this protective function in relation to depression, first by Brown and Harris (1978) and subsequently by many others. So for instance, Parry and Shapiro (1986) interviewed women with low incomes and at least one young child. Of those who did not suffer any life event or difficulty, 5 percent of those with an intimate relationship and 10 percent of those without one broke down with major depression. But of those who did suffer a severe event or difficulty, 10 percent of those with an intimate relationship, but 30 percent of those without one, broke down with major depression. In a study by Solomon and Bromet (1982), mothers with small children were studied after the severe event of the accident at Three Mile Island nuclear power plant in Pennsylvania, which released large quantities of radioactivity into the atmosphere. Here too there was a similar pattern. The general pattern is that social support has a small effect on its own, but that it is protective against adverse life events and difficulties when these occur (Cohen & Wills, 1985).

With the impact of adverse life events, the factor of social support continues to be investigated in different populations, such as men who have suffered unemployment (Bolton & Oatley, 1987), adolescents (Stice et al., 2004), women outpatients (Ali, Oatley, & Toner, 2002), and men with HIV (Johnson et al., 2001). In general, the pattern that social support reduces the power of adverse life events to cause depression is established.

Social support has been a fundamental concept in understanding the psychological impact of life events (Stroebe & Stroebe, 1996). Typical social support measures include having a confidant, lack of interpersonal friction, interpersonal appreciation, integration in a social network, and practical assistance. Thoits (1986) has identified social support as assistance from other people in coping with the slings and arrows of life. Sarason et al. (1987) compared various measures of social support, and concluded that though they focus on different aspects of relationships, high social support generally indicates whether a person is accepted, loved, and involved in relationships where communication is open.

In this book we have argued that human beings are social creatures, and that most of our important emotions concern our social relationships. The study of life events and depression throws additional light on these issues because, first, the events that induce depression are typically losses of relationship, and second, that social support – strong bonds with others – can protect against any one loss. Not only are relationships the source of most of life's meaning for us human beings, but with loss of important relationships, some of life's meaning drains away. We lose part of our self. A life lived with the support of strong bonds of attachment and affiliation with a number of family members, friends, and colleagues means that a loss of one relationship may produce profound sadness, but will not entirely deplete life of its meaning.

Figure 13.3 Woman leaving home to drop her child off at day care before going to work. Brown and Harris (1978) found that a job outside the home protected women from depression.

Factors in recovery and in prolongation

An emphasis in research in the past 40 years has been on what causes emotional disorders. Almost as important are questions of what can resolve an episode so that the person can return to ordinary life, and of what may prolong episodes. Recovery from an episode is associated with fresh starts, with positive evaluations of self (Brown, Lemyre, & Bifulco, 1992), and with new plans coming to fruition (Oatley & Perring, 1991). Recovery may involve a new relationship, a new role, a new life project to replace what was lost, that enables a person to feel worthwhile and purposeful.

The important study on the length of depressive episodes is the National Institute of Mental Health Collaborative Depression Study in which it was found that most episodes of depression did resolve. Thus, within a year of the onset of depression, about 70 percent of patients had recovered. But by five years 12 percent of people remained in depressive episodes that had not resolved (Mueller et al., 1996) and by ten years 7 percent of episodes had not resolved (Keller & Boland, 1998). A continuing episode is known as chronic depression.

Both sadness and anxiety states can maintain themselves because they can make people more sad or anxious: they can set up vicious cycles that are self-sustaining and that make it more difficult to recover from the impact of an adversity. There are several kinds of process.

Cognitive processes

The most favored cognitive explanation of prolonged depression and anxiety is that of **biases** (Mineka & Gilboa, 1998; Williams et al., 1997). It is an idea that links emotional disorders closely to properties of normal emotions and moods. In chapter 7 we showed that emotions change the organization of the brain and hence produce biases of processing. Because depressed people have a tendency to recall memories of loss and failure, Teasdale (1988) has suggested that these memories in turn tend to lower mood, and prolong depression (see figure 13.4). Depressed people are usually capable of performing at normal levels in various tasks if they are given an appropriate plan, but if left to themselves they may fail to discover such a plan (Hertel & Hardin, 1990). They tend to lack initiative. They also tend to interpret the future in a more pessimistic way, focusing on negative events and rarely attending to positive events (Pyszczynski & Greenberg, 1987). If these biases extend to being less able to generate new life plans, then this lack of initiative too could contribute to extending periods of depression.

Negative attributional style (discussed above) is not only a vulnerability factor for depression, but it is a symptom of depression that can prolong an episode. For instance, in a longitudinal study of recovery from diagnosed depression, Oatley and Perring (1991) found that attributions about the

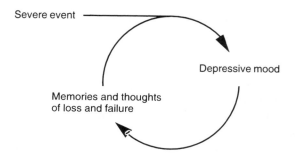

Figure 13.4   A vicious circle: depression caused by a life event may elicit memories of previous losses and failures, which in turn tend to make the person more depressed, and so on.

event that caused the breakdown were the largest predictor of whether symptoms persisted six to eight months later.

In a well-regarded set of studies Susan Nolen-Hoeksema and her colleagues have investigated the psychology of **rumination**. To ruminate is to dwell on symptoms of distress and what caused them in a passive and repetitive manner, rather than in a problem-solving way (Nolen-Hoeksema, 2000).

Nolen-Hoeksema and Morrow (1991) found that, as compared with people who did not ruminate, people who ruminated about a natural disaster – the earthquake in the San Francisco Bay area on October 17, 1989 that killed 62 and left 12,000 people homeless – had lower mood 10 days later, and also seven weeks after the disaster. In a study of people who had a close relative who had died in a hospice, Nolen-Hoeksema et al. (1994) found that the mood of people with a ruminative style was no lower than that of others a month after bereavement, but six months after their relative's death their mood was still low, whereas that of non-ruminators had started to lift.

Women tend more frequently than men to have a ruminative style of coping with adversities. Men are more likely to cope by distraction (Nolen-Hoeksema, Morrow, & Fredrickson, 1993). Nolen-Hoeksema and Jackson (2001) and Nolen-Hoeksema, Larson, and Grayson (1999) report that a gender difference in rumination has been found in self-reports, in interviews, and in laboratory studies. They have found, too, that when differences in rumination are controlled for, the gender difference in rates of depression becomes non-significant. (Consider how this work links to individual differences in emotion regulation and reappraisal, discussed in chapter 11.)

Biases of processing are also thought to help maintain anxiety states in vicious cycles, once they have begun – and anxiety states are more likely than depression to become chronic. For instance, fear makes one avoid certain situations. In disabling chronic anxiety disorders, such as agoraphobia and social phobias, the unfamiliar is avoided (Mathews, Gelder, & Johnson, 1981). This makes what is avoided more threatening, and further diminishes self-confidence. This in turn prolongs anxiety and avoidance.

Whereas the cognitive mechanism for sustaining depression is thought to be influenced strongly by memory, cognitive mechanisms that sustain anxiety tend to be based on attention (Mogg & Bradley, 1999; Williams et al., 1997). People with anxiety traits and disorders have attentional biases toward events that cause anxiety, especially their own particular kind of anxiety (Mathews, 1993). So a person anxious about health, or with hypochondriacal concerns, attends to bodily events thinking them to be symptoms of illness (Stretton & Salovey, 1998). Such a person will tend to notice newspaper items about health, and attend to reports of other people's health, building up mental schemas and habits of mind that serve to make anxiety more likely, and to heighten its intensity. Here too, the cognitive organization set up by an emotional state is such as to bring to mind events that are likely to intensify and prolong that emotional state. So fear produces more fear. Following the 2001 attack on the World Trade Center in New York, as well as depression, symptoms of post-traumatic stress disorder have occurred among those who were closely involved (Galea et al., 2002). Fear that derived from the attack caused further anxiety symptoms, some of which made it impossible for some sufferers to return to work, and caused disruptions of personal relationships.

A new theory of psychological illnesses augments this kind of analysis. Johnson-Laird, Mancini, and Gangemi (2005) propose that what begins disorders such as depression, obsessional-compulsive disorder, phobia, and hypochondria are elicitations of basic emotions such as sadness and fear, derived from the automatic and unconscious appraisals that we have discussed. The elicitations are not inappropriate in terms of what emotions occur. They are only inappropriate in their intensity. This intensity – which remains cognitively impenetrable – triggers trains of thinking, which as we have just discussed, tend to prolong and intensify the emotions. Evidence for this theory comes from a survey of the emotions experienced at first onset by sufferers. These were mostly basic emotions, such as sadness in depression, and anxiety in obsessional-compulsive disorders and phobias. In addition, the reasoning of patients about events related to their disorder was found not to be illogical (as claimed by some researchers) but tended to be superior to the reasoning of non-sufferers.

Interpersonal effects

Alongside cognitive explanations, a second important kind of explanation of how depression is prolonged has been proposed by Constance Hammen and her colleagues (Daley et al., 1997; Hammen, 1991, 1999), and by Joiner (2002). This explanation is in terms of relationships. Depression tends to make relationships deteriorate, which then tends to prolong depression. This process can, however, also draw on cognitive factors: for instance, Goddard, Dritschel, and Burton (1996) have found that changes in depressed people's access to memories can result in decreased social skills. As compared with the non-depressed, depressed people express more negative affect including sadness and anger (Biglan et al., 1985). Such negative emotions are often aversive to other people, and this results in partners being more hostile to them (Coyne, 1976, 1999). Hokanson et al. (1991) tracked mood and interactions between roommates at college. They had three groups of pairs. In one group one member of the pair had a prolonged depressed mood as indicated by a continuously high score on the Beck Depression Inventory (Beck, Steer, & Garbin, 1988). In the second group one person scored high on the Beck Inventory on one occasion but low subsequently. In the third group one person was generally cheerful, with a continuously low score on the Beck Inventory. As compared with roommates of cheerful people, those living with the continuously depressed people showed an increase in their own levels of depression over the course of the year. They reported becoming more managerial of their roommate, and saw their roommate as becoming more dependent.

There is a strong association between **poor marriage** and depression (Whisman, 2001). Poor marriages are difficulties (in the sense recognized by Brown and Harris, 1978) of the kind that provoke onsets of depression. For instance, Whisman and Bruce (1999) found in a community sample in New Haven, Connecticut, that people who were not depressed at the outset of the study but who were dissatisfied with their marriages were, within a year, nearly three times as likely as satisfied spouses to develop a major depressive disorder. In general, when a difficulty such as a bad marriage continues, so too does the depression it has provoked (Brown, Adler, & Bifulco, 1988). Miller et al. (1992) followed up psychiatric in-patients diagnosed as depressed. Those living in dysfunctional families showed a significantly higher level of symptoms a year after discharge than patients returning to functional families. Poor marriages also make episodes more likely to recur. Hooley and Teasdale (1989) found that depressed patients were more likely to relapse within nine months of discharge if they reported marital difficulties and a spouse who was critical of them.

We have already discussed how supportive relationships can protect against negative life events. In contrast, people who are prone to depression can create negative social networks for themselves, thereby increasing both their risk of depression, and the risk of depression being maintained. For instance, Coyne et al. (1987) found that 40 percent of spouses of depressed patients show clinically significant symptoms, compared to 17 percent of spouses of women not suffering from a disorder. Coyne et al. (1991) suggest that people who are susceptible to depression may choose partners who are themselves vulnerable. It has been found that depressed young women often marry men who have disorders (Hammen et al., 1999). Poor relationships with caregivers in childhood may set people on a trajectory in which they are socially unskilled, or in which they feel unconfident, and this makes it harder to enter relationships in which good social support is available in adulthood.

Mind over matter?

Despite the fact that some depressions and anxiety states can become chronic, Parrott and Sabini (1990) point out that most people do not get trapped in inescapable cycles forever. People can regulate their moods, and some memories that come to mind, even when one is low, are not depressing or fear-producing. We might say that after an episode of depression or intense anxiety, as people start to reconceptualize their lives, although they may be affected by episodes from the past, for some at least, it is also possible to make plans for the future.

Emotions and mental health beyond depression and anxiety

We now consider two further areas of health in which emotions have been implicated.

Expressed Emotion and relapse in schizophrenia

Whereas emotional disorders are largely provoked by the adversities of life, psychotic conditions such as **schizophrenia** are more closely determined by genetics. Symptoms of schizophrenia include delusions, certain kinds of hallucinations, disorganized behavior, and deteriorating relationships. For a diagnosis according to DSM-IV-TR (American Psychiatric Association, 2000) a disturbance has to last for at least six months, and to cause severe dysfunction socially and at work.

People with schizophrenia have difficulties with social skills, and independently, as Salem and Kring (1999) have shown, they also have flattened affect. Flack et al. (1999) have argued that the lack of emotional expression by schizophrenic people also contributes, by means of William James's theory of emotions, to attenuation of their own emotions. At the extreme, a person with schizophrenia can be catatonic: that is to say be absolutely immobile for hours on end, and this state has recently been analyzed as an extreme fear response, derived evolutionarily from freezing when confronted with a large carnivore. Moscowitz (2004) argues that it may represent an end state of people who feel faced with doom.

Although schizophrenia has a strong genetic component, the emotions of family members affect its course and relapse rate. In the 1960s Brown and his colleagues demonstrated a relationship between relapse of schizophrenic people and the emotional tone in the family in which they lived. Relapse in a patient who had returned home from psychiatric hospitalization could be predicted from three features of an interview with a close relative (spouse or parent with whom the patient lived) about the patient: (a) the number of critical comments made by the relative, for instance "he just keeps smoking, smoking, smoking," (b) the degree of hostility both in nonverbal

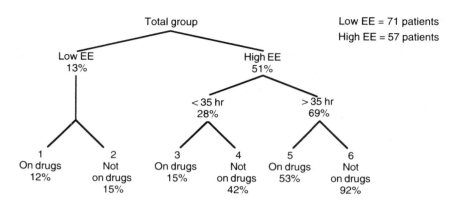

Figure 13.5 Percentages of schizophrenic patients relapsing within nine months of leaving hospital, as a function of High and Low Expressed Emotion of the families to whom they returned of whether they spent less or more than 35 hours per week with this family, and of whether they took their anti-psychotic medication (Vaughn & Leff, 1976).

aspects such as tone of voice, and in content, for instance "I wish he were dead," and (c) the degree of over-involvement, such as treating the patient as a child, or as in "I'd lost so much weight, I couldn't sleep for worry" (Brown, Birley, & Wing, 1972). These three (a, b, & c) were combined into an index that became known as Expressed Emotion.

In a study that built on this work, Vaughn and Leff (1976) followed up schizophrenic patients who had been discharged from psychiatric hospital to see what factors (from the Expressed Emotion interview) predicted whether they would relapse and be back in hospital again within the next nine months. Frequency of critical comments in the interview was the best predictor. Two groups of families were defined: High Expressed Emotion families in which relatives made six or more critical comments, and Low Expressed Emotion families in which fewer than six such comments were recorded.

Results are shown in figure 13.5. For patients who returned to a family that was low in Expressed Emotion, irrespective of whether the patients took their anti-psychotic medication, there was a low rate of relapse. But of those returning to a High Expressed Emotion family, who spent more than 35 hours a week with them, and did not take their medication, 92 percent relapsed within nine months.

Can families with High Expressed Emotion learn to decrease their anger and hostility to a patient and, if so, will the relapse rate diminish? A typical study on this question is by Hogarty et al. (1986) who worked with 90 High Expressed Emotion families of schizophrenic patients. One group of patients had only medication (*n* = 29); of these 41 percent relapsed within a year. By contrast, in the group (*n* = 20) that had treatment for the families plus social skills training for the patient (who also took medication) none relapsed within one year. Barbato and D'Avanzo (2000) reviewed 25 intervention studies, and concluded that although there were methodological problems in many of them, family interventions were generally found to be effective in reducing relapse rates.

Expressed Emotion is not just any emotion. It is interpersonal anger, contempt, and criticism of someone unable to escape: "she just follows me everywhere," said one patient (Kuipers & Bebbington, 1988, p. 905). It is the opposite of warmth and affection. It has been found that schizophrenic patients (Sturgeon et al., 1984; Tarrier et al., 1988), and also children with disruptive behavior disorder (Hibbs et al., 1992), respond with increased bodily arousal when High Expressed Emotion relatives, but not Low Expressed Emotion relatives, are in the room with them.

There have now been many studies of Expressed Emotion in families. Two broad conclusions have been reached as a result of a meta-analysis of these studies by Butzlaff and Hooley (1998). One is that the effect of High Expressed Emotion is associated with relapse of schizophrenia, and Low Expressed Emotion is associated with prevention of relapse. All but three of the 27 studies that reached methodological criteria for inclusion showed the effect. The mean effect size was equivalent to about $r = 0.31$, which translates into some 65 percent of patients relapsing who were in High Expressed Emotion families, and 35 percent relapsing who were in Low Expressed Emotion families. Butzlaff and Hooley's second broad conclusion is that it is now well established that the Expressed Emotion concept works well, also, for families whose members have disorders other than schizophrenia. In the studies they reviewed, the effect size was higher ($r = 0.39$) for relapse of depressive disorders, and higher still ($r = 0.51$) for relapse of eating disorders such as anorexia.

Measures of Expressed Emotion are ways of taking the emotional temperature of a family. There is some suggestion that in cultures other than English-speaking ones, different factors may be important. For instance, Lopez et al. (2004) found that in Mexican families, family warmth was more important as a protection against relapse than family hostility was as a provocation of relapse.

Psychiatric disorders are not just disturbances of the patients. They are disturbing to others. A lesson of Expressed Emotion research is that with acceptance of the patient's condition and some flexibility in coping with it, not only may the lives of families with schizophrenic and other disorders become easier, but the cycle of provoking the patient into ever more difficult behavior and relapse may be cut.

Psychosomatic illness

As well as causing emotional disorders, stresses of the kind discussed earlier in this chapter contribute to onset and maintenance of at least some kinds of physical illness. The relation of mind to bodily ills is called psychosomatic medicine, and several traditions contribute to it. One, based on psychoanalytic ideas, is that inner conflict can give rise to illness (Alexander, 1950). A more recent idea is that people who barely express or experience emotions – a trait known as **alexithymia** – tend to have more bodily symptoms and a greater susceptibility to illness than people who do experience and express emotions (Luminet et al., 2004; Taylor, Bagby, & Parker, 1997). Bermond, Bleys, and Stoffels (2005) have recently found evidence that alexithymic people have more active left hemispheric processing, than do non-alexithymic people. The main line of research on psychosomatic illness, however, has been based on the idea first proposed by Selye (1936), that stresses challenge the psycho-physiological system. He thought that intense or long-lasting stresses may exhaust physiological resources and the exhaustion would predispose to illness.

Much of the research on psychosomatic illness now involves the **immune system**, which extends throughout the body and includes the bone marrow, spleen, thymus, lymph nodes, and the white cells of the blood such as lymphocytes and macrophages. The study of psychological effects on this system is known as psychoneuroimmunology. The recommended book is Rabin (1999).

One kind of immunity is innate. It consists of the acute response of inflammation and repair at the site of a wound or infection and the migration of white blood cells called macrophages to ingest foreign particles and debris. The second kind of immunity is acquired, because its effectiveness improves after contact with particular foreign invaders of a disease. The proteins of these invaders are called antigens. They are recognized by the immune system, and then destroyed. Central to this response are white blood cells called T-lymphocytes. Each has on its surface receptors each of which recognizes and bonds to a single type of antigen. Since there are thought to be a million billion (10^{15}) different kinds of receptor, it follows that in any one person there can only be a tiny number of T-lymphocytes that can bond to any given antigen. The immune response includes proliferation of a clone of T-lymphocytes with receptors for the invading antigen, until there are enough to kill all the invading antigens of an infective agent such as a virus. Once a response has occurred, memory T-cells for that antigen are created to give a faster response next time that antigen is encountered. Another kind of lymphocyte, the Natural Killer (NK) cell, also proliferates during an immune response. NK cells can destroy virally infected body cells and some kinds of cancer cells.

There are three main kinds of changes of immune function that affect illness. First, an impaired immune system can fail to recognize and destroy antigens of bacteria, fungi, and viruses. Second, an impaired immune system may fail to recognize and destroy malignant cancer cells. Third, changes can occur in the immune system's recognition of the body's own tissue, so that in some diseases, called autoimmune diseases, such as rheumatoid arthritis, this recognition fails.

Janice Kiecolt-Glaser and her colleagues (2002) present evidence that negative emotions are risk factors, and supportive relationships are protective in a range of illnesses. They distinguish between short-term (acute) stress and long-term (chronic) stress. Over ten years Kiecolt-Glaser has developed a series of studies on acute stress, taking as a model students' acute anxiety and stress at exams. She and her colleagues have found that acute stress decreases immune response to vaccinations (Glaser et al., 1998), and that students who have a surgical wound three days before an exam have a 40 percent lower rate of healing than those with the same kind of wound made during the summer vacation (Maroucha, Kiecolt-Glaser, & Favegehi, 1998). As to chronic stressors: those that last more than a month have been found to be the strongest predictors of developing a cold when inoculated with cold viruses (Cohen et al., 1998). The persisting symptoms of post-traumatic stress syndrome have been found to be associated with impairment of the immune response system, as found by Ironson et al. (1997) who investigated people who were closely associated with the destruction caused by Hurricane Andrew.

A second kind of psychosomatic effect is on coronary heart disease, which is a leading cause of death in the USA, where each year some 450,000 people die from it. The disease occurs when fatty accumulations occur inside the arteries that supply the muscles of the heart (the coronary arteries). When these arteries become narrowed by these accumulations, and when certain transient effects occur that further narrow the arteries, as for instance during exercise, the area of the heart that is supplied by a narrowed artery suffers ischemia, a shortage of oxygen. If a coronary artery becomes completely blocked the area of the heart it supplies completely loses its oxygen supply: a heart attack, which can be fatal. To start with, in research on psychological and social factors that predicted coronary heart disease, the emphasis was on the so-called Type-A personality: a personality type characterized by impatience and hostility (Rosenman et al., 1975). Some research continues to support this kind of explanation; for instance, Siegman et al. (2000) found that behavioral ratings of social dominance and of hostility were independently associated with coronary heart disease. But other results have been mixed. It has, however, been found that in people who already have narrowing of their coronary arteries, the arousal of anger can cause ischemia (Gabbay et al., 1996). More generally, it has been established that a range of factors can adversely affect coronary heart conditions, see Smith and Ruiz (2002) for a review. These factors often involve negative emotions, and they are similar to those that provoke, or predispose to, depression (as discussed above). As an example, in the Stockholm Female Coronary Risk Study, Orth-Gomer et al. (2000) found that women who already had coronary heart disease who were maritally distressed were three times more likely than married but undistressed women to experience a new coronary event.

Cancer is another leading cause of death in industrialized societies. Are there social and emotional effects that affect it? It has been established that cancers do not occur solely because of genetics or age. Doll and Peto (1981) have shown that some 80 percent of cancers are attributable to lifestyle and environment, hence could be avoided. Tobacco smoking accounts for 30 percent of the death rate in Western nations, mostly but not wholly from lung cancer. In addition, for reasons that are not well understood, perhaps associated with amounts of fat and fiber, diet contributes another

35 percent. Laboratory studies, and studies of steps in the process leading to human cancer, show that stress can adversely affect mechanisms involved in cancer. At the same time, many of the results of direct effects of stress on human cancer are mixed or suggestive rather than conclusive (Kiecolt-Glaser et al., 2002). Complicating the analyses is the likelihood of indirect effects of stress on lifestyle and diet.

Overall, then, in psychosomatic medicine, knowledge is growing that indicates that for many conditions the same stresses that cause negative emotions and emotional disorders, as well perhaps as the presence of emotional disorders themselves, are associated with risks to physical health. Explorations continue.

Summary

In this chapter we discussed how depression and anxiety are related to sadness and fear: they are emotional disorders. Together they are the most common psychiatric conditions in Western populations, with women being nearly twice as frequently afflicted as men. By contrast, men suffer more often than women from disorders of the abuse of alcohol, and from persistent antisocial behavior that continues the externalizing disorders of childhood. We described findings that the first episode of major depression and/or clinical anxiety is usually caused by a stress, which is typically a severely adverse event or difficulty, along with at least one other factor such as a genetic predisposition, a personal history of childhood neglect, a certain kind of cognitive style, or lack of social support in the immediate environment. An episode of major depression itself makes further episodes of depression more likely. We found that as with emotions and moods, the social world is the occasion for many emotional disorders and, just as with emotions and moods, emotional disorders also affect people's relationships. Sometimes these relationships can help to prolong a disorder. We also learned that critical and hostile emotions in the family can provoke relapse in schizophrenia and other disorders. Finally we discussed how psychosomatic illnesses, such as susceptibility to infections and exacerbations of coronary heart disease, are affected by the same kinds of stresses that provoke depression and anxiety.

Further reading

One of the most important books published in adult psychiatry and engaging to read is:

George W. Brown & Tirril Harris (1978). *Social origins of depression: A study of psychiatric disorder in women*. London: Tavistock.

A fine article on the relation of fear to anxiety states is by:

Arne Öhman & Susan Mineka (2001). Fears, phobias, and preparedness: Towards an evolved module of fear and fear learning. *Psychological Review, 108*, 483–522.

Very useful for understanding depression is:

Ian Gotlib & Constance Hammen (Eds.). (2002). _Handbook of depression_. New York: Guilford.

An interesting and comprehensive article on health in relation to emotions is:

Janice Kiecolt-Glaser et al. (2002). Emotions, morbidity, and mortality: New perspectives from psychoneuroimmunology. _Annual Review of Psychology, 53,_ 83–107.

Psychotherapy, Consciousness, and Well-being

> *There is, I assure you, a medical art for the soul. It is philosophy, whose aid need not be sought, as in bodily diseases, from outside ourselves. We must endeavor with all our resources and all our strength to become capable of doctoring ourselves.*
>
> ***Cicero:** Tusculan* **Disputations**, *III*, 6

Contents

Figure 14.0 Ronald De Sousa used these pictures for his book *The Rationality of Emotions.* They are from Thomas Hill's (1885) book on etiquette – a making conscious of how to perform social customs.

Psychological therapies and the emotions

Emotions can take over our lives. Sometimes they make us do things we do not understand, or that we regret. Emotions can be vague and unformed, with meanings that only become clear as we express them to others. At the same time we sense that our emotions are our guides to our most authentic selves. They are at the center of many religious practices and rituals, of drama and other literature, and of psychotherapy. It is as if, in the religions, literatures, and psychotherapeutic practices of the world, human **consciousness** has struggled to find a right relation with the emotions. And, if emotions are signals of events that affect our deepest concerns and our most important relationships, we might expect that this would be so.

In the East the tenor of emotional life is thought to be best modulated by practices such as meditation, and by attitudes such as non-attachment to worldly things (Armstrong, 2001). Recently, mindfulness meditation has been found to have effects on the brain similar to those of positive emotions, shifting activation to the left hemisphere (Davidson et al., 2003a) and – with East meeting West - mindfulness has been developed into a form of psychological therapy (Segal, Williams, & Teasdale, 2002).

In the West the idea of transformation of the self was of interest to the classical Greeks and to the Hebrews. Such ideas were thought to derive from ancient Egyptian sources. They flourished in dozens of sects in the Middle East. They were incorporated into Christianity, and became a driving force in the Renaissance (Jonas, 1958; Yates, 1964). Here is one version: At the core of each of us is a little piece of divine substance, the soul, that has been detached from God, and contained inside a human body. Our task on earth is to see through the veils of bodily existence, and undertake a spiritual journey. Helped by a mentor, we relinquish whatever obscures our vision, undergo spiritual rebirth, and struggle out of darkness to the light, so that our soul may reunite with the divine. Emotions are part of the obscuring veil, first to be recognized and owned, then transcended.

Consider the Roman Catholic practice of confession, as one expression of this theme, and notice its relation to the emotions. Early in the Christian tradition confession was made before a group of neighbors. By early medieval times it was performed privately with a priest, and this practice continues. Throughout, it has had several components. First comes a confession not just of general sinfulness but of some specific sin, perhaps an occasion of immoderate anger or of improper lust. Second must come the emotions of shame and remorse for this sin. Third, there needs to be some restitution for the wrong. A fourth part was then anticipated – the amendment of life. Confession was never something that could be done alone because the church fathers understood the eyes of at least one other person to be an essential part of inducing shame, and repudiating the sin along with the shameful previous version of the self who committed it.

In many societies comparable practices exist that may be classed broadly as psychotherapeutic. The general pattern is this. Any of us can fall out of a right relation with ourselves, with our families and communities, with the society in which we live, or with the gods. Signs of wrong relations can include strong and disturbed emotions. Practices and rituals are followed that center on the disordered emotion. The societal practices may involve manipulating and interpreting particular states of consciousness or inducing them. They may involve going to a sequestered place, privation, meditation, and, in some societies, drugs. There are typically meetings with others such as mentors, gurus, priests, shamans, and also with the members of the immediate community (Kleinman, 1988; Tseng & McDermott, 1981). The aim is healing (the root meaning of the Greek term "therapy") – which means making the self whole – and reintegration of the individual with society. As we might expect, many of these same elements exist in modern secular practices of psychotherapy.

In all the different tributaries of this stream, at the center of the process of change are the emotions (Greenberg & Safran, 1987; Neu, 1977). Let us first approach this topic from a direction that has become familiar in the West: from the direction of psychoanalytic therapy, which both stands in a long line of therapies from different cultures (Prince, 1980) and has been the origin of most modern Western approaches to psychotherapy. In this approach, the therapist tries to work with the client to make sense of emotion-based symptoms. This is in contrast to the medical approach of trying directly to relieve the suffering and anguish of such symptoms.

The basic idea of psychoanalytic therapy

Sigmund Freud's first form of psychotherapy focused on emotionally traumatic events in a patient's earlier life. We presented a prototype in chapter 1: Freud's case of Katharina (reported in Freud & Breuer, 1895). Freud's therapy was aimed at recalling the trauma, enabling it to become conscious, allowing the emotions associated with it to be experienced and expressed, thus freeing the patient from the trauma's continuing harmful effects. Not long after he had published his first papers on hysteria, however, Freud came to believe he had been mistaken in thinking that disorder was necessarily caused by childhood sexual abuse. The center of his new idea, formed in the final few years of the nineteenth century, was that neurotic people suffer from **inner conflict**; for instance, both feeling sexually attracted to someone and feeling at the same time inhibited by the prohibitions of society.

Historical figure: Sigmund Freud

Sigmund Freud was born in 1856 of an impecunious wool merchant and his wife, and from the age of four until a year before he died he lived in Vienna. Soon after qualifying as a doctor in 1881, he met Martha Bernays, fell deeply in love, and began a chaste four-year engagement, the frustrations of which may have contributed to his theories of sexuality. After various more or less unsuccessful attempts to make his way in biology and neurology, Freud started treating patients by hypnosis, at which he said he was not very good, so he began the treatment that has become famous as psychoanalysis. In 1902 Freud was promoted to professor extraordiarius (equivalent to associate professor) at the University in Vienna. Although he was always touchy about the recognition he felt he deserved, in retrospect one can see that from this time his fortunes improved, and his influence spread until in his own lifetime he became the world's most famous psychologist. In 1938, Freud and his family fled from the Nazis to England. His last year, before he died of cancer in September 1939, was spent in London. Freud's work was foundational not only to psychology and psychiatry, but important in art and literature. He affected the very texture of twentieth-century thinking. (Biographical information: Gay, 1988; Sulloway, 1979.)

Figure 14.1 Almost all forms of therapy involve a therapist listening to a client talking about his or her emotional life.

Almost from the beginning, psychoanalysis attracted both adherents and detractors. Detractors argued that psychoanalysis was less a therapeutic procedure, more a matter for the police! This debate continues: psycho-analytic therapy continues to flourish and has become part of Western culture. Recent attackers include Crews (1994) and Grünbaum (1986). Among other issues, Freud's reputation is being questioned in controversies surrounding cases in which people report having recovered memories of childhood sexual-emotional traumas and abuse (see Bekerian & Goodrich, 1999; Ochsner & Schachter, 2003) that perhaps have been repressed, or perhaps have been suggested by therapists.

Most enduringly, Freud proposed a therapy of listening carefully, with respect, and with what he called "evenly hovering attention," to patients who suffered from emotional disorders such as anxiety disorders and depression. In Western psychiatric practice, all psychological therapies with individuals owe something to this practice of active listening.

Therapy's focus on the emotions

There are now many different kinds of psychological therapy. In 1986, Kazdin counted 400 variants. Many clinical psychologists and psychiatrists would describe themselves as eclectic, which means they incorporate selected aspects from different variants into their practice (Davidson & Neale, 2001; Lambert, 2004). Most therapies involve a close relationship with a therapist, talk, and suggestion. Nearly all involve emotions in a more-or-less explicit way (Greenberg & Safran, 1987; Greenberg & Safran, 1989). Therapy, then, is an interaction with another person in which, as a patient or client, one can discover some of the properties of one's emotion schemas – most typically schemas of anxiety, anger, and despair – and can to some extent change how these schemas operate. Therapy provides the context of a relation-ship, in which one may experience one's emotion schemas, understand them better, take responsibility for them, and modify some aspects of one's behavior accordingly. Though all psychological therapy is concerned with the emotions, we present here three kinds of therapy that focus on them.

Psychoanalysis: unconscious schemas of relating

The distinctive feature of psychoanalytic therapy is the recognition of **transference** of the client to the therapist. The idea of transference was discussed by Freud (1905) in the case of Ida Bauer, to whom Freud gave the pseudonym "Dora." She came every day except Sunday to see him at his consulting rooms at Berggasse 19, in Vienna (Bernheimer & Kahane, 1985). In his case history of Dora, Freud explained his new method: the patient was asked to lie on a couch, narrate the story of her life, and say whatever else came to mind. In turn, Freud suggested interpretations to fill the gaps in the story. One of the gaps Dora left was that as she denounced her father for having an affair with another woman, Frau K., she omitted to say that, partly facilitated by her father's affair, she herself was enjoying the courtly attentions of Herr K., the woman's husband.

Transference is the manifestation of emotion schemas, mental models that embody ways of relating to others that have become habitual. It is perhaps best thought of as a set of emotional attitudes toward significant others, from the past, such as parents. Such attitudes and emotions are projected onto people in the present, including the therapist. "What are transferences?" asked Freud (1905). "They are new editions or facsimiles of the impulses and phantasies which . . . replace some earlier person [such as a parent] by the person of the physician" (p. 157). Thus Dora, in Freud's case, said her father "always preferred secrecy and roundabout ways." That is to say, she did not trust him. For instance, when he started his affair with Frau K., he diverted Dora's attention from it by arranging for Herr K. to pay courtly attention to her. In her analysis, Dora began to treat Freud as she had treated her father: with distrust. She took this to the point of dumping Freud by leaving therapy after three months, just as she had emotionally detached herself from her father.

Transference has been studied experimentally by Susan Andersen and Serena Chen (2002). They use the term relational self for the beliefs and emotions of selfhood that derive from earlier relationships. Their general procedure was to ask participants to write 14 sentences of description of themselves in relation with two significant others, one for whom they had positive feelings, and one for whom they had negative feelings. Typically such others were parents, siblings, friends, and lovers. The experimenters looked to see how far these relational traits from the past might affect a relationship with a person the participant met for the first time. Anderson, Reznik, and Manzella (1996) showed people a description of a new person that resembled their own previous description of a significant other. Their facial expressions were of more positive emotions when the description was reminiscent of a significant other they liked, than for when the description resembled a significant other they did not like.

In a further study, Berk and Anderson (2000) asked 120 people to write descriptions of significant others. Two weeks later these people (called perceivers) returned to the laboratory for what they thought was an unrelated experiment, in which they were asked to talk on an intercom for eight minutes with another person (called a target). There were 120 different targets, one for each perceiver, and they did not know the purpose of the experiment. The experimenters gave the perceivers information that purported to be about the target, and asked them to get to know the target person in order to provide a balanced assessment of him or her. When the target's traits (as the perceivers had been told) resembled those of the perceiver's positive (as compared with negative) significant other, the target exhibited more positive emotion in the conversation over the intercom. In other words, when positive transference from the perceiver was received, this made the target happier than when negative transference was received. For targets in control groups, no differences in positive emotions were found. In terms of themes of this book, we would say that a transference of positive emotions invites the other into a warm and cooperative relationship, and the other then is often able to respond warmly in return.

Psychoanalytic therapy is designed to recognize transferences, and to bring them to consciousness. Transference occurs in many kinds of relationship (Singer & Singer, 1992). It occurs in almost every consultation with a physician, as we find ourselves hoping he or she will protect and look after us, make everything better, as once a caregiver could. It occurs, as even therapists who are not analysts admit, in almost every kind of psychological therapy. It occurs in relationships of students with teachers. It occurs in encounters with people who have power or influence of most kinds, so-called authority figures. It occurs in romantic relationships, in which we may be needy, or demanding, or irritable, or unavailable, or controlling, as we once were with our parents. These transferential styles have been demonstrated by the attachment styles of infancy carrying forward into adulthood (Waters et al., 2000), as we discussed in chapter 11.

The idea of psychoanalytic therapy is that our relationships are so fundamental to every aspect of life, including our mental health, that if they are based on figures from the past rather than on real people in the present, there will at best be misunderstanding, and at worst intractable problems. Emotional schemas that are problematic are often based on intense wishes bound tightly to beliefs that people hold about what is wrong with them, or how they can never be satisfied (Dahl, 1991). So a woman might have an emotion schema derived from childhood in which she knows only bad things ever happen if she is angry. She tries more or less unsuccessfully to suppress her anger, perhaps restricting her life so that occasions for anger occur infrequently, but then finds her life narrow and unsatisfying. Or from experiences with his parents, a man may feel it too dangerous to have any strong emotion because of the likelihood of losing control, and his overcontrolled personality becomes rigid, like a stone. Yet another person may long for intimacy but be terrified of being taken over by the other.

The idea of psychoanalysis as the interpretation of transference is that effects of the emotion-relational schema are brought directly into the therapeutic relationship. As Strachey (1934) has written, from the viewpoint of the therapist:

> Instead of having to deal as best we may with conflicts of the remote past, which are concerned with dead circumstances and mummified personalities, and whose outcome is already determined, we find ourselves involved in an actual and immediate situation in which we and the patient are the principal characters (p. xx).

Then, as Strachey continues, there is the possibility that when the partly unconscious terms of the schema in which the client is lodged become conscious, the client can choose a new solution in the relationship with the therapist, and this kind of new solution can generalize to other relationships outside therapy.

There have been several attempts empirically to study transference in therapy. Among such studies are those of Luborsky and Crits-Christoph (1990) who have devised a method to recognize what they call Core Conflictual Relationship Themes in transference. They have gone some way to showing that when therapists recognize and interpret occurrences of these themes, the patient makes better progress in therapy (Henry et al., 1994).

Cognitive-behavioral therapy: changing emotions by thought

The idea that we can change our emotions by thinking about them in the right way can be traced back to the **Epicureans** and **Stoics**, two schools of ethical philosophy in which, following Aristotle, emotions were understood as evaluations of events in relation to desires or goals (Nussbaum, 2001; Oatley, 2004c). The founder of Epicureanism was Epicurus who lived near Athens, around 300 BCE, in a community of like-minded friends. Stoicism got its name from the *stoa*, in which the philosophers of this school taught.

Figure 14.2 A *stoa* (portico) that runs alongside the *agora* (marketplace) in Athens. It was in such a place that the Stoics met to teach their system of managing emotions. (The *stoa* in this picture is not the original but one constructed a century after the founding of Stoicism, and rebuilt in the 1930s.)

Though the dictionaries tell us that epicurean now means "devoted to the pursuit of pleasure," and stoic means "indifferent to pleasure or pain," these meanings are far from their origins. In fact, philosophers of Epicurean and Stoic schools developed subtle and profound understandings of emotions. Their influence crossed from the Greek to the Roman world, and was current for about 600 years: one could say they were the first emotions researchers in the West. The doctrines of these schools had an important influence in the development of Western society. The Epicureans, for instance, developed ideas of natural human sociality that influenced both the American and French Revolutions. The idea that human beings have a right to the pursuit of happiness is distinctively Epicurean, as is the idea of living naturally, in harmony with an environment of which we are stewards. The ideas of the Stoics are thought to have influenced the acceptance of Christianity by the Romans following the conversion of the Emperor Constantine.

Nussbaum (1994) argues that the Epicureans were the first in the West to discover the unconscious. They pointed out, for instance, that people fear death, although it must surely be irrational to do so. They argued that if we are dead we would have no more consciousness than we had before we were born. Though the process of dying might be painful, to fear death as such is irrational. It must therefore depend on reasons of which we are unconscious. Perhaps we fear that when dead we will no longer be the object of anyone's attention. The Epicureans taught that one should live in a simple way, and enjoy simple pleasures, like food and the enjoyment of friendship, rather than chasing after things that either make one anxious, like wealth, or are unnatural, like luxuries, or are ephemeral, like fame. To allow ourselves to have such goals can only lead to painful emotions: anger when someone frustrates one's will, greed at wanting more and more, envy at someone having something we do not. They recommended shifts in attention, from such irrational desires to more worthwhile ones. In terms of modern psychology, this theme has been explored in terms of regulation of the emotions by Gross and his colleagues (Gross, 2002; Gross & John, 2003), discussed in chapter 11.

The Stoics were yet more radical than the Epicureans. They thought that because emotions derive from desires, therefore to free oneself from crippling and destructive emotions, one should extirpate almost all desires. The only values that are outside the vagaries of chance or the will of others, and therefore are under one's control, are one's own rationality and good character. The Stoic understanding was that most emotions, especially such emotions as anger, anxiety, and lust, are damaging to the self and to society, and so should be extirpated. Just as medicine sought a cure for bodily ills, so the Epicureans and Stoics thought of philosophy as a cure for the soul, and focused on emotions as the chief sources of the soul's diseases. One may get lovely insights into Stoic thinking from the Roman writers Marcus Aurelius (*c*.170) and Epictetus (*c*.100), one an emperor and the other a former slave. In the Roman world, as Christianity took over the heritage of the Stoics, the bad desires and bad thoughts which the Stoics sought to extirpate became the seven deadly sins (Sorabji, 2000).

Just as the ancient Epicureans and Stoics took thought about how to avoid being influenced by desires that were worthless or unworthy, so there is a modern form of psychotherapy that works on thoughts in a comparable way. It was developed by Beck (1976) and it is called cognitive-behavioral therapy. It is based on teaching people how to recognize and avoid errors of evaluation about the incidents that lead to emotions. Other kinds of cognitive therapy are based on similar formulations. For instance, clients who suffer anxiety and depression are asked to keep a diary. In it, when they suffer an episode of negative emotion, they are to write in their diary what incident preceded the upset, descriptions of emotions that occurred and the thoughts that accompanied them, and then some alternative thoughts. In this way clients can gain some distance on their emotions, see some of the repetitive causes, and understand some of the cycles of thoughts-causing-emotions that bring to mind thoughts that cause more of the same emotions (Teasdale, 1988). Writing, it turns out, has, in all cultures that have used it, become one of the main means for reflecting on, and becoming conscious of, the meanings of emotions.

In his therapy, Beck (1976; Beck et al., 1979) has argued that the patterns of appraisal that cause anxiety and depression tend to involve contextual evaluations that are arbitrary, absolute, and personalizing: if clients can make evaluations of other kinds – attributions that are external rather than internal, local rather than global, impermanent rather than stably permanent – about events then different emotions can occur that will break vicious cycles. Cognitive therapy then allows revision both of core beliefs, and of plans changing the answer to the question that Stein et al. (1994) propose as central to context evaluation: "What can I do about it?"

Among recent therapies related to those discussed in this section we might count the proposal of cognitive psychologist Keith Stanovich (2004) whose book is subtitled "Finding meaning in the age of Darwin." He argues that much of what we do is driven by our genes, which set preferences for the benefits of their replication, which are not necessarily purposes of ours. For instance we like sweet foods. But this preference is genetically prompted and is contributing to an epidemic of obesity: not a human purpose at all. Many of the automatic primary appraisals of emotions (the Stoic first movements) that we discussed in chapter 7 are due simply to the promptings of genes. Sometimes genetic purposes and human purposes coincide, and that is fine. For instance the genetic imperative for reproduction coincides with purposes that we agree are human, such as love for our children. But we do not want to be mere robots controlled by our genes. Asserting human purposes over those that are merely genetic requires thought, in cognitive terms metacognition, to work out what human purposes might be, and – which is even more difficult – to choose accordingly. Stanovich's approach, of subjecting genetically based propensities to analysis and prioritization, continues the arguments of the Stoics and the cognitive-behavioral therapists. What we are searching for is rationality and meaning according to a complex range of worldwide human purposes, rather than allowing ourselves to be beckoned only by purposes of selfish genes which tend to focus on the immediate. Our search for rational living has come some way in the philosophies of both East and West, but it still has a long way to go.

Emotion-focused therapy: changing emotions by emotions

Why have emotions such a central role in therapy? Greenberg (1993) argues that making emotions explicit confers on the schemas, on which they are based, a sense of clarity and possibility of control. Greenberg (2002) cites Spinoza (1661–1675) as saying that the only way to change an emotion is by means of another emotion, and this may be taken as the goal of emotion-focused therapy. In therapy, emotions can be explored. For instance, a person who in life and in therapy, is angry, angry, angry, may suddenly find her anger change to sadness, as she realizes that she too has been partly responsible for some of what she is angry about, and that she too has suffered losses.

In the course of life we take on many goals, many projects. Some, like attachment, are formed without words. Others formed later may have arisen more explicitly, but without us realizing how our goals may affect each other, so some of their implications may be unconscious. Emotions signal that some goal or concern is affected. If it is only partly known, an emotion may be our best clue to the importance of this concern. One of the tasks of emotion-focused therapy, then, is to work on such clues to build some consciously comprehended model of our goal structure as part of our sense of self.

Part of the task of therapy, and life, is to recognize emotions that we have not allowed ourselves to experience fully enough. Therapy, in this case, consists of encouraging a fuller experience of such emotions, which Greenberg (2002) calls primary emotions. So clients may recognize that they are angry, although they had not allowed themselves to be so, or full of grief that they had not recognized. With recognition and expression, primary emotions and their origins become more comprehensible. They become, as philosophers say, more intentional, and the implications for relationships become clearer.

In addition, however, clients tend to experience some emotions too much. Greenberg calls these secondary emotions. They are what psychoanalysts call defenses. They are the emotions clients often report as troublesome. Secondary emotions derive from, or have been changed from, or have emerged to cover up, certain primary emotions that were unacceptable. So women who have been taught to be submissive may feel sad when really they are angry, but then their feeling of impotence makes them despairing, and yet more sad. Men who have been brought up never to be afraid may have covered up their fear with anger, and their angry disposition has distanced them from others, and become a cause of isolation. Often when primary emotions are not known, or accepted, they can metamorphose into secondary emotions rather easily (cf. Elster, 1999). Here the therapeutic task is not to encourage clients to experience secondary emotions – they do that too much already – but to understand that these emotions conceal something more authentic. A third category is of instrumental emotions: the emotions that people have learned will help them get their way – the tears that elicit sympathy, the easy irritation that makes others hesitate to challenge or to be close.

In a way, all forms of therapy revolve around emotions, and the relationships to which they give structure. As our understanding grows, it is likely that emotions will become more central to theories of psychotherapy.

Outcomes of therapy

But does therapy work? We live in an era of what has come to be called evidence-based interventions, and empirically supported psychotherapies (Kendall, 1998). Neither insurance companies nor other kinds of health care delivery system are willing to devote resources to treatments for which there is no evidence of effectiveness.

There have now been thousands of trials of different kinds of psychotherapy, assigning clients randomly to groups, comparing outcomes for people who received therapy with those in a control group. Still one of the best of such studies was that of Sloane et al. (1975). One of the first applications of the statistical technique of meta-analysis was by Mary Lee Smith, Gene Glass, and Thomas Miller (1980) who used it to estimate the effects of psychotherapy. Smith et al. found that in over 475 studies, the average effect size over a range of kinds of psychotherapy was 0.85 of a standard deviation. What this means is that the average person receiving therapy was better off than 80 percent of the members of control groups who did not receive therapy. In a review of meta-analyses of psychotherapeutic trials and of educational interventions, Lipsey and Wilson (1993) broadly confirmed these results. In comparison with educational interventions, a relatively modest amount of time in psychotherapy – typically of the order of a dozen sessions – has been found to be more effective than the majority of educational interventions designed, for instance, to produce more effective learning of mathematics. Ten years after this finding, Lambert and Ogles (2004) offered an extensive review of meta-analyses of different kinds of psychotherapy, and came to similar conclusions. Outcome studies have been performed for many established psychological therapies, usually with positive results. Despite partisan commitments, therapists of different persuasions often produce effects of similar size.

These results are rather general, and are averaged across many clients. But not all therapy is effective and not all therapists are helpful. Just as psychotherapy can do good, it can do harm. Orlinsky and Howard (1980) reviewed case files of 143 women seen by 23 therapists. Six therapists were good: overall 84 percent of the clients they saw were improved at the end of therapy and none were worse. Five therapists were not good: for these people less than 50 percent of their clients were improved and

10 percent were worse. A recent review of the outcome literature by Westen, Novotny, and Thompson-Brenner (2004), moreover, concludes that even with empirically supported therapies, many patients do not get better, and many more do not maintain the gains they make.

What about particular kinds of therapy? **Antidepressant** and **tranquilizer** medications, which we discussed in chapter 6, are aimed respectively at decreasing the intensity of depression and anxiety states for the average patient. They are still the treatments of choice for many psychiatrists because they are relatively cheap and not labor intensive for the clinician. Medically qualified practitioners obey the ancient medical injunction: relieve suffering. The intent is different from that of most psychological therapies, which is to understand the anguish, despair, and other emotions, and by understanding reconnect them to the more voluntary aspects of life. In this kind of way, the client may be freed from the involuntary actions and emotions that had become disabling.

Psychoanalysis remains controversial. Even supporters such as Fonagy (2000) and Bateman (2004) express concern that, because of the reluctance of its adherents to subject its practices to scientific scrutiny, its influence has declined. The situation for psychoanalysis may be improving, however, because good studies of treatment effects have now been conducted. For shorter durations, eight or sixteen sessions, psychodynamic therapy has been found to be effective for emotional disorders. It has produced effects of much the same size as cognitive-behavioral therapy (Barkham et al., 1996; Shapiro et al., 1995). Longer-term psychoanalysis has been difficult to evaluate because it can take years. The problem has, however, been largely solved by a study in Stockholm, Sweden, of over 400 patients who received national insurance funded psychodynamic treatment for up to three years: either full psychoanalysis, five times a week, or what is called psychoanalytic psychotherapy, once or twice a week. Methodologically, the authors argued that looking at outcomes as a function of the duration and frequency of treatment was equivalent to assigning people randomly to treatment groups (Sandell, Blomberg, & Lazar, 2002). The general finding (Blomberg, Lazar, & Sandell, 2001) was that the greater the amount of psychodynamic treatment, the better the outcome for the patients. Follow-ups after three years of full psychoanalysis of 156 patients, who were symptomatic when they started, showed substantial improvement with treatment. These patients continued to improve after treatment to the point where their mental health scores had become the same as those of a non-clinical sample.

The kind of therapy that is most widely respected by psychologists, partly because it has a well-formulated theoretical base, and partly because the studies of its effectiveness have been performed repeatedly and convincingly, especially for depression and anxiety, is cognitive-behavioral therapy (Hollon & Beck, 2004). Gloaguen et al. (1998) found in a meta-analysis that in cases of depression it was more effective than antidepressant medication, and associated with a lower rate of relapse. Emotion-focused therapy is newer than cognitive-behavioral therapy, so consequently there is less research here. It, too, however, has been found in outcome studies to produce gains of approximately the same size as those of cognitive-behavioral therapy (Elliott, Greenberg, & Lietaer, 2004).

Psychotherapy without professionals

A serious problem for therapy is its availability. Look at the prevalence of psychiatric disorder in USA, described by Kessler et al. (1994), that we discussed in chapter 13. Consider the most common disorders, anxiety and depression. Now do some arithmetic: multiply the prevalence rates by the population of the USA, say 300 million, more than half of whom are between 15 and 54, the age-band of these prevalence figures. You will conclude that each year several tens of millions of Americans suffer from clinically significant anxiety or depression, or both. Even in such a highly resourced society there are just not enough mental health professionals to go round. Kessler et al. indeed, found that in any year in which people suffered a disorder, only about a fifth of them consulted a professional, and for only about half of those was this a mental health professional. Psychoanalysis, four or five times a week for several years, is obviously available only to the few. Even short treatments such as behavioral and cognitive therapy of 8 to 12 sessions are not available to all.

So what is the answer? One is that alongside ideas of individual therapy developed by psychologists and psychiatrists there was also another kind of therapy that involved people meeting in groups. Its founders included Jane Addams who opened a house for group social work in 1889 and was later awarded a Nobel Prize. Not many years later Joseph Pratt discovered that tuberculosis patients, whom he arranged to meet together in groups of 20 or so, formed supportive social structures among themselves that had important therapeutic effects on the course of illness. In terms of outcomes, group therapy, like individual therapy, has generally been found effective (Lambert & Ogles, 2004; Tillitski, 1990). Many self-help organizations such as Alcoholics Anonymous base their practices on group processes arranged around emotionally salient issues.

Still, however, there is not enough to go round. It is therefore not surprising that when people are surveyed about those to whom they turn in times of emotional crisis, they name a wide variety of persons, including priests, rabbis, doctors – but principally friends. Recall from chapter 13 that the factor most widely found to be protective against emotional disorder is relationships with other people – close relationships with relatives and friends, known as social support.

An important finding in this context is that of Bernard Rimé and his colleagues (Rimé et al., 1998) who have found that when people experience an emotion that is salient enough to remember a few hours after it has occurred, on 90 percent of occasions they will have discussed it with one or more other people. Rimé calls this **social sharing** of emotions. At the beginning of this research Rimé et al. (1991) thought that such sharing would diminish the intensity of emotions that were shared as compared with those that were unshared, but no such difference was found. One can understand this: when an injustice has been experienced, talking about it does not diminish the anger one feels! People do want to share their emotions, and when asked they say they receive benefits from doing so. We suggest the benefit comes from being able in conversation to make meaningful sense of their emotions. This sense includes the implications of the emotions for the speaker and others, as seen both from the inside, and from the outside in terms of implications of the commentary of the friend or relative. It seems likely that this is an important aspect of social support.

Among the aims of psychiatric health care, then, should be that of enabling civil society to evolve so that it is hard rather than easy for people to become socially marginalized. At the same time, where practices have been discovered by mental health professionals that have been helpful in therapy for emotional suffering then, arguably, rather than distributing these services for fees, the job of mental health professionals might better be seen as giving them away, diffusing them into the community.

Consciousness and making sense of emotions

Sharing an emotion with a friend and sharing one's emotional concerns with a therapist have common features, not least in that in both cases we tend to talk in the form of narrative. We tell stories about ourselves. Bruner (1986) has said that narrative is that distinctive form of human thinking by which we strive to understand ourselves and others as people who act in the world to pursue intentions that meet vicissitudes. Vicissitudes, or problems with goals and intentions, as we have explained throughout this book, are events that cause emotions. Bruner contrasts the narrative mode of thinking with what he calls the paradigmatic mode, which is used in science, and in explanations. Narrative, of course, is also the stuff of novels and of movies. So, could it be, as Bruner maintains, that meaning is made precisely by casting emotional events into the terms of narrative? Freud (e.g. 1905) asked Dora and his other patients to tell the story of their lives. When we confide an emotion to a friend, we do it in narrative terms. It seems likely therefore that, as Bruner suggests, narrative is the principal human activity of **meaning-making**. And this is not just turning over emotions with a therapist or friend, but reading novels and poetry, watching plays and movies, which can also, at least in some circumstances, have consciousness-raising functions.

Emotions can be mere stirrings, vague excitements, unshaped movements of the mind, even when they are acutely persecuting, painful, or tumultuous. We have presented evidence that there is a biological basis for emotions. But if that were all, we would be left solely with emotions that are like those of our relatives the apes. We human beings are born not just into the biological world, but into society. Each society includes individuals to whom we become attached in friendship, or with whom we become involved in conflict. In every society, in every community, in every famiiy, a history forms, with its characters, its traditions of custom: human meanings about what we people are up to with each other. In such traditions, emotions and our understandings of them are the pivotal points.

As human beings we are conscious. By taking thought we can become conscious that we are conscious. But what difference does this make? What is it that we do that could not be done without being conscious? Many forms of therapy are based on the idea of making our emotional lives more conscious, and earlier in this chapter we gave reasons why this may be helpful. Leventhal (1991) has argued that emotions are represented at several different layers, as reflex-like phenomena, as schemas, and as concepts. Only the concepts are easily open to consciousness and to (more or less) voluntary change, so an abiding question is what kinds of conceptual changes might we accomplish, and which of them might also affect schemas and other lower-level structures. Asking this another way: In what ways can we influence our mental and emotional lives (Wegner & Pennebaker, 1993)?

The idea that we in part create ourselves by conscious reflection can be traced to Shakespeare. Bloom (1989) put it like this: the greatest of Shakespeare's originalities, one that was so original but so complete in its cultural effects that we now do not notice it, or notice that someone began it, was "the representation of change by showing people pondering their own speeches and being altered through that consideration" (Bloom, 1989, p. 54). If Bloom is right, for us moderns, becoming conscious helps to make us who we are. Let us therefore look briefly at how conscious reflection upon ourselves has emerged in the history of Western literature.

Becoming conscious of emotions in literature

"There is no history of mankind, there is only an indefinite number of histories of all kinds of aspects of human life," wrote Karl Popper. The history most of us learn at school, he continued, is largely "the history of power politics [which] is nothing but the history of international crime" (Popper, 1962b, p. 270). Among the many histories that would be more edifying – the history of ideas, the history of technology, the history of the family – might be counted the history of consciousness and of the emotions. This can be approached via written stories where emotions and their effects are typically at the center of the narrative.

From the earliest times to the present, it is extraordinary that at the focus of poetic, fictional, and folk-historical narratives have been the emotions. From the Sumerians come epics dating from more than 4,000 years ago about Gilgamesh and Enkidu, and their troubles, including an episode in which Gilgamesh become recognizably depressed at the death of Enkidu. From Egypt come many writings allowing a picture of ancient life to be drawn. Among them is: "The dispute between a man and his soul," dating from about 3,700 years ago, in which a man complains of his misery, longs for death, and is answered by his soul becoming a bit irritated with this grumbling, and saying that death will occur in due time (Lichtheim, 1973).

From the Hebrews come the first five books of the Bible written about 2,800 years ago, with their theme of a family history in which the protagonists, Adam, Eve, Abraham, Sarah, Jacob, Isaac, and the rest oscillate between fear and hopeful dependence on their god Yahweh (Rosenberg & Bloom, 1990). From the Greeks comes the *Iliad*, contemporary with the first books of the Bible. Its first words are: "Of rage sing, goddess." It is a tale of the repercussions of Achilles' sulking during the long and angry war triggered by the abduction of Helen by the Trojan prince Menelaos (Homer, 850 BCE). So, from the first, we find writing in the West struggling to understand, and reflect upon, emotions and our consciousness of them.

In chapter 3 we argued that one difference between us and the apes is that our emotions are more intentional, more conscious. The principal way in which we become conscious – at least conscious of ourselves – is in being able to give accounts in narrative form as we confide emotional incidents in conversation, as we discussed above. We can also write about emotionally troubling issues. Pennebaker et al. (1988) had 50 students write either about such issues, or about superficial topics, for 20 minutes on four consecutive days. Those who wrote about disturbing emotional issues showed improvements in immune function in the form of higher lympho-cyte response to an antigen challenge, and fewer medical consultations at the University Health Center. Although participants who wrote about emotionally important issues found the actual writing more distressing than did the control participants, three months later they were significantly happier than the controls and, looking back, they viewed the experience of confronting the emotional issues about which they wrote as a positive experience. These effects have been replicated many times, both in Pennebaker's laboratory and by other research groups. Pennebaker has found therapeutic effects of confronting traumatic experiences, by writing or by talking. He understands the process in terms of alleviating a debilitation caused by suppressing traumatic experiences. He has concluded that the debilitation is relieved by confiding and by confronting the experience and its emotions (Pennebaker, 1989, 1997, 2002; Pennebaker, Mehl, & Niederhoffer, 2003; Pennebaker & Seagal, 1999).

A speculation: just as therapy is successful when a client comes to take responsibility for his or her emotions and actions, so literature offers a world in which the brute facts of cause and effect in the physical world are replaced by actions for which selves (our own and others') are responsible, despite the outcomes of such actions not always being as expected, and despite the world turning out to be not as we had hoped. Written narrative liter-ature, from ancient times to the present, concentrates on our emotional lives and on problematics of this kind – as if story telling and story listen-ing have always been attempts to understand these matters. The activity is satisfying because stories provide possibilities of vicarious action, as well as pieces of solutions to the problems of how to act and how to be a person in the society. Publicly available stories give members of society common exemplars of action of emotion and of responsibility. They help us to reflect on and become part of the cultural tradition in which we live.

Emotions and art

A conversation in which we try to understand how someone did not show up for a date, or how someone at work has been insulting, is ephemeral. The words hover for a moment between the people who are talking and then disperse into the air. Like other kinds of art, stories can persist in time and can travel beyond the place of their inception (Oatley, 2003). Since the beginning of the Romantic era in literary theory (Abrams, 1953) discussed in chapters 3 and 4, a consensus has developed that art is the expression of emotions in different media: music, poetry, novels, painting. Why is this idea important for those who seek to understand emotions? It is because emotions are, as it were, protean. They are often raw materials rather than finished products. We humans shape these inchoate feelings. In children's stories, as well as in novels, plays, news, and movies, we are given examples of actions and events leading up to emotions, and the consequences emotions have.

The biological bases of emotions have effects that are often powerful but loosely specified. With such raw materials, it seems that artists from the beginning of recorded time have worked to articulate emotions in their individuality. Emotions are depicted as emerging when we encounter vicissitudes, problems, uncertainties, when we do not know how to act. They tell us something is happening to which we should pay attention. Artists bring these vague feelings, the conflicts with others and within the self, the uncertainties that they represent, into awareness.

Emotional creativity

If emotions are like a paints on a painter's palette, materials for elaboration, how can one be creative about the emotions? Averill and Thomas-Knowles (1991) and Averill (1999) have researched this question and concluded that emotions are indeed favorable sources for creativity. To use another simile: the biologically based emotions are like modes of locomotion that we are innately given: crawling on all fours, walking, running, jumping. But these have been creatively elaborated by individuals in cultures: in dancing, skating, gymnastics, and so forth.

Averill and Nunley (1992) propose that one of the great examples of emotional creativity was the poet Dante. He fell in love with Beatrice in 1274. It does not seem an exaggeration to say that the European and American notion of falling in love, and being in love, has been affected by him and his writing ever since. Dante first met Beatrice when he was nine and she was eight – at that moment he fell in love. He did not speak to Beatrice until nine years later, when one day they met on a street in Florence. Dante's only contacts with Beatrice seemed to be in public places, and though she died at the age of 24, his love for her had become and remained the main preoccupation of his poetry.

Dante made love the ultimate meaning. In his early poems, in _La vita nuova_ (The new life, 1295) he writes of his love, and also of his despair. In one poem he writes about being mocked by other women for swooning in the presence of Beatrice, and of how he resolved to seek peace of mind rather than tormenting himself with Beatrice's goodness and beauty. The poem he wrote next after this resolve was, says Reynolds in her introduction to these poems, a turning point for Dante and for European literature: it "opened up vistas and depths in which the human experience of love was glimpsed as being ultimately one with the power by which the universe is governed" (p. 160). By the time Dante came to write his masterpiece, _The Divine Comedy_ (Dante Alighieri, 1307–1321), his love for Beatrice had become transformed into a pilgrimage first to the depths of hell – as we might say, into the human unconscious – then through purgatory in which we reflect on our life and its meaning, and finally to paradise where Beatrice becomes his guide.

Dante did not invent the Romantic ideal of cultivating a love for someone idealized, or of becoming good on that person's behalf, but he found a solution to the contradictions of courtly love that we discussed in chapter 3. Though his love was never consummated sexually, his writing had profound cultural implications.

For any of us in Western society the very existence of the erotic is an opportunity for a highly personal creativity. Some people may express this in poetry. Others are moved to different kinds of expressions that they have previously felt incapable of. Indeed in the West loving someone may be one of life's most truly creative events, responding to that change in which the self expands to include another, when doors of understanding may open. Building a self without this much-mythologized experience may be yet more challenging.

Emotions in drama, ritual, and art

In all societies people enact rituals that include such group activities as singing, dancing, processions. In many societies, there is theater or its equivalent. In all there is the telling of stories, many that are historical but also many that are fictional. Some stories – including love stories and stories of conflict in which the good are assailed but finally triumph – occur worldwide (Hogan, 2003). With literacy came the writing down of stories (Olson, 1994), and in some cultures, such as the Jewish one and that of the Christian Protestants after the reformation, there is explicit understanding that the written text as such is to be interpreted and reflected upon. Just as emotions are at the center of the psychotherapies which are modern secular descendants of some of the rituals and societal practices of religion, emotions too are at the center of narrative literature. Just as the experiencing of primary emotions (Greenberg, 2002) is a central event in emotion-focused therapy, so _katharsis_, as Aristotle called it – clarifying the relation of emotions to human action (Nussbaum, 1986, p. 391) – is central at the theater, or in listening to a story, or in reading a novel.

How do we understand this? One explanation is given by Scheff (1979). He argues that all these societal practices – explicit therapy, informal therapy, ritual, drama, stories – have at their center the possibility not just of experiencing emotions but of experiencing them at what he calls a best aesthetic distance. Scheff argues that if emotionally damaging events or difficulties are experienced as overwhelming (as in a trauma), or if we distance ourselves from them too much (as when we defend ourselves against our emotions), then we accumulate a kind of emotional arrears, which distorts our emotional lives. What ritual, drama, and narrative do, argues Scheff, is to provide memory cues that will bring emotions of our own to mind, but in a safe context where we can experience them at a best aesthetic distance. (See Cupchik, 2002, for history and explanation of the idea of aesthetic distance.)

> When we cry over the fate of Romeo and Juliet, we are reliving our own personal experiences of overwhelming loss, but under new and less severe conditions. The experience of vicarious loss, in a properly designed drama, is sufficiently distressful to reawaken the old distress. It is also sufficiently vicarious, however, that the emotion does not feel overwhelming (Scheff, 1979, p. 13).

Scheff proposes that in experiencing emotions in this way – and (as Pennebaker, Zech, and Rimé, 2001, suggest) in confiding and writing about them – we can assimilate them to our understanding with therapeutic effect. We have argued that the supply of therapeutic help in Western society is too limited to meet the need. But narrative, recounted, heard, and read, is not in short supply in any society. Such forms, moreover, are more under the control of the person involved than are many kinds of therapy – we can use them as and when we wish. Cupchik and László (1994), for instance, found that passages of fiction that provided insight were read more slowly and reflectively than other kinds of passages.

But the issue does not end here, because literature requires that the reader or the watcher of a film or play creates for him or herself the space and events that are experienced, enters this space, and becomes engaged in it. It is a space of imagination, not just of the writer who supplies mere suggestions, but of the watcher or reader. This is the same kind of space in adulthood as play is in childhood (Winnicott, 1971). People often listen to music, play or watch sport, read novels, go to the movies for enjoyment. People in general enjoy such things even when the emotions they experience are negative, as in a thriller. We humans seem to prefer being in an emotional state to not being in one. Why do we find the experiencing of emotions entertaining? Perhaps it is because when we experience emotions they engage us, and enjoyment is another word for being fully engaged (Goffman, 1961).

But art can be transformative. Events in a novel, play, or film are not experienced in quite the same way as they are in quotidian life, but in a kind of simulation that runs not on computers but on minds (Oatley, 1999,

2004b), or as an older metaphor had it, in a kind of dream (Miall & Kuiken, 2002). In this imaginative space we experience emotions, not those of the characters, but our own (Oatley, 2002). And just as we change somewhat when we arrive at work, or join a group of friends, or enter the office of a therapist, we may be changed when we enter a space of emotional imagination. So just as we are careful whom we choose as a friend or a therapist, we should be judicious about what we read (Booth, 1988), and what movies we see.

Cultures of understanding

In the nineteenth century, novels such as those by Gustave Flaubert and Émile Zola in France, by Jane Austen and George Eliot in England, by Leo Tolstoy and Fyodor Dostoevsky in Russia, by Herman Melville and Harriet Beecher Stowe in America, came to be means of enjoyment, ways of experiencing emotions so that they could be assimilated (as proposed by Scheff), and ways of identification with others so that the experiences of taking part emotionally in lives beyond the boundaries of our personal lot could become, as George Eliot put it, "the raw material for moral sentiment" (Pinney, 1963, p. 270).

Soon after the close of the century a change began. This occurred partly by the new movement of psychoanalysis, in which the patient was asked "to give . . . the whole story of his life and illness" (Freud, 1905, p. 16). A parallel movement was taking place within literature, as in Marcel Proust's novel *Remembrance of Things Past* (1913–27) in which the reader is invited to become the writer.

By the 1920s novels had become more inward, and the idea – not new but beginning at least with Shakespeare – became common that becoming a whole person was concerned with being able to understand oneself in terms of a narrative of one's life. As Marcus (1984) has put it, in relation to psychoanalytic therapy, at the end of successful therapy "one has come into possession of one's own story . . . a fictional construction which is at the same time satisfactory to us in the form of the truth, and as the form of the truth" (p. 62). By "fictional" here Marcus does not mean "untrue." He means, rather, that such a history of oneself necessarily is a con-struction, a creative interpretation from fragmentary elements, as Bartlett (1932) showed, and as we discussed in chapter 10.

Marcus then continues with an extraordinary passage on the psycho-therapy initiated by Freud:

> No larger tribute has ever been paid to a culture in which the various narrative and fictional forms had exerted for centuries both moral and philosophical authority and which had produced as one of its chief climaxes the great bourgeois novels of the nineteenth century. Indeed, we must see Freud's writings – and method – as themselves part of this culmination, and at the same moment, along with the great modernist novels of the first half

of the twentieth century, as the beginning of the end of this tradition and its authority. (p. 62)

Is there a new tradition and a new authority? Could they derive from understanding our emotions in both a scientific and a narrative way?

Happiness and well-being

The American Declaration of Independence speaks of inalienable rights, among which are "life, liberty, and the pursuit of happiness." But what is happiness?

One way to approach this question is to ask what makes for pleasurable experiences. In their research, Fredrickson and Kahneman (1993) have had people watch pleasurable film clips, such as a comedy routine or a puppy playing with a flower. As they watched, participants rated their pleasure continuously by using a pointer and a dial. The moment-by-moment ratings were then correlated with the participants' overall ratings of their pleasure at watching each film clip. This is one of a number of studies that indicate that when remembering pleasurable experiences the peak moment of pleasure predicts well how pleasurably the whole event is remembered. A second predictor of the whole experience is the end of the event. The implication is that if you want to have fond memories of an event, such as a date or a vacation, you should plan to make the last part the most pleasurable. Somewhat surprisingly, the length of a pleasurable experience is unrelated to overall memories of pleasure. This phenomenon is known as duration neglect, and it seems to imply that it matters less whether less you have a ten-minute massage or a one-hour massage, than whether the peaks and the last moments were pleasurable.

Do we know what will make us happy? Daniel Gilbert and colleagues have studied this question in terms of what they call affective forecasting (e.g., Gilbert et al., 2000). In one study, Gilbert et al. (1998) asked people who had not experienced a breakup of a romantic relationship how they thought they would feel two months after a romantic breakup. They compared these estimates with those of people who had actually broken up with a partner two months previously. The people making the prediction thought that they would be much less happy than those who had suffered a breakup actually were. The inference is that we overestimate the effect of specific events of emotional importance.

Most of us would predict that we would be happy if we acquired a large sum of money, and devastated if we lost the use of our legs. But, Brickman, Coates, and Janoff-Bulman (1978) studied people who won a lottery, and people who lost the use of their legs in an accident. The lottery winners were only marginally happier than people in a comparison group, and those who had lost the use of their legs only a little less happy than those in the comparison group. It seems that we overvalue particular things, and can adapt to many kinds of circumstance.

Wilson et al. (2000) also found that people tend to focus too much on selected events of importance in the future: taking GREs, getting married, being hired into a good position. We tend to think that if such events turn out well, we will be truly happy. Just as when we take what we think will be the ideal vacation, we tend to think of what we will like about it, the mountains perhaps, or the beach, or the absence of phone calls. But we tend not to imagine the other things that can happen: the bad case of diarrhea that lasts for days, difficulty with finding a good place to stay, perhaps even a quarrel with our partner. These too will have effects.

Flow

Can happiness be taken simply as if it were a matter of pleasure, as if life were made up of Mars Bars or Mercedes cars? An ancient tradition holds differently. Happiness is a matter of right action. Aristotle's conclusion in his _Politics_ was: "If we are right in our view and happiness is assumed to be acting well, the active life will be the best" (Book VII, 1325b). His word for happiness, _eudaimonia_, meant acting in the world, acting rightly, and being engaged in what one is doing. In their review of the psychology of happiness, nearly 2,400 years later, based on an assessment of recent evidence, Averill and More (2000) agree. Among the kinds of recent evidence is that of Mihalyi Csikszentmihalyi (1990) who used experience sampling augmented by interviewing.

Csikszentmihalyi found that although many people's emotions were principally affected by the accidents of life, others conceived the world quite differently. Rico Medelin, for instance, worked on an assembly line in a factory that made movie projectors. His task was supposed to take 43 seconds, and he had to do it some 600 times a day. Although we could probably imagine grumbling if we had to earn our living at such a job, and had been doing it for as long as Rico – five years – the samples of his experience on the production line were of happiness. He had analyzed his task and worked out how to use his tools to become better and faster. His best average for the day was 28 seconds per unit. "It is better than anything else," said Rico. "It's better than watching TV" (pp. 39–40).

Through Rico and people like him, Csikszentmihalyi discovered a state he called flow. Another of his participants, who lived in the Italian Alps, enjoyed tending her cows and her orchard. She said, "I find a special satisfaction in caring for the plants. I like to see them grow each day" (p. 55). A dancer described how in a performance her attention was very complete, without any wandering of the mind. She was completely involved in what she was doing. A young mother described the time she and her small daughter spent together in similar ways.

Csikszentmihalyi also calls the state of flow optimal experience, and says it is characterized by a sense of creativity, of purpose, of being **fully engaged** so that self and the activity merge. We cannot control where we are born, or affect many of the other accidents of life. As the Stoics had pointed out many centuries previously, what this means is that we are wise to concentrate on those things over which we have some influence. We can choose to do what we are doing, turn it into a project in which we are engaged. Csikszentmihalyi has described some of the conditions for doing this, and for achieving the state of engagement. It is not a matter of waiting for pleasurable events in the world. One needs to be creative (Csikszentmihalyi, 1996). One has to accept or choose an activity and make it meaningful. Most typically this will involve a goal, solving problems, learning skills, paying careful attention to feedback that allows one to evaluate how one is doing. But as Averill and More (2000) point out, we cannot expect optimal experience all the time. It is probably as silly to strive for such a thing as to hope for a life full of all the pleasures one can imagine.

Positive emotions and subjective well-being

In recent times, there has been a leap of interest in the psychology of happiness. As we discussed in chapter 7, Fredrickson (1998) has argued that positive emotions have been neglected in comparison with negative emotions, and has presented evidence that they enable us to broaden our conceptions and to build schemas. She and her colleagues (Fredrickson et al., 2003) have also argued that positive emotions can be important in resilience in times of crisis, such as the one that occurred with the September 11, 2001, attack on the World Trade Center in New York.

Fredrickson and Losada (2005) have asked how positive and negative emotions might be related. They relate their work to that of Gottman (1993a, 1993b) which we discussed in chapter 9, in which he found that people in long-lasting marriages maintained ratios of at least 5 to 1 emotionally positive to emotionally negative interactions with their partners (see figure 14.3). Fredrickson and Losada propose that a state of mental heath, which they call flourishing, as opposed to languishing, involves maintaining a ratio of at least 2.9 to 1 positive to negative emotions in one's life. This does not mean we should try to make every emotion positive. That would be banal. It means that when negative emotions predominate, our selves, our relationships, and possibly our health tend to suffer. If we have been right in our proposal in this book that emotions set up relationships, maintaining a predominance of positive as compared with negative emotions means making more invitations into cooperative relationships, based on the social motivations of attachment and affiliation, than into conflicts based on assertion and status.

A psychology of the causes of **well-being**, and of who is and is not happy, has recently been explored (Kahneman, Diener, & Schwarz, 1999; Lykken, 1999; MacLeod & Conway, 2005; Myers, 2000). A graph in the May issue of *Scientific American* in 1996, presented by David Myers and Ed Diener, shows the combined results of 916 surveys of subjective well-being of 1.1 million people in 45 countries, transferred onto a 0 to 10 scale with 5 being neutral and 10 being the extreme of happiness. This histogram has

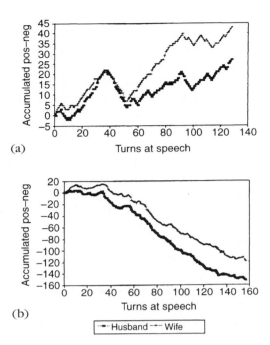

Figure 14.3 Cumulative graphs of two couples (Gottman & Levenson, 1992). The top graph (a) is of a couple who exchange more positive than negative interactions in a discussion. The bottom graph (b) is of a couple whose negative emotional interactions exceed positive ones.

a mean of 6.75. Some commentators understand this by saying that most people are happy. But we need to put this in a context of a world in which each day 25,000 people (the number in a medium-sized university) die from contaminated water alone (Ponting, 1991). Each year millions are subjected to the violence of war and displacement from their homes. A recent report by UNICEF *Childhood under threat: The state of the world's children 2005* (December 9, 2004) said that more than half the world's children had no access to at least one of seven essential resources: shelter, water, sanitation, schooling, information, health care, and food, and were thus being denied ordinary rights of childhood.

Civilizations have collapsed in the past by depleting their resources (Diamond, 2005; Ponting, 1991; Tainter, 1988), and their collapse has typically been hastened by competitive warfare. Civilization is now global, and human profligacy is unsurpassed, so we are rapidly depleting the resources of the whole planet (Wright, 2004). Too many of our pleasures are satisfactions only of the immediate, perhaps just the promptings of our selfish genes as Stanovich (2004) observed. To say most people are happy might seem to be like remarking that a group is to be seen happily eating and drinking as their raft drifts toward a huge waterfall.

Surveys are predominantly of literate people. There are large differences in reported subjective well-being in different countries. Denmark's average reported life satisfaction has been around 8 on the 0 to 10 scale, whereas Japan's has hovered around 6 (Diener, Oishi, & Lucas, 2003). Though individualist societies, including the USA and many countries in Western Europe, value subjective happiness, more collectivist societies such as Japan regard matters such as the well-being of others as more important. In general, among nations, reports of average subjective well-being correlate with national wealth, with human rights, with equality, with individualism, and with life expectancy (Diener & Biswas-Diener, 2002). In the slums of Calcutta, Biswas-Diener and Diener (2001) interviewed 83 people in three groups – those living in slum housing, prostitutes who lived in brothels, and homeless people who lived on the streets. They found a strong correlation of 0.45 between reported subjective well-being and income. These people were not happy on the whole. They had substantially lower life satisfaction than a comparison group of students. Even so, they reported a surprising amount of satisfaction in relationships with family and friends.

In developed countries, the correlation between subjective well-being and income is small (Myers, 2000), because after reaching a certain point – despite what the advertisements of our consumer society imply – having yet more stuff makes one scarcely any happier. What is more important, as Myers has emphasized, is living a life that is meaningful, that is to say with meaningful relationships.

This brings us to the close of our book. Although one can sometimes read, in the pages of psychology, implications that negative emotions are to be avoided, and that positive emotions are to be thought of as pleasures that one might acquire in a consumer society, if what we have written about in this book is on the right lines, this must be a misapprehension. If emotions are the joints and sinews of our relationships, if they are the deepest clues to our identity, and if they are signals of how things are going between one person and another, they are not to be treated as pieces of bitter gall or delicious chocolates. They are the means by which we articulate our lives with each other.

Summary

In this chapter we saw that psychological therapies have existed in the religious practices and rituals of many societies. In general they aim to reintegrate people who have become disrelated with their community. In such practices emotions play a central role. We discussed how, in the twentieth century, the secular practice arose of psychoanalytic therapy in which a patient tells the story of his or her life to a therapist within the structure of a relationship. In this form of therapy, issues compiled into the patient's emotion schemas are replayed in transference. There are many forms of psychotherapy, and most have an emotional base. In some it is thought beneficial to express emotions, in others it is more important to understand habitual or defensive emotions, in yet others the aim is to encourage new ways of behaving and thinking that do not carry the burdens of familiar anguish. Emotions are at the center of therapy because they point to our goals or concerns, including concerns of the deepest aspects of ourselves. In therapy it is often possible to make fresh starts with some of the concerns that are most important to us. We learned that benefits of therapy have been demonstrated empirically, though not every therapist is helpful with every client. It is clear from therapy, and from the narrative literature that has been written down during the past 4,000 years, that emotions are not fixed, but are a matter for creativity. We discussed how they arise when problems occur in individual lives, so that they pose, as it were, challenges to how to deal with these problems. Most kinds of therapy involve the client telling the therapist some kind of narrative about his or her life, in which emotions are prominent. It is probably not accidental that the fictional literatures of the world also consist of stories, the most common of which involve a protagonist who has some aim or concern, who forms a plan which then meets a problem of some kind, and results in the protagonist experiencing emotions, which may prompt creative solutions to the problem. Conscious understanding of our emotions involves becoming more knowledgeable about the narratives that we and others tell about the self and its doings. We concluded with a discussion of happiness and well-being, and with the proposal that consciousness might include the idea that positive emotions, in general, invite others into cooperative relationships with us.

Further reading

Psychotherapy has a useful handbook, which includes chapters on different therapeutic approaches, on therapy in different settings, and on outcomes of therapy.
Michael Lambert (2004). *Bergin and Garfield's handbook of psychotherapy and behavior change, fifth edition*. New York: Wiley.

For an engaging discussion about the relation of psychotherapy to autobiographical memory, emotions, and narratives of the self:
Jeff Singer & Peter Salovey (1993). *The remembered self: Emotion and memory in personality*. New York: Free Press.

On emotions and creativity, see:
James Averill (1999). Creativity in the domain of emotion. In T. Dalgleish & M. Power (Eds.), *Handbook of cognition and emotion* (pp. 765–82). Chichester: Wiley.

On emotions and the arts, see:
Keith Oatley (2003). Creative expression and communication of emotion in the visual and narrative arts. In R. J. Davidson, K. R. Scherer, & H. H. Goldsmith (Eds.), *Handbook of affective sciences* (pp. 481–502). New York: Oxford University Press.

Glossary

Action readiness. As proposed by Nico Frijda: the fundamental process of an emotion that establishes a priority and a readiness to act in a certain kind of way.

Adaptation. Modification of characteristics of a biological organism to fit an environmental niche.

Adreno-corticoid hormones. Hormones released from the outside part (the cortex) of the adrenal glands.

Affect. General term used to include emotions, moods, and preferences.

Affection. Feeling of warmth and cooperativeness toward another person.

Affiliation. Association with other people; used in this book to denote a social motivation of cooperation and friendliness.

Aggression. Action of conflict with another, or of hurting, or intending to overcome the other. The term is usually used in relation to physical violence, but also as a metaphor: e.g., aggression in argument.

Alexithymia. Reduced language of emotions, or a difficulty in identifying emotions verbally and in talking about them.

Amygdala. Part of the limbic system implicated in emotions. Joseph LeDoux has proposed that the amygdala conducts appraisals of danger.

Anthropology. Study of different human ways of life throughout the world.

Antidepressant. Drug designed to relieve depression.

Antisocial behavior (antisocial personality). Behavior that is aggressive and indifferent to the welfare of others. When it causes harm it is not followed by guilt or remorse. Antisocial personality is a diagnosis of someone who commits such behavior repeatedly. This diagnosis has replaced the older concept of "psychopath."

Anxiety. Mood of fear, apprehension, worry, or dread. Also a name for a group of emotional disorders that includes panic, phobia, obsessive-compulsive disorder, post-traumatic stress disorder, and generalized anxiety disorder.

Appraisal. Evaluation of an event according to a number of criteria. A set of appraisals determines what emotion (if any) is produced by the event.

Arousal. Alertness, with the nervous system including the sympathetic division of the autonomic nervous system activated, and the body prepared for action.

Assertion. The act of putting oneself forward, or of maintaining one's status. Used here to denote a social motivation of conflict with others, often in relation to power or status.

Assessment. Measurement of a person's traits, attributes, or accomplishments.

Attachment. Term introduced by John Bowlby to describe a bio-behavioral system in which the infant and caregiver maintain proximity to one another, for the safety of the infant.

Attachment style. Classification of children into secure, ambivalent, and avoidant categories, on the basis of Mary Ainsworth's Strange Situation test.

Attribution. Assigning causes to, or giving explanations of, an event. Internal attribution means assigning the cause to oneself. External attribution means assigning it to something outside the self.

Attunement. Style of interaction in which the emotions and actions of a parent and infant are synchronized with each other.

Autonomic nervous system. Part of the nervous system concerned with the inside of the body, and thought by William James to be important in the production of emotions as perceptions of bodily change. It has two divisions: the parasympathetic and sympathetic.

Basic emotions. Hypothesis that humans are equipped biologically with a small number of emotions that are basic, and that other emotions are elaborations or combinations of these.

"Big five" personality factors. Five fundamental factors or traits of personality, namely aggreeableness, conscientiousness, extraversion, neuroticism, and openness.

Bi-polar disorder. Emotional disorder with periods of depression and at least one period of mania. This disorder used to be called manic-depressive psychosis.

Broaden and build. Barbara Fredrickson's postulation of effects of positive emotions in widening the scope of cognitive processes and building schemas.

Bullying. Victimization based on a power imbalance in which a person with lesser power is humiliated and/or hurt by a person of greater power, usually repeatedly.

Caregiver. Parent or other person responsible for the care of a child.

Catharsis. Recognition and modification of an emotion by expressing it in psychotherapy, in drama, or in ritual.

Central nervous system. Brain and spinal cord.

Cerebral hemispheres. Hemispherical parts of the brain, one on each side, that comprise the larger part of the forebrain in humans.

Chromosome. Elongated structure, in the nuclei of cells, that carries genes. There are 23 pairs of chromosomes in body cells of humans. One member of each pair derives from the individual's mother and the other from the father.

Cognitive. Having to do with the representation and use of knowledge.

Cognitive behavior therapy. Form of therapy founded by Aaron Beck, in which thought is used to change emotions. Clients come to understand how their emotions are elicited in everyday life, and come to think more rationally about them. This therapy has some affinities to the teachings of Epicureans and Stoics.

Cognitive bias. Tendency toward a particular style of mental processing.

Complex emotion. Emotion with several parts, one of which is typically an evaluation in relation to the self.

Componential theories of emotion. Theories that emotions are made up of components that are not themselves emotions, such as features of appraisal.

Conditioning (classical conditioning). Learning to associate an event with pleasure or pain. It was discovered by Ivan Pavlov who found that the pleasurable anticipatory response of salivation by a dog could be learned in relation to a bell that signaled the delivery of meat powder into a dog's mouth.

Conduct disorder. Externalizing disorder of childhood and adolescence in which others' rights, or social norms, are often violated. It usually includes aggression that causes harm to others, damage to property, deceitfulness, and theft.

Continuity. Continuation of patterns of response or behavior over months or years.

Core affect. Central core of an emotional experience with dimensions of positivity and arousal, as proposed by James Russell.

Correlation. Statistical term for association between two variables. For instance, if emotions include both physiological and expressive components, one would expect these to be correlated. Correlation does not indicate the direction of relationship, nor does it show any necessary causal link between the variables. The correlation coefficient is r.

Cortex (neocortex). Outer part of the enlarged forebrain that is prominent in humans.

Cortisol. Hormone secreted by the adrenal cortex, and associated with stress.

Cross-sectional study. Study done at a single point in time.

Culture. Pattern of ideas, customs, and traditions shared within a particular society or language group.

Depression (or major depression). Set of symptoms including a low or sad mood for at least two weeks, together with at least four other symptoms such as: loss of pleasure, weight loss, insomnia, retardation, fatigue, feelings of worthlessness or guilt, difficulties of concentration, suicidal thoughts.

Diagnosis. Determination of the presence of a particular disorder in an individual, on the basis of the presence of a set of symptoms.

Diencephalon. Part of the forebrain, sometimes used interchangeably with "hypothalamus."

Differential parenting. Discrepancy of parental behavior directed to different children in the same family.

Discrete emotions. Particular emotions such as happiness, sadness, anger, and so on. The idea that the emotions are discrete is usually contrasted with the idea that emotional life is best characterized on dimensions such as positivity and arousal.

Display rules. Implicit rules, proposed by Paul Ekman and Wallace Friesen, of what emotions can and cannot be expressed in particular circumstances.

DNA (deoxyribonucleic acid). Spiral molecules in the chromosomes, which carry the genetic code.

Dominance. Control over others, or striving by assertion of power to rise above others in a social hierarchy.

Double blind method. Method for assessing the effectiveness of a treatment, for instance of a psychoactive drug, in which effects of the drug are compared with those of a placebo (inactive compound), so that neither participants nor those who administer treatments or assessments know which participants had the active drug and which the placebo.

DSM (Diagnostic and Statistical Manual of the American Psychiatric Association). This manual, now in its fourth revision (DSM-IV-TR), sets criteria for diagnosis of mental (psychiatric) disorders, including emotional disorders.

Dynamic systems theory. A theory which, in the study of emotions, is most usually applied to development, in which emotions are made up of components that become arranged into self-organizing systems as the person develops in interaction with his or her environment.

Electroencephalogram (EEG). Electrical pattern recorded from the surface of the brain, summing the activity of many millions of nerve cells.

Elicitor. Event that starts some emotion, or some action.

Emotion. Typically a multi-component response to a challenge or an opportunity that is important to an individual's goals. Components include (a) a conscious mental state with a recognizable quality of feeling directed toward some object, (b) a bodily change, (c) recognizable expressions of face, tone of voice, and gesture, (d) a readiness for a certain kind of action or social interaction.

Emotional bias. Likelihood of responding with one kind of emotion more than another.

Emotional disorder. Disorder or disturbance of experience and action that involves emotions such as anxiety, sadness, and anger, in extreme or long-lasting forms that are disabling to ordinary life. The most prevalent emotional disorders in adulthood are anxiety states and depression.

Emotionality. Way in which individuals differ from one another in experience and expression of emotions; the emotional component of personality.

Emotion-focused therapy. Form of therapy founded by Leslie Greenberg. As compared with cognitive-behavioral therapy in which thought is intended to change emotions, here emotions are used to change emotions.

Emotion regulation. Implicit and explicit maneuvers to modify the intensity and duration of emotional experiences and emotional behavior.

Emotion schema. Pattern of emotional response, based on previous experience of emotion in relationships, that is carried into new circumstances.

Empathy. Emotion that mirrors the emotion of another person.

Environment of evolutionary adaptedness (of humans). Hypothetical environment, probably of nomadic scavenging and gathering in small social groups, to which evolution human beings were fitted during most of the past six million years.

Epicurean. Follower of the Greek ethical philosopher Epicurus, who taught the value of enjoying pleasures that are simple and natural such as those of friendship, rather than prioritizing goals that cause anxiety such as the pursuit of wealth, or that are ephemeral and artificial such as the pursuit of fame.

Epidemiology. Study of diseases and disorders in a community, in terms of frequency (prevalence) and rate of onset (incidence).

Epistemology. Study of knowledge, and of how one can know things.

Ethnography. Description of ethnic groups, cultures, and customs.

Ethology. Study of behavior of animals in natural settings, with explanations typically given in relation to the theory of evolution.

Evaluation. Term used by Aristotle and his followers as the central component of an emotion, assigning a value to an event in relation to a goal.

Evolution. Charles Darwin's theory of how species developed by small modifications according to three principles: the production of more offspring than are needed merely to maintain numbers of a population, the random production among offspring of variations that can be inherited, and selection of certain traits because some variations enable individuals to survive and reproduce better than others.

Experience sampling. Method of asking a participant to respond to an electronic signal several times a day, by recording current mood and other variables.

Experiment. In psychology, a method in which a researcher manipulates a variable, for instance by randomly assigning participants to an experimental or a control group, in order to determine if a particular treatment has a causal effect on an outcome.

Expressed Emotion. Hostility and over-involvement, expressed in a family toward one of its members.

Expression. Charles Darwin's term for the more-or-less involuntary changes of face, voice, and posture that are observable signs of an emotion.

Externalizing disorder. Pattern of psychological disturbance in children characterized by antisocial behavior such as opposition, destructiveness, and aggression. (See Conduct disorder and Oppositional defiant disorder.)

Facial feedback hypothesis. The idea that information from facial movements creates or intensifies emotions.

Fixed action pattern. Term introduced by ethologists to describe a genetically specified pattern of behavior. It has now been replaced by "species-characteristic pattern."

Flow. Mihaly Csikszentmihalyi's term for a state of optimal experience, being fully and creatively engaged in what one is doing.

Folk psychology (folk theory). Ordinary understanding of psychological matters generally accepted, often implicitly, in a cultural group.

Forebrain. Most recently evolved part of the mammalian brain; the largest part of the brain in mammals.

Free-floating. Description applied to an emotion or mood as being without an object, or as being undirected to a specific person or event.

Frontal lobe. Front part of the cortex in humans.

Galvanic skin reflex. Change in electrical conductance of the skin due to minute amounts of sweat being secreted: an indication of autonomic change thought of as an important part of an emotion.

Gender difference. Difference, for instance in the frequency of emotional attributes, as a function of gender.

Gene. Length of DNA in a particular place on a specific chromosome, in which the orderings of the four bases of the DNA molecule (adenine, thymine, cytosine, and guanine) carry genetic meaning, rather as words carry meaning by means of the ordering of letters.

Genetics. The study of the effects of genes and heredity, especially of the variation of genetic traits among individuals.

Genomics. Science of functions of specific genes.

Gesture. Movement made for a communicative reason, or that is expressive of an emotion or intention.

Goal. Aim or objective, not necessarily consciously known.

Goal corrected partnership. John Bowlby's term for the partnership between child and parent, based on each being able to represent the goals of the other.

Grooming. Activity of primates in which individuals sit with each other in pairs sorting through the other's fur for twigs and parasites. Primates spend as much as 20 percent of their time grooming. It is a principal means of maintaining co-operative relationships.

Group therapy. Psychological therapy in groups (usually of between about 5 and 12 people).

Habituation. Response that decreases with repeated exposure to the same stimulus.

Heart rate. Measure of emotional arousal.

Heritability. Extent to which a pattern of behavior is attributable to genetic factors.

Heuristic. Plan or bias, often a short-cut, used when there is no guaranteed solution to a problem.

Hierarchy. Arrangement of status or power within a group of individuals, often with a clear leader, the alpha, and others of lesser status ranged below.

Hormone. Chemical substance that travels in the blood to affect the brain and other parts of the body. Examples are estrogen, oxytocin, testosterone, cortisol.

Human universals. Characteristics shared by all human beings.

Humors. Four fluid substances that, according to a theory that persisted from ancient times to the Renaissance, were responsible for persisting dispositions. The humors are blood, bile, black bile, and phlegm. Corresponding dispositions or moods are sanguine, choleric, melancholy, and phlegmatic.

Hunter-gatherer. Nomadic way of life based on traveling among naturally occurring food sources to gather roots and other foods, with supplementation by hunting.

Hypercognition/hypocognition. Cultural emphasis (hypercognition) or de-emphasis (hypocognition) in language and thinking about some particular state such as an emotion. In the USA today fear, for instance of terrorism, tends to be hypercognized, while shame tends to be hypocognized.

Hypothalamus. Part of the forebrain vital for the control of the autonomic nervous system and the pituitary gland. It is also implicated in species-characteristic behaviors of eating, drinking, sex, and attack.

Imitation. Action to mimic actions of another individual.

Immune system. Part of the body's system of defense against infections and cancers.

Imprinting. A species-characteristic pattern of learning that occurs during a time-limited period in infancy of some animals. For instance, when exposed to a moving, sound-producing object during this developmental phase, the infant follows this object and acts as if it were its mother.

Incidence. Term used in epidemiology to indicate the frequency with which new cases of some particular disorder occur in a population.

Individual differences. Differences among people of behavior, cognition, or emotional state.

Individualism. Cultural feature of Western societies: the individual is thought ideally to be autonomous and independent.

Induction (mood induction). Causing a mood in participants by having them watch a carefully chosen segment of a movie to make them sad, happy, etc., or by having them listen to a particular a piece of music, or in other ways.

Infancy. Early part of life, in humans roughly the first two years.

In-group/out-group. In-group is a group of which a person is a member, and with which that person identifies. Out-group is a group of which a person is not a member, and to which the person feels competitive or hostile.

Inner conflict. Contradiction between inner goals.

Instinct. Genetically specified pattern of motivated action in a species. The term has now been replaced by "species-characteristic pattern."

Institutionalized children. Children brought up in an institution such as an orphanage, in which opportunities for attachment are typically less than ideal.

Intentional. Philosophical term to describe mental states as about something. So beliefs are always intentional, and emotions are typically intentional.

Interdependence. Norm that stresses relatedness and mutual dependence of each on others. It is said to be characteristic of many non-Western societies, and to contrast with Western ideals of individualism and autonomy.

Internalizing disorder. Pattern of disturbance in children, characterized by social withdrawal, anxiety, fears, and unhappiness.

Interpretation. Suggestion in psychoanalytic therapy of an unrecognized goal that might explain an emotion or other mental state.

Interview. Conversation; in research it takes place between a researcher and a participant in which the researcher asks prepared questions to gather data.

Kindling hypothesis. Idea that a person becomes depressed more easily, and with less dependence on external stress, with each successive episode of depression.

Lateralization. Differential function on different sides of the brain. For instance, in right-handed people language tends to be lateralized to the left.

Lesion. Damage or local destruction of tissue. In neuroscience, typically damage to a part of the brain.

Lexicon. Vocabulary in a field. The emotion lexicon is the set of words that denote emotions in a society, or in the vocabulary of a person.

Life event or difficulty. Life event is an external event that changes a person's life. Severely negative life events, for instance bereavements, are stressors. A difficulty is a long-lasting stressor, for instance living in poverty.

Limbic system. Part of the forebrain that includes the amygdala. This system is thought to be especially important for emotions.

Longitudinal study. Study in which measurements are taken at two or more points in time.

Male provisioning hypothesis. Hypothesis, due to Owen Lovejoy, that with human pair bonding, which is thought to have come into being with the evolutionary emergence of upright walking, the male devotes economic input (provisioning) to a particular female, and to her young which he is likely to have fathered.

Mania. State of high excitement, enthusiasm, confidence, strong positive mood, and hyperactivity, together with impairment of judgment.

Meta-analysis. Statistical method applied to measures from a large number of studies, in which the measures are converted into standard scores and added to estimate the average effect of a particular intervention or variable.

Metaphor. Term derived from literary theory, sometimes used to designate a mode of thought in which a concept from one domain is mapped onto a concept from another. For example, in the idea that anger is hot, an emotion is mapped onto the domain of temperature.

Mirror neurons. Neurons discovered in monkeys by Giacomo Rizzolatti, Vittorio Gallese, and their colleagues, which respond both when the monkey makes an intended movement such as picking up a raisin, and when it sees a comparable intended movement made by someone else.

Misattribution. Attribution of a mood to an object other than that which caused it; thus anxiety can sometimes be misattributed to sexual attraction.

Modeling. Process of learning that occurs through observation and imitation.

Mood. Maintained state of emotion, or a disposition to respond emotionally in a particular way, that may last for hours or days, perhaps at a low level, and perhaps without the person knowing what started it.

Mood-congruent recall. Preferential recall of emotional episodes when the person is in the same mood as when the episode was experienced.

Motivation. State of having, consciously or unconsciously, some goal, aim, or purpose.

Neglect. Parental ignoring of a child, so that the warmth and control necessary for good parenting are not given.

Neocortex. See Cortex.

Neurochemicals. Chemicals that play active roles in the brain; for instance, transmitter substances, peptides, hormones.

Neuroimaging. Display and analysis of images of brain processes, derived from scanning the brain and making computational constructions of specific brain activities.

Neuron. Nerve cell.

Norm. Convention to which people in a society tend to conform.

Object. Used in this book to denote the object of an emotion, as in the phrase "the object of my affections."

Obsessions and compulsions. Obsessions are repeated, involuntary, intrusive thoughts or images, such as doubts, fears, and urges to count things. Compulsions are repetitive actions such as washing the hands. Obsessional-compulsive disorder is an anxiety disorder in which obsessive thoughts and/or compulsive actions become disabling to ordinary life.

Oppositional defiant disorder. Externalizing disorder of childhood, based on a pattern of angry, disobedient, and sometimes destructive behavior.

Panic (panic disorder). Sudden and intense feeling of extreme anxiety or dread, often accompanied by severe autonomic disturbance. Panic disorders are clinical anxiety states that include panics.

Parasympathetic nervous system. One of two divisions of the autonomic nervous system. Action of the parasympathetic system tends toward quieting and recuperation.

Passion. Term used in ancient texts for emotion. It means literally to suffer some state such as sorrow, in contrast to being an active agent. The term now tends to mean extreme emotion.

Passionate love. Term introduced by Elaine Hatfield for sexual love, or the state of longing for union with the other.

Peptide. Chemical substance, with a molecule made up of several amino acids, that diffuses to affect neural functions of the brain.

Peripheral. Used in neuroanatomy in contrast to "central." The peripheral nervous system is made up of the nerves running between the brain or spinal cord, and the skin, muscles, and other organs.

Personality. Stable pattern of a person's behavioral dispositions, thinking, and emotions.

Phobia. Intense fear of a situation or object that leads to avoidance; usually recognized by the person as irrational.

Post-traumatic stress disorder. Anxiety disorder that includes involuntary flash-backs and avoidance, and that typically involves the overturning of a personal value system. It follows a severe trauma, which might be personal, as when a person has been raped, or civil as with hurricanes and earthquakes, or military as in warfare.

Prevalence. Number of people suffering from a certain disorder in a population.

Prognosis. Likely outcome of a disorder.

Protective factors. Factors in people's lives (like having a close friend) that keep people from developing a disorder when they undergo major stress.

Prototype. Characteristic example of a concept. Thus anger is a prototypical emotion, whereas consternation is not.

Psychiatry. Care that medical practitioners provide for people's disordered emotions, thoughts, or behavior.

Psychoactive drugs. Drugs that affect mood, behavior, and/or thought processes.

Psychoanalysis. Method of inquiry and therapy developed by Sigmund Freud, in which behaviors and emotions are understood in the light of unconscious processes, typically those that developed in childhood. The analyst listens and occasionally offers interpretations to make sense of what the patient is saying or feeling.

Psychological therapy. Therapy means healing, making whole. Psychological therapy involves meeting with a therapist to discuss understandings of psychological distress or emotional disorder, sometimes to acquire insights, sometimes to receive advice, sometimes to receive suggestions for behavior. (See Cognitive behavior therapy, Emotion-focused therapy, Psychoanalysis.)

Psychology. Study of mental processes and of behavior.

Psychopathology. Psychologically disordered states and the study and understanding of these states.

Psychosis. Severe mental disorder, such as schizophrenia and bi-polar disorder, in which the person is typically deluded and disturbing to others, but has little insight into the seriousness of his or her condition.

Psychosomatic illness. Physical illness that is caused, maintained, or exacerbated by psychological causes.

Questionnaire. Sheet or computer screen designed to gather data in which there is a set of written questions, or statements with which participants are asked to agree or disagree.

Rasa. Sanscrit term for aesthetic emotion, that is to say an emotion experienced by a spectator or reader in drama or literature, which has affinities to a corresponding everyday emotion, but which can be more deeply understood.

Reflex. Discrete action, based on a neural pathway that connects a stimulus to a response.

Regulation (emotion regulation). Modulation or moderation of the intensity and/or duration of an emotion.

Reinforcement. Following a behavior with something rewarding or punishing, thereby changing the probability that the behavior will occur again.

Risk (risk factor). Factor statistically associated with a particular disorder, that predicts its occurrence.

RNA (Ribonucleic acid). Complex molecule that acts as an intermediate between genes and the making of proteins and other constituents of cells.

Role. Term derived from the theater, indicating a performance of a particular social function, like being a mother, or a student, or a friend. Performance in roles attracts commentary from others, thus giving a basis for morality in any culture.

Romantic love. Sexual love; it involves idealization of the other, often expression in poetry or song, and sometimes secrecy and suspension of rules of ordinary conduct.

Romantic period, Romanticism (in the arts). Period that started around 1750 in Europe, in which primacy of the natural and of the emotions was stressed, as compared with the artificial and with the dictates of convention.

Rumination. Mentally dwelling on emotions, or on adverse events and their consequences, without necessarily trying to solve problems associated with them.

Schema. Coherent structure stored in memory that is a representation of people, events, and objects, on which systematic perception and action are based.

Schizophrenia. Psychotic disorder characterized by disturbances of emotion, and of thought and perception such as delusions and hallucinations.

Script. Stored outline of a sequence of actions that achieves a goal.

Selection (natural selection). Process by which Charles Darwin hypothesized that traits that were adaptive in a particular environment were selected and hence preserved, to be passed to subsequent generations (see Evolution).

Self (self-concept). Self is a person's mental model of who he or she is, in terms of dispositions, emotions, abilities, values, and relationships.

Septal region. Part of the limbic system which, when stimulated electrically in rats, is associated with pleasure and reward.

Significance. Statistical term: a significance level is expressed as a probability, p. If p is less than 0.05, this means that there is less than a 5 percent probability that an outcome in a study was due to chance variations, and that therefore it was more likely to have been due to causes hypothesized in the study.

Socialization. Manner in which parents and teachers induct children into appropriate behaviors and emotions of a culture.

Social referencing. Child's monitoring of emotional expressions of an adult to see how to act in relation to an unfamiliar object or event.

Social support. Relationships that are supportive to the individual at times of stress.

Socio-emotional. Term that implies the closeness of emotional and social development.

Sociology. Study of society and its institutions.

Somatic marker. Antonio Damasio's term for gut feeling: a body-based image (somatic means having to do with the body, marker indicates an image) that signals an emotional state, typically a state of fear.

Species-characteristic pattern. Extended pattern of goal-directed behavior acquired genetically and characteristic of a species.

Split brain. Condition in which the corpus callosum (large bundle of nerve fibers that connects left and right cerebral hemispheres) has been severed in a surgical procedure to alleviate epilepsy, so that left and right cerebral hemispheres function independently of each other.

Status. Position in a hierarchy, or standing in some informal or formal social group.

Stoic. Follower of a Greek school of ethical philosophy in which it was taught that goals that depend on outside circumstances are worthless, as well as harmful because their pursuit causes destructive emotions such as anger. The alternative taught by the Stoics is the pursuit of virtue and rationality that cannot be affected by outside circumstances.

Strange Situation. Test developed by Mary Ainsworth to examine infants' reactions to separation from, and reunion with, their caregivers.

Stress (stressor). An event or living condition that challenges a person's capacity to cope.

Stress-diathesis. Theoretical idea that psychiatric disorders are based on a life event or difficulty (stress) to which the person has a vulnerability, genetic or learned (diathesis).

Striatal system. Part of the forebrain concerned with scheduling daily activities.

Stroop test. Test invented by John Stroop in which, although a participant is asked to name the color in which a word is printed, there is a tendency instead to read the word, which can then interfere with color naming. In the emotional Stroop test, meanings of color-printed words have emotional significance that can attract attention, and slow down the color naming.

Subcortical regions. Brain regions below the cortex, such as the regions of the limbic system.

Sympathetic nervous system. One of the two divisions of the autonomic nervous system. Action of the sympathetic system tends toward arousal, and preparation for fight or flight.

Sympathy. Appreciation or concern for the emotional state of another individual or group.

Symptom (psychiatric symptom). Individual piece of emotional experience or behavior that is problematic for a person, and can contribute to the criteria for diagnosing whether a disorder exists.

Temperament. Aspect of behavioral propensity and emotionality that is stable over time, and that has a genetic basis.

Temporal lobe. Part of the cortex close to the limbic system.

Trait. Characteristic that is stable over time.

Tranquilizer. Anti-anxiety drug.

Transference. Term derived from psychoanalysis. Pattern of a person's behavior, relating, emotional responses, and beliefs, directed toward a therapist or other person, based on an earlier relationship, such as that with a parent.

Transmitter substance. Chemical substance secreted by neurons to communicate with other neurons by diffusing across the minute gaps of the synapses. Several dozen transmitter substances are known; examples are acetyl choline, noradrenaline, serotonin, dopamine.

Trauma. Damaging event of emotional significance, such as sexual or physical abuse in childhood, or a civil or military disaster that closely affects a person.

Twin studies. Studies of twins to separate relative effects of genes and environment. In typical designs the similarity (concordance) of some trait in pairs of monozygotic (identical) twins who share 100 percent of their genes is compared with the similarity of the trait in pairs of dizygotic twins, who share on average 50 percent of their genes.

Unconscious. State of being unaware of mental processes. One type of unconscious is that, as Hermann von Helmholtz pointed out, we are not aware of most processes that occur in the brain, only of the conclusions of these processes that are delivered to consciousness. Another sense, proposed by Sigmund Freud, is that we can have unconscious goals or intentions that can become conscious in the course of therapy, or by other means.

Vulnerability factor. Aspect of life that makes it more likely that a person will succumb to emotional disorder when exposed to a major stressor.

Warmth. Affectionate atmosphere in a family or a relationship, marked by happiness and a lack of tension.

Well-being. Good emotional state, marked by a general sense of happiness and life satisfaction.

References

References are for the most part cited in the format recommended by the American Psychological Association, except that for older books we cite the date of the original publication in the text, and in this reference list we generally give the date of a publication available in libraries and/or bookshops as (current edition 19xx) at the end of the reference.

Abe, J. A. A., Beetham, M., & Izard, C. E. (2002). What do smiles mean? An analysis in terms of differential emotions theory. In M. H. Abel (Ed.), *An empirical reflection on the smile*. New York: Edwin Mellen Press.

Abe, J. A. A., & Izard, C. E. (1999). The developmental functions of emotions: An analysis in terms of differential emotions theory. *Cognition and Emotion, 13*, 523–549.

Abrams, M. H. (1953). *The mirror and the lamp: Romantic theory and the critical tradition*. Oxford: Oxford University Press.

Abramson, L. Y., Metalsky, G. I., & Alloy, L. B. (1989). Hopelessness depression: A theory-based subtype of depression. *Psychological Review, 96*, 358–372.

Abramson, L. Y., Seligman, M. E. P., & Teasdale, J. D. (1978). Learned helplessness in humans: Critique and reformulation. *Journal of Abnormal Psychology, 87*, 49–74.

Abu-Lughod, L. (1986). *Veiled sentiments*. Berkeley: University of California Press.

Abu-Lughod, L., & Lutz, C. A. (1990). *Introduction to language and the politics of emotion*. New York: Cambridge University Press.

Achenbach, T. M., & Edelbrock, C. S. (1984). Psychopathology of childhood. *Annual Review of Psychology, 35*, 227–256.

Achenbach, T. M., Howell, C. T., Quay, H. C., & Conners, C. K. (1991). National survey of problems and competencies among four to sixteen year olds. *Monographs of the Society for Research in Child Development, 56* (3, Serial No. 225).

Aggleton, J. P. (Ed.) (2000). The amygdala (2nd ed.). Oxford: Oxford University Press.

Agmo, A., Barreau, S., & Lemaire, V. (1997). Social motivation in recently weaned rats is modified by opiates. *Developmental Neuroscience, 19*, 505–520.

Aguilar, B., Sroufe, A., Edgland, B., & Carlson, E. (2000). Distinguishing the early-onset persistent and adolescence-onset antisocial behavior types: From birth to 16 years. *Development and Psychopathology, 12*, 109–132.

Aharon, I., Etcoff, N., Ariety, D., Chabris, C., O'Connor, E., & Breiter, H. (2001). Beautiful faces have variable reward value: fMRI and behavioral evidence. *Neuron, 32*, 537–551.

Ainsworth, M. D. S. (1967). *Infancy in Uganda: Infant care and the growth of love*. Baltimore, MD: Johns Hopkins Press.

Ainsworth, M. D. S. (1992). Obituary: John Bowlby (1907–1990). *American Psychologist, 47*, 668.

Ainsworth, M. D. S., & Bells, S. M. (1970). Attachment, exploration, and separation: Illustrated by the behavior of one-year-olds in a stranger situation. *Child Development, 41*, 49–67.

Ainsworth, M. D. S., Blehar, M. C., Walters, E., & Wall, S. (1978). *Patterns of attachment: A psychological study of the strange situation*. Hillsdale, NJ: Erlbaum.

Alexander, F. (1950). *Psychosomatic medicine*. New York: Norton.

Ali, A., Oatley, K., & Toner, B. (2002). Life stress, self-silencing, and domains of meaning in unipolar depression: An investigation of an outpatient sample of women. *Journal of Social and Clinical Psychology, 21*, 669–685.

Allen, J., McElhaney, K. B., Land, D., et al. (2003). A secure base in adolescence: Markers of attachment security in the mother–adolescent relationship. *Child Development, 74*, 282–307.

Allik, J., & Realo, A. (1997). Emotional experience and its relation to the five-factor model in Estonian. *Journal of Personality, 65*, 625–647.

Alloy, L., Abramson, L. Y., Hogan, M. E., et al. (2000). The Temple-Wisconsin cognitive vulnerability to depression (CVD) project: Lifetime history of Axis-I psychopathology in individuals at high and low cognitive risk for depression. *Journal of Abnormal Psychology, 109*, 403–418.

Alloy, L., Abramson, L. Y., Murray, L. A., Whitehouse, W. G., & Hogan, M. E. (1997). Self-referent information processing in individuals at high and low cognitive risk for depression. *Cognition and Emotion, 11*, 539–568.

Als, H., Tronick, E., & Brazelton, T. B. (1980). Affective reciprocity and the development of autonomy. The study of a blind infant. *Journal of Child Psychiatry, 19*, 22–40.

Altshuler, L. L., Bartzokis, G., Grieder, T., Curran, J., & Mintz, J. (1998). Amygdala enlargement in bipolar disorder and hippocampal reduction in schizophrenia: An MRI study demonstrating neuroanatomic specificity. *Archive of General Psychiatry, 55*, 663–664.

Ambadar, Z., Schooler, J., & Cohn, J. F. (2005). Deciphering the ambiguous face. *Psychological Science, 16*, 403–410.

American Psychiatric Association (2000). *Diagnostic and statistical manual of mental disorders, Fourth edition, Text revision (DSM-IV-TR)*. Washington, DC: American Psychiatric Association.

Andalmann, P. K., & Zajonc, R. B. (1989). Facial efference and the experience of emotion. *Annual Review of Psychology, 40*, 249–280.

Anderson, A. K., & Phelps, E. A. (2000). Expression without recognition: Contributions of the human amygdala to emotional communication. *Psychological Science, 11*, 106–111.

Anderson, A. K., & Phelps, E. A. (2002). Is the human amygdala critical for the subjective experience of emotion?: Evidence of intact dispositional affect in patients with amygdala lesions. *Journal of Cognitive Neuroscience, 14*, 709–720.

Anderson, J. C., Williams, S., McGee, R., & Silva, P. A. (1987). DSM-III disorders in preadolescent children: Prevalence in a large sample from the general population. *Archives of General Psychiatry, 44*, 69–76.

Anderson, S. M., & Chen, S. (2002). The relational self. *Psychological Review, 109*, 619–645.

Anderson, S. M., Reznik, I., & Manzella, L. M. (1996). Eliciting facial affect, motivation, and expectancies in transference: Significant other representations in social relations. *Journal of Personality and Social Psychology, 71*, 1108–1129.

Andrew, R. J. (1963). The origin and evolution of the calls and facial expressions of the primates. *Behavior, 20*, 1–109.

Andrew, R. J. (1965, October). The origin of facial expressions. *Scientific American, 213*, 88–94.

Angold, A. (1988). Childhood and adolescent depression: I. Epidemiological and aetiological aspects. *British Journal of Psychiatry, 152*, 501–507.

Anisfeld, E., Casper, V., Nozyce, M., & Cunningham, N. (1990). Does infant carrying promote attachment? An experimental study of the increased physical contact on the development of attachment. *Child Development, 61*, 1617–1627.

Ardrey, R. (1966). *The territorial imperative*. New York: Dell.

Aristotle (1984). *Complete works. Revised Oxford translation in 2 volumes* (J. Barnes, Ed.). Princeton, NJ: Princeton University Press.

Armstrong, K. (2001). *Buddha*. London: Penguin.

Arnold, M. B., & Gasson, J. A. (1954). Feelings and emotions as dynamic factors in personality integration. In M. B. Arnold & S. J. Gasson (Eds.), *The human person* (pp. 294–313). New York: Ronald.

Aron, A., & Aron, E. N. (1997). Self-expansion motivation and including the other in self. In S. Duck (Ed.), *Handbook of personal relationships: Theory, research, and interventions* (2nd ed., pp. 251–270). Chichester: Wiley.

Aron, A., & Aron, E. N. (1998). Love and sexuality. In K. S. McKinney (Ed.), *Sexuality and close relationships* (pp. 25–48). Hillsdale, NJ: Lawrence Erlbaum.

Aron, A., Aron, E. N., & Allen, J. (1989). *The motivation for unrequited love: A self-expansion perspective*. Paper presented at the International Conference on Personal Relationships, Iowa City, IA.

Aron, A., Aron, E. N., Tudor, M., & Nelson, G. (1991). Close relationships as including other in self. *Journal of Personality and Social Psychology, 60*, 241–253.

Arsenio, W. F., & Lemerise, E. A. (2004). Aggression and moral development: Integrating social information processing and moral domain models. *Child Development, 75*, 987–1002.

Astington, J. W. (1993). *The child's discovery of the mind*. Cambridge, MA: Harvard University Press.

Astington, J. W., & Jenkins, J. M. (1995). Theory of mind development and social understanding. *Cognition and Emotion*, 9, 151–165.

Atkinson, L., Goldberg, S., Raval, V., et al. (2005). On the relation between maternal state of mind and sensitivity in the prediction of infant attachment security. *Developmenal Psychology*, 41, 42–53.

Atkinson, R. L., Atkinson, R. C., Smith, E. E., & Bem, D. M. (1989). *Introduction to Psychology* (10th edn). Belmont, CA: Wadsworth.

Aubé, M., & Senteni, A. (1996). Emotions as commitments operators: A foundation for control structure in multi-agents systems. In W. V. de Velde & J. W. Perram (Eds.), *Agents breaking away: Proceedings of the 7th European Workshop on MAAMAW, Lecture notes on artificial intelligence, No. 1038* (pp. 13–25). Berlin: Springer.

Augustine (c.400). *Confessions* (R. S. Pine-Coffin, Trans.). Harmondsworth: Penguin (current edition 1960).

Aureli, F., Preston, S. D., & De Waal, F. B. M. (1999). Heart rate responses to social interactions in Free-moving Rhesus Macaques (*Macaca mulatta*): A pilot study. *Journal of Comparative Psychology*, 133, 59–65.

Aurelius, M. (c.170). *Meditations* (M. Staniforth, Trans.). London: Penguin (1964).

Averill, J. R. (1982). *Anger and aggression. An essay on emotion*. New York: Springer.

Averill, J. R. (1985). The social construction of emotion: With special reference to love. In K. J. Gergen & K. E. Davis (Eds.), *The social construction of the person* (pp. 89–109). New York: Springer Verlag.

Averill, J. R. (1999). Creativity in the domain of emotion. In T. Dalgleish & M. Power (Eds.), *Handbook of cognition and emotion* (pp. 765–782). Chichester: Wiley.

Averill, J. R., & More, T. A. (2000). Happiness. In M. Lewis & J. Haviland-Jones (Eds.), *Handbook of emotions, second edition* (pp. 663–676). New York: Guilford.

Averill, J. R., & Nunley, E. P. (1992). *Voyages of the heart: Living an emotionally creative life*. New York: Free Press.

Averill, J. R., & Thomas-Knowles, C. (1991). Emotional creativity. In K. T. Strongman (Ed.), *International review of studies on emotion* (pp. 269–299). Chichester: Wiley.

Axelrod, R. (1984). *The evolution of cooperation*. New York: Basic Books.

Bachorowski, J. A. (1999). Vocal expression and perception of emotion. *Current Directions in Psychological Science*, 8, 53–57.

Bachorowski, J. A., & Owren, M. J. (2001). Not all laughs are alike: Voiced by not voiced laughter readily elicits positive affect. *Psychological Science*, 12, 252–257.

Bachorowski, J. A., Smoski, M. J., & Owren, M. J. (2001). The acoustic features of human laughter. *Journal of Acoustic Society of America*, 110, 1581–1597.

Bakermans-Kranenburg, M., Van Ijzendoorn, M. H., & Juffer, F. (2003). Less is more: Meta-analyses of sensitivity and attachment interventions in early childhood. *Psychological Bulletin*, 129, 195–215.

Bakhtin, M. (1963). *Problems of Dostoevsky's poetics* (C. Emerson, Trans.). Minneapolis: University of Minneapolis Press (current edition 1984).

Baldwin, M. (1992). Relational schemas and the processing of social information. *Psychological Bulletin*, 112, 461–484.

Bamber, J. H. (1979). *The fears of adolescence*. London: Academic Press.

Bandura, A., Caprara, G. V., Barbaranelli, C., et al. (2003). Role of affective self-regulatory efficacy in diverse spheres of psychosocial functioning. *Child Development*, 74, 769–782.

Banse, R., & Scherer, K. (1996). Acoustic profiles in vocal emotion expression. *Journal of Personality and Social Psychology*, 70, 614–636.

Barbato, A., & D'Avanzo, B. (2000). Family interventions in schizophrenia and related disorders: A critical review. *Acta Psychiatrica Scandinavica*, 102, 81–97.

Bard, P. (1928). A diencephalic mechanism for the expression of rage with special reference to the sympathetic nervous system. *American Journal of Physiology*, 84, 490–513.

Bard, P., & Rioch, D. M. (1937). A study of four cats deprived of neocortex and additional portions of the forebrain. *Johns Hopkins Medical Journal*, 60, 73–153.

Barkham, M., Rees, A., Shapiro, D. A., Stiles, W. B., Agnew, R. M., Halstead, J., et al. (1996). Outcomes of time-limited psychotherapy in applied settings: Replicating the second Sheffield psychotherapy project. *Journal of Consulting and Clinical Psychology*, 64, 1079–1085.

Baron, R. A. (1987). Interviewer's mood and reaction to job applicants. *Journal of Applied Social Psychology, 17*, 911–926.

Barrett, D. H., Resnick, H. S., Foy, D. W., et al. (1996). Combat exposure and adult psychosocial adjustment among US Army veterans serving in Vietnam, 1965–1971. *Journal of Abnormal Psychology, 105*, 575–581.

Bartlett, F. C. (1932). *Remembering: A study in experimental and social psychology*. Cambridge: Cambridge University Press.

Bateman, A. (2004). Psychoanalysis and psychiatry – Is there a future? *Acta Psychiatrica Scandinavica, 109*, 161–163.

Bates, J. E., Olson, S., Pettit, G., & Bayles, K. (1982). Dimensions of individuality in the mother-infant relationship at six months of age. *Child Development, 53*, 446–461.

Bateson, P. (1990). Obituary: Konrad Lorenz (1903–1989). *American Psychologist, 45*, 65–66.

Bateson, P. P. G. (1983). *Mate choice*. Cambridge: Cambridge University Press.

Batson, C. D., Engel, C. L., & Fridell, S. R. (1999). Value judgments: Testing the somatic-marker hypothesis using false physiological feedback. *Personality and Social Psychology Bulletin, 25*, 1021–1032.

Batson, C. D., & Shaw, L. L. (1991). Evidence for altruism: Toward a pluralism of prosocial motives. *Psychological Inquiry, 2*, 107–122.

Battaglia, M., Oglliari, A., Nanoni, A., et al. (2004). Children's discrimination of expressions of emotions: Relationship with indices of social anxiety and shyness. *Journal of the American Academy of Child and Adolescent Psychiatry, 43*, 358–365.

Bauer, D. H. (1976). An exploratory study of developmental changes in children's fear. *Journal of Child Psychology and Psychiatry, 17*, 69–74.

Baumeister, R. F., Bratslavsky, E., Finkenauer, C., & Vohs, K. D. (2001). Bad is stronger than good. *Review of General Psychology, 5*, 323–370.

Baumeister, R. F., Stillwell, A. M., & Heatherton, T. F. (1994). Guilt: An interpersonal approach. *Psychological Bulletin, 115*, 243–267.

Baxter, M. G., & Murray, E. A. (2002). The amygdala and reward. *Nature Reviews Neuroscience, 3*, 563–574.

Bear, D. (1979). The temporal lobes: An approach to the study of organic behavioral changes. In M. S. Gazzaniga (Ed.), *Handbook of behavioral neurobiology, Vol. 2. Neuropsychology* (pp. 75–95). New York: Plenum.

Beauregard, M., Levesque, J., & Bourgouin, P. (2001). Neural correlates of conscious self-regulation of emotion. *The Journal of Neuroscience, 21*, 1–6.

Bechara, A., Damasio, H., Tranel, D., & Damasio, A. (1997). Deciding advantageously before knowing the advantageous strategy. *Science, 275*, 1293–1295.

Beck, A. T. (1976). *Cognitive therapy and the emotional disorders*. New York: Meridian.

Beck, A. T. (1983). Cognitive therapy of depression: New perspectives. In P. J. Clayton & P. E. Barrett (Eds.), *Treatment of depression: Old controversies, new approaches* (pp. 265–284). New York: Raven Press.

Beck, A. T., & Emery, G. (1985). *Anxiety disorders and phobias: A cognitive perspective*. New York: Basic Books.

Beck, A. T., Rush, A. J., Shaw, B. F., & Emery, G. (1979). *Cognitive therapy of depression*. New York: Guilford.

Beck, A. T., Steer, R., & Garbin, M. (1988). Psychometric properties of the Beck Depression Inventory: Twenty-five years of evaluation. *Clinical Psychology Review, 8*, 77–100.

Beeghly, M., Bretherton, I., & Mervis, C. B. (1986). Mothers' internal state language to toddlers. *British Journal of Developmental Psychology, 4*, 247–61.

Beer, J. S. (2002). Self-regulation of social behavior. *Unpublished dissertation*. University of California, Berkeley.

Beer, J., Heerey, E. A., Keltner, D., Knight, R., & Scabini, D. (2003). The regulatory function of self-conscious emotion: Insights from patients with orbitofrontal damage. *Journal of Personality and Social Psychology, 85*, 594–604.

Beier, E. G., & Sternberg, D. P. (1977). Marital communication. *Journal of Communication, 27*, 92–97.

Bekerian, D. A., & Goodrich, S. J. (1999). Forensic applications of theories of cognition and emotion. In T. Dalgleish & M. Power (Eds.), *Handbook of cognition and emotion* (pp. 783–798). Chichester: Wiley.

Bellak, L. (1986). *The thematic apperception test* (4th ed.). Larchmont: Grune & Stratton.

Belsky, J., & Fearon, R. M. P. (2004). Early attachment security, subsequent maternal sensitivity, and later child development: Does continuity in development depend upon continuity of caregiving? *Attachment and Human Development, 4*, 361–387.

Belsky, J., Fish, M., & Isabella, R. (1991). Continuity and discontinuity in infant negative and positive emotionality: Family antecedents and attachment consequences. *Developmental Psychology*, *27*, 421-431.

Belsky, J., Jaffee, S. R., Sligo, J., Woodward, L., & Slva, P. (2005). Intergenerational transmission of warm-sensitive-stimulating parenting: A prospective study of mothers and fathers of 3-year-olds. *Child Development*, *76*, 384-396.

Ben-Ze'ev, A. (2000). *The subtlety of emotions*. Cambridge, MA: MIT Press.

Ben Ze'ev, A., & Oatley, K. (1996). The intentional and social nature of human emotions: Reconsideration of the distinctions between basic and non-basic emotions. *Journal for the Theory of Social Behaviour*, *26*, 81-92.

Bennett, D. S., Bendersky, M., & Lewis, M. (2002). Facial expressivity at 4 months: A context by expression analysis. *Infancy*, *3*, 97-113.

Bentler, P. M., & Newcomb, M. D. (1978). Longitudinal study of marital success and failure. *Journal of Consulting and Clinical Psychology*, *46*(5), 1053-1070.

Berk, M. S., & Anderson, S. M. (2000). The impact of past relationships on interpersonal behavior: Behavioral confirmation in the social-cognitive process of transference. *Journal of Personality and Social Psychology*, *79*, 546-562.

Berkowitz, L. (1989). The frustration-aggression hypothesis: An examination and reformulation. *Psychological Bulletin*, *106*, 59-73.

Berkowitz, L. (1990). On the formation and regulation of anger and aggression: A cognitive-neoassociationistic analysis. *American Psychologist*, *45*, 494-503.

Berkowitz, L. (2003). Affect, aggression, and antisocial behavior. In R. J. Davidson, K. R. Scherer, & H. H. Goldsmith (Eds.), *Handbook of affective sciences* (pp. 804-823). New York: Oxford University Press.

Berkowitz, L., Cochran, S., & Embree, M. (1981). Physical pain and the goal of aversively stimulated aggression. *Journal of Personality and Social Psychology*, *40*, 687-700.

Bermond, B., Bleys, J. W., & Stoffels, E. J. (2005). Left hemispheric preference and alexithymia: A neuropsychological investigation. *Cognition and Emotion*, *19*, 151-160.

Bermond, B., Fasotti, L., Nieuwenhuyse, B., & Schuerman, J. (1991). Spinal cord lesions, peripheral feedback and intensities of emotional feelings. *Cognition and Emotion*, *5*, 201-220.

Bernheimer, C., & Kahane, C. (1985). *In Dora's case: Freud - hysteria - feminism*. New York: Columbia University Press.

Bernstein, G. A., & Borchardt, C. M. (1991). Anxiety disorders of childhood and adolescence: A critical review. *Journal of the American Academy of Child and Adolescent Psychiatry*, *30*, 519-532.

Berntson, G. G., Cacioppo, J. T., & Quigley, K. S. (1993). Respiratory sinus arrhythmia: Autonomic origins, physiological mechanisms, and psychophysiological implications. *Psychophysiology*, *30*, 183-196.

Berridge, K. C. (2000). Taste reactivity: Measuring hedonic impact in human infants and animals. *Neuroscience and Biobehavioral Reviews*, *24*, 173-198.

Berridge, K. C. (2003). Comparing the emotional brains of humans and other animals. In R. J. Davidson, K. Scherer, & H. H. Goldsmith (Eds.), *Handbook of affective sciences* (pp. 25-51). New York: Oxford University Press.

Berry, D. S., & Willingham, J. K. (1997). Affective traits, responses to conflict, and satisfaction in romantic relationships. *Journal of Research in Personality*, *31*, 564-576.

Berscheid, E. (1985). Interpersonal attraction. In G. Lindzey & E. Aronson (Eds.), *Handbook of social psychology* (3rd ed., pp. 413-484). New York: Random House.

Berscheid, E. (1988). Some comments on love's anatomy; Or, whatever happened to old-fashioned lust? In R. J. Sternberg & M. L. Barnes (Eds.), *The psychology of love* (pp. 359-374). New Haven, CT: Yale University Press.

Bharata Muni (200 BCE). *Natyasastra; English translation with critical notes* (A. Rangacharya, Trans.). Bangalore: IBH Prakashana (current edition 1986).

Biehl, M., Matsumoto, D., Ekman, P., Hearn, V., Heider, K., Kudoh, T., & Ton, V. (1997). Matsumoto and Ekman's Japanese and Caucasian Facial Expressions of Emotion (JACFEE): Reliability data and cross-national differences. *Journal of Nonverbal Behavior*, *21*, 3-21.

Biglan, A., Hops, H., Sherman, L., Friedman, L. S., Arthus, J., & Osteen, V. (1985). Problem-solving interactions of depressed women and their husbands. *Behavior Therapy*, *16*, 431-451.

Bird, H. R., Canino, G., & Rubio-Stipec, M. (1988). Estimates of the prevalence of childhood maladjustment in a community survey in Puerto Rico. *Archives of General Psychiatry*, *45*, 1120-1126.

Birdwhistell, R. L. (1970). *Kinesics and context*. Philadelphia: University of Pennsylvania Press.

Biswas-Diener, R., & Diener, E. (2001). Making the best of a bad situation: Satisfaction in the slums of Calcutta. *Social Indicators Research, 55*, 329–352.

Blair, R. J. R., & Cipolotti, L. (2000). Impaired social response reversal: A case of acquired sociopathy. *Brain, 123*, 1122–1141.

Blair, R. J. R., Morris, J. S., Frith, C. D., Perrett, D. I., & Dolan, R. (1999). Dissociable neural responses to facial expressions of sadness and anger. *Brain, 122*, 883–893.

Blascovich, J., & Mendes, W. B. (2000). Challenge and threat appraisals: The role of affective cues. In J. Forgas (Ed.), *Feeling and thinking: The role of affect in social cognition* (pp. 59–82). Cambridge: Cambridge University Press.

Blascovich, J., Spencer, S., Quinn, D., & Steele, C. (2001). African-Americans and high blood pressure: The role of stereotype threat. *Psychological Science, 12*, 225–229.

Blazer, D., Hughes, D., & George, L. K. (1987). Stressful life events and the onset of a generalized anxiety syndrome. *American Journal of Psychiatry, 144*, 1178–1183.

Bless, H., Clore, G. L., Schwarz, N., Golisano, V., Rabe, C., & Wölk, M. (1996). Mood and the use of scripts: Does a happy mood really lead to mindlessness? *Journal of Personality and Social Psychology, 71*(4), 665–679.

Bless, H., Mackie, D. M., & Schwarz, N. (1992). Mood effects on attitude judgments: Independent effects of mood before and after message elaboration. *Journal of Personality and Social Psychology, 63*(4), 585–595.

Bless, H., Schwarz, N., & Wieland, R. (1996). Mood and the impact of category membership and individuating information. *European Journal of Social Psychology, 26*, 935–959.

Block, J. H., Block, J., & Gjerde, P. F. (1986). The personality of children prior to divorce: A prospective study. *Child Development, 57*, 827–840.

Blomberg, J., Lazar, A., & Sandell, R. (2001). Long-term outcome of long-term psychoanalytically oriented psychotherapies: First findings of the the Stockholm outcome of psychotherapy and psychoanalysis project. *Psychotherapy Research, 11*, 361–382.

Bloom, H. (1989). *Ruin the sacred truths: Poetry and belief from the Bible to the present*. Cambridge, MA: Harvard University Press.

Bloom, L. (1989). Developments in expression: Affect and speech. In N. L. Stein, B. Leventhal, & T. Trabasso (Eds.), *Psychological and biological approaches to emotion* (pp. 215–245). Hillsdale, NJ: Erlbaum.

Bodenhausen, G. V., Kramer, G. P., & Susser, K. (1994). Happiness and stereotypic thinking in social judgment. *Journal of Personality and Social Psychology, 66*, 621–632.

Bodenhausen, G., Sheppard, L., & Kramer, G. (1994). Negative affect and social judgment: The different impact of anger and sadness. *European Journal of Social Psychology, 24*, 45–62.

Bodiford, C. A., Eisenstadt, T. H., Johnson, J. H., & Bradlyn, A. S. (1988). Comparison of learned helplessness cognitions and behavior in children with high and low scores on the children's depression inventory. *Journal of Abnormal Child Psychology, 17*, 152–158.

Boesch, C., & Boesch, H. (1989). Hunting behavior of wild chimpanzees in the Tai National Park. *American Journal of Physical Anthropology, 78*, 547–573.

Bokhorst, C., Bakermans-Kranenburg, M., Fearon, R. M. P., et al. (2003). The importance of shared environment in mother–infant attachment security: A behavioral genetic study. *Child Development, 74*, 1769–1782.

Boldizar, J. P., Perry, D. G., & Perry, L. C. (1989). Outcome values and aggression. *Child Development, 60*, 571–579.

Bolger, N., & Schilling, E. A. (1991). Personality and the problems of everyday life: The role of neuroticism in exposure and reactivity to daily stressors. *Journal of Personality, 59*, 355–386.

Bolger, N., Davis, A., & Rafaeli, E. (2003). Diary methods: Capturing life as it is lived. *Annual Review of Psychology, 54*, 579–616.

Bolton, W., & Oatley, K. (1987). A longitudinal study of social support and depression in unemployed men. *Psychological Medicine, 17*, 453–460.

Bonanno, G. A., & Keltner, D. (2004). The coherence of emotion systems: Comparing "on-line" measures of appraisal and facial expressions, and self-report. *Cognition and Emotion, 18*, 431–444.

Bongers, I. L., Koot, H. M., Van der Ende, J., & Verhulst, F. C. (2004). Developmental trajectories of externalizing behaviors in childhood and adolescence. *Child Development, 75*, 1523–1537.

Boole, G. (1854). An investigation of the laws of thought. Dover: New York.

Booth, W. C. (1988). *The company we keep: An ethics of fiction*. Berkeley, CA: University of California Press.

Borod, J. C. (1992). Interhemispheric and intrahemispheric control of emotion: A focus on unilateral brain damage. *Journal of Consulting and Clinical Psychology, 60*, 339–348.

Boucher, J. D., & Brandt, M. E. (1981). Judgment of emotion: American and Malay antecedents. *Journal of Cross-Cultural Psychology, 12*, 272–283.

Bouton, M. E., Mineka, S., & Barlow, D. H. (2001). A modern learning theory perspective on the etiology of panic disorder. *Psychological Review, 108*, 4–32.

Bower, G. H. (1981). Mood and memory. *American Psychologist, 36*, 129–148.

Bower, G. H., Gilligan, S. G., & Monteiro, K. P. (1981). Selectivity of learning caused by affective states. *Journal of Experimental Psychology: General, 110*, 451–473.

Bowlby, J. (1951). *Maternal care and mental health*. Geneva: World Health Organization (textual quotes from shorter version 1953 published as *Child care and the growth of love*, Harmondsworth: Penguin).

Bowlby, J. (1971). *Attachment and loss, Vol. 1. Attachment*. London: Hogarth Press (current edition Penguin 1978).

Bowlby, J. (1979). *The making and breaking of affectional bonds*. London: Tavistock.

Bowlby, J. (1988). *A secure base: Clinical applications of attachment theory*. London: Routledge.

Bowlby, J. (1991). *Charles Darwin: A new life*. New York: Norton.

Bowman, E., Aigner, T. & Richmond, B. (1996). Neural signals in the monkey ventral striatum related to motivation for juice and cocaine rewards. *Journal of Neurophysiology, 75*, 1061–1073.

Boyle, M. (1991). Child health in Ontario. In R. Barnhorst & L. C. Johnson (Eds.), *The state of the child in Ontario*. Toronto: University of Toronto Press.

Boyle, M. H., & Lipman, E. (2002). Do places matter? Socioeconomic disadvantage and behavior problems of children in Canada. *Journal of Consulting and Clinical Psychology, 70*, 378–389.

Boyle, M. H., Jenkins, J. M., Georgiades, K., Cairney, J., Duku, E., & Racine, Y. (2004). Differential-maternal parenting behavior: Estimating within- and between-family effects on children. *Child Development, 75*, 1457–1476.

Bradley, M. M. (1994). Emotional memory: A dimensional analysis. In S. H. M. Van Goozen, N. E. V. De Poll, & J. A. Sergeant (Eds.), *Emotions: Essays on emotion theory* (pp. 97–134). Hillsdale, NJ: Erlbaum.

Bradwejn, J. (1993). Neurobiological investigations into the role of cholecystokinin in panic disorder. *Journal of Psychiatry and Neuroscience, 18*, 178–188.

Brazier, M. A. B. (1959). The historical development of neurophysiology. In *Handbook of physiology Section 1* (Vol. 1, pp. 1–58). Bethesda, MD: American Physiological Association.

Breiter, H. C., Etcoff, N. L., Whalen, P. J., et al. (1996). Response and habituation of the human amygdala during visual processing of facial expression. *Neuron, 17*, 875–887.

Breiter, H., Aharon, I., Kahneman, D., Dale, A., & Shizgal, P. (2001). Functional imaging of neural responses to expectancy and experience of monetary gains and losses. *Neuron, 30*, 619–639.

Bremner, J. G., & Slater, A. (Eds.). (2004). *Theories of infant development*. New York: Blackwell.

Brennan, S. (1985). The caricature generator. *Leonardo, 18*, 59–87.

Bretherton, I., Fritz, J., Zahn-Waxler, C., & Ridgeway, D. (1986). Learning to talk about emotions: A functionalist perspective. *Child Development, 57*, 529–548.

Brewin, C. R., Andrews, B., & Gotlib, I. H. (1993). Psychopathology and early experience: A reappraisal of retrospective reports. *Psychological Bulletin, 133*, 82–98.

Brewin, C. R., Dalgleish, T., & Joseph, S. (1996). A dual representation theory of posttraumatic stress disorder. *Psychological Review, 103*, 670–686.

Brickman, P., Coates, D., & Janoff-Bulman, R. (1978). Lottery winners and accident victims: Is happiness relative? *Journal of Personality and Social Psychology, 37*, 917–927.

Briggs, J. (2000). Emotions have many faces: Inuit lessons. *Anthropologica (New Series), 42*, 157–164.

Briggs, J. L. (1970). *Never in anger: Portrait of an Eskimo family*. Cambridge, MA: Harvard University Press.

Broadbent, D. E., & Broadbent, M. (1988). Anxiety and attentional bias: State and trait. *Cognition and Emotion, 2*, 165–183.

Brody, L., R., & Hall, J. A. (2000). Gender, emotion, and expression. In M. Lewis & J. Haviland-Jones (Eds.), *Handbook of emotions, second edition* (pp. 338–349). New York: Guilford.

Broidy, L. M., Nagin, D., Tremblay, R. E., et al. (2003). Developmental trajectories of childhood disruptive behaviors and adolescent delinquency: A six-site, cross-national study. *Developmental Psychology, 39*, 222-245.

Brooks-Gunn, J., & Lewis, M. (1982). Affective exchanges between normal and handicapped infants and their mothers. In T. Field & A. Fogel (Eds.), *Emotion and early interaction*. Hillsdale, NJ: Erlbaum.

Brown, D. E. (1991). *Human universals*. Philadelphia: Temple University Press.

Brown, G. W., & Harris, T. O. (1978). *Social origins of depression: A study of psychiatric disorder in women*. London: Tavistock.

Brown, G. W., & Harris, T. O. (1993). Aetiology of anxiety and depressive disorders in an inner-city population. 1. Early adversity. *Psychological Medicine, 23*, 143-154.

Brown, G. W., & Moran, P. (1994). Clinical and psychosocial origins of chronic depressive episodes. 1. A community study. *British Journal of Psychiatry, 165*, 447-456.

Brown, G. W., & Moran, P. (1998). Emotion and the etiology of depressive disorders. In W. F. Flack & J. D. Laird (Eds.), *Emotions in psychopathology: Theory and research* (pp. 171-184). New York: Oxford University Press.

Brown, G. W., & Rutter, M. (1966). The measurement of family activities and relationships. *Human Relations, 19*, 241-262.

Brown, G. W., Adler, Z., & Bifulco, A. (1988). Life events, difficulties and recovery from chronic depression. *British Journal of Psychiatry, 152*, 487-498.

Brown, G. W., Birley, J. L. T., & Wing, J. K. (1972). Influence of family life on the course of schizophrenic disorders. *British Journal of Psychiatry, 121*, 241-258.

Brown, G. W., Harris, T. O., & Hepworth, C. (1995). Loss, humiliation and entrapment among women developing depression: A patient and non-patient comparison. *Psychological Medicine, 25*, 7-21.

Brown, G. W., Lemyre, L., & Bifulco, A. (1992). Social factors and recovery from anxiety and depressive disorders: A test of specificity. *British Journal of Psychiatry, 161*, 44-54.

Bruner, J. (1986). *Actual minds, possible worlds*. Cambridge, MA: Harvard University Press.

Bruner, J. S. (2003). Do not pass go. Review of *The culture of control: Crime and social order in contemporary society*, by David Garland. *New York Review of Books, 50*, September 25.

Buck, R. (1999). The biology of affects: A typology. *Psychological Review, 106*, 301-336.

Buck, R. (2002). The genetics and biology of true love: Prosocial biological affects and the left hemisphere. *Psychological Review, 109*, 739-744.

Buck, R., & Ginsberg, B. E. (1997). Communicative genes and the evolution of empathy: Selfish and social emotions as voices of selfish and social genes. In C. S. Carter, I. I. Lederhendler, & B. Kirkpatrick (Eds.), *The integrative neurobiology of affiliation* (pp. 481-483). New York: New York Academy of Sciences.

Buck, R. W., & Parke, R. D. (1972). Behavioral and physiological response to the presence of a friendly or neutral person in two types of stressful situations. *Journal of Personality and Social Psychology, 24*, 143-153.

Burgess, E. W., & Wallin, P. (1953). *Engagement and marriage*. Philadelphia, PA: Lippincott.

Burnam, M. A., Stein, J. A., Golding, J. M., Siegel, J. M., Sorenson, S. B., Forsythe, A. B., & Telles, C. A. (1988). Sexual assault and mental disorders in a community population. *Journal of Consulting and Clinical Psychology, 56*, 843-850.

Buss, A. H., & Plomin, R. (1984). *Temperament: Early developing personality traits*. Hillsdale, NJ: Erlbaum.

Buss, D. (1992). Mate preference mechanisms: Consequences for partner choice and intrasexual competition. In J. H. Barkow, L. Cosmides, & J. Tooby (Eds.), *The adapted mind* (pp. 267-288). New York: Oxford University Press.

Buss, D. M. (1994). *The evolution of desire: Strategies of human mating*. New York: Basic Books.

Buss, D. M., Larsen, R., Westen, D., & Semmelroth, J. (1992). Sex differences in jealousy: Evolution, physiology, and psychology. *Psychological Science, 3*, 251-255.

Buss, K. A., & Kiel, E. J. (2004). Comparison of sadness, anger, and fear facial expressions when toddlers look at their mothers. *Child Development, 75*, 1761-1773.

Butler, E. A., Egloff, B., Wilhelm, F. H., Smith, N. C., Erickson, E. A., & Gross, J. J. (2003). The social consequences of expressive suppression. *Emotion, 3*, 48-67.

Butzlaff, R. L., & Hooley, J. M. (1998). Expressed emotion and psychiatric relapse: A meta-analysis. *Archives of General Psychiatry, 55*, 547-552.

Cacioppo, J. T., & Gardner, W. L. (1999). Emotion. *Annual Review of Psychology, 50*, 191–214.

Cacioppo, J. T., Klein, D. J., Berntson, G. C., & Hatfield, E. (1993). The psychophysiology of emotion. In M. Lewis & J. M. Haviland (Eds.), *Handbook of emotions* (pp. 119–142). New York: Guilford.

Caine, S., & Koob, G. (1993). Modulation of cocaine self-administration in the rat through D-3 dopamine receptors. *Science, 260*, 1814–1816.

Calhoun, C., & Solomon, R. (1984). What is an emotion? In C. Calhoun & R. Solomon (Eds.), *Readings in philosophical psychology*. New York: Oxford University Press.

Calkins, S. D., Dedmon, S. E., & Gill, K. L. (2002). Frustration in infancy: Implications for emotion regulation, physiological processes, and temperament. *Infancy, 3*, 175–197.

Campos, J. J., Barrett, K. C., Lamb, M. E., Goldsmith, H. H., & Stenberg, C. (1983). Socioemotional development. In M. M. Haith & J. J. Campos (Eds.), *Handbook of child psychology* (pp. 783–915). New York: Wiley.

Campos, J. J., Campos, R. G., & Barrett, K. C. (1989). Emergent themes in the study of emotional development and emotion regulation. *Developmental Psychology, 25*, 394–402.

Campos, J. J., Frankel, C. B., & Camras, L. (2004). On the nature of emotion regulation. *Child Development, 75*, 377–394.

Campos, J. J., Kermoian, R., & Zumbahlen, M. R. (1992). Socioemotional transformations in the family system following infant crawling onset. In N. Eisenberg & R. A. Fabes (Eds.), *Emotion and its regulation in early development. (New Directions in Child Development No. 55)* (pp. 25–40). San Francisco: Jossey-Bass.

Campos, J. J., Thein, S., & Owen, D. (2003). A Darwinian legacy to understanding human infancy: Emotional expressions as behavior regulators. *Annals of the New York Academy of Sciences, 1000*, 1–26.

Camras, L. (2000). Surprise! Facial expressions can be coordinative motor structures. In M. D. Lewis & I. Granic (Eds.), *Emotion, development, and self-organization: Dynamic systems approaches to emotional development* (pp. 101–124). New York: Cambridge University Press.

Camras, L. A. (1992). Expressive development and basic emotions. *Cognition and Emotion, 6*, 269–283.

Camras, L., Meng, Z., Ujiie, T., et al. (2002). Observing emotion in infants: Facial expression, body behavior, and rater judgments of responses to an expectancy-violating event. *Emotion, 2*, 179–193.

Canli, T., Zhao, Z., Desmond, J. E., et al. (1999). FMRI identifies a network of structures correlated with retention of positive and negative emotional memory. *Psychology, 27*, 441–462.

Cannon, W. B. (1927). The James–Lange theory of emotion: A critical examination and an alternative theory. *American Journal of Psychology, 39*, 106–124.

Cannon, W. B. (1929). *Bodily changes in pain, hunger, fear and rage* (2nd ed.). New York: Appleton.

Cannon, W. B. (1931). Again the James–Lange and the thalamic theories of emotion. *Psychological Review, 38*, 281–295.

Carlson, E., Sroufe, A., & Egeland, B. (2004). The construction of experience: A longitudinal study of representation and behavior. *Child Development, 75*, 66–83.

Carlson, N. (2004). *Foundations of physiological psychology* (6th edn). Boston, MA: Allyn & Bacon.

Carlson, V., Barnett, D., Chichetti, D., & Braunwald, K. (1989). Disorganized/disoriented attachment relationships in maltreated infants. *Developmental Psychology, 25*, 525–531.

Carmichael, M. S., Dixen, J., Palmisano, G., et al. (1987). Plasma oxytocin increses in the human sexual response. *Journal of Clinical Endocrinology and Metabolism, 64*(1), 27–31.

Carr, A. (1999). *The handbook of child and adolescent clinical psychology: A contextual approach*. London: Routledge.

Carstensen, L. A. L., Fung, H., & Charles, S. (2003). Socioemotional selectivity theory and the regulation of emotion in the second half of life. *Motivation and Emotion, 27*, 103–123.

Carter, C. S. (1992). Oxytocin and sexual behavior. *Neuroscience and Biobehavioral Reviews, 16*, 131–144.

Carter, C. S. (1998). Neuroendocrine perspectives on social attachment and love. *Psychoneuroendocrinology, 23*(8), 779–818.

Carter, C. S., & Altemus, M. (1997). Integrative functions of lactational hormones in social behavior and stress management. In C. S. Carter & I. I. Lederhendler (Eds.), *Annals of The New York Academy of Sciences, 807*, 164–174.

Cartwright, F. F. (1977). *A social history of medicine*. London: Longman.

Caspi, A., Elder, G. H., & Bem, D. J. (1987). Moving against the world: Life course patterns of explosive children. *Developmental Psychology, 23*, 308–313.

Caspi, A., Elder, G. H., & Bem, D. J. (1988). Moving away from the world: Life-course patterns of shy children. *Developmental Psychology, 24*, 824–831.

Caspi, A., McClay, J., Moffitt, T. E., Mill, J., Martin, J., Craig, I. W., et al. (2002). Role of genotype in the cycle of violence in maltreated children. *Science, 297*, 851–854.

Caspi, A., Moffitt, T. E., Morgan, J., et al. (2004). Maternal expressed emotion predicts children's anti-social behavior problems: Using monozygotic-twin differences to identify environmental effects on behavior development. *Developmental Psychology, 40*, 149–162.

Caspi, A., Sugden, K., Moffitt, T. E., Taylor, A., Craig, I. W., Taylor, A., et al. (2003). Influence on life stress on depression: Moderation by a polymorphism in the 5-HTT gene. *Science, 301*, 386–389.

Cassidy, J. (1994). Emotion regulation: Influences of attachment relationships. In N. A. Fox (Ed.), *Monographs of the Society for Research in Child Development, 59 (Serial number 240). The development of emotion regulation* (pp. 228–249).

Chagnon, N. A. (1968). *Yanomamö: The fierce people*. New York: Holt, Rinehart & Winston.

Chaiken, S., Lieberman, A., & Eagly, A. H. (1989). Heuristic and systematic information processing within and beyond the persuasion context. In J. S. Uleman & J. A. Bargh (Eds.), *Unintended thought: Limits of awareness, intention and control* (pp. 212–252). New York: Guilford.

Chamberlain, P., & Reid, J. B. (1998). Comparison of two community alternatives to incarceration for chronic juvenile offenders. *Journal of Consulting and Clinical Psychology, 66*, 624–633.

Cherlin, A. J., Furstenberg, F. F., Chase-Lansdale, P. L., Kiernan, K. E., & Robins, P. K. (1991). Longitudinal studies of effects of divorce on children in Great Britain and the United States. *Science, 252*, 1386–1389.

Chess, S., & Thomas, A. (1990). Continuities and discontinuities in temperament. In L. Robins & M. Rutter (Eds.), *Straight and devious pathways from childhood to adulthood* (pp. 205–220). Cambridge: Cambridge University Press.

Chetkovich, K. (2004). Envy. In L. Menand (Ed.), *The best American essays, 2004* (pp. 9–29). Boston: Houghton Mifflin.

Cheyney, D. L., & Seyfarth, R. M. (1990). *How monkeys see the world: Inside the mind of another species*. Chicago: University of Chicago Press.

Chojnacki, J. T., & Walsh, W. B. (1990). Reliability and concurrent validity of the Sternberg Triangular Love Scale. *Psychological Reports, 67*, 219–224.

Chong, S. C. F., Werker, J. F., Russell, J. A., & Carroll, J. M. (2003). Three facial expressions mothers direct to their infants. *Infant and Child Development, 12*, 211–232.

Chrétien De Troyes (1180). The knight of the cart. In D. Staines (Ed.), *The complete romances of Chrétien de Troyes* (pp. 170–256). Bloomington: Indiana University Press (1990).

Christian, D. (2004). *Maps of time: An introduction to big history*. Berkeley, CA: University of California Press.

Christianson, S.-Å. (Ed.). (1992). *The handbook of emotion and memory: Research and theory*. Hillsdale, NJ: Erlbaum.

Christianson, S.-Å., & Loftus, E. (1991). Remembering emotional events: The fate of detailed information. *Cognition and Emotion, 5*, 81–108.

Cicchetti, D. (1990). The organization of socioemotional, cognitive, and representational development: Illustrations through a developmental psychopathology perspective on Down syndrome and child maltreatment. In R. A. Thompson (Ed.), *Socioemotional development* (pp. 259–366). Lincoln: University of Nebraska Press.

Cicchetti, D., & Beeghly, M. (1987). Symbolic development in maltreated youngsters: An organizational perspective. *New Directions for Child Development, 36*, 47–68.

Cicchetti, D., Ganiban, J., & Barnett, D. (1991). Contributions from the study of high-risk populations to understanding the development of emotion regulation. In J. Garber & K. A. Dodge (Eds.), *The development of emotion regulation and dysregulation* (pp. 15–48). New York: Cambridge University Press.

Cicero (45 BCE). *Tusulan Disputations*. Loeb ed., Cicero Vol. 18. (Ed. and Trans. J. E. King). Cambridge, MA: Harvard University Press (current edition 1927).

Clark, C. (1990). Emotions and the micropolitics in everyday life: Some patterns and paradoxes of "Place". In T. D. Kemper (Ed.), *Research agendas in the sociology of emotions* (pp. 305–334). Albany, NY: State University of New York Press.

Clark, M. S., & Finkel, E. J. (2005). Willingness to express emotion: The impact of relationship type, communal orientation, and their interaction. *Personal Relationships*, *12*, 169–180.

Clark, M. S., & Williamson, G. M. (1989). Moods and social judgments. In H. Wagner & A. Manstead (Eds.), *Handbook of social psychophysiology* (pp. 347–370). Chichester: Wiley.

Clark, M. S., Fitness, J., & Brissette, I. (2004). Understanding people's perceptions of relationships is crucial to understanding their emotional lives. In M. Brewer & M. Hewstone (Eds.), *Emotion and motivation. Perspectives on social psychology* (pp. 21–46). Malden, MA: Blackwell.

Clore, G. L. (1992). Cognitive phenomenology: Feelings and the construction of judgment. In L. L. Martin & A. Tesser (Eds.), *The construction of social judgment* (pp. 133–163). Hillsdale, NJ: Erlbaum.

Clore, G. L., & Gasper, K. (2000). Feeling is believing: Some affective influences on belief. In N. H. Frijda, A. S. R. Manstead, & S. Bem (Eds.), *Emotions and beliefs: How feelings influence thoughts* (pp. 10–44). Cambridge: Cambridge University Press.

Clore, G. L., & Parrott, W. G. (1991). Moods and their vicissitudes: Thoughts and feelings as information. In J. Foras (Ed.), *Emotion and social judgment* (pp. 107–123). Oxford: Pergamon.

Clore, G. L., Gasper, K., & Garvin, E. (2001). Affect as information. In J. P. Forgas (Ed.), *Handbook of affect and social cognition* (pp. 121–144). Nahwah, NJ: Erlbaum.

Cohen, S., & Wills, T. A. (1985). Stress, social support, and the buffering hypothesis. *Psychological Bulletin*, *98*, 310–357.

Cohen, S., Frank, E., Doyle, W. J., et al. (1998). Types of stressors that increase susceptibility to the common cold in healthy adults. *Health Psychology*, *17*, 214–223.

Cohn, J. F., & Tronick, E. Z. (1983). Three-month-old infants' reaction to simulated maternal depression. *Child Development*, *54*, 185–193.

Coie, J. D., & Kupersmidt, J. D. (1983). A behavioral analysis of emerging social status in boys' groups. *Child Development*, *54*, 1400–1416.

Cole, P. M., Martin, S. F., & Dennis, T. (2004). Emotion regulation as a scientific concept: Methodological challenges and directions for child development research. *Child Development*, *75*, 317–333.

Cole, P. M., Zahn-Waxler, C., Fox, N. A., et al. (1996). Individual differences in emotion regulation and behavior problems in preschool children. *Journal of Abnormal Psychology*, *105*, 518–529.

Collingwood, R. G. (1938). *The principles of art*. Oxford: Oxford University Press.

Collins, N. L. (1996). Working models of attachment: Implications for explanation, emotion, and behavior. *Journal of Personality and Social Psychology*, *71*, 810–832.

Collins, N. L., & Feeney, B. C. (2000). A safe haven: An attachment theory perspective on support seeking and caregiving in intimate relationships. *Journal of Personality and Social Psychology*, *78*, 1053–1073.

Collins, R. C. (1990). Stratification, emotional energy, and the transient emotions. In T. D. Kemper (Ed.), *Research agendas in the sociology of emotions* (pp. 27–57). Albany, NY: The State University of New York Press.

Conway, M. A. (1990). Conceptual representation of emotions: The role of autobiographical memories. In K. J. Gilhooly, M. T. G. Keene, R. H. Logie, & G. Erdos (Eds.), *Lines of thinking: Reflections on the psychology of thought, Vol. 2. Skills, emotion, creative processes, individual differences and teaching thinking*. Chichester: Wiley.

Conway, M. A., & Bekerian, D. A. (1987). Situational knowledge and emotions. *Cognition and Emotion*, *1*, 145–191.

Cooper, M. L., Shaver, P., & Collins, N. L. (1998). Attachment styles, emotion regulation, and adjustment in adolescence. *Journal of Personality and Social Psychology*, *74*, 1380–1397.

Corter, C. M., & Fleming, A. S. (1990). Maternal responsiveness in humans: Emotional, cognitive, and biological factors. *Advances in the Study of Behavior*, *19*, 83–136.

Costa, P. T., & McCrae, R. R. (1996). Mood and personality in adulthood. In C. Magai & S. H. McFadden (Eds.), *Handbook of emotion, adult development, and aging* (pp. 369–383). San Diego: Academic Press.

Costello, E. J. (1989). Developments in child psychiatric epidemiology. *Journal of the American Academy of Child and Adolescent Psychiatry*, *28*, 836–841.

Coyne, J. C. (1976). Depression and response to others. *Journal of Abnormal Psychology*, *85*, 186–193.

Coyne, J. C. (1994). Self-reported distress: Analog or ersatz depression. *Psychological Bulletin*, *116*, 29–45.

Coyne, J. C. (1999). Thinking interactionally about depression: A radical restatement. In T. Joiner & J. C. Coyne (Eds.), *The interactional nature of depression* (pp. 365–392). Washington, DC: American Psychological Association.

Coyne, J. C., & Gotlib, I. H. (1983). The role of cognition in depression: A critical appraisal. *Psychological Bulletin, 94,* 472–505.

Coyne, J. C., Kessler, R. C., Tal, M., Turnbull, J., Wortman, C., & Greden, J. (1987). Living with a depressed person: Burden and psychological distress. *Journal of Consulting and Clinical Psychology, 55,* 347–352.

Coyne, J. C., & Whiffen, V. E. (1995). Issues in personality as diathesis for depression: The case of sociotropy-dependency and autonomy-self criticism. *Psychological Bulletin, 118,* 358–378.

Craddock, N., & Jones, I. (1999). Genetics of bipolar disorder. *Journal of Medical Genetics, 36,* 585–594.

Crews, F. (1994, November 18). The unknown Freud. *New York Review of Books, 40,* 55–66.

Criss, M. M., Pettit, G. S., Bates, J. E., Dodge, K. A., & Lapp, A. L. (2002). Family adversity, positive peer relationships, and children's externalizing behavior: A longitudinal perspective on risk and resilience. *Child Development, 73,* 1220–1237.

Crockenberg, S. (1986). Are temperamental differences in babies associated with predictable differences in care giving? In J. V. Lerner & R. M. Lerner (Eds.), *New directions in child development: Temperament and social interaction in infants and children* (Vol. 31, pp. 53–74). San Francisco: Jossey-Bass.

Cronin, H. (1991). *The ant and the peacock.* New York: Cambridge University Press.

Crowell, J., Treboux, D., & Waters, E. (2002). Stability of attachment representations: The transition to marriage. *Developmental Psychology, 38,* 467–479.

Csikszentmihalyi, M. (1990). *Flow: The psychology of optimal experience.* New York: Harper Collins.

Csikszentmihalyi, M. (1996). *Creativity: Flow and the psychology of discovery and invention.* New York: Harper Collins.

Cummings, E. M. (1987). Coping with background anger in early childhood. *Child Development, 58,* 976–984.

Cummings, E. M., Davies, P. T., & Campbell, S. T. (2000). Developmental psychopathology and family process: Theory, research, and clinical implications. New York: Guilford.

Cupchik, G. C. (2002). The evolution of psychical distance as an aesthetic concept. *Culture and Psychology, 8,* 155–187.

Cupchik, G., & László, J. (1994). The landscape of time in literary reception: Character experience and narrative action. *Cognition and Emotion, 8,* 297–312.

Cutlip, W. D., II, & Leary, M. R. (1993). Anatomic and physiological bases of social blushing: Speculations from neurology and psychology. *Behavioural Neurology, 6,* 181–185.

Cyrnanowski, J. M., Frank, E., Young, E., & Shear, M. K. (2000). Adolescent onset of gender difference in lifetime rates of major depression – A theoretical model. *Archives of General Psychiatry, 57,* 21–27.

Dahl, H. (1991). The key to understanding change: Emotions as appetitive wishes and beliefs about their fulfillment. In J. D. Safran & L. S. Greenberg (Eds.), *Emotions, psychotherapy, and change* (pp. 130–165). New York: Guilford.

Daley, S. E., Hammen, C. L., & Rao, U. (2000). Predictors of first onset and recurrence of major depression in young women during the 5 years following high school graduation. *Journal of Abnormal Psychology, 109,* 525–533.

Daley, S. E., Hammen, C. L., Burge, D., et al. (1997). Predictors of the generation of episodic stress: A longitudinal study of late adolescent women. *Journal of Abnormal Psychology, 105,* 251–259.

Daly, M., & Wilson, M. (1997). Crime and conflict: Homicide in evolutionary psychological perspective. *Crime and Justice, 22,* 251–300.

Damasio, A. R. (1994). *Descartes' error.* New York: Putnam.

Damasio, A. R. (2003). *Looking for Spinoza: Joy, sorrow, and the feeling brain.* Orlando, FL: Harcourt.

Damasio, A. R., Grabowski, T. J., Bechara, A., et al. (2000). Subcortical and cortical brain activity during the feeling of self-generated emotions. *Nature Neuroscience, 3,* 1049–1056.

Damasio, H., Grabowski, T., Frank, R., Galaburda, A. M., & Damasio, A. R. (1994). The return of Phineas Gage: The skull of a famous patient yields clues about the brain. *Science, 264,* 1102–1105.

Dante Alighieri (1295). *La vita nuova (The new life)* (Ed. & Trans. B. Reynolds). Harmondsworth: Penguin (1969).

Dante Alighieri (1307–1321). *La divina comedia (The divine comedy)* (Ed. & Trans. M. Musa). Harmondsworth: Penguin (1984).

Darwin, C. (1859). *On the origin of species by means of natural selection.* London: Murray.

Darwin, C. (1872). *The expression of the emotions in man and animals*. Chicago: University of Chicago Press (current edition 1965).

Darwin, C. (1872/1998). *The expression of emotions in man and animals* (3rd ed.). New York: Oxford University Press.

Davidson, G. C., & Neale, J. M. (2001). *Abnormal psychology, eighth edition*. New York: Wiley.

Davidson, R. J. (1992). Anterior cerebral asymmetry and the nature of emotion. *Brain and Cognition, 20,* 125–151.

Davidson, R. J. (1993). The neuropsychology of affective style. In M. Lewis & J. M. Haviland (Eds.), *Handbook of emotions* (pp. 143–154). New York: Guilford.

Davidson, R. J., & Fox, N. A. (1989). Frontal brain asymmetry predicts infants' response to maternal separation. *Journal of Abnormal Psychology, 98,* 127–131.

Davidson, R. J., & Irwin, W. (1999). The functional neuroanatomy of emotion and affective style. *Trends in Cognitive Sciences, 3,* 11–21.

Davidson, R. J., Ekman, P., Saron, C. D., Senulis, J. A., & Friesen, W. V. (1990). Approach–withdrawal and cerebral asymmetry: Emotional expression and brain physiology I. *Journal of Personality and Social Psychology, 58,* 330–341.

Davidson, R. J., Jackson, D. C., & Kalin, N. H. (2000). Emotion, plasticity, context, and regulation. *Psychological Bulletin, 126,* 890–906.

Davidson, R. J., Kabat-Zinn, J., Schumacher, J., Rosenkrantz, M., Muller, D., Santorelli, S. F., et al. (2003a). Alterations in brain and immune function produced by mindfulness meditation. *Psychosomatic Medicine, 65,* 564–570.

Davidson, R. J., Pizzagalli, D., Nitschke, J. B., & Kalin, N. H. (2003b). Parsing the subcomponents of emotion and disorders: Perspectives from affective neuroscience. In R. J. Davidson, K. Scherer & H. H. Goldsmith (Eds.), *Handbook of affective sciences* (pp. 8–24). New York: Oxford University Press.

Dawkins, R. (1986). *The blind watchmaker*. New York: Norton.

De Castro, B. O., Veerman, J. W., Koops, W., et al. (2002). Hostile attribution of intent and aggressive behavior: A meta-analysis. *Child Development, 73,* 916–934.

De Lorris, G., & De Meun, J. (1237–1277). *The romance of the rose* (H. W. Robbins, Trans.). New York: Dutton (current edition 1962).

De Sousa, R. (1987). *The rationality of emotions*. Cambridge, MA: MIT Press.

De Sousa, R. (2004). Emotions: What I know, what I'd like to think I know, and what I'd like to think. In R. C. Solomon (Ed.), *Thinking about feeling: Contemporary philosophers on emotions* (pp. 61–75). New York: Oxford University Press.

De Waal, F. (1982). *Chimpanzee politics*. New York: Harper & Row.

De Waal, F. (1989). Peacemaking among primates. Cambridge, MA: Harvard University Press.

De Waal, F. (1996). *Good natured: The origins of right and wrong in humans and other animals*. Cambridge, MA: Harvard University Press.

De Waal, F. B. M. (1995). Bonobo sex and society. *Scientific American, 272*(March), 82–88.

De Waal, F. B. M. (2000). Primates: A natural heritage of conflict resolution. *Science, 289,* 586–590.

De Waal, F., & Lanting, F. (1997). *Bonobo: The forgotten ape*. Berkeley, CA: University of California Press.

Denham, S. A. (1986). Social cognition, prosocial behavior, and emotion in preschoolers: Contextual validation. *Child Development, 57,* 194–201.

Denham, S. A., Blair, K. A., DeMulder, E., et al. (2003). Preschool emotional competence: Pathway to social competence? *Child Development, 74,* 238–256.

Dentan, R. K. (1968). *The Semai: A nonviolent people of Malaya*. New York: Holt, Rinehart & Winston.

Depue, R. A., & Collins, P. F. (1999). Neurobiology of the structure of personality: Dopamine, facilitation of incentive motivation, and extraversion. *Behavioral and Brain Sciences, 22,* 491–569.

Depue, R. A., & Morrone-Strupinsky, J. V. (2005 in press). A neurobehavioral model of affiliative bonding: Implications for conceptualizing a human trait of affection. *Behavioral and Brain Sciences.*

Descartes, R. (1649). Passions of the soul. In E. L. Haldane & G. R. Ross (Eds.), *The philosophical works of Descartes*. New York: Dover (current edition 1911).

DeOliveira, C. A., Moran, G., & Pederson, D. R. (2005). Understanding the link between maternal adult attachment classifications and thoughts and feelings about emotions. *Attachment and Human Development, 7,* 153–170.

DeSteno, D. A., & Salovey, P. (1996). Jealousy and the characteristics of one's rival: A self-evaluation maintenance perspective. *Personality and Social Psychology, 22,* 920–932.

DeSteno, D., Petty, R. E., Rucker, D. D., Wegener, D. T., & Braverman, J. (2004). Discrete emotions and persuasion: The role of emotion-induced expectancies. *Journal of Personality and Social Psychology, 86*, 43–56.

DeSteno, D., Petty, R., Wegener, D., & Rucker, D. (2000). Beyond valence in the perception of likelihood: The role of emotion specificity. *Journal of Personality and Social Psychology, 78*, 397–416.

Dewey, J. (1895). The theory of emotions: II. The significance of emotions. *Psychological Review, 2*, 13–32.

Di Ciano, P., Blaha, C. D., & Phillips, A. G. (1998). Conditioned changes in dopamine oxidation currents in the nucleus accumbens of rats by stimuli paired with self-administration or yoked-administration of d-amphetamine. *European Journal of Neuroscience, 10*(3), 1121–1127.

Diamond, J. (1997). *Guns, germs, and steel: The fates of human societies*. New York: Norton.

Diamond, J. (2005). *Collapse: How societies choose to fail or succeed*. New York: Viking.

Diamond, L. M. (2003). What does sexual orientation orient?: A biobehavioral model distinguishing romantic love and sexual desire. *Psychological Review, 110*(1), 173–192.

Diener, E., & Biswas-Diener, R. (2002). Will money increase subjective well-being? A literature review and guide to needed research. *Social Indicators Research, 57*, 119–169.

Diener, E., Oishi, S., & Lucas, R. E. (2003). Personality, culture, and subjective well-being: Emotional and cognitive evaluations of life. *Annual Review of Psychology, 2003, 54*, 403–425.

Dimberg, U., & Öhman, A. (1996). Behold the wrath: Psychophysiological responses to facial stimuli. *Motivation and Emotion, 20*, 149–182.

Dimberg, U., Thunberg, M., & Elmehed, K. (2000). Unconscious facial reactions to emotional facial expressions. *Psychological Science, 11*, 86–89.

Dimberg, U., Thunberg, M., & Grunedal, S. (2002). Facial reactions to emotional stimuli: Automatically controlled emotional responses. *Cognition and Emotion, 16*, 449–471.

Dishion, T. J., McCord, J., & Poulin, F. (1999). When interventions harm: Peer groups and problem behavior. *American Psychologist, 54*, 755–764.

Dix, T. (1991). The affective organization of parenting: Adaptive and maladaptive processes. *Psychological Bulletin, 110*, 3–25.

Djikic, M., & Oatley, K. (2004). Love and personal relationships: Navigating on the border between the ideal and the real. *Journal for the Theory of Social Behaviour, 34*, 199–209.

Dodge, K. A., & Coie, J. D. (1987). Social-information-processing factors in reactive and proactive aggression in children's peer groups. *Journal of Personality and Social Psychology, 53*, 1146–1158.

Dodge, K. A., Bates, J. E., & Pettit, G. S. (1990). Mechanisms in the cycle of violence. *Science, 250*, 1678–1683.

Dodge, K. A., Lansford, J. E., Burks, V. S., et al. (2003). Peer rejection and social information-processing factors in the development of aggressive behavior problems in children. *Child Development, 74*, 374–393.

Dohrenwend, B. P., Link, B. C., Kern, R., Shrout, P. E., & Markowitz, J. (1990). Measuring life events: The problem of variablity within event categories. *Stress Medicine, 6*, 179–187.

Doi, T. (1973). *The anatomy of dependence* (J. Beste, Trans.). Tokyo: Kodansha.

Doll, R., & Peto, R. (1981). *The causes of cancer*. Oxford: Oxford University Press.

Dollard, J., Doob, L. W., Miller, N. E., Mowrer, O. H., & Sears, R. R. (1939). *Frustration and aggression*. New Haven: Yale University Press.

Dostoevsky, F. (1955). Introduction by D. Magarshak (Trans.). *The Idiot*. Harmondsworth: Penguin.

Dowdney, G., & Coyne, J. C. (1990). Children of depressed parents. *Psychological Bulletin, 108*, 50–76.

Dozois, D. J. A., & Dobson, K. S. (Eds.). (2004). *The prevention of anxiety and depression: Theory, research, and practice*. Washington, DC: American Psychological Association.

Drevets, W. C., Videen, T. O., Price, J. L. Preskorn, S. H., Carmichael, S. T., & Raichle, M. E. (1992). A functional anatomical study of unipolar depression. *Journal of Neuroscience, 12*, 3628–3641.

Dumont, M., Yzerbyt, V. Y., Wigboldus, D., & Gordijn, E. (2003). Social categorization and fear reactions to the September 11th terrorist attacks. *Personality and Social Psychology Bulletin, 29*, 1509–1520.

Dunbar, K. (1993). How scientists really reason: Scientific reasoning in real-world laboratories. In R. J. Sternberg & J. Davidson (Eds.), *Mechanisms of insight*. Cambridge, MA: MIT Press.

Dunbar, R. I. M. (1993). Coevolution of neocortical size, group size, and language in humans. *Behavioral and Brain Sciences, 16*, 681–735.

Dunbar, R. I. M. (1996). *Grooming, gossip and the evolution of language*. London: Faber & Faber.

Dunbar, R. I. M. (2001). Brains on two legs: Group size and the evolution of intelligence. In F. B. M. De Waal (Ed.), *Tree of origin: What primate behavior can tell us about human social evolution* (pp. 173–191). Cambridge, MA: Harvard University Press.

Dunbar, R. I. M. (2003). The social brain: Mind, language, and society in evolutionary perspective. *Annual Review of Anthropology, 32*, 163–181.

Dunbar, R. I. M. (2004). *The human story: A new history of mankind's evolution*. London: Faber.

Dunn, J. (1987). Understanding feelings: The early stages. In J. Bruner & H. Haste (Eds.), *Making sense: The child's construction of the world* (pp. 26–40). London: Methuen.

Dunn, J. (2000). Mind-reading, emotion understanding, and relationships. *International Journal of Behavioral Development, 24*, 142–144.

Dunn, J. (2003). Emotional development in early childhood: A social relationship perspective. In R. J. Davidson, K. R. Scherer, & H. H. Goldsmith (Eds.), *Handbook of affective sciences* (pp. 332–346). New York: Oxford University Press.

Dunn, J. (2004). The development of individual differences in understanding emotion and mind: Antecedents and sequillae. In N. H. Frijda, A. S. R. Manstead, & A. Fischer (Eds.), *Feelings and emotions: The Amsterdam Symposium* (pp. 303–320). New York: Cambridge University Press.

Dunn, J., & Brown, J. (1991). Relationships, talk about feelings, and the development of affect regulation in early childhood. In J. Garber & K. Dodge (Eds.), *The development of emotion regulation and dysregulation* (pp. 89–108). Cambridge: Cambridge University Press.

Dunn, J., Bretherton, I., & Munn, P. (1987). Conversations about feeling states between mothers and their young children. *Developmental Psychology, 23*, 132–139.

Dunn, J., Brown, J., & Beardsall, L. (1991). Family talk about feeling states and children's later understanding of others' emotions. *Developmental Psychology, 27*(3), 448–455.

Dutton, D. G., & Aron, A. P. (1974). Some evidence for heightened sexual attraction under conditions of high anxiety. *Journal of Personality and Social Psychology, 30*, 510–517.

Eagly, A., & Wood, W. (1999). The origins of sex differences in human behavior: Evolved dispositions versus social roles. *American Psychologist, 54*, 408–423.

Eales, M. J. (1992). Shame and guilt: Instincts and their vicissitudes in human evolution. Unpublished manuscript.

Easterling, D. V., & Leventhal, H. (1989). Contribution of concrete cognition to emotion: Neutral symptoms as elicitors of worry about cancer. *Journal of Applied Psychology, 74*, 787–796.

Edelbrock, C., & Costello, A. J. (1988). Structured psychiatric interviews for children. In M. Rutter, A. H. Tuma, & I. S. Lann (Eds.), *Assessment and diagnosis in child psychopathology* (pp. 87–112). London: David Fulton.

Edelbrock, C., Costello, A. J., Dulcan, M. K., Kalas, R., & Conover, N. C. (1985). Age differences in the reliability of the psychiatric interview of the child. *Child Development, 56*, 265–275.

Edelmann, R. J. (1990). Embarrassment and blushing: A component-process model, some initial descriptive and cross-cultural data. In W. R. Crozier (Ed.), *Shyness and embarrassment: Perspectives from social psychology* (pp. 205–229). Cambridge: Cambridge University Press.

Edelmann, R. J., & Hampson, S. E. (1979). Changes in nonverbal behavior during embarrassment. *British Journal of Social and Clinical Psychology, 18*, 385–390.

Edelmann, R. J., & Hampson, S. E. (1981). Embarrassment in dyadic interaction. *Social Behavior and Personality, 9*, 171–177.

Eibl-Eibesfeldt, I. (1970). *Ethology: The biology of behavior*. New York: Holt, Rinehart & Winston.

Eibl-Eibesfeldt, I. (1979). *The biology of peace and war* (E. Mosbacher, Trans.). New York: Viking.

Eibl-Eibesfeldt, I. (1989). *Human ethology*. New York: Aldine de Gruyter.

Eich, E., & Macaulay, D. (2000). Fundamental factors in mood-dependent memory. In J. Forgas (Ed.), *Feeling and thinking: The role of affect in social cognition* (pp. 109–130). New York: Cambridge University Press.

Eich, E., Macaulay, D., & Ryan, L. (1994). Mood dependent memory for events of the personal past. *Jounrnal of Experimental Psycholoigy (General), 123*, 201–215.

Eisenberg, N. (1992). *The caring child*. Cambridge, MA: Harvard University Press.

Eisenberg, N. (2000). Empathy and sympathy. In M. Lewis & J. M. Haviland-Jones (Eds.), *Handbook of emotions, second edition* (pp. 677–691). New York: Guilford.

Eisenberg, N., & Fabes, R. A. (1994). Mothers' reactions to children's negative emotions: Relations to children's temperament and anger behavior. *Merrill-Palmer Quarterly, 40*, 138–156.

Eisenberg, N., Fabes, R. A., Miller, P. A., Fultz, J., Shell, R., Mathy, R. M., & Reno, R. R. (1989). Relation of sympathy and distress to prosocial behavior: A multimethod study. *Journal of Personality and Social Psychology, 57*, 55–66.

Eisenberg, N., Sadovsky, A., Spinrad, T., et al. (2005). The relations of problem behavior status to children's negative emotionality, effortful control, and impulsivity: Concurrent relations and prediction of change. *Developmental Psychology, 41*, 193–211.

Ekman, P. (1972). Universals and cultural differences in facial expressions of emotion. In J. Cole (Ed.), *Nebraska Symposium on Motivation, 1971* (pp. 207–283). Lincoln: University of Nebraska Press.

Ekman, P. (1984). Expression and the nature of emotion. In K. R. Scherer & P. Ekman (Eds.), *Approaches to emotion* (pp. 319–344). Hillsdale, NJ: Erlbaum.

Ekman, P. (1992). An argument for basic emotions. *Cognition and Emotion, 6*, 169–200.

Ekman, P. (1993). Facial expression and emotion. *American Psychologist, 48*, 384–392.

Ekman, P. (1994). Strong evidence for universals in facial expressions: A reply to Russell's mistaken critique. *Psychological Bulletin, 115*, 268–287.

Ekman, P., & Friesen, W. V. (1969). The repertoire of nonverbal behavior: categories, origins, usage and coding. *Semiotica, 1*, 49–98.

Ekman, P., & Friesen, W. V. (1971). Constants across culture in the face and emotion. *Journal of Personality and Social Psychology, 17*, 124–129.

Ekman, P., & Friesen, W. V. (1975). *Pictures of facial affect*. Palo Alto, CA: Consulting Psychologists Press.

Ekman, P., & Friesen, W. V. (1978). *Facial action coding system: A technique for the measurement of facial movement*. Palo Alto, CA: Consulting Psychologists Press.

Ekman, P., & Friesen, W. V. (1984). *Emotion facial action coding system (EM-FACS)*. Obtainable from Paul Ekman, University of California, San Franciso.

Ekman, P., Friesen, W. V., & Ellsworth, P. C. (1982). *Emotion in the human face*. Cambridge: Cambridge University Press.

Ekman, P., Levenson, R. W., & Friesen, W. V. (1983). Autonomic nervous system activity distinguishes among emotions. *Science, 221*, 1208–1210.

Ekman, P., & Rosenberg, E. L. (1997). *What the face reveals*. New York: Oxford University Press.

Ekman, P., Sorenson, E. R., & Friesen, W. V. (1969). Pan-cultural elements in the facial displays of emotions. *Science, 164*, 86–88.

Eley, T. C., Lichtenstein, P., & Moffitt, T. E. (2003). A longitudinal behavioral genetic analysis of the etiology of aggressive and nonaggressive antisocial behavior. *Development and Psychopathology, 15*, 383–402.

Eley, T. C., Lichtenstein, P., & Stevenson, J. (1999). Sex differences in the etiology of aggressive and nonaggressive antisocial behavior: Results from two twin studies. *Child Development, 70*, 155–168.

Elfenbein, H. A., & Ambady, N. (2002). On the universality and cultural specificity of emotion recognition: A meta-analysis. *Psychological Bulletin, 128*, 203–235.

Elfenbein, H. A., & Ambady, N. (2003). Universals and cultural differences in recognizing emotions. *Current Directions in Psychological Science, 12*, 159–164.

Elias, N. (1939). *The history of manners: The civilization process, Vol. 1* (E. Jephcott, Trans.). New York: Pantheon (1978).

Eliot, G. (1860). *The mill on the Floss*. Edinburgh: Blackwood (current edition Penguin, 1973).

Eliot, G. (1871–1872). *Middlemarch: A study of provincial life*. Edinburgh: Blackwood (current edition Penguin, 1965).

Elliott, R., Greenberg, L. S., & Lietaer, G. (2004). Research on experiential psychotherapies. In M. J. Lambert (Ed.), *Bergin and Garfield's handbook of psychotherapy and behavior change, fifth edition* (pp. 493–539). New York: Wiley.

Ellis, H. B., Fisher, P. A., & Zaharie, S. (2004). Predictors of disruptive behavior, developmental delays, anxiety, and affective symptomatology among institutionally reared Romanian children. *Journal of the American Academy of Child and Adolescent Psychiatry, 43*, 1283–1292.

Ellsworth, P. (1991). Some implications of cognitive appraisal theories of emotion. In K. T. Strongman (Ed.), *International review of studies on emotion* (pp. 143–161). Chichester: Wiley.

Ellsworth, P. C., & Smith, C. A. (1985). Patterns of cognitive appraisal in emotion. *Journal of Personality and Social Psychology, 48*, 813–838.

Ellsworth, P. C., & Smith, C. A. (1988). From appraisal to emotion: Differences among unpleasant feelings. *Motivation and Emotion, 12*, 271–302.

Elmadjian, F. J., Hope, M., & Lamson, E. T. (1957). Excretion of E and NE in various emotional states. *Journal of Clinical Endocrinology, 17*, 608–620.

El-Sheikh, M., & Elmore-Staton, L. (2004). The link between marital conflict and child adjustment: Parent–child conflict and perceived attachments as mediators, potentiators, and mitigators of risk. *Development and Psychopathology, 16*, 631–648.

Elster, J. (1999). *Alchemies of the mind: Rationality and the emotions*. Cambridge: Cambridge University Press.

Emde, R. N., Izard, C., Huebner, R., Sorce, J. F., & Klinnert, M. (1985). Adult judgments of infant emotions: Replication studies within and across laboratories. *Infant Behavior and Development, 8*, 79–88.

Emde, R. N., Plomin, R., Robinson, J., Corley, R., DeFries, J., Fulker, D. W., Reznick, J. S., Campos, J., Kagan, J., & Zahn-Waxler, C. (1992). Temperament, emotion, and cognition at fourteen months: The MacArthur Longitudinal Twin Study. *Child Development, 63*, 1437–1455.

Emery, N. J., & Amaral, D. G. (2000). The role of the amygdala in primate social cognition. In R. D. Lane & L. Nadel (Eds.), *Cognitive neuroscience of emotion* (pp. 156–191). New York: Oxford University Press.

Emery, R. E. (1988). *Marriage, divorce and children's adjustment*. Newbury Park, CA: Sage.

Emery, R. E., Fincham, F. D., & Cummings, E. M. (1992). Parenting in context: The role of the family in child psychotherapy. *Journal of Consulting and Clinical Psychology, 60*, 909–912.

Emmons, R. A., & Diener, E. (1985). Personality correlates of subjective well-being. *Personality and Social Psychology Bulletin, 11*(1), 89–97.

Emmons, R. A., & Diener, E. (1986). An interactional approach to the study of personality and emotion. *Journal of Personality, 54*(2), 371–384.

Epictetus (c.100). *Discourses and Encheiridion* (English translation by W. A. Oldfather). Cambridge, MA: Loeb-Harvard University Press (1998).

Erikson, E. H. (1950). *Childhood and society*. London: Penguin (reissued 1965).

Erikson, E. H. (1959). Identity and the life cycle. *Psychological Issues, 1*, 1–171.

Eser, D., Di Michele, F., Zwanger, P., et al. (2005). Panic induction with cholecystokinin-tetrapeptide (CCK-4) increases plasma concentrations of the neuroactive steroid 3, 5 tetrahydrodeoxycorticosterone (3, 5-THDOC) in healthy volunteers. *Neuropsychopharmacology, 30*, 192–195.

Esquivel, L. (1992). *Like water for chocolate* (T. & C. Christensen, Trans.). New York: Doubleday.

Esser, G., Schmift, M. H., & Woerner, W. (1990). Epidemiology and course of psychiatric disorders in school aged children: Results of a longitudinal study. *Journal of Child Psychology and Psychiatry, 31*, 243–263.

Esteves, F., Dimberg, U., & Öhman, A. (1994). Automatically elicited fear: Conditioned skin conductance responses to masked facial expressions. *Cognition and Emotion, 8*, 393–413.

Etcoff, N. L. (1989). Asymmetries on recognition of emotion. In F. Boller & J. Grafman (Eds.), *Handbook of neuropsychology* (Vol. 3, pp. 363–382). Amsterdam: Elsevier.

Etcoff, N. L., & Magee, J. J. (1992). Categorical perception of facial expressions. *Cognition, 44*, 227–240.

Etcoff, N. L., Ekman, P., Frank, M., Magee, J., & Torreano, L. (1992). Detecting deception: Do aphasics have an advantage? Paper presented at conference of International Society for Research on Emotions, Carnegie Mellon University, Pittsburgh, PA, August.

Eysenck, H. J. (1990). Biological determinants of personality. In L. A. Pervin (Ed.), *Handbook of personality* (pp. 244–276). New York: Guilford.

Eysenck, M. W. (1992). *Anxiety: The cognitive perspective*. Howe: Erlbaum.

Fabes, R. A., Eisenberg, N., Nyman, M., & Michealieu, Q. (1991). Young children's appraisals of others' spontaneous emotional reactions. *Developmental Psychology, 27*, 858–866.

Fagot, B. I., & Kavanagh, K. (1990). The prediction of antisocial behavior from avoidant attachment classifications. *Child Development, 61*, 864–873.

Fauber, R. L., & Long, N. (1992). Children in context: The role of the family in child psychotherapy. *Journal of Consulting and Clinical Psychology, 59*, 813–820.

Feeney, B. C., & Collins, N. L. (2001). Predictors of caregiving in adult intimate relationships: An attachment theoretical perspective. *Journal of Personality and Social Psychology, 80*, 972–994.

Fehr, B., & Russell, J. A. (1984). Concept of emotion viewed from a prototype perspective. *Journal of Experimental Psychology: General, 113*, 464–486.

Fehr, B., & Russell, J. A. (1991). The concept of love viewed from a prototype perspective. *Journal of Personality and Social Psychology, 60,* 425–438.

Feigeson, N., Park, J., & Salovey, P. (2001). The role of emotions in comparative negligence judgments. *Journal of Applied Social Psychology, 31,* 576–603.

Feldman, R., & Klein, P. S. (2003). Toddlers' self-regulated compliance to mothers, caregivers, and fathers: Implications for theories of socialization. *Developmental Psychology, 39,* 680–692.

Feldman-Barratt, L., Quigley, K. S., Bliss-Moreau, E., & Aronson, K. R. (2004). Interoceptive sensitivity and self-reports of emotional experience. *Journal of Personality and Social Psychology, 87,* 684–697.

Feldman-Barrett, L. (1997). The relationship among momentary emotional experiences, personality descriptions, and retrospective ratings of emotion. *Personality and Social Psychology Bulletin, 23,* 1100–1110.

Feldman-Barrett, L., & Barrett, D. J. (2001). Computerized experience-sampling: How technology facilitates the study of conscious experience. *Social Science Computer Review, 19,* 175–185.

Feldman-Barrett, L., & Russell, J. A. (1999). Structure of current affect. *Current Directions in Psychological Science, 8,* 10–14.

Fergusson, D. (2002). Tobacco consumption during pregnancy and its impact on child development. In R. E. Tremblay, R. G. Barr, & R. Peters (Eds.), *Encyclopaedia on early childhood development (online).* Montreal: Centre of Excellence for Early Childhood Development. www.excellence-earlychildhood.ca/documents/FergussonANGxp.pdf

Fernald, A. (1989). Intonation and communicative intent in mothers' speech to infants: Is the melody the message? *Child Development, 60,* 1497–1510.

Fernald, A. (1992). Human maternal vocalizations to infants as biologically relevant signals: An evolutionary perspective. In J. H. Barkow, L. Cosmides, & J. Tooby (Eds.), *The adapted mind* (pp. 391–428). New York: Oxford University Press.

Fernald, A. (1993). Approval and disapproval: Infant responsiveness to vocal affect in familiar and unfamiliar languages. *Child Development, 64,* 657–674.

Fernandez-Dols, J. M., & Ruiz-Belda, M. A. (1995). Are smiles a sign of happiness? Gold medal winners at the Olympic Games. *Journal of Personality and Social Psychology, 69,* 1113–1119.

Fernandez-Dols, J. M., & Ruiz-Belda, M. A. (1997). Spontaneous facial behavior during intense emotional episodes: Artistic truth and optical truth. In J. A. Russell & J. M. Fernandez-Dols (Eds.), *The psychology of facial expression* (pp. 255–294). Cambridge: Cambridge University Press.

Ferrari, M., & Koyama, E. (2002). Meta-emotions about anger and *amae. Consciousness and Emotion, 3,* 197–212.

Fiedler, K. (2001). Affective states trigger processes of assimilation and accommodation. In L. L. Martin & G. L. Clore (Eds.), *Theories of mood and cognition: A user's guidebook.* Mahwah, NJ: Lawrence Erlbaum Associates.

Field, J. (1934). *A life of one's own.* Harmondsworth: Penguin (current edition 1952).

Field, T. (1994). The effects of mother's physical and emotional unavailability on emotion regulation. In N. A. Fox (Ed.), *The development of emotion regulation. Monographs of the Society for Child Development, 59* (2–3, Serial No. 240), 208–227.

Field, T. (2001). *Touch.* Cambridge, MA: MIT Press.

Field, T., Healy, B., Goldstein, S., Perry, S., Bendell, D., Schanberg, S., Zimmerman, E. A., & Kuhn, C. (1988). Infants of depressed mothers show "depressed" behavior even with nondepressed adults. *Child Development, 59,* 1569–1579.

Finkenauer, C., Engels, R., & Baumeister, R. F. (2005). Parenting behaviour and adolescent behavioural and emotional problems: The role of self-control. *International Journal of Behavioral Development, 29,* 58–69.

Finlay-Jones, R. (1989). Anxiety. In G. W. Brown & T. O. Harris (Eds.), *Life events and illness* (pp. 95–112). London: Unwin Hyman.

Fiorino, D. F., Coury, A., & Phillips, A. G. (1997). Dynamic changes in nucleus accumbens dopamine efflux during the Coolidge effect in male rats. *Journal of Neuroscience, 17*(12), 4849–4855.

Fischer, A. H. (2000). *Gender and emotion: Social psychological perspectives.* Cambridge: Cambridge University Press.

Fischer, A. H., & Manstead, A. S. R. (2000). The relation between gender and emotions in different cultures. In A. H. Fischer (Ed.), *Gender and emotion: Social psychological perspectives* (pp. 71–93). Cambridge: Cambridge University Press.

Fisher, H. E. (1992). *Anatomy of love.* New York: Norton.

Fiske, A. P. (1991). *Structures of social life.* New York: Free Press.

Fiske, A. P., Kitayama, S., Markus, H. R., & Nisbett, R. E. (1998). The cultural matrix of social psychology. In D. T. Gilbert, S. T. Fiske, & G. Lindzey (Eds.), *Handbook of social psychology* (4th ed., pp. 915–981). Boston: McGraw-Hill.

Fivush, R. (1989). Exploring sex differences in the emotional content of mother–child conversations about the past. *Sex Roles, 20*, 675–691.

Flack, W. F., & Laird, J. D. (Eds.). (1998). *Emotions in psychopathology: Theory and research.* New York: Oxford University Press.

Flack, W. F., Laird, J. D., Cavallaro, L. A., & Miller, D. R. (1998). Emotional expression and experience: A psychosocial perspective on schizophrenia. In W. F. Flack & J. D. Laird (Eds.), *Emotions in psychopathology: Theory and research* (pp. 315–322). New York: Oxford University Press.

Fleming, A. S., & Corter, C. (1995). Psychobiology of maternal behavior in nonhuman mammals: Role of sensory, experiential and neural factors. In M. Bornstein (Ed.), *Handbook of parenting.* Hillsdale, NJ: Erlbaum.

Fleming, A. S., Kraemer, G. W., Gonzalez, A., et al. (2002). Mothering begets mothering: The transmission of behavior and its neurobiology across generations. *Pharmacology, Biochemistry and Behavior, 73*, 61–75.

Fleming, J. E., Boyle, M. E., & Offord, D. R. (1993). The outcome of adolescent depression in the Ontario Child Health Study follow-up. *Journal of the American Academy of Child and Adolescent Psychiatry, 32*, 28–33.

Florian, V., Mikulincer, M., & Bucholtz, I. (1995). Effects of adult attachment style on the perception and search for social support. *Journal of Psychology, 126*, 665–676.

Foa, E. B., Feske, U., Murdoch, T. B., Kozak, M. J., & McCarthy, P. R. (1991). Processing of threat-related information in rape-victims. *Journal of Abnormal Psychology, 100*, 156–162.

Fogel, A., Nwokah, E., Dedo, J. Y., Messinger, D., Dickson, K. L., Matusov, E., & Holt, S. A. (1992). Social process theory of emotion: A dynamic systems approach. *Social Development, 2*, 122–142.

Fonagy, P. (2000). The outcome of psychoanalysis: The hope of a future. *The Psychologist, 13*, 620–623.

Fonagy, P., Steele, H., & Steele, M. (1991). Maternal representations of attachment during preganancy predict the organization of infant–mother attachment at one year of age. *Child Development, 62*, 891–905.

Ford, T., Goodman, R., & Meltzer, H. (2004). The relative importance of child, family, school, and neighbourhood correlates of childhood psychiatric disorder. *Social Psychiatry and Psychiatric Epidemiology, 39*, 487–496.

Forgas, J. (1994). Sad and guilty. Affective influences on the explanation of conflict episodes. *Journal of Personality and Social Psychology, 66*, 56–68.

Forgas, J. (Ed.). (2000). *Feeling and thinking: The role of affect in social cognition.* Cambridge: Cambridge University Press.

Forgas, J., & Laham, S. M. (2005). The interaction between affect and motivation in social judgments and behavior. In J. Forgas, K. Williams, et al. (Eds.), *Social motivation: Conscious and unconscious processes* (pp. 168–193). New York: Cambridge University Press.

Forgas, J. P. (1995). Mood and judgment: The affect infusion model (AIM). *Psychological Review, 117*, 39–66.

Forgas, J. P. (1998). On being happy and mistaken: Mood effects on the fundamental attribution error. *Journal of Personality and Social Psychology, 75*(2), 318–331.

Forgas, J. P. (2003). Affective influences on attitudes and judgments. In R. J. Davidson, K. R. Scherer, & H. H. Goldsmith (Eds.), *Handbook of affective sciences* (pp. 596–618). New York: Oxford University Press.

Forgas, J. P., & Moylan, S. (1987). After the movies: The effect of mood on social judgments. *Personality and Social Psychology Bulletin, 13*, 465–477.

Foster, C. A., Witcher, B. S., Campbell, W. K., & Green, J. D. (1998). Arousal and attraction: Evidence for automatic and controlled processes. *Journal of Personality and Social Psychology, 74*, 86–101.

Fox, N., & Davidson, R. A. (1987). Electroencephalogram asymmetry in response to the approach of a stranger and maternal separation in 10-month-old infants. *Developmental Psychology, 23*, 233–240.

Fox, R. (1991). Aggression then and now. In M. H. Robinson & L. Tiger (Eds.), *Man and beast revisited* (pp. 81–93). Washington, DC: Smithsonian Institute Press.

Fraley, R. C., & Shaver, P. R. (1998). Airport separations: A naturalistic study of adult attachment dynamics in separating couples. *Journal of Personality and Social Psychology, 75*, 1198–1212.

Francis, D., & Meaney, M. J. (1999). Maternal care and the development of stress responses. *Development, 9*, 128–134.

Frank, M., Ekman, P., & Friesen, W. V. (1993). Behavioral markers and recognizability of the smile of enjoyment. *Journal of Personality and Social Psychology, 64,* 83-93.

Frank, M. G., & Stennet, J. (2001). The forced-choice paradigm and the perception of facial expressions of emotion. *Journal of Personality and Social Psychology, 80,* 75-85.

Frank, R. H. (1988). *Passions within reason: The strategic role of the emotions.* New York: W. W. Norton & Co.

Fredrickson, B. L. (1998). What good are positive emotions? *Review of General Psychology, 2,* 1-20.

Fredrickson, B. L. (2003). The value of positive emotions. *American Scientist, 91,* 330-335.

Fredrickson, B. L., & Branigan, C. (2005). Positive emotions broaden the scope of attention and thought-action repertoires. *Cognition and Emotion, 19,* 313-332.

Fredrickson, B. L., & Kahneman, D. (1993). Duration neglect in retrospective evaluations of affective episodes. *Journal of Personality and Social Psychology, 65,* 45-55.

Fredrickson, B. L., & Levenson, R. W. (1998). Positive emotions speed recovery from the cardiovascular sequelae of negative emotions. *Cognition and Emotion, 12,* 191-220.

Fredrickson, B. L., & Losada, M. (2005, in press). Positive affect and the complex dynamics of human flourishing. *American Psychologist.*

Fredrickson, B. L., Tugade, M. M., Waugh, C. E., & Larkin, G. R. (2003). What good are positive emotions in crises? A prospective study of resilience and emotions following the terrorist attacks on the United States on September 11th 2001. *Journal of Personality and Social Psychology, 84,* 365-376.

Freedman, J. L. (1978). *Happy people: What happiness is, who has it, and why.* New York: Harcourt Brace Jovanovich.

Freud, A. (1937). *The ego and the mechanisms of defense.* London: Hogarth Press.

Freud, S. (1901). *The psychopathology of everyday life. The Pelican Freud Library, Vol. 5* (J. Strachey, A. Richards, & A. Tyson, Eds., A. Tyson, Trans.). Harmondsworth: Penguin (current edition 1975).

Freud, S. (1904/1985). Psychopathic characters on the stage. In A. Dickson (Ed.), *The Pelican Freud Library, Vol. 14. Art and literature* (pp. 119-127). London, England: Penguin.

Freud, S. (1905). *Fragment of an analysis of a case of hysteria (Dora). The Pelican Freud Library, Vol. 9.*

Case histories, II (J. Strachey & A. Richards, Eds.). Harmondsworth: Penguin (current edition 1979).

Freud, S. (1920). *Beyond the pleasure principle. The Pelican Freud Library, Vol. 11. On metapsychology: The theory of psychoanalysis* (J. Strachey & A. Richards, Eds.) (pp. 1-64). Harmondsworth: Penguin (current edition 1974).

Freud, S., & Breuer, J. (1895). *Studies on hysteria. The Pelican Freud Library, Vol. 3* (J. Strachey, A. Strachey, & A. Richards, Eds.). Harmondsworth: Penguin (current edition 1974).

Frick, P. J., & Morris, A. S. (2004). Temperament and developmenal pathways to conduct problems. *Journal of Clinical Child and Adolescent Psychology, 33,* 54-68.

Fridlund, A. J. (1992). The behavioral ecology and sociality of human faces. *Review of Personality and Social Psychology, 13,* 90-121.

Fridlund, A. J. (1994). *Human facial expression: An evolutionary view.* San Diego: CA Academic Press.

Friesen, W. V. (1972). *Cultural differences in facial expressions in a social situation. An experimental test of the concept of display rules.* Doctoral thesis, University of California, San Francisco.

Frijda, N. (1993a). Moods, emotion episodes, and emotions. In M. Lewis & J. M. Haviland (Eds.), *Handbook of emotions* (pp. 381-403). New York: Guilford.

Frijda, N. H. (1986). *The emotions.* Cambridge: Cambridge University Press.

Frijda, N. H. (1988). The laws of emotion. *American Psychologist, 43,* 349-358.

Frijda, N. H. (1994). The Lex Talionis: On vengeance. In S. H. M. Van Goozen, N. E. Van der Poll, & J. A. Sergeant (Eds.), *Emotions: Essays on emotion theory* (pp. 263-289). Hillsdale, NJ: Erlbaum.

Frijda, N. H. (2005). Emotion experience. *Cognition and Emotion, 19,* 473-497.

Frijda, N. H. (Ed.). (1993b). Appraisal and beyond: The issue of cognitive determinants of emotion. *Cognition and Emotion, 7,* 225-387.

Frijda, N. H., & Mesquita, B. (1994). The social rules and functions of emotions. In S. Kitayama & H. R. Markus (Eds.), *Emotion and culture: Empirical studies of mutual influence* (pp. 51-87). Washington, DC: American Psychological Association.

Frijda, N. H., Kuipers, P., & ter Schure, E. (1989). Relations among emotion, appraisal, and emotional action readiness. *Journal of Personality and Social Psychology, 57,* 212-228.

Fyer, A., Mannuzza, S., & Coplan, J. D. (1996). Panic disorders and agoraphobia. In H. I. Kaplan & B. J. Saddock (Eds.), *Comprehensive textbook of psychiatry, 6th edition* (Vol. 1, pp. 1191–1204). Baltimore: Williams & Wilkins.

Gabbay, F. H., Krantz, D. S., Kop, W., et al. (1996). Triggers of myocardial ischemia during daily life in patients with coronary artery disease: Physical and mental activities, anger, and smoking. *Journal of the American College of Cardiology, 27*, 585–592.

Gabrielsson, A., & Juslin, P. N. (2003). Emotional expression in music. In R. Davidson, K. Scherer, & H. H. Goldsmith (Eds.), *Handbook of affective sciences* (pp. 503–534). London: Oxford University Press.

Galambos, N. L., Barker, E. T., & Almeida, D. M. (2003). Parents do matter: Trajectories of change in externalizing and internalizing problems in early adolescence. *Child Development, 74*, 578–594.

Galea, S., Ahern, J., Resnick, H., Kilpatrick, D., Bucuvalas, M., Gold, J., et al. (2002). Psychological sequelae of the September 11 terrorist attacks in New York City. *New England Journal of Medicine, 346*, 982–987.

Gallese, V., Keysers, C., & Rizzolatti, G. (2004). A unifying view of the basis of social cognition. *Trends in Cognitive Sciences, 8*, 396–403.

Garber, J., & Dodge, K. A. (1991). *The development of emotion regulation and dysregulation*. Cambridge: Cambridge University Press.

Garber, J., Braafladt, N., & Zeman, J. (1991). The regulation of sad affect: An information processing perspective. In J. Garber & K. A. Dodge (Eds.), *The development of emotion regulation and dysregulation* (pp. 208–240). Cambridge: Cambridge University Press.

Gardner, F., Ward, S., Burton, J., & Wilson, C. (2003). The role of mother–child joint play in the early development of children's conduct problems: A longitudinal observational study. *Social Development, 12*, 361–378.

Gardner, H. (1993). *Creating minds: An anatomy of creativity seen through the lives of Freud, Einstein, Picasso, Stravinsky, Eliot, Graham, and Ghandi*. New York: Basic Books.

Gasper, K., & Clore, G. L. (1998). The persistent use of negative affect by anxious individuals to estimate risk. *Journal of Personality and Social Psychology, 74*, 1350–1363.

Gasper, K., & Clore, G. L. (2000). Do you have to pay attention to your feelings in order to be influenced by them? *Personality and Social Psychology Bulletin, 26*, 698–711.

Gay, P. (1988). *Freud: A life for our time*. London: Dent.

Gazelle, H., & Rudolph, K. (2004). Moving toward and away from the world: Social approach and avoidance trajectories in anxious solitary youth. *Child Development, 75*, 829–849.

Gazzaniga, M. S. (1985). *The social brain*. New York: Basic Books.

Gazzaniga, M. S. (1988). Brain modularity: Towards a philosophy of conscious experience. In A. J. Marcel & E. Bisiach (Eds.), *Consciousness in contemporary science* (pp. 218–238). Oxford: Oxford University Press.

Gazzaniga, M. S., Ivry, R. B., & Mangun, G. R. (2002). *Cognitive neuroscience*. New York: Norton.

Geertz, C. (1973). *The interpretation of cultures*. New York: Basic Books.

George, C., Kaplan, N., & Main, M. (1985). The Berkeley Adult Attachment Interview. Unpublished protocol. Department of Psychology, University of California, Berkeley.

Gerard, J., & Buehler, C. (2004). Cumulative environmental risk and youth maladjustment: The role of youth attributes. *Child Development, 75*, 1832–1849.

Gewertz, D. (1981). A historical reconsideration of female dominance among the Chambri of Papua New Guinea. *American Ethnologist, 8*, 94–106.

Gibbs, E. L., Gibbs, F. A., & Fuster, B. (1948). Psychomotor epilepsy. *Archives of Neurology and Psychiatry, 60*, 331–339.

Gilbert, D. T., Brown, R. P., Pinel, E. C., & Wilson, T. D. (2000). The illusion of external agency. *Journal of Personality and Social Psychology, 79*, 690–700.

Gilbert, D. T., Pinel, E. C., Wilson, T. D., Blumberg, S. J., & Wheatley, T. P. (1998). Immune neglect: A source of durability bias in affective forecasting. *Journal of Personality and Social Psychology, 75*, 617–638.

Gilbert, P. (1998). What is shame? Some core issues and controversies. In P. Gilbert & B. Andrews (Eds.), *Shame: Interpersonal behavior, psychopathology, and culture* (pp. 3–38). New York: Oxford University Press.

Gilbert, P. (2000). The relationship of shame, social anxiety and depression: The role of the evaluation of social rank. *Clinical Psychology and Psychotherapy, 7*, 174–189.

Gilliom, M., & Shaw, D. S. (2004). Codevelopment of externalizing and internalizing problems in early childhood. *Development and Psychopathology*, *16*, 313–333.

Givens, D. B. (1983). *Love signals: How to attract a mate*. New York: Crown.

Gladwell, M. (2005). *Blink*. New York: Little, Brown & Co.

Glaser, R., Kiecolt-Glaser, J. K., Malarkey, W. B., & Sheridan, J. F. (1998). The influence of psychological stress on the immune response to vaccines. *Annals of the New York Academy of Sciences*, *840*, 656–663.

Gleick, J. (1988). *Chaos: Making of new science*. New York: Viking.

Glickman, S. E., & Schiff, B. B. (1967). A biological theory of reinforcement. *Psychological Review*, *74*, 81–109.

Gloaguen, V., Cottraux, J., Cucherat, M., & Blackburn, I. (1998). A meta-analyisis of the effects of cognitive therapy in depressed patients. *Journal of Affective Disorders*, *49*, 59–72.

Goethe, J. W. von (1774). *The sorrows of young Werther* (M. Hulse, Trans.). Harmondsworth: Penguin (current edition 1989).

Goffman, E. (1961). *Encounters: Two studies in the sociology of interaction*. Indianapolis, IN: Bobbs-Merrill.

Goldberg, S. (2000). *Attachment and development*. London: Arnold.

Goldberg, S., Grusec, J. E., & Jenkins, J. M. (1999). Confidence in protection: Arguments for a narrow definition of attachment. *Journal of Family Psychology*, *13*, 475–483.

Goldberg, S., MacKay, S., & Rochester, M. (1994). Affect, attachment, and maternal responsiveness. *Infant Behavior and Development*, *17*, 335–339.

Goldsmith, H. H. (1993). Temperament: Variability in developing emotion systems. In M. Lewis & J. M. Haviland (Eds.), *Handbook of emotions* (pp. 353–364). New York: Guilford.

Goldsmith, H. H. (2003). Genetics of emotional development. In R. Davidson, J. K. R. Scherer & H. H. Goldsmith (Eds.), *Handbook of affective sciences* (pp. 295–319). New York: Oxford University Press.

Goldsmith, H. H., & Alansky, J. A. (1987). Maternal and infant temperamental predictors of attachment: A meta-analytic review. *Journal of Consulting and Clinical Psychology*, *55*, 805–816.

Goleman, D. (1995). *Emotional intelligence*. New York: Bantam.

Golombok, S., & Fivush, R. (1994). *Gender development*. Cambridge: Cambridge University Press.

Gombrich, E. H. (1972). *The story of art* (12th ed.). London: Phaidon.

Gonzaga, G. C., Keltner, D., Londahl, E. A., & Smith, M. (2001). Love and the commitment problem in romantic relations and friendship. *Journal of Personality and Social Psychology*, *81*, 247–262.

Gonzaga, G. C., Turner, R., Campos, B., et al. (2005, in press). Romantic love and sexual desire: Distinctions in nonverbal display and neurohormonal response. *Emotion*.

Goodall, J. (1986). *The chimpanzees of Gombe: Patterns of behavior*. Cambridge, MA: Harvard University Press.

Goodall, J. (1992). Unusual violence in the overthrow of an alpha male chimpanzee at Gombe. In T. Nishida, W. C. McGrew, P. Marler, M. Pickford, & F. B. M. De Waal (Eds.), *Topics in primatology, Vol. 1. Human origins* (pp. 131–142). Tokyo: University of Tokyo Press.

Goodenough, F. C. (1931). *Anger in young children*. Minneapolis: University of Minnesota Press.

Gottfried, J. A., O'Doherty, J., & Dolan, R. J. (2003). Encoding predictive reward value in human amygdala and orbitofrontal cortex. *Science*, *301*, 1104–1107.

Gottman, J. M. (1993a). *Why marriages succeed or fail*. New York: Simon & Schuster.

Gottman, J. M. (1993b). The roles of conflict engagement, escalation, and avoidance in marital interaction: A longitudinal view of five types of couples. *Journal of Consulting and Clinical Psychology*, *61*, 6–15.

Gottman, J. M. (1998). *Raising an emotionally intelligent child*. New York: Simon & Schuster.

Gottman, J. M. (2002). *The marriage clinic: A scientifically based marital therapy*. New York: Norton.

Gottman, J. M., & Levenson, R. W. (1992). Marital processes predictive of later dissolution: Behavior, physiology and health. *Journal of Personality and Social Psychology*, *63*, 221–233.

Gottman, J. M., & Levenson, R. W. (2000). The timing of divorce: Predicting when a couple will divorce over a 14-year period. *Journal of Marriage and the Family*, *62*, 737–745.

Gottman, J. M., & Notarius, C. (2000). Decade review: Observing marital interaction. *Journal of Marriage and the Family*, *60*, 927–947.

Gottman, J. M., Coan, J., Carrere, S., & Swanson, C. (1998). Predicting marital happiness and stability from newlywed interactions. *Journal of Marriage and the Family, 60*, 5–22.

Gowers, W. R. (1881). *Epilepsy and other chronic convulsive diseases: Their causes, symptoms, and treatment*. New York: William Wood.

Graham, P. J. (1979). Epidemiological studies. In H. C. Quay & J. S. Werry (Eds.), *Psychopathological disorders of childhood*. New York: Wiley.

Gray, L., Watt, L., & Blass, E. M. (2000). Skin-to-skin contact is analgesic in healthy newborns. *Pediatrics, 105*, 1–6.

Green, D. P., Goldman, S. L., & Salovey, P. (1993). Measurement error masks bipolarity in affect ratings. *Journal of Personality and Social Psychology, 64*, 1029–1041.

Greenberg, L. S. (1993). Emotion and change processes in psychotherapy. In M. Lewis & J. M. Haviland (Eds.), *Handbook of emotions* (pp. 499–508). New York: Guilford.

Greenberg, L. S. (2002). *Emotion focused therapy: Coaching clients to work through their feelings*. Washington: American Psychological Association.

Greenberg, L. S., & Safran, J. D. (1987). *Emotion in psychotherapy*. New York: Guilford.

Greenberg, L. S., & Safran, J. D. (1989). Emotion in psychotherapy. *American Psychologist, 44*, 19–29.

Greenberg, M. T., Lengua, L., Coie, J. D., & Pinderhughes, E. E. (1999). Predicting developmental outcomes at school entry using a multiple-risk model: Four American communities. The Conduct Problems Prevention Research Group. *Developmental Psychology, 35*, 403–417.

Greene, J. D., Sommerville, R. B., Nystrom, L. E., Darley, J. M., & Cohen, J. D. (2001). An fMRI investigation of emotional engagement in moral judgment. *Science, 75*, 2105–2108.

Greene, J., & Haidt, J. (2002). How (and where) does moral judgment work? *Trends in Cognitive Sciences, 6*, 517–523.

Griffiths, P. E. (1997). *What emotions really are*. Chicago: University of Chicago Press.

Grinker, R. R., & Spiegel, J. P. (1945). *Men under stress*. New York: Blakiston.

Gross, J. J. (2002). Emotion regulation: Affective, cognitive, and social consequences. *Psychophysiology, 39*, 281–291.

Gross, J. J., & John, O. P. (2003). Individual differences in two emotion regulation processes: Implications for affect, relationships, and well-being. *Journal of Personality & Social Psychology, 85*, 348–362.

Gross, J. J., Fredrickson, B. L., & Levenson, R. W. (1994). The psychophysiology of crying. *Psychophysiology, 31*, 460–468.

Gross, J. J., Sutton, S. K., & Ketelaar, T. (1998). Relations between affect and personality: Support for the affect-level and affective-reactivity views. *Personality and Social Psychology Bulletin, 24*(3), 279–288.

Grossmann, K. E., Grossmann, K., Winter, M., & Zimmerman, P. (2002). Attachment relationships and appraisal of partnership: From early experience of sensitive support to later relationship representation. In L. Pulkkinen & A. Caspi (Eds.), *Paths to successful development: Personality in the life course* (pp. 73–105). New York: Cambridge University Press.

Grossmann, K., Grossmann, K. E., Spangler, G., Suess, G., & Unzner, L. (1985). Maternal sensitivity and newborn orientation responses as related to quality of attachment in northern Germany. *Monographs of the Society for Research in Child Development, 50* (1–2, Serial no. 209), 233–256.

Gruber, H. E., & Barrett, P. H. (1974). *Darwin on man: A psychological study of scientific creativity, together with Darwin's early and unpublished notebooks*. New York: Dutton.

Grunbaum, A. (1986). Precis of *The foundations of psychoanalysis: A philosophical critique*. *Behavioral and Brain Sciences, 9*, 217–284.

Grych, J., & Fincham, F. (1992). Marital conflict and children's adjustment: A cognitive contextual framework. *Psychological Bulletin, 101*, 267–290.

Guerra, N. G., Huessman, L. R., & Spindler, A. (2003). Community violence exposure, social cognition, and aggression among urban elementary school children. *Child Development, 74*, 1561–1576.

Haidt, J. (2001). The emotional dog and its rational tail: A social intuitionist approach to moral judgment. *Psychological Review, 108*, 814–834.

Haidt, J. (2003). The moral emotions. In R. Davidson, K. Scherer, & H. H. Goldsmith (Eds.), *Handbook of affective sciences* (pp. 852–870). London England, Oxford University Press.

Haidt, J., & Keltner, D. (1999). Culture and facial expression: Open ended methods find more faces and a gradient of universality. *Cognition and Emotion, 13*, 225–266.

Haidt, J., Koller, S. H., & Dias, M. G. (1993). Affect, culture, and morality, or Is it wrong to eat your dog? *Journal of Personality and Social Psychology, 65*, 613–628.

Haight, G. S. (1968). *George Eliot: A biography*. Oxford: Oxford University Press.

Haight, G. S. (Ed.). (1985). *Selections from George Eliot's letters*. New Haven, CT: Yale University Press.

Hales, R., Yudovsky, S. C., & Talbott, J. A. (1999). *The American Psychiatric Press textbook of psychiatry, 3rd edition*. Washington, DC: American Psychiatric Press.

Hamilton, C. E. (2000). Continuity and discontinuity of attachment from infancy through adolescence. *Child Development, 71*, 690–694.

Hamm, A. O., Vaitl, D., & Lang, P. J. (1990). Fear conditioning, meaning and belongingness: A selective association analysis. *Journal of Abnormal Psychology, 98*, 395–406.

Hamman, S. G., Ely, T. D., Grafton, S. T., & Kilts, C. D. (1999). Amygdala activity related to enhanced memory for pleasant and unpleasant stimuli. *Nature Neuroscience, 2*, 289–293.

Hammen, C., Rudolph, K., Weisz, J., Rao, U., & Burge, D. (1999). The context of depression in clinic-referred youth: Neglected areas in treatment. *Journal of the American Academy of Child and Adolescent Psychiatry, 38*, 64–71.

Hammen, C. (1991). Generation of stress in the course of unipolar depression. *Journal of Abnormal Psychology, 100*, 555–561.

Hammen, C. (1999). The emergence of an interpersonal approach to depression. In T. Joiner & J. C. Coyne (Eds.), *The interactional nature of depression* (pp. 21–35). Washington, DC: American Psychological Association.

Hammen, C., Burge, D., Burney, E., & Adrian, C. (1990). Longitudinal study of diagnoses in children of women with unipolar and bipolar affective disorder. *Archives of General Psychiatry, 47*, 1112–1117.

Hammen, C., Ellicott, A., Gitlin, M., & Jamison, K. R. (1989). Sociotropy/autonomy and vulnerability to specific life events in patients with unipolar depression and bipolar disorders. *Journal of Abnormal Psychology, 98*, 154–160.

Hankin, B., Abramson, L. Y., Miller, N., & Haeffel, G. J. (2004). Cognitive vulnerability-stress theories of depression: Examining affective specificity in the prediction of depression versus anxiety in three prospective studies. *Cognitive Therapy and Research, 28*, 309–345.

Hardt, J., & Rutter, M. (2004). Validity of adult retrospective reports of adverse childhood experiences: review of the evidence. *Journal of Child Psychology and Psychiatry, 45*, 260–273.

Harker, L. A., & Keltner, D. (2001). Expressions of positive emotion in women's college yearbook pictures and their relationship to personality and life outcomes across adulthood. *Journal of Personality and Social Psychology, 80*, 112–124.

Harkness, S., & Super, C. M. (1985). Child–environment interactions in the socialization of affect. In M. Lewis & C. Saarni (Eds.), *The socialization of emotions* (pp. 21–36). New York: Plenum Press.

Harlow, H. F. (1959, June). Love in infant monkeys. *Scientific American, 200*, 68–74.

Harris, C. R. (2001). Cardiovascular responses of embarassment and effects of emotional suppression in a social setting. *Journal of Personality and Social Psychology, 81*, 886–897.

Harris, C. R. (2003). A review of sex differences in sexual jealousy, including self-report data, psychophysiological responses, interpersonal violence, and morbid jealousy. *Personality and Social Psychology Review, 7*, 102–128.

Harris, C. R., & Christenfeld, N. (1996). Gender, jealousy, and reason. *Psychological Science, 7*, 364–366.

Harris, P. L. (1989). *Children and emotion: The development of psychological understanding*. Oxford: Blackwell.

Harris, P. L. (2000). *The work of the imagination*. Oxford: Blackwell.

Harris, P. L., & Saarni, C. (1989). Children's understanding of emotion: An introduction. In C. Saarni & P. L. Harris (Eds.), *Children's understanding of emotion* (pp. 3–24). Cambridge: Cambridge University Press.

Harris, P. L., Donnelly, K., Guz, G. R., & Pitt-Watson, R. (1986). Children's understanding of the distinction between real and apparent emotion. *Child Development, 57*, 895–909.

Harris, P. L., Johnson, C. N., Hutton, D., Andrews, G., & Cooke, T. (1989). Young children's theory of mind and emotion. *Cognition and Emotion, 3*, 379–400.

Harrison, P. J. (2002). The neuropathology of primary mood disorder. *Brain, 125*, 1428–1449.

Harro, J., Vasar, E., & Bradwejn, J. (1993). CCK in animal and human research on anxiety. *Trends in Pharmacological Science, 14*, 244–249.

Hart, A. J., Whalen, P. J., Shin, L. M., et al. (2000). Differential response of the human amygdala to racial outgroup vs. ingroup face stimuli. *Neuroreport, 11*, 2351–2354.

Harter, S. (1999). *The construction of the self*. New York: Guilford.

Harter, S., & Buddin, B. (1987). Children's understanding of the simultaneity of two emotions: A five-stage developmental acquisition sequence. *Developmental Psychology, 23*, 388–439.

Harter, S., Marold, D., Whitesell, N. R., & Cobbs, G. (1996). A model of the effects of parent and peer support on adolescent false self behavior. *Child Development, 67*, 360–374.

Hatfield, E., & Rapson, R. L. (2002). Passionate love and sexual desire: Cultural and historical perspectives. In A. L. Vangelista, H. T. Reis, & M. A. Fitzpatrick (Eds.), *Stability and change in relationships* (pp. 306–324). New York: Cambridge University Press.

Hatfield, E., Cacioppo, J. T., & Rapson, R. L. (1994). *Emotional contagion.* Cambridge: Cambridge University Press.

Hauser, M. D. (1996). *The evolution of communication.* Cambridge, MA: MIT Press.

Hazan, C., & Shaver, P. (1987). Romantic love conceptualized as an attachment process. *Journal of Personality and Social Psychology, 52*, 511–524.

Healy, D. (2004). *Let them eat Prozac: The unhealthy relationship between the pharmaceutical industry and depression.* New York: New York University Press.

Heelas, P. (1986). Emotion talk across cultures. In R. Harré (Ed.), *The social construction of emotions* (pp. 234–266). Oxford: Blackwell.

Hejmadi, A., Davidson, R. J., & Rozin, P. (2000). Exploring Hindu Indian emotion expressions: Evidence for accurate recognition by Americans and Indians. *Psychological Science, 11*, 183–187.

Henley, N. M. (1973). Status and sex: Some touching observations. *Bulletin of the Psychonomic Society, 2*, 91–93.

Henriques, J. B., & Davidson, R. J. (1991). Left frontal hypoactivation in depression. *Journal of Abnormal Psychology, 100*, 535–545.

Henry, W. P., Strupp, H. H., Schacht, T. E., & Gaston, L. (1994). Psychodynamic approaches. In A. E. Bergin & S. L. Garfield (Eds.), *Handbook of psychotherapy and behavior change* (4th ed., pp. 467–508). New York: Wiley.

Hertel, P. T., & Hardin, T. S. (1990). Remembering with and without awareness in a depressed mood. *Journal of Experimental Psychology: General, 119*, 45–59.

Hertenstein, M. J. (2002). Touch: Its communicative functions in infancy. *Human Development, 45*, 70–94.

Hertenstein, M. J., & Campos, J. (2004). The retention effects of an adult's emotional displays on infant behavior. *Child Development, 75*, 595–613.

Hertenstein, M. J., Keltner, D., & Apps, B. (2005). The communication of emotion through touch. Unpublished manuscript.

Hess, U., Adams, R. B., & Kleck, R. E. (2005). Who may frown and who should smile? Dominance, affiliation, and the display of happiness and anger. *Cognition and Emotion, 19*, 515–536.

Hess, U., Banse, R., & Kappas, A. (1995). The intensity of facial expression is determined by underlying affective states and social situations. *Journal of Personality and Social Psychology, 69*, 280–288.

Hess, W. R. (1950). Function and neural regulation of internal organs. In K. Akert (Ed.), *Biological order and brain organization: Selected works of W. R. Hess* (pp. 17–32). Berlin: Springer-Verlag (current edition 1981).

Hess, W. R., & Brügger, M. (1943). Subcortical center of the affective defense reaction. In K. Akert (Ed.), *Biological order and brain organization: Selected works of W. R. Hess* (pp. 183–202). Berlin: Springer-Verlag (current edition 1981).

Heurer, F., & Reisberg, D. (1992). Emotion, arousal, and memory for detail. In S. Christianson (Ed.), *The handbook of emotion and memory: Research and theory* (pp. 151–180). Hillsdale, NJ: Erlbaum.

Hiatt, S., Campos, J. J., & Emde, R. N. (1979). Facial patterning and infant facial expression: Happiness, surprise, and fear. *Child Development, 50*, 1020–1035.

Hibbs, E. D., Zahn, T. P., Hamburger, S. D., Kruesi, M. J. P., & Rapoport, J. L. (1992). Parental expressed emotion and psychophysical reactivity in disturbed and normal children. *British Journal of Psychiatry, 160*, 504–510.

Higgins, E. T. (1987). Self discrepancy: A theory relating self and affect. *Psychological Review, 94*, 319–340.

Hilton, S. M., & Zbrozyna, A. W. (1963). Amygdaloid region for defense reactions and its efferent pathway to the brainstem. *Journal of Physiology, 165*, 160–173.

Hinde, R. (1976). On describing relationships. *Journal of Child Psychology and Psychiatry, 17*, 1–19.

Ho, A. P., Gillin, J. C., Buchsbaum, M. S., Wu, J. C., Abel, L., & Bunney, W. E., Jr. (1996). Brain glucose metabolism during non-rapid eye movement sleep in major depression. A positron emission tomography study. *Archives of General Psychiatry, 53*, 645–652.

Hochschild, A. R. (1983). *The managed heart: Commercialization of human feeling*. Berkeley, CA: University of California Press.

Hochschild, A. R. (1990). Ideology and emotion management. In T. D. Kemper (Ed.), *Research agendas in the sociology of emotions* (pp. 117–142). Albany, NY: The State University of New York Press.

Hockett, C. F. (1973). *Man's place in nature*. New York: McGraw-Hill.

Hoffman, M. L. (2000). *Empathy and moral development: Implications for caring and justice*. New York: Cambridge University Press.

Hofstede, G. (1980). *Culture's consequences: International differences in work-related values*. Beverley Hills, CA: Sage.

Hogan, P. C. (2003). *The mind and its stories*. Cambridge: Cambridge University Press.

Hogarty, G. E., Anderson, C. M., Reiss, M. A., et al. (1986). Family psychoeducation, social skills training, and maintenance chemotherapy in the aftercare treatment of schizophrenia. One-year effects of a controlled study of relapse and Expressed Emotion. *Archives of General Psychiatry, 43*, 633–642.

Hohmann, G. W. (1966). Some effects of spinal cord lesions on experienced emotional feelings. *Psychophysiology, 3*, 143–156.

Hokanson, J. E., Hummer, J. T., & Butler, A. C. (1991). Interpersonal perceptions by depressed college students. *Cognitive Therapy and Research, 15*, 443–457.

Hollon, S. D., & Beck, A. T. (2004). Cognitive and cognitive-behavioral therapies. In M. J. Lambert (Ed.), *Bergin and Garfield's handbook of psychotherapy and behavior change, fifth edition* (pp. 447–492). New York: Wiley.

Holman, S. D., & Goy, R. W. (1995). Experiential and hormonal correlates of care-giving in rhesus macaques. In C. R. Pryce & R. D. Martin (Eds.), *Motherhood in human and nonhuman primates: Biosocial determinants* (pp. 87–93). Basel: Karger.

Holmes, T. H., & Rahe, R. H. (1967). The social readjustment rating scale. *Journal of Psychosomatic Research, 11*, 213–218.

Hom, H. L., & Arbuckle, B. (1988). Mood induction effects upon goal setting and performance in young children. *Motivation and Emotion, 12*, 113–122.

Homer (*c.*850 BCE). *The Iliad* (Ed. and Trans. M. Hammond). Harmondsworth: Penguin (current edition 1987).

Hooley, J. M., & Teasdale, J. D. (1989). Predictors of relapse in unipolar depressives: Expressed emotion, marital distress and perceived criticism. *Journal of Abnormal Psychology, 98*, 229–237.

Hooven, C., Gottman, J. M., & Katz, L. F. (1995). Parental meta-emotion structure predicts family and child outcomes. *Cognition and Emotion, 9*, 229–264.

Hops, H., Biglan, A., Sherman, L., Arthur, J., Friedman, L., & Osteen, V. (1987). Home observations of family interactions of depressed women. *Journal of Consulting and Clinical Psychology, 55*, 341–346.

Howell, S. (1981). Rules not words. In P. H. A. Lock (Ed.), *Indigenous psychologies: The anthropology of the self* (pp. 133–143). London: Academic Press.

Hrdy, S. B. (1999). *Mother nature*. New York: Ballantine Publishing.

Hsu, H.-C., & Fogel, A. (2003). Stability and transitions in mother–infant face-to-face communication during the first 6 months: A microhistorical approach. *Developmental Psychology, 39*, 1061–1082.

Huesmann, L. R., Eron, L. D., Lefkowitz, M., & Walder, L. O. (1984). Stability of aggression over time and generations. *Developmental Psychology, 20*, 1120–1134.

Hughes, C., & Dunn, J. (2002). 'When I say a naughty word'. A longitudinal study of young children's accounts of anger and sadness in themselves and close others. *British Journal of Developmental Psychology, 20*, 515–535.

Hughlings-Jackson, J. (1959). *Selected writings of John Hughlings-Jackson* (J. Taylor, Ed.). New York: Basic Books.

Hupka, R. B. (1991). The motive for the arousal of romantic jealousy: Its cultural origin. In P. Salovey (Ed.), *The psychology of jealousy and envy* (pp. 252–270). New York: Guilford.

Huxley, A. (1932). *Brave new world*. London: Chatto & Windus.

Hyson, M. C., & Izard, C. E. (1985). Continuities and changes in emotion expressions during brief separation at 13 and 18 months. *Developmental Psychology, 21*, 1165–1170.

Insel, T. (1992). Oxytocin – A neuropeptide for affiliation: Evidence from behavioral, receptor autoradiographic, and comparative studies. *Psychoneuroendocrinology, 17*(1), 3–35.

Insel, T. R. (1993). Oxytocin and the Neuroendocrine basis of affiliation. In J. Schulkin (Ed.), *Hormonally induced changes in mind and brain* (pp. 225–251). San Diego: Academic Press.

Insel, T. R., & Harbaugh, C. R. (1989). Lesions of the hypothalamic paraventricular nucleus disrupt the initiation of maternal behavior. *Physiology and Behavior, 45*, 1033–1041.

Insel, T., Young, L., & Wang, Z. (1997). Molecular aspects of monogamy. *Annals of The New York Academy of Sciences, 807*, 302–316.

Ironson, G., Wynings, C., Schneiderman, N., et al. (1997). Post traumatic stress symptoms, intrusive thoughts, loss and immune function after Hurricane Andrew. *Psychosomatic Medicine, 59*, 128–141.

Isabella, R. A., Belsky, J., & Von Eye, A. (1989). Origins of infant–mother attachment: An examination of interactional synchrony during the infant's first year. *Developmental Psychology, 25*, 12–21.

Isen, A. (1970). Success, failure, attention and reactions to others: The warm glow of success. *Journal of Personality and Social Psychology, 15*, 294–301.

Isen, A. M. (1987). Positive affect, cognitive processes and social behavior. In L. Berkowitz (Ed.), *Advances in experimental social psychology* (vol. 20, pp. 203–253). New York: Academic Press.

Isen, A. M. (1993). Positive affect and decision making. In M. Lewis & J. M. Haviland (Eds.), *Handbook of emotions* (pp. 261–278). New York: Guilford.

Isen, A. M., Daubman, K. A., & Nowicki, G. P. (1987). Positive affect facilitates creative problem solving. *Journal of Personality and Social Psychology, 52*, 1122–1131.

Isen, A. M., Shalker, T., Clark, M., & Karp, L. (1978). Affect, accessibility of material in memory and behavior: A cognitive loop? *Journal of Personality and Social Psychology, 36*, 1–12.

Ito, T. A., Larsen, J. T., Smith, N. K., & Cacioppo, J. T. (1998). Negative information weighs more heavily on the brain: The negativity bias in evaluative categorizations. *Journal of Personality and Social Psychology, 75*, 887–900.

Izard, C. E. (1971). *The face of emotion.* New York: Appleton-Century Crofts.

Izard, C. E. (1977). *Human emotions.* New York: Plenum Press.

Izard, C. E. (1979). *The maximally discriminative facial movement coding system (MAX).* Newark, DE: University of Delaware, Office of Instructional Technology.

Izard, C. E. (1991). *The psychology of emotions.* New York: Plenum.

Izard, C. E. (1993). Four systems for emotion activation: Cognitive and non-cognitive processes. *Psychological Review, 100*, 68–90.

Izard, C. E. (1994). Innate and universal facial expressions: Evidence from developmental and cross-cultural research. *Psychological Bulletin, 115*, 288–299.

Izard, C. E. (2002). Translating emotion theory and research into preventive interventions. *Psychological Bulletin, 128*, 796–824.

Izard, C. E. (2004). The generality-specificity issue in infants' emotion responses: A comment on Bennett, Bedersky, and Lewis (2002). *Infancy, 6*, 417–423.

Izard, C. E., & Malatesta, C. Z. (1987). Perspectives on emotional development I: Differential emotions theory of early emotional development. In J. D. Osofsky (Ed.), *Handbook of infant development* (pp. 494–554). New York: Wiley.

Izard, C. E., Dougherty, L. M., & Hembree, E. A. (1983). *A system for identifying affect expressions by holistic judgments (AFFEX).* Newark, DE: University of Delaware, Office of Instructional Technology.

Izard, C. E., Fine, S., Mostow, A., et al. (2002). Emotion processes in normal and abnormal development and preventive intervention. *Development and Psychopathology, 14*, 761–787.

Izard, C. E., Hembree, E. A., & Huebner, R. R. (1987). Infants' emotion expressions to acute pain: Developmental change and stability of individual differences. *Developmental Psychology, 23*, 105–113.

James, W. (1884). What is an emotion? *Mind, 9*, 188–205.

James, W. (1890). *The principles of psychology.* New York: Dover (current edition 1950).

Jamison, K. R. (1993). *Touched with fire: Manic-depressive illness and the artistic temperament.* New York: Free Press.

Jamison, K. R. (1995). *An unquiet mind.* New York: Knopf.

Jamner, L. D., Alberts, J., Leigh, H., & Klein, L. C. (1998, March). Affiliative need and endogenous opioids. Paper presented at the annual meeting of the Society of Behavioral Medicine. New Orleans, LA.

Janig, W. (2003). The autonomic nervous system and its coordination by the brain. In R. Davidson, K. Scherer, & H. H. Goldsmith (Eds.), *Handbook of affective sciences* (pp. 135–186). London: Oxford University Press.

Jankowiak, W. R., & Fischer, E. F. (1992). A cross-cultural perspective on romantic love. *Ethos, 31*, 149–155.

Jaynes, J. (1990). *The origin of consciousness in the breakdown of the bicameral mind*. London: Penguin Books Ltd.

Jenike, M. A. (1996). Obsessive-compulsive disorder. In H. I. Kaplan & B. J. Saddock (Eds.), *Comprehensive textbook of psychiatry, 6th edition* (Vol. 1, pp. 1218–1227). Baltimore: Williams & Wilkins.

Jenkins, J. M. (1992). Sibling relationships in disharmonious homes. In F. Boer & J. Dunn (Eds.), *Children's sibling relationships: Developmental and clinical issues* (pp. 125–136). Hillsdale, NJ: Erlbaum.

Jenkins, J. M. (2000). Marital conflict and children's emotions: The development of an anger organization. *Journal of Marriage and the Family, 62*, 723–736.

Jenkins, J. M., & Ball, S. (2000). Distinguishing between negative emotions: Children's understanding of the social-regulatory aspects of emotion. *Cognition and Emotion, 14*, 261–282.

Jenkins, J. M., & Greenbaum, R. (1999). Intention and emotion in child psychopathology: Building cooperative plans. In P. D. Zelazo, J. W. Astington & D. R. Olson (Eds.), *Developing theories of intention: Social understanding and self control* (pp. 269–291). Mahwah, NJ: Erlbaum.

Jenkins, J. M., & Oatley, K. (1996). Emotional episodes and emotionality through the life span. In C. Magai & S. H. McFadden (Eds.), *Handbook of emotion, adult development, and aging* (pp. 421–441). San Diego: Academic Press.

Jenkins, J. M., & Oatley, K. (1998). The development of emotion schemas in children: The processes underlying psychopathology. In W. F. Flack & J. D. Laird (Eds.), *Emotions and psychopathology* (pp. 45–56). New York: Oxford University Press.

Jenkins, J. M., & Oatley, K. (2000). Psychopathology and short-term emotion: The balance of affects. *Journal of Child Psychology and Psychiatry, 41*, 463–472.

Jenkins, J. M., & Smith, M. A. (1990). Factors protecting children living in disharmonious homes: Maternal reports. *Journal of the American Academy of Child and Adolescent Psychiatry, 29*, 60–69.

Jenkins, J. M., & Smith, M. A. (1991). Marital disharmony and children's behaviour problems: Aspects of a poor marriage which affect children adversely. *Journal of Child Psychology and Psychiatry, 32*, 793–810.

Jenkins, J. M., Dunn, J., O'Connor, T. G., Rasbash, J., & Simpson, A. (2005a). The mutual influence of marital conflict and children's behavior problems: Shared and non-shared family risks. *Child Development*.

Jenkins, J. M., Franco, F., Dollins, F., & Sewell, A. (1995). Toddlers' reactions to negative emotion displays: Forming models of relationships. *Infant Behavior and Development, 18*, 273–281.

Jenkins, J. M., Rasbash, J., & O'Connor, T. (2003). The role of the shared family context in differential parenting. *Developmental Psychology, 39*, 99–113.

Jenkins, J. M., Simpson, A., Dunn, J., Rasbash, J., & O'Connor, T. G. (2005b). The mutual influence of marital conflict and children's behavior problems: Shared and non-shared family risks. *Child Development, 76*, 24–39.

Jenkins, J. M., Smith, M. A., & Graham, P. (1989). Coping with parental quarrels. *Journal of the American Academy of Child and Adolescent Psychiatry, 28*, 182–189.

Jenkins, J. M., Turrell, S., Kogushi, Y., et al. (2003). A longitudinal investigation of the dynamics of mental state talk in families. *Child Development, 74*, 905–920.

Jenson, P. S., Xenakis, S. N., Davis, H., & Degroot, J. (1988). Child psychopathology rating scales and interrater agreement: II. Child and family characteristics. *Journal of the American Academy of Child and Adolescent Psychiatry, 27*, 451–461.

John, O. P. (1990). The "big five" factor taxonomy: Dimensions of personality in the natural language and in questionnaires. In L. A. Pervin (Ed.), *Handbook of personality* (pp. 66–100). New York: Guilford.

John, O. P., & Gross, J. (2004). Healthy and unhealthy emotion regulation: Personality processes, individual differences, and life span development. *Journal of Personality, 72*, 1301–1333.

John, O. P., & Srivastava, S. (1999). The big five trait taxonomy: History, measurement, and theoretical perspectives. In L. A. Pervin & O. P. John (Eds.), *Handbook of Personality: Theory and Research* (2nd ed., pp. 102–138). New York: Guilford.

Johnson, E. J., & Tversky, A. (1983). Affect, generalization, and the perception of risk. *Journal of Personality and Social Psychology, 45*, 20–31.

Johnson, J. G., Alloy, L., Panzarella, C., et al. (2001). Hopelessness as a mediator of the association between social support and depressive symptoms: Findings of a study of men with HIV. *Journal of Consulting and Clinical Psychology, 69*, 1056–1060.

Johnson, S. L., & Kizer, A. (2002). Bipolar and unipolar depression: A comparison of clinical phenomenology and psychosocial predictors. In

I. H. Gotlib & C. L. Hammen (Eds.), *Handbook of depression* (pp. 141–165). New York: Guilford.

Johnson-Laird, P. N., & Oatley, K. (1989). The language of emotions: An analysis of a semantic field. *Cognition and Emotion*, *3*, 81–123.

Joiner, T. (2002). Depression in its interpersonal context. In I. H. Gotlib & C. L. Hammen (Eds.), *Handbook of depression* (pp. 295–313). New York: Guilford.

Jonas, H. (1958). *The gnostic religion: The message of the alien God and the beginnings of Christianity*. Boston: Beacon.

Jung, C. G. (1925). Marriage as a psychological relationship. In J. Campbell (Ed.), *The portable Jung* (pp. 163–177). New York: Viking-Penguin (current edition 1971).

Juslin, P. N., & Laukka, P. (2003). Communication of emotions in vocal expression and music performance: Different channels, same code? *Psychological Bulletin*, *129*, 770–814.

Kagan, J. (1982). Heart rate and heart rate variability as signs of temperamental dimensions in infancy. In C. E. Izard (Ed.), *Measuring emotions in infants and children*. Cambridge: Cambridge University Press.

Kagan, J., Reznick, J. S., & Snidman, N. (1988). Biological bases of childhood shyness. *Science*, *240*, 167–171.

Kahneman, D., Diener, E., & Schwartz, N. (Eds.). (1999). *Well-being: The foundations of hedonic psychology*. New York: Russell Sage Foundation.

Kaler, S. R., & Freeman, B. J. (1994). Analysis of environmental deprivation: Cognitive and social development in Romanian orphans. *Journal of Child Psychology and Psychiatry*, *35*, 769–781.

Kandel, E. R., Schwartz, J. H., & Jessell, T. M. (1991). *Principles of neural science* (3rd ed.). Norwalk, CT: Appleton & Lange.

Kane, F., Coulombe, D., & Miliaressis, E. (1991). Amygdaloid self-stimulation: A movable electrode mapping study. *Behavioral Neuroscience*, *105*, 926–932.

Kano, T. (1992). *The last ape: Pygmy chimpanzee behavior and ecology* (E. O. Vineberg, Trans.). Stanford, CA: Stanford University Press.

Kappas, A., Bherer, F., & Thériault, M. (2000). Inhibiting facial expressions: Limitations to the voluntary control of facial expressions of emotion. *Motivation and Emotion*, *24*, 259–270.

Kashani, J. H., & Orvaschel, H. (1988). Anxiety disorders in mid-adolescence. *American Journal of Psychiatry*, *145*, 960–964.

Kashani, J. H., & Orvaschel, H. (1990). A community study of anxiety in children and adolescents. *American Journal of Psychiatry*, *147*, 313–318.

Katkin, E. S. (1985). Blood, sweat, and tears: Individual differences in autonomic self-perception. *Psychophysiology*, *22*, 125–137.

Katkin, E. S., Blascovich, J., & Godband, S. (1981). Empirical assessment of visceral self-perception: Individual and sex differrences in the acquisition of heart rate discrimination. *Journal of Personality and Social Psychology*, *40*, 1095–1101.

Katz, L. F., & Gottman, J. M. (1997). Buffering children from marital conflict and dissolution. *Journal of Clinical Child Psychology*, *26*, 157–171.

Kazdin, A. E. (1986). Comparative outcome studies of psychotherapy: Methodological issues and strategies. *Journal of Consulting and Clinical Psychology*, *54*, 95–105.

Kazdin, A. E. (2004). Psychotherapy for children and adolescents. In M. J. Lambert (Ed.), *Bergin and Garfield's handbook of psychotherapy and behavior change, 5th edition* (pp. 543–589). Hoboken, NJ: Wiley.

Keegan, J. (1994). *A history of warfare*. New York: Vintage.

Keller, M. B., & Boland, R. J. (1998). Implications of failing to achieve successful long term maintenance treatment of recurrent unipolar major depression. *Biological Psychiatry*, *44*, 348–360.

Keller, M., Gummerum, M., Wang, X. T., & Lindsey, S. (2004). Understanding perspectives and emotions in contract violation: Development of deontic and moral reasoning. *Child Development*, *75*, 614–635.

Kelly, E. L., & Conley, J. J. (1987). Personality and compatibility: A prospective analysis of marital stability and marital satisfaction. *Journal of Personality and Social Psychology*, *52*(1), 27–40.

Keltner, D. (1995). Signs of appeasement: Evidence for the distinct displays of embarrassment, amusement, and shame. *Journal of Personality and Social Psychology*, *68*, 441–454.

Keltner, D. (2004). The compassionate instinct. *Greater Good*, *1*, 6–9.

Keltner, D., & Anderson, C. (2000). Saving face for Darwin: Functions and uses of embarrassment. *Current Directions in Psychological Science*, *9*, 187–191.

Keltner, D., & Bonanno, G. A. (1997). A study of laughter and dissociation: The distinct correlates of laughter and smiling during bereavement. *Journal of Personality and Social Psychology*, *73*, 687–702.

Keltner, D., & Buswell, B. (1996). Evidence for the distinctness of embarrassment, shame, and guilt: A study of recalled antecedents and facial expressions of emotion. *Cognition and Emotion, 10*(2), 155–172.

Keltner, D., & Buswell, B. N. (1997). Embarrassment: Its distinct form and appeasement functions. *Psychological Bulletin, 122*, 250-270.

Keltner, D., & Gross, J. J. (1999). Functional accounts of emotions. *Cognition and Emotion, 13*, 467–480.

Keltner, D., & Haidt, J. (1999). Social functions of emotions at four levels of analysis. *Cognition and Emotion, 13*, 505–521.

Keltner, D., & Haidt, J. (2001). Social functions of emotions. In T. Mayne & G. Bonanno (Eds.), *Emotions: Current issues and future directions* (pp. 192–213). New York: Guilford.

Keltner, D., & Haidt, J. (2003). Approaching awe, a moral, spiritual, and aesthetic emotion. *Cognition and Emotion, 17*(2), 297-314.

Keltner, D., & Harker, L. A. (1998). The forms and functions of the nonverbal display of shame. In P. Gilbert & B. Andrews (Eds.), *Interpersonal approaches to shame* (pp. 78-98). Oxford, England: Oxford University Press.

Keltner, D., & Kring, A. (1998). Emotion, social function, and psychopathology. *General Psychological Review, 2*, 320-342.

Keltner, D., & Shiota, M. N. (2005). New facial displays of emotions. Unpublished manuscript.

Keltner, D., Capps, L. M., Kring, A. M., Young, R. C., & Heerey, E. A. (2001). Just teasing: A conceptual analysis and empirical review. *Psychological Bulletin, 127*, 229-248.

Keltner, D., Ekman, P., Gonzaga, G. C., & Beer, J. (2003). Facial expression of emotion. In R. Davidson, K. Scherer, & H. H. Goldsmith (Eds.), *Handbook of affective sciences* (pp. 415-432). London: Oxford University Press.

Keltner, D., Ellsworth, P. C., & Edwards, K. (1993). Beyond simple pessimism: Effects of sadness and anger on social perception. *Journal of Personality and Social Psychology, 64*, 740-752.

Keltner, D., Gruenfeld, D. H., & Anderson, C. (2003). Power, approach and inhibition. *Psychological Review, 110*(2), 265-284.

Keltner, D., Haidt, J., & Shiota, M. (in press). Social functionalism and the evolution of emotions.

Keltner, D., Locke, K. D., & Audrain, P. C. (1993). The influence of attributions on the relevance of negative emotions to personal satisfaction. *Personality and Social Psychology Bulletin, 19*, 21-29.

Keltner, D., Young, R. C., Heerey, E. A., Oemig, C., & Monarch, N. D. (1998). Teasing in hierarchial and intimate relations. *Journal of Personality and Social Psychology, 75*, 1231-1247.

Keltner, D., Young, R., & Buswell, B. N. (1997). Appeasement in human emotion, personality, and social practice. *Aggressive Behavior, 23*, 359-374.

Kemper, T. D. (1978). *A social-interactional theory of emotions.* New York: Wiley.

Kendall, P. C. (1998). Empirically supported psychological therapies. *Journal of Consulting and Clinical Psychology, 66*, 3-6.

Kendler, K. S., Heath, A., Martin, A., & Eaves, I. J. (1986). Symptoms of anxiety and depression in a volunteer twin population. *Archives of General Psychiatry, 43*, 213-221.

Kendler, K. S., Hettema, J. M., Butera, F., Gardner, C. O., & Prescott, C. A. (2003). Life event dimensions of loss, humiliation, entrapment, and danger. *Archives of General Psychiatry, 60*, 789-796.

Kendler, K. S., Neale, M. C., Kessler, R. C., Heath, A. C., & Eaves, L. J. (1993a). A twin study of recent life events. *Archives of General Psychiatry, 50*, 789-796.

Kendler, K. S., Neale, M. C., Kessler, R. C., Heath, A. C., & Eaves, L. J. (1993b). A longitudinal twin study of 1-year prevalence of major depression in women. *Archives of General Psychiatry, 50*, 843-852.

Kendler, K. S., Thornton, L. M., & Gardner, C. O. (2000). Stressful life events and previous episodes in the etiology of major depression in women: An evaluation of the "kindling" hypothesis. *American Journal of Psychiatry, 157*, 1243-1251.

Kendler, K. S., Thornton, L. M., & Gardner, C. O. (2001). Genetic risk, number of previous episodes, and stressful life events in predicting onset of major depression. *American Journal of Psychiatry, 158*, 582-586.

Kessler, R. C. (1997). The effects of stressful life events on depression. *Annual Review of Psychology, 1997*(48), 191-214.

Kessler, R. C., McGonagle, K. A., Zhao, S., Nelson, C. P., Hughes, M., Eshleman, S., Wittchen, H.-U., & Kendler, K. S. (1994). Lifetime and 12-month prevalence of DSM-III-R psychiatric disorders in the United States: Results from the National Comorbidity Survey. *Archives of General Psychiatry, 51*, 8-19.

Kessler, R. C., Zhao, S., Blazer, D. G., & Swarz, M. (1997). Prevalence, correlates, and course of minor depression and major depression in the national comorbidity study. *Journal of Affective Disorders, 45,* 19–30.

Ketelaar, T. (2004). Ancestral emotions, current decisions: Using evolutionary game theory to explore the role of emotions in decision-making. In C. Crawford & C. Salmon (Eds.), *Evolutionary psychology, public policy and personal decisions* (pp. 145–168). Mahwah, NJ: Erlbaum.

Ketelaar, T. (2005, in press). Emotions and economic decision-making: The role of moral sentiments in experimental economics. In D. DeCremer, K. Murnighan, &. M. Zeelenberg (Eds.), *Social psychology and experimental economics.* Hillsdale, NJ: Lawrence Erlbaum Publishers.

Ketelaar, T. & Au, W. T. (2003). The effects of guilty feelings on the behavior of uncooperative individuals in repeated social bargaining games: An affect-as-information interpretation of the role of emotion in social interaction. *Cognition and Emotion, 17,* 429–453.

Ketelaar, T. & Clore, G. L. (1997). Emotions and reason: The proximate effects and ultimate functions of emotions. In G. Matthews (Ed.), *Advances in personality* (pp. 355–396). Amsterdam: Elsevier.

Keverne, E. B. (1996). Psychopharmacology of maternal behaviour. *Journal of Psychopharmacology, 10,* 16–22.

Keverne, E. B., Nevison, C. M., & Martel, F. L. (1997). Early learning and the social bond. In C. S. Carter, I. I. Lederhendler, & B. Kirkpatrick (Eds.), *The integrative neurobiology of affiliation, Vol. 807.* New York: New York Academy of Sciences.

Kiecolt-Glaser, J. K., Robles, T. F., Heffner, K. L., Loving, T. J., & Glaser, R. (2002). Psycho-oncology and cancer: Psychoneuroimmunology and cancer. *Annals of Oncology, 13 (Supplement 4),* 166–169.

Kim, J. K., Conger, R. D., Lorenz, F. O., & Elder, G. H. (2001). Parent–adolescent reciprocity in negative affect and its relation to early adult social development. *Developmental Psychology, 37,* 775–790.

Kim, K. J., Conger, R. D., Elder, G. H., & Lorenz, F. O. (2003). Reciprocal influences between stressful life events and adolescent internalizing and externalizing problems. *Child Development, 74,* 127–143.

Kim-Cohen, J., Moffitt, T. E., Caspi, A., & Taylor, A. (2004). Genetic and environmental processes in young children's resilience and vulnerability to socioeconomic deprivation. *Child Development, 75,* 651–668.

Kitayama, S., Karasawa, M., & Mesquita, B. (2003). Collective and personal processes in regulating emotions: Emotion and self in Japan and the United States. In P. Philipott & R. S. Feldman (Eds.), *The regulation of emotion.* Hillsdale, NJ: Erlbaum.

Kitayama, S., Markus, H. R., & Kurokawa, M. (2000). Culture, emotions, and well-being: Good feelings in Japan and the United States. *Cognition and Emotion, 14,* 93–124.

Klasmeyer, G., & Sendlmeier, W. F. (1999). Voice and emotional states. In R. Kent & M. Ball (Eds.), *Voice quality measurement* (pp. 339–359). San Diego, CA: Singular Publishing.

Klaus, M. H., & Kennell, J. H. (1976). *Maternal-infant bonding.* St Louis: Mosby.

Kleinman, A. (1988). *Rethinking psychiatry: From cultural category to personal experience.* New York: Free Press.

Klinnert, M. D., Emde, R. N., Butterfield, P., & Campos, J. J. (1986). Social referencing: The infant's use of emotional signals from a friendly adult with mother present. *Developmental Psychology, 22,* 427–432.

Klüver, H., & Bucy, P. C. (1937). "Psychic blindness" and other symptoms following bilateral temporal lobectomy. *American Journal of Physiology, 119,* 352–353.

Knutson, B. (1996). Facial expressions of emotion influence interpersonal trait inferences. *Journal of Nonverbal Behavior, 20,* 165–182.

Knutson, B., Burgdorf, J., & Panksepp, J. (2002). Ultrasonic vocalizations as indices of affective states in rats. *Psychological Bulletin, 128,* 961–977.

Knutson, B., Wolkowitz, O. M., Cole, S. W., et al. (1998). Selective alteration of personality and social behavior by serotonergic intervention. *American Journal of Psychiatry, 155,* 373–379.

Kochanska, G., & Aksan, N. (2004). Development of mutual responsiveness between parents and their young children. *Child Development, 75,* 1657–1676.

Kochanska, G., Aksan, N., Knaack, A., & Rhines, H. (2004). Maternal parenting and children's conscience: Early security as moderator. *Child Development, 75,* 1229–1242.

Kochanska, G., Forman, D. R., Aksan, N., & Dunbar, S. B. (2005). Pathways to conscience: Early mother-child mutually responsive orientation and children's moral emotion, conduct, and cognition. *Journal of Child Psychology and Psychiatry, 46*, 19–34.

Kopp, C. B. (1989). Regulation of distress and negative emotions: A developmental view. *Developmental Psychology, 25*(3), 343–354.

Kopp, C. B. (1992). Emotional distress and control in young children. In N. Eisenberg & R. A. Fabes (Eds.), *Emotion and its regulation in early development (New Directions in Child Development, No. 55)* (pp. 41–56). San Francisco: Jossey Bass.

Kopp, C. B., & Neufeld, S. J. (2003). Emotional development during infancy. In R. J. Davidson, K. R. Scherer, & H. H. Goldsmith (Eds.), *Handbook of affective sciences* (pp. 347–374). New York: Oxford University Press.

Kosfeld, M., Heinrichs, M., Zak, P., Fischenbacher, U., & Fehr, E. (2005). Oxytocin increases trust in humans. *Nature, 435*, 673–676.

Kövesces, Z. (2003). *Metaphor*. London: Oxford University Press.

Kraemer, G. W. (1992). A psychobiological theory of attachment. *Behavioral and Brain Sciences, 15*, 493–541.

Kraemer, G. W. (1997). Psychobiology of early social attachment in rhesus monkeys: Clinical implications. *Annals of the New York Academy of Sciences, 807*, 401–418.

Kraepelin, E. (1899). Psychiatrie: Ein Lehrbuch für Studirende und Aerzte, 2nd edition. Leipzig: Barth.

Kramer, P. D. (1993). *Listening to Prozac*. New York: Viking.

Kraut, R. E., & Johnson, R. E. (1979). Social and emotional messages of smiling: An ethological approach. *Journal of Personality and Social Psychology, 37*, 1539–1553.

Krebs, J. R., & Davies, N. B. (1993). *An introduction to behavioural ecology.* Oxford: Blackwell.

Kreitler, H., & Kreitler, S. (1972). Psychology and the arts. Durham, NC: Duke University Press.

Kring, A., & Werner, K. H. (2004). Emotion regulation and psychopathology. In P. Philippot & R. S. Feldman (Eds.), *The regulation of emotion* (pp. 359–385). Mahwah, NJ: Erlbaum.

Krpan, K., Coombs, R., Zinga, D., et al. (2005). Experiential and hormonal correlates of maternal behavior in teen and adult mothers. *Hormones and Behavior, 47*, 112–122.

Kuipers, L., & Bebbington, P. (1988). Expressed emotion research in schizophrenia: Theoretical and clinical implications. *Psychological Medicine, 18*, 893–909.

La Bar, K. S., & LeDoux, J. E. (2003). Emotional learning circuits in animals and humans. In R. J. Davidson, K. R. Scherer, & H. H. Goldsmith (Eds.), *Handbook of affective sciences* (pp. 52–65). New York: Oxford University Press.

La Rochefoucauld (1665). *Maxims* (L. Tancock, Trans.). Harmondsworth: Penguin (current edition 1959).

Lacourse, E., Nagin, D., Tremblay, R. E., et al. (2003). Developmental trajectories of boys' delinquent group membership and facilitation of violent behaviors during adolescence. *Development and Psychopathology, 15*, 183–197.

Lagattuta, K. H., Wellman, H. M., & Flavell, J. (1997). Preschoolers' understanding of the link between thinking and feeling: Cognitive cuing and emotional change. *Child Development, 68*, 1081–1104.

Lambert, A. J., Khan, S. R., Lickel, B. A., & Fricke, K. (1997). Mood and the correction of positive versus negative stereotypes. *Journal of Personality and Social Psychology, 72*, 1002–1016.

Lambert, M. J. (2004). *Bergin and Garfield's handbook of psychotherapy and behavior change, fifth edition.* New York: Wiley.

Lambert, M. J., & Ogles, B. M. (2004). The efficacy and effectiveness of psychotherapy. In M. J. Lambert (Ed.), *Bergin and Garfield's handbook of psychotherapy and behavior change, fifth edition* (pp. 139–193). New York: Wiley.

Lambie, J., & Marcel, A. J. (2002). Consciousness and emotion experience: A theoretical framework. *Psychological Review, 109*, 219–259.

Lancaster, J. B., & Kaplan, H. (1992). Human mating and family formation strategies: The effects of variability among males in quality and the allocation of mating effort and parental investment. In T. Nishida, W. C. McGrew, et al. (Eds.), *Topics in primatology, Vol. 1. Human origins* (pp. 21–33). Tokyo: University of Tokyo Press.

Lane, R. D., Fink, G. R., Chau, P. M., & Dolan, R. J. (1997). Neural activation during selective attention to subjective emotional responses. *Neuroreport, 8*, 3969–3972.

Lang, P. J., Greenwald, M. K., Bradley, M. M., & Hamm, A. O. (1993). Looking at pictures: Affective, facial, visceral, and behavioral reactions. *Psychophysiology, 30*, 261–273.

Lange, C. (1885). The emotions. In E. Dunlap (Ed.), *The emotions*. Baltimore, MD: Williams & Wilkins (current edition 1922).

Langer, S. K. (1957). *Philosophy in a new key: A Study in the Symbolism of Reason, Rite, and Art.* Cambridge, MA: Harvard University Press,

Larsen, R. J., Kasimatis, M., & Frey, K. (1992). Facilitating the furrowed brow: An unobtrusive test of the facial feedback hypothesis applied to unpleasant affect. *Cognition and Emotion, 6,* 321–338.

Larsen, R. J., & Ketelaar, T. (1991). Personality and susceptibility to positive and negative emotional states. *Journal of Personality and Social Psychology, 61*(1), 132–140.

Larsen, R., Moneta, G., Richards, M., & Wilson, S. (2002). Continuity, stability, and change in daily emotional experience across adolescence. *Child Development, 73,* 1151–1165.

Last, C. G., Perrin, S., Hersen, M., & Kazdin, A. E. (1992). DSM-III-R anxiety disorders in children: Sociodemographic and clinical characteristics. *Journal of the American Academy of Child and Adolescent Psychiatry, 31,* 1070–1076.

Lawler, K. A., Younger, J. W., Piferi, R. L., Billington, E., Jobe, R., Edmondson, K., et al. (2003). A change of heart: Cardiovascular correlates of forgiveness in response to interpersonal conflict. *Journal of Behavioral Medicine, 26,* 373–393.

Lawton, M. P. (2001). Emotion in later life. *Current Directions in Psychological Science, 10,* 120–123.

Lazarus, R. S. (1991). *Emotion and adaptation.* New York: Oxford University Press.

Lazarus, R. S., & Lazarus, B. N. (1994). *Passion and reason: Making sense of our emotions.* New York: Oxford University Press.

Leakey, R., & Lewin, R. (1991). *Origins.* Harmondsworth: Penguin.

Leary, M. R., Britt, T. W., Cutlip, W. D., & Templeton, J. L. (1992). Social blushing. *Psychological Bulletin, 112,* 446–460.

Leary, M. R., Rejeski, W. J., & Britt, T. W. (1990, June). Distinguishing embarrassment from social anxiety. Paper presented at the 2nd Annual Meeting of the American Psychological Society, Dallas.

Leary, M. R., Rejeski, W. J., Britt, T., & Smith, G. E. (1994). Physiological differences between embarrassment and social anxiety. Manuscript submitted for publication.

Lebra, T. S. (1983). Shame and guilt: A psychological view of the Japanese self. *Ethos, 11,* 192–209.

LeDoux, J. (1996). *The emotional brain: The mysterious underpinnings of emotional life.* New York: Simon & Schuster.

LeDoux, J. E. (1993). Emotional networks in the brain. In M. Lewis & J. M. Haviland (Eds.), *Handbook of emotions* (pp. 109–118). New York: Guilford.

Lee, R. B. (1984). *The Dobe !Kung.* New York: Holt, Rinehart & Winston.

Leick, G. (2001). *Mesopotamia: The invention of the city.* London: Penguin.

Lerner, J. S., & Keltner, D. (2001). Fear, anger, and risk. *Journal of Personality and Social Psychology, 81,* 146–159.

Lerner, J. S., Goldberg, J. H., & Tetlock, P. E. (1998). Sober second thoughts: The effects of accountability, anger, and authoritarianism on attributions of responsibility. *Personality and Social Psychology Bulletin, 24,* 563–574.

Levenson, R. W. (1999). The intrapersonal functions of emotion. *Cognition and Emotion, 13,* 481–504.

Levenson, R. W. (2003). Autonomic specificity and emotion. In R. J. Davidson, K. R. Scherer, & H. H. Goldsmith (Eds.), *Handbook of affective sciences* (pp. 212–224). New York: Oxford University Press.

Levenson, R. W., Carstensen, L. L., Friesen, W. V., & Ekman, P. (1991). Emotion, physiology, and expression in old age. *Psychology and Aging, 6,* 28–35.

Levenson, R. W., Ekman, P., & Friesen, W. V. (1990). Voluntary facial action generates emotion-specific autonomic nervous system activity. *Psychophysiology, 27,* 363–384.

Levenson, R. W., Ekman, P., Heider, K., & Friesen, W. V. (1992). Emotion and autonomic nervous system activity in the Minangkabau of West Sumatra. *Journal of Personality and Social Psychology, 62,* 972–988.

Leventhal, H. (1991). Emotion: Prospects for conceptual and empirical development. In R. J. Lister & H. J. Weingartner (Eds.), *Perspectives on cognitive neuroscience* (pp. 325–348). New York: Oxford University Press.

Levesque, J., Eugene, F., Joanette, Y., Paquette, V., Mensour, B., Beaudoin, G., Leroux, J. M., Bourgouin, P., & Beauregard, M. (2003). Neural circuitry underlying voluntary suppression of sadness. *Biological Psychiatry, 53,* 502–510.

Levi, P. (1958). *If this is a man* (S. Woolf, Trans.). London: Sphere (current edition 1987).

Levine, L. (1997). Reconstructing memory for emotions. *Journal of Experimental Psychology: General, 126,* 165–177.

Levine, L. J., & Burgess, S. L. (1997). Beyond general arousal: Effects of specific emotions on memory. *Social Cognition, 15,* 157–181.

Levine, L. J., & Safer, M. A. (2002). Sources of bias in memory for emotions. *Current Directions in Psychological Science, 11*, 169–173.

Levine, L., & Pizarro, D. (2004). Emotion and memory research: A grumpy overview. *Social Cognition, 22*, 530–554.

Levine, L., Stein, N. L., & Liwag, M. (1999). Remembering children's emotions: Sources of concordant and discordant accounts between parents and children. *Developmental Psychology, 35*, 790–801.

Levine, S., & Stanton, M. E. (1984). The hormonal consequences of mother–infant contact in primates and rodents. In C. C. Brown (Ed.), *The many facets of touch: The foundation of experience, its importance through life, with initial emphasis for infants and young children* (pp. 51–58). Skillman, NJ: Johnson & Johnson Baby Products Co.

Levy, R. J. (1984). Emotion, knowing, and culture. In R. A. Shweder & R. A. Levine (Eds.), *Culture theory: Essays on mind, self, and emotion* (pp. 214–237). Cambridge: Cambridge University Press.

Lewis, C. S. (1936). *The allegory of love: A study in medieval tradition*. Oxford: Oxford University Press.

Lewis, Marc D. (2005, in press). Bridging emotion theory and neurobiology through dynamic systems modeling. *Behavioral and Brain Sciences.*

Lewis, Marc D., & Ramsay, D. (2005). Infant emotional and cortisol responses to goal blockage. *Child Development, 76*, 518–530.

Lewis, Marc D., & Douglas, L. (1998). A dynamic systems approach to cognition-emotion interactions in development. In M. F. Masculo & S. Griffin (Eds.), *What develops in emotional development* (pp. 159–188). New York: Plenum.

Lewis, Marc D., & Granic, I. (Eds.). (2000). *Emotion, development, and self-organization: Dynamic systems approaches to emotional development.* New York: Cambridge University Press.

Lewis, Michael (1990). Models of developmental psychopathology. In M. Lewis & S. M. Miller (Eds.), *Handbook of Developmental Psychopathology* (pp. 15–28). New York: Plenum.

Lewis, Michael (2002). Early emotional development. In A. Slater & M. Lewis (Eds.), *Introduction to infant development* (pp. 192–209). Oxford: Oxford University Press.

Lewis, Michael, Alessandri, S. M., & Sullivan, M. W. (1990). Violation of expectancy, loss of control and anger expressions in young infants. *Developmental Psychology, 26*(5), 745–751.

Lewis, Michael, & Ramsay, D. (2002). Cortisol response to embarrassment and shame. *Child Development, 73*, 1034–1045.

Lewis, Michael, Sullivan, M. W., Stanger, C., & Weiss, M. (1989). Self-development and self-conscious emotions. *Child Development, 60*, 146–156.

Li, J., Wang, L., & Fischer, K. W. (2004). The organization of Chinese shame concepts. *Cognition and Emotion, 18*, 767–797.

Li, M., & Fleming, A. S. (2003). The nucleus accumbens shell is critical for normal expression of pup-retrieval in postpartum female rats. *Behavioural Brain Research, 145*, 99–111.

Lichtheim, M. (1973). *Ancient Egyptian literature: Vol. 1. The Old and Middle Kingdoms*. Berkeley, CA: University of California Press.

Liebowitz, M. R. (1983). *The chemistry of love*. Boston: Little, Brown.

Lindsley, D. B. (1951). Emotions. In S. S. Stevens (Ed.), *Handbook of experimental psychology* (pp. 473–516). New York: Wiley.

Lipps, T. (1962). Empathy, inner imitation, and sense feeling. In M. Rader (Ed.), *A modern book on esthetics: An anthology, 3rd edition* (pp. 374–382). New York: Holt, Rinehart & Winston.

Lipsey, M. W., & Wilson, D. B. (1993). The efficacy of psychological, educational, and behavioral treatment. *American Psychologist, 48*, 1181–1209.

Liu, J., Raine, A., Venables, P. H., & Mednick, S. A. (2004). Malnutrition at age 3 years and externalizing behavior problems at ages 8, 11, and 17 years. *American Journal of Psychiatry, 161*, 2005–2013.

Loftus, E. F., & Doyle, J. M. (1987). *Eyewitness testimony: Civil and criminal*. New York: Kluwer.

Loftus, E., & Ketcham, K. (1994). *The myth of repressed memory: False memories and allegations of sexual abuse*. New York: St. Martin's Press.

Londerville, S., & Main, M. (1981). Security of attachment, compliance, and maternal training methods in the second year of life. *Developmental Psychology, 17*, 289–299.

Lopez, S. R., Nelson-Hipke, K., Polo, A. J., Jenkins, J. H., et al. (2004). Ethnicity, expressed emotion, attributions, and course of schizophrenia: Family warmth matters. *Journal of Abnormal Psychology, 113*, 428–439.

Lorenz, K. (1935). Der Kumpan in der Umwelt des Vogels. *Journal of Ornithology, 83*, 137–213. [Companionship in bird life.] In C. Schiller (Ed. & Trans.), *Instinctive behavior: Development of a modern concept* (pp. 83–128). London: Methuen.

Lorenz, K. (1937). Über die Bildung des Instinktbegriffes. *Die Naturwissenschaften, 25,* 289–331. [The conception of instinctive behavior.] In C. Schiller (Ed. & Trans.), *Instinctive behavior: Development of a modern concept* (pp. 176–208). London: Methuen.

Lorenz, K. (1967). *On aggression* (M. Latzke, Trans.). London: Methuen.

Lorenz, K., & Tinbergen, N. (1938). Taxis und Instinkthandlung in der Eirollbewegung der Graugans. *Zeitschrift für Tierpsychologi, 2,* 1–29. [Taxis and instinctive action in the egg-retrieving behavior of the greylag goose.] In C. Schiller (Ed. & Trans.), *Instinctive behavior: Development of a modern concept* (pp. 176–208). London: Methuen.

Lovejoy, C. O. (1981). The origin of man. *Science, 211,* 341–350.

Lowenstein, G., & Lerner, J. S. (2003). The role of affect in decision making. In R. J. Davidson, K. R. Scherer, & H. H. Goldsmith (Eds.), *Handbook of affective sciences* (pp. 619–642). New York: Oxford University Press.

Luborsky, L., & Crits-Christoph, P. (1990). *Understanding transference.* New York: Basic Books.

Luminet, O., Rimé, B., Bagby, R. M., & Taylor, G. J. (2004). A multimodal investigation of emotional responding in alexithymia. *Cognition and Emotion, 18,* 741–766.

Lutkenhaus, P., Grossmann, K. E., & Grossmann, K. (1985). Infant–mother attachment at twelve months and style of interaction with a stranger at the age of three years. *Child Development, 56,* 1538–1542.

Lutz, C. (1990). Engendered emotion: Gender, power, and the rhetoric of emotional control in American discourse. In C. A. Lutz & L. Abu-Lughod (Eds.), *Language and the politics of emotions* (pp. 69–91). New York: Cambridge University Press.

Lutz, C., & White, G. M. (1986). The anthropology of emotions. *Annual Review of Anthropology, 15,* 405–436.

Lutz, C. A. (1988). *Unnatural emotions: Everyday sentiments on a Micronesian atoll and their challenge to Western theory.* Chicago: University of Chicago Press.

Lykken, D. (1999). *Happiness: The nature and nurture of joy and contentment.* New York: St. Martin's Griffin.

Lyons-Ruth, K., Alpern, L., & Repacholi, B. (1993). Disorganized infant attachment classification and maternal psychosocial problems as predictors of hostile-aggressive behavior in the preschool classroom. *Child Development, 64,* 572–585.

Lyons-Ruth, K., Connell, D. B., Grunebaum, H. U., & Botein, S. (1990). Infants at social risk: Maternal depression and family support services as mediators of infant development and security of attachment. *Child Development, 61,* 85–98.

Lytton, H. (1990). Child and parent effects in boys' conduct disorder. A reinterpretation. *Developmental Psychology, 26,* 683–704.

Maccoby, E. E., & Martin, J. (1983). Socialization in the context of the family: Parent-child interaction. In P. H. Mussen (Ed.), *Handbook of child psychology.* New York: Wiley.

MacDonald, K. (1992). Warmth as a developmental construct: An evolutionary analysis. *Child Development, 63,* 753–773.

Macintyre, M. (1986). Female autonomy in a matrilineal society. In N. Grieve & A. Burns (Eds.), *Australian women: New feminist perspectives* (pp. 248–256). Melbourne: Oxford University Press.

Mackie, D. M., Devos, T., & Smith, E. R. (2000). Intergroup emotions: Explaining offensive action tendencies in an intergroup context. *Journal of Personality and Social Psychology, 79,* 602–616.

Mackie, D. M., & Worth, L. T. (1989). Processing deficits and the mediation of positive affect in persuasion. *Journal of Personality and Social Psychology, 57,* 27–40.

Mackie, D. M., & Worth, L. T. (1991). Feeling good but not thinking straight: The impact of positive mood on persuasion. In J. P. Forgas (Ed.), *Emotion and Social Judgments* (pp. 181–200). Oxford: Pergamon Press.

Maclean, K. (2003). The impact of institutionalization on child development. *Development and Psychopathology, 15,* 853–884.

MacLean, P. D. (1949). Psychosomatic disease and the "visceral brain": recent developments bearing on the Papez theory of emotion. *Psychosomatic Medicine, 11,* 338–353.

MacLean, P. D. (1990). *The triune brain in evolution.* Plenum: New York.

MacLean, P. D. (1993). Cerebral evolution of emotion. In M. Lewis & J. M. Haviland (Eds.), *Handbook of emotions* (pp. 67–83). New York: Guilford.

MacLeod, A., & Conway, C. (2005). Well-being and the anticipation of future positive experiences: The role of income, social networks, and planning ability. *Cognition and Emotion, 19,* 357–374.

Magai, C., & Haviland-Jones, J. (2002). *The hidden genius of emotion: Lifespan transformations of personality*. New York: Cambridge University Press.

Magai, C., & McFadden, S. H. (1995). *The role of emotions in social and personality development*. New York: Plenum.

Magai, C., & McFadden, S. H. (Eds.). (1996). *Handbook of emotion, adult development, and aging*. San Diego: Academic Press.

Main, M. (1990). Parental aversion to infant-initiated contact is correlated with the parent's own rejection during childhood: The effects of experience on signals of security with respect to attachment. In K. E. Barnard & T. B. Brazelton (Eds.), *Touch: The foundation of experience* (pp. 461–495). Madison, CT: International Universities Press, Inc.

Main, M., Kaplan, N., & Cassidy, J. (1985). Security in infancy, childhood, and adulthood: A move to the level of representation. In I. Bretherton & E. Waters (Eds.), *Growing points of attachment theory and research. Monographs of the Society for Research in Child Development, 50* (1-2, Serial No. 209), 65–106.

Main, M., & Solomon, J. (1986). Discovery of a disorganized/disoriented attachment pattern. In M. W. Brazelton (Ed.), *Affective development in infancy* (pp. 95–124). Norwood, NJ: Ablex.

Main, M., & Solomon, J. (1990). Procedures for identifying infants as disorganized/disoriented during the Ainsworth Strange Situation. In M. Greenberg, D. Cicchetti, & E. M. Cummings (Eds.), *Attachment in the preschool years: Theory, research and intervention* (pp. 121-160). Chicago: University of Chicago Press.

Main, M., & Stadtman, J. (1981). Infant response to rejection of physical contact by the mother. *Journal of the American Academy of Child Psychiatry, 20,* 292-307.

Malatesta, C. Z. (1990). The role of emotions in the development and organization of personality. In R. A. Thompson (Ed.), *Nebraska Symposium on Motivation, Vol. 36. Socioemotional development* (pp. 1-56). Lincoln: University of Nebraska Press.

Malatesta, C. Z., Culver, C., Tesman, J. R., & Shepard, B. (1989a). *The development of emotion expression during the first two years of life. Monographs of the Society for Research in Child Development, 54* (1-2, Serial No. 219), 1-103.

Malatesta, C. Z., Grigoryev, P., Lamb, C., Albin, M., & Culver, C. (1986). Emotion socialization and expressive development in preterm and full term infants. *Child Development, 57,* 316-330.

Malatesta, C. Z., & Haviland, J. M. (1982). Learning display rules: the socialization of emotion expression in infancy. *Child Development, 53,* 991-1003.

Mandler, G. (1964). The interruption of behavior. In *Nebraska Symposium on Motivation* (Vol. 12). Lincoln, NB: Nebraska University Press.

Mandler, G. (1984). *Mind and body: Psychology of emotions and stress*. New York: Norton.

Manstead, A. S. R., & Wagner, H. L. (1981). Arousal, cognition, and emotion: An appraisal of two-factor theory. *Current Psychological Reviews, 1,* 35-54.

Marcus, S. (1984). Freud and Dora: Story, history, case history (originally published Winter, 1974, in *Partisan Review*). In S. Marcus (Ed.), *Freud and the culture of psychoanalysis* (pp. 42-86). New York: Norton.

Marks, J. (1992). The promises and problems of molecular anthropology in hominid origins. In T. Nishida, W. C. McGrew, P. Marler, M. Pickford, & F. B. M. De Waal (Eds.), *Topics in primatology, Vol. 1. Human origins* (pp. 441-453). Tokyo: University of Tokyo Press.

Markus, H. R., & Kitayama, S. (1991). Culture and the self. Implications for cognition, emotion, and motivation. *Psychological Review, 98,* 224-253.

Markus, H. R., & Kitayama, S. (1994). The cultural construction of self and emotion: Implications for social behavior. In S. Kitayama & H. R. Markus (Eds.), *Emotion and culture: Empirical studies of mutual influence* (pp. 89-130). Washington, DC: American Psychological Association.

Maroucha, P. T., Kiecolt-Glaser, J. K., & Favegehi, M. (1998). Mucosal wound healing is impaired by examination stress. *Psychosomatic Medicine, 60,* 362-365.

Marshall, L. (1976). *The !Kung of Nyae Nyae*. Cambridge, MA: Harvard University Press.

Martin, L. L. (2000). Moods do not convey information: Moods in context do. In J. Forgas (Ed.), *Feeling and thinking: The role of affect in social cognition* (pp. 153-177). New York: Cambridge University Press.

Martin, L. L., & Clore, G. L. (2001). *Theories of mood and cognition: A user's guidebook*. Mahwah, NJ: Erlbaum.

Martini, T., Root, C., & Jenkins, J. M. (2004). Low and middle income mothers' regulation of negative emotion: Effects of children's temperament and situational emotional responses. *Social Development, 13,* 515-530.

Mason, W. A., & Mendoza, S. P. (Eds.). (1993). *Primate social conflict*. Albany, NY: State University of New York Press.

Matas, L., Arend, R. A., & Sroufe, L. A. (1978). Continuity of adaptation in the second year: The relationship between quality of attachment and later competence. *Child Development, 49*, 547–556.

Matheson, M. D., & Bernstein, I. S. (2000). Grooming, social bonding, and agonistic aiding in rhesus monkeys. *American Journal of Primatology, 51*, 177–186.

Mathews, A. (1993). Biases in emotional processing. *The Psychologist: Bulletin of the British Psychological Society, 6*, 493–499.

Mathews, A., Gelder, M. G., & Johnson, D. W. (1981). *Agoraphobia: Nature and treatment*. London: Tavistock.

Mathews, A., & Klug, F. (1993). Emotionality and interference with color-naming in anxiety. *Behavior Research and Therapy, 29*, 147–160.

Mathews, A., & MacLeod, C. (1994). Cognitive approaches to emotion and emotional disorders. *Annual Review of Psychology, 45*, 25–50.

Mathews, A., Yiend, J., & Lawrence, A. (2004). Individual differences in the modulation of fear-related brain activation by attentional control. *Journal of Cognitive Neuroscience, 16*, 1683–1694.

Matsumoto, D. (1987). The role of facial response in the experience of emotion: More methodological problems and a meta-analysis. *Journal of Personality & Social Psychology, 52*(4), 769–774.

Matsumoto, D. (1989). Cultural influences on the perception of emotion. *Journal of Cross-Cultural Psychology, 20*(1), 92–105.

Matsumoto, D. (1990). Cultural similarities and differences in display rules. *Motivation & Emotion, 14*(3), 195–214.

Matsumoto, D. (2002). Methodological requirements to test a possible ingroup advantage in judging emotions across cultures: Comments on Elfenbein and Ambady and evidence. *Psychological Bulletin, 128*(2), 236–242.

Matsumoto, D., Consolacion, T., Yamada, H., Suzuki, R., Franklin, B., Paul, S., Ray, R., & Uchida, H. (2002). American-Japanese cultural differences in judgments of emotional expressions of different intensities. *Cognition & Emotion, 16*(6), 721–747.

Matsumoto, D., & Ekman, P. (1989). American-Japanese cultural differences in intensity ratings of facial expressions of emotion. *Motivation & Emotion, 13*(2), 143–157.

Matsumoto, D., & Ekman, P. (2004). The relationship between expressions, labels, and descriptions of contempt. *Journal of Personality and Social Psychology, 87*(4), 529–540.

Matsumoto, D., Kasri, F., & Kooken, K. (1999). American-Japanese cultural differences in judgments of expression intensity and subjective experience. *Cognition & Emotion, 13*, 201–218.

Matsumoto, D., Takeuchi, S., Andayani, S., Kouznetsova, N., & Krupp, D. (1998). The contribution of individualism-collectivism to cross-national differences in display rules. *Asian Journal of Social Psychology, 1*, 147–165.

Matsumoto, D., Weissman, M., Preston, K., Brown, B., & Kupperbusch, C. (1997). Context-specific measurement of individualism-collectivism on the individual level: The IC Interpersonal Assessment Inventory (ICIAI). *Journal of Cross-Cultural Psychology, 28*, 743–767.

Maughan, B., Rowe, R., Messer, J., et al. (2004). Conduct disorder and oppositional defiant disorder in a national sample: Developmental epidemiology. *Journal of Child Psychology and Psychiatry, 45*, 609–621.

Mauro, R., Sato, K., & Tucker, J. (1992). The role of appraisal in human emotions: A cross-cultural study. *Journal of Personality and Social Psychology, 62*, 301–317.

Mauss, I. B., Levenson, R. W., McCarter, L., et al. (2005). The tie that binds? Coherence among emotion experience, behavior, and physiology. *Emotion, 5*, 175–190.

Mayberg, H. S., Liotti, M., Brannan, S. K., et al. (1999). Reciprocal limbic cortical function and negative mood: Converging PET findings in depression and normal sadness. *American Journal of Psychiatry, 156*, 675–682.

Mayer, J. D., Gaschke, Y. N., Braverman, D. L., & Evans, T. W. (1992). Mood-congruent judgment is a general effect. *Journal of Personality and Social Psychology, 63*, 119–132.

Mayer, J. D., Salovey, P., & Caruso, D. R. (2004). Emotional intelligence: Theory, findings, and implications. *Psychological Inquiry, 15*, 197–215.

McCrae, R. R. (1992). The five factor model: issues and applications. *Journal of Personality and Social Psychology (Special issue), 60*(2).

McCullough, M. E. (2000). Forgiveness as human strength: Theory, measurement, and links to well-being. *Journal of Social and Clinical Psychology, 19*, 43–55.

McCullough, M. E., Sandage, S. J., & Worthington, E. L. J. (1997). *To forgive is human*. Downers Grove, NJ: InterVarsity.

McCullough, M. E., Tsang, J., & Emmons, R. A. (2004). Gratitude in "intermediate affective terrain": Grateful moods and their links to personality and daily life events. *Journal of Personality and Social Psychology, 86*, 295–309.

McCullough, M. E., Kilpatrick, S. D., Emmons, R. A., & Larson, D. B. (2001). Is gratitude a moral affect? *Psychological Bulletin, 127*, 249–266.

McFarland, C., & Ross, M. (1987). The relation between current impressions and memories of self and dating partners. *Personality & Social Psychology Bulletin, 13*, 228–238.

McGee, R., Feehan, M., Williams, S., et al. (1990). DSM-III disorders in a large sample of adolescents. *Journal of the American Academy of Child and Adolescent Psychiatry, 29*, 611–619.

McGrath, C. (2004). Wolfe's world. *New York Times, Magazine Section*, Oct 31, pp. 34–39.

McGuffin, P., & Sargeant, M. P. (1991). Genetic markers and affective disorder. In P. McGuffin & R. Murray (Eds.), *The new genetics of mental illness* (pp. 165–181). Oxford: Butterworth-Heinemann.

McNally, R. J. (1999). Panic and phobias. In T. Dalgleish & M. Power (Eds.), *Handbook of cognition and emotion* (pp. 479–496). Chichester: Wiley.

McNally, R. J. (2003). Progress and controversy in the study of posttraumatic stress disorder. *Annual Review of Psychology, 54*, 229–252.

McNally, R. J., Kaspi, S. P., Riemann, B. C., & Zeitlin, S. B. (1990). Selective processing of threat cues in posttraumatic stress disorder. *Journal of Abnormal Psychology, 99*, 398–402.

McNeill, D. (Ed.). (2000). *Language and gesture*. New York: Cambridge University Press.

McQuaid, J. R., Monroe, S. M., Roberts, J. E., Kupfer, D. J., & Frank, E. (2000). A comparison of two life stress assessment approaches: Prospective prediction of treatment outcome in recurrent depression. *Journal of Abnormal Psychology, 109*, 787–791.

Meaney, M. J. (2001). Maternal care, gene expression, and the transmission of individual differences in stress reactivity across generations. *Annual Review of Neuroscience, 24*, 1161–1192.

Melzoff, A. N. (1993). The centrality of motor coordination and proprioception in social and cognitive development. In G. J. P. Savelsbergh (Ed.), *The development of coordination in infancy* (pp. 463–496). Amsterdam: Elsevier.

Menon, U., & Shweder, R. A. (1994). Kali's tongue: Cultural psychology, cultural consensus and the meaning of "shame" in Orissa, India. In H. Markus & S. Kitayama (Eds.), *Emotion and culture: Empirical studies of mutual influence* (pp. 241–284). Washington DC: American Psychological Association.

Mesquita, B. (2001). Culture and emotion: Different approaches to the question. In T. J. Mayne & G. A. Bonanno (Eds.), *Emotions: Current issues and future directions. Emotions and social behavior* (pp. 214–250). New York: Guilford.

Mesquita, B. (2003). Emotions as dynamic cultural phenomena. In J. Davidson Richard, K. R. Scherer, & H. H. Goldsmith (Eds.), *Handbook of affective sciences* (pp. 871–890). New York: Oxford University Press.

Mesquita, B., & Ellsworth, P. C. (2001). The role of culture in appraisal. In K. R. Scherer & A. Schorr (Eds.), *Appraisal processes in emotion. Theory, methods, research*. New York: Oxford University Press.

Mesquita, B., & Frijda, N. (1992). Cultural variations in emotions: A review. *Psychological Bulletin, 112*, 179–204.

Mesquita, B., Frijda, N. H., & Scherer, K. R. (1997). Culture and emotion. In P. R. Dasen & T. S. Saraswathi (Eds.), *Handbook of cross-cultural psychology, Vol. 2: Basic processes and human development* (pp. 255–297). Boston: Allyn & Bacon.

Mesquita, B., & Markus, H. R. (2004). Culture and emotion: Models of agency as sources of cultural variation in emotion. In N. H. Frijda, A. S. R. Manstead, & A. Fischer (Eds.), *Feelings and emotions: The Amsterdam Symposium* (pp. 341–358). New York: Cambridge University Press.

Messinger, D. (2002). Positive and negative: Infant facial expressions and emotions. *Current Directions in Psychological Science, 11*, 1–6.

Miall, D. S., & Kuiken, D. (2002). A feeling for fiction: Becoming what we behold. *Poetics, 30*, 221–241.

Mikulincer, M., & Shaver, P. R. (2003). The attachment behavioral system in adulthood: Activation, psychodynamics, and interpersonal processes. In M. P. Zanna (Ed.), *Advances in Experimental Social Psychology*. New York: Academic Press.

Mikulincer, M., & Shaver, P. R. (2005). Attachment theory and emotions in close relationships: Exploring the attachment-related dynamics of emotional reactions to relational events. *Personal Relationships, 12*, 149–168.

Miller, E. K., & Cohen, J. D. (2001). An integrative theory of prefrontal cortex function. *Annual Review of Neuroscience, 24*, 167–202.

Miller, I. W., Keitner, G. I., Whisman, M. A., Ryan, C. E., Epstein, N. B., & Bishop, D. S. (1992). Depressed patients with dysfunctional families: Description and course of illness. *Journal of Abnormal Psychology, 101*, 637–646.

Miller, R. S. (1992). The nature and severity of self-reported embarrassing circumstances. *Personality and Social Psychology Bulletin, 18*, 190–198.

Miller, R. S. (1995). On the nature of embarrassability: Shyness, social-evaluation, and social skill. *Journal of Personality, 63*, 315–339.

Miller, R. S., & Leary, M. R. (1992). Social sources and interactive functions of embarrassment. In M. Clark (Ed.), *Emotion and social behavior*. New York: Sage.

Miller, R. S., & Tangney, J. P. (1994). Differentiating embarrassment from shame. *Journal of Social and Clinical Psychology, 13*, 273–287.

Miller, W. L. (1994). The politics of emotion display in heroic society. In N. Frijda (Ed.), *Proceedings of the 8th conference of the International Society for Research on Emotions*, Cambridge, 14–17 July. Storrs, CT: ISRE Publications (pp. 43–46).

Minde, K., Goldberg, S., Perrotta, M., Washington, J., Lojkasek, M., Corter, C., & Parker, K. (1989). Continuities and discontinuities in the development of 64 very small premature infants to 4 years of age. *Journal of Child Psychology and Psychiatry, 30*, 391–404.

Mineka, S., & Cook, M. (1993). Mechanisms involved in the observational conditioning of fear. *Journal of Experimental Psychology: General, 122*, 24–38.

Mineka, S., & Gilboa, E. (1998). Cognitive biases in anxiety and depression. In W. F. Flack & J. D. Laird (Eds.), *Emotions in psychopathology: Theory and research* (pp. 216–228). New York: Oxford University Press.

Mineka, S., Rafeali, E., & Yovel, I. (2003). Cognitive biases in emotional disorders: Information processing and social-cognitive perspectives. In R. J. Davidson, K. R. Scherer, & H. H. Goldsmith (Eds.), *Handbook of affective sciences* (pp. 976–1009). New York: Oxford University Press.

Minuchin, S., Rosman, B. L., & Baker, L. (1978). *Psychosomatic families: Anorexia nervosa in context*. Cambridge, MA: Harvard University Press.

Mischel, W., & Shoda, Y. (1995). A cognitive-affective system theory of personality: Reconceptualizing situations, dispositions, dynamics, and invariance in personality structures. *Psychological Review, 102*, 244–268.

Mitchell, S. A. (1988). *Relational concepts in psychoanalysis*. Cambridge, MA: Harvard University Press.

Mithen, S. (1996). *The prehistory of the mind: The cognitive origins of art and science*. London: Thames and Hudson.

Mithen, S. (2001). The evolution of imagination: An archeological perspective. *SubStance* (# 94/95), 28–54.

Miyake, K., Campos, J., Kagan, J., & Bradshaw, D. L. (1986). Issues in socioemotional development. In H. Stevenson, H. Azuma, & K. Hakuta (Eds.), *Child development and education in Japan* (pp. 239–261). New York: Freeman.

Miyake, K., Chen, S.-J., & Campos, J. J. (1985). Infant temperament, mother's mode of interaction, and attachment in Japan: An interim report. In I. Bretherton & E. Waters (Eds.), *Growing points of attachment theory and research. Monographs of the Society for Research in Child Development, 50 (1–2, Serial No. 209)* (pp. 276–297).

Moffitt, T. E., Caspi, A., Harrington, H., & Milne, B. J. (2002). Males on the life-course-persistent and adolescence-limited antisocial pathways: Follow-up at age 26 years. *Development and Psychopathology, 14*, 179–207.

Mogg, K., & Bradley, B. P. (1999). Selective attention and anxiety: A cognitive-motivational perspective. In T. Dalgleish & M. Power (Eds.), *Handbook of cognition and emotion* (pp. 145–170). Chichester: Wiley.

Moldoveanu, M., & Nohria, N. (2002). Master passions: Emotion, narrative, and the development of culture. Cambridge, MA: MIT Press.

Monroe, S. M., & Hadjiyannakis, K. (2002). The social environment and depression. In I. H. Gotlib & C. L. Hammen (Eds.), *Handbook of depression* (pp. 314–340). New York: Guilford.

Monroe, S. M., & Simons, A. D. (1991). Diathesis stress in the context of life stress research: Implications for the depressive disorders. *Psychological Bulletin, 110*, 406–425.

Monroe, S. M., & Wade, S. L. (1988). Life events. In C. G. Last & M. Hersen (Eds.), *Handbook of anxiety disorders* (pp. 293–305). New York: Pergamon Press.

Montague, D., & Walker-Andrews, A. S. (2002). Mothers, fathers, and infants: The role of person familiarity and parental involvement in infants' perception of emotion expressions. *Child Development, 73*, 1339–1352.

Montepare, J. M., Goldstein, S. B., & Clausen, A. (1987). The identification of emotions from gait information. *Journal of Nonverbal Behavior, 11*, 33–42.

Moore, G. A., & Calkins, S. D. (2004). Infants' vagal regulation in the still-face paradigm is related to dyadic coordination of mother–infant interaction. *Developmetnal Psychology, 40*, 1068–1080.

Morris, D., Collett, P., Marsh, P., & O'Shaughnessy, M. (1979). *Understanding emotions from gestures: Their origin and distribution.* London: Cape.

Mortimore, P., Sammons, P., Stoll, L., Lewis, D., & Ecob, R. (1988). *School matters.* Berkeley, CA: University of California Press.

Moskowitz, A. K. (2004). "Scared stiff": Catatonia as an evolutionary based fear response. *Psychological Review, 111*, 984–1002.

Mueller, T. I., Keller, M. B., Leon, A., Solomon, D. A., Shea, M. T., Coryell, W., et al. (1996). Recovery after five years of unremitting major depressive disorder. *Archives of General Psychiatry, 53*, 794–799.

Mumme, D. L., & Fernald, A. (2003). The infant as onlooker: Learning from emotional reactions observed in a television scenario. *Child Development, 74*, 221–237.

Munoz, R. F., Mrazek, P. J., & Haggerty, R. J. (1995). Institute of Medicine report on prevention of mental disorders: Summary and commentary. *American Psychologist, 51*, 1116–1122.

Murphy, M. R., Seckl, J. R., Burton, S., Checkley, S. A., & Lightman, S. L. (1987). Changes in oxytocin and vasopressin secretion during sexual activity in men. *Journal of Clinical Endocrinology and Metabolism, 65*(4), 738–742.

Murphy, S. T., & Zajonc, R. B. (1993). Affect, cognition, and awareness: Affective priming with optimal and suboptimal stimulus exposures. *Journal of Personality and Social Psychology, 64*, 723–739.

Murray, C. J. L., & Lopez, A. D. (Eds.). (1996). *The global burden of disease: A comprehensive assessment of mortality and disability from diseases, injuries, and risk factors in 1990 and projected to 2020.* Cambridge, MA: Harvard University Press.

Murray, S. L., & Holmes, J. G. (1993). Seeing virtues in faults: Negativity and the transformation of interpersonal narratives in close relationships. *Journal of Personality and Social Psychology, 65*, 707–723.

Murray, S. L., & Holmes, J. G. (1997). A leap of faith? Positive illusions: Idealization and the construction of satisfaction in close relationships. *Journal of Personality and Social Psychology, 70*, 79–98.

Myers, D. G. (2000). The funds, friends, and faith of happy people. *American Psychologist, 55*, 56–67.

Myers, D. G., & Diener, E. (1996). The pursuit of happiness. *Scientific American, 274*(May), 54–56.

Myers, S. A., & Berscheid, E. (1997). The language of love: The difference a preposition makes. *Personality and Social Psychology Bulletin, 23*, 347–362.

Nakota, T., & Trehub, S. (2004). Infants' responsiveness to maternal speech and singing. *Infant Behavior and Development, 27*, 455–464.

Nance, J. (1975). *The gentle Tasaday.* New York: Harcourt Brace Jovanovich.

Neff, K. D., & Harter, S. (2003). Relationship styles of self-focused autonomy, other-focused connectedness. *Journal of Social and Personal Relationships, 20*, 81–99.

Nelson, E., & Panksepp, J. (1996). Oxytocin mediates acquisition of maternally associated odor preferences in preweaning rat pups. *Behavioral Neuroscience, 110*(3), 583–592.

Nelson, E. E., & Panksepp, J. (1998). Brain substrates of infant–mother attachment: Contributions of opioids, oxytocin, and norepinephrine. *Neuroscience and Biobehavioral Reviews, 22*(3), 437–452.

Nesse, R. (2000). Is depression an adaptation? *Archives of General Psychiatry, 57*, 14–20.

Nesse, R. M. (1990). Evolutionary explanations of emotions. *Human Nature, 1*, 261–283.

Neu, J. (1977). *Emotion, thought and therapy.* London: Routledge & Kegan Paul.

Niedenthal, P. M., & Halberstadt, J. H. (2000). Grouding categories in emotional response. In J. Forgas (Ed.), *Feeling and thinking: The role of affect in social cognition* (pp. 357–386). New York: Cambridge University Press.

Niedenthal, P. M., & Setterlund, M. B. (1994). Emotion congruence in perception. *Personality and Social Psychology Bulletin, 20*, 401–411.

Nishida, T., Hasegawa, T., Hayaki, H., Takahata, Y., & Uehara, S. (1992). Meat-sharing as a coalition strategy by an alpha male chimpanzee. In T. Nishida, W. C. McGrew, P. Marler, M. Pickford, & F. B. M. De Waal (Eds.), *Topics in primatology, Vol. 1. Human origins* (pp. 159–174). Tokyo: University of Tokyo Press.

Nofzinger, E. A., Nichols, T. E., Meltzer, C. C., et al. (1999). Changes in forebrain function from waking to REM sleep in depression: Preliminary analysese of [18F] FDG PET studies. *Psychiatry Research, 91,* 59–78.

Nolen-Hoeksema, S. (2000). The role of rumination in depressive disorders and mixed anxiety/depressive symptoms. *Journal of Abnormal Psychology, 109,* 504–511.

Nolen-Hoeksema, S. (2002). Gender differences in depression. In I. H. Gotlib & C. L. Hammen (Eds.), *Handbook of depression* (pp. 492–509). New York: Guilford.

Nolen-Hoeksema, S., & Jackson, B. (2001). Mediators of the gender difference in rumination. *Psychology of Women Quarterly, 25,* 37–47.

Nolen-Hoeksema, S., Larson, J., & Grayson, C. (1999). Explaining the gender difference in depression. *Journal of Personality and Social Psychology, 77,* 1061–1072.

Nolen-Hoeksema, S., & Morrow, J. (1991). A prospective study of depression and post traumatic stress symptoms after a natural disaster: The 1989 Loma Prieta earthquake. *Journal of Personality and Social Psychology, 61,* 115–121.

Nolen-Hoeksema, S., Morrow, J., & Fredrickson, B. J. (1993). Response styles and the duration of episodes of depressed mood. *Journal of Abnormal Psychology, 102,* 20–28.

Nolen-Hoeksema, S., Parker, L. E., & Larson, J. (1994). Ruminative coping with depressed mood following loss. *Journal of Personality and Social Psychology, 67,* 92–104.

Nomura, Y., Wikramaratne, P., Warner, V., et al. (2002). Family discord, parental depression and psychopathology in offspring: Ten-year follow-up. *Journal of the American Academy of Child and Adolescent Psychiatry, 41,* 402–409.

Nussbaum, M. (2001). *Upheavals of thought: The intelligence of emotions.* New York: Cambridge University Press.

Nussbaum, M. C. (1986). *The fragility of goodness: Luck and ethics in Greek tragedy and philosophy.* Cambridge: Cambridge University Press.

Nussbaum, M. C. (1994). *The therapy of desire: Theory and practice in Hellenistic ethics.* Princeton, NJ: Princeton University Press.

O'Connell, P., Pepler, D., & Craig, W. (1999). Peer involvement in bullying: Insights and challenges for intervention. *Journal of Adolescence, 22,* 437–452.

O'Connor, T., Dunn, J., Jenkins, J. M., et al. (2001a). Family settings and children's adjustment: Differential adjustment within and across families. *British Journal of Psychiatry, 179,* 110–115.

O'Connor, T., Jenkins, J. M., Hewitt, J., DeFries, J., & Plomin, R. (2001b). Longitudinal connections between parenting and peer relationships in adoptive and biological families. *Marriage and Family Review, 33,* 251–271.

O'Connor, T., McGuire, S., Reiss, D., et al. (1998). Co-occurrence of depressive symptoms and anti-social behavior in adolescence: A common genetic liability. *Journal of Abnormal Psychology, 107,* 27–37.

O'Connor, T. G., Marvin, R. S., Rutter, M., et al. (2003). Child–parent attachment following early institutional deprivation. *Development and Psychopathology, 15,* 19–38.

O'Doherty, J., Kringelbach, M., Rolls, E., et al. (2001). Abstract reward and punishment representations in the human orbitofrontal cortex. *Nature Neuroscience, 4,* 95–102.

Oatley, K. (1988). Life events, social cognition and depression. In S. Fisher & J. Reason (Eds.), *Handbook of life stress, cognition and health* (pp. 543–557). New York: Wiley.

Oatley, K. (1992). *Best laid schema: The psychology of emotions.* New York: Cambridge University Press.

Oatley, K. (1999). Why fiction may be twice as true as fact: Fiction as cognitive and emotional simulation. *Review of General Psychology, 3,* 101–117.

Oatley, K. (2002). Emotions and the story worlds of fiction. In M. C. Green, J. J. Strange, & T. C. Brock (Eds.), *Narrative impact: Social and cognitive foundations* (pp. 39–69). Mahwah, NJ: Erlbaum.

Oatley, K. (2003). Creative expression and communication of emotion in the visual and narrative arts. In R. J. Davidson, K. R. Scherer, & H. H. Goldsmith (Eds.), *Handbook of affective sciences* (pp. 481–502). New York: Oxford University Press.

Oatley, K. (2004a). From the emotions of conversation to the passions of fiction. In A. S. R. Manstead, N. Frijda, & A. Fischer (Eds.), *Feelings and emotions: The Amsterdam Symposium* (pp. 98–115). Cambridge: Cambridge University Press.

Oatley, K. (2004b). Scripts, transformations, and suggestiveness, of emotions in Shakespeare and Chekhov. *Review of General Psychology, 8,* 323–340.

Oatley, K. (2004c). *Emotions: A brief history.* Malden, MA: Blackwell.

Oatley, K., & Bolton, W. (1985). A social-cognitive theory of depression in reaction to life events. *Psychological Review, 92,* 372–388.

Oatley, K., & Duncan, E. (1992). Incidents of emotion in daily life. In K. T. Strongman (Ed.), *International review of studies on emotion* (pp. 250–293). Chichester: Wiley.

Oatley, K., & Duncan, E. (1994). The experience of emotions in everyday life. *Cognition and Emotion*, 8, 369–381.

Oatley, K., & Jenkins, J. M. (1992). Human emotions: Function and dysfunction. *Annual Review of Psychology*, 43, 55–85.

Oatley, K., & Johnson-Laird, P. N. (1987). Towards a cognitive theory of emotions. *Cognition and Emotion*, 1, 29–50.

Oatley, K., & Johnson-Laird, P. N. (1995). The communicative theory of emotions: Empirical tests, mental models, and implications for social interaction. In L. L. Martin & A. Tesser (Eds.), *Striving and feeling: Interactions among goals, affect, and self-regulation* (pp. 363–393). Mahwah, NJ: Erlbaum.

Oatley, K., & Perring, C. (1991). A longitudinal study of psychological and social factors affecting recovery from psychiatric breakdown. *British Journal of Psychiatry*, 158, 28–32.

Ochsner, K. N. (2000). Are affective events richly recollected or simply familiar? The experience and process of recognizing feelings past. *Journal of Experimental Psychology: General*, 129, 242–261.

Ochsner, K. N., Bunge, S. A., Gross, J. J., & Gabrieli, J. D. E. (2002). Rethinking feelings: An fMRI study of the cognitive regulation of emotion. *Journal of Cognitive Neuroscience*, 14, 1215–1229.

Ochsner, K., & Schachter, D. (2003). Remembering emotional events: A social cognitive and neuroscience apprroach. In R. J. Davidson, K. R. Scherer, & H. H. Goldsmith (Eds.), *Handbook of affective sciences* (pp. 643–660). New York: Oxford University Press.

Oenguer, D., & Price, J. L. (2000). The organization of networks within the orbital and medial prefrontal cortex of rats, monkeys, and humans. *Cerebral Cortex*, 10(3), 206–219.

Offord, D. R., Boyle, M. H., Racine, Y. A., et al. (1992). Outcome, prognosis and risk in a longitudinal follow-up study. *Journal of the American Academy of Child and Adolescent Psychiatry*, 31, 916–923.

Offord, D. R., Boyle, M. H., Szatmari, P., et al. (1987). Ontario Child Health Study: II. Six-month prevalence of disorder and rates of service utilization. *Archives of General Psychiatry*, 44, 832–836.

Öhman, A. (1986). Face the beast and fear the face: Animal and social fears as prototypes for evolutionary analyses of emotion. *Psychophysiology*, 23, 123–145.

Öhman, A. (2000). Fear and anxiety: Evolutionary, cognitive, and clinical perspectives. In M. Lewis & J. Haviland-Jones (Eds.), *Handbook of emotions, Second Edition* (pp. 573–593). New York: Guilford.

Öhman, A., & Dimberg, U. (1978). Facial expressions as conditioned stimuli for electrodermal responses: A case of "preparedness"? *Journal of Personality and Social Psychology*, 36, 1251–1258.

Öhman, A., & Mineka, S. (2001). Fears, phobias, and preparedness: Towards an evolved module of fear and fear learning. *Psychological Review*, 108, 483–522.

Öhman, A., & Soares, J. J. F. (1994). "Unconscious anxiety": Phobic responses to masked stimuli. *Journal of Abnormal Psychology*, 103, 231–240.

Olds, D. (2002). Prenatal and infancy home visiting by nurses: From randomized trials to community replication. *Prevention Science*, 3, 153–172.

Olds, D., Henderson, C. R., Cole, R., et al. (1998). Long term effects of nurse home visitiation on children's criminal and antisocial behavior: 15-year follow up of a randomized controlled trial. *Journal of the American Medical Association*, 280, 1271–1273.

Olds, J. (1955). Physiological mechanisms of reward. In M. R. Jones (Ed.), *Nebraska symposium on motivation* (pp. 73–134). Lincoln, NE: University of Nebraska Press.

Olds, J., & Milner, P. (1954). Positive reinforcement produced by electrical stimulation of septal area and other regions of rat brain. *Journal of Comparative and Physiological Psychology*, 47, 419–427.

Ollendick, T. (Ed.). (2004). *Phobic and anxiety disorders in children and adolescents: A clinician's guide to effective psychosocial and pharmacological interventions*. Oxford: Oxford University Press.

Olson, D. R. (1994). *The world on paper*. New York: Cambridge University Press.

Oltmanns, T. F. (2003). *Case studies in abnormal psychology, sixth edition*. New York: Wiley.

Olweus, D. (1979). Stability of aggressive reaction patterns in males: A review. *Psychological Bulletin*, 86, 852–875.

Olweus, D. (1980). Familial and temperamental determinants of aggressive behavior in adolescent boys: A causal analysis. *Developmental Psychology*, 16, 644–660.

Olweus, D. (1993). *Bullying at school: What we know and what we can do*. Oxford: Blackwell.

Olweus, D., Limber, S., & Mihalic, S. F. (1999). *Blueprints for violence prevention, book nine: Bullying prevention program*. Boulder, CO: Center for the Study and Prevention of Violence.

Orlinsky, D. E., & Howard, K. I. (1980). Gender and psychotherapeutic outcome. In A. M. Brodsky & R. T. Hare-Martin (Eds.), *Women and psychotherapy* (pp. 3–34). New York: Guilford.

Orth-Gomer, K., Wamala, S. P., Horsten, M., et al. (2000). Marital stress worsens prognosis in women with coronary heart disease: The Stockholm Female Coronary Risk Study. *Journal of the American Medical Association, 284*, 3008–3014.

Ortony, A., & Turner, T. J. (1990). What's basic about basic emotions? *Psychological Review, 74*, 431–461.

Ortony, A., Clore, G., & Collins, A. (1988). *The cognitive structure of emotions*. New York: Cambridge University Press.

Osgood, C. E., May, W. H., & Miron, M. S. (1975). *Cross-cultural universals of affective meaning*. Urbana, IL: Illinois University Press.

Oster, H. (2003). Emotion in the infant's face: Insights from the study of infants with facial anomalies. *Annals of the New York Academy of Sciences, 1000*, 197–204.

Oster, H., Hegley, D., & Nagel, L. (1992). Adult judgments and fine-grained analysis of infant facial expressions: testing the validity of a priori coding formulas. *Developmental Psychology, 28*, 1115–1131.

Oveis, C., Horberg, L., & Keltner, D. (2005). Compassion, similarity of self to other, and vagal tone. Unpublished manuscript. University of California-Berkeley.

Oveis, C., Sherman, S., & Haidt, J. (2004). Elevation and vagal tone. Unpublished manuscript. University of Virginia.

Owren, M. J., & Bachorowski, J. (2001). The evolution of emotional expression: A "selfish-gene" account of smiling and laughter in early hominids and humans. In T. J. Mayne & G. A. Bonanno (Eds.), *Emotions: Current issues and future directions* (pp. 152–191). New York: Guilford.

Oxford, M., Cavell, T. A., & Hughes, J. N. (2003). Callous/unemotional traits moderate the relation between ineffective parenting and child externalizing problems: A partial replication and extension. *Journal of Clinical Child and Adolescent Psychology, 32*, 577–585.

Ozer, D. J., & Reise, S. P. (1994). Personality assessment. *Annual Review of Psychology, 45*, 357–388.

Page, D. (1955). *Sappho and Alceus: An introduction to the study of ancient Lesbian poetry*. Oxford: Oxford University Press.

Panksepp, J. (1993). Neurochemical control of moods and emotions: Amino acids to neuropeptides. In M. Lewis & J. M. Haviland (Eds.), *Handbook of emotions* (pp. 87–107). New York: Guilford.

Panksepp, J. (1998). *Affective neuroscience: The foundations of human and animal emotions*. Oxford: Oxford University Press.

Panksepp, J. (2001). The neuro-evolutionary cusp between emotions and cognitions: Implications for understanding consciousness and the emergence of a unified mind science. *Evolution and Cognition, 7*, 141–163.

Panksepp, J. (2005). Affective consciousness: Core emotional feelings in animals and humans. *Consciousness and Cognition, 14*, 30–80.

Panksepp, J., Nelson, E., & Bekkedal, M. (1997). Brain systems for the mediation of social separation-distress and social-reward. Evolutionary antecedents and neuropeptide intermediaries. In C. S. Carter, I. I. Lederhendler, & B. Kirkpatrick (Eds.), *The integrative neurobiology of affiliation, Vol. 807* (pp. 78–100). New York: New York Academy of Sciences.

Papez, J. W. (1937). A proposed mechanism of emotion. *Archives of Neurology and Psychiatry, 38*, 725–743.

Papousek, H., Jürgens, U., & Papousek, M. (Eds.). (1992). *Non-vocal communication: Comparative and developmental approaches*. New York: Cambridge University Press.

Parkinson, B. (1996). Emotions are social. *British Journal of Psychology, 87*, 663–683.

Parkinson, B., & Manstead, A. S. R. (1992). Appraisal as a cause of emotion. In M. S. Clark (Ed.), *Emotion*. Newbury Park, CA: Sage.

Parkinson, B., Fischer, A. H., & Manstead, A. S. R. (2004). *Emotion in social relations: Cultural, group, and interpersonal processes*. Philadelphia, PA: Psychology Press.

Parrott, W. G., & Sabini, J. (1990). Mood and memory under natural conditions: Evidence for mood incongruent recall. *Journal of Personality and Social Psychology, 59*, 321–336.

Parrott, W. G., & Spackman, M. P. (2000). Emotion and memory. In M. Lewis & J. Haviland-Jones

(Eds.), *Handbook of emotions, second edition* (pp. 476–490). New York: Guilford.

Parrott, W. G., & Smith, S. F. (1991). Embarrassment: Actual vs. typical cases and classical vs. prototypical representations. *Cognition and Emotion, 5,* 467–488.

Parry, G., & Shapiro, D. A. (1986). Social support and life events in working-class women. *Archives of General Psychiatry, 43,* 315–323.

Pascalis, O., & Slater, A. (Eds.) (2003). *The development of face processing in infancy and early childhood: Current perspectives.* New York: Nova Science.

Paster, G. K., Rowe, K., & Floyd-Wilson, M. (Eds.) (2004). *Reading the passions: Essays on the cultural history of emotion.* Philadelphia: University of Pennsylvania Press.

Patel, V., Araya, R., De Lima, M., et al. (1999). Women, poverty and common mental disorders in four restructuring societies. *Social Science and Medicine, 49,* 1461–1471.

Patterson, G. R. (1982). *Coercive family process.* Eugene, OR: Castalia.

Patterson, G. R. (1985). A microsocial analysis of anger and irritable behavior. In M. A. Chesney & R. H. Rosenman (Eds.), *Anger and hostility in cardiovascular and behavioral disorders.* Washington, DC: Hemisphere Publishing Corporation.

Patterson, G. R. (1986). Performance models for antisocial boys. *American Psychologist, 41,* 432–444.

Patterson, G. R., Capaldi, D., & Bank, L. (1991). The early starter model for predicting delinquency. In D. J. Pepler & K. H. Rubin (Eds.), *The development and treatment of childhood aggression.* Hillsdale, NJ: Erlbaum.

Patterson, G. R., Furgatch, M. S., Voerger, K. L., & Stoolmiller, M. (1998). Variables that initiate and maintain an early onset trajectory of offending. *Development and Psychopathology, 10,* 531–547.

Patterson, S. B., & Albers, A. B. (2001). Effects of poverty and maternal depression on early child development. *Child Development, 72,* 1794–1813.

Pavlov, I. P. (1927). *Conditioned reflexes* (G. V. Anrep, Trans.). New York: Dover (current edition 1960).

Pavot, W., Diener, E., & Fujita, F. (1990). Extraversion and happiness. *Personality and Individual Differences, 11*(12), 1299–1306.

Pecina, S., & Berridge, K. C. (2000). Opioid site in nucleus accumbens shell mediates eating and hedonic "liking" for food: Map based on microinjection Fos plumes. *Brain Research, 863,* 71–86.

Pedersen, C. (1997). Oxytocin control of maternal behavior. Regulation by sex steroids and offspring stimuli. *Annals of the New York Academy of Sciences, 807,* 126–145.

Pellegrini, A. D. (2002). Rough and tumble play from childhood through adolescence: Development and possible functions. In P. K. Smith & C. H. Hart (Eds.), *Blackwell handbook of childhood social development* (pp. 437–453). Malden, MA: Blackwell.

Pellegrini, A. D. (2003). Perceptions and functions of play and real fighting in early adolescence. *Child Development, 74,* 1522–1533.

Pellegrini, A. D., & Bjorkland, D. F. (2004). The ontogeny and phylogeny of children's object and fantasy play. *Human Nature, 15,* 23–43.

Peng, K., & Nisbett, R. (1999). Culture, dialectics, and reasoning about contradiction. *American Psychologist, 54,* 741–754.

Peng, K., Ames, D., & Knowles, E. (2001). Culture and human inference: Perspectives from three traditions. In D. Masumoto (Ed.), *Handbook of culture and psychology.* New York: Oxford University Press, pp. 243–263.

Pennebaker, J. W. (1989). Confession, inhibition, and disease. In L. Berkowitz (Ed.), *Advances in experimental social psychology* (Vol. 22, pp. 211–244). San Diego: Academic Press.

Pennebaker, J. W. (1997). Writing about emotional experiences as a therapeutic process. *Psychological Science, 8,* 162–166.

Pennebaker, J. W. (2002). Writing, social processes, and psychotherapy: From past to future. In S. J. Lepore & J. M. Smyth (Eds.), *The writing cure: How expressive writing promotes health and emotional well-being* (pp. 281–291). Washington, DC: American Psychological Association.

Pennebaker, J. W., Kiecolt-Glaser, J. K., & Glaser, R. (1988). Disclosure of traumas and immune function: Health implications of psychotherapy. *Journal of Consulting and Clinical Psychology, 56,* 239–245.

Pennebaker, J. W., Mehl, M. R., & Niederhoffer, K. G. (2003). Psychological aspects of natural language use: Our words, our selves. *Annual Review of Psychology, 54,* 547–577.

Pennebaker, J. W., & Seagal, J. D. (1999). Forming a story: The health benefits of narrative. *Journal of Clinical Psychology, 55,* 1243–1254.

Pennebaker, J. W., Zech, E., & Rimé, B. (2001). Disclosing and sharing emotion: psychological, social, and health consequences. In M. S. Stroebe, R. O. Hansson, W. Stroebe, & H. Schut (Eds.), *Handbook of bereavement research: consequences, coping, and care* (pp. 517-543). Washington, DC: American Psychological Association.

Perper, T. (1985). *Sex signals: The biology of love.* Philadelphia: ISI Press.

Perrow, C. (1984). *Normal accidents: Living with high-risk technologies.* New York: Basic Books.

Peters-Martin, P., & Wachs, T. (1984). A longitudinal study of temperament and its correlates in the first 12 months. *Infant behavior and development, 7,* 285-298.

Peterson, G., Mehl, L., & Leiderman, H. (1979). The role of some birth related variables in father attachment. *American Journal of Orthopsychiatry, 40,* 330-338.

Pettit, G. S., & Bates, J. E. (1989). Family interaction patterns and children's behavior problems from infancy to 4 years. *Developmental Psychology, 25,* 413-420.

Petty, R., & Cacioppo, J. (1986). The elaboration likelihood model of persuasion. In L. Berkowitz (Ed.), *Advances in experimental social psychology* (Vol. 19, pp. 124-205). New York: Academic Press.

Phan, K. L., Taylor, S. F., Welsh, R. C., Ho, S.-H., Britton, J. C., & Liberzon, I. (2004). Neural correlates of individual ratings of emotional salience. *Neuroimage, 21,* 768-780.

Phillips, A. G., Blaha, C. D., Pfaus, J. G., & Blackburn, J. R. (1992). Neurobiological correlates of positive emotional states: Dopamine, anticipation, and reward. In K. T. Strongman (Ed.), *International review of studies on emotion* (Vol. 2, pp. 31-50). New York: John Wiley.

Phillips, A. T., Wellman, H. M., & Spelke, E. S. (2002). Infants' ability to connect gaze and emotional expression to intended action. *Cognition, 85,* 53-78.

Phillips, M. L., Young, A. W., Senior, C., et al. (1997). A specific neural substrate for perceiving facial expressions of disgust. *Nature, 389,* 495-498.

Pickles, A., Rowe, R., Simonoff, E., et al. (2001). Child psychiatric symptoms and psychosocial impairment: Relationship and prognostic significance. *British Journal of Psychiatry, 179,* 230-235.

Pilowsky, I., & Katsikitis, M. (1994). The classification of facial emotions: A computer based taxonomic approach. *Journal of Affective Disorders, 30,* 61-71.

Pinney, T. (Ed.) (1963). *Essays of George Eliot.* New York: Columbia University Press.

Pittam, J., & Scherer, K. R. (1993). Vocal expression and communication of emotion. In M. Lewis & J. M. Haviland (Eds.), *Handbook of emotions* (pp. 185-197). New York: Guilford.

Plato (375 BCE). *The republic.* London: Penguin (current edition 1955).

Plomin, R. (1988). *Development, genetics and psychology.* Hillsdale, NJ: Erlbaum.

Plomin, R., & Bergeman, C. S. (1991). The nature of nurture: Genetic influence on environmental measures. *Behavioral and Brain Sciences, 14,* 373-427.

Plomin, R., & Caspi, A. (1998). DNA and personality. *European Journal of Personality, 12,* 387-407.

Plomin, R., Chipuer, H. M., & Loelin, J. C. (1990). Behavioral genetics and personality. In L. A. Pervin (Ed.), *Handbook of personality* (pp. 225-243). New York: Guilford.

Plomin, R., Lichtenstein, P., Pedersen, N., McClearn, G. E., & Nesselroade, J. R. (1990). Genetic influences on life events during the last half of the life span. *Psychology of Aging, 5,* 25-30.

Plomin, R., & McGuffin, P. (2003). Psychopathology in the postgenomic era. *Annual Review of Psychology, 54,* 205-228.

Plutchik, R. (1980). *Emotion: A psychobioevolutionary synthesis.* New York: Harper & Row.

Polya, G. (1957). *How to solve it: A new aspect of mathematical method* (2nd ed.). Garden City, NY: Doubleday.

Pomerantz, E. M., & Rudolph, K. (2003). What ensues from emotional distress? Implications for competence estimation. *Child Development, 74,* 329-345.

Ponting, C. (1991). *A green history of the world: The environment and the collapse of great civilizations.* London: Sinclair-Stevenson.

Popper, K. R. (1962a). *Conjectures and refutations.* New York, NY: Basic Books.

Popper, K. R. (1962b). *The open society and its enemies* (Vol. 2, 4th ed.). London: Routledge & Kegan Paul.

Porges, S. (1998). Love: An emergent property of the mammalian autonomic nervous system. *Pychoendocrinology, 23,* 837-861.

Porges, S. P. (1995). Orienting in a defensive world: Mammalian modifications of our evolutionary heritage. A polyvagal theory. *Psychophysiology, 32,* 301-318.

Power, M., & Dalgleish, T. (1997). *Cognition and emotion: From order to disorder.* Hove: Psychology Press.

Prince, R. (1980). Variations in psychotherapeutic procedures. In H. C. Triandis & J. G. Draguns (Eds.), *Handbook of cross-cultural psychology. Vol. 6. Psychopathology* (pp. 291–349). Boston: Allyn & Bacon.

Prior, M., Smart, D., Sanson, A., & Oberklaid, F. (1993). Sex differences and psychological adjustment from infancy to eight years. *Journal of the American Academy of Child and Adolescent Psychiatry, 32*, 291–304.

Profet, M. (1992). Pregnancy sickness as adaptation: A deterrent to maternal ingestion of teratogens. In J. H. Barlow, L. Cosmides, & J. Tooby (Eds.), *The adapted mind* (pp. 327–366). New York: Oxford University Press.

Proust, M. (1913–1927). *A la recherche du temps perdu* [Remembrance of things past] (C. K. Scott-Moncreiff, T. Kilmartin, & A. Mayor, Trans.). London: Chatto & Windus (current edition 1981).

Provine, R. R. (1992). Contagious laughter: Laughter is a sufficient stimulus for laughs and smiles. *Bulletin of the Psychonomic Society, 30*, 1–4.

Provine, R. R. (1993). Laughter punctuates speech: Linguistic, social, and gender contexts of laughter. *Ethology, 95*, 291–298.

Provine, R. R., & Fischer, K. R. (1989). Laughing, smiling, and talking: Relation to sleeping and social context in humans. *Ethology, 83*, 295–305.

Purkis, J. (1985). *A preface to George Eliot.* London: Longman.

Putnam, H. (1975). The meaning of meaning. In K. Gunderson (Ed.), *Language, mind and knowledge. Minnesota studies in the philosophy of science* (Vol. 7). Minneapolis, MN: University of Minnesota Press.

Putnam, S. P., & Stifter, C. A. (2005). Behavioral approach-inhibition in toddlers: Prediction from infancy, positive and negative affective components, and relations with behavior problems. *Child Development, 76*, 212–266.

Pynoos, R. S., & Nader, K. (1989). Children's memory and proximity to violence. *Journal of the American Academy of Child and Adolescent Psychiatry, 28*, 236–241.

Pyszczynski, T., & Greenberg, J. (1987). Self-regulatory perseveration and the depressive self-focusing style: A self-awareness theory of reactive depression. *Psychological Bulletin, 102*, 122–138.

Quigley, B., & Tedeschi, J. (1996). Mediating effects of blame attributions on feelings of anger. *Personality and Social Psychology Bulletin, 22*, 1280–1288.

Quinton, D., & Rutter, M. (1988). *Parenting breakdown: The making and breaking of inter-generational links.* Aldershot: Avebury.

Quinton, D., Rutter, M., & Liddle, C. (1984). Institutional rearing, parental difficulties, and marital support. *Psychological Medicine, 14*, 107–124.

Rabin, B. S. (1999). *Stress, immune function, and health: The connection.* New York: Wiley.

Radke-Yarrow, M., Cummings, E. M., Kuczynski, L., & Chapman, M. (1985). Patterns of attachment in two and three-year-olds in normal families and families with parental depression. *Child Development, 56*, 884–893.

Radke-Yarrow, M., Richters, J., & Wilson, W. E. (1988). Child development in a network of relationships. In R. A. Hinde & J. Stevenson-Hinde (Eds.), *Relationships within families* (pp. 48–67). Oxford: Clarendon Press.

Raine, A. (2002). Biosocial studies of antisocial and violent behavior in children and adults: A review. *Journal of Abnormal Child Psychology, 30*, 311–326.

Reisenzein, R. (1983). The Schachter theory of emotion: Two decades later. *Psychological Bulletin, 94*, 239–264.

Reisenzein, R. (1992a). A structuralist reconstruction of Wundt's three-dimensional theory of emotion. In H. Westmeyer (Ed.), *The structuralist program in psychology: foundations and applications* (pp. 141–189). Toronto: Hopgrefe & Huber.

Reisenzein, R. (1992b). Stumpf's cognitive-evaluative theory of emotion. *American Psychologist, 47*, 34–45.

Rholes, W. S., Simpson, J. A., & Orina, M. M. (1999). Attachment and anger in an anxiety-provoking situation. *Journal of Personality and Social Psychology, 76*, 940–957.

Richards, I. A. (1925). *Principles of literary criticism.* New York: Harcourt Brace Jovanovich.

Richards, M. P. M., & Bernal, J. (1972). An observational study of mother–infant interaction. In N. Blurton-Jones (Ed.), *Ethological studies of child behavior.* New York: Cambridge University Press.

Richman, N., Stevenson, J., & Graham, P. J. (1982). *Preschool to school.* London: Academic Press.

Rimé, B., Finkenauer, C., Luminet, O., Zech, E., & Philippot, P. (1998). Social sharing of emotion: New evidence and new questions. *European Review of Social Psychology, 9*, 145–189.

Rimé, B., Mesquita, B., Philippot, P., & Boca, S. (1991). Beyond the emotional event: Six studies on the social sharing of emotions. *Cognition and Emotion, 5,* 435–465.

Rimé, B., Philippot, P., & Cisamolo, D. (1990). Social schemata of peripheral changes in emotion. *Journal of Personality and Social Psychology, 59,* 38–49.

Rinn, W. E. (1984). The neuropsychology of facial expression: A review of the neurological and psychological mechanisms for producing facial expressions. *Psychological Bulletin, 95,* 52–77.

Ritchie, S., & Howes, C. (2003). Program practices, caregiver stablity, and child–caregiver relationships. *Journal of Applied Developmental Psychology, 24,* 497–516.

Rizzolatti, G., Fadiga, L., Gallese, V., & Fogassi, L. (1996). Premotor cortex and the recognition of motor action. *Cognitive Brain Research, 3,* 131–141.

Roberts, R. E., Attkisson, C. C., & Rosenblatt, A. (1998). Prevalence of psychopathology among children and adolescents. *American Journal of Psychiatry, 155,* 715–725.

Roberts, T. A., & Pennebaker, J. W. (1995). Gender differences in perceiving internal state: Toward a his-and-hers model of perceptual cue use. In M. Zanna (Ed.), *Advances in experimental social psychology* (Vol. 27, pp. 143–176). New York: Academic Press.

Roberts, W., & Strayer, J. (1987). Parent responses to the emotional distress of their children: Relations with children's competence. *Developmental Psychology, 23,* 415–425.

Robins, L. N., & Regier, D. A. (1991). *Psychiatric disorders in America: The epidemiologic catchment area study.* New York: Free Press.

Rogers, C. R. (1972). My personal growth. In A. Burton et al. (Eds.), *Twelve therapists* (pp. 28–77). San Francisco: Jossey-Bass.

Rogers, H. E. (1965). A wife's eye view of Carl Rogers. *Voices, 1,* 93–98.

Rolls, E. T. (1997). Taste and olfactory processing in the brain and its relation to the control of eating. *Critical Reviews in Neurobiology, 11*(4), 263–287.

Rolls, E. T. (1999). *The brain and emotion.* New York: Oxford University Press.

Rolls, E. T. (2000). The orbitofrontal cortex and reward. *Cerebral Cortex, 10,* 284–294.

Rolls, E. T., & Bayliss, L. L. (1994). Gustatory, olfactory, and visual convergence within the primate orbitofrontal cortex. *Journal of Neuroscience, 14*(9), 1532–1540.

Rolls, E. T., Hornak, J., Wade, D., & McGrath, J. (1994). Emotion related learning in patients with social and emotional changes associated with frontal lobe damage. *Journal of Neurology, Neurosurgery and Psychiatry, 57,* 1518–1524.

Romney, A. K., Moore, C. C., & Rusch, C. D. (1997). Cultural universals: Measuring the semantic structure of emotion terms in English and Japanese. *Proceedings from the National Academy of Sciences, 94,* 5489–5494.

Rosaldo, M. (1980). *Knowledge and passion: Ilongot notions of self and social life.* Cambridge: Cambridge University Press.

Roseman, I. J. (1984). Cognitive determinants of emotion: A structural theory. In P. Shaver (Ed.), *Review of personality and social psychology, Vol. 5. Emotions, relationships and health* (pp. 11–36). Beverley Hills, CA: Sage.

Rosenbaum, J. F., Biederman, J., & Gersten, M., et al. (1988). Behavioral inhibition in children with parents with panic disorder and agoraphobia. *Archives of General Psychiatry, 45,* 463–470.

Rosenberg, D., & Bloom, H. (1990). *The book of J.* New York: Grove Weidenfeld.

Rosenberg, E. (1998). Levels of analysis and the organization of affect. *Review of General Psychology, 2,* 247–270.

Rosenberg, E. L., & Ekman, P. (1994). Coherence between expressive and experiential systems in emotion. *Cognition and Emotion, 8,* 201–229.

Rosenman, R. H., Brand, R. J., Jenkins, C. D., Friedman, M., Straus, R., & Wurm, M. (1975). Coronary heart disease in the Western collaborative group study. *Journal of the American Medical Association, 233,* 872–877.

Ross, E. D. (1984). Right hemisphere's role in language, affective behavior, and emotion. *Trends in Neuroscience, 7,* 342–346.

Rothbart, M. K. (1986). Longitudinal observation of infant temperament. *Developmental Psychology, 22,* 356–365.

Rothbart, M., Ellis, L. K., & Posner, M. (2004). Temperament and self-regulation. In R. F. Baumeister & K. Vohs (Eds.), *Handbook of self-regulation: Research, theory, and applications* (pp. 357–370). New York: Guilford.

Rothbart, M., Ellis, L. K., Rueda, M. R., & Posner, M. (2003). Developing mechanisms of temperamental effortful control. *Journal of Personality, 71,* 1113–1143.

Rothbart, M. K., Ziaie, H., & O'Boyle, C. G. (1992). Self regulation and emotion in infancy. In N. Eisenberg & R. A. Fabes (Eds.), *Emotion and its regulation* in early development (New Directions in Child Development, No. 55) (pp. 7–24). San Francisco: Jossey-Bass.

Rousseau, J.-J. (1755). Discourse on the origin and basis of inequality among men. In *The essential Rousseau* (pp. 125–201). New York: Penguin (current edition 1975).

Rousseau, J.-J. (1762). The social contract, or principles of political right. In *The essential Rousseau* (pp. 1–124). New York: Penguin.

Rozin, P., & Fallon, A. E. (1987). A perspective on disgust. *Psychological Review, 94,* 23–41.

Rozin, P., & Kalat, J. (1971). Specific hungers and poison avoidance as adaptive specialization of learning. *Psychological Review, 78,* 459–486.

Rozin, P., & Royzman, E. B. (2001). Negativity bias, negativity dominance, and contagion. *Personality and Social Psychology Review, 5,* 296–320.

Rozin, P., Haidt, J., & McCauley, C. R. (1993). Disgust. In M. Lewis & J. M. Haviland (Eds.), *Handbook of emotions* (pp. 575–594). New York: Guilford.

Rozin, P., Lowery, L., Imada, S., & Haidt, J. (1999). The CAD triad hypothesis: A mapping between three moral emotions (contempt, anger, and disgust), and three moral codes (community, autonomy, divinity). *Journal of Personality and Social Psychology, 66,* 870–881.

Rubin, K. H. (1993). The Waterloo longitudinal project: Correlates and consequences of social withdrawal from childhood to adolescence. In K. H. Rubin & J. Asendorpf (Eds.), *Social withdrawal, inhibition and shyness in childhood* (pp. 291–314). Hillsdale, NJ: Erlbaum.

Ruch, W. (1993). Exhilaration and humor. In M. Lewis & J. M. Haviland (Eds.), *Handbook of emotion* (pp. 605–616). New York: Guilford.

Rusbult, C. E. (1980). Commitment and satisfaction in romantic associations: A test of the investment model. *Journal of Experimental Social Psychology, 17,* 172–186.

Rusbult, C. E. (1983). A longitudinal test of the investment model: The development (and deterioration) of satisfaction and commitment in heterosexual involvements. *Journal of Personality and Social Psychology, 45,* 101–117.

Russell, J. A. (1991b). In defense of a prototype approach to emotion concepts. *Journal of Personality and Social Psychology, 60,* 37–47.

Russell, J. A. (1994). Is there universal recognition of emotion from facial expression? A review of methods and studies. *Psychological Bulletin, 115,* 102–141.

Russell, J. A. (2003). Core affect and the psychological construction of emotion. *Psychological Review, 110,* 145–172

Russell, J. A., Bachorowski, J. A., & Fernandez-Dols, J. M. (2003). Facial and vocal expression of emotion. *Annual Review of Psychology, 54,* 329–349.

Russell, J. A., & Fernandez-Dols, J. M. (1997). What does a facial expression mean? In J. A. Russell & J. M. Fernandez-Dols (Eds.), *The psychology of facial expression* (pp. 3–30). New York: Cambridge University Press.

Rutter, M. (1972). *Maternal deprivation reassessed.* Harmondsworth: Penguin.

Rutter, M. (1979). Protective factors in children's responses to stress and disadvantage. In M. W. Kent & J. E. Rolfs (Eds.), *Primary prevention in psychopathology, Vol. 3: Social competence in children* (pp. 49–74). Hanover, NH: University Press of New England.

Rutter, M. (1992). Psychosocial resilience and protective mechanisms. In J. E. Rolf, D. Masten, D. Cicchetti, K. Nuechterlein, & S. Wientraub (Eds.), *Risk and protective factors in the development of psychopathology.* New York: Cambridge University Press.

Rutter, M. (2002). Nature, nurture, and development: From evangelism through science towards policy and practice. *Child Development, 73,* 1–21.

Rutter, M. (2005). Environmentally mediated risks for psychopathology: Research strategies and findings. *Journal of the American Academy of Child and Adolescent Psychiatry, 44,* 3–18.

Rutter, M., & Giller, H. (1983). *Juvenile delinquency: Trends and perspectives.* Harmondsworth: Penguin.

Rutter, M., Giller, H., & Hagell, A. (1998). *Antisocial behavior by young people.* New York: Cambridge University Press.

Rutter, M., Graham, P., Chadwick, O., & Yule, W. (1976). Adolescent turmoil: Fact or fiction? *Journal of Child Psychology and Psychiatry, 17,* 35–56.

Rutter, M., Silberg, J., O'Connor, T. G., & Simonoff, E. (1999). Genetics and child psychiatry: II. Empirical research findings. *Journal of Child Psychology and Psychiatry, 40,* 19–55.

Rutter, M., & Taylor, E. (Eds.). (2002). *Child and adolescent psychiatry, 4th edition.* Oxford: Blackwell.

Rutter, M., Tizard, J., & Whitmore, K. (1970). *Education, health and behavior.* London: Longmans.

Rutter, M., Tuma, A. H., & Lann, I. S. (1988). *Assessment and diagnosis in child psychopathology*. London: David Fulton.

Rutter, M., Yule, B., Quinton, D., Rowlands, O., Yule, W., & Berger, M. (1975). Attainment and adjustment in two geographical areas: III. Some factors accounting for area differences. *British Journal of Psychiatry, 126*, 520-533.

Rydell, A.-M., Berlin, L., & Bohlin, G. (2003). Emotionality, emotion regulation, and adaptation among 5- to 8-year-old children. *Emotion, 3*, 30-47.

Saarni, C. (1984). An observational study of children's attempts to monitor their expressive behavior. *Child Development, 55*, 1504-1513.

Saarni, C. (1999). *The development of emotional competence*. New York: Guilford.

Sacks, O. (1973). *Awakenings*. London: Duckworth.

Safer, M. A., Bonanno, G. A., & Field, N. P. (2001). It was never that bad: Biased recall of grief and long-term adjustment to the death of a spouse. *Memory, 9*, 195-204.

Sagi, A., Lamb, M. E., Lewkowicz, K. S., Shoham, R., Dvir, R., & Estes, D. (1985). Security of infant-mother, -father, and -metapelet attachments among kibbutz-reared Israeli children. *Monographs of the Society for Research in Child Development, 50* (1-2, Serial No. 209), 257-276.

Salaman, E. (1982). A collection of moments. In U. Neisser (Ed.), *Memory observed: Remembering in natural contexts* (pp. 49-63). San Francisco: Freeman.

Salem, J. E., & Kring, A. (1999). Flat affect and social skills in schizophrenia: Evidence for their independence. *Psychiatry Research, 87*, 159-167.

Salovey, P. (1991). *The psychology of jealousy and envy*. New York: Guilford.

Salovey, P., & Mayer, J. M. (1990). Emotional intelligence. *Imagination, cognition and personality, 9*, 185-211.

Sandell, R., Blomberg, J., & Lazar, A. (2002). Time matters: On temporal interactions in long term follow-up of long term psychotherapies. *Psychotherapy Research, 12*, 39-58.

Sapolsky, R. M. (1994). *Why zebras don't get ulcers*. New York: Freeman.

Sarason, B. R., Shearin, E. N., Pierce, G. R., & Sarason, G. R. (1987). Interrelations of social support measures: Theoretical and practical implications. *Journal of Personality and Social Psychology, 52*, 813-832.

Scarr, S., & Salapatek, P. (1970). Patterns of fear development during infancy. *Merrill-Palmer Quarterly, 16*, 53-90.

Schachter, S., & Singer, J. (1962). Cognitive, social and physiological determinants of emotional state. *Psychological Review, 69*, 379-399.

Schank, R., & Abelson, R. (1977). *Scripts, plans, goals and understanding: An inquiry into human knowledge structures*. Hillsdale, NJ: Erlbaum.

Schechner, R. (2001). Rasaesthetics. *The Drama Review, 43*, 27-50.

Scheff, T. J. (1979). *Catharsis in healing, ritual, and drama*. Berkeley: University of California Press.

Scheff, T. J. (1997). *Emotions, the social bond, and human reality: Part/whole analysis*. New York: Cambridge University Press.

Scherer, J. F., True, W. R., Xian, H., Lyons, M. J., Eisen, S. A., Goldberg, J., et al. (2000). Evidence for genetic influences common and specific to symptoms of generalized anxiety and panic. *Journal of Affective Disorders, 57*, 25-35.

Scherer, K. R. (1986). Vocal affect expression: A review and a model for future research. *Psychological Bulletin, 99*, 143-165.

Scherer, K. R. (1988). Criteria for emotion antecedent appraisal: A review. In V. Hamilton, G. H. Bower, & N. H. Frijda (Eds.), *Cognitive perspectives on emotion and motivation* (pp. 89-126). Dordrecht: Kluwer.

Scherer, K. R. (1997). The role of culture in emotion antecedent appraisal. *Journal of Personality and Social Psychology, 73*, 902-922.

Scherer, K. R., Johnstone, T., & Klasmeyer, G. (2003). Vocal expression of emotion. In R. J. Davidson, K. R. Scherer, & H. H. Goldsmith (Eds.), *Handbook of affective sciences* (pp. 433-456). New York: Oxford University Press.

Scherer, K. R., Zentner, M. R., & Stern, D. (2004). Beyond surprise: The puzzle of infants' expressive reactions to expectancy violation. *Emotion, 4*, 389-402.

Schiff, B. B., & Lamon, M. (1989). Inducing emotion by unilateral contraction of facial muscles: A new look at hemispheric specialization and the experience of emotion. *Neuropsychologia, 27*, 923-935.

Schiff, B. B., & Lamon, M. (1994). Inducing emotion by unilateral contraction of hand muscles. *Cortex, 30*, 247-254.

Schimmack, U. (1996). Cultural influences on the recognition of emotion by facial expressions:

Individualistic or Caucasian cultures? *Journal of Cross-Cultural Psychology, 27,* 37–50.

Schimmack, U., Oishi, S., & Diener, E. (2002). Cultural influences on the relation between pleasant emotions and unpleasant emotions: Asian dialectic philosophies or individualism-collectivism? *Cognition and Emotion, 16,* 705–719.

Schimmack, U., Oishi, S., & Diener, E. (2005). Individualism: A valid and important dimension of cultural differences between nations. *Personality and Social Psychology Review, 9,* 17–31.

Schultz, W., Dayan, P., & Montague, P. R. (1997). A neural substrate of prediction and reward. *Science, 275,* 1593–1599.

Schwarz, N. (1990). Feelings as information: Informational and motivational functions of affective states. In E. T. Higgins & R. M. Sorrentino (Eds.), *Handbook of motivation and cognition, Volume 2* (pp. 527–561). New York: Guilford.

Schwarz, N., & Clore, G. L. (1983). Mood, misattribution, and judgments of well-being: Informative and directive functions of affective states. *Journal of Personality and Social Psychology, 45,* 513–523.

Sebeok, T. A., & Umiker-Sebeok, J. (1983). "You know my method": A juxtaposition of Charles S. Peirce and Sherlock Holmes. In U. Eco & T. A. Sebeok (Eds.), *The sign of three: Dupin, Holmes, Peirce* (pp. 11–54). Bloomington: Indiana University Press.

Segal, Z. V., Williams, J. M. G., & Teasdale, J. D. (2002). *Mindfulness based cognitive therapy for depression: A new approach to preventing relapse.* New York: Guilford.

Segal, Z. V., Williams, J. M. G., Teasdale, J. D., & Gemar, M. (1996). A cognitive science perspective on kindling and episode sensitization in recurrent affective disorder. *Psychological Medicine, 26,* 371–380.

Selye, H. (1936). A syndrome produced by diverse nocuous agents. *Nature, 138,* 32.

Serrano, J. M., Iglesias, J., & Loaches, A. (1995). Infants' responses to adult static facial expressions. *Infant Behavior and Development, 18,* 477–482.

Seyfarth, R. M., & Cheney, D. L. (1992). Meaning and mind in monkeys. *Scientific American, 267,* 122–129.

Shakespeare, W. (1600). *Hamlet.* London: Methuen (current edition 1981).

Shakespeare, W. (1623). As you like it. In A. Harbage (Ed.), *The complete Pelican Shakespeare: Comedies and romances* (pp. 200–229). Harmondsworth: Penguin (current edition 1969).

Shakespeare, W. (1623). *The Norton Shakespeare* (Ed. S. Greenblatt). New York: Norton (modern edition 1997).

Shapiro, D. A., Rees, A., Barkham, M., Hardy, G., Reynolds, S., & Startup, M. (1995). Effects of treatment duration and severity of depression on the maintenance of gains after cognitive-behavioral and psychodynamic interpersonal psychotherapy. *Journal of Consulting and Clinical Psychology, 63,* 378–387.

Shaver, P. R., & Brennan, K. A. (1992). Attachment style and the "big five" of personality traits: Their connections with each other and with romantic relationship outcomes. *Personality and Social Psychology Bulletin, 18,* 536–545.

Shaver, P. R., & Mikulincer, M. (2002). Attachment-related psychodynamics. *Attachment and human development, 4,* 133–161.

Shaver, P., Hazan, C., & Bradshaw, D. (1988). Love as attachment: The integration of three behavioral systems. In R. J. Sternberg & M. L. Barnes (Eds.), *The psychology of love* (pp. 68–99). New Haven, CT: Yale University Press.

Shaver, P., Schwartz, J. C., Kirson, D., & O'Connor, C. (1987). Emotion knowledge: Further exploration of a prototype approach. *Journal of Personality and Social Psychology, 52,* 1061–1086.

Shay, J. (1995). *Achilles in Vietnam: Combat trauma and the undoing of character.* New York: Simon & Schuster.

Shearn, D., Bergman, E., Hill, K., Abel, A., & Hinds, L. (1990). Facial coloration and temperature responses in blushing. *Psychophysiology, 27,* 687–693.

Shearn, D., Bergman, E., Hill, K., Abel, A., & Hinds, L. (1992). Blushing as a function of audience size. *Psychophysiology, 29,* 431–436.

Shelley, M. (1818). *Frankenstein, or modern Prometheus.* Harmondsworth: Penguin (current edition 1985).

Sherif, M. (1956, November). Experiments in group conflict. *Scientific American, 195,* 54–58.

Sherif, M., & Sherif, C. W. (1953). *Groups in harmony and in tension.* New York: Harper & Row.

Shields, A., & Ciccetti, D. (2001). Parental maltreatment and emotion disregulation as risk factors for bullying and victimization in middle childhood. *Journal of Clinical Child Psychology, 30,* 349–363.

Shields, S. A. (2002). *Speaking from the heart: Gender and the social meaning of emotion*. Cambridge: Cambridge University Press.

Shikibu, M. (*c.*1000). *The tale of Genji* (R. Tyler, Trans.). New York: Viking Penguin (2001).

Shostrom, E. L. P. (1966). *Three approaches to psychotherapy* (film). Santa Ana, CA: Psychological Films.

Shrout, P. E., Link, B. G., Dohrenwend, B. P., Skodal, A. E., Stueve, A., & Mirtznik, J. (1989). Characterizing life events as risk factors for depression: The role of fateful loss events. *Journal of Abnormal Psychology*, 98, 460–467.

Shweder, R. (1990). In defense of moral realism: Reply to Gabannesch. *Child Development*, 61, 2060–2067.

Shweder, R. A., & Haidt, J. (2000). The cultural psychology of the emotions: Ancient and new. In M. Lewis & J. M. Haviland-Jones (Eds.), *Handbook of emotions, second edition* (pp. 397–414). New York: Guilford.

Shweder, R. A., Much, N. C., Mahapatra, M., & Park, L. (1997). The "big three" of morality (autonomy, community, divinity), and the "big three" explanations of suffering. In A. Brandt & P. Rozin (Eds.), *Morality and health* (pp. 119–169). New York: Routledge.

Sibley, C., & Ahlquist, J. E. (1984). The phylogeny of the hominid primates, as indicated by DNA–RNA hybridization. *Journal of Molecular Evolution*, 20, 2–15.

Siegman, A. W., Townsend, S. T., Civilek, A. C., et al. (2000). Antagonistic behavior, dominance, hostility, and coronary heart disease. *Psychosomatic Medicine*, 62, 248–257.

Silk, J. B., Alberts, S. C., & Altmann, J. (2003). Social bonds of female baboons enhance infant survival. *Science*, 302, 1231-1234.

Silk, J. S., Steinberg, L., & Morris, A. S. (2003). Adolescents' emotion regulation in daily life: Links to depressive symptoms and problem behavior. *Child Development*, 74, 1869–1880.

Simon, H. A. (1967). Motivational and emotional controls of cognition. *Psychological Review*, 74, 29–39.

Simons, R. L., Whitbeck, L. B., Conger, R. D., & Chyi-In, W. (1991). Inter-generational transmission of harsh parenting. *Developmental Psychology*, 27(1), 159–171.

Simpson, J. A., & Kenrick, D. T. (1998). *Evolutionary social psychology*. Hillsdale, NJ: Lawrence Erlbaum.

Simpson, J. A., Ickes, W., & Grich, J. (1999). When accuracy hurts: Reactions of anxious-ambivalent dating partners to a relationship-threatening situation. *Journal of Personality and Social Psychology*, 76, 754–769.

Simpson, J. A., Rholes, W. S., & Phillips, D. (1996). Conflict in close relationships: An attachment perspective. *Journal of Personality and Social Psychology*, 71, 899–914.

Singer, J. A., & Salovey, P. (1993). *The remembered self: Emotion and memory in personality*. New York: Free Press.

Singer, J. A., & Singer, J. L. (1992). Transference in psychotherapy and daily life: Implications of current memory and social cognition research. In J. W. Barron, M. N. Eagle, & D. L. Wolinsky (Eds.), *Interface of psychoanalysis and psychology* (pp. 516–538). Washington, DC: American Psychological Association.

Singer, T., Seymour, B., O'Doherty, J., et al. (2004). Empathy for pain involves the affective but not sensory components of pain. *Science*, 303, 1157–1162.

Slaby, R. G., & Guerra, N. G. (1988). Cognitive mediators of aggression in adolescent offenders: 1. Assessment. *Developmental Psychology*, 24, 580–588.

Slater, A., & Lewis, M. (2002). *Introduction to infant development*. Oxford: Oxford University Press.

Sloane, R. B., Staples, F. R., Cristol, A. H., Yorkston, N. J., & Whipple, K. (1975). *Psychotherapy versus behavior therapy*. Cambridge, MA: Harvard University Press.

Smith, A. (1759). *The theory of moral sentiments*. Oxford: Oxford University Press (1976).

Smith, C., & Ellsworth, P. (1985). Patterns of cognitive appraisal in emotion. *Journal of Personality and Social Psychology*, 48, 813–838.

Smith, E. R. (1993). Social identity and social emotions: Toward new conceptualizations of prejudice. In D. M. Mackie & D. L. Hamilton (Eds.), *Affect, cognition, and stereotyping* (pp. 297–315). New York: Academic Press.

Smith, M. L., Glass, G. V., & Miller, T. I. (1980). *The benefits of psychotherapy*. Baltimore, MD: Johns Hopkins University Press.

Smith, P. K. (1982). Does play matter? Functional and evolutionary aspects of animal and human play. *Behavioral and Brain Sciences*, 5, 139–184.

Smith, T. W., & Ruiz, J. M. (2002). Psychosocial influences on the development and course of coronary heart disease: Current status and implications for research and practice. *Journal of Consulting and Clinical Psychology*, 70, 548–568.

Smoski, M. J., & Bachorowski, J.-A. (2003). Antiphonal laughter between friends and strangers. *Cognition and Emotion, 17*, 327–340.

Smuts, B. B. (1985). *Sex and friendship in baboons.* New York: Aldine.

Snowdon, C. T. (2003). Expression of emotion in non-human animals. In R. Davidson, K. Scherer, & H. H. Goldsmith (Eds.), *Handbook of affective sciences* (pp. 457–480). London: Oxford University Press.

Snyder, C. R., & Heinze, L. S. (2005). Forgiveness as a mediator of the relationship between PTSD and hostility in survivors of childhood abuse. *Cognition and Emotion, 19*, 413–431.

Snyder, J., & Patterson, G. R. (1986). The effects of consequences on patterns of social interaction: A quasi-experimental approach to reinforcement in natural interaction. *Child Development, 57*, 1257–1268.

Sober, E., & Wilson, D. S. (1998). *Unto others: The evolution and psychology of unselfish behavior.* Cambridge, MA: Harvard University Press.

Sogon, S., & Masutani, M. (1989). Identification of emotion from body movements. *Psychological Reports, 65*, 35–46.

Solomon, R. C. (1977). *The passions.* New York: Anchor.

Solomon, R. C. (2004). Emotions, thoughts, and feelings: Emotions as engagements with the world. In R. C. Solomon (Ed.), *Thinking about feeling: Contemporary philosophers on emotions* (pp. 76–88). New York: Oxford University Press.

Solomon, Z., & Bromet, E. (1982). The role of social factors in affective disorder: An assessment of the vulnerability model of Brown and his colleagues. *Psychological Medicine, 12*, 125–130.

Sood, B., Delaney-Black, V., Covington, C., et al. (2001). Prenatal alcohol exposure and childhood behavior at age 6 to 7 years: I. Dose–response effect. *Pediatrics, 108*, 1–9.

Sorabji, R. (2000). *Emotion and peace of mind: From Stoic agitation to Christian temptation.* Oxford: Oxford University Press.

Sorce, J. F., Emde, R. N., Campos, J., & Klinnert, M. D. (1985). Maternal emotional signaling: Its effect on the visual cliff behavior of 1-year-olds. *Developmental Psychiatry, 21*, 195–200.

Spangler, G., & Grossmann, K. E. (1993). Biobehavioral organization in securely and insecurely attached infants. *Child Development, 64*, 1439–1450.

Spielberger, C. D. (1983). *State-Trait Anxiety Inventory for Adults.* Palo Alto: Mind Garden.

Spielberger, C. D. (1996). *Manual for the State-Trait Anger Expression Inventory (STAXI).* Odessa, FL: Psychological Assessment Resources.

Spinoza, B. (1661–1675). On the improvement of the understanding, The ethics, and Correspondence (R. H. M. Elwes, Trans.). New York: Dover (current edition 1955).

Spock, B. (1945). *The common sense book of baby and child care.* New York: Dell, Sloan & Pearce.

Sroufe, A. (1978). The ontogenesis of emotion. In J. Osofsky (Ed.), *Handbook of infancy* (pp. 462–516). New York: Wiley.

Sroufe, L. A., Schork, E., Motti, E., Lawroski, N., & LaFreniere, P. (1984). The role of affect in emerging social competence. In C. Izard, J. Kagan, & R. Zajonc (Eds.), *Emotion, cognition and behavior* (pp. 289–319). New York: Cambridge University Press.

Stack, D. M. (2001). The salience of touch and physical contact during infancy: Unraveling some of the mysteries of the somesthetic sense. In G. Bremner & A. Fogel (Eds.), *Blackwell handbook of infant development* (pp. 351–378). Malden, MA: Blackwell.

Staines, J. (2004). Compassion in the public sphere of Milton and King Charles. In G. K. Paston, K. Rowe, & M. Floyd-Wilson (Eds.), *Reading the early modern passions: Essays in the cultural history of emotion* (pp. 89–110). Philadelphia: University of Pennsylvania Press.

Stanislavski, C. (1965). *An actor prepares* (E. R. Habgood, Trans.). New York: Theater Arts Books.

Stanovich, K. E. (2004). *The robot's rebellion: Finding meaning in the age of Darwin.* Chicago: University of Chicago Press.

Starkstein, S. E., & Robinson, R. G. (1991). The role of the frontal lobes in affective disorder following stroke. In H. S. Levin, H. M. Eisenberg, & A. L. Benton (Eds.), *Frontal lobe function and dysfunction* (pp. 288–303). New York: Oxford University Press.

Stattin, H., Romelsjo, A., & Stenbacka, M. (1997). Personal resources as modifiers of the risk for future criminality: An analysis of protective factors in relation to 18-year-old boys. *British Journal of Criminology, 37*, 198–223.

Stearns, P. N., & Haggarty, T. (1991). The role of fear: Transitions in American emotional standards for children, 1850–1950. *The American Historical Review, 96*, 63–94.

Steelman, L. M., Assel, M. A., Swank, P. R., et al. (2002). Early maternal warm responsiveness as a predictor of child social skills: Direct and indirect paths of influence over time. *Journal of Applied Developmental Psychology*, *23*, 135-156.

Stein, N., Folkman, S., Trabasso, T., & Richards, T. A. (1997). Appraisal and goal processes as predictors of psychological well-being in bereaved caregivers. *Journal of Personality and Social Psychology*, *72*, 872-884.

Stein, N. L., & Albro, E. (2001). The origins and nature of arguments: Studies in conflict understanding, emotion, and negotiation. *Discourse Processes*, *32*, 113-133.

Stein, N. L., & Levine, L. J. (1989). The causal organization of emotional knowledge. *Cognition and Emotion*, *3*, 343-378.

Stein, N. L., Liwag, M., & Trabasso, T. (1995). Remembering the distant past: Understanding and remembering emotional events. Paper presented to the Biennial Meeting of the Society for Research In Child Development. Indianapolis, March 30–April 2.

Stein, N. L., Trabasso, T., & Liwag, M. (1994). The Rashomon phenomenon: Personal frames and future-oriented appraisals in memory for emotional events. In M. M. Haith, J. B. Benson, R. J. Roberts, & B. F. Pennington (Eds.), *Future oriented processes*. Chicago: University of Chicago Press.

Steiner, J. E., Glaser, D., Hawilo, M. E., & Berridge, K. C. (2001). Comparative expression of hedonic impact: Affective reactions to taste by human infants and other primates. *Neuroscience and Biobehavioral Reviews*, *25*, 53-74.

Steinhauer, P. D. (1991). The least detrimental alternative: A systematic guide to case planning and decision making for children in care. Toronto: University of Toronto Press.

Stemmler, D. G. (1989). The autonomic differentiation of emotions revisited: Convergent and discriminant validation. *Psychophysiology*, *26*, 617-632.

Stemmler, G. (2003). Methodological considerations in the psychophysiological study of emotion. In R. J. Davidson, K. R. Scherer, & H. H. Goldsmith (Eds.), *Handbook of affective sciences* (pp. 225-255). New York: Oxford University Press.

Stern, D. (1985). *The interpersonal world of the infant*. New York: Basic Books.

Stern, D. (1994). One way to build a clinically relevant baby. *Infant Mental Health Journal*, *15*, 9-25.

Sternberg, K. J., Lamb, M. E., Greenbaum, C., Cicchetti, D., Dawud, S., Cortes, R. M., Krispin, O., & Lorey, F. (1993). Effects of domestic violence on children's behavior problems and depression. *Developmental Psychology*, 44-52.

Sternberg, R. J. (1997). Construct validation of a triangular love scale. *European Journal of Social Psychology*, *27*, 313-335.

Stevenson, R. L. (1886). *Dr Jekyll and Mr Hyde*. Harmondsworth: Penguin (current edition 1979).

Stice, E., Ragan, J., & Randall, P. (2004). Prospective relations between social support and depression: Differential direction of effects for parent and peer support. *Journal of Abnormal Psychology*, *113*, 155-159.

Strachey, J. (1934). The nature of the therapeutic action in psychoanalysis. *International Journal of Psychoanalysis*, *15*, 127-159.

Strack, F., Martin, L. L., & Stepper, S. (1988). Inhibiting and facilitating conditions of the human smile: A nonobtrusive test of the facial feedback hypothesis. *Journal of Personality and Social Psychology*, *54*, 768-777.

Strakowski, S. M., DelBello, M. P., Sax, K. W., Zimmerman, M. E., Shear, P. K., Hawkins, J. M., & Larson, E. R. (1999). Brain magnetic resonance imaging of structural abnormalities in bipolar disorder. *Archives of General Psychiatry*, *56*, 254-260.

Strauss, E., & Moscovitch, M. (1981). Perception of facial expressions. *Brain and Language*, *13*, 308-332.

Strayer, F. F. (1980). Social ecology of the preschool peer group. In W. A. Collins (Ed.), *Development of cognition affect and social relations: Minnesota symposia in child development*. Hillsdale, NJ: Erlbaum.

Stretton, M. S., & Salovey, P. (1998). Cognitive and affective components of hypochondriacal concerns. In W. F. Flack & J. D. Laird (Eds.), *Emotions in psychopaathology: Theory and research* (pp. 265-279). New York: Oxford University Press.

Striano, T. (2004). Direction of regard and the still-face effect in the first year: Does intention matter? *Child Development*, *75*, 468-479.

Stringer, C., & Gamble, C. (1993). *In search of the Neanderthals*. New York: Thames and Hudson.

Stroebe, W., & Stroebe, M. S. (1996). The social psychology of social support. In E. T. Higgins & A. W. Kruglanski (Eds.), *Social psychology: Handbook of basic principles* (pp. 597-521). New York: Guilford.

Stroop, J. R. (1935). Studies of interference in serial verbal reactions. *Journal of Experimental Psychology*, *18*, 643-662.

Stubbe, D. E., Zahner, G. E. P., Goldstein, M. J., & Leckman, J. F. (1993). Diagnostic specificity of a brief measure of expressed emotion: A community study of children. *Journal of Child Psychology and Psychiatry, 34,* 139–154.

Sturgeon, D., Turpin, D., Kuipers, L., Berkowitz, R., & Leff, J. (1984). Psychophysiological responses of schizophrenic patients to high and low Expressed Emotion relatives: A follow-up study. *British Journal of Psychiatry, 145,* 62–69.

Stuss, D. T., & Benson, D. F. (1984). Neuropsychological studies of the frontal lobes. *Psychological Bulletin, 95,* 3–28.

Sullivan, M. W., & Lewis, M. (2003). Contextual determinants of anger and other negative expressions in young infants. *Developmental Psychology, 39,* 693–705.

Sullivan, M. W., Lewis, M., & Alessandri, S. M. (1992). Cross-age stability in emotional expressions during learning and extinction. *Developmental Psychology, 28,* 58–63.

Sullivan, P. F., Neale, M. C., & Kendler, K. S. (2000). The genetic epidemiology of major depression: A review and a meta-analysis. *American Journal of Psychiatry, 157,* 1552–1562.

Sulloway, F. J. (1979). *Freud, biologist of the mind: Beyond the psychoanalytic legend.* New York: Basic Books.

Suomi, S. J. (1999). Developmental trajectories, early experiences, and community consequences. In D. P. Keating & C. Hertzman (Eds.), *Developmental health and the wealth of nations: Social, biological, and educational dynamics* (pp. 185–200). New York: Guilford.

Suomi, S. J., & Harlow, H. F. (1972). Social rehabilitation of isolate reared monkeys. *Developmental Psychology, 6,* 487–496.

Sutton, S. K., & Davidson, R. J. (1997). Prefrontal brain asymmetry: A biological substrate of the behavioral approach and inhibition systems. *Psychological Science, 8,* 204–210.

Svejda, M. J., Campos, J. J., & Emde, R. N. (1980). Mother–infant "bonding": Failure to generalize. *Child Development, 56,* 775–779.

Svejda, M. J., Pannabecker, B. J., & Emde, R. N. (1982). Parent-to-infant attachment: A critique of the the early "bonding" model. In R. N. Emde & R. J. Harmon (Eds.), *The development of attachment and affiliative systems* (pp. 83–93). New York: Plenum.

Szechtman, H., & Woody, E. (2004). Obsessive-compulsive disorder as a disturbance of security motivation. *Psychological Review, 111,* 111–127.

Tainter, J. A. (1988). *The collapse of complex societies.* Cambridge: Cambridge University Press.

Tajfel, H., & Turner, J. (1979). An integrative theory of intergroup conflict. In W. G. Austin & S. Worchel (Eds.), *The social psychology of intergroup relations.* Monterey, CA: Brooks Cole.

Tan, E. S. (1996). *Emotion and the structure of film: Film as an emotion machine.* Mahwah, NJ: Erlbaum.

Tangney, J. P. (1990). Assessing individual differences in proneness to shame and guilt: Development of the self-conscious affect and attribution inventory. *Journal of Personality and Social Psychology, 59,* 102–111..

Tangney, J. P. (1992). Situational determinants of shame and guilt in young adulthood. *Personality and Social Psychology Bulletin, 18,* 199–206.

Tangney, J. P., Miller, R. S., Flicker, L., & Barlow, D. H. (1996). Are shame, guilt, and embarrassment distinct emotions? *Journal of Personality and Social Psychology, 70,* 1256–1264.

Tannen, D. (1991). *You just don't understand: Women and men in conversation.* New York: Ballantine.

Tarrier, N., Barrowclough, C., Porceddu, K., & Watts, S. (1988). The assessment of psychophysiological reactivity to the Expressed Emotion of the relatives of schizophrenic patients. *British Journal of Psychiatry, 152,* 618–624.

Taylor, G. J., Bagby, R. M., & Parker, J. D. A. (1991). The alexithymia construct: A potential program for psychosomatic medicine. *Psychosomatics, 32,* 153–164.

Taylor, S. E. (1991). Asymmetrical effects of positive and negative events: The mobilization-minimization hypothesis. *Psychological Bulletin, 110,* 67–85.

Taylor, S. E., Klein, L. C., Lewis, B. P., Gruenewal, T. L., Gurung, R. A. R., & Updegraff, J. A. (2000). Biobehavioral responses to stress in females: Tend-and-befriend, not fight-or-flight. *Psychological Review, 107,* 411–429.

Teasdale, J. (1988). Cognitive vulnerability to persistent depression. *Cognition and Emotion, 2,* 247–274.

Tellegen, A. (1985). Structures of mood and personality and their relevance to assessing anxiety, with an emphasis on self-report. In A. Hussain Tuma & J. D. Maser (Eds.), *Anxiety and the anxiety disorders* (pp. 681–706). Hillsdale, NJ: Lawrence Erlbaum.

Terwogt, M. M., Schene, J., & Harris, P. L. (1986). Self-control of emotional reactions by young children. *Journal of Child Psychology and Psychiatry, 27,* 357–366.

Thoits, P. (1985). Self-labeling processes in mental illness: The role of emotional deviance. *American Journal of Sociology, 91,* 617–632.

Thoits, P. A. (1986). Social support as coping assistance. *Journal of Consulting and Clinical Psychology, 54,* 416–423.

Thoits, P. A. (1995). Identity-relevant events and psychological symptoms: A cautionary tale. *Journal of Health and Social Behavior, 36,* 72–82.

Thomas, E. M. (1989). *The harmless people* (revised ed.). New York: Random House.

Thompson, R. A. (1994). Emotion regulation: A theme in search of definition. *Monographs of the Society for Research in Child Development (Serial No. 240), 59*(2-3), 25–52.

Tiedens, L. Z. (2000). Powerful emotions: The vicious cycle of social status positions and emotions, *Emotions in the workplace: Research, theory, and practice* (pp. 72–81). Westport, CT: Quorum Books/Greenwood Publishing.

Tiedens, L., & Leach, C. W. (Eds.). (2004). *The social life of emotions.* New York: Cambridge University Press.

Tiedens, L. Z. (2001). Anger and advancement versus sadness and subjugation: The effect of negative emotion expressions on social status conferral. *Journal of Personality & Social Psychology, 80*(1), 86–94.

Tillitski, C. J. (1990). A meta-analysis of estimated effect sizes for group versus individual versus control treatments. *International Journal of Group Psychotherapy, 40,* 215–224.

Tinbergen, N. (1951). *The study of instinct.* Oxford: Oxford University Press.

Tizard, B., & Hodges, J. (1978). The effect of early institutional rearing on the development of eight year old children. *Journal of Child Psychology and Psychiatry, 19*(2), 99–118.

Tolstoy, L. (1877). *Anna Karenina* (R. Pevear & L. Volokonsky, Trans.). London: Penguin (2000).

Tomasello, M. (1999). *The cultural origins of human cognition.* Cambridge, MA: Harvard University Press.

Tomasello, M., Carpenter, M., Call, J., Behne, T., & Moll, H. (2005, in press). Understanding and sharing intentions: The origins of cultural cognition. *Behavioral and Brain Sciences.*

Tomkins, S. S. (1962). *Affect, imagery, consciousness, Vol. 1. The positive affects.* New York: Springer.

Tomkins, S. S. (1963). *Affect, imagery, consciousness, Vol. 2. The negative affects.* New York: Springer.

Tomkins, S. S. (1970). Affect as the primary motivational system. In M. B. Arnold (Ed.), *Feelings and emotions: The Loyola symposium* (pp. 101–110). New York: Academic Press.

Tomkins, S. S. (1979). Script theory: Differential magnification of affects. In H. E. Howe & R. A. Dienstbier (Eds.), *Nebraska symposium on motivation, 1978* (pp. 201–236). Lincoln: University of Nebraska Press.

Tomkins, S. S. (1995). *Exploring affect: The selected writings of Sylvan S. Tomkins* (Ed. E. V. Demos). New York: Cambridge University Press.

Tomkins, S. S. (1984). Affect theory. In K. Scherer & P. Ekman (Eds.), *Approaches to emotion* (pp. 163–195). Hillsdale, NJ: Erlbaum.

Tooby, J., & Cosmides, L. (1990). The past explains the present: Emotional adaptations and the structure of ancestral environments. *Ethology and Sociobiology, 11,* 375–424.

Tracy, J. L., & Robins, R. W. (2004). Show Your Pride: Evidence for a Discrete Emotion Expression. *Psychological Science, 15,* 94–97.

Tranel, D. (1994). "Acquired sociopathy?": The development of sociopathic behavior following focal brain damage. In D. Fowles (Ed.), *Progress in experimental personality and psychopathology research.* New York: Springer.

Tranel, D., & Damasio, H. (1994). Neuroanatomical correlates of electrodermal skin conductance responses. *Psychophysiology, 31,* 427–438.

Treboux, D., Crowell, J., & Waters, E. (2004). When "new" meets "old": Configurations of adult attachment representations and their implications for marital functioning. *Developmental Psychology, 40,* 295–314.

Tremblay, R. E. (1999). When children's social development fails. In D. Keating & C. Hertzman (Eds.), *Developmental health and the wealth of nations* (pp. 55–71). New York: Guilford.

Tremblay, R. E. (2004). Decade of Behavior Distinguished Lecture: Development of physical aggression during infancy. *Infant Mental Health Journal, 25,* 399–407.

Trevarthen, C. (1979). Communication and co-operation in early infancy. In M. Bullowa (Ed.), *Before speech: The beginning of interpersonal communication* (pp. 321–347). Cambridge: Cambridge University Press.

Triandis, H. (1972). *The analysis of subjective culture.* New York: Wiley.

Triandis, H. C. (1989). The self and social behavior in differing cultural contexts. *Psychological Review, 96,* 269–289.

Triandis, H. C. (1994). *Culture and social behavior.* New York: McGraw-Hill.

Triandis, H. C. (1995). *Individualism and collectivism.* Boulder: Westview Press.

Trivers, R. L. (1971). The evolution of reciprocal altruism. *Quarterly Review of Biology, 46,* 35–57.

Tronick, E. Z. (1989). Emotions and emotional communications in infants. *American Psychologist, 44,* 112–119.

Tronick, E. Z., Cohn, J., & Shea, E. (1986). The transfer of affect between mothers and infants. In T. B. Brazelton & M. W. Yogman (Eds.), *Affective development in infancy.* Norwood, NJ: Ablex.

Tropp, M. (1976). *Mary Shelley's monster.* Boston: Houghton Mifflin.

Tsai, J. L., & Levenson, R. W. (1997). Cultural influences on emotional responding: Chinese American and European American dating couples during interpersonal conflict. *Journal of Cross-Cultural Psychology, 28,* 600–625.

Tsai, J. L., & Chentsova-Dutton, Y. (2002). Understanding depression across cultures. In I. H. Gotlib & C. L. Hammen (Eds.), *Handbook of depression* (pp. 467–491). New York: Guilford.

Tsai, J. L., Chentsova-Dutton, Y., Friere-Bebeau, L. H., & Przymus, D. (2002). Emotional expression and physiology in European Americans and Hmong Americans. *Emotion, 2,* 380–397.

Tsai, J. L., Levenson, R. W., & Carstensen, L. L. (2000). Autonomic, expressive, and subjective responses to emotional films in older and younger Chinese American and European American adults. *Psychology and Aging, 15,* 684–693.

Tsai, J. L., Simenova, D., & Watanabe, J. (2004). Somatic and social: Chinese Americans talk about emotion. *Personality and Social Psychology Bulletin, 30,* 1226–1238.

Tseng, W.-S., & McDermott, J. F. (1981). *Culture, mind, and therapy: An introduction to cultural psychiatry.* New York: Brunner-Mazel.

Tucker, D. M., & Frederick, S. L. (1989). Emotion and brain lateralization. In H. Wagner & A. Manstead (Eds.), *Handbook of social psychophysiology* (pp. 27–70). Chichester: Wiley.

Turner, R. A., Altemus, M., Enos, T., Cooper, B., & McGuinness, T. (1999). Preliminary research on plasma oxytocin in normal cycling women: Investigating emotion and interpersonal distress. *Psychiatry: Interpersonal & Biological Processes, 62,* 97–113.

Turner, R. A., Altemus, M., Yip, D. N., Kupferman, E., Fletcher, D., Bostrom, A., et al. (2002). Effects of emotion on oxytocin, prolactin, and ACTH in women. *Stress: The International Journal on the Biology of Stress, 5,* 269–276.

UNICEF (2004). *Childhood under threat: The state of the world's children 2005.* www.unicef.org/sowc05/english/fullreport.html

Uvnas-Moberg, K. (1994). Role of efferent and afferent vagal nerve activity during reproduction: Integrating function of oxytocin on metabolism and behaviour. *Psychoneuroendocrinology, 19,* 687–695.

Uvnas-Moberg, K. (1997). Physiological and endocrine effects of social contact. In C. S. Carter, I. I. Lederhendler, and B. Kirkpatrick (Eds.), *The integrative neurobiology of affiliation, Vol. 807* (pp. 146–163). New York: New York Academy of Sciences.

Uvnas-Moberg, K. (1998). Oxytocin may mediate the benefits of positive social interaction and emotions. *Psychoneuroendocrinology, 23*(8), 819–835.

Vaccarino, F. J., Schiff, B. B., & Glickman, S. E. (1989). A biological view of reinforcement. In S. B. Klein & R. R. Mowrer (Eds.), *Contemporary learning theories.* Hillsdale, NJ: Erlbaum.

Vaillancourt, T., Brendgen, M., Boivin, M., & Tremblay, R. E. (2003). A longitudinal confirmatory factor analysis of indirect and physical aggression: Evidence of two factors over time. *Child Development, 74,* 1628–1638.

Vaish, A., & Striano, T. (2004). Is visual reference necessary? Contributions of facial versus vocal cues in 12-month-olds' social referencing behavior. *Developmental Science, 7,* 261–269.

Valiente, C., Eisenberg, N., Shepard, S., et al. (2004). The relations of mothers' negative expressivity to children's experience and expression of negative emotion. *Journal of Applied Developmental Psychology, 25,* 215–235.

Van Bezooijen, R., Van Otto, S. A., & Heenan, T. A. (1983). Recognition of vocal dimensions of emotion: A three-nation study to identify universal characteristics. *Journal of Cross-Cultural Psychology, 14,* 387–406.

Van den Berghe, P. L. (1979). *Human family systems: An evolutionary view.* Amsterdam: Elsevier.

Van Ijzendoorn, M. H. (1992). Intergenerational transmission of parenting: A review of studies in nonclinical populations. *Developmental Review*, *12*, 76–99.

Van Ijzendoorn, M. H., & Bakermans-Kranenburg, M. (1997). Intergenerational transmission of attachment: A move to the contextual level. In L. Atkinson & K. Zucker (Eds.), *Attachment and psychopathology* (pp. 135–170). New York: Guilford.

Van Sommers, P. (1988). *Jealousy*. Harmondsworth: Penguin.

Vaughn, C. E., & Leff, J. P. (1976). The influence of family and social factors on the course of psychiatric illness: A comparison of schizophrenic and depressed patients. *British Journal of Psychiatry*, *129*, 125–137.

Veblen, T. (1899). *The theory of the leisure class: An economic study of institutions*. New York: Macmillan.

Velez, C. N., Johnson, J., & Cohen, P. (1989). A longitudinal analysis of selected risk factors for childhood psychopathology. *Journal of the American Academy of Child and Adolescent Psychiatry*, *28*, 861–864.

Verhulst, F. C., Koot, H. M., & Berden, G. F. M. (1990). Four year follow up of an epidemiological sample. *Journal of the American Academy of Child and Adolescent Psychiatry*, *29*, 440–448.

Visalberghi, E., & Sonetti, M. G. (1994). Lorenz's concept of aggression and recent primatological studies on aggressive and reconciliatory behaviors. *La Nuova Critica*, Nuova serie, 23–24, 57–67.

Von Uexküll, J. (1934). A stroll through the worlds of animals and men. In C. H. Schiller (Ed.), *Instinctive behavior: Development of a modern concept* (pp. 5–80). London: Methuen (current edition 1957).

Vygotsky, L. S. (1987). Emotions and their development in childhood. In R. W. Rieber & A. S. Carton (Eds.), *Collected works of L. S. Vygotsky* (Vol. 1, pp. 325–337). New York: Plenum.

Waganaar, W. A. (1986). My memory: A study of autobiographical memory over six years. *Cognitive Psychology*, *18*, 225–252.

Wagner, H. L., MacDonald, C. J., & Manstead, A. S. R. (1986). Communication of individual emotions by spontaneous facial expression. *Journal of Personality and Social Psychology*, *50*, 737–743.

Wainwright, N. W. J., & Surtees, P. G. (2002). Childhood adversity, gender and depression over the life course. *Journal of Affective Disorders*, *72*, 33–44.

Wakschlag, L. S., Pickett, K. E., Cook, E., et al. (2002). Maternal smoking during pregnancy and severe antisocial behavior in offspring: A review. *American Journal of Public Health*, *92*, 966–974.

Walden, T. A., & Ogan, T. A. (1988). The development of social referencing. *Child Development*, *59*, 1230–1240.

Walker-Andrews, A. S. (1986). Intermodal perception of expressive behaviors: Relation of eye and voice? *Developmental Psychology*, *22*, 373–77.

Walker-Andrews, A. S. (1997). Infants' perception of expressive behaviors: Differentiation of multimodal information. *Psychological Bulletin*, *121*, 437–456.

Wallbott, H. G., & Scherer, K. (1986). How universal and specific is emotional experience? Evidence from 27 countries on five continents. *Social Science Information*, *25*, 763–795.

Washburn, S. L. (1991). Biochemical insights into our ancestry. In M. H. Robinson & L. Tiger (Eds.), *Man and beast revisited* (pp. 61–73). Washington, DC: Smithsonian Institute Press.

Waters, E., Hamilton, C. E., & Weinfield, N. S. (2000). The stability of attachment-security from infancy to adolescence and early adulthood: General introduction. *Child Development*, *71*, 678–683.

Waters, E., Merrick, S., Treboux, D., Crowell, J., & Albersheim, L. (2000). Attachment security in infancy and early adulthood: a twenty-year longitudinal study. *Child Development*, *71*, 684–689.

Watson, D. (1988). Intraindividual and interindividual analyses of positive and negative affect: Their relation to health complaints, perceived stress, and daily activities. *Journal of Personality and Social Psychology*, *54*(6), 1020–1030.

Watson, D., & Clark, L. (1992). On traits and temperament: General and specific factors of emotional experience and their relation to the five-factor model. *Journal of Personality*, *60*(2), 441–476.

Watson, D., & Tellegen, A. (1985). Towards a consensual structure of mood. *Psychological Bulletin*, *98*, 219–235.

Watson, D., Clark, L. A., & Tellegen, A. (1988). Development and validation of brief measures of positive and negative affect: The PANAS scales. *Journal of Personality and Social Psychology*, *54*, 1063–1070.

Watson, D., Clark, L., McIntyre, C. W., & Hamaker, S. (1992). Affect, personality, and social activity. *Journal of Personality and Social Psychology*, *63*(6), 1011–1025.

Weaver, I., Cervoni, N., Champagne, F., et al. (2004). Epigenetic programming by maternal behavior. *Nature Neuroscience*, *7*, 847–854.

Weber, M. (1947). *The theory of social and economic organization* (A. M. Henderson & Talcott Parsons, Trans.). London: Hodge.

Wegner, D. M., & Pennebaker, J. W. (Eds.). (1993). *Handbook of mental control.* Englewood Cliffs, NJ: Prentice Hall.

Weiner, B. (1985). An attributional theory of achievement motivation and emotion. *Psychological Review, 92,* 548-573.

Weiner, B. (1986). *An attributional theory of motivation and emotion.* New York: Springer-Verlag.

Weiner, B., & Graham, S. (1989). Understanding the motivational role of affect: Lifespan research from an attributional perspective. *Cognition and Emotion, 3,* 401-419.

Weinfield, N. S., Sroufe, A., & Egeland, B. (2000). Attachment from infancy to early adulthood in a high risk sample: Continuity, discontinuity, and their correlates. *Child Development, 71,* 695-702.

Weisfeld, G. E. (1980). Social dominance and human motivation. In D. R. Omark, E. F. Strayer, & D. G. Freedman (Eds.), *Dominance relations: An ethological view of human conflict and social interaction* (pp. 273-286). New York: Garland.

Weisfeld, G. E., & Beresford, J. M. (1982). Erectness of posture as an indicator of dominance or success in humans. *Motivation and Emotion, 6,* 113-131.

Weiskrantz, L. (1956). Behavioral changes associated with ablation of the amygdaloid complex in monkeys. *Journal of Comparative and Physiological Psychology, 49,* 381-391.

Weiss, S. J., Wilson, P., Hertenstein, M. J., & Campos, R. (2000). The tactile context of a mother's caregiving: Implications for attachment of low birth weight infants. *Infant Behavior and Development, 23,* 91-111.

Weissman, M. M., Bland, R., Canino, G. J., et al. (1996). Cross-national epidemiology of major depression and bipolar disorder. *Journal of the American Medical Association, 24,* 293-299.

Weissman, M. M., Gammon, G. D., John, K., et al. (1987). Children of depressed parents: Increased psychopathology and early onset of major depression. *Archives of General Psychiatry, 44,* 847-853.

Weisz, J. R., Suwanlert, S., Chaiyasit, W., & Walter, B. A. (1987). Over- and undercontrolled clinic referral problems among Thai and American children and adolescents: The wat and wai of cultural differences. *Journal of Consulting and Clinical Psychology, 55,* 719-726.

Wellman, H. M. (1995). Young children's conception of mind and emotion: Evidence from English speakers. In J. Russell, J.-M. Fernandez-Dols, A. S. R. Manstead, & J. Wellenkamp (Eds.), *Everyday concepts of emotion* (NATO ASI series D, Vol. 81) (pp. 289-313). Dordrecht: Kluwer.

Wellman, H. M., & Lagattuta, K. H. (2004). Theory of mind for learning and teaching: the nature and role of explanation. *Cognitive Development, 19,* 479-497.

Werner, E. E. (1989, April). Children of the Garden Island. *Scientific American, 260,* 106-111.

Werner, E. E., & Smith, R. S. (1982). *Vulnerable but invincible: A longitudinal study of resilient children and youth.* New York: McGraw-Hill.

Westen, D., Novotny, C. M., & Thompson-Bremner, H. (2004). The empirical status of empirically supported therapies: Assumptions, findings, and reporting in controlled clinical trials. *Psychological Bulletin, 130,* 631-663.

Whalen, P. J., Rauch, S. L., Etcoff, N. L., McInerney, S. C., Lee, M. B., & Jenike, M. A. (1998). Masked presentations of emotional facial expressions modulate amygdala activity without explicit knowledge. *Journal of Neuroscience, 18,* 411-418.

Whisman, M. A. (2001). The association between depression and marital dissatisfaction. In S. R. H. Beach (Ed.), *Marital and family processes in depression: A scientific foundation for clinical practice* (pp. 3-24). Washington, DC: American Psychological Association.

Whisman, M. A., & Bruce, M. L. (1999). Marital dissatisfaction and incidence of major depressive episode in a community sample. *Journal of Abnormal Psychology, 108,* 674-678.

Whitbeck, L. B., Hoyt, R. L., Simons, R. L., Conger, R. D., Elder, G. H., Lorenz, F. O., & Huck, S. (1992). Intergenerational continuity of parental rejection and depressed affect. *Journal of Personality and Social Psychology, 63,* 1036-1045.

Whitesell, N. R., & Harter, S. (1996). The interpersonal context of emotion: Anger with close friends and classmates. *Child Development, 67,* 1345-1359.

Whitley, B. E. (1993). Reliability and aspects of the construct validity of Sternberg's Triangular Love Scale. *Journal of Social and Personal Relationships, 10,* 475-483.

Wicker, B., Keysers, C., Plailly, J., et al. (2003). Both of us disgusted in my insula: The common neural basis of seeing and feeling disgust. *Neuron, 40,* 655-664.

Wickramaratne, P. J., & Weissman, M. M. (1998). Onset of psychopathology in offspring by developmental phase and parental depression. *Journal of the American Academy of Child and Adolescent Psychiatry*, 37, 933–942.

Widen, S. C., & Russell, J. A. (2003). A closer look at preschoolers' freely produced labels for facial expressions. *Developmental Psychology*, 39, 114–128.

Wierzbicka, A. (1999). *Emotions across languages and cultures: Diversity and universals*. Cambridge: Cambridge Unversity Press.

Williams, J. M. G., Watts, F. N., MacLeod, C., & Mathews, A. (1997). *Cognitive psychology and emotional disorders, 2nd edition*. Chichester: Wiley.

Williams, J. R., Insel, T. R., Harbaugh, C, R., & Carter, C. S. (1994). Oxytocin administered centrally facilitates formation of a partner preference in female prairie voles (Microtus Ochrogaster). *Journal of Neuroendocrinology*, 6, 247–250.

Williams, S., Anderson, J., McGee, R., & Silva, P. A. (1990). Risk factors for behavioral and emotional disorder in preadolescent children. *Journal of the American Academy of Child and Adolescent Psychiatry*, 29, 413–419.

Willis, F. N., & Briggs, L. F. (1992). Relationship and Touch in Public Settings. *Journal of Nonverbal Behavior*, 16, 55–63.

Willis, F. N., & Hamm, H. K. (1980). The use of interpersonal touch in securing compliance. *Journal of Nonverbal Behavior*, 5, 49–55.

Wills, T. A., & Dishion, T. J. (2004). Temperament and adolescent substance use: A transactional analysis of emerging self-control. *Journal of Clinical Child and Adolescent Psychology*, 33, 69–81.

Wilson, A. C., & Cann, R. L. (1992, April). The recent African genesis of humans. *Scientific American*, 266, 68–73.

Wilson, M. I., & Daly, M. (1996). Male sexual proprietariness and violence against wives. *Current Directions in Psychological Science*, 5, 2–7.

Wilson, T. D., Wheatley, T. P., Meyers, J. M., Gilbert, D. T., & Asson, D. (2000). Focalism: A source of durability bias in affective forecasting. *Journal of Personality and Social Psychology*, 78, 821–836.

Winkielman, P., Zajonc, R., & Schwartz, N. (1997). Subliminal affective priming resists attributional intervention. *Cognition and Emotion*, 11, 433–465.

Winnicott, D. W. (1958). *Through paediatrics to psychoanalysis*. London: Tavistock.

Winnicott, D. W. (1965). Ego distortion in terms of true and false self. In J. D. Sutherland (Ed.), *D. W. Winnicott: The maturational process and the facilitating environment: Studies in the theory of emotional development* (pp. 140–152). London: Hogarth Press.

Winnicott, D. W. (1971). *Playing and reality*. London: Tavistock.

Witt, D. M., Carter, C., & Walton, D. (1990). Central and peripheral effects of oxytocin administration. *Physiology and Behavior*, 37, 63–69.

Witt, D. M., Winslow, J. T., & Insel, T. (1992). Enhanced social interaction in rats following chronic, centrally infused oxytocin. *Pharmacology, Biochemistry, and Behavior*, 43, 855–861.

Witvliet, C., Ludwig, T. E., & Vander Laan, K. L. (2001). Granting forgiveness or harboring grudges: Implications for emotion, physiology, and health. *Psychological Science*, 12, 117–123.

Woolf, V. (1965). *Jacob's Room*. Harmondsworth: Penguin.

Wordsworth, W. (1802). Preface to *Lyrical Ballads* of 1802. In S. Gill (Ed.), *William Wordsworth*. Oxford: Oxford University Press (1984).

World Health Organization (1983). *Depressive disorders in different cultures*. Geneva, Switzerland: World Health Organization.

World Health Organization. (2003). *International Classification of Diseases, Tenth Revision, Clinical Modification (ICD-10-CM) Pre-release draft*. Geneva: World Health Organization (available at www.cdc.gov/nchs/about/otheract/icd9/icd10cm.htm).

Worobey, J., & Blajda, V. M. (1989). Temperament ratings at 2 weeks, 2 months, and 1 year: Differential stability of activity and emotionality. *Developmental Psychology*, 25, 257–263.

Worth, L. T., & Mackie, D. M. (1987). Cognitive mediation of positive affect in persuasion. *Social Cognition*, 5, 76–94.

Worthington, E. L. J. (1998). Empirical research in forgiveness: Looking backward, looking forward. In J. E. L. Worthington (Ed.), *Dimensions of forgiveness* (pp. 321–339). Philadelphia, PA: Templeton Foundation Press.

Wrangham, R. (2001). Out of the *Pan*, into the fire: How our ancestors' evolution depended on what they ate. In F. B. M. De Waal (Ed.), *Tree of origin: What primate behavior can tell us about human social evolution* (pp. 121–143). Cambridge, MA: Harvard University Press.

Wright, M. R. (1981). *Empedocles, the extant fragments*. New Haven, CT: Yale University Press.

Wright, R. (1992). *Stolen continents: The "New World" through Indian eyes*. Toronto: Penguin.

Wright, R. (2004). *A short history of progress*. Toronto: Anansi.

Wright, T. (1604). *The passions of the minde in generall* (reprint edited by T. O. Sloan). Urbana: University of Illinois Press (1971).

Wyvell, C. L. & Berridge, K. C. (2000). Intra-accumbens amphetamine increases the conditioned incentive salience of sucrose reward: Enhancement of reward "wanting" without enhanced "liking" or response reinforcement. *Journal of Neuroscience, 20*, 8122–8130.

Yates, F. A. (1964). *Giordano Bruno and the Hermetic tradition*. London: Routledge & Kegan Paul.

Yuille, J. C., & Cutshall, J. L. (1986). A case study of eyewitness testimony to a crime. *Journal of Applied Psychology, 71*, 291–301.

Yzerbyt, V. Y., Dumont, M., Wigboldus, D., & Gordijn, E. (2003). I feel for us: The impact of categorization and identification on emotions and action tendencies. *British Journal of Social Psychology, 42*, 533–549.

Zahn-Waxler, C., & Kochanska, G. (1990). Origins of guilt. In R. Thompson (Ed.), *Socioemotional development. Nebraska Symposium on Motivation* (pp. 183–258). Lincoln: University of Nebraska Press.

Zahn-Waxler, C., Radke-Yarrow, M., & King, R. A. (1979). Child rearing and children's prosocial initiations towards victims of distress. *Child Development, 50*, 319–330.

Zahn-Waxler, C., Radke-Yarrow, M., Wagner, E., & Chapman, M. (1992). Development of concern for others. *Developmental Psychology, 28*, 126–136.

Zajonc, R. B. (1980). Feeling and thinking: Preferences need no inferences. *American Psychologist, 35*, 151–175.

Zajonc, R. B., Murphy, S. T., & Inglehart, M. (1989). Feeling and facial efference: Implications of the vascular theory of emotion. *Psychological Review, 96*, 395–416.

Zald, D. (2003). The human amygdala and the emotional evaluation of sensory stimuli. *Brain Research Reviews, 41*, 88–123.

Zald, D. H., Lee, J. T., Fluegel, K. W., & Pardo, J. V. (1998). Aversive gustatory stimulation activates limbic circuits in humans. *Brain, 121*, 1143–1154.

Zeanah, C. H., & Fox, N. A. (2004). Temperament and attachment disorders. *Journal of Clinical Child and Adolescent Psychology, 33*, 32–41.

Zillman, D. (1978). Attribution and misattribution of excitatory reactions. In J. H. Harvey, W. J. Ickes, & R. F. Kidd (Eds.), *New directions in attribution research* (Vol. 2, pp. 335–368). Hillsdale, NJ: Erlbaum.

Zillman, D. (1988). Cognitive excitation interdependencies in aggressive behavior. *Aggressive Behavior, 14*, 51–64.

Zillmann, D. (1989). Effects of prolonged consumption of pornography. In D. Zillman & J. Bryand (Eds.), *Pornography: Research advances and early policy considerations*. Hillsdale, NJ: Erlbaum.

Zillmann, D., & Vorderer, P. (Eds.) (2000). *Media entertainment: The psychology of its appeal*. Mahwah, NJ: Erlbaum.

Subject Index

Author Index